M000290686

# UNIVERSITY CASEBOOK SERIES

### EDITORIAL BOARD

## ROBERT C. CLARK
DIRECTING EDITOR
Distinguished Service Professor and Austin Wakeman Scott
Professor of Law and Former Dean of the Law School
Harvard University

## DANIEL A. FARBER
Sho Sato Professor of Law and Director, Environmental Law Program
University of California at Berkeley

## OWEN M. FISS
Sterling Professor of Law
Yale University

## SAMUEL ISSACHAROFF
Bonnie and Richard Reiss Professor of Constitutional Law
New York University

## HERMA HILL KAY
Barbara Nachtrieb Armstrong Professor of Law and
Former Dean of the School of Law
University of California at Berkeley

## SAUL LEVMORE
William B. Graham Distinguished Service Professor of Law and
Former Dean of the Law School
University of Chicago

## THOMAS W. MERRILL
Charles Evans Hughes Professor of Law
Columbia University

## ROBERT L. RABIN
A. Calder Mackay Professor of Law
Stanford University

## CAROL M. ROSE
Gordon Bradford Tweedy Professor Emeritus of Law and Organization and
Professorial Lecturer in Law
Yale University
Lohse Chair in Water and Natural Resources
University of Arizona

## KATHLEEN M. SULLIVAN
Stanley Morrison Professor of Law and
Former Dean of the Law School
Stanford University

CASES, PROBLEMS AND MATERIALS

# SALES TRANSACTIONS: DOMESTIC AND INTERNATIONAL LAW

FOURTH EDITION

*by*

CURTIS R. REITZ
Algernon Sydney Biddle Professor of Law Emeritus
University of Pennsylvania Law School

FOUNDATION PRESS
2011

THOMSON REUTERS

This publication was created to provide you with accurate and authoritative information concerning the subject matter covered; however, this publication was not necessarily prepared by persons licensed to practice law in a particular jurisdiction. The publisher is not engaged in rendering legal or other professional advice and this publication is not a substitute for the advice of an attorney. If you require legal or other expert advice, you should seek the services of a competent attorney or other professional.

Nothing contained herein is intended or written to be used for the purposes of 1) avoiding penalties imposed under the federal Internal Revenue Code, or 2) promoting, marketing or recommending to another party any transaction or matter addressed herein.

© 1992, 2001, 2006 FOUNDATION PRESS
© 2011 By THOMSON REUTERS/FOUNDATION PRESS

     1 New York Plaza, 34th Floor

     New York, NY 10004

     Phone Toll Free 1–877–888–1330

     Fax 646–424–5201

     foundation–press.com

Printed in the United States of America

**ISBN** 978–1–59941–887–2

Mat #41059268

*To the memory of*

*John O. Honnold*
*1915–2011*

*Father of the Vienna Convention*

# PREFACE TO THE FOURTH EDITION

About 100 years ago, in this country, the law of sales contracts split off from the broad common-law field of general contract law. The split was the unintended consequence of codification of the law of sales, which occurred, it is said, as part of a broader movement to unify the laws of the states of the United States. Other sectors of contract law were not codified and remained common-law subjects. Common law governed real estate contracts, contracts for services, construction contracts, insurance contracts, and so forth.

Other areas of early 20th century codification involved various kinds of intangible property that were created, sometimes by bi-lateral agreement, but the key legal issues involved the arrangement of property rights among the initial parties and subsequent parties who came to have interest in the property. Typically this involved pieces of paper, like promissory notes, drafts, and documents of title. These laws could be better characterized as laws regarding personal property more than contracts. Even the Uniform Sales Act was largely focused on determining when title passed to goods sold. Passing of title was the fulcrum for deciding many legal issues.

About 50 years ago, a second wave of codification occurred in the country, resulting in the Uniform Commercial Code. The property-like fields comprised the major part of the Code. The Article on Sales, however, took on a predominantly contract orientation. The Code retained title-passing provisions, but they were isolated from the rest of the Article. The fundamental premise of Article 2 was that issues between buyers and sellers should be resolved primarily by reference to their agreements. An array of contract-type provisions were added to the codified law. In many instances, the stated purpose of the new provisions was to overrule judicial decisions that the drafters of Article 2 deemed to be "uncommercial."

After Article 2 went into effect, a major effort was made to revise the common law of contracts to incorporate some of the contract law reforms that had been codified in that Article. This was accomplished by promulgation of a revision of the Restatement of the Law of Contracts, a publication of considerable influence on common-law courts. Notwithstanding this development, the codified law of sales contracts differs significantly from the common law of contracts generally.

About 25 years ago, a new body of positive law of sales was created. The purpose was to provide a legal platform for international sales of goods. This code is the product of an international convention, drafted under the auspices of the United Nations, the Convention on Contracts for the International Sale of Goods. This Convention was ratified by the President with the advice and consent of the Senate and is part of the law of the United States and of more than 80 other countries. Under the Supremacy Clause of the US Constitution, the Convention is part of the laws of the several states.

The effects on legal education of these 20th century events have been severe. It appears that teachers of first-year contracts courses differ widely on whether to incorporate UCC Article 2 or the UN Convention into those courses and, if so, how and to what extent. Teachers of upper-level commercial law courses differ on the proper syllabus for teaching the law of sales.

These materials, like previous editions, have been compiled on a number of pedagogical premises. The first is to rely on the expectation that issues of contract formation, including formation of sales contracts, will have been addressed in the basic contracts course. The second is that the focus of a modern course in sales law should be on issues that are giving rise to serious controversy and, as a result, to litigation of sufficient gravity that it reaches appellate courts. The third is that a course on sales law today should encompass both the domestic law of the United States and the UN Convention. The materials are structured to be of use in a course that is devoted primarily or solely to the domestic law of the United States.

John O. Honnold, co-editor of three previous editions of this book and of five editions of earlier commercial law casebooks, died in January 2011. Professor Honnold played major roles in the development of UCC Sales Article 2 and of the UN Convention on Contracts for the International Sale of Goods. Indeed, he is widely described as the Father of that Convention. He will be missed by all who knew him and loved him, but the products of his life-long work endure.

CURTIS R. REITZ

Philadelphia PA
February 2011

# SUMMARY OF CONTENTS

# SUMMARY OF CONTENTS

# TABLE OF CONTENTS

**CHAPTER 3. Title: Sellers' Responsibility and Buyers' Rights** ------------------------------------------------------ 82

# TABLE OF CASES

Principal cases are in bold type. Non-principal cases are in roman type. References are to Pages.

# TABLE OF CASES

Principal cases are in bold type. Non-principal cases are in roman type. References are to Pages.

CASES, PROBLEMS AND MATERIALS

# SALES TRANSACTIONS: DOMESTIC AND INTERNATIONAL LAW

PART I

# GENERAL INTRODUCTION

CHAPTER 1

# COMMERCIAL LAW

## 1. NATURE AND SIGNIFICANCE OF COMMERCIAL LAW

To understand commercial law, one must first consider commercial transactions. A free market economy is an economy in which independent actors exchange things of value. Each side makes its own determination of the value of what is to be received compared to the value of what is to be given up. Agreement occurs when both sides perceive that the exchange will make them better off, the paradigmatic win-win situation.[1] Basic exchange transactions involve a transfer of a thing of value for a price. The things exchanged include goods, services, investment securities, intellectual property, other intangible property, or real property (or combinations of these) in exchange for a price. The price side of exchange transactions is usually expressed in terms of money.

Some exchange transactions occur in "spot" markets. Transactors meet, negotiate their bargain, and promptly complete the exchange. This simple type of transaction can occur if both parties have the thing of value they propose to exchange at the time of contracting. Frequently, however, one or both parties to a commercial transaction cannot perform "on the spot." Thus, a transferor may obligate itself to produce or acquire the thing of value to be exchanged. Familiar examples include contracts for goods to be manufactured or acquired, crops to be raised, and real estate improvements to be constructed. Most contracts for services necessarily contemplate a time period, after contract formation, during which the service providers prepare for and deliver performance.

On the payment side, the purchaser may not have enough ready money to pay the full price, but may be able to pay over a period of time. The extent to which potential purchasers can obtain credit, that is, can defer

---

**1.** Transactions of exchange can and do occur within a single firm or enterprise, between actors that are elements of the firm rather than independent economic entities. Intra-firm activities are, of course, not market transactions. Managers of the firm determine whether such exchanges occur and the terms of them. Prices, for example, are set administratively and are often described as "administered prices."

In management theories of the business firm, one of the most basic determinations is the "make or buy" decision. A "make" choice is to provide the thing needed from sources inside the firm. "Make" choices may lead to vertical integration of activities within a single firm. A "buy" choice is to go into the market and enter into an exchange transaction with one of the providers of the thing desired.

The distinction between intra-firm transactions and market transactions blurs when strong commercial relationships are established. Independent entities may become interdependent as a result of a pattern of transactions with each other.

payment of the full price, is a significant determinant of the level of exchange activity that occurs. Extension of credit is, itself, an exchange transaction, a transaction in which a credit provider gives up present value in exchange for the credit recipient's later payment of larger amount; the difference is usually called "interest.".

Another type of exchange transaction involves transfer of risk. Property owners may contract to transfer risk of loss of or damage to their property to insurers in exchange for payment of money, the insurance "premium." Persons whose activities may expose them to potential legal liability may contract to transfer that risk to insurers. Other common forms of insurance involve transfer of the risk of individuals' death, illness or incapacity. In credit transactions, lenders have the risk that their borrowers may default; a charge for such risk is often part of the "interest" amount.

The primary focus of this course is on transactions that involve goods. Other kinds of commercial transactions will be addressed only tangentially. Contracts for sales of goods are part of the larger body of general Contract law that you studied previously, but as we will learn, there are many unique aspects to the law of sales.

Commercial law provides the essential legal infrastructure that makes exchange transactions feasible. The law functions in several ways. Commercial law is, in part, *facilitative*. It assists diverse transactors to achieve their respective objectives and thereby advances the societal value of private ordering. Commercial law can simplify the task of bargaining by providing, for recurring transaction-types, reasonable terms that the parties to a particular transaction can incorporate into their bargain without significant *ex ante* negotiation costs. Commercial law can guide the parties when issues arise in the course of performance that they had not fully planned for. Commercial law is in part *evaluative and remedial*. Although most exchange transactions are completed without significant controversy, not all transactions conclude satisfactorily to both sides. When disputes arise, commercial law determines the respective rights and duties and, in the cases of breach, the remedies that are available to the aggrieved parties. Commercial law is also in part *regulative*. Thus it may forbid use of certain terms or it may shape transactions to deny the effectiveness of terms that are unjust or unfair or otherwise contravene public policy. Such provisions are invoked, typically, as part of *ex post* controversies over disputed performance.

## 2. DEVELOPMENT OF COMMERCIAL LAW

The history of commercial law is important for understanding of the present. It is helpful to know the roots from which this branch of the law has grown and the manner in which it evolved. Early on, commercial law began to develop on an international level, but soon national courts and legislatures acted to domesticate and divide the field with their separate national laws. During the nineteenth century, parts of the commercial laws of the United States and Great Britain were codified into statutory form.

One of the areas codified was the law of sales of goods. The consequences of these developments have been profound.

### a.  MERCANTILE CUSTOM

Until the seventeenth century a large share of commercial law was merchants' law—a body of customs made and administered by the merchants themselves without regard to the laws of the countries in which they lived. Many of the rules were international in scope: maritime insurance policies still bear the marks of customs from Genoa and Antwerp. Merchant courts also decided controversies that developed at the international fairs which were the centers for much of early trade. The court governed important staple commodities (such as wool). A "mayor of the staple," skilled in mercantile practice, presided over this court along with a jury of merchants.

### b.  NATIONALIZATION OF THE LAW

In late seventeenth century, the English King's judges shouldered the law of the merchant courts to one side. In 1666 they proclaimed that "the law of merchants is the law of the land"[2]—a hollow claim when made but that was later fulfilled in part by the work of a renowned Scotsman, William Murray, who in 1756 was made Chief Justice of the King's Bench and given the title of Lord Mansfield. In controversies between merchants, Mansfield made it a point to ascertain and apply the customs of the trade. One of his tools for this work was a special group of merchants who acted as a jury in commercial cases and gave him advice on commercial practice.[3] Mercantile custom was not fully imported into the law of sales of goods.[4] This was an accident: the sales cases that could have been the basis for development of the law did not come to Mansfield, but went rather to judges of a different bent who were content to decide mercantile transactions on the basis of legal concepts that had been developed for the British land economy. And it may be that most of the mercantile customs within the wide field of sales were, even then, too varied to be frozen into general rules of law. At any rate, a body of British common-law doctrine developed to govern sales of goods.

In the early nineteenth century United States, the law "received" from Great Britain after the American Revolution prevailed among the settled states along the Eastern seaboard. A more difficult problem emerged as new states were carved out of the wilderness. Frontier law was rough and ready, marked by a shortage of law books and legal education, and a

---

**2.**  Woodward v. Rowe, 2 Keb. 132, 84 Eng.Rep. 84 (1666).

**3.**  A brief and readable account of Mansfield's work may be found in Holdsworth, Some Makers of English Law 160–175 (1938). For more detail, see Fifoot, Lord Mansfield (1936). Chapter IV (82–117) is devoted to commercial law. Mansfield's Scottish background is not irrelevant, for it may explain his receptiveness to civil law doctrines prevalent in Scotland.

**4.**  K. Llewellyn, Across Sales on Horseback, 52 Harv.L.Rev. 725 (1939). This article, in spite of its title, is no pony for sales law. There was a sequel called The First Struggle to Unhorse Sales, in 52 Harv.L.Rev. 873 (1939), which calls for the same comment.

cheerful willingness to improvise.[5] The rapidly developing commerce of the new world lacked uniform, or even ascertainable, rules of law.

In 1842, the great American jurist, Justice Story wrote the United States Supreme Court opinion holding that federal courts, unhampered by divergent state court decisions, could declare uniform rules for "general commercial law." Indeed the opinion opened up wider vistas: Lord Mansfield and Cicero were cited for the proposition that commercial law was "in a great measure, not the law of a single country only, but of the commercial world."[6] Federal courts continued to declare rules of "general commercial law," infrequently,\ and with decreasing effectiveness, until 1938. In that year, such federal judicial law-making was held to be unconstitutional by the Supreme Court.[7]

### c.  NINETEENTH CENTURY CODIFICATION

In the nineteenth century codification of law was in the air throughout the Western world. A Civil Code supplanted local rules and customs in France in 1804. Napoleon carried the Civil Code to much of Europe with his conquering armies. Even after Napoleon was driven out of other countries, the Civil Code remained. Most of Latin America and substantial parts of Africa and Asia followed the Civil Code. In Great Britain, despite the efforts of writers like Jeremy Bentham, the common-law system remained in place, although Scots law differed in certain respects from English law.[8] In the middle of the century, Britain undertook to transplant a great deal of its common-law jurisprudence to India in the form of codes drafted by common-law lawyers for that part of the British Empire.

Near the end of the nineteenth century, a renewed movement for codification of British law led to several statutory enactments in particular commercial fields. Contributing significantly to this movement were individuals who had participated in drafting Indian Codes. Among these was the remarkable Mackensie Chalmers. He had returned from India and was eager for the task of codifying parts of the common law of the Mother Country. With the support of influential government officials and members of the banking community, Chalmers embarked on a series of codification projects.

---

**5.**   R. Pound, The Formative Era of American Law 7–12 (1938).

**6.**   Swift v. Tyson, 16 Pet. (41 U.S.) 1, 18, 10 L.Ed. 865 (1842). See G. Gilmore, Commercial Law in the United States: Its Codification and Other Misadventures, in Ziegel and Foster, Aspects of Comparative Commercial Law, 449, 452–457 (1969).

**7.**   Erie Railroad Co. v. Tompkins, 304 U.S. 64, 58 S.Ct. 817, 82 L.Ed. 1188 (1938). See C. Hackman, Uniform Commercial Law in the Nineteenth Century Federal Courts, 27 Emory L.J. 45 (1978).

**8.**   Scots law had derived from Roman law. Adherence to this tradition differentiated the law of Scotland from the law of England. These differences continued into the nineteenth century. In 1855, a Royal Commission issued a report on the ways in which "the Mercantile Laws in the different parts of the United Kingdom of Great Britain and Ireland may be advantageously assimilated." Second Report of the Commissioners on Mercantile Laws of the United Kingdom, 354 Parliamentary Papers (1855). In 1856, Parliament enacted legislation to deal with some of those divergences. Mercantile Law Amendment Act, Scotland, 1856, 19 & 20 Viced. c. 60; Mercantile Law Amendment Act, 1856, 19 & 20 Viced. c. 97.

In 1882, Parliament enacted Chalmers' first effort, a law that dealt with instruments for the payment of money. The Sale of Goods Act followed and was enacted in 1893. When Chalmers presented his draft codes to Parliament, he stated that they did not change the law as it had been developed by common-law judges; rather his goal was to set the law down in a clear and coherent manner. After several other projects, the codification movement came to an end in Britain as Chalmers went on to other work.

Similar legislative activity followed in the United States, but for entirely different political and economic reasons. In the United States, the general commercial law of the federal courts espoused by Justice Story had not developed very far. Most commercial law remained a matter of state law, expressed in common-law decisions of state courts. The aggregate of these decisions left much of the law unsettled, and differences existed among state courts' decisions that had been handed down. Uncertainty about the law existed where courts had not spoken. Business activity, led by emerging large corporations, was increasingly national in scope. The absence of an adequate base of law was hindering the development of interstate commerce. Legislation was seen as the answer to the difficulty of sparse and non-uniform law. If all the states enacted the same commercial law statute, then legislation could make the law uniform across the country. The same process could make the law more certain. The National Conference of Commissioners on Uniform State Laws was established to draft and promulgate such statutes.[9] The primary legislative goals for the work of the Conference were stability, clarity and uniformity of the laws of the states.

In 1895 the Conference promulgated its first commercial law product, the Uniform Negotiable Instruments Law. The law was patterned on Chalmers' Bills of Exchange Act. By 1906 a Uniform Sales Act, based on Chalmers' Sale of Goods Act, had been drafted. The Sales Act was not completely successful. While over thirty states adopted it, many southern states did not. Other Conference products followed over the years.

### d.  THE U.S. UNIFORM COMMERCIAL CODE

The American economy that emerged in mid-twentieth century found the early products of the Conference inadequate. Those acts had been based on nineteenth century precepts from Chalmers' era. Modernization of

---

**9.**  The Conference was formed through enactment of legislation, by every state, to create a uniform state law commission for that state. The number of commissioners and the method of their selection is provided by that state's law. The commissioners of all the states meet annually in a Conference of Commissioners, a meeting that typically lasts eight working days. Between annual meetings, drafting committees made up of commissioners and aided by reporters prepare drafts for submission to an annual meeting. Under Conference procedures, no act can be approved unless it has been "read" and debated at two annual meetings. Much of each annual meeting is conducted in the form of a committee of the whole, in which commissioners speak and vote as individuals. Final approval of acts occurs by "vote of the states," a process in which each state has one vote. See W. Armstrong, Jr., A Century of Service: A Centennial History of the National Conference of Commissioners on Uniform State Laws (1991).

commercial law was required. One possible pathway could have been replacement of uniform state laws with federal legislation for the entire country. The U.S. Supreme Court had recently opened that pathway by recognizing that Congress had broad legislative powers under the Commerce Clause of the U.S. Constitution. A move to federalize U.S. commercial began but soon stalled and the initiative remain with the states.[10] The Uniform State Law Conference, in 1940, started work on a Revised Sales Act to supersede the 1906 Sales Act.The Conference was soon joined in this project by the American Law Institute (ALI).[11] The scope of the effort expanded to the other areas of commercial law. The result was the Uniform Commercial Code (the "UCC" or sometimes simply the "Commercial Code").

UCC Articles 2 and 3 took the place of the Uniform Sales Act and the Negotiable Instruments Law. In other articles, the UCC created commercial laws for which there were no historic statutory counterparts. The most innovative of these was a broad, unified body of law for secured credit transactions in which lenders' goods or other personal property were made collateral assuring creditors against lenders' defaults on their obligations to repay loans. This became UCC Article 9. This article superseded many diverse legal arrangements, including some uniform acts some non-uniform laws, and some common-law arrangements.

The first version of the Commercial Code, released in 1952, was promptly enacted in Pennsylvania and nowhere else. Further enactments were deferred pending action by New York, where consideration of adoption by the New York legislature was deferred pending major studies by the New York Law Revision Commission. These studies led the Uniform Law Conference and the American Law Institute to make substantial revisions of the UCC, which were embodied in the 1957 and 1958 Official Texts.[12] The Official Texts of 1962 and 1966 corrected a few errors.[13] By 1968 the

---

**10.** In 1936, the New York Merchants' Association launched a movement to modernize sales law and proposed the adoption by Congress of a Federal Sales Act to govern foreign and interstate trade. The movement made some limited progress, but was set aside as the nation entered World War II.

**11.** The American Law Institute (ALI) was established in 1923. The initiative for the Institute came from William Draper Lewis, Dean of the University of Pennsylvania Law School. The original purpose was to clarify and simplify the law and better adapt it to the needs of life. The ALI is well known for its many "Restatements of the Law," products that it continues to revise, and for the Model Penal Code. In 1942, the ALI entered into a joint effort with the National Conference of Commissioners on Uniform State Laws to develop the Uniform Commercial Code. See The American Law Institute: Seventy–Fifth Anniversary 1923–1998 (1998).

**12.** For further details and references see the New York Law Revision Commission, Study of Uniform Commercial Code, Vol. 1, 348 (1955). (Herein cited N.Y.L.Rev.Comm., Study of UCC.)

**13.** Useful insights into the drafting of the UCC are provided in the twenty-three volumes of Uniform Commercial Code Drafts (E. Kelly ed. 1984) (the "Kelly Drafts"). Revealing and amusing comments on the making of the UCC appear in Symposium: Drafters Reflect on the Code, 43 Ohio St.L.J. 537–642 (1982).

original UCC had been adopted by all states.[14] Congress had adopted the Code on behalf of the District of Columbia.

The extraordinarily innovative Secured Transaction Article proved to be the least durable part of the Code. It was modified substantially in 1972. Within a few years, more changes occurred. In the 1980s, two articles were added to the Code: Article 2A on Leases (1987 with 1990 amendments) and Article 4A on Funds Transfers (1989).

Another revision of the entire Commercial Code was undertaken in the 1990s. Revisions were completed in: Article 3 (Negotiable Instruments), with related changes in Article 4 (Bank Deposits and Collections) (1991), Article 5 (Letters of Credit), and Article 8 (Investment Securities) (1994). Another revision of Article 9 (Secured Transactions) was promulgated in 1998. Revisions of Article 1 (General Provisions) and Article 7 (Documents of Title) were completed in the early 2000s.[15] The Commercial Code that is provided to law students as part of their course materials is this modern version.

Proposed revisions of Article 2 (Sales) and Article 2A (Leasing) were completed in 2003. These proposals have not been enacted by any state and prospects for enactments have become exceedingly slight.[16]

The Secured Transactions Article continues to be open to revision. Another version is scheduled to be considered by the Uniform Law Conference and the American Law Institute in 2010.

*e.   INTERNATIONAL COMMERCIAL CONVENTIONS: THE U.N. CONVENTION ON INTERNATIONAL CONTRACTS FOR THE SALE OF GOODS*

Economic activity is being rapidly and deeply globalized. The global economy needs an infrastructure of modern and uniform commercial law to undergird this activity. Three international organizations have taken on this mission. They are the United Nations Commission on International Trade Law (UNCITRAL),[17] the International Institute for the Unification of Private Law (UNIDROIT), also known as the Rome Institute,[18] and the

---

**14.** Louisiana adopted most of the Articles of the original UCC in 1975. Omitted were Articles 2 and 7 (Documents of Title).

**15.** The part of the proposed revision of Article 1that deals with the power of parties to choose the law governing their transactions has been controversial. Legislatures that have acted so far have not enacted proposed 1–301, which was drawn to give parties great flexibility; rather state legislatures have retained the more restrictive provision in former 1–105.

**16.** The proposed revision of Article 2 has drawn substantial criticism, particularly from manufacturers of durable consumer goods.

**17.** UNCITRAL's membership, limited by the United Nations to 60 States, elected by the General Assembly. The United States has been a member from the outset, and has played an active role in UNCITRAL's work. The headquarters are in Geneva, Switzerland. The web site is www.uncitral.org.

**18.** UNIDROIT is an independent inter-governmental organization, founded in 1926 and composed currently of 63 Member States. The United States is a member. The headquarters of the Institute and its secretariat are located in Rome, Italy. The web site is www.unidroit.org.

Hague Conference on Private International Law, usually referred to as the Hague Conference.[19] There is no world legislative body to enact international private law for the global economy. The task falls to nations, sometimes called nation-states. Most efforts to develop international commercial law have been in the form of international conventions, multilateral agreements comparable to treaties that nations can adopt. Nations that ratify an international convention incorporate the content of the convention into their national laws. The object of efforts to develop international private law in this manner is to create uniform bodies of national law that supersede the various domestic laws of ratifying nations that would otherwise be applicable.[20]

This manner of development, internationally, of uniform commercial law by nations ratifying conventions mirrors the development, domestically, of uniform commercial state law in the United States where state legislatures enact products of the Uniform Law Conference. But major differences must be noted. U.S. states that enact uniform commercial legislation are, for the most part, states that shared\ a common legal history. (That is also true in other nations that upgrade their domestic commercial laws.) International conventions, however, bridge nations with many different domestic legal systems, derived from common-law and civil law traditions. Domestic commercial codes supplement existing bodies of domestic law regarding contracts and property and are expected to be interpreted and applied by domestic courts familiar with that nation's remedial jurisprudence. There is no body of international private law dealing broadly with matters of contract and property on which international commercial conventions can be based. There are no international tribunals to provide definitive interpretations of those conventions in contested situations. Development of international private law is a daunting challenge given the absence of global legislative and judicial institutions.

Notwithstanding the difficulties, a number of international commercial conventions have been created and are beginning the development of international private law. One of the earliest areas of developments dealt with ocean transport of goods where territorially limited national laws do not apply. UNCITRAL has been active in this field for more than forty years. Its most recent product, completed in 2008,[21] has not yet gone into force, but the prospects for success are strong.

---

**19.** Despite being named a "conference," the Hague Conference is a permanent intergovernmental body with its headquarters at The Hague in the Netherlands. Founded in the 19th century, the Conference was originally composed of European nations. The Hague Conference currently has 69 members from around the globe. The United States has been a member since 1964. The web site is www.hcch.org.

**20.** In the absence of *international commercial law*, the governing law will be the domestic law of one nation. In transnational transactions, more than one nation's law might be invoked. Which nation's domestic law would apply would be determined by the choice of law rules for such transactions. Choice of law is a matter generally described as private international law. Relegating transnational transactions to diverse national laws is, for obvious reasons, problematic. The domestic commercial laws of 200—plus nations are not uniform, and in many instances the domestic law of a particular nation may be unclear or inadequate.

**21.** The United Nations Convention on Contracts for the International Carriage of Goods Wholly or Partially by Sea—the "Rotterdam Rules."

For the purposes of this course, the most notable development is the United Nations Convention of International Contracts for the Sale of Goods, known familiarly as CISG.[22] This Convention is an UNCITRAL product from the 1980s. The Convention went into force among eleven nation-states, including the United States, on January 1, 1988. By 2010, the Convention had been ratified by 74 nations, including nations on each continent and with diverse legal and economic systems.

CISG is comparable to the Sales article. Article 2, of the U.S. Commercial Code, but there are significant differences. CISG applies to sales contracts between commercial entities with places of business in different countries, that is to international trade in goods. Unlike the Commercial Code. CISG does not apply to sales of goods to consumers, even if those transactions are international is scope. Another important difference is the power granted by CISG to parties in business-to-business transactions to opt out of convention and to have their transactions governed instead by some nation's domestic law. Such opt-out power is a unique aspect of international private law. It has no counterpart in Article 2 of the Commercial Code. The terminology of CISG is different from that of the Commercial Code and, indeed, different from the terminology of other systems of domestic law. The drafters, who were quite diverse in their individual legal backgrounds, chose intentionally to avoid language and legal concepts that had particular meanings only in some existing legal systems. CISG is written in six languages, all equally authoritative in accordance with the practice of the United Nations. English is the only official language of the Commercial Code.

International private law for secured transactions has begun to develop. In the last decade, under the auspices of UNIDROIT and UNCITRAL, two major conventions have been completed. One deals with secured transactions in which the property taken as collateral is equipment that moves around the world.[23] Protocols to this conventions deal with specific kinds of property. The first protocols cover large civil aircraft and railway equipment. This convention is in effect. The other convention will allow secured lenders to take as collateral accounts receivable generated in international commercial transactions, if and when it takes effect.[24] Inter-

---

**22.** CISG was preceded by earlier, less successful conventions on the same subject. In 1964, the Hague Conference finalized conventions establishing a Uniform Law on the International Sale of Goods (ULIS) and a Uniform Law on the Formation of Contracts for the International Sale of Goods (ULF). By 1972 sufficient ratifications, primarily by countries of western Europe, had occurred to bring these conventions into force. The United States did not ratify either convention.

**23.** Convention on International Interests in Mobile Equipment (Cape Town 2001). This convention went into force on March 1, 2006. As of 2010, there are 34 parties to this convention. The United States is a party.

**24.** United Nations Convention on the Assignment of Receivables in International Trade, 2001. The receivables convention is not in force. As of 2010, no nation has ratified this convention.

national developments in secured transactions law have not followed the example of UCC Article 9, which has a scope that extends to all forms of secured transactions.

For complete and current information on international commercial conventions, visit the web sites of UNCITRAL, UNIDROIT and the Hague Conference. On these sites, you will find texts and status reports of completed conventions along with information regarding work in progress.

## f. INTERNATIONAL PROJECTS TO HARMONIZE DOMESTIC LAWS; THE UNIDROIT PRINCIPLES

Some international commercial law projects have aimed at seeking convergence of national domestic laws toward a common set of rules or principles. The object of this process is commonly referred to as seeking to harmonize national laws, i.e., to reduce or eliminate differences that may exist. Several notable examples of harmonization projects are found in the work of UNCITRAL and UNIDROIT.

The UNIDROIT Principles of International Commercial Contracts (2004)enunciate rules that are common to most existing domestic legal systems, but that are best adapted to the special requirements of international trade.[25] The Principles deal with a number of matters that are either completely excluded from CISG or not sufficiently covered in that Convention. The format resembles that used by the American Law Institute in its Restatements of the Law. Like the Restatements, the Principles are addressed to primarily to tribunals and to private sector parties. The Principles can be applied when contracting parties have agreed to be governed by them, but are also offered to tribunals as guides to solving issues when the tribunals cannot ascertain the relevant applicable law.[26]

UNCITRAL has promulgated a number of model laws that are addressed to national legislatures. UNCITRAL products of this kind deal with electronic commerce, government procurement and infrastructrure development, and insolvency.

## 3. UNITED STATES COMMERCIAL LAW

## a. SUBSTANTIVE LAW

The center piece of the commercial law of the United States is the Uniform Commercial Code, but commercial law is much more than the Code. This segment considers other sources of domestic commercial law. Some of those sources are state law, others federal or national law. Rarely can a question of commercial law be answered by looking only at the Commercial Code. As many commercial law teachers have said: The first task is to persuade students to look *at* the Code, to wrestle seriously with the precise terms of the statute, but the second task is to get them to look *up* from the Code, to consider other applicable law.

---

**25.** The Principles can be found on the UNIDROIT web site.

**26.** There is a link on the UNIDROIT web site to a data base of citations to the Principles and a selected bibliography.

The Commercial Code, by its own terms, floats on the surface of a vast and deep body of state common law, only some of which is, in the Code's language, "displaced by the particular provisions of the Uniform Commercial Code." UCC 1–103(b). Unless displaced, all of the broad "principles of law and equity" apply. All states have statutory provisions other than the Commercial Code that may apply. Notable among these are the Uniform Electronic Transactions Act and non-uniform statutes protecting consumers from deceptive acts and practices. Laws to protect consumers usually define consumers as individuals who buy for personal, family or household purposes.

At the national level, a most significant body of commercial law is the Bankruptcy Code. When a party to a commercial transaction becomes bankrupt, federal law determines the rights and duties of the parties. The Bankruptcy Code often relies upon provisions of state law, but that is not required. Congress also enacted the Consumer Credit Protection Act and the Magnuson–Moss Warranty Act, two pieces of legislation intended to protect consumers against certain kinds of overreaching in the marketplace. Some federal agencies have promulgated regulations that deal with aspects of commercial law and consumer protection. The Federal Trade Commission issued several important regulations for the protection of consumers, most notably the Holder-in-Due–Course Regulation of 1975.

### b. ENFORCEMENT OF THE LAW; REMEDIES

Enforcement of the Commercial Code and other aspects of commercial law other than the Bankruptcy Code is left to the general system of state and federal courts. The idea of establishing courts devoted exclusively or primarily to handling commercial disputes has been raised from time to time, but legislatures have not chosen to create such courts, except for the federal bankruptcy court system. The result is that commercial cases are decided by judges sitting in courts of general jurisdiction where other kinds of cases predominate. In trial courts of general jurisdiction, parties have the right to trial by jury, but this right is frequently waived in commercial cases.

In the United States, there are overlapping systems of federal and state courts. By and large federal judges deal with matters of federal law while state law is the province of state courts. A major exception allows civil litigants to disputes governed entirely by state law to invoke the jurisdiction of a federal court if the litigants are citizens of different states and the amount in controversy is at least $75,000.[27] A plaintiff can chose to file its claim in state court even if entitled to invoke the "diversity" jurisdiction of a federal court, but the defendant can "remove" the case to federal court. In "diversity" cases, federal trial judges are obligated to apply the state law of the state in which the court sits, which would include the relevant version of Commercial Code. Lawyers representing parties in commercial controversies frequently take them to federal courts when they can do so.

---

**27.** Congress raises the amount in controversy from time to time. The current provision dates from 2007.

As we shall see, much of the judicially created jurisprudence regarding the Commercial Code is the product of federal courts. Much of the most important judicial construction of the Code is therefore the work of the eleven federal Courts of Appeals, the highest federal courts to which cases can be appealed as of right. (The U.S. Supreme Court elects not to hear "diversity" cases.)

American law is now generally hospitable to arbitration of commercial disputes, if parties to those transactions agree. Arbitral awards can be enforced by the system for enforcement of judgments of courts. By long-standing tradition, commercial arbitrators do not prepare opinions in domestic cases and their awards are confidential. (In labor law, a different tradition exists.) In some states, relatively small disputes are routinely referred by state courts preliminarily to a form of arbitration known as court-annexed arbitration. Therefore, domestic commercial arbitration, to the extent it is used, has added little to the corpus of jurisprudence regarding the Commercial Code.

One consequence of the pattern for adjudication and arbitration of commercial disputes is that there is no tribunal of highest or ultimate authority regarding the interpretation of the Commercial Code (or of any other state-law aspect of commercial law). In selecting the cases for these materials, the editors have intentionally given priority to opinions of the highest courts of states or, to opinions of federal courts of appeals in "diversity" cases. As you will learn, courts are invariably sensitive to the duty to enforce the law of a particular state. The extent to which they may find persuasive decisions of other courts regarding the law of other states varies.

### c.  *OVERSIGHT BODY: UCC PERMANENT EDITORIAL BOARD*

The Uniform Law Conference and the American Law Institute, sponsors of the Uniform Commercial Code, established a Permanent Editorial Board to monitor development of new legal issues arising under the Code. The PEB has no authority to propose amendments to the text of the Code, but has undertaken to propose proper interpretations of the text in Commentaries that the PEB issues from time to time. In some instances, the Commentaries have resulted in amendments to the Official Comments.

### 4.  COMMERCIAL LAW FOR INTERNATIONAL TRANSACTIONS

### a.  *SUBSTANTIVE LAW*

As we learned previously, modern international law for commercial transactions is national law. "Law merchant" was customary law that emerged outside national law but was "adopted" as domestic law by British courts.[28] Far more developed as a part of international commercial law was a set of principles for choosing which nation's domestic law governed

---

**28.** Some scholars assert that the "law merchant" continues to exist independent of national law, but there is little agreement as to the content of such law. The Commercial Code, Article 1–103(b), refers to the "law merchant" as part of the principles of law and equity that are the foundation for the Code.

international transactions. This body of law, known as "private international law," was enunciated by courts and scholars and was sometimes incorporated into international conventions. The Hague Conference on Private International Law developed conventions of this kind.[29]

Nation-states create substantive international commercial law when they ratify conventions like CISG, the United Nations Convention on Contracts for International Sale of Goods. CISG is not law by virtue of the actions of UNCITRAL and the U.N. General Assembly. There is no international legislature empowered to enact international commercial law. Likewise there is no body of uncodified substantive international commercial law that are the foundation for conventions like CISG.

CISG addresses the problem by a general provision for questions concerning matters governed by the Convention which are "not settled in it." Article 7(2) provides that such matters shall be settled "in conformity with the general principles on which it [the Convention] is based or, in the absence of such principles, in conformity with the [domestic] law applicable by virtue of the rules of private international law." Although this provision has been discussed by scholars, it has had little practical effect.

*b.   ENFORCEMENT OF THE LAW; REMEDIES*

Enforcement of international commercial law, when disputes arise, can be sought through litigation or arbitration. There is no international court system. CISG disputes must be litigated in national courts, subject to national laws regarding jurisdiction over subject matter and personal jurisdiction over defendants. Litigation involving CISG that occurs in the United States has been mostly in the federal court system.

Arbitration is a long-standing method of dispute resolution used in international commerce. Unlike domestic U.S. commercial arbitration practice, international arbitrators prepare written opinions that explain their awards. Several established systems are available to parties who elect to arbitrate. These systems provide methods for selection of arbitrators and procedures for conduct of the proceedings.

One of these exists pursuant to rules and procedures of the International Chamber of Commerce (ICC), which established in 1923 what is now called the International Court of Arbitration (ICA). Its headquarters are in Paris, France. Most ICA decisions are unreported. However, since 1974, selected arbitral opinions and awards have been published. The initial collection spanned eleven years. Since 1976, the International Council for Commercial Arbitration has been publishing Yearbooks of Commercial Arbitration containing selected of arbitral awards and other materials. Published ICA cases are redacted so as not to identify the parties to the disputes or the names of the arbitrators.

Several United States organizations offer to support international commercial arbitration. Among them is the American Arbitration Associa-

---

**29.** The 1986 Convention on the Law Applicable to Contracts for the International Sale of Goods is one of these conventions of pertinence to this course. Although ratified by only a few nations, this convention is sometimes relied upon as useful expression of private international law.

tion, which is also very prominent in domestic arbitration in various fields. Like the ICA, the AAA published some decisions involving international disputes in redacted form.

Since 1994, China offers a government-supported arbitration system through the China International Economic and Trade Commission (CIETAC). CIETAC has its headquarters in Beijing, but also has subcommissions in Shanghai and Shenzhen. CIETAC rules require that arbitration panels submit drafts of their awards to the Commission so that the Commission "may remind the tribunal of the issues in the award on the condition that the tribunal's independence of decision is not affected."[30]

Another arbitration system devoted substantially to arbitration of international commercial disputes is the London Court of International Arbitration (LCIA). The LCIA, which has been in existence for more than a century, is a corporation under the control of its constituent bodies, the Corporation of the City of London, the London Chamber of Commerce, and the Chartered Institute of Arbitrators. Since the United Kingdom is not a party to CISG, the LCIA role in enforcement of the Convention may be limited.

International commercial law with regard to judicial enforcement of arbitration awards is well developed. The United Nations Convention on the Recognition and Enforcement of Foreign Arbitral Awards, commonly known as the "New York Convention," commits signatory nations to enforcement of arbitration awards. The United States is a party to the New York Convention and fulfills its obligation through chapter 2 of the Federal Arbitration Act.

### c. *OVERSIGHT BODY: CISG ADVISORY GROUP*

UNCITRAL, the organization that developed CISG, does not purport to monitor the Convention in application. In the absence of an official follow-up mechanism, a group of self-selected international sales law scholars organized themselves into the International Sales Convention Advisory Council.[31] The Council is made up of scholars from around the world. It discusses and renders opinions on unsettled questions of interpretation of CISG. Although the Council is an unofficial body, its work is gaining respect.[32] The Council has a website, www.cisgac.com, where its opinions may be found.

### d. *EXTENT TO WHICH CISG CURRENTLY APPLIES IN INTERNATIONAL TRADE*

The application of CISG to international trade is determined by several factors. The first of these is the extent to which countries of the world have

---

**30.** CIETAC web site, visited Feb. 2, 2010.

**31.** The Advisory Council is jointly sponsored by the Institute of International Commercial Law at Pace University School of Law in New York and the Centre for Commercial Law Studies at Queen Mary, University of London.

**32.** See J. Karton & L. de Germiny, Has the CISG Advisory Council Come of Age?, 27 Berkeley J. Int'l L. 448 (2009).

ratified the Convention. As noted earlier, CISG does not have the force of law by virtue of the actions of UNCITRAL and the U.N. General Assembly. It becomes law when ratified by a nation. Ratification makes ai international convention part of the law of the ratifying nation. Among ratifying nations, the law takes on the character of international law, but its application is limited to the jurisdictions of the ratifying nations. As of 2010, the number of nations that have ratified CISG is 74.

The second factor is the effect of an option in CISG. A ratifying country could make CISG applicable to international whenever, under choice of law principles of private international law, the law governing an international transaction is the law of the ratifying country. This option is set forth in CISG 1. But that Article also allows a ratifying country to provide that CISG applies to an international sales transaction only if both countries in which the parties have their principal places of business have ratified the Convention. Most nations have elected the requirement of reciprocity. Therefore, CISG applies to transactions among traders whose principal places of business are in the 74 ratifying nations.

From the perspective of the United States, CISG has been ratified by all of that country's important trading partners, with one major exception. CISG was ratified by Canada and Mexico and therefore covers all of North America, the NAFTA region. In Europe, every major country except the United Kingdom is a party to CISG. It has wide impact within the European Community. (Prospects for ratification by the U.K. are slim.) In Asia, China, Japan, and South Korea are CISG parties, but India is not; Japan's ratification took effect in August 2009.(Taiwan and Hong Kong are not recognized as nation-states by the international community and, therefore, are not eligible to become parties to CISG.[33]) Complete and up-to-date information on the status of CISG can be found on the UNCITRAL web site.

The third factor determining the coverage of CISG is the result of the Convention provision that allows parties to sales transactions to elect to be governed by law other than CISG. In the process of drafting CISG, the choice was made to allow parties to contracts for international sales to opt out of the Convention. The opt-out clause is found in CISG 6: "The parties may exclude the application of this Convention...." The rationale for including the opt-out clause was entirely political. The drafters knew that the Convention would face opposition from some officials and enterprises in the process of national governments' deciding whether to become parties to the Convention. Hoping for broadest adoption of the Convention, the drafters saw the opt-out clause as a device to soften opposition to ratification and thereby to increase the number of nations that would become parties to the Convention.

---

**33.** Hong Kong is a Special Administrative District of the Peoples Republic of China (PRC). The PRC became a CISG Contracting Party in 1997. The PRC could have but elected not to include Hong Kong. This action was permitted by CISG 93(1). See Innotex Precision Ltd. v. Horei Image Products, Inc., 679 F. Supp. 2d 1356 (N.D. Ga. 2009).

The CISG drafters could not know what the practical effect of Article 6 would be in countries that became CISG parties. After more than two decades of experience, published studies indicate that the effect has been substantial. A 2009 study reports: "The evidence varies, but we have data for a few jurisdictions. For the US, somewhere in the range of 55–71% of lawyers 'typically/generally' opt out. In Germany that figure is probably around 45% of lawyers who 'generally/predominantly' opt out. In Switzerland it seems the figure is around 41%, while for Austrian lawyers, it is around 55%. Some 37% or less of Chinese lawyers typically opt out."[34]

To put these numbers in perspective, note that they reflect only international commercial transactions in which lawyers were actively involved in the negotiation stage of contracting. An opt-out requires agreement of both parties and must be part of the terms of the original contracts. Many commercial transactions are "unlawyered" at the formation stage.This would be less likely if the parties are large corporations with in-house legal offices. Small and medium-sized business entities do not typically have in-house counsel and the expense may make impractical retaining counsel to advise on contract negotiation. It may be that, for some time, CISG will have its greatest effect on transactions between small and medium-sized businesses, not transactions is which large national or transnational enterprises are a party. It should be no surprise, therefore, that the parties to reported CISG litigation appear to be predominantly smaller enterprises.[35]

## 5.   WORKING WITH THE UNIFORM COMMERCIAL CODE

Studying and working with the Uniform Commercial Code requires some special lawyer skills. Like all statutes, there is a text, but attached to each section of text there are comments. There is a subtle and nuanced relationship between the text and comments to be understood. The Code is a large body of commercial law that spans a number of fields, but purports to one integrated Code with an overarching set of purposes and themes. The Uniform Commercial Code is law only to the extent that it has been enacted by state legislatures. In that multi-state enactment process, some uniformity has been lost. The Code has now been through a number of revisions. These and other issues pose interesting challenges to the art of studying and working with the Code.

---

**34.**  L. Spagnola, A Glimpse Through the Kaleidoscope: Choices of Law and the CISG (Kaleidoscope Part I), 13 Vindobona J. 135, 135–36 (2009). An updated version of this paper is L. Spagnola, Green Eggs and Han: The CISG, Path Dependence, and the Behavioral Economics of Lawyers' Choices of Law in International Sales Contracts, http://ssrn.com/abstract=1664168 (2010).

**35.**  International trade in commodities is often influenced by international associations or conferences of traders in those products. Many of these organizations promulgate standard form agreements which their members commonly use. Quite often these standard forms provide that the governing law is the law of the United Kingdom. The U.K. is nor a CISG Contracting Party. Whatever the reason, CISG appears to have little role currently in international commodities trading.

### a.   *THE OFFICIAL TEXT*

The text of the Uniform Commercial Code is a product of its two sponsoring organizations and the source of legislation in all states of the United States. They call their product the "official text." Many legislatures have chosen not to adopt that text exactly as promulgated by the Uniform State Laws Conference and the American Law Institute. The law in place is substantially the text proposed for uniform enactment, but lawyers and law students must keep in mind that the "Official Text" may have been varied by the legislature whose law governs a particular transaction. In law school commercial law courses, statutory supplements provide students with the Official Text of the Code, but do not (and cannot) catalogue state-by-state variations. Judicial opinions, on the other hand, always refer to the actual law of one state, the state whose law governs the transaction in question. These are difficulties, but years of experience shows that they are not insurmountable difficulties.

Law school statutory supplements provide, for the most part, only the most recent version of the Official Text that have had significant adoptions by state legislatures. However, enactments are incomplete and ongoing. A state-by-state status table must be consulted for an accurate current account. Many cases decided under earlier versions of the Commercial Code remain instructive. Two Articles remain essentially in the form that they took early on in the original generation of the Code. These are Article 2 (Sales) and Article 2A (Leases). Proposed revisions of these Articles have not be enacted, but they too are instructive and are commonly included in statutory supplements to course materials.

Interpretation of a uniform statute is a process of applying its provisions of general applicability to the facts of particular situations, regardless of otherwise applicable state law. That process for the Code is in some respects the same as the process of interpretation of other statutes, but in other respects it differs. Unlike most domestic statutes, the UCC has within itself statements on its proper interpretation. The very first substantive provision states: "This Act shall be liberally construed and applied to promote its underlying purposes and policies." UCC 1–103(a).[36] Subsection (a) describes the "underlying purposes and policies" in three branches:

(1) to simplify, clarify and modernize the law governing commercial transactions;

(2) to permit the continued expansion of commercial practices through custom, usage and agreement of the parties;

(3) to make uniform the law among the various jurisdictions

Section 1–103 reveals the Code's basic attitude toward the arrangements made by actors in the private sector. It implies that the law's primary purpose is to facilitate market transactions. Simplicity and clarity of rules enable actors to act expeditiously with an understanding of the

---

**36.** The provisions found in Article 1 are "general provisions" that apply to all of the other Articles.

background legal environment. Uniformity of law facilitates interstate commerce by eliminating concerns for conflicts of law in interstate transactions. Modernization involves casting off anachronistic rules that no longer fit current market practices.[37]

Section 1–103 says nothing about regulation of the marketplace. There is no suggestion that the Code is intended to address market failures or intervene to change the balance of the market power of private actors. Some commentators have criticized the Code drafters as lacking the willingness to make moral or ideological judgments about the nature of a just society and to shape the Code toward such objectives.[38] Others contend that Sales Article of the Code not only enables but directs courts to impose their understanding of commercial morality on the market place.[39] They refer to the Code's general obligation of "honesty" in the performance and enforcement of any contract or duty together with the Article 2 provisions that expanded this obligation to include "observance of reasonable commercial standards of fair dealing in the trade" and empowered courts to strike down "unconscionable" contracts or contract terms.[40]

### b.  THE OFFICIAL COMMENTS

Hazardous for the lazy mind, but helpful to the responsible lawyer, are the Official Comments which follow each section of the Code. Few statutes have this kind of auxiliary material, though it is standard practice to have comments attached to proposed uniform laws promulgated by the Uniform Law Conference. Troublesome problems about their significance in the Code system cannot be avoided.

---

**37.** At the time of drafting the original Code, the 1906 Sales Act was seen as an anachronism:

> In nineteenth-century commerce, the prototypical sales transaction was the face-to-face sale in which the buyer paid cash and took her goods home. [The picture of a commercial transaction in the Sales Act . . . is typified "by the horseman who stops at the saddler's door to buy a new saddle."] . . . In the modern world of sales, . . . most commercial sellers and buyers . . . contract for a sale in the future; their agreement is usually on the buyer's or seller's printed form; their sale is on credit; and their relationship has just begun. In addition, there may be one or more middlemen between the seller-manufacturer and the buyer, who may be buying for resale or use. Both the commercial structure of a sale and the needs of the parties to it will vary markedly depending on whether it is a sale to a business buyer for resale or use, or to a consumer.

> By the late 1930s, Llewellyn was not alone in seeing problems of obsolescence in the Uniform Sales Act. Indeed, the merchants were the first to complain, followed by the academic community and the commercial bar.

**38.** See, e.g., R. Danzig, A Comment on the Jurisprudence of the Uniform Commercial Code, 27 Stan. L. Rev. 621, 635 (1975).

**39.** See e.g., J. Murray, The Article 2 Prism: The Underlying Philosophy of Article 2 of the Commercial Code, 21 Washburn L.J. 1 (1981); Z. Wiseman, The Limits of Vision: Karl Llewellyn and the Merchant Rules, 100 Harv. L. Rev. 465, 475–477 (1987).

**40.** Revised Article 1–304 extended the obligation to observe reasonable commercial standards of fair dealing, originally only in the Sales Article, to all of the Articles of the Code except the Article on Letters of Credit. The original (and current) Sales Article provision, 2–103(1)(b), applied only to merchants, but the revised Article 1 provision does not.

The most obvious point about the Comments is the one which, curiously enough, is most often overlooked. The text to the Code was enacted by legislatures, the Comments were not. One is tempted to ignore this point because the Comments, written in an explanatory and non-statutory style, are easier to read. *Facilis est descensus Averno.*

But the tempter will whisper: The drafters wrote these Comments, didn't they? If they say what the Code does, that's bound to be right, isn't it? Why bother then with this prickly statutory language? (You may find it easier to resist these temptations if you put yourself in the role of a judge to whom this argument has been made and then imagine your comments to that hapless attorney.)

The problem of measuring the force of the Comments is sufficiently important to justify some background. Versions of the Code prior to 1957 included a significant provision about the Comments in the general provisions of Article 1. Section 1–102(3) then stated:

> (f) The Comments of the National Conference of Commissioners on Uniform State Laws and the American Law Institute may be consulted in the construction and application of this Act but if text and comment conflict, text controls.

In 1956 the sponsoring organizations released a document entitled "1956 Recommendations of the Editorial Board for the Uniform Commercial Code," recommending widespread revisions which, for the most part, are reflected in the current version of the Code. These "1956 Recommendations" called for the deletion of the above-quoted provision of Section 1–102(3)(f) and did not substitute any new provision on the status of the Comments. The question immediately arises: Does this deletion imply the rejection of the idea behind the deleted provision so that reference to the Comments has become illegitimate?

An answer appears in the Comments to the 1956 Recommendations. The reasons for this and other changes were only briefly stated. The explanation for this change was as follows: "paragraph (3)(f) was deleted because the old comments were clearly out of date and it was not known when new ones could be prepared."[41]

Revised comments accompanied the 1957 and all subsequent versions of the Code, but without any statutory provision referring to them. In some states the revised Comments had not yet been drafted at the time of the Code's adoption. In others it is highly doubtful that the Comments were laid before the legislators in the form of a committee report explaining the legislation which the legislators were asked to adopt.

It would be wrong, however, to conclude that the Comments are without value to lawyers and to courts. We shall read many opinions in which the Comments are given substantial weight in the reasoning of the

---

**41.** 1956 Recommendations, page 3. Perhaps we face here an engineering problem: How high can the comments lift themselves by their own bootstraps? Are the editors violating their own principles in quoting this comment? See R. Braucher, The Legislative History of the Uniform Commercial Code, 58 Colum.L.Rev. 798, 808–810 (1958).

courts. Surely the Comments may be given at least as much weight as a scholarly article or treatise commenting on the Code. It should be equally clear that the Comments do not approach the weight of legislation. If the statutory provisions adopted by the legislature contradict or fail to support the Comments, those Comments should be examined with care to determine what weight they be given.

The point is significant. We shall see some instances where the Comments contradict the statute. More frequent are instances of enthusiastic discussion in the Comments of significant problems on which the statute is silent.

A thorough job construing the Code calls for using the Comments to make sure one has found the pertinent language of the statute, as a double-check on a tentative construction, and as a secondary aid where the language of the statute is ambiguous. However, students should follow the practice of referring to Comments only **after** the pertinent statutory language has been identified and carefully examined.

## c.  DEFINITIONS

The Official Text of the Code uses words, of course, and the meanings of those words are for the most part not unique, but many words in the Code are defined specially by the Code itself. Anyone working with the Code must have a method of discerning when there may be a special Code definition of a word or phrase. Fortunately, the Code contains ingenious devices to aid users of the Code to recognize specially defined terms and where to find those definitions. A fast and easy way to find many of these definitions is by the list of ''Definitional Cross References'' at the end of the Comments. However, a careful lawyer will not rely on the completeness of these references in the Comments. For a thorough job, one will check Article 1, which contains important provisions applicable to the Code as a whole; Section 1–201 contains the definitions of a great many terms used throughout the Code. In addition, one will check the definitions specially applicable to each Article, usually collected in one of the early sections of an article.

## 6.  WORKING WITH INTERNATIONAL CONVENTIONS

## a.  GENERAL RULES OF INTERPRETATION

Unlike the Uniform Commercial Code, which is part of the jurisprudence of a single nation, international commercial conventions are legally stateless. United States lawyers and judges can approach the Commercial Code from within a recognized American tradition of the construction and application of statutes generally. The special aspects of giving meaning to the UCC, discussed above, are not fundamental departures from the general jurisprudence of statutory interpretation in the United States. International conventions have no similar context.

The Vienna Convention on the Law of Treaties contains standards for interpretation of all treaties, regardless of subject matter.[42] Articles 31 and 32 of that convention are most salient in this regard:

### Article 31 General rule of interpretation

1.   A treaty shall be interpreted in good faith in accordance with the ordinary meaning to be given to the terms of the treaty in their context and in the light of its object and purpose.

2.   The context for the purpose of the interpretation of a treaty shall comprise, in addition to the text, including its preamble and annexes:

(a) any agreement relating to the treaty which was made between all the parties in connexion with the conclusion of the treaty;

(b) any instrument which was made by one or more parties in connexion with the conclusion of the treaty and accepted by the other parties as an instrument related to the treaty.

3.   There shall be taken into account, together with the context:

(a) any subsequent agreement between the parties regarding the interpretation of the treaty or the application of its provisions;

(b) any subsequent practice in the application of the treaty which establishes the agreement of the parties regarding its interpretation;

(c) any relevant rules of international law applicable in the relations between the parties.

4.   A special meaning shall be given to a term if it is established that the parties so intended.

### Article 32 Supplementary means of interpretation

Recourse may be had to supplementary means of interpretation, including the preparatory work of the treaty and the circumstances of its conclusion, in order to confirm the meaning resulting from the application of article 31, or to determine the meaning when the interpretation according to article 31:

(a) leaves the meaning ambiguous or obscure; or

(b) leads to a result which is manifestly absurd or unreasonable.

Typically, the preparatory work that occurred during the drafting and negotiation of international conventions is recorded and preserved. Under accepted principles of public international law, this kind of record (*travaux préparatoires*) may be used as a guide to interpretation of conventions. This is evident in Article 32, and in Article 31(2)(b), of the Vienna Convention.

Commentaries written by respected scholars are a traditional source of international law. Uniform interpretation of international commercial law

---

**42.**   1155 U.N.T.S. 331, 8 I.L.M. 679. This convention was prepared under the aegis of the United Nations. It went into force in 1980. The United States has not ratified this convention.

conventions may be achieved through the work of such scholars whose works are known and respected generally.

When international conventions are negotiated, the product is usually stated in multiple languages and each version is declared to be equally official. International agreements prepared under the auspices of the United Nations are always drafted in six official languages. The Hague Conference and UNIDROIT normally use only two languages, English and French, but sometimes more. The interpretation problems generated by this common form of international law making are a potentially severe impediment to finding a single proper reading of the provisions of the law.

### b. APPLICATION AND INTERPRETATION OF CISG

A problem with comprehending the Convention on Contracts for the International Sale of Goods (CISG) is the absence of captions for the 101 substantive Articles. There are titles for the major divisions of the Convention, Parts, Chapters and Sections, but the Articles are identified only by numbers. There is, therefore, no official detailed table of contents. For anyone working with the Convention, this is a handicap, but that problem is exacerbated in first encounters with the Convention. To alleviate this problem, unofficial tables of contents have been prepared. Your professor may distribute a table of contents prepared by Professor John Honnold, who had a leading role at UNCITRAL when the Convention was negotiated. Another source is a CISG web site maintained by the Pace University Law School.

More than 70 nations are parties to CISG. The jurisprudence of statutory construction within those nations' domestic legal systems are quite diverse. If CISG or any body of international law were viewed through prisms of domestic legal systems, the meaning of the international law would vary with the background of the observer. That result is, of course, inconsistent with the fundamental idea of law as uniform **international** law.

Drafters of CISG included a one-sentence provision on interpretation of the Convention. "In the interpretation of this Convention, regard is to be had to its international character and the need to promote uniformity in its application and the observance of good faith in international trade." CISG 7(1). Reference to the Convention's *international character* and appeal for *uniformity* constitute a rhetorical effort that tries to remind judges and arbitrators not to use parochial approaches to statutory construction in the interpretation of this body of law. Professor Honnold wrote: "To read the words of the Convention with regard for their 'international character' requires that they be projected against an international background. With time, a body of international experience will develop through international case law and scholarly writing."[43] Notwithstanding CISG 7(1), national

---

**43.** J. Honnold, Uniform Law for International Sales § 88 (3d ed. 1999). Professor Honnold suggested that the provisions on interpretation of treaties in the Vienna Convention on the Law of Treaties were not appropriate to CISG provisions that deal with relations

courts applying CISG to international sales sometimes refer to their domestic laws for guidance on the meaning of Articles of the Convention. This "homeward bias" toward domestic laws undermines the CISG objective of uniformity of international sales law since the domestic sales laws vary considerably in substance.[44]

A very useful and influential compilation of the preparation of CISG through many drafts and negotiating rounds is John Honnold, Documentary History of the Uniform Law for International Sales (1989).

A number of highly regarded commentaries on CISG have been published. See, e.g., J. Honnold, Uniform Law for International Sales Under the 1980 United Nations Convention (3d ed. 1999); P. Schlectriem & I. Schwenzer, Commentary on the UN Convention on the International Sale of Goods (2d ed. 2005). Another source of guidance is the CISG Advisory Council, an international group of scholars organized by the Centre for Commercial Law Studies, Queen Mary, University of London and the Institute of International Commercial Law at Pace University Law School. The Advisory Council issues reports on the meaning of selected CISG provisions.

## 7. COMMERCIAL LAWYERS' ROLES AND TASKS

Lawyers play several roles in bringing commercial law to bear on commercial transactions. Lawyers in private practice, commonly organized into law firms, are retained by clients to provide professional services. Similar services may be provided to organization by salaried lawyers such as the lawyers on a corporation's legal staff. Clients retain or employ lawyers to handle commercial legal matters in different ways. A key distinction is between lawyers who serve as advocates and lawyers who serve as advisors and counselors. Lawyer-advocates, sometimes called commercial litigators, represent their clients with respect to contracts or commercial transactions that failed. Lawyer-counselors who represent clients at earlier stages of commercial transactions serve in different ways. In the period when transactions are being negotiated, lawyers may serve as negotiators or drafters of documents, or may provide assistance in countless ways to "close the deal." If transactions later threaten to break down, lawyers may be called on to give counsel on how to deal with the turbulence.

From clients' standpoint, lawyer-counselors or lawyer-litigators earn their fees or their salaries by providing services of value to the clients.

---

between commercial parties because, in his view, the Vienna Convention applied only to treaty obligations of States. Id. § 86.

**44.** Another provision of CISG refers tribunals to domestic law. CISG 7(2) deals with legal issues that arise in transactions that are within the scope of the Convention but for which the Convention has no governing rule. CISG 7(2) provides that tribunals should try to fill the gaps, first, by referring to the general principles on which the Convention is based. If that fails, the fall-back is to refer to domestic law, as determined by the choice-of-law rules of private international law. For discussion of CISG 7(2), see A. Janssen & S. Kiene, The CISG and Its General Principles, in CISG Methodology (Janssen & Meyer, eds. 2009) at 261.

Lawyer-counselors can add significant value by enabling the clients to obtain all or much of the benefits the clients had anticipated when deals were made. Clients appreciate lawyers who can keep them out of controversy or, when controversy arises, can extricate them from the trouble without becoming embroiled in law suits. Lawyer-advocates, on the other hand, rarely add value, even when their advocacy succeeds and their clients prevail in the legal proceedings. Litigants are usually seeking to avoid or limit loss. The transaction costs, delays, and uncounted other negative aspects of being a party to a legal dispute mean that neither side is likely to come out ahead. Even the prevailing parties in commercial disputes are likely to count the transactions as net losses. Lawyers who specialize in commercial litigation cannot expect that most clients will be satisfied with the outcomes. They are likely to be relieved rather than happy about the experience.

Commercial law is one of the tools that is used by lawyer-counselors and by lawyer-advocates. In studying and evaluating the content of commercial law, one can get considerable insight by considering how a tool works for counselors and how it works for litigators. For example, consider how important it may be whether a statutory provision states a "bright line" rule that has clear meaning and sharp edges or broadly states a general principle that must be construed in light of the unique facts and circumstances of particular transactions. Deal makers, it is said, have a greater need for legal certainty, a need that expands when more than two parties are or may become involved. Dispute resolvers have a greater need for rules that achieve just and fair results. The tension between law as a planning device and law as an instrument of justice, while not unique to commercial law, is nonetheless pervasive in that domain. It is a tension that can never be resolved perfectly.

A major part of the grist for study of commercial law consists of reported decisions of courts or arbitrators. Underlying every such opinion is a failed contract or transaction. One sees in these decisions an application of commercial law to resolve disputes. When evaluating decisions in such cases, one's understanding can be deepened by rolling the narratives back to the earlier stages when the deals were set up and when the deals began to break down Very important lessons can be learned by considering when lawyers were first brought into the matter, what the lawyers did, and whether some different professional conduct, at earlier stages, might have produced better outcomes.

Another way of putting the point is this: the professional work of the most valued commercial lawyers is unlikely ever to be seen in the reported judicial opinions. To learn how to be a successful lawyer-counselor in commercial matters, one can be a legal pathologist, searching the remains of failed transactions for ways to avoid such failures in the future.

# PART II

# SALES TRANSACTIONS: DOMESTIC AND INTERNATIONAL LAW

# CHAPTER 2

# BASIC PRINCIPLES

## (A) DOMESTIC UNITED STATES LAW

Principles of law are basic if they are broad and deep in their application. In the United States law of sales, one of the most fundamental problems is the relationship between codified law and common law. Another set of fundamental problems in the law of sales centers on the relationship between the law and the marketplace. In this chapter we consider both sets of basic legal problems.

A number of principles address the problem of the scope of application of Article 2 of the Commercial Code. The first of these to be considered is the extent to which Article 2 has displaced common law, and the nature of that displacement. The initial question can be framed this way: What transactions (or parts of transactions) are governed by the Sales Article and what transactions are governed by other law, usually the common law of contracts?

Article 2 is primarily facilitative in nature. Overwhelmingly, the Article is intended to assist parties to exchange transactions, but broad regulatory provisions overlay the Code. Two of the most important of these are the transcendent obligation that all parties act in good faith in the performance and enforcement of sales contracts and the power of courts to strike down contracts or contract terms that are unconscionable.

## 1. SCOPE OF UNIFORM COMMERCIAL CODE ARTICLE 2

UCC 2–102 declares that it "applies to transactions in goods." The principal transaction, reflected in the title of Article 2, is "sales." The principal actors are "buyers," defined somewhat tautologically in UCC 2–103(1)(a), and "sellers," similarly defined in (1)(d). The core meaning of "sale" is "the passing of title [to goods] from the seller to the buyer for a price." UCC 2–106(1). "Sales" result from "contracts for sale," defined in the same section and divided into "present sales" and "future sales." For the most part, these elementary concepts have clear meanings that do not often blur at the edges.[1]

The same cannot be said of "goods," the object of "sales." The Code defines "goods" as "all things (including specially manufactured goods) which are movable at the time of identification to the contract for sale other than the money in which the price is to be paid, investment securities (Article 8) and things in action." UCC 2–105(1). The manifest rationale for

---

**1.** Revised UCC Article 2 does not change these basic provisions.

using the concept of movability in the definition is to distinguish goods from realty.[2] "Goods" has a clear core of meaning but bristles with difficulties in many settings.[3]

Why does it matter whether or not a contract is for "goods" as defined by Article 2? That question can be answered on multiple levels. As a matter of jurisprudence, it matters because the legislators said so; they exercised their power to establish a body of law for a certain set of commercial transactions, sales of goods, not sales of services, or of intellectual property, or of intangibles, or of real estate, etc. The legislatures determined that the Article was appropriate for transactions in goods, but they made no determination that the Article would be appropriate in other transactions.

That is not an entirely satisfying answer to the pragmatist who asks what is the practical effect of a ruling that a particular transactions is or is not governed by Article 2. For the most part, sales transactions that are not governed by Article 2 are governed by common law. So the question becomes: how different is Article 2 from common law? The answer is complex. Drafters of Article 2 did not set out to make wholesale departures from common law. The stated goal was to simplify, clarify and modernize the law and to give greater deference to commercial practices.[4] The most recent edition of the Restatement of the Law of Contracts, largely a restatement of common law, was written after the Commercial Code had been widely enacted. The drafters of the Restatement were influenced by parts of Article 2. Comment 1 to 1–103 notes that, before the Commercial Code, courts often found that policies of a uniform act were applicable in reason to transactions not expressly covered by the act, and concludes: "Nothing in the Uniform Commercial Code stands in the way of the continuance of such action by the courts." The more that Article 2 and common law converge, the less that the scope provision will have practical effect.

As we will see, judicial disputes about the scope of Article 2 are not rare. Wherever you find cases in which the issue of scope is contested, you can be reasonably sure that there is a significant difference between the applicable provision in Article 2 and the common law. The advocates for the parties are seeking to gain some litigation advantage by doing so. One recurrent situation that arises is the limitations period, the time after which a claim is barred as untimely. The Article 2 limitations period in 2–725 is significantly shorter than the period for common-law contracts.[5] In

---

**2.** Things that are embedded in or attached to realty may be extracted or severed from the real property and thereby become movable. The definition sections of the Article provide that the disattached or severed property becomes goods. 2–105(1) (second sentence), 2–107.

**3.** See, e.g., Annot., What constitutes "goods" within the scope of UCC Article 2, 4 ALR 4th 912.

**4.** UCC 1–103.

**5.** A recent example is Fab–Tech Inc. v. E.I. du Pont de Nemours & Co., 311 Fed. Appx. 443 (2d Cir. 2009). The trial court found that the contract was for services and therefore that the claim was not time-barred. The appellate court found that the contract was within Article 2 and therefore part of the claim was time-barred.

the cases that follow, you will see other instances where the outcomes are similarly affected.

Disputes about the scope of Article 2 often arise in fact patterns where the contracts involve goods plus something else. In this chapter we will consider several of the most commonly contested situations.

*a. GOODS AND SERVICES*

Many familiar transactions require one party to deliver goods and render services for a single price. Would UCC Article 2 or common law govern the whole agreement? Should the contracts be divided, with different law governing its parts, or should transactions treated by the parties as indivisible be placed entirely under or outside of Article 2? The Code gives no guidance to the parties or the courts.[6]

# BMC Industries, Inc. v. Barth Industries, Inc.

United States Court of Appeals, Eleventh Circuit, 1998.
160 F.3d 1322.

■ TJOFLAT, CIRCUIT JUDGE:

This appeal arises from a contract entered into between BMC Industries, Inc., and Barth Industries, Inc., for the design, manufacture, and installation of equipment to automate BMC's production line for unfinished eyeglass lenses. Eighteen months after the delivery date set out in the contract had passed, BMC filed suit against Barth for breach of contract. Barth, in turn, counterclaimed for breach of contract. . . .

A jury resolved the breach of contract and promissory estoppel issues in favor of BMC, and returned a verdict of $3 million against Barth. . . . Barth . . . appealed. We affirm the district court's decision denying Barth judgment as a matter of law. We conclude, however, that the court erroneously instructed the jury on the contract issues, and therefore vacate the judgment against Barth and remand the case for a new trial on these issues. . . .

I.

A

BMC, through its Vision–Ease division, manufactures semi-finished polymer ophthalmic lenses that are used in the production of eyeglasses. These lenses are created by an assembly-line process. First, an employee fills a mold assembly with a monomer fluid, and places the mold assembly on a conveyor. Next, the assembly is inspected and then heated and cured until the monomer solidifies into a plastic lens. Finally, the lens is removed from the mold assembly through a process called "de-clipping and de-gasketing"; an employee removes the spring clip holding the mold assembly

---

**6.** See Annot., Applicability of UCC Article 2 to mixed contracts for sale of goods and services, 5 ALR 4th 501.

together and slices open the rubber gasket that holds the lens. The lens is then packaged and sold to a finished eyeglass retailer.

In order to decrease labor costs, and thereby remain competitive with other lens manufacturers who were utilizing cheaper foreign labor, BMC decided to become the first company to automate portions of its lens manufacturing process. Consequently, in early 1986, BMC commissioned Barth to complete a preliminary design and feasibility study. Barth's subcontractor, Komech, finished the study in June 1986. Based on this study, Barth and BMC entered into a contract (the "Contract") which provided that Barth would "design, fabricate, debug/test and supervise field installation and start up of equipment to automate the operations of mold assembly declipping, clip transport, mold assembly clipping, and mold filling." The Contract, which stated that it was governed by Florida law, listed a price of $515,200 and provided for delivery of four automated production lines by June 1987. The Contract also stated that time was of the essence.

On November 4, 1986, Barth and BMC executed a written amendment to the Contract, extending the delivery date by one month. In February 1987, Barth terminated Komech as design subcontractor, and hired another engineering company, Belcan, in its place. Belcan subsequently redesigned the automation equipment, which delayed Barth's progress and led the parties to execute the second (and last) written amendment, which extended the delivery date to "October 1987."

After this second amendment, Barth continued to experience technical problems and design difficulties that caused repeated delays. The parties did not extend the delivery date beyond October 1987 to accommodate these delays, however. Instead, Barth and BMC each demonstrated a willingness to continue performance under the Contract.

One such delay, for example, occurred in June 1987, when Belcan decided that the equipment design posed a risk of explosion because of the proximity of certain chemicals to electrical components. Although BMC perceived no such risk, it told Barth and Belcan to "go ahead" and redesign the equipment. Barth revised its estimated delivery schedule to account for the resulting delay, listing December 1987 as the new delivery deadline. It sent this schedule to BMC with a cover letter that stated: "Please look over the attached & let me know what you think." BMC's response, if any, is not contained in the record.

This design problem was only one of many technical difficulties that developed; other problems arose with the filling nozzles and mold assembly springs, among other components. Consequently, by October 1987, the amended Contract's delivery deadline, Barth estimated that it could not deliver the equipment until April 1988. BMC executives were still anxious, however, to continue the automation project. Thus, during the spring of 1988, although they protested Barth's failure to deliver the equipment on time, these executives encouraged Barth to continue working on the project.

In June 1988, Barth completed the four automated de-clip/de-gasket machines and delivered them to BMC. Without the entire automated system, however, BMC could not fully test these machines; the whole production line had to be in place.

By August 1988, BMC's mounting apprehension about Barth's ability to perform led it to seek assurance that Barth would be able to complete performance under the Contract. In an effort to obtain such assurance, BMC executives met with Robert Tomsich, a Barth officer (and director).... According to these executives, Tomsich ensured them that Barth would perform the Contract....

Although BMC had considered terminating the Contract and suing Barth for breach, BMC took neither step. Instead, it continued to lead Barth ... to believe that it was determined to finish the project; BMC collaborated with Barth's engineers to overcome difficulties, suggested design changes, and asked Barth whether more money (presumably provided by BMC) would help it complete the equipment in less time.

By January 1989, Barth still had not produced a functioning automation system. Due to time and cost overruns, Barth had invested over $1 million of its own money in the project. BMC previously had agreed to compensate Barth for these additional expenses; consequently, during that month, Tomsich asked BMC for $250,000 to cover some of Barth's cost overruns. One month later, BMC responded with a $100,000 payment, along with a letter stating that BMC was "insisting on Barth's adherence to the projected schedule," and was "not waiving any rights or remedies" for any breach, including "Barth's failure to meet the delivery dates specified in the contract." Barth's latest schedule called for delivery in June 1989.

Barth's delays and setbacks continued throughout the spring of 1989; but while BMC encouraged Barth to carry on, and continued to cooperate with Barth's engineers to solve problems, BMC also became increasingly impatient. In March, and again in April 1989, BMC pointed out Barth's unacceptable failure to meet deadlines.

Near the end of May 1989, Barth notified BMC that it had finally completed the mold assembly filling machine and that it would deliver the equipment F.O.B. Barth's dock in accordance with the Contract. BMC refused delivery of the mold assembly filler, and instead filed this lawsuit on June 5, 1989.

### B.

BMC's breach of contract count alleged that the second written amendment to the Contract established October 1987 as the deadline for Barth's performance. Because Barth failed to deliver the automated equipment by that date, Barth was in default of its contractual obligations. BMC sought damages for Barth's breach in the sum of $6.4 million. Two separate injuries suffered by BMC comprised this measure of damages. First, BMC sought to recover the labor costs that it would have saved had it been able to use the automated equipment rather than pay employees to produce the lenses manually. Because BMC executives predicted that the automated equipment would have a useful life of ten years, BMC sought these lost labor savings for the ten year period from October 1987 until October 1997. Second, BMC sought compensation for what it termed the "working capital effect." This effect is an estimate of the money BMC lost because its capital was tied up paying higher labor costs rather than being used for investment or being used to pay off the company's debt (and thus reducing the interest BMC paid to its creditors).

As an affirmative defense to BMC's breach of contract claim, Barth asserted that BMC's conduct after the October 1987 delivery date had passed amounted to a waiver of the delivery date under Article 2 of the Uniform Commercial Code ("UCC"). Although Barth failed to deliver the machines by October 1987, Barth argued, BMC executives urged Barth to keep working, BMC engineers continued to assist Barth in overcoming technical problems, and BMC executives agreed to increase the purchase price. Therefore, Barth claimed, BMC waived its entitlement to delivery of the machines in October 1987.

Additionally, Barth counterclaimed against BMC for breach of contract. Barth repeated its argument that BMC's conduct amounted to a waiver of the October 1987 delivery date, and asserted that the delivery deadline therefore became indefinite. Because Barth tendered the machines within a reasonable amount of time, Barth substantially performed its contractual obligations. Consequently, Barth claimed, BMC's refusal to accept delivery of the machines in May 1989 constituted breach of the Contract. Barth sought damages totaling $1.13 million, which consisted of the original purchase price of $515,200 specified in the Contract, plus Barth's cost overruns that BMC had agreed to reimburse.

\* \* \*

As an affirmative defense, Barth responded that BMC fraudulently failed to inform Barth of problems BMC was unable to solve in its manual lens production process, and that BMC misrepresented that problems experienced by the automated equipment did not occur when BMC produced lenses manually. Barth claimed that it would not have entered into the Contract had BMC not made these misrepresentations; BMC's own fraud, therefore, barred BMC from recovery on its claims against Barth. Barth also counterclaimed against BMC for fraud, and sought both compensatory and punitive damages.

\* \* \*

At the pretrial conference, the district court concluded that the Contract was predominantly a transaction in services rather than goods, and therefore held that Article 2 of the UCC did not apply. Instead, Florida common law would govern the Contract. That law does not recognize a waiver of a contract term unless the waiver is supported by detrimental reliance or consideration. Consequently, in order to establish a waiver of the October 1987 delivery date, Barth would have to show that it detrimentally relied on, or gave consideration for, BMC's waiver of the delivery date.

. . . The court submitted the . . . issues to the jury using a special verdict form that contained eight interrogatories. In response to the first interrogatory, which asked, "Did Barth breach its contract with BMC?" the jury answered affirmatively, and awarded BMC $3,001,879 in damages. . . . The jury responded "No" to the remaining interrogatories, which asked whether BMC was liable on Barth's counterclaims.

C.

On appeal, Barth contends that the district court erred when it concluded that the UCC did not apply to the Contract, and thus did not govern the waiver issue. Had the court applied the UCC, Barth argues, it would have concluded that BMC waived the October 1987 delivery date, and therefore breached the Contract by refusing to accept delivery in May 1989. Having reached that conclusion, the court would have granted Barth's motion for judgment as a matter of law on the breach of contract issues, and awarded Barth damages in the sum of $1.13 million. Assuming a dispute of material fact on the waiver issue, Barth contends alternatively that BMC's judgment on the breach of contract count should be vacated, and the case remanded for a new trial on that count and its breach of contract counterclaim.

* * *

II.

A.

The district court held that the Contract was predominantly for services rather than goods, and that the UCC was therefore inapplicable. We disagree.

The UCC's Article 2 only applies to "transactions in goods." Fla. Stat. ch. 672–102 (1997). Goods are defined as "all things (including specially manufactured goods) which are movable at the time of identification to the contract for sale other than the money in which the price is to be paid, investment securities . . . and things in action." Fla. Stat. ch. 672.105(1) (1997). A contract that is exclusively for services, therefore, is not governed by Article 2. Courts are frequently faced, however, with contracts involving both goods and services—so-called "hybrid" contracts. Most courts follow the "predominant factor" test to determine whether such hybrid contracts are transactions in goods, and therefore covered by the UCC, or transactions in services, and therefore excluded. See Bonebrake v. Cox, 499 F.2d 951, 960 (8th Cir.1974). Under this test, the court determines "whether their predominant factor, their thrust, their purpose, reasonably stated, is the rendition of service, with goods incidentally involved (e.g., contract with artist for painting) or is a transaction of sale, with labor incidentally involved (e.g., installation of a water heater in a bathroom)." Id. (footnotes omitted). At least one Florida court has implicitly adopted the predominant factor test. See United States Fidelity & Guar. Co. v. North Am. Steel Corp., 335 So. 2d 18, 21 (Fla. 2d DCA 1976) ("Since the predominate nature of the transaction was the furnishing of a product rather than services, we believe that the fabricated pipe could properly be characterized as goods.").

Although courts generally have not found any single factor determinative in classifying a hybrid contract as one for goods or services, courts find several aspects of a contract particularly significant. First, the language of the contract itself provides insight into whether the parties believed the goods or services were the more important element of their agreement. Contractual language that refers to the transaction as a "purchase," for example, or identifies the parties as the "buyer" and "seller," indicates that the transaction is for goods rather than services. See Bonebrake, 499 F.2d at 958 (stating that language referring to "equipment" is peculiar to goods rather than services); Bailey v. Montgomery Ward & Co., 690 P.2d 1280, 1282 (Colo.Ct.App.1984) (holding that a contract that identifies the transaction as a "purchase" and one of the parties as the "customer" signals a transaction in goods); Meeker v. Hamilton Grain Elevator Co., 442 N.E.2d 921, 923 (Ill. App. Ct. 1982) (stating that a contract that calls the parties "seller" and "purchaser" indicates a contract for goods).

Courts also examine the manner in which the transaction was billed; when the contract price does not include the cost of services, or the charge for goods exceeds that for services, the contract is more likely to be for goods. See Triangle Underwriters, Inc. v. Honeywell, Inc., 604 F.2d 737, 743 (2d Cir.1979) (stating that a bill that does not include services indicates a contract for goods); Lincoln Pulp & Paper Co. v. Dravo Corp., 436 F. Supp. 262, 275 & n. 15 (D.Me.1977) (holding that the contract at issue was for services after noting that the bill did not allocate costs between services and goods, and the evidence showed that the cost of the goods was less than half of the contract price).

Movable goods is another hallmark of a contract for goods rather than services. The UCC's definition of goods makes clear the importance of mobility in determining whether a contract is for goods; the UCC states that goods are "all things (including specially manufactured goods) which are movable at the time of identification to the contract for sale." Fla. Stat. ch. 672.105(1) (1997). Noting the importance of mobility, one Florida court held that a contract to edit and publish printed materials was a contract for goods after stating that "the items allegedly furnished by the appellant were specially produced or manufactured and were movable." Lake Wales Publ'g Co. v. Florida Visitor, Inc., 335 So. 2d 335, 336 (Fla. 2d DCA 1976); see also Smith v. Union Supply Co., 675 P.2d 333, 334 (Colo.Ct.App.1983) (holding that a contract to provide the materials and labor for installation of a new roof was a contract for goods because "[t]he materials to be installed ... were 'movable at the time of identification to the contract for sale.' " (quoting Colorado's version of the UCC)).

In this case, the district court relied primarily on Lincoln Pulp & Paper for its conclusion that the contract was for services rather than goods. The contract at issue in Lincoln Pulp & Paper involved the design and construction of a heat and chemical recovery unit in a pulp mill. The district court noted that, similar to Lincoln Pulp & Paper, the Contract obligated Barth to design, manufacture, test, and construct equipment, and also that the Contract's price did not allocate expenses between services and materials. The district court concluded that this case was sufficiently analogous to Lincoln Pulp & Paper to warrant the same result: a determination that the Contract was for services rather than goods.

The question whether a contract is predominantly for goods or services is generally one of fact. See Allmand Assocs., Inc. v. Hercules Inc., 960 F. Supp. 1216, 1223 (E.D.Mich.1997). When there is no genuine issue of material fact concerning the contract's provisions, however, a court may determine the issue as a matter of law. See id. Concluding that there are no material issues of fact as to the terms of the contract, the district court decided as a matter of law that the contract was for services. We review questions of law de novo. See Preserve Endangered Areas of Cobb's History, Inc. v. United States Army Corps of Eng'rs, 87 F.3d 1242, 1246 (11th Cir.1996).

Applying the "predominant factor" test to the Contract, we conclude that it was predominantly a transaction in goods. We reach this conclusion based on the contractual language, the circumstances surrounding the Contract, and the nature of the goods at issue.

Our starting point is the language of the Contract itself, which provides a number of indicia that the parties intended a contract for goods rather than services. First, the Contract is titled "PURCHASE ORDER," a reference that is used repeatedly throughout the document. This title is most instructive, as the parties have chosen to identify their agreement with a name that is almost exclusively used for transactions in goods. Second, the parties refer to themselves in the Contract as the "Buyer" and "Seller." Third, the Contract states that it is a purchase order "for the fabrication and installation of automated *equipment*." (emphasis added). All of this contractual language is "peculiar to goods, not services," Bonebrake, 499 F.2d at 958, and indicates that the parties had a contract for goods in mind.

Additionally, the Contract involves movable goods. Barth designed and fabricated the automated equipment in its own facilities, and planned to move the equipment to BMC's plant only once it was completed. Barth's original offer, which was incorporated into the Contract, included the term "F.O.B. Barth dock," meaning that the equipment was tendered to BMC once it was delivered to Barth's loading dock. Consequently, although Barth was still obligated to install and debug the equipment, it was clearly movable at the time it was identified to the Contract.

Lincoln Pulp & Paper is distinguishable from this case. The district court stated that the Contract price, similar to Lincoln Pulp & Paper, does not allocate costs between services and goods. The district court failed to note, however, that the Contract allocates payments according to delivery of automated equipment; the Contract's payment schedule calls for the delivery and acceptance of each automated equipment line to be met by a $70,050 payment from BMC. If the Contract price were being paid predominantly for Barth's design and engineering services as BMC claims, then the parties would have pegged payments to completion of the engineering and design services, not to the delivery of equipment. Furthermore, while the cost of services made up over half of the contract price in Lincoln Pulp & Paper, the opposite appears to be true in this case. A total of $280,200, which is over half of the contract price, is pegged to the delivery of equipment.

Finally, we note that the court in Lincoln Pulp & Paper stated that "[a] sale of equipment is not removed from the scope of Article 2 merely because the equipment was specially designed and manufactured before delivery or installed by the supplier." 436 F. Supp. at 276 n. 16. In fact, it is not surprising that the Barth–BMC Contract included such a significant services element (i.e., design and manufacturing). Because no other company had successfully automated its eyeglass lens production, Barth had to spend considerable time designing this first-of-its-kind machinery. This necessary services element, however, does not remove the Contract from the category of agreements for specially designed and manufactured equipment to which Article 2 applies.

The other two cases on which BMC relies are also inapposite. Both cases involved parties that clearly contemplated a contract for services. The first case, Wells v. 10–X Mfg. Co., 609 F.2d 248 (6th Cir.1979), involved the production of cloth hunting shirts. In that case, however, the buyer provided all of the materials (except thread) that the manufacturer used to produce the clothing. Id. at 252. Consequently, the manufacturer did not sell goods, only the service of turning the materials into a finished product.

The other case BMC cites, Inhabitants of the City of Saco v. General Elec. Co., 779 F. Supp. 186 (D.Me.1991), involved a contract for the design and construction of a solid waste disposal facility. That case is also distinguishable because it involved a typical construction contract for a non-movable product—the disposal facility. The only movable goods were the materials that were used to construct the immobile structure. Even more significantly, the contractual language in that case clearly identified the contract as a transaction in services. The contract stated that its purpose was "for the furnishing of services in Phase I of the project, and 'to establish the conditions on which Contractor [GE] will propose to furnish services under Phase II'." Id. at 197 (first and second emphases added). Not only did the language state that the contract was for services, it also referred to one of the parties as the "Contractor," a term typically used in services transactions.

### B.

Having determined that the UCC governs this case, we must next apply Article 2's waiver provision to the Contract. The UCC waiver provision states in relevant part:

(2) A signed agreement which excludes modification or recession except by a signed writing cannot be otherwise modified or rescinded. . . .

(4) Although an attempt at modification or rescission does not satisfy the requirements of subsection (2) or (3) [regarding the statute of frauds] it can operate as a *waiver.*

(5) A party who has made a waiver affecting an executory portion of the contract may retract the waiver by reasonable notification received by the other party that strict performance will be required of any term waived, unless the retraction would be unjust in view of a material change of position in reliance on the waiver.

Fla. Stat. ch. 672.209 (1997) (emphasis added).

### 1.

Although the UCC does not specifically lay out the elements of waiver, we have stated that waiver requires "(1) the existence at the time of the waiver a right, privilege, advantage, or benefit which may be waived; (2) the actual constructive knowledge thereof; and (3) an intention to relinquish such right, privilege, advantage, or benefit." Dooley v. Weil (In re Garfinkle), 672 F.2d 1340, 1347 (11th Cir. 1982). Conduct may constitute waiver of a contract term, but such an implied waiver must be demonstrated by clear evidence. See American Somax Ventures v. Touma, 547 So. 2d 1266, 1268 (Fla. 4th DCA 1989). Waiver may be implied when a party's actions are inconsistent with continued retention of the right. See First Pa. Bank, N.A. v. Oreck, 357 So. 2d 743, 744 (Fla. 4th DCA 1978).

As an initial matter, we must determine whether, under the UCC, waiver must be accompanied by detrimental reliance. Although it is settled that waiver under Florida common law must be supported by valid consideration or detrimental reliance, see Masser v. London Operating Co., 106 Fla. 474, 145 So. 72 (1932), courts disagree on whether the UCC retains this requirement. We conclude, however, that the UCC does not require consideration or detrimental reliance for waiver of a contract term.

Our conclusion follows from the plain language of subsections 672.209(4) and (5). While subsection (4) states that an attempted modification that fails may still constitute a waiver, subsection (5) provides that the waiver may be retracted unless the non-waiving party relies on the waiver. Consequently, the statute recognizes that waivers may exist in the absence of detrimental reliance—these are the retractable waivers referred to in subsection (5). Only this interpretation renders meaning to subsection (5), because reading subsection (4) to require detrimental reliance for all waivers means that waivers would never be retractable. See Wisconsin Knife Works v. National Metal Crafters, 781 F.2d 1280, 1291 (7th Cir.1986) (Easterbrook, J., dissenting) (noting that reading a detrimental reliance requirement into the UCC would eliminate the distinction between subsections (4) and (5)). Subsection (5) would therefore be meaningless.

At least one Florida court implicitly agrees with this conclusion; in Linear Corp. v. Standard Hardware Co., 423 So.2d 966 (Fla. 1st DCA 1982), the court held that a contract term had been waived despite the absence of any facts showing detrimental reliance. The court in Linear addressed a contract between a manufacturer and a retailer for the sale of electronic security devices. The contract included a provision stating that the manufacturer would not repurchase any devices the retailer was unable to sell, and another term providing that contract modifications must be in writing. Despite this contractual language, the retailer filed suit claiming that the manufacturer subsequently made an oral agreement to repurchase unsold devices, but failed to adhere to this oral agreement.

Citing chapter 672.209(4), the court concluded that the parties' conduct demonstrated that they had waived the requirement that modifications be in writing, and therefore gave effect to the oral modification. See id. at 968. The court recognized this waiver despite the apparent absence of any detrimental reliance by the retailer—in fact the court never even mentioned any reliance requirement for waiver under the UCC. Consequently, the court implicitly held that a contract term could be waived without the existence of detrimental reliance by the non-waiving party.

Although other courts have held that waiver requires reliance under the UCC, those courts have ignored the UCC's plain language. The leading case espousing this view of waiver is Wisconsin Knife Works v. National Metal Crafters, 781 F.2d 1280 (7th Cir.1986) (addressing section 2–209 of the model version of the UCC, from which Florida adopted section 672.209 verbatim), in which a panel of the Seventh Circuit addressed a contract that included a term prohibiting oral modifications, and considered whether an attempted oral modification could instead constitute a waiver. Writing for the majority, Judge Posner concluded that the UCC's subsection (2), which gives effect to "no oral modification" provisions, would become superfluous if contract terms could be waived without detrimental reliance. Judge Posner reasoned that if attempted oral modifications that were unenforceable because of subsection (2) were nevertheless enforced as waivers under subsection (4), then subsection (2) is "very nearly a dead letter." Id. at 1286. According to Judge Posner, there must be some difference between modification and waiver in order for both subsections (2) and (4) to have meaning. This difference is waiver's detrimental reliance requirement.[19]

---

**19.** Contrary to our reasoning above, Judge Posner claims that reading a reliance requirement into waiver under subsection (4) is not inconsistent with subsection (5). According to Judge Posner, subsection (5) is broader than subsection (4), covering waivers other than mere attempts at oral modification. Judge Posner argues as an example that subsection (5) covers express waivers that are written and signed. See id. at 1287. In dissent, however, Judge Easterbrook convincingly dissects this argument. As Judge Easterbrook explains, subsection (5) is narrower than subsection (4)—limiting the effect of waivers that are not detrimentally relied upon—not the reverse as Judge Posner claims. Furthermore, Judge Easterbrook demonstrates that subsection (5) cannot cover express written and signed waivers because such writings are not waivers, but rather effective written modifications under subsection (2). See id. at 1291 (Easterbrook, J., dissenting).

Judge Posner, however, ignores a fundamental difference between modifications and waivers: while a party that has agreed to a contract modification cannot cancel the modification without giving consideration for the cancellation, a party may unilaterally retract its waiver of a contract term provided it gives reasonable notice. The fact that waivers may unilaterally be retracted provides the difference between subsections (2) and (4) that allows both to have meaning. We therefore conclude that waiver under the UCC does not require detrimental reliance. Consequently, without reaching the issue of detrimental reliance, we consider whether BMC waived the Contract's October 1987 delivery date.

2.

Applying the elements of waiver to the facts before us, we hold as a matter of law that BMC waived the October 1987 delivery date. The October 1987 delivery date was a waivable contract right, of which BMC had actual knowledge. We also conclude that BMC's conduct impliedly demonstrated an intent to relinquish that right.

* * *

BMC argues, however, that while it agreed to delay enforcing its rights against Barth ..., it did not waive those rights. BMC's argument defies logic. ...

BMC's own complaint buttresses our conclusion that BMC waived the October 1987 delivery date. According to BMC's complaint, [Barth's parent company] promised "that Barth would *meet dates*, performance and reliability criteria under the agreement, as amended," and that [the parent] "ensured that the equipment was *timely* completed and delivered to BMC in Florida." (emphasis added). Because the October 1987 delivery date had already passed, however, Barth could not "meet dates" or "timely" complete the equipment unless the delivery date had been extended.

Furthermore, BMC's course of dealing with Barth evidenced BMC's waiver of the October 1987 delivery date, because BMC failed timely to demand compliance with that contract term or terminate the Contract and file suit. When a delivery date passes without the seller's delivery, the buyer must object within a reasonable time and warn the seller that it is in breach. See KLT Indus., Inc. v. Eaton Corp., 505 F. Supp. 1072, 1079 (E.D.Mich.1981); see also Harrison v. City of Tampa, 247 F. 569, 572 (S.D.Fla.1918) ("I do not recognize any principle by which one party to a contract, after a breach by the other party, may continue acting under such contract to some future time, and then abrogate the contract by reason of such former breach.").

Although BMC maintained at trial that Barth breached the contract as of October 1987, BMC did not tell Barth it intended to terminate the contract and hold Barth liable for the breach until May 1989. In fact, the earliest indication from BMC that it was considering termination was August 1988, when BMC executives met with Tomsich to seek assurance that Barth would perform. As we have already stated, however, the result of that meeting was a waiver of the October 1987 delivery date, not a timely exercise of BMC's right to terminate the Contract. BMC did not warn Barth in earnest of its intent to terminate until February 1989, when BMC sent Barth a letter along with $100,000 of the $250,000 payment Tomsich had requested at the August 1988 meeting. This letter warned Barth that BMC was not waiving its rights and remedies for Barth's failure to meet contractual delivery dates. BMC warned Barth again in March when it sent a letter advising of its intent to "hold [Barth] responsible, both for the initial breach and for all failures to meet subsequently promised dates."

Until 1989, however, BMC continued to act as though both parties were bound by the Contract and that Barth was not in default of its obligations: the October 1987 delivery date passed without comment from BMC; engineers from BMC frequently provided advice or assistance to help Barth personnel overcome technical problems; BMC executives frequently visited Barth's production facilities and encouraged Barth to continue working to complete the equipment; BMC even continued to spend money on the project—in December 1987, over one month after the October 1987 delivery date had passed, BMC purchased an additional $71,075 worth of springs and tooling for the machines. In sum, rather than terminating the Contract, or at least warning Barth that it was in breach after the October 1987 delivery date had passed, BMC continued to act as though the Contract remained in effect.

This is not to say that BMC never complained that Barth had missed deadlines; BMC executives frequently expressed their concern and disappointment that the project was so far behind schedule. On April 5, 1988, for example, the Chairman, President, and CEO of BMC sent a letter to Barth in which he stated: "The project is well behind schedule, and each day of delay represents lost savings for Vision–Ease. I hope that Barth will exert every effort to ensure the speedy completion and installation of the equipment and avoid any further delay." But while BMC complained of delays, it never declared Barth in default or terminated the contract—instead, BMC told Barth to keep working. After Barth had spent an additional eighteen months of time and money and, according to Barth, was prepared to deliver the machines, however, BMC suddenly decided to terminate the Contract. This BMC could not do.

The UCC states that when a contractual delivery date is waived, delivery must be made within a reasonable time. See Fla. Stat. ch. 672.309(1) (1997); KLT Indus., Inc. v. Eaton Corp., 505 F. Supp. 1072, 1079 (E.D.Mich.1981). Consequently, because BMC waived the October 1987 delivery date, Barth was only obligated to deliver the machines within a reasonable time period. We remand this case to the district court for a new trial on the question of whether Barth tendered the machines within a reasonable time period.[23]

* * *

---

**23.** On remand, if the jury concludes that Barth did not deliver the machines within a reasonable time period, then BMC will prevail on its breach of contract claim against Barth.

IV.

For the foregoing reasons, we hold that the district court erred in concluding that the UCC did not apply to the Contract. Furthermore, we conclude that BMC waived the October 1987 delivery date. We therefore VACATE the district court's judgment against Barth and REMAND the case to the district court for retrial of BMC's claims against Barth as well as Barth's counterclaims in accordance with the UCC. . . .

## NOTES

**(1) The "Predominant Factor" Test.** Lacking a statutory standard, courts have created a test to determine whether hybrid contracts for goods and services are covered—in entirety—by Article 2 or by common law, the so-called "predominant factor" test. Is that a sound solution? Why not apply Article 2 only to the goods portion of the contract? As we will see in coming chapters, Article 2 contains a set of provisions that protect a buyer's title to goods and another set of provisions that govern a seller's obligation as to the quality of goods. Neither seems to apply to the service portions of hybrid contracts. Other Article 2 provisions and their common-law counterparts seem to apply necessarily to the contract as a whole. It does not make sense, for example, to apply different rules on the length of the limitations period or the requirement of a writing or the admission of parol evidence to only the goods or only the services portion of hybrid contracts. The issue in *BMC Industries* was whether the buyer had waived the seller's duty to deliver by a specified date. Is that an issue that could have been decided separately for goods and services?

The Court of Appeals decided first that the transaction was governed by Article 2 (II–A of the opinion) and, after that, addressed the particular issue of waiver (II–B). Should the decision on whether the governing law is the Code or common law be sensitive to the nature of the particular issue before the court? If this seller's delay was predominantly caused by difficulty in solving design problems, should that have lead the court to apply the Florida common-law to the waiver issue?

In applying its version of the "predominant factor" test, the Court of Appeals relied heavily on the parties' choice of words in their agreement, the payment terms, and that fact that the equipment would be movable. What language could the parties have used that would have signaled to a court that they viewed the transaction as predominantly one for services? How were the payment terms inconsistent with the possibility that this seller's purported ability to design a novel piece of equipment was the major factor that led to the agreement? Why was it relevant to the choice of law for this hybrid contract that, in the end, the equipment would be movable?

---

BMC's damages should then be calculated according to Fla. Stat. ch. 672.713 (1997). If instead, however, the jury finds that BMC terminated the contract before a reasonable time had passed, then Barth will prevail on its counterclaim. BMC has stipulated that Barth is entitled to recover $1.13 million if it prevails.

**(2) "Specially Manufactured Goods."** The Article 2 definition of goods provides, parenthetically, that the definition includes "specially manufactured goods."[7] The Court of Appeals quoted that language, but did not rely on it in its analysis. Instead the court applied the judicially formulated "predominant factor" test. Should the court have given more weight to the statutory language?

**(3) Waiver.** The drafters of Article 2 elected to treat some matters of contract law. Among these were the rules regarding contract modification and waiver of contract rights. As to modification, the drafters intentionally modified the common law by eliminating the requirement of consideration so that a modification of only one party's obligations would be enforceable, 2–209(1). They reset the law regarding a contract term that purported to preclude oral modification or rescission, 2–209(2), and clarified the application of the statute of frauds to modification agreements, 2–209(3). The impact of the provisions of (2) and (3) would make some purported modification agreements unenforceable. This apparently led the drafters to provide that evidence that might otherwise have established a modification might be sufficient to show a contract waiver, 2–209(4). Is there any indication that the drafters intended thereby to change the common law on waiver? Is the provision on retraction of waivers, 2–209(5), a departure from common law? Is Comment 5 helpful?

**(4) The Uniform Commercial Code: Which Version?** The NCCUSL and the ALI, sponsors of the Uniform Commercial Code, are not legislatures empowered to create law. An Article of the Commercial Code takes effect only when duly enacted as a state or federal statute. In that process, legislatures may—and sometimes do—depart from the Official Text in a non-uniform way. A practicing lawyer or judge, applying the Code, must use a version enacted into law and in force when the disputed transaction occurred. In *BMC Industries*, the federal court, acting under diversity of citizenship jurisdiction, applied the Florida version of the Code as well as the Florida common-law waiver.[8] Throughout the course, you will see citations to state-enacted versions of the Code in the opinions of federal and state courts.[9]

Because of possible variations among the state-enacted versions of the Code, it is sometimes a necessary step in litigation to identify which state's version governs the issue arising in a dispute. The Commercial Code's

---

**7.** A similar term appeared in § 5 of the Sale of Goods Act and in § 5 of the Uniform Sales Act, 19th century laws drafted in the early stage of the Industrial Revolution, when commercial practices may have differed substantially from those found today.

**8.** Federal courts have subject-matter jurisdiction to entertain cases in which the parties are from different jurisdictions, including a foreign litigant suing a United States party. In these so-called "diversity cases," federal district courts are required to apply the law of the state in which they sit. Erie Railroad Co. v. Tompkins, 304 U.S. 64, 58 S.Ct. 817, 82 L.Ed. 1188 (1938).

**9.** The Eleventh Circuit Court disagreed with a decision of the Seventh Circuit on the meaning of 2–209(4). In doing so, the Eleventh Circuit described the Seventh Circuit as having applied "the model version of the UCC." Careful reading of the Seventh Circuit majority and dissenting opinions makes clear that that court was applying the Wisconsin version of 2–209. Both Wisconsin and Florida had enacted the Official Text without variation.

general choice of law provision is found in UCC 1–301. In *BMC Industries*, the contract of the parties specified that Florida law governed.

**(5) Litigation: Which Court?** A contract may provide that disputes must be resolved in a particular court or must be submitted to arbitration. Absent such terms, the aggrieved party may initiate proceedings in a court of its choosing, so long as that court is authorized to hear the submitted dispute (commonly referred to as jurisdiction over the subject matter) and is able to compel the defendant to respond to the complaint (jurisdiction over the person of the defendant). Subject-matter jurisdiction is determined by the domestic law of the place of the forum. Personal jurisdiction is a more complex matter, only partly determined by domestic law. In the United States, the extent of personal jurisdiction is restricted by the standard of due process of law in the Fourteenth Amendment of the U.S. Constitution.[10] In *BMC Industries* the plaintiff brought suit in a United States federal district court in Florida.

———

*Construction contracts.* Improvement of real estate takes many forms. The most common are construction and repair of buildings. Another kind of

———

**10.** See Vermeulen v. Renault, U.S.A. Inc., 965 F.2d 1014 (11th Cir.1992). A Georgia resident sued Regie Nationale Des Usines Renault (RNUR), the French automobile manufacturer of LeCar, and other defendants, for serious injuries sustained as a result of negligent manufacture and design of the LeCar passenger restraint system. Defendants removed the case from the state court, where the plaintiff had filed, to federal district court. That court granted the French corporation's motion to dismiss for lack of personal jurisdiction. The Court of Appeals for the Eleventh Circuit reversed.

At that time, RNUR sold its automobiles to American Motors Corporation (AMC), which resold them in the United States through one of its subsidiaries. The RNUR–AMC master agreement stated that title to the vehicles passed to AMC in France and that AMC would take full responsibility for marketing and distributing RNUR vehicles in the United States. The agreement also contemplated that RNUR would be involved in decisions affecting marketing and could advise on suggested retail prices for RNUR vehicles, that RNUR would provide assistance in training AMC personnel on servicing and repair of RNUR vehicles, and that RNUR retained the full and exclusive ownership of the ''Renault'' trademark. The AMC subsidiary provided retail warranties to U.S. buyers of RNUR vehicles, but RNUR agreed to reimburse AMC for warranty work performed by AMC or authorized dealers.

The Eleventh Circuit held that RNUR had purposefully availed itself of the privilege of conducting business in Georgia because (1) it had designed its vehicles to accommodate the American market, and (2) RNUR had taken some part with AMC's conducting of a nationwide advertising campaign in the U.S., and (3) that RNUR had played a role in AMC's establishment of Renault dealerships in the U.S., including six dealerships in Georgia, and (4) RNUR retained ultimate control of the U.S. distribution network through various provisions in the master agreement with AMC.

Compare Asahi Metal Industry Co., Ltd. v. Superior Court of California, 480 U.S. 102, 107 S.Ct. 1026, 94 L.Ed.2d 92 (1987) (indemnity suit by Taiwanese tire manufacturer, which had sold tires in California, against Japanese manufacturer of valve incorporated into the tire for which tire manufacturer had incurred liability in California. The Court held that exercise of jurisdiction did not comport with traditional notions of fair play and substantial justice and therefore violated the Due Process Clause); cf. World–Wide Volkswagen Corp. v. Woodson, 444 U.S. 286, 100 S.Ct. 559, 62 L.Ed.2d 490 (1980).

improvement is the construction of roads and bridges, railroads, airports, etc. Contractors engaged to do this kind of work will need a lot of materials, as well as labor. Construction contracts are not within the scope of Article 2 if the obligation of the contractors is to provide a completed improvement. Thus, contracts to build a house or a "turn key" facility are not deemed to involve transactions in goods. Even though the materials to be incorporated into the improvement were originally goods and, in the completed project, may retain their identity as goods that have been affixed to the real estate, contractors do not "sell" goods; what the contractors commit to provide is not movable. See UCC 2–105(1).

A construction project is likely to have a congeries of lesser contracts, some of which are indisputably contracts for sales of goods. A contract by a lumber yard to supply lumber or bricks to a builder is an Article 2 contract between those parties. Sometimes, however, materials suppliers also engage to do work with the materials at the site of an improvement. As with equipment acquisition transactions, the value of the additional work may begin to eclipse the value of the materials. A case of this kind arose in New York, soon after Article 2 had been adopted there. The contract was to supply and install the structural steel necessary for a bridge. Three levels of the New York courts struggled inconclusively with the question of characterization. In the end, the Court of Appeals (the highest court of that state) bypassed the issue on the view that the questions presented in that case would be decided the same way whether Article 2 or the common law applied. Schenectady Steel Co. v. Bruno Trimpoli General Construction Co., 34 N.Y.2d 939, 316 N.E.2d 875, 359 N.Y.S.2d 560 (1974).

*Service contracts.* Many service providers deliver products in connection with performance of their service functions. At common law, service of food in a restaurant was considered an "uttering" and not a sale. Article 2 does not purport to reverse the characterization generally, but declares that such a transaction is a sale for purpose of one section of Article 2, the section on the implied warranty of merchantable quality, 2–314. Lawyers prepare and deliver to their clients, documents such as contract forms, wills and trust instruments. Physicians and surgeons administer medications and insert medical devices in patients. Architects and engineers prepare and deliver drawings and specifications. Are any of these transactions in goods?

### b.  GOODS AND INFORMATION

We live today in what is often called the Age of Information.[11] Much of what people buy and sell is information, knowledge, know-how, and the like. Education and entertainment (there is a difference) involve transfers of information. Technology is the heart of the process of economic growth and development. Currently, rapid advances in information technology are reshaping the economy in fundamental ways. One application of information technology is the input of amounts of information into products. A set

---

11.  See M. Castells, The Information Age: Economy, Society and Culture (1996).

of legal principles fashioned in the 19th century is hard pressed to deal with transactions in which a core value in an exchange is information.

Information tends to become a commodity when it is packaged and delivered. It is easy to characterize printed and bound books as "goods." With the advent of digitalization of information, vast amounts of data can be installed into chips and diskettes and other devices or can be delivered directly (downloaded) from one computer to another without ever being embodied in a tangible object. One kind of such information that often comes in a device is "software."

As transactions in information proliferated, with some transaction failures that led to litigation, lawyers and judges had to characterize the transactions in order to identify the governing law. Some argued that these transactions should be governed by Article 2 of the Uniform Commercial Code. Others contended that the common law should apply. The following early case is illustrative.

## Advent Systems Limited v. Unisys Corp.

United States Court of Appeals, Third Circuit, 1991.
925 F.2d 670.

■ WEIS, C.J.

In this diversity case we conclude that computer software is a good within the Uniform Commercial Code; in the circumstances here a non-exclusive requirements contract complies with the statute of frauds; and expert testimony on future lost profits based on prior projections is suspect when actual market performance data are available. Because the district court ruled that the Code did not apply, we will grant a new trial on a breach of contract claim. . . .

Plaintiff, Advent Systems Limited, is engaged primarily in the production of software for computers. As a result of its research and development efforts, by 1986 the company had developed an electronic document management system (EDMS), a process for transforming engineering drawings and similar documents into a computer data base.

Unisys Corporation manufactures a variety of computers. As a result of information gained by its wholly-owned United Kingdom subsidiary during 1986, Unisys decided to market the document management system in the United States. In June 1987 Advent and Unisys signed two documents, one labeled "Heads of Agreement" (in British parlance "an outline of agreement") and, the other, "Distribution Agreement."

In these documents, Advent agreed to provide the software and hardware making up the document systems to be sold by Unisys in the United States. Advent was obligated to provide sales and marketing material and manpower as well as technical personnel to work with Unisys employees in building and installing the document systems. The agreement was to continue for two years, subject to automatic renewal or termination on notice.

During the summer of 1987, Unisys attempted to sell the document system to ARCO, a large oil company, but was unsuccessful. Nevertheless, progress on the sales and training programs in the United States was satisfactory, and negotiations for a contract between Unisys (UK) and Advent were underway.

The relationship, however, soon came to an end. Unisys, in the throes of restructuring, decided it would be better served by developing its own document system and in December 1987 told Advent their arrangement had ended. Unisys also advised its UK subsidiary of those developments and, as a result, negotiations there were terminated.

Advent filed a complaint in the district court alleging ... breach of contract.... The district court ruled at pretrial that the Uniform Commercial Code did not apply because although goods were to be sold, the services aspect of the contract predominated.

A jury ... awarded damages to Advent in the sum of $4,550,000 on the breach of contract claim....

On appeal ... Unisys contends that the relationship between it and Advent was one for the sale of goods and hence subject to the terms of the statute of frauds in the Uniform Commercial Code. Because the agreements lacked an express provision on quantity, Unisys insists that the statute of frauds bans enforcement. In addition, Unisys contends that the evidence did not support the damage verdict.

\* \* \*

## II.  SOFTWARE AND THE UNIFORM COMMERCIAL CODE

The district court ruled that as a matter of law the arrangement between the two parties was not within the Uniform Commercial Code and, consequently, the statute of frauds was not applicable. As the district court appraised the transaction, provisions for services outweighed those for products and, consequently, the arrangement was not predominantly one for the sale of goods.

In the "Heads of Agreement" Advent and Unisys purported to enter into a "joint business collaboration." Advent was to modify its software and hardware interfaces to run initially on equipment not manufactured by Unisys but eventually on Unisys hardware. It was Advent's responsibility to purchase the necessary hardware. "In so far as Advent has successfully completed [some of the processing] of software and hardware interfaces," Unisys promised to reimburse Advent to the extent of $150,000 derived from a "surcharge" on products purchased.

Advent agreed to provide twelve man-weeks of marketing manpower, but with Unisys bearing certain expenses. Advent also undertook to furnish an experienced systems builder to work with Unisys personnel at Advent's prevailing rates, and to provide sales and support training for Unisys staff as well as its customers.

The Distribution Agreement begins with the statement, "Unisys desires to purchase, and Advent desires to sell, on a non-exclusive basis, certain of Advent hardware products and software licenses for resale worldwide." Following a heading "Subject Matter of Sales," appears this sentence, "(a) Advent agrees to sell hardware and license software to Unisys, and Unisys agrees to buy from Advent the products listed in Schedule A." Schedule A lists twenty products, such as computer cards, plotters, imagers, scanners and designer systems.

Advent was to invoice Unisys for each product purchased upon shipment, but to issue separate invoices for maintenance fees. The cost of the support services "was set at 3% per annum of the prevailing Advent user list price of each software module for which Unisys is receiving revenue from a customer." Services included field technical bulletins, enhancement and maintenance releases, telephone consultation, and software patches, among others. At no charge to Unisys, Advent was to provide publications such as installation manuals, servicing and adjustment manuals, diagnostic operation and test procedures, sales materials, product brochures and similar items. In turn, Unisys was to "employ resources in performing marketing efforts" and develop "the technical ability to be thoroughly familiar" with the products.

In support of the district court's ruling that the U.C.C. did not apply, Advent contends that the agreement's requirement of furnishing services did not come within the Code. Moreover, the argument continues, the "software" referred to in the agreement as a "product" was not a "good" but intellectual property outside the ambit of the Uniform Commercial Code.

Because software was a major portion of the "products" described in the agreement, this matter requires some discussion. Computer systems consist of "hardware" and "software." Hardware is the computer machinery, its electronic circuitry and peripheral items such as keyboards, readers, scanners and printers. Software is a more elusive concept. Generally speaking, "software" refers to the medium that stores input and output data as well as computer programs. The medium includes hard disks, floppy disks, and magnetic tapes.

In simplistic terms, programs are codes prepared by a programmer that instruct the computer to perform certain functions. When the program is transposed onto a medium compatible with the computer's needs, it becomes software. . . .

The increasing frequency of computer products as subjects of commercial litigation has led to controversy over whether software is a "good" or intellectual property. The Code does not specifically mention software.

In the absence of express legislative guidance, courts interpret the Code in light of commercial and technological developments. The Code is designed "to simplify, clarify and modernize the law governing commercial transactions" and "to permit the continued expansion of commercial practices." 13 Pa. Cons. Stat. Ann. § 1102 (Purdon 1984). As the Official Commentary makes clear:

> This Act is drawn to provide flexibility so that, since it is intended to be a semi-permanent piece of legislation, it will provide its own machinery for expansion of commercial practices. It is intended to make it possible for the law embodied in this Act to be developed by the courts in the light of unforeseen and new circumstances and practices.

Id. comment 1.

The Code "applies to transactions in goods." 13 Pa. Cons. Stat. Ann. § 2102 (Purdon 1984). Goods are defined as "all things (including specially manufactured goods) which are movable at the time of the identification for sale." Id. at § 2105. The Pennsylvania courts have recognized that " 'goods' has a very extensive meaning" under the U.C.C. Duffee v. Judson, 251 Pa. Super. 406, 380 A.2d 843, 846 (1977); see also Lobianco v. Property Protection, Inc., 292 Pa. Super. 346, 437 A.2d 417 (1981) ("goods" under U.C.C. embraces every species of property other than real estate, choses in action, or investment securities.).

Our Court has addressed computer package sales in other cases, but has not been required to consider whether the U.C.C. applied to software per se. See Chatlos Systems, Inc. v. National Cash Register Corp., 635 F.2d 1081 (3d Cir.1980) (parties conceded that furnishing the plaintiff with hardware, software and associated services was governed by the U.C.C.); see also Carl Beasley Ford, Inc. v. Burroughs Corporation, 361 F.Supp. 325 (E.D.Pa.1973) (U.C.C. applied without discussion), aff'd, 493 F.2d 1400 (3d Cir.1974). Other Courts of Appeals have also discussed transactions of this nature. RRX Industries, Inc. v. Lab–Con, Inc., 772 F.2d 543 (9th Cir.1985) (goods aspects of transaction predominated in a sale of a software system); Triangle Underwriters, Inc. v. Honeywell, Inc., 604 F.2d 737, 742–43 (2d Cir.1979) (in sale of computer hardware, software, and customized software goods aspects predominated; services were incidental).

Computer programs are the product of an intellectual process, but once implanted in a medium are widely distributed to computer owners. An analogy can be drawn to a compact disc recording of an orchestral rendition. The music is produced by the artistry of musicians and in itself is not a "good," but when transferred to a laser-readable disc becomes a readily merchantable commodity. Similarly, when a professor delivers a lecture, it is not a good, but, when transcribed as a book, it becomes a good.

That a computer program may be copyrightable as intellectual property does not alter the fact that once in the form of a floppy disc or other medium, the program is tangible, movable and available in the marketplace. The fact that some programs may be tailored for specific purposes need not alter their status as "goods" because the Code definition includes "specially manufactured goods."

The topic has stimulated academic commentary[2] with the majority espousing the view that software fits within the definition of a "good" in the U.C.C.

Applying the U.C.C. to computer software transactions offers substantial benefits to litigants and the courts. The Code offers a uniform body of law on a wide range of questions likely to arise in computer software disputes: implied warranties, consequential damages, disclaimers of liability, the statute of limitations, to name a few.

The importance of software to the commercial world and the advantages to be gained by the uniformity inherent in the U.C.C. are strong policy arguments favoring inclusion. The contrary arguments are not persuasive, and we hold that software is a "good" within the definition in the Code.

The relationship at issue here is a typical mixed goods and services arrangement. The services are not substantially different from those generally accompanying package sales of computer systems consisting of hardware and software. See Chatlos Systems, Inc. v. National Cash Register Corp., 479 F. Supp. 738, 741 (D.N.J.1979); Beasley Ford, 361 F. Supp. at 328.

Although determining the applicability of the U.C.C. to a contract by examining the predominance of goods or services has been criticized, we see no reason to depart from that practice here. As we pointed out in De Filippo v. Ford Motor Co., 516 F.2d 1313, 1323 (3d Cir.), cert. denied, 423 U.S. 912 (1975), segregating goods from non-goods and insisting "that the Statute of Frauds apply only to a portion of the contract, would be to make the contract divisible and impossible of performance within the intention of the parties."

We consider the purpose or essence of the contract. Comparing the relative costs of the materials supplied with the costs of the labor may be helpful in this analysis, but not dispositive. Compare RRX, 772 F.2d at 546 ("essence" of the agreement) with Triangle, 604 F.2d at 743 ("compensation" structure of the contract).

In this case the contract's main objective was to transfer "products." The specific provisions for training of Unisys personnel by Advent were but a small part of the parties' contemplated relationship.

The compensation structure of the agreement also focuses on "goods." The projected sales figures introduced during the trial demonstrate that in

---

**2.** Among the articles and notes that have reviewed extant case law are: Boss & Woodward, Scope of the Uniform Commercial Code; Survey of Computer Contracting Cases, 43 Bus. Law. 1513 (1988); Owen, The Application of Article 2 of the Uniform Commercial Code To Computer Contracts, 14 N. Kentucky L. Rev. 277 (1987); Rodau, Computer Software: Does Article 2 of the Uniform Commercial Code Apply, 35 Emory L.J. 853 (1986); Holmes, Application of Article Two of the Uniform Commercial Code to Computer System Acquisitions, 9 Rutgers Computer & Technology L.J. 1 (1982); Note, Computer Software As A Good Under the Uniform Commercial Code: Taking a Byte Out of the Intangibility Myth, 65 B.U.L. Rev. 129 (1985); Note, Computer Programs as Goods Under the U.C.C., 77 Mich. L. Rev. 1149 (1979).

the contemplation of the parties the sale of goods clearly predominated. The payment provision of $150,000 for developmental work which Advent had previously completed, was to be made through individual purchases of software and hardware rather than through the fees for services and is further evidence that the intellectual work was to be subsumed into tangible items for sale.

We are persuaded that the transaction at issue here was within the scope of the Uniform Commercial Code and, therefore, the judgment in favor of the plaintiff must be reversed.

## III.   THE STATUTE OF FRAUDS

This brings us to the Unisys contention that the U.C.C. statute of frauds bars enforcement of the agreement because the writings do not contain a quantity term.

Section 2–201(a) provides that a contract for the sale of goods of $500 or more is not enforceable unless in writing. "[A] contract . . . is not enforceable . . . unless there is some writing sufficient to indicate that a contract for sale has been made. . . . A writing is not insufficient because it omits . . . a term agreed upon but the contract is not enforceable . . . beyond the quantity of goods shown in such writing." 13 Pa. Cons. Stat. Ann. § 2201(a) (Purdon 1984). The comment to this section states that although the required writing need not contain all the material terms "there are three definite and invariable requirements as to the memorandum," one of which is that "it must specify a quantity." Id. comment 1.

\* \* \*

The circumstances here do not require us to adopt an open-ended reading of the statute but permit us to apply a narrower holding. Nothing in the Code commands us to ignore the practicality of commercial arrangements in construing the statute of frauds. Indeed, the Code's rule of construction states that the language "shall be liberally construed and applied to promote its underlying purposes and policies." 13 Pa. Cons. Stat. Ann. § 1102(a). As noted earlier, Comment 1 to that section observes that the Code promotes flexibility in providing "machinery for expansion of commercial practices." Following this guidance, we look to the realities of the arrangement between the parties.

In the distribution agreement, Unisys agreed to engage in the business of selling identified document systems during the two-year term of the contract and to buy from Advent on stated terms the specified products necessary to engage in that venture. The detailed nature of the document, including as it does, such provisions as those for notice of breach, opportunity for cure, and termination leaves no doubt that the parties intended to create a contract.

The parties were obviously aware that they were entering a new, speculative market and some uncertainty was inevitable in the amount of sales Unisys could make and the orders it would place with Advent. Consequently, quantity was not stated in absolute terms. In effect, the parties arrived at a non-exclusive requirements contract, a commercially useful device. We do not consider that in the circumstances here the arrangement raises the statute of frauds bar.

The Code recognizes exclusive requirements contracts in section 2–306, and imposes on the parties to such agreements a duty of good faith. For present purposes, the salient factor is that exclusive requirements contracts satisfy the quantity requirements of the statute of frauds, albeit no specific amount is stated. . . .

The reasons for excepting exclusive requirements contracts from the strictures of the statute of frauds are strong. The purchasing party, perhaps unable to anticipate its precise needs, nevertheless wishes to have assurances of supply and fixed price. The seller, on the other hand, finds an advantage in having a steady customer. Such arrangements have commercial value. To deny enforceability through a rigid reading of the quantity term in the statute of frauds would run contrary to the basic thrust of the Code—to conform the law to business reality and practices.

By holding that exclusive requirements contracts comply with the statute of frauds, courts have decided that indefiniteness in the quantity term is acceptable. If the agreement here does not satisfy the statute of frauds because of indefiniteness of a quantity term, then neither does an exclusive requirements contract. We find no reason in logic or policy to differentiate in the statute of frauds construction between the contract here and an exclusive requirements arrangement.

The same reasons that led courts to dispense with a specific and certain quantity term in the exclusive requirements context apply equally when a continuing relationship is non-exclusive. The same regulating factor—good faith performance by the parties—applies and prevents the contracts from being illusory. The writings here demonstrate that the parties did not articulate a series of distinct, unrelated, simple buy and sell arrangements, . . . but contemplated what resembles in some respects a joint venture or a distributorship.

A construction of the statute of frauds which does not recognize the quite substantial difference between a simple buy and sell agreement and what occurred here is unduly restrictive. Section 2–306 in recognizing exclusive requirements and output contracts does not purport to treat them as the only permissible types of open quantity agreements. We do not read section 2–306 as an exclusionary measure, but rather as one capable of enlargement so as to serve the purposes of the Code.

\* \* \*

In sum, we hold that the writings here satisfy the statute of frauds.

## IV.  ENFORCEABILITY

Having concluded that the statute of frauds is not a bar, we now confront the issue of enforceability.

Section 2–204 provides that a contract does not fail for indefiniteness even though one or more terms have been left open if the parties intended to make a contract and there is a reasonably certain basis for giving an appropriate remedy. 13 Pa. Cons. Stat. Ann. § 2204(c) (Purdon 1984). As Professor Murray has explained:

> Rather than focusing upon what parties failed to say, the Code and RESTATEMENT 2d focus upon the overriding question of whether the parties manifestly intended to make a binding arrangement. If that manifestation is present, the only remaining concern is whether the terms are definite enough to permit courts to afford an appropriate remedy. The second requirement assists courts to determine the degree of permissible indefiniteness.

J. Murray, Murray On Contracts § 38, at 85 (3d ed. 1990).

Unlike the statute of frauds issue discussed earlier, the definiteness required to provide a remedy rests on a very solid foundation of practicality. A remedy may not be based on speculation and an award cannot be made if there is no basis for determining if a breach has occurred.

Unisys argues that since there are specific non-exclusive stipulations in the agreement, they negate the implication found in most exclusive requirements contracts that a "best efforts clause" is included. That may be so, but that does not nullify the obligation of the parties to deal in good faith.

Section 1–203 of the Code provides that contracts require a "good faith performance." This requires the parties to observe "reasonable commercial standards of fair dealing in the trade."

The Pennsylvania Superior Court has concluded that in the absence of any express language, the law will imply an agreement by the parties to do those things that "according to reason and justice they should do in order to carry out the purposes for which the contract was made and to refrain from doing anything that would destroy or injure the other party's right to receive the fruits of the contract." Slater v. Pearle Vision Center, Inc., 376 Pa. Super. 580, 546 A.2d 676, 679 (1988). See Restatement (Second) of Contracts § 205 (1979). . . .

The terms of the agreement between Unisys and Advent lend themselves to imply a good faith obligation on the parties of at least some minimal effort: "A fundamental assumption of both parties is that throughout the term of this agreement, Unisys will employ resources in performing marketing efforts involving Advent Products and will develop the technical capability to be thoroughly familiar with these products."

On remand, Advent may be able to show that it was inconsistent with good faith for a party that has committed itself to engage in particular business for a specified period of time to cease devoting any resources to that venture prior to the end of the stated period. . . . We leave open the possibility that the performance of the parties following signing of the documents and perhaps pre-contractual expectations will provide evidence to satisfy the requirements of section 2–204. See §§ 2–208, 1–205 (course of performance, usage of trade).

On the other hand, it may be that the reason Unisys decided to devote no resources to the project of selling document systems is relevant to whether the standard of fair dealing in the trade was breached. Simply because no resources were devoted, does not mean in and of itself that there was a breach of the covenant of good faith. See, e.g., Angelica Uniform Group, Inc. v. Ponderosa Systems, Inc., 636 F.2d 232, 232 (8th Cir.1980); R.A. Weaver & Assoc., Inc. v. Asphalt Construction, Inc., 587 F.2d 1315, 1321–22 (D.C.Cir.1978); Southwest Natural Gas Co. v. Oklahoma Portland Cement Co., 102 F.2d 630, 632–33 (10th Cir. 1939); 1 J. White & R. Summers, Uniform Commercial Code § 3–8, at 169 (3d ed. 1988).

Whether Advent can establish the definiteness required to sustain a remedy is a serious question. The record before us consists of evidence submitted on the basis of the pretrial ruling denying application of the U.C.C. Our contrary holding will require the parties to reassess the proofs necessary to meet the Code. We are in no position to anticipate the evidence that may appear in further proceedings and, thus, at this juncture cannot rule whether the agreement between Unisys and Advent is enforceable.

\* \* \*

The judgment in favor of the defendant on the tortious interference claim will be affirmed. The judgment in favor of the plaintiff on the breach of contract claim will be reversed and the case will be remanded for further proceedings.

## NOTES

**(1) Information as Goods.** The Court of Appeals reversed the court below and held that computer software is a good within the Uniform Commercial Code. It is instructive to examine closely the court's reasoning and the rapidly developing context in which it was decided. Since this was a diversity case, the court was applying Pennsylvania law.

The court quoted the Pennsylvania statutory definition of "goods," and several paragraphs later said that "once in the form of a floppy disc or other medium, the [computer] program is tangible, movable and available in the marketplace." At the time of this decision, there was no practical way to transfer software other than by implanting it into a physical medium and transferring the medium. The Internet (World Wide Web) did not become widely known until 1996, five years after this court's opinion.

The court found little traction in precedent[12] or academic commen-

---

**12.** The court said that Pennsylvania courts had found that " 'goods' has a very extensive meaning" and cited two cases. Neither involved computer software. The court cited two of its own prior decisions in which some software was involved, but noted that the litigants in those cases had not contested the application of Article 2. The court cited two cases in other Courts of Appeals in which the "goods aspects" of the transactions had predominated, but did not discuss either case.

tary.[13] The court proceeded to reasoning by analogy. Software was compared with CDs and books, both of which the court deemed to be goods although no authority was cited. Today, music and books can be purchased and transferred without implanting the information into a physical medium, but those developments were very far off in 1991.

What seemed most persuasive to the court was what it called "policy argument." "The importance of software to the commercial world and the advantages to be gained by the uniformity inherent in the U.C.C. are strong policy arguments favoring inclusion." Buttressing this argument was the court's conclusion that, in the absence of legislative guidance, courts interpret the Code in light of commercial and technological developments to modernize the law and permit the continued expansion of commercial practices. For this the court relied on UCC 1–102 and a Comment to that provision.

Evaluate the analysis as of 1991. Would such a case be decided differently today?

**(2) License or Sale.** Commonly, owners of software copyright or patent the program and, when they market their intellectual property, they only "license" others to use it; license agreement typically provide that licensees may not sell or transfer the program, and may not decompile or reverse engineer it or modify it without permission of the licensor. To this extent, the transaction does not fit the "passing of title" element in the UCC 2–106(1) definition of "sale." Should that have been given more weight in the court's decision on the applicability of Article 2?[14]

**(3) No Contract; No Enforceable Contract.** The litigation strategy of Unisys was framed to try to avoid large damages for Unisys's decision to abort the arrangement with Advent Systems. There were two elements to the strategy: there was no contract, or the contract, if it existed, was unenforceable.

The latter of these was based on the statute of frauds, which provides that certain kinds of contracts are not enforceable unless the defendant has a signed writing that meets the statute's requirements. The statute of frauds applies to contracts for the sale of goods, but does not apply to sale (or license) of information. The ancient statute of frauds is restated with some modifications in UCC 2–201, which appears to provide that the writing must contain a tem that specified quantity. To try to get the litigation benefit of quantity term requirement of UCC 2–201, Unisys had to persuade the court that the transaction was governed by Article 2. That led Unisys to raise the scope issue.

Unisys's no-contract defense is a based on rules of contract formation, which exist at common law under the doctrine of indefiniteness. The

---

**13.** The court noted that academic commentary was divided, but that a majority of writers espoused the view that software fits within the definition of goods in the Code.

**14.** Note that the title of Article 2 is "Sales," but the scope provision in UCC 2–102 refers to "transactions in goods," not merely to "sales of goods." What might explain the use of the broader term, "transactions," instead of the more specific term?

drafters of Article 2 disapproved common-law decisions that failed to enforce agreements on the ground of indefiniteness in UCC 2–204. By contending for the application of Article 2, Unisys may have weakened its no-contract defense.

Unisys won the battle but lost the war. The Court of Appeals held that Article 2 governed the transaction, but rejected both the no-contract and the no-enforceable-contract defenses, one definitively. The court's reasoning is worth close analysis. Note the important role that "good faith" played in both.

**(4) Domestic Law: Which Nation's?** The seller in *Advent Systems*, a United Kingdom company, contracted with a United States company, whose headquarters were in Pennsylvania, just outside Philadelphia. The courts applied Pennsylvania law to the contract dispute. The probable explanation is that the contract had a specific choice of law clause to that effect. In the bargaining stage for contracts, how important are the terms of a choice-of-law clause likely to be to the representatives of the parties? Would a party be likely to use much of its bargaining leverage, e.g., give up something of economic value, to prevail on this clause? Absent a choice-of-law clause in the contract, the court or tribunal in which the dispute is pending would have to choose the governing law. The principles used for this purpose are referred to as private international law.

This is the first international sales contract we have considered. It preceded the effective date of the CISG, which was therefore not a consideration in the case.

**(5) Subsequent Development of the Law Regarding Information.** In the mid–1990s, the Uniform Law Conference and the American Law Institute launched a project to add an article to the Commercial Code that would deal with transactions in computer information. It was to be Article 2B. The project was contentious and, in 1999, the two sponsors parted ways on the project. The Conference continued the work as a free-standing uniform act, the Uniform Computer Information Transactions Act. The Conference promulgated UCITA in 2002. It was adopted in Virginia and Maryland, but was rejected by every other state legislature that considered it. The Conference has ceased effort to promote enactments. In 2009, after several years of work, the ALI published a restatement-like product, the Principles of the Law of Software Contracts, which do not contemplate legislation. The primary objective of UCITA and the Principles was to formulate a full body of law for transactions in information. A major difficulty is the matter of scope, because the marketplace is now full of consumer goods and commercial equipment that contain computers and software as integral components.

———

*c. GOODS AND REAL PROPERTY*

The line between real property and goods is necessarily somewhat artificial. Movability, the essential characteristic of things defined to be goods, is not uncharacteristic of land. Rocks and soil can be moved; top soil, gravel and "fill" are regularly bought and sold. The Code brings into Article 2 some things that are, by the terms of a contract, to be severed by the seller, including specifically minerals, growing crops, and timber. UCC 2–107(1). See, e.g., Manchester Pipeline Corp. v. Peoples Natural Gas Co., 862 F.2d 1439 (10th Cir.1988).

The Code is also helpful in characterizing transactions that go the other way, goods that are, by terms of a contract, to be affixed to realty. So long as the things are movable at the time of identification to a contract for sale, they are "goods" under UCC 2–105(1). The time of "identification" is set forth in UCC 2–501(1). Under this provision, a thing to be affixed to real estate is almost certain to be identified to the goods contract while still movable. The two Pennsylvania cases relied upon by the court in concluding that Article 2 applied in *Advent Systems* arose out of transactions of this kind.

Contracts may involve transfer of both real estate and goods for a single price, the analogue of transactions in goods and services. Consider, for example, the sale of a new house in which the builder-developer has installed a stove, a refrigerator, other appliances and fixtures. Real estate sales are governed by common law.[15] Should Article 2 apply to any part of the contract?

### d.   DISTRIBUTORSHIP AND FRANCHISE AGREEMENTS

Some manufacturers of trade-marked goods market their goods through independent distributors or franchisees. Typically a master agreement is made between the manufacturer and distributor or franchisee. That agreement determines the essential nature of the relationship and contemplates future sales of goods from time to time. An agreement may allot an exclusive territory to the distributor or franchisee and obligate it to develop the market for the manufacturer's goods in that region. Are such master agreements within Article 2? See Watkins & Son Pet Supplies v. The Iams Co., 254 F.3d 607 (6th Cir. 2001); Sally Beauty Co., Inc. v. Nexxus Products Co., 801 F.2d 1001, 1005 (7th Cir. 1986) ("the rule in the majority of jurisdictions is that distributorship (both exclusive and non-exclusive) are to be treated as sale of goods contracts under the UCC.")

### e.   SALE OF THE ASSETS OF A BUSINESS

Suppose the owner of a business, such as an automobile tire store, contracts to sell all of the assets of the business, including the inventory, the display cases, the accounts receivable, the trade name under which the store has operated and other "goodwill," and the balance of a lease on the building. Should the contract be governed by Article 2? See Stewart v. Lucero, 121 N.M. 722, 918 P.2d 1 (1996); Knoxville Rod & Bearing, Inc. v. Bettis Corp., 672 S.W.2d 203 (Tenn.App.1983); Melms v. Mitchell, 266 Or. 208, 512 P.2d 1336 (1973).

---

**15.**  The Commissioners on Uniform State Laws promulgated a Uniform Land Transactions Act in 1977. No state has adopted this act.

## 2.   THE RELATIONSHIP OF ARTICLE 2 AND COMMON LAW OF CONTRACTS

One of the manifest purposes of the drafters of Article 2 was to create body of law for sales that was better than the common law (and better than the Uniform Sales Act). At the same time the drafters accepted much of the common law of contracts, in part by explicit codification of some common-law doctrines and in part by acceptance of the base of common law that supplements the provisions in the statute. UCC 1–103. The importance of UCC 1–103 cannot be overstated. The application of this section to disputes that arise, in part, under Article 2 is virtually universal.[16] This section considers a number of issues on which the Code has deliberately superseded common law.

### a.   *"NO CONTRACT" AND "NO ENFORCEABLE CONTRACT" DEFENSES*

Drafters of Article 2 of the Commercial Code, notably Chief Reporter Karl Llewellyn, were critical of the extent to which some courts, as a matter of common law, had adopted a formalistic approach in the analysis of legal issues arising in sales transactions. One manifestation of this formalism was evident in the success of the defense, in actions for breach of sales contracts, that no contract had been formed even though both parties had taken some action to perform their parts of the bargain. A number of the provisions in Part 2 of Article 2 were designed to override decisions of this kind when the "no contract" contention was not commercially reasonable. Another manifestation was evident in the success of the defense that enforcement was barred because the defendant had not signed a contract writing that stated the terms of the contract. Successful invocation of the Statute of Frauds does not establish that no contract was formed, but only that the claimant is not entitled to enforcement.[17] (If the defense fails, the claimant must still prove the existence of the contract.) The Article 2 version of the Statute of Frauds retained this defense, but narrowed it significantly.

*Offer and acceptance.* One reform was to jettison the notion that contracts could be formed only by the dialectic process of a communication by one party that constituted an "offer" and response by the other party that constituted an "acceptance." In the informal, messy real world of commercial transactions, it was often impossible to identify an offer and an acceptance, but the parties' conduct was indicative that both believed that a contract existed. If the "no contract" defense is upheld when a contract had been substantially performed before a dispute arose, the parties' reasonable expectations would be disappointed. Indeed, the possibility of a

---

**16.**   For discussion of the interaction of common law and the Code, see R. Hillman, J. McDonnell and S. Nickels, Common Law and Equity Under the UCC (1984 and Supp.).

**17.**   The distinction between "no contract" and "no enforceable contract" may have resulted from the way the Statute of Frauds was drafted. In its original 1677 incarnation, the law was known as the Statute for the Prevention of Frauds and Perjuries. Its manifest purpose was to counter spurious claims of contracts in a period when the actual parties to an alleged contract were not allowed to testify.

successful "no contract" defense invited strategic behavior by transactions looking to escape from deals no longer seen as desirable, perhaps based on advice of counsel that an escape door was available. UCC 2–204(1) and (2) dispensed with the need to find an offer and acceptance in contracts for the sale of goods. A related provision, addressed to transactions in which an offer could be identified, relaxed the requirements of a verbal acceptance that was communicated in a particular manner or medium. UCC 2–206, among other things, validates seller's performance conduct as an acceptance.

*Statute of Frauds.* The Article 2 version of the Statute of Frauds, in UCC 2–201, narrowed the defense considerably. UCC 2–201(1) minimized the required content of a sufficient writing. UCC 2–201(2) dispensed with the requirement of the defendant's signature if a sufficient writing had the plaintiff's signature, in transaction where both parties were merchants (a defined term). More fundamentally, UCC 2–201(3)(c) eliminated the defense after contracts had been performed. UCC 2–201(3)(a) eliminated the defense of buyers in executory contracts for goods to be specially manufactured after the sellers had commenced performance, if the circumstances indicate that the goods were for the buyers and were not suitable for sale to others in the ordinary course of business.

While all parts of the Statute of Frauds have been tested in litigation, the text of UCC 2–201 created special uncertainty about the quantity term of contracts. Some read the statute to say that a contract that lacks a quantity term cannot be enforced. An alternative reading of the same sentence of the statute is that a quantity term in the writing is not essential, but—if a quantity term is present—it forecloses proof that the contract was for a larger quantity. Which is the better reading of the text? Comment 1 declares that a quantity term "must appear." What weight should that have if the alternative reading of the text is more sound?[18]

### b.  ESTABLISHING THE TERMS OF THE CONTRACTS

The legislative move that allows courts to find contracts from conduct had the consequence of giving rise to disputes about the content of contracts. When contract formation follows from exchange of offers and acceptances that are "mirror images" of each other, the terms would be a matter of expressed agreement. If the expressed terms did not include a term that a court thought to be essential, the court would tend to hold that there was no contract.[19] If the expressed terms of the parties differed, usually because they used different standard forms, courts would find that no contract had been formed.

---

**18.** The Commercial Code has a Statute of Frauds, found in Article 1, that applies to contracts for the sale of "personal property" other than goods. UCC 1–206.

**19.** A highpoint of cases of this kind was the decision of the then highly respected New York Court of Appeals, in an opinion by then Judge Cardozo, that the parties' failure to fix the price term was fatal to the process of contract formation. Sun Printing & Publishing Ass'n v. Remington Paper & Power Co., 235 N.Y. 338, 139 N.E. 470 (1923).

*Gap fillers.* Article 2 overruled these common law requirements. One approach was to provide by statute terms that would be incorporated into contracts where there were gaps in the express agreements. Many of the "gap fillers" are found in Part 3 of Article 2. Thus, UCC 2–305 deals with absence of an agreed price term, and UCC 2–308 and 2–309 with the absence of terms for place and time of delivery. "Gap fillers," in many guises, are found throughout Article 2. The difference between "agreement" and "contract," as defined by the Code, is largely the terms that are supplied by Article 2. See UCC 1–201(3) and (12).

*Indefiniteness.* Another approach was to enact a general principle on the required degree of specificity of agreements. This principle declares that "even though one or more terms are left open a contract does not fail for indefiniteness if the parties intended to have a contract and there is a reasonably certain basis for giving an appropriate remedy." UCC 2–204(3).

*Battle of the forms.* Another problem, known as the *battle of the forms,* was, in a sense, exacerbated by Article 2. Unlike transactions in which the parties were insufficiently expressive, transactions with battling forms contained too much expressive content, albeit expressions that do not coincide. The chief purpose of UCC 2–207 was to recognize that contracts may be formed despite the parties' use of non-matching forms. Its success in that regard has stimulated the use of standard forms by parties who engage in frequent, repetitive transactions. Typically these transactions involve the sale of supplies or equipment by one business entity to another. Not enough is at stake in any one of these transactions to justify using lawyers and negotiators, but it is feasible for the entities to use lawyers to draft "standard" terms that can be deployed, over and over, by employees unaware of and unconcerned with the "boilerplate" legal provisions. This scenario is a recipe for contractual disaster.

The difficulty is to find the terms of the contracts formed by exchange of forms. The kindest thing to say is that, on this matter, Article 2 is muddled. Several very different approaches emerged in a welter of litigated cases, but two became dominant. One is called the "knock out" rule and other is called the "last shot" rule. The "knock out" rule, based on UCC 2–207(3), is premised on the finding that a contract was formed by the parties' conduct and finds the terms of that contract in the expressed terms, to the extent they agree, and for the rest turns to the "gap fillers" of Article 2. The "last shot" rule, based in part on UCC 2–206(1), is premised on the finding that no contract was formed until the party receiving the last of the battling forms had "accepted" it; the terms are those in the last form, plus any needed "gap fillers." A "first shot" rule, of sorts, can be discerned in UCC 2–207(1) and (2).

Lawyers drafting these forms found a way to escalate the difficulty by including provisions declaring that there could be no contract formed except on the terms in the form. "My way or the highway" clauses, ignored of course by the people transacting business, began to show up in litigation. In due course, all standard forms will have such clauses, but for a time the original users of such forms may extract some legal advantage, the equivalent to the last shot rule. The mess is not likely to be cleaned up satisfactorily under the current version of Article 2. Most of these deformed agreements will be recognized as enforceable contracts, but dispute as to their terms will continue.

*Written agreements and parol evidence.* The negotiated terms of agreements in commercial transactions are often set down in writings. The circumstances for this vary from carefully crafted writings created for that purpose by the parties to standard forms in which most of the terms were not negotiated. However created, both parties to a contract frequently sign the writing as the final expression of their agreement. Later, one of the parties may declare that the writing did not contain all of the agreed terms or that some term is not accurately stated in the record. If the other party stands on the writing as both correct and complete, the dispute that results is a matter for the parol evidence rule.

The parol evidence rule is a major piece of the common law of contracts and reflects an important societal value that respects the integrity of writings as the best evidence of what the parties to commercial transactions agreed to. Some people even refer to the *sanctity* of writings in this respect. The drafters of Article 2 were not content to leave the sales contracts to the common law parol evidence rule, perhaps because there was no consensus as to the rule at common law. Among the several differences was a fundamental disagreement over the way to determine whether a writing was complete. Some espoused the view that a writing's completeness could be inferred from looking at it, the so-called "four corners" rule. This approach gave the greatest weight to a clause in the writing that declared the writings completeness, often called a "merger clause." Others contended that completeness of a writing could be found only after considering all proffered evidence, including testimony of witnesses. Even "merger clauses" could be overridden by other evidence.[20]

UCC 2–202 displaced the common law on parol evidence, but did not choose clearly between the competing views. The text provides that additional terms are admissible unless the court finds the writing to have been intended as a complete and exclusive statement of the terms of the agreement, but is silent on how that critical finding is to be made. Comment 3 suggests that a decision can be made on the face of the writing, but the decision must allow the additional evidence unless the terms, if agreed upon, "would certainly have been included in the document." A criterion phrased in certainty would have little exclusionary effect. To see the effect, substitute "probably" for "certainly." Neither the text nor the Comment refers to merger clauses.

*Terms incorporated from context.* The terms of agreements can be expressed by the parties or implied from the context of their transaction. Implied terms can arise from several sources. If an agreement contemplates

---

**20.** The "four corners" rule was attributed to Samuel Williston; the consider-all-the-evidence rule was attributed to Arthur Linton Corbin. Both were renowned contracts teachers and scholars in the early part of the 20th century.

repeated occasions for performance by a party and the other party, with knowledge of the nature of the performance and opportunity to object to it, accepts that performance or acquiesces in it, terms implied by the *course of performance* may become part of the contract between the parties. UCC 1–303(a). If the parties have a history of previous agreements, terms may be implied by their *course of dealing* in previous transactions. UCC 1–303(b). A *usage of trade* is a practice from which terms may be implied if the practice has such regularity of observance among parties to similar transactions as to justify an expectation that it will be observed in the transaction in question. UCC 1–303(c).

### c.   *MODIFICATION AND WAIVER*

In the performance (or post-agreement) stage of many contracts of sale, the parties may individually or jointly change the deal. Common-law contract doctrines were not well suited to this commercial flexibility. Article 2 therefore includes provisions that permit parties to accomplish their commercial purposes.

UCC 2–209(1) declares that an agreement to modify a contract needs no consideration to be binding. One important effect is to enforce agreements that modify the obligation of one party without any change in the obligation of the other.

Waiver is another method by which flexibility can be introduced into the performance of contracts of sale. Under common-law contract doctrine, if a promise is subject to a condition, the promisor can waive the condition with the result that the promise can be enforced even if the condition was not fulfilled. Article 2 deals with the law of waiver only with respect to the effect of retractions of waivers. UCC 2–209(5).

### 3.   REGULATION OF PRIVATE CONDUCT

Most of the provisions in Article 2 are subject to contrary agreement by the parties to sales contracts. In that sense, most of Article 2 is not regulatory in nature. But there are some provisions in Article 2 that do have broad regulatory effect. Key provisions of this kind apply to different phases of sales contracts. One applies to the contract formation stage and the other to the stages of performance and enforcement. If a contract, as formed, is unconscionable in whole or in part, the aggrieved party may persuade a court to refuse to enforce the unconscionable agreement. The relevant time frame is the period of contract formation. Another regulatory provision has no application to the formation of sales contracts, but applies at a later stage. An obligation of good faith applies to the performance and enforcement of these contracts.

### a.   *UNCONSCIONABLE CONTRACTS OR TERMS*

A striking provision of UCC 2–302 authorizes courts to deny enforcement to ''unconscionable'' agreements. The section provides:

(1) If the court as a matter of law finds the contract or any clause of the contract to have been unconscionable at the time it was made

the court may refuse to enforce the contract, or it may enforce the remainder of the contract without the unconscionable clause, or it may so limit the application of any unconscionable clause as to avoid any unconscionable result.

(2) When it is claimed or appears to the court that the contract or any clause thereof may be unconscionable the parties shall be afforded a reasonable opportunity to present evidence as to its commercial setting, purpose and effect to aid the court in making the determination.

The most difficult (and intriguing) problem is the lack of any textual definition of the key concept of "unconscionability." By implication, subsection (2) indicates that the meaning of the word is derived from "commercial setting, purpose and effect," but these references do not specify what is to be found in setting, purpose and effect.

Comment 1 to UCC 2–302 seeks to meet the gap in the text. At one point the Comment refers to the "basic test" of whether the clause is "one-sided," at another the Comment states that "the principle is one of the prevention of oppression and unfair surprise (cf. Campbell Soup Co. v. Wentz, 172 F.2d 80 (3d Cir. 1948), and not of "disturbance of allocation of risks because of superior bargaining power." Can these two comments be reconciled? Are "oppression" and "surprise" commensurate concepts? The former seems concerned with substantive fairness, the latter with procedural regularity.

The Comment states that "the underlying basis of the section is illustrated by the results in cases such as the following. ..." The Comment then summarizes the holdings of ten cases. Five of these involved narrow construction of clauses disclaiming implied warranties of quality; the Code deals with this problem specifically in Section 2–316. The remaining five cases limited the impact of clauses restricting remedies for breach, a problem covered in Sections 2–718 and 2–719. Thus, even if these Comments are influential in construing the Code, the possible scope of Section 2–302, in areas not duplicated by Sections 2–316, 2–718 and 2–719, was left for case-law development.[21]

Although the precise meaning of unconscionability may be obscure, the Commercial Code is quite clear on the process of wielding the power to refuse enforcement. The issue is not one for determination by a jury. Redundantly, UCC 2–302 refers to "the court" and "as a matter of law" to eliminate any doubt that the issue cannot be given to a jury for determination.

### b. *THE OBLIGATION OF GOOD FAITH*

A good faith obligation, stated in revised Article 1, spans the entire Commercial Code. UCC 1–304 provides that: "Every contract or duty

---

**21.**  The unconscionability provision has been much discussed by academic scholars and treatise writers. One early and still influential analysis identified the difference between procedural and substantive unconscionability. A. Leff, Unconscionability and the Code—The Emperor's New Clause, 115 U. Pa. L. Rev. 485 (1967).

within [the Uniform Commercial Code] imposes an obligation of good faith in its performance or enforcement." Supplementing this provision in Article 1 is the definition of "good faith," "honesty in fact and the observance of reasonable commercial standards of fair dealing." UCC 1–201(20).[22] Similar provisions are found in Article 2. UCC 2–103(1)(b).[23]

"Good faith" is used in Article 2 in provisions that allow one contracting party to make choices that are binding on the other. One of those is the provision that allows parties to conclude a sales contract with the price term left open, to be fixed later by one of the parties. UCC 2–305.[24] Subsection (2) requires that party to fix the price "in good faith." Another provision deals with agreements that leave the quantity term unspecific, the amount to be determined by either the buyer's requirements or the seller's output. UCC 2–306(1). The party with discretion must act in "good faith."

The statutory obligation of UCC 1–304 applies only to "performance and enforcement" of contracts. There is, by clear implication, no statutory obligation of good faith in negotiation of contracts. What might explain that legislative policy choice?

## 4.   REFERENCES

There are many resources for further study of the law of sales under UCC Article 2. For a compilation of statutory variations as enacted in various states, reported cases, and index, see Pike & Fischer, Uniform Commercial Code Reporting Service.

## (B)   INTERNATIONAL SALES LAW

This segment of the chapter deals primarily with the Convention on Contracts for the International Sale of Goods (CISG). CISG is not, of course, the only body of international sales law, but it has a central role in that sphere. CISG is analogous in many ways to the Uniform Commercial Code. Basic legal issues similar to those that we considered under the Code arise under CISG.

## 1.   SCOPE OF CISG

### a.   INTERNATIONALITY OF TRANSACTIONS

CISG applies to transactions that have a prescribed international character. The most important CISG prescription is found in Article 1(a).

---

**22.** Not all of the states that enacted revised Article 1 adopted the revised provision on good faith. Some retained the former provision that was limited to honesty in fact.

**23.** The overlap resulted from the failure of the proposed revision of Article 2. That revision was drafted contemporaneously with the successful revision of Article 1 and would have reconciled the provisions in the two articles.

**24.** By allowing contracts to be formed with an open price term, Article 2 overruled some common-law decisions which held that a sales transaction that lacked an agreed price term was incomplete and not a contract.

That provision declares that the Convention applies to contracts of sale of goods between parties whose places of business are in different nations when both of the nations have are parties to the Convention. CISG 1(a).

Conventions are written in the terminology of public international law. Nations are called "States" or "Nation–States." (The normal capitalization of "States" is helpful for people where "state" refers to sub-national entities, as in the 50 states of the United States.) A nation that adopts a convention is called a "Contracting State." A nation becomes a Contracting State by ratification, acceptance, approval or accession, terms that have distinctive meanings in public international law, but the differences are not important for our purposes. Thus CISG Article 1(a) refers to States and Contracting States.

The trigger for application of CISG is international diversity in the places of business of the parties to transactions. It is very important to note that CISG does not refer to the place of incorporation or registration as the determinant of the Convention's scope. Some parties to international sales contracts have only one place of business, but increasingly enterprises have places of business in more than one nation. One of the most dramatic changes occurring in the global economy is the explosive development of transnational enterprises (TNE), sometimes called multinational enterprises or multinational corporations. The national identity of a large TNE may be hard to find.[25] CISG is not concerned with the national identity of an enterprise, nor with the number of its places of business. When a party to a contract has more than one place of business, CISG refers to the place "which has the closest relationship to the contract and its performance." CISG 10(a).[26]

CISG has been in force for some nations since January 1, 1988.[27] The number of Contracting Parties continues to grow. For enterprises with places of business in the United States, it is useful to know that almost all of that nation's trading partners are now parties to CISG. The major exception is the United Kingdom. The potential application of CISG 1(a) to international trade involving United States enterprises is very large.

CISG 1 has a second provision that was intended to cover the situation where one of the parties to an international sales transaction had its place of business in a Contracting State but the other party did not. Absent the Convention, international sales are governed by domestic law of some nation. Which nation's domestic law applies is determined by the rules of private international law. CISG's drafters provided in Article 1(b) that, if private international law pointed to the law of a Contracting State, then

---

**25.** The enterprise that resulted from the merger of the Chrysler Corporation and Daimler Benz, although registered under German law, is formally a German enterprise.

**26.** If a party has no place of business, applicability is determined by the party's "habitual residence." CISG 10(b).

**27.** Commercial conventions commonly provide that they go into effect when a prescribed number of nations have become Contracting States. CISG 99(1) set the number at 10. That number was reached by January 1, 1988. The United States was one of the original parties.

the transaction could be governed by CISG rather than by that country's domestic sales law even though the counter-party's place of business was not in a Contracting State. Thus, in a transaction between parties with places of business respectively the U.S and the U.K., if the choice of law arrow pointed to the U,K, U.K. domestic law would apply, but if the arrow pointed to the U.S., CISG would apply.

CISG 1(b) is not mandatory. Nations that become Contracting States are allowed to opt out. CISG 95. As countries ratified CISG, Article 95 opt-outs were rare, but the United States did so. Thus, in the example above, if the choice of law arrow pointed to the U.S., the governing law would be the Article 2 of the Commercial Code, not the Convention. As the number of non-Contracting States diminished, the significance of the U.S. opt out has waned.

**Problem 1.** Seller, whose place of business is in the United Kingdom and Buyer, whose place of business is in the United States, are negotiating a contract for sale of goods. Buyer and Seller reach impasse on the choice of law clause. Seller prefers that the contract be governed by the U.K. Sale of Goods Act, while Buyer prefers Article 2 of the Uniform Commercial Code. To resolve the matter, both agree to a clause in their agreement that the contract was to be governed by CISG. Should a United States court, or a United Kingdom court, or an international arbitrator conclude that the clause be given effect? What body of law is relevant?

### b.   GOODS, SELLER AND BUYER

CISG applies to "contracts for the sale of goods" (CISG 1), but the Convention offers no definition of "goods." (Indeed, the Convention defines none of the terms used in it.) The Convention does not apply to all goods. One important exception is the provision that excludes from coverage sales of goods "bought for personal, family or household use." CISG 2(a).[28] Although ships, vessels, hovercraft or aircraft are probably "goods," the Convention excludes sales of them from its scope. CISG 2(e). Investment securities, negotiable instruments and money are unlikely to be deemed "goods," but sales of these types of "paper property" are also expressly excluded by CISG 2(d). Contracts for the sale of electricity, whether or not goods, are excluded by CISG 2(f).

The Convention defines neither "seller" nor "buyer," but sales by auction, on execution or otherwise by authority of law, are expressly excluded from its scope. CISG 2(b) and (c).

### c.   GOODS AND SERVICES

The Convention expressly recognizes contracts for mixed goods and services and provides for inclusion of some of them. The Convention does not apply if "the preponderant part of the obligations of the party who furnishes the goods consists in the supply of labour and other services." CISG 3(2). By implication, the Convention does apply if supply of materials

---

**28.** Contracts for consumer goods may be governed by the Convention if the seller neither knew nor ought to have known that they were bought for that purpose.

is the preponderant part of a seller's obligation. Like the Commercial Code, CISG includes within its scope contracts for the supply of goods to be manufactured or produced, with an important proviso that excludes any contract in which the buyer supplies a substantial part of the materials necessary for such manufacture or production. CISG 3(1).[29]

### d.   GOODS AND INFORMATION

CISG does not mention transactions in information or intellectual property. It provides no guidance on applicability of the Convention to transactions that are combinations of goods (hardware) and information (software). For an analysis of the issue under CISG and the U.K. Sale of Goods Act, see S. Green & D. Saidov, Software as Goods, Journal of Business Law 161 (March 2007).

### e.   GOODS AND REAL PROPERTY

The Convention is silent on contracts for extraction or severance of property from real estate or for affixing property to real estate. Professor Honnold finds: "Contracts requiring the seller to extract and sever corporeal objects from land and make them available to the buyer seem to be covered by Article 3(1). ... On the other hand, a contract permitting a party to come on land and mine, drill or cut timber does not call for one party to deliver goods to the other; crucial provisions of the Convention on conformity of goods (art. 35), delivery, shipment (Arts. 31–33) and risk of loss (Arts. 66–70) do not address the special circumstances of contracts for mining or other extraction activities."[30]

### f.   DISTRIBUTORSHIP AND FRANCHISE AGREEMENTS

An agreement establishing a distributorship was held not within the scope of the Convention. Amco Ukrservice & Prompriladamco v. American Meter Co., 312 F. Supp. 2d 681 (E.D. Pa. 2004).

### g.   INTERNATIONAL TRANSACTIONS OUTSIDE CISG; CHOICE OF LAW

If an international transaction is a contract for the sale of goods, but is outside CISG because the transaction lacks the requisite internationality of the parties, the governing law would be the domestic law of a nation, chosen by operation of the principles of private international law. Often contracting parties include choice of law clauses in their agreements. Absent agreement, courts refer to general principles of customary interna-

---

**29.**  For discussion of these provisions and caselaw decisions, see CISG Advisory Council Opinion No. 4, Contracts for Sale of Goods to Be Manufactured or Produced and Mixed Contracts (CISG Art. 3), 24 Oct. 2004, www.cisgw3.law.pace.edu.

**30.**  J. Honnold, Uniform Law for International Sales § 56 (3d ed.1999). A French Court of Appeal (Grenoble) held that an international contract for the dismantling and delivery of a warehouse building was a transaction within the scope of CISG. CLOUT Case 152 (26 April 1995). The analysis in the abstract does not consider the building as real property; it is focused entirely on the relative importance of the services, dismantling and delivery, and the warehouse. The court concluded, under CISG 3(2), that the supply of services did not constitute the preponderant part of the obligations.

tional law. A court might apply the Hague Convention on the Law Applicable to International Sales of Goods, 15 June 1955. Seven European nations, not including Germany or the U.K., ratified this convention. It went into effect in 1964.

## 2.  THE RELATIONSHIP OF CISG TO UNDERLYING LAW

CISG, like the Commercial Code, is an incomplete body of law. International commercial law conventions inevitably presuppose that other law will govern on matters that are not within the ambit of the convention or, if within the ambit of a convention, that are not addressed therein. With international conventions, the inevitable problem of incompleteness is exacerbated by the nature of the other law that will be invoked. The interface between a convention and other law is likely to be a discontinuity involving the international law with a nation's domestic law. There is no general body in international commercial law that underlies and supplements international agreements.

CISG's treatment of the problem of incompleteness is, first, to invite tribunals to fashion particular solutions from the Convention's general principles. CISG 7(2).

> Questions concerning matters governed by this Convention which are not expressly settled in it are to be settled in conformity with the general principles on which it is based. . . .

The Convention's approach reflects that established for civil law codes, which were designed to displace an entire body of pre-existing law. As the Convention was being drafted, some representatives objected that, since these general principles had not been articulated, reference to them in the Convention injected a high degree of uncertainty as to its meaning. This objection was met with the argument that filling gaps by turning to the domestic law of some nation, was a worse solution that would produce even greater uncertainty and, further, undermine the effort to produce a body of uniform international law.

Proponents of a "general principles" statement prevailed in the provision of CISG 7(2) quoted above, but the objectors prevailed in seeking a subordinate reference to some nation's domestic law if a needed general principle cannot be found. Article 7(2) continues:

> . . . or, in the absence of such principles, in conformity with the law applicable by virtue of the rules of private international law.

The "rules of private international law" are the choice-of-law rules that exist apart from the Convention and that designate the domestic law that governs any particular contract dispute.

Professor Honnold outlined an approach to implementation of this provision. He first discussed three problem areas to illustrate how the Convention's "general principles" may be ascertained: reliance on representations of the other party, the duty to communicate information needed by the other party, and the obligation to take steps to avoid unnecessary hardship for the other party. He then propounds a general approach:

> This approach responds to the reference in Article 7(2) to the principles on which the Convention is based by requiring that general principles to deal with new situations be moored to premises that underlie specific provisions of the Convention. Thus, like the inductive approach employed in case law development, the first step is the examination of instances regulated by specific provisions of the Convention. The second step is to choose between these two conclusions: (a) The Convention deliberately rejected the extension of these specific provisions; (b) The lack of a specific provision to govern the case at hand results from a failure to anticipate and resolve the issue. If the latter alternative applies, the third step is to consider whether the cases governed by the specific provisions of the Convention and the case at hand are so analogous that a lawmaker would not have deliberately chosen discordant results for the group of similar situations. In this event, it seems appropriate to conclude that the general principle embracing these situations is authorized by Article 7(2). In sum, the approach involves the analogical application of specific provisions of the Convention.

See J. Honnold, Uniform Law for International Sales § 102 (3d ed. 1999).

Under the domestic law the United States, where transactions fall outside the scope of Article 2 of a state's version of the Commercial Code, those transactions are governed by the common law of that state. There is no body of "common law" underlying and surrounding CISG. The UNIDROIT Principles of International Commercial Contracts, first promulgated in 1994 and revised in 2004, are a step in that direction.

Drafters of CISG had no occasion to use legislation to overrule or supersede existing international sales law. The grand purpose of CISG was to displace the wide variety of national laws that might apply to international sales transactions with a single, uniform body of law. It is impossible, in these materials, to canvas the various domestic commercial laws that exist around the world in order to comprehend the extent to which the provisions of CISG depart from some or all variations of domestic law. The treatment of writings, in contract formation and contract interpretation, is a good example of the CISG's approach to underlying domestic laws.

*a. THE "NO CONTRACT" AND "NO ENFORCEABLE CONTRACT" DEFENSES*

*Offer and acceptance.* Contract formation is governed by Part II of the Convention, Articles 14 through 24. A critical question is the requirement for a response to an offer to be effective in forming a contract. CISG 23 provides that "a contract is concluded at the moment when an acceptance of an offer becomes effective in accordance with the provisions of this Convention." CISG 18(1) declares that a response is an "acceptance" if is an "assent to the offer" and that "silence or inactivity does not in itself amount to acceptance." The Convention has several provisions specifying when a communication containing an offer or acceptance is effective, the time period for making an acceptance, the circumstances in which a late acceptance may be effective, and the circumstances in which an offer or an acceptance can be withdrawn.

*Statute of Frauds.* The Convention's primary position on the requirement of a writing as a condition to enforcement of a sales contract was to eschew such a requirement. CISG 11 provides that a contract need not be concluded in or evidenced by a writing. During the preparation of the Convention, representatives of some nations objected to the omission of a requirement of a writing. To meet this objection, CISG 12 was added to permit nations to obviate Article 11 by so declaring at the time of ratification. CISG 96.[31]

*Indefiniteness.* The Convention's standard for a sufficiently definite agreement is found in its definition of an "offer." A proposal is sufficiently definite "if it indicates the goods and expressly or implicitly fixes or makes provision for the quantity and the price." CISG 14(1). This suggests that negotiations that lack an express price term could not form a contract, but that implication is countered by the Convention's provision on "open price" terms, CISG 55.

### b. ESTABLISHING THE TERMS OF THE CONTRACT

*Gap fillers.* CISG contains many provisions that supply contract terms if the express agreements of the parties so not deal with those terms. The general obligation of sellers and buyers is found in the requirements of "the contract and this Convention." CISG 30, 53. Many of the "gap fillers" are found in Part III. Thus, CISG 55 deals with the absence of an agreed price term, and CISG 31 and 33 with the absence of terms for place and time of delivery. "Gap fillers" appear throughout the Convention.

*Battle of the forms.* CISG does not require communications looking to contract formation to meet the "mirror image" standard. A response to an "offer" may be effective if (I) it "purports to be an acceptance" and (ii) contains "additional or different" terms that "do not materially alter the terms of the offer." CISG 19(2). Absent objection by the offeror, the terms of the contract are those in the offer "with the modifications contained in the acceptance."The extent of this flexibility is sharply narrowed by the Convention's meaning of material alteration. A provision "relating to price, payment, quality and quantity of the goods, place and time of delivery, extent of one party's liability to the other or the settlement of disputes" is deemed a material alteration. CISG 19(3). There are no examples of the kind of term that might be an immaterial alteration.

*Terms implied from context.* In determinations of the terms of sales contracts, the Convention gives primacy to the expressions of the parties and the construction of those expressions, CISG 8(1) and (2), but the Convention directs tribunals to consider contextual sources as well. Thus

---

**31.** For the nations that exercised this power, see the UNCITRAL web site, www. uncitral.org/status of texts.

CISG 8(3) provides that "due consideration is to be given to all relevant circumstances of the case including ... any practices which the parties have established between themselves, usages and any subsequent conduct of the parties."

*Written agreements and parol evidence.* The Convention approach to the admissibility of evidence of contract terms that add to a written agreement is quite liberal. CISG 11 declares that a contract may be proved by any means, including witnesses. CISG 8 may also be relevant. The following case is instructive.

## MCC–Marble Ceramic Center v. Ceramica Nuova d'Agostino

United States Court of Appeals, Eleventh Circuit, 1998.
144 F.3d 1384.

■ BIRCH, CIRCUIT JUDGE:

This case requires us to determine whether a court must consider parol evidence in a contract dispute governed by the United Nations Convention on Contracts for the International Sale of Goods ("CISG"). The district court granted summary judgment on behalf of the defendant-appellee, relying on certain terms and provisions that appeared on the reverse of a pre-printed form contract for the sale of ceramic tiles. The plaintiff-appellant sought to rely on a number of affidavits that tended to show both that the parties had arrived at an oral contract before memorializing their agreement in writing and that they subjectively intended not to apply the terms on the reverse of the contract to their agreements. The magistrate judge held that the affidavits did not raise an issue of material fact and recommended that the district court grant summary judgment based on the terms of the contract. The district court agreed with the magistrate judge's reasoning and entered summary judgment in the defendant-appellee's favor. We REVERSE.

### BACKGROUND

The plaintiff-appellant, MCC–Marble Ceramic, Inc. ("MCC"), is a Florida corporation engaged in the retail sale of tiles, and the defendant-appellee, Ceramica Nuova d'Agostino S.p.A. ("D'Agostino") is an Italian corporation engaged in the manufacture of ceramic tiles. In October 1990, MCC's president, Juan Carlos Mozon, met representatives of D'Agostino at a trade fair in Bologna, Italy and negotiated an agreement to purchase ceramic tiles from D'Agostino based on samples he examined at the trade fair. Monzon, who spoke no Italian, communicated with Gianni Silingardi, then D'Agostino's commercial director, through a translator, Gianfranco Copelli, who was himself an agent of D'Agostino. The parties apparently arrived at an oral agreement on the crucial terms of price, quality, quantity, delivery and payment. The parties then recorded these terms on one of D'Agostino's standard, pre-printed order forms and Monzon signed the contract on MCC's behalf. According to MCC, the parties also entered into a requirements contract in February 1991, subject to which D'Agostino agreed to supply MCC with high grade ceramic tile at specific discounts as long as MCC purchased sufficient quantities of tile. MCC completed a number of additional order forms requesting tile deliveries pursuant to that agreement.

MCC brought suit against D'Agostino claiming a breach of the February 1991 requirements contract when D'Agostino failed to satisfy orders in April, May, and August of 1991. In addition to other defenses, D'Agostino responded that it was under no obligation to fill MCC's orders because MCC had defaulted on payment for previous shipments. In support of its position, D'Agostino relied on the pre-printed terms of the contracts that MCC had executed. The executed forms were printed in Italian and contained terms and conditions on both the front and reverse. According to an English translation of the October 1990 contract, the front of the order form contained the following language directly beneath Monzon's signature:

> The buyer hereby states that he is aware of the sales conditions stated on the reverse and that he expressly approves of them with special reference to those numbered 1–2–3–4–5–6–7–8.

R2–126, Exh. 3 P 5 ("Maselli Aff."). Clause 6(b), printed on the back of the form states:

> Default or delay in payment within the time agreed upon gives D'Agostino the right to . . . suspend or cancel the contract itself and to cancel possible other pending contracts and the buyer does not have the right to indemnification or damages.

Id. P 6.

D'Agostino also brought a number of counterclaims against MCC, seeking damages for MCC's alleged nonpayment for deliveries of tile that D'Agostino had made between February 28, 1991 and July 4, 1991. MCC responded that the tile it had received was of a lower quality than contracted for, and that, pursuant to the CISG, MCC was entitled to reduce payment in proportion to the defects. D'Agostino, however, noted that clause 4 on the reverse of the contract states, in pertinent part:

> Possible complaints for defects of the merchandise must be made in writing by means of a certified letter within and not later than 10 days after receipt of the merchandise. . . .

Maselli Aff. P 6. Although there is evidence to support MCC's claims that it complained about the quality of the deliveries it received, MCC never submitted any written complaints.

MCC did not dispute these underlying facts before the district court, but argued that the parties never intended the terms and conditions printed on the reverse of the order form to apply to their agreements. As evidence for this assertion, MCC submitted Monzon's affidavit, which claims that MCC had no subjective intent to be bound by those terms and that D'Agostino was aware of this intent. MCC also filed affidavits from

Silingardi and Copelli, D'Agostino's representatives at the trade fair, which support Monzon's claim that the parties subjectively intended not to be bound by the terms on the reverse of the order form. The magistrate judge held that the affidavits, even if true, did not raise an issue of material fact regarding the interpretation or applicability of the terms of the written contracts and the district court accepted his recommendation to award summary judgment in D'Agostino's favor. MCC then filed this timely appeal.

## DISCUSSION

We review a district court's grant of summary judgment de novo and apply the same standards as the district court. . . .

The parties to this case agree that the CISG governs their dispute because the United States, where MCC has its place of business, and Italy, where D'Agostino has its place of business, are both States Party to the Convention. See CISG, art. 1. Article 8 of the CISG governs the interpretation of international contracts for the sale of goods and forms the basis of MCC's appeal from the district court's grant of summary judgment in D'Agostino's favor. MCC argues that the magistrate judge and the district court improperly ignored evidence that MCC submitted regarding the parties' subjective intent when they memorialized the terms of their agreement on D'Agostino's pre-printed form contract, and that the magistrate judge erred by applying the parol evidence rule in derogation of the CISG.

### I.   Subjective Intent Under the CISG

Contrary to what is familiar practice in United States courts, the CISG appears to permit a substantial inquiry into the parties' subjective intent, even if the parties did not engage in any objectively ascertainable means of registering this intent. Article 8(1) of the CISG instructs courts to interpret the "statements . . . and other conduct of a party . . . according to his intent" as long as the other party "knew or could not have been unaware" of that intent. The plain language of the Convention, therefore, requires an inquiry into a party's subjective intent as long as the other party to the contract was aware of that intent.

In this case, MCC has submitted three affidavits that discuss the purported subjective intent of the parties to the initial agreement concluded between MCC and D'Agostino in October 1990. All three affidavits discuss the preliminary negotiations and report that the parties arrived at an oral agreement for D'Agostino to supply quantities of a specific grade of ceramic tile to MCC at an agreed upon price. The affidavits state that the "oral agreement established the essential terms of quality, quantity, description of goods, delivery, price and payment." . . . The affidavits also note that the parties memorialized the terms of their oral agreement on a standard D'Agostino order form, but all three affiants contend that the parties subjectively intended not to be bound by the terms on the reverse of that form despite a provision directly below the signature line that expressly and specifically incorporated those terms.[9]

The terms on the reverse of the contract give D'Agostino the right to suspend or cancel all contracts in the event of a buyer's non-payment and require a buyer to make a written report of all defects within ten days. As the magistrate judge's report and recommendation makes clear, if these terms applied to the agreements between MCC and D'Agostino, summary judgment would be appropriate because MCC failed to make any written complaints about the quality of tile it received and D'Agostino has established MCC's non-payment of a number of invoices amounting to $108,389.40 and 102,053,846.00 Italian lira.

Article 8(1) of the CISG requires a court to consider this evidence of the parties' subjective intent. Contrary to the magistrate judge's report, which the district court endorsed and adopted, article 8(1) does not focus on interpreting the parties' statements alone. Although we agree with the magistrate judge's conclusion that no "interpretation" of the contract's terms could support MCC's position,[10] article 8(1) also requires a court to consider subjective intent while interpreting the conduct of the parties. The CISG's language, therefore, requires courts to consider evidence of a party's subjective intent when signing a contract if the other party to the contract was aware of that intent at the time. This is precisely the type of evidence that MCC has provided through the Silingardi, Copelli, and Monzon affidavits, which discuss not only Monzon's intent as MCC's representative but also discuss the intent of D'Agostino's representatives and their knowledge that Monzon did not intend to agree to the terms on the reverse of the form contract. This acknowledgment that D'Agostino's representatives were aware of Monzon's subjective intent puts this case squarely within article 8(1) of the CISG, and therefore requires the court to consider MCC's evidence as it interprets the parties' conduct.[11]

---

**9.** MCC makes much of the fact that the written order form is entirely in Italian and that Monzon, who signed the contract on MCC's behalf directly below this provision incorporating the terms on the reverse of the form, neither spoke nor read Italian. This fact is of no assistance to MCC's position. We find it nothing short of astounding that an individual, purportedly experienced in commercial matters, would sign a contract in a foreign language and expect not to be bound simply because he could not comprehend its terms. We find nothing in the CISG that might counsel this type of reckless behavior and nothing that signals any retreat from the proposition that parties who sign contracts will be bound by them regardless of whether they have read them or understood them. See e.g., Samson Plastic Conduit and Pipe Corp. v. Battenfeld Extrusionstechnik GMBH, 718 F. Supp. 886, 890 (M.D.Ala.1989) ("A good and recurring illustration of the problem ... involves a person who is ... unfamiliar with the language in which a contract is written and who has signed a document which was not read to him. There is all but unanimous agreement that he is bound....")

**10.** The magistrate judge's report correctly notes that MCC has not sought an interpretation of those terms, but rather to exclude them altogether.

**11.** Without this crucial acknowledgment, we would interpret the contract and the parties' actions according to article 8(2), which directs courts to rely on objective evidence of the parties' intent. On the facts of this case it seems readily apparent that MCC's affidavits provide no evidence that Monzon's actions would have made his alleged subjective intent not

## II.   Parol Evidence and the CISG

Given our determination that the magistrate judge and the district court should have considered MCC's affidavits regarding the parties' subjective intentions, we must address a question of first impression in this circuit: whether the parol evidence rule, which bars evidence of an earlier oral contract that contradicts or varies the terms of a subsequent or contemporaneous written contract, plays any role in cases involving the CISG. We begin by observing that the parol evidence rule, contrary to its title, is a substantive rule of law, not a rule of evidence. . . . As such, a federal district court cannot simply apply the parol evidence rule as a procedural matter—as it might if excluding a particular type of evidence under the Federal Rules of Evidence, which apply in federal court regardless of the substantive rule of decision.[13]

The CISG itself contains no express statement on the role of parol evidence. See Honnold, Uniform Law [for International Sales Under the 1980 United Nations Convention] § 110 at 170 [2d ed. 1991] . . . It is clear, however, that the drafters of the CISG were comfortable with the concept of permitting parties to rely on oral contracts because they eschewed any statutes of fraud provision and expressly provided for the enforcement of oral contracts. Compare CISG, art. 11 (a contract of sale need not be concluded or evidenced in writing) with U.C.C. § 2–201 (precluding the enforcement of oral contracts for the sale of goods involving more than $500). Moreover, article 8(3) of the CISG expressly directs courts to give "due consideration . . . to all relevant circumstances of the case including the negotiations . . ." to determine the intent of the parties. Given article 8(1)'s directive to use the intent of the parties to interpret their statements and conduct, article 8(3) is a clear instruction to admit and consider parol evidence regarding the negotiations to the extent they reveal the parties' subjective intent.

Despite the CISG's broad scope, surprisingly few cases have applied the Convention in the United States, see Delchi Carrier SpA v. Rotorex Corp., 71 F.3d 1024, 1027–28 (2d Cir.1995) (observing that "there is virtually no case law under the Convention"), and only two reported decisions touch upon the parol evidence rule, both in dicta. One court has concluded, much as we have above, that the parol evidence rule is not viable in CISG cases in light of article 8 of the Convention. In Filanto, a district court addressed the differences between the UCC and the CISG on the issues of offer and acceptance and the battle of the forms. See 789 F. Supp. at 1238. After engaging in a thorough analysis of how the CISG applied to the dispute before it, the district court tangentially observed that article 8(3) "essentially rejects . . . the parol evidence rule." Id. at 1238 n.7. Another court, however, appears to have arrived at a contrary conclusion. In Beijing

---

to be bound by the terms of the contract known to "the understanding that a reasonable person . . . would have had in the same circumstances." CISG, art. 8(2).

**13.**   An example demonstrates this point. The CISG provides that a contract for the sale of goods need not be in writing and that the parties may prove the contract "by any means, including witnesses." CISG, art. 11. . . .

Metals & Minerals Import/Export Corp. v. American Bus. Ctr., Inc., 993 F.2d 1178 (5th Cir.1993), a defendant sought to avoid summary judgment on a contract claim by relying on evidence of contemporaneously negotiated oral terms that the parties had not included in their written agreement. The plaintiff, a Chinese corporation, relied on Texas law in its complaint while the defendant, apparently a Texas corporation, asserted that the CISG governed the dispute. Id. at 1183 n.9. Without resolving the choice of law question, the Fifth Circuit cited Filanto for the proposition that there have been very few reported cases applying the CISG in the United States, and stated that the parol evidence rule would apply regardless of whether Texas law or the CISG governed the dispute. Beijing Metals, 993 F.2d at 1183 n.9. The opinion does not acknowledge Filanto's more applicable dictum that the parol evidence rule does not apply to CISG cases nor does it conduct any analysis of the Convention to support its conclusion. In fact, the Fifth Circuit did not undertake to interpret the CISG in a manner that would arrive at a result consistent with the parol evidence rule but instead explained that it would apply the rule as developed at Texas common law. See id. at 1183 n.10. As persuasive authority for this court, the Beijing Metals opinion is not particularly persuasive on this point.

As one scholar has explained:

> The language of Article 8(3) that "due consideration is to be given to all relevant circumstances of the case" seems adequate to override any domestic rule that would bar a tribunal from considering the relevance of other agreements. ... Article 8(3) relieves tribunals from domestic rules that might bar them from "considering" any evidence between the parties that is relevant. This added flexibility for interpretation is consistent with a growing body of opinion that the "parol evidence rule" has been an embarrassment for the administration of modern transactions.

Honnold, Uniform Law § 110 at 170–71. Indeed, only one commentator has made any serious attempt to reconcile the parol evidence rule with the CISG. See David H. Moore, Note, The Parol Evidence Rule and the United Nations Convention on Contracts for the International Sale of Goods: Justifying Beijing Metals & Minerals Import/Export Corp. v. American Business Center, Inc., 1995 BYU L. Rev. 1347. Moore argues that the parol evidence rule often permits the admission of evidence discussed in article 8(3), and that the rule could be an appropriate way to discern what consideration is "due" under article 8(3) to evidence of a parol nature. Id. at 1361–63. He also argues that the parol evidence rule, by limiting the incentive for perjury and pleading prior understandings in bad faith, promotes good faith and uniformity in the interpretation of contracts and therefore is in harmony with the principles of the CISG, as expressed in article 7. Id. at 1366–70. The answer to both these arguments, however, is the same: although jurisdictions in the United States have found the parol evidence rule helpful to promote good faith and uniformity in contract, as well as an appropriate answer to the question of how much consideration to give parol evidence, a wide number of other States Party to the CISG have rejected the rule in their domestic jurisdictions. One of the primary factors motivating the negotiation and adoption of the CISG was to provide parties to international contracts for the sale of goods with some degree of certainty as to the principles of law that would govern potential disputes and remove the previous doubt regarding which party's legal system might otherwise apply. See Letter of Transmittal from Ronald Reagan, President of the United States, to the United States Senate, reprinted at 15 U.S.C. app. 70, 71 (1997). Courts applying the CISG cannot, therefore, upset the parties' reliance on the Convention by substituting familiar principles of domestic law when the Convention requires a different result. We may only achieve the directives of good faith and uniformity in contracts under the CISG by interpreting and applying the plain language of article 8(3) as written and obeying its directive to consider this type of parol evidence.

This is not to say that parties to an international contract for the sale of goods cannot depend on written contracts or that parol evidence regarding subjective contractual intent need always prevent a party relying on a written agreement from securing summary judgment. To the contrary, most cases will not present a situation (as exists in this case) in which both parties to the contract acknowledge a subjective intent not to be bound by the terms of a pre-printed writing. In most cases, therefore, article 8(2) of the CISG will apply, and objective evidence will provide the basis for the court's decision. See Honnold, Uniform Law § 107 at 164–65. Consequently, a party to a contract governed by the CISG will not be able to avoid the terms of a contract and force a jury trial simply by submitting an affidavit which states that he or she did not have the subjective intent to be bound by the contract's terms. . . . Moreover, to the extent parties wish to avoid parol evidence problems they can do so by including a merger clause in their agreement that extinguishes any and all prior agreements and understandings not expressed in the writing.

Considering MCC's affidavits in this case, however, we conclude that the magistrate judge and the district court improperly granted summary judgment in favor of D'Agostino. Although the affidavits are, as D'Agostino observes, relatively conclusory and unsupported by facts that would objectively establish MCC's intent not to be bound by the conditions on the reverse of the form, article 8(1) requires a court to consider evidence of a party's subjective intent when the other party was aware of it, and the Silingardi and Copelli affidavits provide that evidence. This is not to say that the affidavits are conclusive proof of what the parties intended. A reasonable finder of fact, for example, could disregard testimony that purportedly sophisticated international merchants signed a contract without intending to be bound as simply too incredible to believe and hold MCC to the conditions printed on the reverse of the contract. Nevertheless, the affidavits raise an issue of material fact regarding the parties' intent to incorporate the provisions on the reverse of the form contract. If the finder of fact determines that the parties did not intend to rely on those provisions, then the more general provisions of the CISG will govern the outcome of the dispute.

MCC's affidavits, however, do not discuss all of the transactions and orders that MCC placed with D'Agostino. Each of the affidavits discusses the parties' subjective intent surrounding the initial order MCC placed with D'Agostino in October 1990. The Copelli affidavit also discusses a February 1991 requirements contract between the parties and reports that the parties subjectively did not intend the terms on the reverse of the D'Agostino order form to apply to that contract either. See Copelli Aff. p. 12. D'Agostino, however, submitted the affidavit of its chairman, Vincenzo Maselli, which describes at least three other orders from MCC on form contracts dated January 15, 1991, April 27, 1991, and May 4, 1991, in addition to the October 1990 contract. See Maselli Aff. P 2, 25. MCC's affidavits do not discuss the subjective intent of the parties to be bound by language in those contracts, and D'Agostino, therefore, argues that we should affirm summary judgment to the extent damages can be traced to those order forms. It is unclear from the record, however, whether all of these contracts contained the terms that appeared in the October 1990 contract. Moreover, because article 8 requires a court to consider any "practices which the parties have established between themselves, usages and any subsequent conduct of the parties" in interpreting contracts, CISG, art. 8(3), whether the parties intended to adhere to the ten day limit for complaints, as stated on the reverse of the initial contract, will have an impact on whether MCC was bound to adhere to the limit on subsequent deliveries. Since material issues of fact remain regarding the interpretation of the remaining contracts between MCC and D'Agostino, we cannot affirm any portion of the district court's summary judgment in D'Agostino's favor.

## CONCLUSION

MCC asks us to reverse the district court's grant of summary judgment in favor of D'Agostino. The district court's decision rests on pre-printed contractual terms and conditions incorporated on the reverse of a standard order form that MCC's president signed on the company's behalf. Nevertheless, we conclude that the CISG, which governs international contracts for the sale of goods, precludes summary judgment in this case because MCC has raised an issue of material fact concerning the parties' subjective intent to be bound by the terms on the reverse of the pre-printed contract. The CISG also precludes the application of the parol evidence rule, which would otherwise bar the consideration of evidence concerning a prior or contemporaneously negotiated oral agreement. Accordingly, we REVERSE the district court's grant of summary judgment and REMAND this case for further proceedings consistent with this opinion.

## NOTES

**(1) Parol Evidence.** The issue in this case was not typical of parol evidence disputes in which one party offers evidence of terms that were not included in the record or evidence that contradicts a term in the record. Buyer's contention here was that the record contained boilerplate terms, in the seller's form, that the parties agreed were not part of their contract.

The issue, framed this way, is whether the parties had adopted the writing in its entirety. This may explain why the court relied primarily on CISG 8 and referred only incidentally, in a footnote, to CISG 11.

**(2) Language of the Agreement.** The contract in this case was negotiated face-to-face in Italy by an American buyer, acting through its president who did not speak or understand Italian, and an Italian seller, who may not have understood English. The parties communicated through a translator, an agent of the seller. The parties agreed on the economic terms of their transaction. The agreed terms were then integrated into a document that contained many terms that were expressed in Italian. Undoubtedly, these printed terms were seen by the buyer. Without understanding what those terms were, the buyer signed the document.

Should the printed terms be excluded from the contract because the buyer did not speak or read Italian, and the seller was aware of this impairment? Buyer's counsel "made much" of this argument. How might counsel have distinguished this argument from the argument that the parties intended to exclude the printed terms from the contract? The Court of Appeals found the argument based on the use of Italian "nothing short of astounding." Was the court correct?

## 3. REGULATION OF PRIVATE CONDUCT

The regulatory-like provisions of UCC Article 2 were the provisions that allow courts to strike unconscionable contracts or terms and the parties' general obligation of good faith in their performance or enforcement of sales contracts. CISG contains neither provision. Moreover, CISG declares that parties to contracts that come within the scope of CISG have unfettered power to modify or vary any of the provisions of the Convention. See CISG 6. If there were regulatory provisions in the Convention, blanket authority to derogate from the Convention would not exist.

CISG does not expressly or impliedly address unconscionability as a defense to enforcement of a contract for international sale of goods. No party to an international sales contract could plausibly assert such a defense as a matter of Convention law.

CISG 4(a) does state, however, that the Convention is "not concerned with" the "validity" of the contract or any of its provisions. CISG does not define "validity." In a transaction governed by the CISG, in which the underlying domestic law is United States law, a contention might be made that a contract or term that is unconscionable under UCC 2–302 is not "valid" within the meaning of that term in CISG 4(a). Although "validity" is not defined in CISG, the meaning of that word in the Convention is a matter of Convention law, not domestic law. Scholars of the Convention generally agree that fraud, illegality and incapacity are issues within the term, but do not agree on whether it also encompasses unconscionability.[32]

---

**32.** Compare J. Honnold, Uniform Law for International Sales, § 67 (3d ed. 1999), with C. Gillette & S. Walt, Sales Law: Domestic and International 162–165 (1999).

CISG does not contain a requirement of good faith in the performance or enforcement of contracts and duties of the kind provided in UCC 1–304 or in other nation's domestic law.[33] Such a provision was included in a draft of the Convention, but that provision was deleted from the final text. Professor Honnold explains: "In 1978, the Commission [UNCITRAL] . . . decided that tliahe obligation of 'good faith' should not be imposed loosely and at large, but should be restricted to a principle for interpreting the provisions of the Convention. This compromise was generally accepted and was embodied in the concluding words of Article 7(1)."[34]

## 4. REFERENCES

A useful research tool on CISG is the web site of UNCITRAL, www.uncitral.org. Case law applying the Convention is collected by the UNCITRAL Secretariat and published on the organization's web site, in the segment on case law (CLOUT). CLOUT contains abstracts of decisions that were rendered by national courts in countries that are parties to the Convention. Reporters in various countries submit the abstracts to the Secretariat. The abstracts are now organized by the Secretariat as annotations to a digest of the Convention.

CISG case law and a great deal of other useful material is being collected by the Institute of International Commercial Law at Pace University Law School. It maintains a web site at www.cisg.law.pace.edu. An index of decisions is organized by the years in which decisions were made and by the countries of the tribunals. Also found on this web site are reports of the CISG Advisory Council, a private organization sponsored by the Institute and by the Centre for Commercial Law Studies, Queen Mary, University of London.

For cross references between the Convention and the UCC, see A. Kritzer, Guide to Practical Applications of the United Nations Convention on Contracts for the International Sale of Goods (1989).

---

**33.** The German Civil Code (§ 242) states: "The debtor is bound to effect performance according to the requirements of good faith, giving consideration to common usage."

**34.** J. Honnold, Uniform Law for International Sales, § 94 (3d ed. 1999).

# CHAPTER 3

# TITLE: SELLERS' RESPONSIBILITY AND BUYERS' RIGHTS

## SECTION 1. INTRODUCTION

This chapter introduces the duality of the laws of property and of contract in sales transactions.

Under the Uniform Commercial Code, the essence of a "sale" is the passing of title from the seller to the buyer for a price. UCC 2–106(1).[1] "Title" is not a tern defined by the Code, but it is a common term in the law of real property and personal property. Our concern here is with personal property in the form of goods. A person with title to goods is entitled to possess, use, consume, or dispose of them. For our purposes in this chapter, the legal significance of a person's having, or not having, title to goods is largely a matter of that person's power to exclude claims of other persons to possess, use or consume, or dispose of those goods. In common parlance, we refer to the person with title as "owner" of the goods.

The property interest in goods can be divided among several persons. The owner can allow someone else to have possession and the right to use goods. The law refers to the most common forms of these arrangements as "bailments" or "leases."[2] The owner of goods can transfer a limited property interest to someone else. A common example is pledge of goods as collateral for a loan; the lender's property interest is a "security interest," a property interest limited to the amount of the debt secured.[3]

Ordinary buyers of goods expect to obtain "good" or "clean" title to the goods they have purchased. There are exceptions. A buyer may agree to

---

**1.** The Uniform Sales Act used the passing of title ("property") as the fulcrum for resolving a number of legal issues that may arise during the performance of sales contracts. The Commercial Code's rules on performance and remedies are not based on title passing. However, passing of title continues to be of primary importance to the parties to sales contracts because legal rights and duties not governed by the Code may turn upon the question of ownership. For example, tax obligations may fall upon the owner of property. In this chapter, we are concerned primarily with the role of title to resolve conflicting ownership claims to the goods.

**2.** Lease of goods is addressed in Article 2A of the Commercial Code. Bailments in which the bailee issues a "document of title" are addressed in Article 7. Other bailments are governed by common law.

**3.** Secured transactions in goods, and in other kinds of personal property, are governed by Article 9 of the Commercial Code.

buy only a fractional interest in the goods, to become a "part-owner" sharing title with the seller or with someone else. A buyer may agree to buy goods that are subject to an encumbrance, such as the right of a lender to foreclose and sell the goods to satisfy a loan secured by a security interest in the goods. The price that a buyer of less than full title agrees to pay will depend, of course, on the buyer's judgment of the value of the goods and on the amount of any other person's interest in them.

In this chapter we consider first a seller's responsibility to "pass" title to a buyer. A seller who fails to meet this responsibility is in breach of contract and may be held accountable for damages in an action by the buyer. The claim is described as a claim for breach of a term of the contract known as the warranty of title in domestic U.S. law. The Convention on Contracts for International Sale of Goods does not use the word "title" and does not define "sale," but the essence of a "sale" under CISG does not differ from the Commercial Code. CISG 41 provides that, ordinarily, a seller must deliver goods that are free from any right or claim of a third party, but adds an exception if the buyer agrees to take the goods subject to the third party's right or claim.[4]

Later in the chapter we will consider property law provisions in domestic U.S. law that deal with the claims of rightful owners or encumbrancers to take possession of the goods and the corollary provisions that allow some buyers (and other "purchasers") to defeat those claims. They may be entitled to keep the goods even though their sellers lacked title. If a buyer is a "good faith purchaser" or a "buyer in the ordinary course of business," the buyer may be able to fend off a previous owner's claim to regain possession and control of the goods. There are no analogous provisions of property law in CISG, which has its focus on matters of contract.

# SECTION 2. WARRANTY OF TITLE

## (A) DOMESTIC UNITED STATES LAW

The concern in this section is with transactions in which buyers, at the time of contracting, are unaware that anyone else has or retains a property interest in the goods and discover later that this is not, or may not be true. That may occur because the seller did not have title to the goods. If the goods were stolen, neither the thief nor anyone whose "chain of title" derives from the thief has title to the goods. If the seller holds the goods subject to a security interest or lien, the seller lacks "good" title and may be able to transfer only the seller's partial interest in the goods. Encumbrances on the title to goods arise sometimes through the voluntary action of an owner, who creates or consents to the creation of an interest in the property. The principal example of this form of encumbrance is a "security interest" under UCC Article 9. Other times, an encumbrance arises by

---

**4.** CISG does not deal expressly with the possibility that a seller might retain a property interest in the goods.

action of a third party, usually against the will of the owner. Thus, a judgment creditor may obtain a lien on property of the judgment debtor by the process of attachment or judgment execution. Alternatively, liens may arise by operation of law without a judgment. Examples are the liens that may be obtained by the Internal Revenue Service for unpaid federal taxes ("tax liens") or by repairers of goods for their services ("mechanics' liens").

Sales of encumbered goods or of stolen goods are the most common circumstances that underlie buyers' claims that their sellers failed to meet the obligation to pass good title to the goods. That kind of claim is characterized in domestic U.S. law as a claim for breach of the warranty of title. A buyer might invoke the warranty as the basis of a claim to obtain compensation or as a defense to seller's claim for payment of the price. As to stolen goods, the UCC 2–312(a) warranty is that the title conveyed shall be good and the transfer rightful. As to encumbered goods, the warranty is that the goods are free of any security interest, lien or encumbrance of which the buyer has no knowledge at the time of contracting UCC 2–312(b).

The warranty of title arises by operation of law. There is no need for an express contract term to create the warranty. However, the contracting parties may agree that the warranty is excluded or modified. UCC 2–312(2). The rationale for this provision is to cover circumstances where the buyer is aware that the seller does not claim to have title to the goods or is selling only such title as he or another person may have. Commercial settings for such sales may include public or private auction sales by sheriffs or executors of decedents' estates.

The following case arose from the sale of a motor vehicle. Automobiles and trucks are registered by states (largely to collect revenues from excise taxes) and are typically covered by "certificates of title" (largely to collect sales taxes), documents issued by states to owners of motor vehicles. One aspect of that body of law is a requirement that each motor vehicle have an identification number (VIN), which all manufacturers stamp into vehicles as they are produced. The relationship between the law regarding certificates of title and general property law will be addressed later.

### Colton v. Decker

Supreme Court of South Dakota, 1995.
540 N.W.2d 172.

■ Konenkamp, Justice.

After his truck was seized by law enforcement officials for having multiple serial numbers the owner sued and recovered damages from the seller. Both parties appeal. We affirm the breach of warranty of title but reverse and remand a portion of the damages award.

FACTS

Lee Decker, an over-the-road trucker, purchased a repossessed 1975 Peterbilt truck, Model 359, from a Minnesota bank in 1984. The truck's history is not completely known, but its rails or frame had apparently been extended from its original length to accommodate a double sleeper and it had also been wrecked at one time. The vehicle identification number (VIN) listed on the Minnesota title was 60596P. Decker transferred the truck's title to South Dakota. Although he claims not to have made any major structural changes, on several occasions Decker has acknowledged he rebuilt the truck "from the frame up."

Over a nine-month period in 1989, John Colton, who worked as a driver for Decker, drove the 1975 Peterbilt nearly 100,000 miles. In late December of that year, he offered to purchase the truck for $22,000. To help obtain financing Decker provided Colton with a list of the truck's features. On the list he wrote, "I spent 3 months rebuilding from the frame up when I first got the truck. 90% of the work was performed by myself." Decker's signature immediately followed. Assured of the truck's good condition, Marquette Bank of Sioux Falls financed Colton's purchase. On March 8, 1990, Decker's South Dakota truck title was transferred to Colton.

On August 22, 1991, Colton was stopped by the Wyoming Highway Patrol near Rock Springs, Wyoming and cited for speeding. After noting discrepancies in his logbook, the trooper inspected the rig and discovered that the VIN stamped on the right frame rail did not match the VIN listed on the registration. Conflicting VINs commonly indicate a stolen vehicle or stolen parts. The truck, but not the loaded trailer, was then impounded. Colton hired another trucker to haul the cargo in his trailer to Salt Lake City and retained a Wyoming attorney, but the attorney could not obtain immediate release of his truck. Colton returned to South Dakota. During the months waiting to recover his vehicle, he found some work driving trucks for other companies.

Meanwhile, Wyoming authorities disassembled Colton's truck in search of other serial numbers. The letter "K" in one conflicting number indicated that a glider kit[2] had been used. A third VIN, stamped with a manufacturer's die, was also discovered. Although more numbers matching the VIN on the title were found at various points on the truck (some hidden beneath paint and body putty), the numbers had not been imprinted by the manufacturer, but had been stamped by hand, apparently with a hardware store die. For example, a VIN matching the title was hand-stamped on a crudely fashioned rectangular piece of tin and affixed to the fire wall just above the clutch pedal.

Upon completing their nine-month investigation, Wyoming authorities determined Colton was indeed the true owner. A Wyoming court ordered a new Wyoming title to be issued clarifying the conflicting serial numbers.

---

**2.** Glider kits are parts used to update and replace older equipment on the truck such as frame rails, hood, drive line, and sleeper.

The truck would then be released upon payment of a $1,000 storage fee. Colton, who was now behind on loan payments, borrowed the money from Marquette Bank, traveled to Wyoming, and paid it. Unfortunately, the truck was inoperable, because while in Wyoming's possession, it remained dismantled and unsheltered throughout the winter. On April 11, 1992, Colton towed the truck from Wyoming back to Sioux Falls.

Once home, Colton placed the truck in storage until he could raise the money to repair it. Despite the court order, Colton was unable to obtain a new title in Wyoming because Marquette Bank refused to surrender the South Dakota title—its collateral—to Wyoming authorities. The bank also refused to exchange the faulty title for a new South Dakota "rebuilder's" title. Colton filed suit against Decker alleging breaches of warranty of title, warranty of merchantability, and express warranty of description. He also sent Decker a notice of intent to rescind the sale of the truck.

At trial on November 4–5, 1993, Decker disputed that his reconstruction of the truck required a rebuilder's title. ... After noting in its memorandum opinion (incorporated into the findings of fact and conclusions of law) that the man who assisted Decker in rebuilding the truck had noticed differing serial numbers, the trial court wrote:

[Decker] bought it as a wrecked truck, tore it down and rebuilt it. Even though he did not replace the parts which bore the different VINs, the discrepancies were obvious and discovered at the time he was rebuilding the vehicle.

The court awarded Colton $27,572.71 for breach of warranty of title. His other alleged breaches and offer to rescind were rejected. ...

### DECISION

I.  Warranty of Title

Wyoming authorities challenged the authenticity of Colton's title as the truck had three different VINs engraved at various points. Under these circumstances Colton averred Decker breached the warranty of title under SDCL 57A–2–312:

(1) Subject to subsection (2) there is in a contract for sale a warranty by the seller that

(a) The title conveyed shall be good, and its transfer rightful; and

(b) The goods shall be delivered free from any security interest or other lien or encumbrance of which the buyer at the time of contracting has no knowledge.

(2) A warranty under subsection (1) will be excluded or modified only by specific language or by circumstances which give the buyer reason to know that the person selling does not claim title in himself or that he is purporting to sell only such right or title as he or a third person may have.

Comment 1 to UCC § 2–312 states a buyer is entitled to "receive a good, clear title transferred ... in a rightful manner so [the buyer] will not be exposed to a lawsuit in order to protect it." A split of authority persists on the scope of § 2–312. Decker relies on those cases which hold that a breach of warranty of title occurs only when an outstanding superior title exists.[3] See, e.g., C.F. Sales, Inc. v. Amfert, Inc., 344 N.W.2d 543 (Iowa 1983); Johnston v. Simpson, 621 P.2d 688 (Utah 1980). Other courts hold that under § 2–312 mere initiation of a colorable challenge, one which is not spurious, regardless of the outcome, is sufficient to violate the warranty of title. Jefferson v. Jones, 286 Md. 544, 408 A.2d 1036, 1042 (Md. 1979) (law enforcement seizure of motorcycle when its VIN did not correspond to VIN in title document was colorable claim thus seller breached title warranty); American Container Corp. v. Hanley Trucking Corp., 111 N.J. Super. 322, 268 A.2d 313 (N.J. 1970) (law enforcement seizure of semi-trailer as stolen sufficient to cast substantial shadow thus violating warranty of good title). "Good title" typically means "the title which the seller gives to the buyer is 'free from reasonable doubt, that is, not only a valid title in fact, but [also] one that can again be sold to a reasonable purchaser ...,' " Jefferson, 408 A.2d at 1040 (quoting Langford v. Berry, 68 Ga. App. 193, 22 S.E.2d 349, 351 (Ga.Ct.App.1942)). We find the latter to be the better rule.

Wyoming Highway Patrol officials questioned Colton's ownership due to contradictory VINs thus casting a colorable challenge to its title. This was sufficient for a breach of title warranty claim. American Container Corp., 268 A.2d at 318; City Car Sales, Inc. v. McAlpin, 380 So. 2d 865 (Ala.Civ.App.1979); Ricklefs v. Clemens, 216 Kan. 128, 531 P.2d 94 (Kan. 1975). Indeed, the majority view holds that a purchaser can recover for a breach of warranty of title by merely showing the existence of a cloud on the title. Maroone Chevrolet, Inc. v. Nordstrom, 587 So. 2d 514, 518 (Fla.Dist.Ct.App.1991). Once breach of good title is established, good faith is not a defense, nor is a lack of knowledge of the defect. James A. White & Robert S. Summers, UNIFORM COMMERCIAL CODE § 9–12 (3d ed. rev. 1993); Smith v. Taylor, 44 N.C. App. 363, 261 S.E.2d 19 (N.C.Ct.App.1979). Purchasers should not be required to enter into a contest on the validity of ownership over a titled motor vehicle. Frank Arnold Contractors v. Vilsmeier Auction Co., Inc., 806 F.2d 462, 464 (3d Cir. 1986); Maroone Chevrolet, 587 So. 2d at 518; American Container, 268 A.2d at 318; Ricklefs, 531 P.2d at 100. As the undisputed facts reveal, Colton was forced into a contest over ownership because of conflicting VINs and an improper title. Thus, we uphold the circuit court's ruling that Decker breached the warranty of title. Maroone Chevrolet, 587 So. 2d at 518.

## II.   Damages

Colton was awarded total damages of $27,572.71, consisting of $14,000 for the value of the truck and $13,572.71 for costs incurred retrieving it

---

**3.** Indeed, the UCC drafters flatly stated "The warranty of quiet possession is abolished." Comment 1 UCC § 2–312. Yet the same comment states, "Disturbance of quiet possession, although not mentioned specifically, is one way, among many, in which the breach of the warranty of title may be established."

from Wyoming and storage. Breach of warranty damages are calculated under SDCL 57A–2–714:

> (2) The measure of damages for breach of warranty is the difference at the time and place of acceptance between the value of the goods accepted and the value they would have had if they had been as warranted, unless special circumstances show proximate damages of a different amount.

> (3) In a proper case any incidental and consequential damages under § 57A–2–715 may also be recovered.

Truck's Diminution in Value

Ample special circumstances take this case out of the "time of acceptance" provision in SDCL 57A–2–714. Here the measure of damages begins with determining the value of the truck at the time of dispossession. Ricklefs, 531 P.2d at 101; John St. Auto Wrecking v. Motors Insurance, 56 Misc. 2d 232, 288 N.Y.S.2d 281 (1968). Testimony established the truck was worth $22,000 when impounded, meaning it apparently did not depreciate in value during the months between Colton's purchase and the impoundment. Dismantled and unprotected from the Wyoming winter, uncontroverted testimony valued the truck at $8,000 in salvage. The trial court properly considered the "special circumstances" of SDCL 57A–2–714(2) to include the devaluation of the vehicle while in the hands of the Wyoming Highway Patrol and awarded the difference to Colton. Was the truck worth less than $22,000 at the time of impound? Could the truck have been worth more than $8,000 at the time it was released? The trial court could not answer those questions, as neither party offered any other estimates. The $14,000 award on the loss of the truck due to the breach is affirmed. Carlson v. Rysavy, 262 N.W.2d 27 (S.D.1978).

Retrieving the Truck

Of the $13,572.71 awarded for impoundment, retrieval, and storage expenses, Decker does not dispute that $4,810.10 of this amount relates to expenses incurred in connection with the seizure of the truck by Wyoming authorities.[4] Decker argues the remaining expenses cannot be upheld as incidental damages pursuant to SDCL 57A2–715(1):

> Incidental damages resulting from the seller's breach include expenses reasonably incurred in inspection, receipt, transportation and care and custody of goods rightfully rejected, any commercially reasonable charges, expenses or commissions in connection with effecting cover and any other reasonable expense incident to the delay or other breach.

---

**4.** This amount is composed of towing fees [in Wyoming], hiring another trucker to haul his load to Salt Lake City, retrieving his trailer from Salt Lake City, retaining a Wyoming attorney to get the truck out of impoundment, postage, a loan from Marquette Bank to pay the storage fee, and the motel and long distance expenses while authorities kept Colton in Wyoming.

Towing back to Sioux Falls was properly allowed as a reasonably foreseeable expense, not only because the truck was inoperable, but also because driving the still defectively-titled vehicle imposed the risk of another seizure along the route home. White & Summers at § 10–4; Gerwin v. Southeastern Cal. Ass'n of Seventh Day Adventists, 14 Cal. App. 3d 209, 92 Cal. Rptr. 111 (1971). An award based upon a bona fide effort to compensate for consequences of defects that establish a breach of warranty is a remedy the UCC seeks to provide. McGrady v. Chrysler Motors Corp., 46 Ill. App. 3d 136, 360 N.E.2d 818, 4 Ill. Dec. 705 (Ill. App. Ct. 1977). Expenses incurred retrieving the truck from Wyoming were reasonable expenses incident to the breach.

Storing the Truck

Colton spent $2,375 to store the truck near Sioux Falls, a truck worth $8,000 in salvage. Here, the causal link between the breach and the damages became so attenuated the damages were no longer incident to the breach. SDCL 57A–2–715(1); White & Summers at § 10–3. This was unreasonable, unexpected and served only to drive up expenses and devalue the truck. Neither does this expense meet the requirements for consequential damages under SDCL 57A–2–715(2):

> (a) Any loss resulting from general or particular requirements and needs of which the seller at the time of contracting had reason to know and which could not reasonably be prevented by cover or otherwise; and
>
> (b) Injury to person or property proximately resulting from any breach of warranty.

The law should not encourage waste. Even though the breach started the chain of events, Colton could not leave the truck in storage for an indefinite time until he had the finances to repair the damage caused in Wyoming. Consequential damages must be reasonably foreseeable by the breaching party at the time of contracting. ... The storage fees fail to qualify as reasonably foreseeable. Once Colton retrieved his truck, his responsibility included mitigating further loss. ... The official comment to UCC § 2–715(2) states recovery is impermissible "unless the buyer could not reasonably have prevented the loss by cover or otherwise."

Attorney Fees

Colton incurred legal fees in South Dakota attempting to clear the title and retrieve the truck from Wyoming. The trial court allowed these fees as damages under SDCL 57A–2–715. As an element of damages, the attorney's fees were reasonable expenses incident to the impoundment for clouded title. ...

In his notice of review Colton argues the trial court erred in not allowing his attorney's fees for prosecuting this suit. Also, Colton contends the trial court should have awarded him the attorney fees his bank incurred. Trying to get the title issue resolved, Marquette Bank paid attorney fees, which it added to Colton's loan balance. Other than referring to the UCC, Colton cites no authority to support these arguments. We conclude the trial court properly declined to award such fees as damages under SDCL 57A–2–715(1) or (2) or as disbursements under SDCL 15–17–38.

\* \* \*

Unawarded Damages

Colton further seeks compensation for repairs to the truck, lost profits, lost investment opportunities, and use of an expert witness. The trial court declined to award these damages or costs. We see no abuse of discretion for omitting these items from incidental and consequential damage consideration. Stormo v. Strong, 469 N.W.2d 816, 820 (S.D.1991).

Affirmed in part, reversed in part and remanded.

■ AMUNDSON, JUSTICE (concurring in part and dissenting in part).

I disagree with the majority's calculation of damages. The truck was impounded on August 22, 1991, and Colton towed the truck from Wyoming on April 11, 1992, however, the majority glosses over the fact that the Wyoming authorities offered release of the truck in January 1992 if Colton would pay $1,000 storage fee and forfeit the South Dakota title so that a new Wyoming title could be issued. It is undisputed that the value of the truck when impounded was $22,000. Colton could not afford the $1,000 fee so he went to his creditor, Marquette Bank. Marquette Bank refused to extend Colton's credit to pay the $1,000 and also refused to surrender the South Dakota title. So, from January until April, the dismantled truck endured the Wyoming winter. Decker should not be responsible for the diminution in value of the truck between January and April.

Colton's proper remedy is recovering this loss from Marquette Bank. Forcing Decker to pay for the unreasonable delay caused by Marquette Bank's actions is unjust. Colton had a duty to mitigate his damages, and any damages resulting from his failure to take reasonable steps to mitigate or prevent damages cannot be recovered from Decker. See Wieting v. Ball Air Spray, Inc., 84 S.D. 493, 173 N.W.2d 272 (1969). SDCL 57A–2–715(2) states in part: "(2) Consequential damages resulting from the seller's breach include: (a) Any loss . . . which could not reasonably be prevented by cover or otherwise[.]" (Emphasis added.) This loss could have been prevented by Marquette Bank's releasing the title in a timely manner. Surrendering the title in order for a new, clearer and correct title to be issued was the logical step for Marquette Bank to take. Unfortunately, logic does not always play a part in today's world.

The buyer's right to recover for damages is not unlimited. Buyer must take reasonable steps to reduce or minimize his damages. . . . However, buyer will be excused from mitigation when his financial condition will not allow him to take mitigating steps. . . .

In this case, however, it was not buyer who refused to take mitigating steps, but buyer's creditor, Marquette Bank, who refused to take the necessary steps. The general rule is that a bank is required to maintain a "duty of good faith and fair dealing toward its customers." Garrett v. BankWest, Inc., 459 N.W.2d 833, 846 n. 9 (S.D.1990). Whether or not Marquette Bank acted in good faith is not at issue here, however, Decker should not be punished for the action or inaction of Marquette Bank. Therefore, we should remand in order for the trial court to assess the correct amount of damages.

NOTES

**(1) Stolen Goods.** If the truck that Decker sold to Colton had been a stolen vehicle, Decker's breach of the warranty of title would have been clear. See Fischer v. Bright Bay Lincoln Mercury, Inc., 234 A.D.2d 586, 651 N.Y.S.2d 625 (1996); Curran v. Ciaramelli, 1998 WL 1095080, 37 UCC Rep. Serv.2d 94 (N.Y. Dist. Ct. 1998). The Wyoming police suspected that Colton was driving a stolen truck. Police routinely impound stolen property that they suspect had been stolen. In other circumstances, buyers voluntarily surrender property to rightful owners. Law suits against sellers of goods that had been stolen are uncommon, possibly because it is impractical to expect to recover monetary damages from those who deal in stolen goods.

**(2) Clouds on Title.** In this case, the police officers' suspicion was eventually determined to have been unfounded. The truck had not been stolen and Colton had the title. Views that goods had been stolen can range from clearly plausible to quite fanciful. Where on this spectrum does a seller's responsibility end? Notwithstanding the ultimate conclusion that Colton had good title to the truck, the South Dakota Supreme Court conclude that this seller was in breach of the warranty of title because the contradictory VINs, for which the seller was responsible, created a "colorable challenge" to buyer's title. The court noted that the courts in other states were divided on what constitutes breach of the warranty of title if the goods were not stolen. Is the court's construction of the UCC 2–312 sound? Is the conclusion supported by the *text* of the section? Is it supported by the Comments? See the third sentence of Comment 1. What is the appropriate legal force of a provision in a Comment that goes beyond the text? Does the Comment have legislative force?[1]

**(3) Remedy for Breach of the Warranty of Title.** The remedy provisions of Article 2, found in the 2–700 sections, do not contain a remedy specific to warranty breach under UCC 2–312. The correct measure of damages for such a breach is disputed. Pursuant to the general principle that damages should put an aggrieved party in the position that performance would have done, often called "expectation damages,"[2] buyers who

---

**1.** The first sentence of the third paragraph of Comment 1 declares that "the warranty of quiet possession is abolished," but adds that disturbance of quiet possession is one way that the warranty of title can be breached. Why would drafters of Article 2 abolish a warranty of quiet possession of goods? Overbreadth?

**2.** This general principle of common law is codified for the Commercial Code in UCC 1–305(a).

have been deprived of the goods altogether should be allowed to recover the value of the goods of which they have been deprived. A difficult question that often arises in breach of title warranty cases is determining the date on which that value to be measured. A defect in title may be unknown to a buyer for a substantial period of time after goods have been purchased. Between the date of delivery and the date buyer loses possession, the market value of the goods may have changed substantially. The direction of change could be down or up, and the rate of change can be slow or fast. For example, durable goods and equipment generally depreciate over time, whereas some works of art appreciate, occasionally precipitously, if the reputation of the artist is growing. Other changes in value may be attributable to modifications or improvements made by the buyers.

The issue is complicated by the fact that Article 2 does contain a remedy provision that, on its face, seems to apply to breach of warranty of title cases, UCC 2–714. The caption and subsection (1) refer to damages for breach in regard to accepted goods. "Acceptance" is a legal concept, defined in UCC 2–606,that we will consider in depth in a later chapter. Most disputes arising from breach of warranty of title arise after the goods have been accepted. UCC 2–714(1) deals with "any non-conformity of tender," a phrase that could be read to include tender of goods with a title defect. Subsection (1) provides a broad standard for measurement of a buyer's damages: "any manner that is reasonable." However, subsection (2) deals expressly with damages for "breach of warranty." Under this subsection damages are the difference between the value of the goods "at the time . . . of acceptance" and the value they would have had if they had been as warranted. There is an exception for cases where "special circumstances show proximate damages of a different amount."

UCC 2–714 clearly provides the basic measure of damages for sellers' breach of warranties of *quality*. We take these up in the next chapters. Does this section apply to damages for breach of the warranty of *title*? Value-at-the-time-of acceptance may be appropriate in measurement of damages for breach of a warranty of quality, but application to warranty of title breach is problematic, primarily because of it fixes a buyer's recovery at the moment of acceptance rather than at the later date (perhaps much later) when buyer loses possession of the goods.

A Maryland court faced the problem in a case arising from sale of certain patterns used to produce hardware. The parties agreed that seller did not have title and the rightful owners took possession of them. The patterns had been used and had depreciated in value while in buyer's possession. Buyer contended that the "difference formula" of UCC 2–714(2) should govern. Under that formula the value of conforming goods would be at least the contract price while the value of the accepted goods was zero since buyer never had a lawful right to possession. The court concluded that buyer's claim was excessive. The court felt compelled to apply UCC 2–714(2), but not to use the "difference formula":

Scholars contend that § 2–714(2) does not regulate damages for breach of warranty of title, but that it in fact relates only to breach of warranty of quality.... This is said to be so because § 2–714(2) is based on § 69(6) and (7) of the Uniform Sales Act; those provisions pertained to breaches of warranty of quality, not title....

It is suggested that because § 2–714(2) does not expressly apply to a breach of warranty of title, a court should look to pre-U.C.C. law in that situation by virtue of the "special circumstances" provision of § 2–714(2) and because the U.C.C. comment to that section indicates it is not intended to provide for the exclusive measure of damages.... Pre–U.C.C. law is not too helpful, however. Under it decisions relating to the measure of damages for breach of warranty of title range from purchase price plus interest to value of the goods at time of disposses-sion, to value without specifying any time of determination, to value at time of sale (which may or may not be the same as the purchase price).
...

Other jurisdictions have faced this problem. They have applied § 2–714(2) to breaches of warranty of title.... We shall do likewise. The statute is plain and unambiguous on its face and should be read according to its clear meaning....

The next question is whether to apply § 2–714(2)'s "difference at the time and place of acceptance between the value of the goods accepted and the value they would have had as warranted" or whether there are "special circumstances [that] show proximate damages of a different amount." We hold that there are special circumstances here.... [Buy-er] had use and possession of the patterns for varying periods of time before it had knowledge of any title defects.

Since we conclude that this case falls within the "special circum-stances" clause of § 2–714(2), we must now decide what measure of damages to apply under it. Courts that have considered the question under the U.C.C. have almost uniformly rejected the view that the purchase price of the goods is the proper measure.... The value of the goods at the approximate date of dispossession, or something akin to that, is the measure of damages generally selected.

Metalcraft, Inc. v. Pratt, 65 Md.App. 281, 292–294, 500 A.2d 329, 335–336 (1985).

In *Metalcraft* the value of the goods at the time of dispossession had diminished from their value at the time of sale. Suppose that the goods, prior to discovery of a title defect, had appreciated significantly in value. Should a court interpret the "special circumstances" clause of UCC 2–714(2) to permit the larger recovery that takes that appreciation into account? See Jeanneret v. Vichey, 693 F.2d 259 (2d Cir.1982); Menzel v. List, 24 N.Y.2d 91, 298 N.Y.S.2d 979, 246 N.E.2d 742 (1969).

In *Colton v. Decker*, buyer was dispossessed of the truck, but only temporarily. There was no defect in seller's title and the buyer eventually regained possession of the truck. What statutory measure of damages did the South Dakota Supreme Court find to be appropriate? What statutory measure of damages would have been applied by the dissenting justice?

Were the actual damages assessed by the majority or avowed by the dissent consistent with UCC 2–714?

————

A security interest is an interest in property. A security interest is an encumbrance on the title. If an obligation to pay a loan secured by a security interest is in default, the secured party may repossess the goods, sell them, and apply the proceeds to the debt. Merchants and farmers commonly borrow money to finance their business activities and those who lend money to them often secure their loans by taking security interests in property, including the goods in inventory. Lenders routinely release their encumbrances on merchants' and farmers' inventory at the time of retail sale. They expect that the loans will be repaid from the proceeds of the sales and therefore authorize the merchants or farmers to sell the goods to buyers free of security interests. This commercial practice is reflected in UCC 9–315(a)(1), which provides that a security interest does not "continue" after authorized sale of the goods.

The following case involves a security interest in several pieces of construction equipment. Unlike inventory financing, equipment financing contemplates that the debtor make instalment payments while using the collateral but not sell it before the loan is repaid. Sometimes, however, equipment is put into a second-hand market while there is an outstanding balance on the debt. Absent a release by the secured party, UCC 9–315(a)(1) provides that the security interest "continues." The secured party has the right to repossess the equipment from the buyer, sell it as provided in Article 9 and use the proceeds to satisfy the borrower's obligation. (If there is a surplus, the secured party must account to the debtor. UCC 9–608(a)(4)). In this case, the debtor contracted with an auctioneer to sell one piece of the equipment.

## Frank Arnold Contractors, Inc. v. Vilsmeier Auction Co. Inc.

United States Court of Appeals, Third Circuit, 1986.
806 F.2d 462.

■ SEITZ, CIRCUIT JUDGE.

Defendant Vilsmeier Auction Company, Inc. ("Vilsmeier") appeals from the final judgment of the district court in favor of plaintiff Frank Arnold Contractors, Inc. ("Arnold").

I.

In August 1980, ITT Industrial Credit Company ("ITT") loaned money to Edward McGinn General Contractors, Inc. ("McGinn"). In return, McGinn gave ITT a security interest in several pieces of construction equipment, including a Caterpillar hydraulic excavator. ITT properly perfected the security interest.

In the summer of 1981, ITT became aware that McGinn was experiencing significant financial problems and had failed to make certain payments to ITT on its loan agreements. While the parties dispute succeeding events, it is clear that following discussions between McGinn and ITT representatives the hydraulic excavator was sold at auction by Vilsmeier in October 1981.

Vilsmeier president Hutchinson admitted that prior to the commencement of the auction, Vilsmeier made a public announcement to the effect that all of the equipment being sold was free and clear of any liens, encumbrances or other security interests. Vilsmeier did not disclaim this warranty of title. Appellee Arnold purchased the hydraulic excavator at the auction for approximately $44,000, and began using it in its business. While it possessed the machine, Arnold invested over $5,000 in repair and maintenance of the excavator.

In May 1983, Arnold learned that ITT was suing it to recover the excavator on the basis of the perfected security interest. Although the suit, filed in federal court, was dismissed for lack of jurisdiction, Arnold incurred legal expenses of over $3100. ITT subsequently filed the same claim against Arnold in state court. On the advice of counsel, Arnold surrendered the excavator to ITT in October 1983. Arnold thereafter purchased a replacement excavator for $41,000.

Arnold later filed this diversity action against both Vilsmeier and ITT. During trial before a jury, the district court directed a verdict as to liability for Arnold and against Vilsmeier. The court also granted ITT's motion for a directed verdict as to liability. The court permitted the jury to determine Arnold's damages. After considering Vilsmeier's and Arnold's evidence on damages, the jury awarded Arnold $52,150.50. The district court subsequently denied Vilsmeier's motion for a new trial, and entered judgment in favor of Arnold. This appeal followed.

II.

Vilsmeier raises two challenges to the proceedings in the district court. We will consider these challenges in turn.

A.

Vilsmeier first contends that the district court erred in directing a verdict of liability in favor of Arnold and against it. Our review of the grant of a directed verdict is plenary and we apply the same standard as would the district court in passing on the motion originally. . . .

Vilsmeier argues that the district court's grant of a directed verdict for Arnold improperly precluded the jury from considering whether ITT had waived its security interest in the excavator purchased by Arnold. Under Vilsmeier's view of the case, if ITT had waived its security interest in the excavator, Vilsmeier sold the excavator without an encumbered title, and Arnold would not be entitled to damages for breach of warranty of title.

The district court rejected Vilsmeier's view of the case. The court determined that whether ITT had actually waived its security interest was irrelevant to Arnold's cause of action, because the excavator had a cloud on its title. The district court held as a matter of law that Vilsmeier breached its warranty of title to Arnold by selling the excavator with a cloud on its title, regardless of whether the title was actually encumbered.

The district court's ruling construes § 2–312 of the Uniform Commercial Code ("UCC"), adopted in Pennsylvania, 13 Pa. Cons. Stat. Ann. § 2312 (Purdon 1984). That provision states that as a general rule, a contract for the sale of goods includes a warranty by the seller that the goods sold are sold without title encumbrances, unless the warranty is disclaimed. Comment 1 to § 2312 explains further that the provision provides for a "buyer's basic needs in respect to a title." 13 Pa. Cons. Stat. Ann. § 2312, Comment 1. A seller accomplishes this objective whenever he transfers to his purchaser "a good clear title . . . in a rightful manner so that [the purchaser] will not be exposed to a lawsuit in order to protect it." *Id.* Finally, Comment 1 notes that "disturbance of quiet possession, although not mentioned specifically, is one way, among many, in which the breach of warranty of title may be established." *Id.*

The parties have not called to our attention any decisions of the Pennsylvania courts construing § 2312 under the circumstances present here, and our research reveals none. Accordingly, we are bound to determine how the Pennsylvania Supreme Court would rule on the matter were the question before it. . . .

While the Pennsylvania courts have not addressed whether a cloud on a title is sufficient to breach a seller's warranty under § 2312, the courts in a number of other states have construed their versions of UCC § 2–312 in these circumstances. In the majority of these cases, the courts have concluded that there need not be an actual encumbrance on the purchaser's title to permit recovery for a breach of warranty of title. Often relying on the above-quoted language from Comment 1, the courts have indicated that so long as there is a "substantial shadow" on the purchaser's title, . . . the protection of § 2–312 "applies to third party claims of title no matter whether eventually determined to be inferior or superior to the buyer's ownership." . . . . This view is supported by the policy that a purchaser should not be required to engage in a contest over the validity of his ownership.

At least two courts have indicated, however, that a purchaser must demonstrate more than a cloud on his title before he will be permitted to recover for a breach of warranty of title. These courts apparently require the purchaser to establish the existence of a superior or paramount title in a third party. . . .

We believe the majority approach is well-reasoned and is firmly grounded in the policy of the statute. For this reason, we believe that were the Pennsylvania Supreme Court confronted with this question, it would hold that a purchaser can recover for a breach of warranty of title when he demonstrates the existence of a cloud on his title, regardless of whether it eventually develops that the third party's title is superior. We need not in this case determine all the circumstances in which a purchaser's title is clouded, ... for ITT's two lawsuits plainly demonstrate the cloud over Arnold's title. Under these circumstances, the district court's entry of directed verdicts in favor of Arnold and against Vilsmeier was not error.

B.

Vilsmeier next contends that the district court erred in refusing to grant a new trial on the ground that the jury's damages verdict was unsupported by the evidence. This court reviews the district court's decision for abuse of discretion. ... Where, as here, an appellant asserts that the jury's assessment of damages is too high, a district court may be said to have abused its discretion only if the amount of damages awarded is "shocking."

Vilsmeier's contention that the jury erred in assessing damages is based on the fact that the jury apparently gave more credence to Arnold's damages evidence than it gave to Vilsmeier's. The record demonstrates, however, that the jury's award was perfectly reasonable. In these circumstances, the district court did not abuse its discretion in denying the motion for a new trial.

III.

For the reasons set forth above, the judgment of the district court will be affirmed.

NOTES

**(1) Free of a Security Interest.** To prevail under UCC 2–312(1)(b), a buyer has to show that the goods it purchased were not free of a security interest. Here, the secured party sued the buyer to recover possession of the equipment. Rather than defend, the buyer surrendered the equipment to the secured party. This was done on advice of counsel. In the title warranty law suit, the auctioneer-seller asserted that there was evidence that the secured party had "waived" the security interest. If the security interest had been waived, the equipment sold at the auction was free of the security interest. The federal trial court granted summary judgment to the buyer without allowing the auctioneer-seller to introduce evidence of waiver. The court decided that the secured party's commencement of legal action to regain possession was sufficient to show a breach of the warranty of title. The appellate court affirmed. Did the secured party's legal action "plainly demonstrate" a cloud on buyer's title?

The court does not describe the suggested evidence of waiver. If a secured party released its security interest in advance of an auction sale of the collateral, it is reasonable to suppose that this would have been done only under an agreement with the auctioneer as to the distribution of the proceeds of the auction sale. There is no indication that the secured party received any of those proceeds. Is that significant?

**(2) Damages.** The opinion indicates that the auctioneer-seller contended that the damages fixed by a jury in the trial court were excessive, but the opinion does not reveal the particulars of the dispute. The jury award is virtually the sum of the amount the buyer paid at the auction sale, the amount of improvements the buyer made while in possession of the equipment, and the amount paid to defend the first law suit by the secured party. Is that consistent with UCC 2–714?

**(3) Auctioneer as Seller.** Auction sales take a variety of forms. Commonly auctioneers collect fees from the owners who authorize the auctioneer to sell them, but the auctioneers do not own the goods. The owners of the goods may or may not be made known to the bidders. It appears that Vilsmeier Auction Co. did not identify the owners of the goods. The form of auction sales with undisclosed owners is, therefore, sales by the auctioneer to the high bidders.[3] There was no way for bidders to determine whether the goods on the block were encumbered by examining the public records in which security interests are filed under the names of the borrowers. This explains the Auction Company's express warranty ro the bidders that the goods being sold were free of liens. Under common-law agency doctrine, one who contracts as agent for another without disclosing the identity of the principal is not merely an agent, but is deemed a "party to the contract." Restatement (Second) of Agency §§ 321–322. See Jones v. Ballard, 573 So.2d 783 (Miss.1990) (warranty of title); cf. Powers v. Coffeyville Livestock Sales Co., 665 F.2d 311 (10th Cir.1981) (warranty of quality). Does this doctrine from common law apply to transactions under UCC Article 2. Recall UCC 1–103(b).

**Problem 1.** Buyer was the winning bidder at an auction sale and agreed to buy 45 head of cattle for $13,000. Unknown to Buyer at the time of the auction sale, there was a valid and perfected security interest in the cattle. Also unknown to Buyer, the secured party had consented to the auction sale of the cattle free and clear of the security interest. Terms of the auction sale required Buyer to pay $1,000 down and the balance within six days. On the day following the auction sale, Buyer was informed by a third party that the cattle were subject to a security interest. Buyer was not informed and did not learn that the secured party had authorized sale of the cattle. Buyer stopped payment on his check for the down payment and refused to take and pay for the cattle. Seller promptly resold the cattle for $3,000 and sued Buyer for $10,000. What should be the result? See Wright v. Vickaryous, 611 P.2d 20 (Alaska 1980). How likely is it that an auction buyer of 45 head of cattle would be so unsophisticated in that marketplace as to be surprised by the information that the secured party authorized the sale? How likely is it that such a buyer would not expect that encumbrances created by the seller would be released?

Does this suggest that the buyer may have overbid in the first auction and, having realized this, wanted a way to escape the obligation to pay the contract price? If this were buyer's motive, would buyer's action be consis-

---

**3.** The procedure for contract formation between the auctioneer and a bidder is set forth in UCC 2–328.

tent with the obligation to act in good faith in the performance of the contract?

**Problem 2.** Charles Creditor held a judgment against Daniel Debtor, and sued out a writ of attachment to levy on Debtor's property. Pursuant to the writ of attachment, Samuel Sheriff seized a tractor in Debtor's possession and sold it at an execution sale; Buyer bought the tractor for $500. Unknown to all parties, the tractor was subject to a security interest held by Leo Lean to secure a $300 debt which Debtor owed Lean. Lean's security interest was not terminated by the sale, and Lean threatens to seize the tractor from Buyer unless Debtor's debt is satisfied. Has Buyer any recourse against Sheriff or Creditor? See UCC 2–312(2); Bogestad v. Anderson, 143 Minn. 336, 173 N.W. 674 (1919). Has Buyer any recourse against Debtor?

————

# Pacific Sunwear of California, Inc. v. Olaes Enterprises, Inc.

Court of Appeal of California, 4th App. Dist., Div. One, 2008.
167 Cal.App.4th 466, 84 Cal.Rptr.3d 182.

■ Irion, J.

In this appeal, clothing retailer Pacific Sunwear of California, Inc. (PacSun), appeals a trial court order granting summary judgment in favor of Olaes Enterprises, Inc. (Olaes), in PacSun's breach of warranty lawsuit. The lawsuit alleges that Olaes breached the warranty contained in section 2312, subdivision (3) of the California Uniform Commercial Code (hereafter section 2312(3)), which requires certain sellers to warrant that their goods are "free of the rightful claim of any third person by way of infringement or the like." (§ 2312(3).) PacSun seeks monetary damages for the alleged breach to compensate it for litigation expenses incurred in defending against a third party trademark infringement lawsuit that arose out of PacSun's sale of T-shirts purchased from Olaes.

The trial court granted Olaes's motion for summary judgment on the ground that the third party claim did not constitute a "rightful claim" of infringement under the California Uniform Commercial Code and thus did not breach the section 2312(3) warranty. The trial court reached this conclusion, as a matter of law, after analyzing a federal district court's ruling on the third party's request for a preliminary injunction in the underlying trademark infringement litigation. In particular, the trial court highlighted the district court's finding that there was not a " 'likelihood of confusion' " between the allegedly infringing T-shirts and the third party's trademark.

As we shall explain, the trial court's interpretation of rightful claim was erroneous. A rightful claim under section 2312(3) is not synonymous with a claim that ultimately will prove successful in litigation. Rather, as we will define for the first time under California law, a rightful claim under section 2312(3) is a nonfrivolous claim of infringement that has any significant and adverse effect on the buyer's ability to make use of the purchased goods. Under this standard, the trial court could not properly conclude on the evidence before it, as a matter of law, that the third party infringement claim against PacSun was not a rightful claim, and consequently we reverse.

FACTS

Olaes supplies PacSun with T-shirts imprinted with graphic designs for resale in PacSun stores. In 2004 PacSun purchased 16,000 "Hot Sauce Monkey" T-shirts from Olaes. These T-shirts depict, on the front, a monkey drinking a bottle of hot sauce and, on the back, the same monkey in apparent pain, expelling fire. Centered underneath each of the images is a two-word caption: on the front, the phrase "Smile Now"; on the back, the phrase "Cry Later."

A.  *The Hawaii Litigation*

On May 14, 2004, clothing maker Smile Now Cry Later Inc. (SNCL) filed a complaint in the United States District Court for the District of Hawaii against another clothing maker, Yakira, LLC (also known as "Ecko"), as well as a subsidiary of PacSun, Pacific Sunwear Stores Corp. (also known as "d.e.m.o."), for trademark infringement. The complaint alleged that Ecko had manufactured shirts that infringed on SNCL's trademark, and d.e.m.o. sold the shirts in its retail stores. SNCL included in its complaint a copy of its registered trademark, which depicts two masks in the style of ancient Greek theater masks. One of the masks is smiling and the other is crying. Underneath the corresponding masks are the words "Smile Now" and "Cry Later." SNCL's complaint also contained an example of the allegedly infringing design manufactured by Ecko.

On January 12, 2005, SNCL amended its complaint in the Hawaii litigation to include PacSun as a defendant and to add an allegation that the Hot Sauce Monkey T-shirts violated SNCL's trademark. In the ensuing litigation, PacSun, with cooperation from Olaes, defended itself, denying that the Hot Sauce Monkey T-shirts infringed SNCL's trademark.

In the course of the trademark litigation, SNCL filed a motion for a preliminary injunction barring further sales of the Hot Sauce Monkey T-shirts. The district court issued a 20–page order denying SNCL's motion. In the order, the federal court analyzed SNCL's trademark infringement claim under an eight-factor test utilized by the Ninth Circuit to determine likelihood of confusion, . . . The district court determined that SNCL failed to carry its burden with respect to five of the eight factors, and had not "established a likelihood of confusion" between the Hot Sauce Monkey T-shirts and SNCL's trademark. In June 2005, all parties to the Hawaii litigation entered into a settlement agreement. The settlement was filed under seal.

B. *The Instant Action*

In May 2006 PacSun filed the instant action in superior court. The complaint alleged a single cause of action: that Olaes breached the statutory warranty that the Hot Sauce Monkey T-shirts were "free of the rightful claim of any third person by way of infringement or the like." (§ 2312(3).) After Olaes answered the complaint, PacSun and Olaes filed cross-motions for summary judgment.

The trial court denied PacSun's summary judgment motion and granted Olaes's summary judgment motion. With respect to Olaes's motion, the court ruled that "SNCL's underlying claims of infringement were not 'rightful claims' under [section] 2312(3) and thus [Olaes] did not breach the warranty provided for under that section." In reaching this conclusion, the court noted that "rightful" was not defined in the California Uniform Commercial Code, and that the parties had failed to present any case law "expressly construing the meaning of that word as it appears in [section] 2312(3)." Consequently, the court examined the "usual and ordinary meaning" of the term "rightful" by reference to various dictionary definitions, such as "valid," "just," "appropriate; fitting; right or proper etc." To determine whether the claim was rightful under these definitions, the court proceeded to review the federal district court's preliminary injunction ruling. Highlighting the fact that the federal district court found that SNCL "failed to meet its burden as to five of the eight factors required to establish a claim of trademark infringement," and that there was not a likelihood of confusion, the trial court concluded "as a matter of law, [that] the underlying claim does not meet the plain meaning of the word 'rightful,' i.e., 'valid'; 'proper'; 'appropriate'; [or] 'just.'" The court also "note[d]" the fact that PacSun continued selling the T-shirts after being put on notice of the infringement claim, suggesting that PacSun itself believed the claim was not ?rightful." PacSun appeals.

DISCUSSION

PacSun contends that the trial court erred in ruling, as a matter of law, that SNCL's trademark infringement claim was not a rightful claim. PacSun argues that, "at the very least," there is a disputed factual issue as to whether the claim is "rightful," precluding summary judgment. We agree.

\* \* \*

At issue in the instant appeal is the applicability of section 2312(3) and, specifically, whether the trial court properly ruled on a motion for summary judgment that the section 2312(3) warranty did not apply because the trademark suit filed by SNCL was not a rightful claim of infringement.

In interpreting section 2312(3), the parties suggest widely divergent definitions of the phrase "rightful claim." Olaes suggests that a rightful claim is a valid claim, i.e., one that has proven, or will likely prove, meritorious in litigation. ... By contrast, PacSun argues that any claim "in the form of litigation" constitutes a rightful claim regardless of its underlying merits. We believe the correct interpretation of section 2312(3) lies somewhere in between these positions. . . .

Despite the widespread adoption of subdivision (3) of section 2–312 of the Uniform Commercial Code, there are few reported cases discussing the provision and little precedent regarding the definition of a rightful claim. . . . There are no California cases on point. Thus we take up the question on a relatively clean slate, applying the familiar rules of statutory interpretation.

(1) . . . The phrase "rightful claim" is not defined in the California Uniform Commercial Code, and is not a legal term of art that can be interpreted by reference to existing California statutory or case law. In addition, due to the multitude of definitions of "rightful" in common usage (as noted by the trial court), the term is ambiguous with respect to its application in the current context. Thus, the phrase is reasonably susceptible to more than one interpretation, and we must turn to " ' "extrinsic aids" ' " to discern its meaning. . . .

(2) The primary extrinsic aid for interpretation of the Uniform Commercial Code is the official commentary to that code. While the statutory text, of course, controls over any inconsistent commentary, courts regularly look to the official commentary to determine the meaning of ambiguous statutory provisions. . . .

(3) As explained below, the commentary to Uniform Commercial Code section 2–312 demonstrates that, contrary to Olaes's position, the term "rightful claim" as used in the statute is intended to broadly encompass any nonfrivolous claim of infringement that significantly interferes with the buyer's use of a purchased good.

Official comment 3 to Uniform Commercial Code section 2–312 states that subdivision (1) creates a duty on the part of the seller "to see that *no claim of infringement* of a patent or trade-mark by a third party will *mar* the buyer's title." . . . (italics added.) The commentary further explains that the subdivision's purpose is to "reject[]" case law that had required a buyer to be "expressly prevented from using the goods" by an infringement claim prior to obtaining relief. . . . The commentary thus explains that under the Uniform Commercial Code, " 'eviction' is not a necessary condition to the buyer's remedy since the buyer's remedy *arises immediately upon receipt of notice of infringement.*" . . . (italics added.) The comment quoted above, by stating that the seller warrants there will be "no claim of infringement," and by asserting that the buyer's remedy arises immediately upon notice of infringement (i.e., well before resolution of the claim), strongly suggests that any significant claim of infringement—whether or not ultimately meritorious—triggers the section 2312(3) warranty.[8] . . .

---

8. At the time of the drafting of the Uniform Commercial Code, the drafters were presented with a request from the New York Patent Law Association "that the phrase 'rightful claim' " be replaced with " 'valid claim.' " (1 Rep. of the N.Y. Law Revision Com. for 1955: Study of the Uniform Commercial Code (1998) p. 738.) The request was supported by

(4) The parameters of the section 2312(3) warranty are further clarified by the official commentary to an analogous warranty in subdivision (1) of Uniform Commercial Code section 2–312.[9] The subdivision (1) warranty requires a seller to warrant that title to a purchased item "shall be good, and its transfer rightful." ... The accompanying commentary states that the requirement that the transfer be "rightful" obligates the seller to ensure that the goods are free from any significant claims against title—not simply those claims that ultimately will prove successful in litigation. ...

(5) The Uniform Commercial Code section 2–312, subdivision (1) warranty thus "makes provision for a buyer's basic needs in respect to a title which he in good faith expects to acquire by his purchase, namely, that he receive a good, clean title transferred to him also in a rightful manner so that he will not *be exposed to a lawsuit* in order to protect it." ... (italics added.)

In line with the above commentary, the majority view of the courts is that the Uniform Commercial Code section 2–312, subdivision (1) warranty is not inapplicable simply because the underlying claim against the buyer's title ultimately lacks merit. (See *Maroone Chevrolet, Inc. v. Nordstrom* (Fla.Dist.Ct.App. 1991) 587 So.2d 514, 518 (*Maroone Chevrolet*) [agreeing with the "majority view" that "there need not be an actual encumbrance on the purchaser's title or actual disturbance of possession to permit a purchaser to recover for a breach of warranty of title," and explaining that this view " 'is supported by the policy that a purchaser should not be required to engage in a contest over the validity of his ownership' "]; *Frank Arnold Contractors v. Vilsmeier Auction Co.* (3d Cir. 1986) 806 F.2d 462, 464–465 (*Frank Arnold Contractors*) [noting that the "majority" of courts hold that "there need not be an actual encumbrance on the purchaser's title to permit recovery for a breach of warranty of title," but rather "a 'substantial shadow' on the purchaser's title" is sufficient, and concluding that "the majority approach is well-reasoned and ... firmly grounded in the policy of the statute"].) This broad interpretation, in the commentary and the case law, of Uniform Commercial Code section 2–312, subdivision (1)'s warranty of a good and rightful transfer of title, carries great weight in our interpretation of the analogous warranty in section 2312(3).[10] ...

---

the argument that the phrase " 'rightful claim' " had "the effect of broadening the scope of the warranty" and encompassed even claims that were "only *prima facie* valid." (*Ibid.*) The drafters did not adopt this proposed change, however, suggesting that a broad interpretation of the term "rightful" was intended.

**9.** The phrase "rightful claim" first appears in the 1949 draft of the Uniform Commercial Code under subdivision (1)(b) of section 2–312. ... Uniform Commercial Code section 2–312, as then written, did not include any language specific to infringement claims. The rightful claim language was later deleted from subdivision (1)(b) and immediately reintroduced in the context of infringement claims, when subdivision (3) was added to section 2–312 of the Uniform Commercial Code in a supplement to the official draft in 1955. ...

**10.** Olaes and PacSun both point to Uniform Commercial Code section 2–607 as providing support for their positions. In fact, however, that section sheds little light on the inquiry. Uniform Commercial Code section 2–607 primarily concerns the notice that must be made by the buyer to the seller regarding infringement claims. It states that with respect to a

(6) As between a buyer and "a seller who is a merchant regularly dealing in goods of the kind" (§ 2312(3)), the burden of infringement claims is most sensibly placed on the seller who will generally have superior knowledge as to the existence of such claims, and a stronger incentive to seek out and resolve potential infringement claims prior to sale. ... The seller's incentive to reduce or eliminate prospective claims of infringement is undermined, however, if the section 2312(3) warranty applies only to meritorious claims, leaving the risk of closely contested, but ultimately unsuccessful, infringement claims to be borne by unsuspecting purchasers.

\* \* \*

(8) ... Finally, if the section 2312(3) warranty were determined by reference to the ultimate success or failure of third party infringement litigation, the buyer would be placed in an untenable position when a third party sues, contending infringement of a trademark, patent or copyright. Only by *losing* the lawsuit—or helping the third party claimant to maintain an appearance of success prior to settlement—would the buyer preserve the right to recover from the seller under Uniform Commercial Code section 2–312.[11] This would create a perverse incentive that would undermine the adversary process—a public policy outcome unlikely to have been intended by California Uniform Commercial Code section 2312's drafters.[12] ...

With respect to Olaes's further contention, echoed by the trial court, that it is also significant that PacSun "continued to sell the T-Shirts" during the Hawaii litigation, we emphasize that the relevance of this factor is specifically refuted by the official commentary to the Uniform Commercial Code, which states that eviction (i.e., prevention of use) is not required

---

"claim" for infringement against the buyer, where "the buyer is sued as a result of such a breach," the buyer "must so notify the seller within a reasonable time after he receives notice of the litigation or be barred from any remedy over for liability established by the litigation." ... The section also states that "[w]here the buyer is sued" for an infringement claim "for which his or her seller is answerable over," the "original seller may demand in writing that the buyer turn over to the seller control of the litigation." ... Olaes contends that the phrases, "answerable over" and "liability established by the litigation" suggest that only claims pursued to a successful verdict trigger the warranty. PacSun argues that the language's equation of a "claim" and "sued" with a breach of the warranty supports its contention that virtually any litigation triggers the warranty. While we can see the merits of *both* arguments, we believe that Uniform Commercial Code section 2–607 ultimately sheds no light on the question presented in this appeal. Uniform Commercial Code section 2–607 is directed at notice, tender of defense, and damages, not the substance of the Uniform Commercial Code section 2–312(3) warranty.

**11.** The Uniform Commercial Code contemplates a potential resolution to this dilemma by providing a mechanism for the seller to assume control of the defense to the third party claim. ... The buyer cannot, however, force the seller to do so. ...

**12.** The difficult nature of the buyer's position—if section 2312(3) is understood as only applying to valid claims—is apparent in this very lawsuit. Olaes contends on appeal that it is "*dispositive*" that PacSun has previously asserted that SNCL's claims in the Hawaii litigation are without merit. (Italics added.) Essentially, Olaes contends that PacSun was required to admit the validity of SNCL's claims against it in order to preserve a warranty claim against Olaes.

to establish a breach of the section 2312(3) warranty. (U. Com. Code com., par. 4) . . .

(9) In sum, it is clear from the official commentary, the statutory scheme and the public policy rationales underlying California Uniform Commercial Code section 2312, that the section 2312(3) warranty covers a broad scope of infringement claims and is not limited to claims that ultimately will prove successful in litigation. . . . As we have explained, the warranty against rightful claims applies to all claims of infringement that have any significant and adverse effect on the buyer's ability to make use of the purchased goods, excepting only frivolous claims that are completely devoid of merit. This exception for frivolous claims comports with the Uniform Commercial Code commentary and policy rationales discussed above, while giving necessary effect to the statutory qualifier "rightful." The seller's warranty under California Uniform Commercial Code section 2312 is broad, but neither the statutory text, nor the policy rationales, can support extension of the seller's warranty to even frivolous claims of infringement. As reflected in the statutory text, a seller cannot reasonably be required to seek out and resolve even meritless claims of infringement prior to sale.

\* \* \*

Applying the above standard to the facts of the instant case, we conclude that the trial court erred in granting Olaes's motion for summary judgment.

\* \* \*

DISPOSITION

The judgment is reversed.

■ BENKE, ACTING P. J., and HUFFMAN, J., concurred.


NOTES

(1) **Rightful Claim.** Section 2–312(3) provides for a warranty that buyers of goods shall have them free of a "rightful claim" of a third person "by way of infringement or the like." Comment 3 indicates that the purpose of the section is to protect buyers from claims that the goods were made by infringement of a patent or trademark. The critical issue before the courts in this case was to give meaning to the term "rightful claim. The lower court held that a rightful claim was an infringement claim that had prevailed.[4] The court of appeal disagreed and held that a claim was rightful if it was non-frivolous. The appellate court relied heavily on language in

---

4. The trademark infringement case (in Hawaii) terminated in a settlement, but the terms of the settlement were placed under seal. What might explain the parties agreement to secrecy? The parties to the warranty case (in California) are well aware of the terms of the settlement but are prohibited from informing the California courts. Can one infer that the terms of the settlement included some payment to the owner of the trademark?

Comment 3 to reach this conclusion. Is the Comment addressed to the meaning of "rightful claim"? The court also relied in part on decisions under UCC 2–312(1). Was that sound use of analogy?

**(2) Merchant–Seller.** Unlike the warranty of title or warranty of freedom from encumbrance, the warranty of non-infringement is made only by a seller that is a "merchant regularly dealing in goods of the kind." Merchant is a Code-defined term.[5] Why should such a distinction be made? Comment 3 declares that a merchant-seller has "a duty to see that no claim of infringement of a patent or trademark by a third party will mar the buyer's title," but a non-dealer does not. What is the source of that "duty"?

**(3) Specifications by Buyer.** Section 2–312(3) excepts a merchant-seller from liability if it supplies goods according to buyer's specifications, if the specifications give rise to the infringement claim. See Bonneau Co. v. AG Industries, Inc., 116 F.3d 155 (5th Cir.1997).

**(4) Smart Goods.** Many goods today are "smart goods," i.e., they contain semiconductors and computer information that enable the goods to carry out complex functions. Information content, such as computer programs, can be protected by the law of copyright. The text and Comment are silent on whether sale of goods that, without license from a copyright holder, incorporate copyrighted information would be covered by this subsection. How should the statute be construed?

**(5) Vouching In.** UCC 2–607(3)(a) requires a buyer to give timely notice of any breach of a sales contract to the seller. This includes breach of any UCC 2–312 warranty. Failure to give notice has the effect of barring buyer from any remedy. Section 2–607 further provides that, when a buyer is sued by a third party who claims infringement, the buyer may give notice to its seller that the seller may take over the defense.[6] Buyer is not required to give this notice, but if it does so and seller elects not to take over, seller becomes legally bound to the outcome of the infringement suit. UCC 2–607(5)(a). Subsection (5)(b), which is limited to infringement suits, gives seller the power to demand that the buyer turn over the defense to the seller even if the buyer chooses not to give a 607(5)(a) notice. Under common law procedure, this process is known generally as vouching in. The court of appeal, in a footnote in this case, found that the procedures under UCC 2–607(5) were not relevant to determining whether a breach of warranty had occurred.

**Problem 3.** Marie Louise Jeanneret, a citizen of Switzerland, is a well-known art dealer in Geneva. Defendants Anna and Luben Vichey, wife and husband, are citizens of the United States. Anna's father, Carlo Frua DeAngeli, had an extensive and internationally recognized private collection of paintings in Milan, Italy. One of these was a painting, Portrait sur

---

**5.** UCC 2–104(1). Although "merchant" is statutorily defined, the word is not listed in the Definitional Cross References at the end of the comments to UCC 2–312. The lesson for students is not to rely exclusively on these cross references to signal defined terms.

**6.** UCC 2–607(5)(a) is not limited to suits for infringement, but probably has most significance in that circumstance.

Fond Jaune, by the renowned French post-impressionist, Henri Matisse, who was born in 1869 and died in 1954. Title to the Matisse painting ultimately vested in Anna Vichey. In 1970 the Matisse painting was brought to Vichey's apartment in New York City. In January 1973 Mme. Jeanneret began negotiations for the purchase of the painting, and an agreement was reached for its sale for 700,000 Swiss francs, then equivalent to approximately $230,000. Luben Vichey delivered the painting to plaintiff in Geneva in March 1973.

Mme. Jeanneret included the Matisse painting in a large exhibit of 20th century masters at her gallery in Geneva. In November 1974, Mme. Jeanneret encountered Signora Bucarelli, superintendent in charge of the export of paintings from Italy, who declared she had been looking for the Matisse painting because she suspected its illegal exportation from Italy under laws designed to protect that nation's cultural heritage. Subsequently, the Assistant Minister of Culture issued a notification declaring the painting "an important work" of "particular artistic and historical interest" within the meaning of Italian law.

Mme. Jeanneret brought suit against the Vicheys for breach of warranty of title. At trial, John Tancock, a vice-president of Sotheby Parke Bernet auction house and head of its Department of Impressionist and Modern Painting and Sculpture, testified that, but for the question of illegal exportation, he would appraise the painting at $750,000. On the other hand, if the painting lacked "the necessary export documents from any country where it had been located," his opinion was that it would be impossible to sell the painting since "[n]o reputable auction house or dealer would be prepared to handle it." Hence, "on the legitimate market its value is zero."

What should be the result of this action under UCC 2–312? Does Italy's cultural heritage law affect the owners' title to objects possessed in Italy that are restricted as to export? Should the UCC 2–312 provision on infringement be invoked by an export restriction? Were sellers "merchants dealing in goods of the kind"? See UCC 2–104(1). If the trade usage of the reputable art dealers is self-imposed, in that they would incur no liability to the Italian government if they did handle such works, should that affect determination of Mme. Jeanneret's claim under UCC 2–312? See Jeanneret v. Vichey, 693 F.2d 259 (2d Cir.1982).

————

**Lease Transactions: Lessor's Warranty.** The supplier of goods in a lease transaction does not contract to pass title to the goods. Under the Commercial Code, " 'lease' means a transfer of the right to possession and use of the goods for a term in return for consideration...." UCC 2A–103(j). The warranty of a lessor analogous to a seller's warranty of title and non-infringement is found in UCC 2A–211:

(1) There is in a lease contract a warranty that for the lease term no person holds a claim or interest in the goods that arose from an act

or omission of the lessor ... which will interfere with the lessee's enjoyment of its leasehold interest.

(2) Except in a finance lease there is in a lease contract by a lessor who is a merchant regularly dealing in goods of the kind a warranty that the goods are delivered free of the rightful claim of any person by way of infringement or the like.

What is the purpose of limiting warranty liability under subsection (1) to "an act or omission of the lessor"? There is no such limitation in UCC 2–312(1). What is the purpose of the exception in subsection (2) for a "finance lease"? The latter is a defined term of considerable importance to the overall pattern of Article 2A. See UCC 2A–103(1)(g). Is it possible that the "act or omission" term in subsection (1) was drafted to apply to financial leases? See the Comment to this section.

## (B)   INTERNATIONAL SALES LAW

**Sellers' Responsibility.** The Convention on Contracts for the International Sale of Goods provides that, absent agreement otherwise, a seller must deliver goods that are "free from any right or claim of a third party." CISG 41. The Convention does not use the word "title." Does the Convention's formulation of the sellers' obligation differ from UCC 2–312 in any substantial way? Note the alternative formulation: right *or* claim. Is this more favorable to buyers than the language of UCC 2–312(1)?

The Convention's provision on sellers' obligation with respect to intellectual property is found in Article 42. This provision is considerably more complex than UCC 2–312(2). CISG 42 limits the responsibility of sellers to industrial and intellectual property rights or claims of which "the seller knew or could not have been unaware." Moreover, CISG 42 points to a single national law that determines whether there is a right or claim in an international sale. What is the explanation for such limitations? See J. Honnold, Uniform Law for International Sales §§ 267–270 (3d ed. 1999). Professor Honnold noted that the issue arose very late in the UNCITRAL drafting process and the Article may have unintended consequences.

The parties in *Jeanneret v. Vichey* were from different nations: United States sellers and a Swiss buyer. The buyer was a dealer who purchased the Matisse painting for resale. If this transaction had occurred after the effective date of CISG, would the transaction be within the scope of the Convention? Assuming that the Convention had applied, what would be the outcome?

## SECTION 3.   GOOD FAITH PURCHASE OF GOODS

## (A)   DOMESTIC UNITED STATES LAW

Buyers threatened with loss of goods purchased to third parties claiming to be the rightful owners or claiming a limited property interest in the goods may have rights alternative to the often illusory right to enforce the warranty of title against their sellers.[1] In some circumstances, buyers may have property rights that are superior to the rights of the claimants. In this section, we consider the principles and the legal rules that determine whether buyers rights in goods purchased prevail over the rights of third-party claimants. Sellers' warranty obligations arise out of their contracts with buyers to whom they sold goods. In circumstances where the law determines the property rights of persons who had no contractual relationship, the determination must be based on property rather than contract.

Although we approach the subject from the perspective of sales of goods, the property law involved here is not limited to goods. A basic problem that arises in connection with the transfer of personal property of various kinds is the extent to which an innocent transferee, who has given something of value in exchange for property, takes the property free of conflicting claims of ownership or a limited property interest asserted by a person other than the transferor. In simple terms, the question is whether a good faith purchaser for value can keep the property purchased even though the claimant was, at an earlier time, the rightful owner of the property? The answer is often Yes. According to Professor Grant Gilmore: "The triumph of the good faith purchaser has been one of the most dramatic episodes in our legal history. In his several guises, he serves a commercial function: he is protected not because of his praiseworthy character, but to the end that commercial transactions may be engaged in without elaborate investigation of property rights by one who offers it for sale...."[2]

The principle of good faith purchase applies to the many different kinds of property. In this section, we will examine the concept of good faith purchase as applied to goods. Before proceeding into that subject, we should review, briefly, some fundamentals of common law that underlie the law of good faith purchase in the fields of law for property, agency, crimes and torts.

**Crimes and Torts.** Owners of property may be deprived of possession by theft or fraud. Actions of this kind violate the basic principle that owners should be secure in control and use of their property. This principle of security of property overlaps sales law only partially. Thieves are not buyers. In criminal law, they commit larceny, robbery, and burglary. Sales law is not germane to the legal relationship between thief and victim. Sales law has more overlap with the law of fraudulent transactions. Fraudulent misstatements can induce owners to enter into sales contracts whereby the

---

**1.** As a practical matter, many buyers have no realistic chance of recovery from their sellers in actions to enforce the warranty of title. When buyers learn that there is a cloud on title, they may not be able to find the sellers. Sellers in the kinds of transactions that give rise to claims for breach of warranty of title, even when they can be found, may lack sufficient assets to allow buyers to satisfy judgments against them.

**2.** G. Gilmore, The Commercial Doctrine of Good Faith Purchase, 63 Yale L.J. 1057 (1954).

owners surrender possession of their goods to "buyers" who do not pay the contract price and have no intention to pay it.

The most practical form of relief for such victims of crime or fraud is to recover their property. The law permits rightful owners specific relief, usually in the form of an action for replevin, that will result in restoration of the goods to the rightful owners if the goods are found in the possession of the wrongdoers. Theoretically, tort victims have claims for damages under the tort theory of conversion; moreover, defrauded owners could "ratify" the fraud-tainted transactions and sue the cheats for the agreed price. Collecting money judgments in these circumstances is highly unlikely.[3]

**Problem 1.** (a) S delivered a large quantity of cotton to B upon B's promise to pay $25,000 in 30 days. At the end of that period, B failed to pay. What remedy or remedies are available to S? Does UCC Article 2 apply to this transaction? Under the Code, S is entitled to recover the unpaid price. See UCC 2–709. May S recover the cotton from B? Article 2 allows sellers to recover goods delivered to buyers in narrowly limited circumstances. See UCC 2–702(2). The problem, as stated, does not assume that B was insolvent when B received goods on credit. The last sentence of UCC 2–702(2) restricts sellers' right to reclaim goods on the basis of fraudulent or innocent misrepresentation of solvency or intent to pay. The problem, as stated, does not assume that B made a misrepresentation of any kind. What policy grounds might explain the absence of a statutory remedy that restores the cotton to sellers when buyers fail or refuse to pay the price?

(b) Should S be entitled to replevy the cotton if S can prove that, at the time the contract was made, B consciously intended not to pay? Knew that there was little or no chance that she could pay? Did B, by her silence, falsely imply that she was ready and willing to pay? Is such conduct distinguishable from B's overt misrepresentation of its identity or credit-worthiness?

Property law and the remedies of replevin and conversion are not limited to wrongdoers. Owners can claim the same relief in actions against transferees from the wrongdoers. The extended reach of these elements of common law to innocent transferees is, of course, basis for the need of the law to protect some innocent transferees.

**Agency.** Generally, the law assures owners of property of security in their ownership, but the law also recognizes that owners may dispose of their property through the actions of others. An owner of property may authorize someone else, an agent acting on behalf of the owner, to enter into transactions to sell the property. The common law of "principal and agent" provides that such a sales transaction may bind the principal convey ownership of the property to the buyer.

The common-law of agency expressly undergirds the Commercial Code. UCC 1–103(b). An agent's common-law power to transfer the property of

---

**3.** Criminal law has been reformed in recent years to increase victims' rights. One aspect of this reform has been to order restitution and reparation as a part of offenders' sentences.

its principal is reflected in UCC 2–403(1) (purchaser acquires all title which his transferor "had power to transfer" and 9–315(a)(1) (security interest continues notwithstanding sale "unless the secured party authorized the disposition free of the security interest")).

The law of agency often binds principals to the consequence of actions of their agents even though the agents exceeded their principals' instructions or acted inconsistently with those instructions. The terms of actual authority cannot be ascertained by persons not privy to the principal-agency relationship. Therefore, a principal is bound in circumstances where an agent had apparent authority as well as circumstances in which a third party had reason to believe that an agent had power to act for its principal. For refinements in the common law of agency, see Restatement, (Third) Agency (2006).

**Property.** We turn now to the law of good faith purchase of goods, an aspect of the law of personal property. A typical sequence of events is as follows: A is the owner of goods. B acquires the goods by theft or fraud such that A has the right to recover the goods from B. B resells the goods to C who is unaware of how B obtained the goods. A seeks to replevy the goods from C, or to hold C liable in damages for conversion.

The traditional legal rule is this: If B did not acquire "title" or "property" in the goods, he cannot transfer property to C: *Nemo dat quod non habet.* This rule is still dominant in Anglo–American law where the goods were stolen from A. On the other hand, for cases where A was induced to deliver the goods to B by fraud, a second rule developed. Where A sold the goods to B because of B's fraud, A could rescind the transaction and recover his property, but B had "voidable title" and A's right to rescind could be "cut off" by resale of the goods to a *bona fide* purchaser.[4] Professor Gilmore summarized the historical development:

> The initial common law position was that equities of ownership are to be protected at all costs; an owner may never be deprived of his property rights without his consent. That worked well enough against a background of local distribution where seller and buyer met face to face and exchanged goods for cash. But as the marketplace became first regional and then national, the misappropriation of goods by a faithless agent in fraud of his principal came to be a recurrent situation. Classical theory required that the principal be protected and that the

---

**4.** The seminal case in the voidable title area is the English case of Parker v. Patrick, 101 Eng. Rep. 99 (K.B. 1793), which was followed in Mowrey v. Walsh, 8 Cowen 238 (N.Y.Sup.Ct.1828). The only reason mentioned by the New York court for distinguishing fraud and theft was the one given by the English court in its one sentence, per curiam opinion—the existence of a statute as to theft. By the time of White v. Garden, 10 Common Bench, 919, 138 Eng. Rep. 364 (Q.B. 1851), however, doctrine had developed to the point that the court could write that where fraud was involved, "the transaction is not absolutely void, except at the option of the seller; that he may elect to treat it as a contract, and he must do the contrary before the buyer has acted as if it were such, and re-sold the goods to a third party." See H. Weinberg, Markets Overt, Voidable Titles, and Feckless Agents: Judges and Efficiency in the Antebellum Doctrine of Good Faith Purchase, 56 Tul. L. Rev. 1, 23–32 (1981).

risks of agency distribution be cast on the purchaser. The market demanded otherwise.

The first significant breach in common law property theory was the protection of purchasers from such commercial agents. The reform was carried out through so-called Factor's Acts, which were widely enacted in the early part of the 19th century. Under these Acts any person who entrusted goods to a factor—or agent—for sale took the risk of the factor's selling them beyond his authority; anyone buying from a factor in good faith, relying on his possession of the goods, and without notice of the limitations on his authority, took good title against the true owner. In time the Acts were expanded to protect people, i.e., banks, who took goods from a factor as security for loans made to the factor to be used in operating the factor's own business. The Factor's Acts, as much in derogation of the common law as it is possible for a statute to be, were restrictively construed and consequently turned out to be considerably less than the full grant of mercantile liberty which they had first appeared to be. Other developments in the law gradually took the pressure off the Factor's Acts, which came to be confined to the narrow area of sales through commission merchants, mostly in agricultural produce markets.

Even while they were cutting the heart out of the Factor's Acts, the courts were finding new ways to shift distribution risks. Their happiest discovery was the concept of "voidable title"—a vague idea, never defined and perhaps incapable of definition, whose greatest virtue, as a principle of growth, may well have been its shapeless imprecision of outline. The polar extremes of theory were these: if $B$ buys goods from $A$, he gets $A$'s title and can transfer it to any subsequent purchaser; if $B$ steals goods from A, he gets no title and can transfer none to any subsequent purchaser, no matter how clear the purchaser's good faith. "Voidable title" in $B$ came in as an intermediate term between the two extremes: if $B$ gets possession of $A$'s goods by fraud, even though he has no right to retain them against $A$, he does have the power to transfer title to a good faith purchaser.

The ingenious distinction between "no title" in $B$ (therefore true owner prevails over good faith purchaser) and "voidable title" in $B$ (therefore true owner loses to good faith purchaser) made it possible to throw the risk on the true owner in the typical commercial situation while protecting him in the noncommercial one. Since the law purported to be a deduction from basic premises, logic prevailed in some details to the detriment of mercantile need, but on the whole voidable title proved a useful touchstone.

The contrasting treatment given to sales on credit and sales for cash shows the inarticulate development of the commercial principle. When goods are delivered on credit, the seller becomes merely a creditor for the price: on default he has no right against the goods. But when the delivery is induced by buyer's fraud—buyer being unable to pay or having no intention of paying—the seller, if he acts promptly after discovering the facts, may replevy from the buyer or reclaim from buyer's trustee in bankruptcy. The seller may not, however, move against purchasers from the buyer, and the term "purchaser" includes lenders who have made advances on the security of the goods. By his fraudulent acquisition the buyer has obtained voidable title and purchasers from him are protected.

G. Gilmore, The Commercial Doctrine of Good Faith Purchase, 63 Yale L.J. 1057–60 (1954).[5]

**Problem 2.** A owned a large quantity of cotton, worth $25,000, which was stored in its warehouse. B broke into the warehouse and stole the cotton. Unaware of the theft, C entered into a contract to buy the cotton from B for $25,000.

(a) After delivery to C and payment to B had occurred, the police discover that C had possession of the cotton that had been stolen from A. B has disappeared with the $25,000. A institutes legal action to replevy the cotton from C. What result? Is the answer found in the Commercial Code? Does UCC 2–403(1) apply?

(b) Before the police traced the cotton to C, C sold and delivered the cotton to D who paid $27,000. A institutes legal action against C for conversion? What result?

(c) A institutes legal action to replevy the cotton from D? What result? Is the answer found in the Commercial Code?

**Problem 3.** A delivered a large quantity of cotton to B upon B's promise to pay $25,000 in 30 days. A delivered the goods to B on credit as a result of B's misrepresentation that he was X, a reputable and creditworthy merchant. At the end of that period, B failed to pay. Meanwhile B sold and delivered the cotton to C who paid B $27,000. A institutes legal action to replevy the cotton from C. What result? Is the answer found in the Commercial Code? See UCC 2–403(1).

Note that the drafters of Article 2 added a third sentence to UCC 2–403(1) that results in protection of good faith purchasers, without using the concept of "voidable title," in four transactional settings. Are there any common elements in these situations?

# Kotis v. Nowlin Jewelry, Inc.

Court of Appeals of Texas, Fourteenth District, Houston, 1992.
844 S.W.2d 920.

■ DRAUGHN, J.

Eddie Kotis appeals from a judgment declaring appellee, Nowlin Jewelry, Inc., the sole owner of a Rolex watch, and awarding appellee attorney's fees. Kotis raises fourteen points of error. We affirm.

---

**5.** Reproduced with permission of the Yale Law Journal.

On June 11, 1990, Steve Sitton acquired a gold ladies Rolex watch, President model, with a diamond bezel from Nowlin Jewelry by forging a check belonging to his brother and misrepresenting to Nowlin that he had his brother's authorization for the purchase. The purchase price of the watch, and the amount of the forged check, was $9,438.50. The next day, Sitton telephoned Eddie Kotis, the owner of a used car dealership, and asked Kotis if he was interested in buying a Rolex watch. Kotis indicated interest and Sitton came to the car lot. Kotis purchased the watch for $3,550.00. Kotis also called Nowlin's Jewelry that same day and spoke with Cherie Nowlin.

Ms. Nowlin told Kotis that Sitton had purchased the watch the day before. Ms. Nowlin testified that Kotis would not immediately identify himself. Because she did not have the payment information available, Ms. Nowlin asked if she could call him back. Kotis then gave his name and number. Ms. Nowlin testified that she called Kotis and told him the amount of the check and that it had not yet cleared. Kotis told Ms. Nowlin that he did not have the watch and that he did not want the watch. Ms. Nowlin also testified that Kotis would not tell her how much Sitton was asking for the watch.

John Nowlin, the president of Nowlin's Jewelry, testified that, after this call from Kotis, Nowlin's bookkeeper began attempting to confirm whether the check had cleared. When they learned the check would not be honored by the bank, Nowlin called Kotis, but Kotis refused to talk to Nowlin. Kotis referred Nowlin to his attorney. On June 25, 1990, Kotis' attorney called Nowlin and suggested that Nowlin hire an attorney and allegedly indicated that Nowlin could buy the watch back from Kotis. Nowlin refused to repurchase the watch.

After Sitton was indicted for forgery and theft, the district court ordered Nowlin's Jewelry to hold the watch until there was an adjudication of the ownership of the watch. Nowlin then filed suit seeking a declaratory judgment that Nowlin was the sole owner of the watch. Kotis filed a counterclaim for a declaration that Kotis was a good faith purchaser of the watch and was entitled to possession and title of the watch. After a bench trial, the trial court rendered judgment declaring Nowlin the sole owner of the watch. The trial court also filed Findings of Fact and Conclusions of Law.

In point of error one, Kotis claims the trial court erred in concluding that Sitton did not receive the watch through a transaction of purchase with Nowlin, within the meaning of TEX. BUS. & COM. CODE ANN. § 2.403(a). . . .

Kotis contends there is evidence that the watch is a "good" under the UCC, there was a voluntary transfer of the watch, and there was physical delivery of the watch. Thus, Kotis maintains that the transaction between

Sitton and Nowlin was a transaction of purchase such that Sitton acquired the ability to transfer good title to a good faith purchaser under § 2.403.

Section 2.403 provides:

A purchaser of goods acquires all title which his transferor had or had power to transfer except that a purchaser of a limited interest acquires rights only to the extent of the interest purchased. A person with voidable title has power to transfer good title to a good faith purchaser for value. When goods have been delivered under a transaction of purchase the purchaser has such power even though

> (1) the transferor was deceived as to the identity of the purchaser, or

> (2) the delivery was in exchange for a check which is later dishonored, or

> (3) it was agreed that the transaction was to be a "cash sale", or

> (4) the delivery was procured through fraud punishable as larcenous under the criminal law.

TEX. BUS. & COM. CODE ANN. § 2.403(a) (Vernon 1968).

Neither the code nor case law defines the phrase "transaction of purchase." "Purchase" is defined by the code as a "taking by sale, discount, negotiation, mortgage, pledge, lien, issue or reissue, gift or any other voluntary transaction creating an interest in property." TEX. BUS. & COM. CODE ANN. § 1.201(32) (Vernon 1968). Thus, only voluntary transactions can constitute transactions of purchase.

Having found no Texas case law concerning what constitutes a transaction of purchase under § 2.403(a), we have looked to case law from other states. Based on the code definition of a purchase as a voluntary transaction, these cases reason that a thief who wrongfully takes the goods against the will of the owner is not a purchaser. . . . On the other hand, a swindler who fraudulently induces the victim to deliver the goods voluntarily is a purchaser under the code. . . .

In this case, Nowlin's Jewelry voluntarily delivered the watch to Sitton in return for payment by check that was later discovered to be forged. Sitton did not obtain the watch against the will of the owner. Rather, Sitton fraudulently induced Nowlin's Jewelry to deliver the watch voluntarily. Thus, we agree with appellant that the trial court erred in concluding that Sitton did not receive the watch through a transaction of purchase under § 2.403(a). We sustain point of error one.

In point of error two, Kotis contends the trial court erred in concluding that, at the time Sitton sold the watch to Kotis, Sitton did not have at least voidable title to the watch. In point of error nine, Kotis challenges the trial court's conclusion that Nowlin's Jewelry had legal and equitable title at all times relevant to the lawsuit. The lack of Texas case law addressing such issues under the code again requires us to look to case law from other states to assist in our analysis.

In Suburban Motors, Inc. v. State Farm Mut. Automobile Ins. Co., the California court noted that § 2.403 provides for the creation of voidable title where there is a voluntary transfer of goods. 268 Cal. Rptr. at 18. Section 2.403(a)(1)–(4) set forth the types of voluntary transactions that can give the purchaser voidable title. Where goods are stolen such that there is no voluntary transfer, only void title results. Id. at 19; Inmi–Etti, 492 A.2d at 921. Subsection (4) provides that a purchaser can obtain voidable title to the goods even if "delivery was procured through fraud punishable as larcenous under the criminal law." TEX. BUS. & COM. CODE ANN. § 2.403(a)(4) (Vernon 1968). This subsection applies to cases involving acts fraudulent to the seller such as where the seller delivers the goods in return for a forged check. See Inmi–Etti, 492 A.2d at 921. Although Sitton paid Nowlin's Jewelry with a forged check, he obtained possession of the watch through a voluntary transaction of purchase and received voidable, rather than void, title to the watch. Thus, the trial court erred in concluding that Sitton received no title to the watch and in concluding that Nowlin's retained title at all relevant times. We sustain points of error two and nine.

In point of error three, Kotis claims the trial court erred in concluding that Kotis did not give sufficient value for the watch to receive protection under § 2.403, that Kotis did not take good title to the watch as a good faith purchaser, that Kotis did not receive good title to the watch, and that Kotis is not entitled to the watch under § 2.403. In points of error four through eight, Kotis challenges the trial court's findings regarding his good faith, his honesty in fact, and his actual belief, and the reasonableness of the belief, that the watch had been received unlawfully.

Under § 2.403(a), a transferor with voidable title can transfer good title to a good faith purchaser. TEX. BUS. & COM. CODE ANN. § 2.403(a) (Vernon 1968). Good faith means "honesty in fact in the conduct or transaction concerned." TEX. BUS. & COM. CODE ANN. § 1.201(19) (Vernon 1968). The test for good faith is the actual belief of the party and not the reasonableness of that belief. La Sara Grain v. First Nat'l Bank, 673 S.W.2d 558, 563 (Tex.1984).

Kotis was a dealer in used cars and testified that he had bought several cars from Sitton in the past and had no reason not to trust Sitton. He also testified that on June 12, 1990, Sitton called and asked Kotis if he was interested in buying a Ladies Rolex. Once Kotis indicated his interest in the watch, Sitton came to Kotis's place of business. According to Kotis, Sitton said that he had received $18,000.00 upon the sale of his house and that he had used this to purchase the watch for his girlfriend several months before. Kotis paid $3,550.00 for the watch. Kotis further testified that he then spoke to a friend, Gary Neal Martin, who also knew Sitton. Martin sagely advised Kotis to contact Nowlin's to check whether Sitton had financed the watch. Kotis testified that he called Nowlin's after buying the watch.

Cherie Nowlin testified that she received a phone call from Kotis on June 12, 1990, although Kotis did not immediately identify himself. Kotis asked if Nowlin's had sold a gold President model Rolex watch with a diamond bezel about a month before. When asked, Kotis told Ms. Nowlin that Sitton had come to Kotis' car lot and was trying to sell the watch. Ms. Nowlin testified that Kotis told her he did not want the watch because he already owned a Rolex. Ms. Nowlin told Kotis that Sitton had purchased the watch the day before. Kotis asked about the method of payment. Because Ms. Nowlin did not know, she agreed to check and call Kotis back. She called Kotis back and advised him that Sitton had paid for the watch with a check that had not yet cleared. When Ms. Nowlin asked if Kotis had the watch, Kotis said no and would not tell her how much Sitton was asking for the watch. Ms. Nowlin did advise Kotis of the amount of the check.

After these calls, the owner of Nowlin's asked his bookkeeper to call the bank regarding Sitton's check. They learned on June 15, 1990 that the check would be dishonored. John Nowlin called Kotis the next day and advised him about the dishonored check. Kotis refused to talk to Nowlin and told Nowlin to contact his attorney. Nowlin also testified that a reasonable amount to pay for a Ladies President Rolex watch with a diamond bezel in mint condition was $7,000.00–$8,000.00. Nowlin maintained that $3,500.00 was an exorbitantly low price for a watch like this.

The trier of fact is the sole judge of the credibility of the witnesses and the weight to be given their testimony. . . . Kotis testified that he lied when he spoke with Cherie Nowlin and that he had already purchased the watch before he learned that Sitton's story was false. The judge, as the trier of fact, may not have believed Kotis when he said that he had already purchased the watch. If the judge disbelieved this part of Kotis' testimony, other facts tend to show that Kotis did not believe the transaction was lawful. For example, when Kotis spoke with Nowlin's, he initially refused to identify himself, he said that he did not have the watch and that he did not want the watch, he refused to divulge Sitton's asking price, and he later refused to talk with Nowlin and advised Nowlin to contact Kotis' attorney. Thus, there is evidence supporting the trial court's finding that Kotis did not act in good faith.

There are sufficient facts to uphold the trial court's findings even if the judge had accepted as true Kotis' testimony that, despite his statements to Nowlin's, he had already purchased the watch when he called Nowlin's. The testimony indicated that Kotis was familiar with the price of Rolex watches and that $3,550.00 was an extremely low price for a mint condition watch of this type. An unreasonably low price is evidence the buyer knows the goods are stolen. . . . Although the test is what Kotis actually believed, we agree with appellee that we need not let this standard sanction willful disregard of suspicious facts that would lead a reasonable person to believe the transaction was unlawful. . . . Thus, we find sufficient evidence to uphold the trial court's findings regarding Kotis' lack of status as a good faith purchaser. We overrule points of error three through eight.

In point of error ten, Kotis contends the trial court erred in concluding that Kotis converted the watch by refusing to return it to Nowlin's and by refusing to allow its return to Nowlin's. In point of error eleven, Kotis claims the trial court erred in concluding that Nowlin's is entitled to a constructive trust over the watch. Kotis' argument under these points depends upon our finding that he was a good faith purchaser. Because we have upheld the trial court's finding that Kotis was not a good faith purchaser, we need not address these points.

In point of error twelve, Kotis challenges the trial court's conclusion that Nowlin's was entitled to possession of the watch and that Kotis is not entitled to possession or title to the watch. Having upheld the trial court's finding that Kotis was not a good faith purchaser, we must also uphold the trial court's finding that Nowlin's, and not Kotis, is entitled to possession and title to the watch. We overrule point twelve.

In point of error thirteen, Kotis challenges the trial court's conclusion that Nowlin's is entitled to recover attorney's fees and post-judgment interest against Kotis. Under the Declaratory Judgment Act, a court may "award costs and reasonable and necessary attorney's fees as are equitable and just." TEX. CIV. PRAC. & REM. CODE ANN. § 37.009 (Vernon 1986). The trial court found that $5,883.57 was a reasonable fee for Nowlin's attorney and there was evidence supporting this amount. We overrule point of error thirteen.

In Kotis' final point of error, he claims the trial court erred in denying his counterclaims for damages for conversion and for attorney's fees and costs. Having upheld the trial court's conclusions that Kotis was not a good faith purchaser and was not entitled to possession and title to the watch, we need not address this point.

We affirm the trial court's judgment.

NOTES

(1) **Voidable Title.** The Texas court found that Sitton had received the Rolex watch in a transaction of purchase and therefore had the power to transfer a good title to the watch under the third sentence of UCC 2–403(1). The court went on to find that Sitton had voidable title. Was this step necessary to the court's judgment? If the third sentence applies, does it matter whether Sitton had voidable title?

(2) **Good Faith Purchaser for Value.** The Texas court held that Kotis could not take advantage of Sitton's power to transfer good title. Under UCC 2–403(1), a buyer receives good title if the buyer is a "good faith purchaser for value." In the court's opinion, what facts rendered Kotis ineligible to be a good faith purchaser for value?

Was Kotis a "purchaser"? See UCC 1–201(b)(29) and (30).

Did Kotis give "value"? See UCC 1–204. Does "for value" in UCC 2–401(1) require that the buyer pay an amount comparable to the market value of the goods in question? Suppose Kotis had promised to pay Sitton $8,000, but had not paid any part of the agreed price when he became aware of the claim of Nowlin's claim. Would the executory promise to pay be "value" under UCC 1–204?

The crux of the matter, in the court's reasoning, was that Kotis did not purchase the watch in "good faith." Did the court give appropriate weight to the statutory definition of "good faith" in UCC 1–201(19)? Is being suspicious or cautious tantamount to being dishonest? The court noted that Kotis was a used car dealer. Should that make applicable the definition of "good faith" that is provided "in the case of a merchant" in UCC 2–103(1)(b)?

Revised UCC Article 1 changed the definition of "good faith" to add "observance of reasonable commercial standards of fair dealing" to the previous definition, "honesty in fact." UCC1–201(b)(20). What is the probable effect of the new definition in cases where a purchaser seeks protection under UCC 2–403(1)?

**(3) Leases and Purchase Transactions.** The good faith purchase doctrine protects buyers, but the doctrine is not limited to buyers. "Purchaser" is defined in UCC 1–201(b)(29) and (30) to include anyone who receives an interest in property through a "voluntary transaction," including donees who take by gift. The value requirement of the good faith purchase doctrine would exclude donees from the protected class, but there are many exchange transactions in which value is given for an interest in property other than full title. Section 2–403(1) refers to purchase of a "limited interest" in property. This leads to the question of the power of a purchaser other than a buyer to transfer "good title" to a "good faith purchaser," who is a purchaser other than a buyer.

Since a lessee is a "purchaser" it seems to follow that one who leases goods from a person with voidable title would be protected in the right to possess and use the goods for the term of the lease by UCC 2–403(1). One would have to infer that the power to create "good title" includes the lesser power to transfer a protected limited interest, but the protection would not extend beyond the limited leasehold interest and the rightful owner would retain the reversion. This would also be true with regard to transfers by persons with the power conferred by the third sentence of UCC 2–403(1).

Suppose, however, that a good faith lessee acquires its interest from a prior lessee rather than from a transferor with title. The third sentence of UCC 2–403(1) might be construed to fit this circumstance, but the matter is more clearly addressed in the article on leases. See UCC 2A–305(1). Lease agreements commonly contain provisions that restrict alienability by the lessee, one effect of which may be to terminate the lease if a transfer is made. For the central provisions dealing with this matter, see UCC 2A–303.

Another set of problems arises when the first transfer is a lease transaction and the lessee then sells the goods to a buyer who meets all the criteria for being a good faith purchaser for value. Does the lessee have "voidable title"? Since a lessee does not acquire any title, it would follow that the lessee does not have a title that may be voidable. However, the third sentence of UCC 2–403(1) operates whenever "goods have been delivered under a transaction of purchase," a phrase that seems clearly to include transfer of possession under a lease. Does a lessee who comes within that provision have power to transfer good title?

**Problem 4.** Lessee of a motor home wrongfully sold it to a dealer, who later resold it to a customer. Lessor subsequently finds the motor home and demands its return. Did either the dealer or the customer obtain good title? These facts were litigated in McDonald's Chevrolet, Inc. v. Johnson, 176 Ind.App. 399, 376 N.E.2d 106 (1978), which held that the lessee did not transfer good title. Counsel for the dealer based his argument on the third sentence of UCC 2–403(1), but inexplicably conceded that his client could prevail only if the lessee had voidable title. The court held that the lease involved no transfer of ownership and, therefore, the lessee lacked voidable title and neither the dealer nor the customer obtained good title. If that concession had not been made, what should have been the result?

The lease term in *McDonald's Chevrolet* was very short, only 13 days. In considering the legal rights of the good faith purchaser, should the length of the lease term matter? Suppose the term of the lease was the full expected useful life of the goods?

The court in *McDonald's Chevrolet* indicated that the lessee had acquired a "limited interest" in the motor home, within the sense of the first sentence of UCC 2–403(1). Does the good faith purchase doctrine contemplate a purchaser having a "voidable limited interest" that would create power to transfer a "good limited interest"? Section 2–403(1) does not so provide, but is that a complete answer. See UCC 2A–305(1). Would this argument have been useful to the dealer?

In many goods leasing transactions, the lessee has an option to purchase the goods at the expiration of the lease term. How should the existence of such an option affect the determination of the rights of a good faith purchaser?

## (B) INTERNATIONAL SALES LAW

Article 4(b) declares that the Convention "is not concerned with the effect which the contract may have on the property in the goods sold." Given CISG 4(b)'s disclaimer of concern with property rights in the goods even between sellers and buyers, not surprisingly the CISG has no provision on the property or ownership rights of third parties. When such issues arise in relation to sales transactions otherwise governed by CISG, private international law rules determine which nation's domestic law applies to resolve conflicting claims to the goods.

Domestic United States law on good faith purchase differs from the domestic law of many other nations. Common law and civil law have taken different paths. Moreover, United States law, while derived from English common law, did not incorporate the doctrine of *market-overt* which was accepted in that country.

The civil law begins with a basic principle very different from the foundation of common law. Under civil law, a good faith purchaser of goods is generally protected against the original owner. The civil law principle is expressed in the phrase *possession vout titre* (possession is equivalent to title). Civil law systems have no need for a special rule that protects good faith purchasers when their sellers had voidable title. But most such systems have an exception for cases in which an owner's goods have been stolen. A victim of theft can reclaim the goods from a good faith purchaser within a short time period, which, in French law, is three years. However, if the good faith purchaser acquired goods at a fair or a market or from a merchant who deals in similar goods, even though the goods had previously been stolen, some civil law systems protect the purchaser. The original owner can reclaim the goods only if the owner reimburses the purchase for the price paid for the goods.[6]

English law has an exception to the principle of *nemo dat quod non habet* for circumstances in which goods are sold in a *market-overt*. A market overt is an open and public market that is recognized as such by usage of trade. Even though the goods sold had been stolen, the rights of buyers in a *market-overt* prevail over the rights of the original owners. See Sale of Goods Act § 23(1). Early in the 19th century, American judges declined to apply the principle of *market-overt* in this country.[7]

## SECTION 4.   "ENTRUSTING" AND "BUYERS IN ORDINARY COURSE"

### (A) DOMESTIC UNITED STATES LAW

The sharpest break with the traditional law of good faith purchase made by UCC Article 2 is found in UCC 2–403(2). Suppose an owner (A) leaves his Rolex watch for repair with a jeweler (B) who both repairs and sells jewelry. The jeweler wrongfully sells and delivers the watch to a customer (C). Who has the right to possession of the watch: the original owner or the customer?

The early common law favored the original owner. Merely entrusting possession of goods to a dealer was not sufficient to clothe the dealer with the authority to sell. "If it were otherwise people would not be secure in sending their watches or articles of jewelry to a jeweler's establishment to be repaired or cloth to a clothing establishment to be made into garments."[1]

---

**6.** Louisiana law, which has roots in the civil law, recognizes *possession vout titre*. In a case tried in the courts of Florida, one of the parties contended that Louisiana law governed the dispute and relied on the civil law principle. The Florida court refused to apply Louisiana law on the ground that the civil law principle "contravenes a positive policy of the law of Florida." Brown & Root, Inc. v. Ring Power Corp., 450 So.2d 1245, 1247 (Fla.App.1984).

**7.** In Wheelwright v. Depeyster, 1 Johns. 471, 480 (N.Y.1806), Chancellor Kent rejected a contention based on the notion of a market overt: "I know of no usage or regulation within this State, no Saxon institution of *market-overt*, which controls or interferes with the application of the common law."

**1.** Levi v. Booth, 58 Md. 305, 315 (1882).

During the nineteenth century, however, many states enacted "Factor's Acts" under which an owner of goods who entrusted them to an agent (or "factor") with limited authority to sell took the risk that the agent might sell them beyond its authority. A good faith purchaser from the agent, relying on the agent's possession of the goods and having no notice that it was exceeding his authority, took good title against the original owner. But the Factor's Acts did not protect the good faith purchaser where, as in the example of the diamond ring, the owner entrusted the goods to another for some purpose other than that of sale. A mere bailee could not pass good title to a good faith purchaser.

Here UCC 2–403(2) goes well beyond the Factor's Acts, since it applies to "[a]ny entrusting," i.e., "any delivery" under (3), regardless of the purpose, to a "merchant who deals in goods of that kind." Who is entitled to the diamond ring under the Code? Note that the protection of UCC 2–403 is extended to a "buyer in the ordinary course of business," a category significantly narrower than "good faith purchaser for value." Compare the scope of "buyer" under UCC 2–103(1)(a) with the definitions of "purchase" and "purchaser" under UCC 1–201(b)(29) and (30). Compare also the specific requirements and limitations of "ordinary course of business" in UCC 1–201(b)(9) with the broader meaning of "good faith" and "value" in UCC R1–201(b)(20) and 1–204.

## Porter v. Wertz

Court of Appeals of New York, 1981.
53 N.Y.2d 696, 439 N.Y.S.2d 105, 421 N.E.2d 500.

[Samuel Porter, an art collector, who owned Utrillo's painting "Chateau de Lion-sur-Mer." Harold Von Maker, who identified himself to Porter as Peter Wertz, an art dealer, approached Porter and expressed an interest in buying the Utrillo for his personal collection. Porter, unaware of Von Maker's real identity or his background of illegal activities, permitted Von Maker to take possession of the Utrillo for the avowed purpose of allowing Von Maker to hang the painting in his home pending his decision as to purchase. Von Maker then delivered the painting to the real Peter Wertz, a delicatessen employee, with instruction to try to sell it to an art gallery. After unsuccessful efforts at sales to other galleries, Peter Wertz sold and delivered the Utrillo to Richard Feigen, a well-known New York City art dealer, doing business as Feigen Gallery. Feigen Gallery in turn sold and delivered the painting to Brenner, who resold it to a third party who took the painting to South America.

[Porter had no knowledge of these transactions at the time they occurred. Porter subsequently discovered what Von Maker, Wertz, and Feigen Gallery had done and brought action for conversion against Feigen Gallery. Feigen Gallery argued that Porter had "entrusted" the painting to Von Maker and as a consequence: (1) Feigen Gallery was protected under UCC 2–403(2) as a "buyer in ordinary course of business," or (2) Porter's claim was barred by equitable estoppel under UCC 2–403(1). The trial court rejected Feigen Gallery's defense under 2–403(2), but upheld the claim of estoppel. The Appellate Division reversed and Feigen Gallery appealed to the Court of Appeals.]

## MEMORANDUM

The judgment appealed from and order of the Appellate Division brought up for review should be affirmed, 68 A.D.2d 141, 416 N.Y.S.2d 254, with costs. We agree with the Appellate Division's conclusion that subdivision (2) of section 2–403 of the Uniform Commercial Code does not insulate defendants from plaintiff Porter's lawful claim to the Utrillo painting. Subdivision (2) of section 2–403 of the Uniform Commercial Code provides: "Any entrusting of possession of goods to a merchant who deals in goods of that kind gives him power to transfer all rights of the entruster to a buyer in ordinary course of business." The "entruster provision" of the Uniform Commercial Code is designed to enhance the reliability of commercial sales by merchants (who deal with the kind of goods sold on a regular basis) while shifting the risk of loss through fraudulent transfer to the owner of the goods, who can select the merchant to whom he entrusts his property. It protects only those who purchase from the merchant to whom the property was entrusted in the ordinary course of the merchant's business.

While the Utrillo painting was entrusted to Harold Von Maker, an art merchant, the Feigen Gallery purchased the painting not from Von Maker, but from one Peter Wertz, who turns out to have been a delicatessen employee acquainted with Von Maker. It seems that Von Maker frequented the delicatessen where Peter Wertz was employed and that at some point Von Maker began to identify himself as Peter Wertz in certain art transactions. Indeed, Von Maker identified himself as Peter Wertz in his dealings with Porter.

Defendants argued that Feigen reasonably assumed that the Peter Wertz who offered the Utrillo to him was an art merchant because Feigen had been informed by Henry Sloan that an art dealer named Peter Wertz desired to sell a Utrillo painting. Feigen therefore argues that for purposes of subdivision (2) of section 2–403 of the Uniform Commercial Code it is as though he purchased from a merchant in the ordinary course of business. Alternatively, he claims that he actually purchased the Utrillo from Von Maker, the art dealer to whom it had been entrusted, because Peter Wertz sold the painting on Von Maker's behalf. Neither argument has merit.

Even if Peter Wertz were acting on Von Maker's behalf, unless he disclosed this fact to Feigen, it could hardly be said that Feigen relied upon Von Maker's status as an art merchant. It does not appear that the actual Peter Wertz ever represented that he was acting on behalf of Von Maker in selling the painting.

As to the argument that Feigen reasonably assumed that Peter Wertz was an art merchant, it is apparent from the opinion of the Appellate Division that the court rejected the fact finding essential to this argument, namely, that Peter Wertz had been introduced to Feigen by Henry Sloan as an art merchant. The court noted that in his examination before trial

Richard Feigen had testified that he could not recall whether Henry Sloan had described Peter Wertz as an art dealer and concluded that this substantially weakened the probative force of Feigen's trial testimony on this point. Indeed, Peter Wertz testified that Von Maker had not directed him to the Feigen Gallery but had simply delivered the painting to Wertz and asked him to try to find a buyer for the Utrillo. Wertz had been to several art galleries before he approached the Feigen Gallery. Thus, the Appellate Division's finding has support in the record.

Because Peter Wertz was not an art dealer and the Appellate Division has found that Feigen was not duped by Von Maker into believing that Peter Wertz was such a dealer, subdivision (2) of section 2–403 of the Uniform Commercial Code is inapplicable for three distinct reasons: (1) even if Peter Wertz were an art merchant rather than a delicatessen employee, he is not the same merchant to whom Porter entrusted the Utrillo painting; (2) Wertz was not an art merchant; and (3) the sale was not in the ordinary course of Wertz' business because he did not deal in goods of that kind (Uniform Commercial Code, § 1–201, subd. [9]).

Nor can the defendants-appellants rely on the doctrine of equitable estoppel. It has been observed that subdivision (1) of section 2–403 of the Uniform Commercial Code incorporates the doctrines of estoppel, agency and apparent agency because it states that a purchaser acquires not only all title that his transferor had, but also all title that he had power to transfer (White & Summers, Uniform Commercial Code, § 3–11, p. 139).

An estoppel might arise if Porter had clothed Peter Wertz with ownership of or authority to sell the Utrillo painting and the Feigen Gallery had relied upon Wertz' apparent ownership or right to transfer it. But Porter never even delivered the painting to Peter Wertz, much less create apparent ownership in him; he delivered the painting to Von Maker for his own personal use. It is true, as previously noted, that Von Maker used the name Peter Wertz in his dealings with Porter, but the Appellate Division found that the Feigen Gallery purchased from the actual Peter Wertz and that there was insufficient evidence to establish the claim that Peter Wertz had been described as an art dealer by Henry Sloan. Nothing Porter did influenced the Feigen Gallery's decision to purchase from Peter Wertz a delicatessen employee. Accordingly, the Feigen Gallery cannot protect its defective title by a defense of estoppel.

The Appellate Division opined that even if Von Maker had duped Feigen into believing that Peter Wertz was an art dealer, subdivision (2) of section 2–403 of the Uniform Commercial Code would still not protect his defective title because as a merchant, Feigen failed to purchase in good faith. Among merchants good faith requires not only honesty in fact but observance of reasonable commercial standards. (Uniform Commercial Code, § 2–103, subd. [1], par. [b]). The Appellate Division concluded that it was a departure from reasonable commercial standards for the Feigen Gallery to fail to inquire concerning the title to the Utrillo and to fail to question Peter Wertz' credentials as an art dealer. On this appeal we have received *amicus* briefs from the New York State Attorney–General urging that the court hold that good faith among art merchants requires inquiry as to the ownership of an *objet d'art,* and from the Art Dealers Association of America, Inc., arguing that the ordinary custom in the art business is not to inquire as to title and that a duty of inquiry would cripple the art business which is centered in New York. In view of our disposition we do not reach the good faith question.

Judgment appealed from and order of the Appellate Division brought up for review affirmed with costs, in a memorandum.

## NOTES

**(1) Entrusting to a Merchant; Agency.** Although UCC 2–403(2) does not use concepts of agency, the operational effect is very similar to the results that might be derived from agency law. Unlike UCC 2–403(1), which has the effect of transferring "good title" to good faith purchasers for value, the effect of section 2–403(2) is to transfer "all rights of the entruster." The entruster is in a position comparable to that of an undisclosed principal who turns over goods to an agent and clothes the agent with apparent power to sell. Those who turn over goods to merchants who deal in goods of that kind should recognize that customers of those merchants may have no way of discerning that the goods are not part of the merchants' inventory.

Porter delivered the Utrillo painting to an individual whom he thought was a merchant. Porter was deceived about Von Maker's business status, but Porter intended to give possession to an art dealer. If Von Maker had been a merchant, what would have been the legal significance of the arrangement that Von Maker was considering making the purchase for his personal collection rather than for his business?

If Von Maker, continuing the deception that he was an art dealer, had sold the Utrillo painting to Feigen Gallery, should the court have reached a different conclusion? The opinion of the court makes much of the fact that the individual to whom Porter entrusted the painting was not the same individual who sold the painting to Feigen Gallery? Since the two intermediaries were collaborators in the fraud, should their separate identities have been given importance?

**(2) Buyers in the Ordinary Course of Business.** Section 2–403(2) protects only persons who qualify as buyers in the ordinary course of business, sometimes known as BIOCOBs. UCC 1–201(b)(9) defines BIOCOB. BIOCOB is narrower than good faith purchaser for value in a number of respects. Study the two sets of concepts and list the differences between the two classes.

Can a merchant buyer be a BIOCOB? Is UCC 2–403(2) part of the body of law that is limited to protecting consumers, i.e., individuals who buy for personal, family or household purposes. Feigen Gallery was clearly not an ordinary consumer, but that alone does not render the Gallery ineligible for protection as a BIOCOB. Were there any circumstances in the sale from

Peter Wertz to Feigen Gallery that could have justified the conclusion that the Gallery was not a BIOCOB of the Utrillo painting?

**(3) Seller Retention of Goods Sold and Resale.** All of the fact situations considered to this point have been linear and involved three or more parties. Each transaction can be diagramed in this form: A→B→C, and so forth. A sells or entrusts goods to B who in turn sells goods to C. The disputants are A and C. Another transaction-type, with similar legal problems, is non-linear. It arises when a seller retains goods it has agreed to sell to buyer #1 and then sells the same goods to buyer #2. Both buyers deal with the same seller. The diagram could be in this form: A←B→C. B first sells but does not deliver goods to A. B then sells and delivers the goods to C. Again the disputants are A and C. What legal rules govern? Acquiescence in seller's retention of possession is "entrusting" by a buyer under UCC 2–403(3). If C qualifies as a BIOCOB, then C can prevail under over A. UCC 2–403(2). Suppose, however, that C is not a BIOCOB. Can you construct a theory for C to prevail over A under UCC 2–403(1)?

Another approach to the contest between A and C is by way of the limited specific remedies that the Commercial Code provides to A in a dispute with its seller. Buyers can replevy goods from their sellers or obtain an injunction or decree of specific performance to compel sellers to deliver goods only in limited circumstances.[2] In circumstances where A could not compel B to deliver the goods retained, should A be able to compel C to turn over the goods?

**(4) Lease Transaction: "Entrusting" and Lessees "In Ordinary Course."** Consider a sale of a power shovel by M, a merchant who deals in goods of that kind, to B who pays for the equipment. With M's consent, B leaves the power shovel with M pending B's need for it on a construction project that is expected to begin shortly. Before B returns to take possession of the power shovel, M leases it to L. B discovers that L has the power shovel and demands that L surrender it to B.

Is L's right to possession protected under UCC 2–403(2)? See the definition of "buyer" in UCC 2–103(1)(a). Is L's right to possession protected under UCC 2A–304(2)? Is L a "subsequent lessee"? The comment to this section provides:

> Section 2A–307(2) resolves the potential dispute between B, M and L. By virtue of B's entrustment of the goods to M and M's lease of the goods to L, B has a cause of action against M under the common law. ... Thus, B is a creditor of M. ... Section 2A–307(2) provides that B, as M's creditor, takes subject to M's lease to L. Thus, if L does not default under the lease, L's enjoyment and possession of the goods should be undisturbed.

Query: Is there legal slight of hand in characterizing B as merely a creditor of M?

---

2. See UCC 2–502, 2–716.

# Madrid v. Bloomington Auto Company, Inc.

Court of Appeals of Indiana, Fourth District, 2003.
782 N.E.2d 386.

■ SHARPNACK, JUDGE

Michael and Pamela Madrid (the "Madrids") appeal the trial court's denial of a motion for summary judgment filed by the Madrids, the trial court's grant of a cross-motion for summary judgment filed by Bloomington Auto Company, Inc., d/b/a Royal Lincoln Mercury Nissan ("Royal"), and the denial of a motion to correct error filed by the Madrids. The Madrids raise two issues, which we restate as:

I. Whether legal title to a motor vehicle is governed by Indiana's Certificate of Title Act or the sales provisions of Indiana's Uniform Commercial Code ("UCC"); and

II. Whether the purchasers of a motor vehicle received legal title to the vehicle pursuant to *Ind. Code § 26–1–2–403*, the entrustment provisions of the UCC.

We reverse and remand.

The relevant facts designated by the parties in their summary judgment motions follow. The Madrids and Michael Madrid's company had previously purchased both new and used vehicles from Gary Pratt University Motors, Inc. ("University Motors"). University Motors is a used car dealer in West Lafayette, Indiana. In May 2001, the Madrids became interested in purchasing a Lincoln Navigator and asked University Motors to locate "one with low miles that was 'loaded.'" ... On June 1, 2001, Gary Pratt located a new 2000–model-year Navigator at Royal's dealership in Bloomington, Indiana. Pratt called Royal's sales manager and stated that he had a customer who was interested in the Navigator. Pratt asked if Royal would bring the Navigator to University Motors so that the customer could inspect the vehicle.

Several times in the past, University Motors had requested that Royal drive a new vehicle to University Motors so that University Motors could show the vehicle to a potential customer. If the customer decided to purchase the vehicle, a Royal employee would fill out the sales paperwork and the customer would pay Royal directly for the vehicle. Royal would then pay University Motors a finder's fee for "putting Royal in contact with the customer." ... Because University Motors is not an authorized Lincoln dealership, it is prohibited from selling new Lincoln vehicles. See *Ind. Code § 9–23–3–4* (1998) ("It is an unfair practice for a dealer to sell any new motor vehicle having a trade name, trade or service mark, or related characteristics for which the dealer does not have a franchise in effect at the time of the sale."). To sell a new Lincoln directly to a customer, University Motors would have to purchase the vehicle from Royal and pay state sales tax. University Motors would then sell the vehicle to a customer, and the customer would also be required to pay state sales tax.

Rather than purchase the vehicle from Royal, University Motors agreed to receive a finder's fee from Royal if University Motors had a customer for the vehicle. A Royal employee drove the Navigator to University Motors on June 2, 2001 so that University Motors could show the Navigator to the Madrids. Royal retained the vehicle's certificate of origin, built-in mobile phone, owner's manuals, and extra keys. The same day, the Madrids came to University Motors to look at the vehicle. Pratt told the Madrids that University Motors had purchased the Navigator for $40,000 and he would like to make $3,000 on the sale to them. They agreed on a purchase price of $41,500. After the Madrids paid the purchase price and took possession of the vehicle, University Motors promised to deliver the title, paperwork, and mobile phone the next day by Federal Express. Despite daily telephone calls from the Madrids, University Motors never delivered any of the documents or vehicle accessories to the Madrids.

Royal also called University Motors for updates regarding the potential sale of the Navigator. Pratt first told Royal that "he was 99% sure that the customers were going to buy the Navigator and that he was going to get a non-refundable deposit for the vehicle." ... Royal reminded Pratt that all payments had to be made to Royal. The next day, Pratt told Royal that the customers were out of town, but would purchase the Navigator when they returned. Pratt continued to give Royal various excuses until June 23, 2001, when Royal learned that there was a police seizure at University Motors. Royal's general manager drove to West Lafayette to retrieve the Navigator, but was informed that the Navigator was not one of the vehicles seized. Pratt informed Royal that the customers had possession of the Navigator.

The Madrids filed a complaint against Royal and University Motors requesting that Royal surrender the title to the Madrids or that the trial court "administratively issue title to the vehicle" to the Madrids. ... The Madrids filed a motion for summary judgment, and Royal filed a cross-motion for summary judgment. The trial court granted Royal's cross-motion for summary judgment and denied the Madrids' motion for summary judgment. Specifically, the trial court found that Royal was entitled to summary judgment under Ind. Code § 9–17, Indiana's Certificate of Title Act, "because Royal preserved its ownership of the vehicle by retaining the [certificate of origin] and, therefore, as a matter of law, the Navigator, or its equivalent monetary value, must be returned to Royal." ... Alternatively, the trial court found that under Ind. Code § 26–1–2, the sales provisions of the UCC, Royal retained ownership of the Navigator because: (1) Royal did not "entrust" the vehicle to University Motors; (2) University Motors was not a "merchant who deals in goods of that kind;" and (3) the Madrids knew or should have known that University Motors was not authorized to sell them the new vehicle and did not own the vehicle. ... The trial court also noted that no Indiana court has discussed the effect of the current Indiana Certificate of Title Act on the sales provisions of the UCC. However, relying upon cases from Ohio and Texas, the trial court held that even assuming that Royal entrusted the Navigator to University Motors within the meaning of the UCC, "Royal is still the owner of the Navigator, because a dealer cannot sell a vehicle without giving the buyer a [certificate of origin]." . . . The Madrids filed a motion to correct error, which the trial court denied.

Our standard of review for a trial court's grant of a motion for summary judgment is well settled. On appeal, the standard of review of a grant or denial of a motion for summary judgment is the same as that used in the trial court: summary judgment is appropriate only where the designated evidence shows that there is no genuine issue of material fact and that the moving party is entitled to a judgment as a matter of law. . . .

I.

The first issue is whether legal title to a motor vehicle is governed by Indiana's Certificate of Title Act or the sales provisions of the UCC. According to the Madrids, two separate motor vehicle certificate of title structures are utilized by states—an "ownership" system and a "registration" system. . . . Under an ownership system, "legal title does not pass until a title certificate passes" and the certificate of title statutes displace standard commercial law with respect to motor vehicle ownership. . . . Under a registration system, standard commercial law governs automobile ownership and a certificate of title only creates a right to register and use a vehicle on public roads.

\* \* \*

We begin with an analysis of Indiana's Certificate of Title Act. Indiana's current Certificate of Title Act, which is found at Ind. Code § 9–17 and was enacted in 1991, provides generally that "a person may not operate or permit to be operated upon the highways a motor vehicle . . . under an Indiana registration number unless a certificate of title has been issued . . . for the motor vehicle. . . ." *Ind. Code § 9–17–2–13* (1998). Within sixty days of becoming an Indiana resident, "a person must obtain a certificate of title for all vehicles owned by the person" that are subject to the motor vehicle excise tax and will be operated in Indiana. *Ind. Code § 9–17–2–1* (Supp. 2001); see also 140 IAC 6–1–2 ("Any person who purchases or otherwise acquires a new or used motor vehicle . . . must apply for a certificate of title in the purchaser's or transferee's name."). If the Bureau of Motor Vehicles "is satisfied that the person applying for a certificate of title is the owner of the vehicle . . . the bureau may issue a certificate of title for the vehicle." *Ind. Code § 9–17–2–10* (1998).

Once a certificate of title is obtained, it "is valid for as long as the vehicle for which the certificate of title has been issued is owned or held by the person who originally held the certificate of title." *Ind. Code § 9–17–3–1* (1998). If a vehicle is sold or the ownership is transferred, the holder of the certificate of title must deliver the certificate of title to the purchaser or transferee at the time of the sale or delivery except under certain circumstances where the certificate of title may be delivered within twenty-one days of the sale or delivery. *Ind. Code § 9–17–3–3* (1998).

If a certificate of title "has not previously been issued for a vehicle in Indiana, an application for a certificate of title must be accompanied by a manufacturer's certificate of origin...." *Ind. Code § 9–17–2–4* (1998). The "certificate of origin" refers "to the original ownership document for a vehicle issued by a manufacturer and provided to the initial purchaser of that vehicle so as to begin the chain of ownership of that vehicle." 140 IAC 3.5–1–6. *Ind. Code § 9–17–8–1* (1998) provides that:

> A manufacturer, converter manufacturer, dealer, or other person may not sell or otherwise dispose of a new motor vehicle to another person, to be used by the other person for purposes of display or resale, without delivering to the other person a manufacturer's certificate of origin under this chapter that indicates the assignments of the certificate of origin necessary to show the ownership of the title to a person who purchases the motor vehicle.

Additionally, *Ind. Code § 9–17–8–2* (1998) provides that "[a] person may not purchase or acquire a new motor vehicle without obtaining from the seller of the motor vehicle a valid manufacturer's certificate of origin." Pursuant to this provision, Royal argues that the Madrids did not obtain legal title to the vehicle because they never received the vehicle's certificate of origin.

To support its argument, Royal relies upon *Saturn of Kings Automall, Inc. v. Mike Albert Leasing, Inc., 92 Ohio St. 3d 513, 2001 Ohio 1274, 751 N.E.2d 1019 (Ohio 2001)*. However, the case is distinguishable. There, the Ohio Supreme Court held that, in determining competing claims of ownership of a motor vehicle, Ohio's Certificate of Motor Vehicle Title Law controls over the provisions of Ohio's Uniform Commercial Code. *751 N.E.2d at 1025*. However, Ohio's Certificate of Motor Vehicle Title Law is substantially different than Indiana's Certificate of Title Act. Ohio's statute provides:

> No person acquiring a motor vehicle from its owner, whether the owner is a manufacturer, importer, dealer, or any other person, *shall acquire any right, title, claim, or interest in or to the motor vehicle until there is issued to the person a certificate of title to the motor vehicle*, or delivered to the person a manufacturer's or importer's certificate for it; and no waiver or estoppel operates in favor of such person against a person having possession of the certificate of title to, or manufacturer's or importer's certificate for, the motor vehicle, for a valuable consideration.

*751 N.E.2d at 1021* (quoting R.C. 4505.04(A) (emphasis added)).

Indiana's Certificate of Title Act provides no such limitation on the passing of "any right, title, claim, or interest" in the vehicle until a certificate of title is issued. Although *Ind. Code § 9–17–8–2* provides that "[a] person may not purchase or acquire a new motor vehicle without obtaining from the seller of the motor vehicle a valid manufacturer's certificate of origin," the statute does not expressly limit the passing of legal title until the certificate of title is issued. Rather, Indiana's Certificate of Title Act expressly conditions issuance of a certificate of title upon ownership of a vehicle. See, e.g., *I.C. § 9–17–2–10* ("If the bureau is satisfied that the person applying for a certificate of title *is the owner of the vehicle* or is otherwise entitled to have the vehicle registered in the person's name, the bureau may issue a certificate of title for the vehicle.") (emphasis added). Thus, we do not find Royal's argument persuasive.

The Madrids argue that the 1991 enactment of the Certificate of Title Act did not change the focus and intent of the prior statute. Prior to 1991, certificates of title were governed by Ind. Code § 9–1–2–1 to –4 (repealed 1991). Ind. Code § 9–1–2–1(j) (repealed 1991) provided that "it is unlawful for a person to operate or permit to be operated upon the public highways a motor vehicle . . . under an Indiana registration number unless a certificate of title has been issued under this section." Further, the Act provided that "if satisfied that the applicant is the lawful owner of the vehicle or is otherwise entitled to have the same registered in the applicant's name, the department may issue an appropriate certificate of title." I.C. § 9–1–2–1(a) (repealed 1991).

The Act further provided that "in the event of the sale or transfer of ownership of such vehicle, for which an original certificate of title has been issued heretofore, the original holder of such certificate shall . . . deliver the same to the purchaser or transferee at the time of the sale or delivery to him of such vehicle." Ind. Code § 9–1–2–2(a) (repealed 1991). However, Ind. Code § 9–1–2–3(a) (repealed 1991) provided that:

> no manufacturer, converter manufacturer, dealer, or other person may sell or otherwise dispose of a new motor vehicle to a dealer or any person, to be used by such dealer or person for purposes of display or resale, without delivering to such dealer a manufacturer's certificate of origin in accordance with the provisions of this chapter and with such assignments thereon as may be necessary to show title to the purchaser thereof. The dealer or person may not purchase or acquire a new motor vehicle without obtaining from the seller a valid manufacturer's certificate of origin.

We do not see significant substantive changes in the relevant portions of the pre–1991 and 1991 statutes. The legislative intent behind P.L. 2–1991, which repealed Ind. Code § 9–1–2–1 to –4, was "to amend the Indiana Code to codify, revise or rearrange laws concerning motor vehicles." The relevant provisions were, for the most part, simply rearranged into separate sections and slightly reworded. The intent behind the pre–1991 and 1991 statutes appears to be the same and cases interpreting the pre–1991 statutes provide guidance in this case. *Weatherholt v. Spencer County, 639 N.E.2d 354, 356 (Ind. Ct. App. 1994)* (holding that current and former versions of a statute were substantially the same and the former statute provided guidance), reh'g denied.

Having discussed the pre–1991 and 1991 Certificate of Title Act, we now briefly turn to the relevant sales provisions of the UCC. *Ind. Code § 26–1–2–401* (Supp. 2001) provides that under the sales provisions of the UCC, "unless otherwise explicitly agreed, title passes to the buyer at the time and place at which the seller completes his performance with reference to the physical delivery of the goods, despite any reservation of a security interest and even though a document of title is to be delivered at a different time or place." Moreover, "any entrusting of possession of goods to a merchant who deals in goods of that kind gives him power to transfer all rights of the entruster to a buyer in ordinary course of business." *Ind. Code § 26–1–2–403* (Supp. 2001). The Madrids contend that they are entitled to legal title to the vehicle under these provisions.

The sales provisions of the UCC do not "impair or repeal" Indiana's Certificate of Title Act. *Ind. Code § 26–1–2–102* (1998). Furthermore, because the UCC is a "general statute intended as a unified coverage of its subject matter, no part of it shall be deemed to be impliedly repealed by subsequent legislation if such construction can reasonably be avoided." *Ind. Code § 26–1–1–104* (1998). Thus, we must attempt to give effect to both the sales provisions of the UCC and the Indiana Certificate of Title Act if such an interpretation is possible.

We have previously discussed the relationship between the pre–1991 Certificate of Title Act and the UCC in the context of motor vehicle sales. Under the pre–1991 statute, we held that ownership of a vehicle is not dependent upon possessing a certificate of title. For example, in *Pekin Ins. Co. v. Charlie Rowe Chevrolet, Inc., 556 N.E.2d 1367, 1370 (Ind. Ct. App. 1990),* we observed that:

> certificate of title is not of itself proof of ownership or legal title to the vehicle.... A person may have legal title in a vehicle even though he does not possess a certificate of title. Because failing to possess a certificate of title does not indicate absolutely that a person does not have legal title to an automobile, the determination of when a person has legal title is controlled by the application of the commercial code.

Thus, under the pre–1991 statutes, legal title to a vehicle was governed by the sales provisions of the UCC rather than the certificate of title statutes.

\* \* \*

Given the correlation between the pre–1991 and 1991 Certificate of Title Acts, we ... conclude that the Madrids are correct that Indiana's current Certificate of Title Act creates a "registration" type system rather than an "ownership" type system. Mindful of *Ind. Code § 26–1–2–102*, which provides that sales provisions of the UCC do not "impair or repeal" Indiana's Certificate of Title Act, we note that our interpretation does not impair the Certificate of Title Act. Rather, this interpretation gives effect to both statutes. Thus, we conclude that the trial court erred when it determined that the legal ownership of the vehicle is determined by Indiana's Certificate of Title Act. Rather, legal ownership of vehicles is determined by the sales provisions of the UCC. ...

## II.

Having determined that legal title to a motor vehicle is governed by the sales provisions of the UCC rather than the Indiana Certificate of Title Act, we must now determine whether the Madrids received legal title to the vehicle pursuant to *Ind. Code § 26–1–2–403*, the entrustment provisions of the UCC. As previously noted, the sales provisions of the UCC provide that "unless otherwise explicitly agreed, title passes to the buyer at the time and place at which the seller completes his performance with reference to the physical delivery of the goods, despite any reservation of a security interest and even though a document of title is to be delivered at a different time or place...." *I.C. § 26–1–2–401(2)*. Further, *Ind. Code § 26–1–2–403(2)* provides that "any entrusting of possession of goods to a merchant who deals in goods of that kind gives him power to transfer all rights of the entruster to a buyer in ordinary course of business." The trial court held that Royal did not entrust the Navigator to University Motors, University Motors was not a merchant who deals in goods of the same kind as Royal, and the Madrids knew or should have known that University Motors was not an authorized Lincoln new car dealer and did not own the vehicle.

The Madrids first argue that the trial court erred by determining that University Motors was not a merchant who deals in goods of the same kind as Royal. *Ind. Code § 26–1–2–403(2)* applies only if the goods are entrusted "to a merchant who deals in goods of that kind...." Royal argues that University Motors was not an authorized Lincoln new car dealer and statutorily could not deal in new Lincoln cars. See *I.C. § 9–23–3–4*. Thus, according to Royal, University Motors was not a merchant who deals in goods of that kind, i.e. a merchant who deals in new Lincoln cars. However, Royal cites no authority for this proposition.

The Madrids contend that Royal's interpretation is too narrow. The Madrids argue that it is sufficient that both University Motors and Royal were car dealers. The Madrids rely upon *Shacket v. Philko Aviation, Inc., 681 F.2d 506 (7th Cir. 1982)*, cert. granted in part, *459 U.S. 1069, 103 S. Ct. 487 (1982)*, rev'd on other grounds, *462 U.S. 406, 103 S. Ct. 2476, 76 L. Ed. 2d 678 (1983)*. In Shacket, a dealer of new airplanes ("Dealer") entrusted possession of a new airplane to dealer of used airplanes ("Seller"). ... The dealer of used airplanes proceeded to "sell" the airplane to two separate buyers. Id. The Seventh Circuit held that even though Seller was only in the business of selling used aircraft, it could still transfer the good title of the Dealer to a buyer. ... "The term 'goods of that kind' is not limited to the same goods but encompasses goods of the same fundamental nature." ... The fact that the Seller "was in the business of selling aircraft on a commercial basis is sufficient to permit [it] to pass good title to a buyer in the ordinary course." ...

We find Shacket to be persuasive. It is sufficient for purposes of *Ind. Code § 26–1–2–403(2)* that University Motors and Royal were both merchants of "goods of the same fundamental nature." ... Thus, even though University Motors sold used vehicles and Royal sold new vehicles, Royal placed the Navigator with "a merchant who deals in goods of that kind" by loaning it to University Motors. ...

The Madrids next argue that the trial court erred by determining that Royal did not entrust the Navigator to University Motors. *Ind. Code § 26–1–2–403(3)* (Supp. 2001) defines "entrusting" to include "any delivery and any acquiescence in retention of possession regardless of any condition expressed between the parties to the delivery or acquiescence and regardless of whether the procurement of the entrusting or the possessor's disposition of the goods have been such as to be theft under the criminal law." The trial court held that the vehicle was not entrusted to University Motors "because the vehicle was only brought to University Motors so the Madrids could inspect the vehicle." . . . However, entrustment expressly includes "any delivery and any acquiescence in retention." *I.C. § 26–1–2– 403(3).* Royal agreed to deliver the vehicle to University Motors so that University Motors could show the vehicle to the Madrids. Royal acquiesced in University Motors' retention of the vehicle despite University Motors' repeated excuses regarding why the Madrids had not yet purchased the vehicle. These actions fall within the definition of entrustment pursuant to *Ind. Code § 26–1–2–403.*

The trial court also held that it was "unlikely that the Madrids took possession of the vehicle without notice of the true owner's identity" and the Madrids "knew, or should have known, that University Motors was not an authorized Lincoln car dealer." . . . The trial court essentially held that the Madrids were not buyers in the ordinary course of business. . . . No evidence was designated that the Madrids knew that the sale violated Royal's rights. Pratt told the Madrids that University Motors had purchased the Navigator. The only evidence designated that raises an inference that the sale was outside the ordinary course of business is the failure of University Motors to provide a certificate of origin at the time of the sale to the Madrids. However, as noted Part I, supra, we held under the pre–1991 statutes that the failure of a buyer to demand a certificate of title at the time of the sale did not result in the buyer losing its status as a buyer in the ordinary course of business. . . . Thus, we conclude that the Madrids were buyers in the ordinary course of business. . . .

\* \* \*

Reversed and remanded.

## NOTES

**(1) Certificates of Title; Certificates of Origin.** State governments maintain records of the owners of motor vehicles. Typically the records are maintained by the Bureau of Motor Vehicles or by the Bureau of Revenue. States impose substantial taxes on transactions of sale of motor vehicles to user/buyers, on sales of new vehicles and on subsequent sales of those "previously owned" vehicles. Administration of this tax system is facilitated by a requirement that each user/buyer must obtain a certificate of title. To facilitate this system, automobile manufacturers issue certificates of origin on vehicles as they leave the plant. These certificates accompany the vehicles through the distribution chain to retail dealers. The certificate contains, among other information, the vehicle identification number (VIN) which the manufacturer has stamped onto the chassis.

As part of the execution of a retail sales transaction, the certificate of origin must be surrendered to the state administrative agency in exchange for the initial certificate of title, commonly referred to as the "A" title. The certificate of title is issued by the agency of the state in which the buyer resides. Retail dealers make arrangements to do this and also to apply for permanent license plates,[3] a separate requirement of state law. Dealers commonly charge buyers a fee for "tags and title" for handling these matters.[4] If owners move to a different state, they must get a certificate from the administrative agency in the new state, within a short time. To obtain the new certificate, they must surrender old certificate. Each time a vehicle is sold, the certificate of title is surrendered for a "B" title, a "C" title, etc.

While the certificate of title acts in force are similar, there is no uniformity among them.[5] One of the aspects on which the acts differ was crucial to the disposition of this case. Compare the Ohio statute with the Indiana statute. Do you agree that the dispute should be decided in favor of the dealer if the events had occurred in Ohio?

**(2) Certificates of Title and Documents of Title.** Commercial law recognizes that certain special documents issued by custodians of goods can be trade ("negotiated") with the effect that a purchaser of a document acquires title to the goods. In the Commercial Code, these documents are called "documents of title." The subject is addressed in Article 7, which provides that the holders of negotiable warehouse receipts or bills of lading,[6] the most common documents of title, to whom the documents have been duly negotiated acquire title to the documents and title to the goods. UCC 7–502(a).[7] The certificates of title for motor vehicles are not documents of title. Certificates of tile are not issued by custodians of the vehicles. Acquiring a certificate of title does not, in itself, convey title to the motor vehicle.

**(3) Construction of UCC 2–403(2).** The Indiana court held that the competing claims of the Madrids and Royal Lincoln Mercury Nissan (Royal) dealership should be decided under UCC 2–403(2). Both had dealt, in different ways, with a used car dealer, Gary Pratt University Motors (Pratt). It is important to keep the facts clearly in mind for purpose of legal analysis. Royal gave Pratt physical possession of the Navigator. There was no contract for sale of the Navigator by Royal to Pratt. Pratt and the Madrids entered into—and partially executed—a contract of sale for the Navigator. Pratt gave physical possession of the vehicle to the Madrids, The Madrids gave $41,500.00 to Pratt. Pratt disappointed both Royal and the

---

3. Dealers issue temporary license plates at the time of delivery. These expire after a short time.

4. If a buyer borrows money to pay part of the price of a vehicle and grants the lender a security interest in the vehicle to assure repayment, the lender's security interest will be noted on the certificate by the state agency. Commonly, lenders require that the certificates be kept in their custody. The law of secured transactions in motor vehicles relies upon notations on certificates of title as the means for perfection of securities interests in the vehicles. UCC 9–311(a)(2) and (3).

5. The National Conference of Commissioners on Uniform State Laws promulgated a proposed uniform act in 1955, but that effort to promote uniformity failed. The Conference revised its proposal in 2006.

6. To be "negotiable," documents of title must have certain terms. UCC 7–104.

7. Analogous provisions for bills of lading used in interstate and international commerce are found in the Federal Bill of Lading Act, 49 U.S.C. §§ 80101–80116.

Madrids and both appear to have multiple causes of action for monetary relief against Pratt. The chances of collecting, however, appear slim.

*Merchant who deals in goods of that kind.* Did Royal "entrust" the Navigator to Pratt? UCC 2–403(3) speaks of delivery of possession. That subsection does not specify the characteristics of the persons making or receiving the delivery. These can be found or inferred in UCC 2–403(2). That subsection assumes that the person making delivery is the owner of goods. If an entruster is a thief, the "rights of the entruster" that might be transferred are nil. The subsection specifies that the person receiving delivery must be a "merchant who deals in goods of that kind." If an entrustee is not such a merchant, it cannot transfer any rights. That was the central issue in *Porter v. Wertz*. Whether Pratt was a "merchant who deals in goods of that kind" requires parsing the phrase. Was Pratt a "merchant," a defined term? See UCC 2–104(1). How broadly or narrowly should "goods of that kind" be read? Did Pratt deal in new cars? Used cars? Cars? The court declared that the answer lies in the "fundamental nature" of the goods. Does that formulation have any basis in the text or the comments of the statute? Does it help to indicate the correct answer?

*Buyer in the ordinary course of business.* Only a BIOCOB can obtain the rights of an entruster. That phrase is a defined term. UCC 1–201(b)(9). The court discussed the first sentence's requirement that a buyer act "without knowledge that the sale violates the rights of another person in the goods." Was the court correct in concluding that the Madrids did not "know" that the sale violated the rights of Royal?[8] The first and second sentence of UCC 1–201(b) refer to "the ordinary course [of business]." The court indicated that the only non-ordinary aspect of the sale was Pratt's failure to give to the Madrids a certificate of origin at the time of sale. As indicated above, it would be unusual for a car dealer to deliver a certificate of origin to a customer.[9] Were there other aspects of the Pratt–Madrids sale that appear to have been outside of "the ordinary course of business".

## (B) INTERNATIONAL SALES LAW

The Convention on Contracts for International Sale of Goods has no provision regarding resolution of conflicting claims to property.

---

## SECTION 5.   LEGAL BARS TO RECOVERY

### (A) DOMESTIC UNITED STATES LAW

#### 1. NOTICE OF BREACH

A buyer must give its seller notice of any breach of contract. UCC 2–607(3)(a). Breach of a warranty of title is breach of one of a seller's

---

**8.** "Knows" is a defined term. UCC 1–202.

**9.** The usual practice is that dealers, for a fee, undertake to obtain certificates of title for their customers. That appears to have been the arrangement made between Pratt and the Madrids.

contractual obligations. Comment 2 to UCC 2–312 affirms that the requirement of notice applies to breach of this warranty. The draconian sanction for buyer's failure to give notice is a bar of any remedy. Id.

The Code requires that notice be given "within a reasonable time" after a buyer discovers or should have discovered the breach. Thus, the reasonable period of time begins to run when a buyer learns or should have learned of the breach. The end of the reasonable period of time is not prescribed in UCC 2–607(3)(a). It is a matter for determination by the trier of fact on a case-by-case basis. Comment 2 to UCC 2–312 states that the length of the reasonable time period should be longer if the seller's breach was "in bad faith." The Comment does not define what constitutes "bad faith."

## 2.  STATUTE OF LIMITATIONS

The law provides generally that a claim for relief becomes time-barred when a specified period of time has elapsed after the claim accrued. In most instances, the period is specified by a statute of limitations. Article 2 of the Commercial Code has a statute of limitations provision. In some circumstances, the time bar is established as a matter of common law. Property law has such a rule in the protection afforded to a person who has possession of property, adverse to the interest of another person, for a period of time. Both kinds of prescription may arise in disputes within this chapter.

*Warranty of title claims.* Under Article 2 of the Commercial Code, an action for breach of any contract of sale must be commenced within four years after the cause of action has accrued, and a "breach of warranty" occurs when tender of delivery is made regardless of the aggrieved party's lack of knowledge of the breach. UCC 2–725(1) and (2). The unqualified language of subsection (2) does not limit that section to breach of a warranty of quality, the more obvious context for that section to apply. This subsection is quite inappropriate to claims for breach of warranty of title, which may be latent for considerable time after buyers take possession.[1] Nevertheless, any attempt to persuade a court that subsection (2) does not apply to suits for breach of a UCC 2–312 warranty is undermined by Comment 2 to UCC 2–312, which declares: "... Section 2–725 provides that the cause of action occurs when the breach occurs. Under the provisions of that section the breach of the warranty of good title occurs when tender of delivery is made since the warranty is not one which extends to 'future performance of the goods.' "

---

**1.** The proposed revision of Article 2 recognized the inappropriateness of UCC 2–725(2) to the situation of suits for breach of warranty of title. The revision contained a new set provisions that deal with this issue. Under the proposal, the limitations period for breach of a UCC 2–312 warranty would not begin to run until a buyer had discovered or should have discovered the breach. See Revised 2–725(3)(d). Failing enactment of the revision, does the proposal provide a basis for advocacy regarding the better construction of current Article 2 in suits for breach of warranty of title?

The limitations period in UCC 2–725 is four years. In some circumstances, the period could have run before a buyer discovered or could have discovered that there was a breach of the title warranty.

*Property claims.* Under the adverse possession common-law doctrine, a possessor who has actual, exclusive, open, notorious, continuous and hostile possession of land under a claim of right for a certain period can take good title and defeat the claim of an original owner. After 1870, a number of courts applied the doctrine to cases involving stolen horses and farm animals. Later cases applied the doctrine to manufactured goods, such as a piano, violin or typewriter. See P. Gerstenblith, The Adverse Possession of Personal Property, 37 Buff. L. Rev. 119 (1988); R. H. Heimholz, Wrongful Possession of Chattels: Hornbook Law and Case Law, 80 Nw. U. L. Rev. 1221 (1986); J. Dawson, Fraudulent Concealment and Statutes of Limitations, 31 Mich. L. Rev. 875 (1933).

Other courts have sought to resolve the timeliness of property claims of aggrieved owners versus innocent possessors by use of conventional statutes of limitations principles. The owners' claims are cut off after the passage of a statutory period. The difficult question, for this purpose, was to fix a date for the period to begin to run. Some courts held that the statutory period begins when the true owner was deprived of the property. Other courts utilized a discovery rule, whereby an owner's cause of action did not accrue until the owner has demanded return of the property and the possessor has refused to comply with the demand. A refinement of the discovery rule dealt with owners who were insufficiently diligent in locating their property or in making demand for its return. DeWeerth v. Baldinger, 836 F.2d 103 (2d Cir.1987); O'Keeffe v. Snyder, 83 N.J. 478, 416 A.2d 862 (1980). See P. Franzese, "Georgia on My Mind"—Reflections on O'Keefe v. Snyder, 19 Seton Hall L. Rev. 1 (1989); J. Petrovich, The Recovery of Stolen Art: Of Paintings, Statues, and Statutes of Limitations, 27 U.C.L.A. L. Rev. 1122 (1980). See also P. Gerstenblith, The Adverse Possession of Personal Property, 37 Buff. L. Rev. 119 (1988); R. H. Heimholz, Wrongful Possession of Chattels: Hornbook Law and Case Law, 80 Nw. U. L. Rev. 1221 (1986); J. Dawson, Fraudulent Concealment and Statutes of Limitations, 31 Mich. L. Rev. 875 (1933).

A third approach was to resolve the property claims by examining the relative blameworthiness of the two contesting parties. In the mid–1960's, a mailroom clerk at the Guggenheim Museum in New York City stole a Marc Chagall watercolor entitled *The Cattle Dealer* from a storage area. In 1967, Jules and Rachel Lubell bought the Chagall from a reputable dealer and hung it in their home. The museum learned of the location of the painting in 1985 and demanded its return. The New York Court of Appeals held that the right to the painting should be determined by comparing the conduct of both the museum and the buyers: The museum had not notified the police or other museums or galleries of the theft; the buyers could have discovered the museum's right to ownership by consulting a catalogue of Chagall's works, but had not done so. Solomon R. Guggenheim Foundation v. Lubell, 77 N.Y.2d 311, 567 N.Y.S.2d 623, 569 N.E.2d 426 (1991). After trial, the parties settled the suit. Mrs. Lubell retained the watercolor, but she and two dealers who had sold the painting paid an undisclosed sum of money to the museum. N.Y. Times, Dec. 29, 1993, B3.

A law review note proposed a special rule for stolen pieces of fine art. Observing that the advent of computer networks and high-quality digitized color imaging made possible creation of an international theft registry, the author concluded that adverse possession and multi-factor balancing tests are no longer suited to the realm of such movable and concealable personal property and hurt diligent owners who have reported thefts but have been unable to find their property. The author advanced this thesis: Victims of art thefts who promptly report the thefts to the police and to an international theft database should never be legally barred from recovering their property since buyers, for a small fee, can search the registry. S. Bibas, The Case Against Statutes of Limitations for Stolen Art, 103 Yale L.J. 2437 (1994).

## (B) INTERNATIONAL SALES LAW

### 1.  NOTICE OF BREACH

The Convention on Contracts for the International Sale of Goods imposes on buyers a strict requirement to give notice of breach of either CISG 41 or CISG 42, the Articles that deal with sellers' obligation to deliver goods free from any right or claim of a third party. Article 43(1) provides that a buyer loses the right to rely on either Article "if he does nor give notice to the seller specifying the nature of the third party within a reasonable time after he has become aware of the right or claim." Sub-article (2) is an exception for circumstances where a seller knew of the right or claim and the nature of it.

A 2006 German decision applied CISG 43 to bar a claim of breach of CISG 41. The transaction was the sale of a used car by a German car dealer to a car dealer in the Netherlands. Four months after delivery, the police seized the car as stolen property. The Netherlands car dealer gave notice to the German car dealer two months later. Subsequently, buyer sued seller for refund of the price. Seller contended that the notice had not been given within a reasonable time. The Bundesgerichtof held that buyer was precluded from relying on CISG 41. CLOUT ABSTRACT no. 822 (2006).

The court also found the notice deficient in substance for failure to inform the seller of the identity of the third party claimant and the steps that the claimant had taken to recover the vehicle.

### 2.  STATUTE OF LIMITATIONS

CISG has no statute of limitations provisions. The international community has addressed this matter in a separate multilateral Convention on the Limitation Period in the International Sale of Goods, which was promulgated several years before CISG.[2] The Limitations Period Conven-

---

**2.**  The United States ratified the Limitations Period Convention effective December 1, 1994.

tion does not explicitly address the issue of claims for breach of warranty of title. The Convention generally fixes a limitations period of four years (Article 8), and specifies that the period begins to run when a claim accrues (Article 9(1)). Article 10 declares:

1.  A claim arising from a breach of contract shall accrue on the date on which such breach occurs.

2.  A claim arising from a defect or other lack of conformity shall accrue on the date on which the goods are actually handed over to, or their tender is refused by, the buyer.

CHAPTER 4

# QUALITY: SELLERS' RESPONSIBILITY AND BUYERS' RIGHTS

## SECTION 1. INTRODUCTION

### 1. HISTORICAL BACKGROUND

The scope of sellers' responsibility for the quality of goods has passed through a remarkable evolution of a curiously cyclical character. In the Middle Ages the authority of the Church and of guilds combined to impose heavy standards of quality upon sellers.[1] Thereafter, as we shall see, English law came to afford but little protection to buyers: *caveat emptor*! This outlook, in turn, has been reversed in modern law, but some of the quaint language found in current statutes cannot be understood without an appreciation of the history.

The law of sales is here, as at so many points, enmeshed with the larger body of contract law. Students of the history of contracts will recall the reluctance of early common-law courts to enforce simple promises; in a static land economy, legal obligations were not to be assumed lightly. Although the specific undertakings in a document bearing the maker's seal received early legal protection, less formal undertakings had to wait for the ancient action "on the case" to develop beyond its tort ancestry into its contractual descendant, the action of special *assumpsit*.

The reluctance to give legal effect to simple informal statements made by sellers is illustrated by the famous 1625 decision of Chandelor v. Lopus[2] in which a buyer brought an action on the case against a goldsmith for affirming that a stone he sold the buyer was a "bezoar" (or "bezar"), a stone found in the alimentary organs of goats and supposed to have remarkable medicinal qualities. The jury found for the plaintiff. (How the plaintiff proved that this was not a "true" bezoar does not appear.) The Exchequer Chamber set aside the verdict and ruled that the declaration based on this affirmation was insufficient: "... the bare affirmation that it was a bezar stone, without warranting it to be so is no cause of action."[3]

---

**1.** W. Hamilton, The Ancient Maxim Caveat Emptor, 40 Yale L.J. 1133 (1931).

**2.** Cro. Jac. 4, 79 Eng. Rep. 3 (1625).

**3.** In view of the peculiar nature of the commodity, it may be worthwhile to record the further statement of the judges that, "... every one in selling wares will affirm that his wares are good, or the horse which he sells is sound."

Just how far the seller had to go to "warrant" was not stated; apparently he had to make an explicit statement like "I warrant that . . ." or "I agree to be bound that. . . ."

It is striking to find this 17th century decision dominating the New York court's thinking in an 1804 commercial case, Seixas v. Woods.[4] A dealer advertised and sold wood as "brazilletto," a wood valuable for manufacturing a chemical used in making dye; in fact the wood was worthless "peachum." A judgment for the buyer was reversed. Chancellor Kent's concurring opinion stated: "The mentioning the word, as Brazilletto wood, in the bill of parcels, and in the advertisement some days previous to the sale, did not amount to a warranty to the plaintiffs. To make an affirmation at the time of the sale, a warranty, it must appear by evidence to be so *intended*, and not to have been a mere matter of judgment and opinion, and of which the defendant had no particular knowledge. Here it is admitted, the defendant was equally ignorant with the plaintiffs, and could have had no such intention."[5]

Later in the 19th century, cases like these were overturned. The *Seixas* ("brazilletto") case was rejected in New York in a 1872 case involving a dealer who bought barrels of "blue vitriol" and innocently resold them as such: when the material proved to be "salzburger vitriol" (a less valuable commodity) the dealer was held liable to the purchaser.[6] The opinions in such cases usually did not discuss the reasons of policy that produced the change in approach, but one may surmise that a greater volume and speed of trade called for firmer protection for contractual expectations. The dealer who resold the goods may have been misled by its supplier, but a rule of law that made the dealer liable to its buyer for its representations would normally give the dealer recourse against its supplier.[7]

When Professor Williston came to draft the Uniform Sales Act,[8] one of his principal targets was the emphasis which some cases placed on the seller's "intent"—an offensive manifestation of a "subjective" view of

---

**4.**  2 Caines 48 (1804).

**5.**  Chief Justice Gibson, of Pennsylvania, used characteristically salty (and extreme) language to similar effect in McFarland v. Newman, 9 Watts 55 (Pa.1839). Gibson also drew a questionable analogy between a sale of goods and the deed for real estate. "A sale is a contract executed, on which, of course, no action can be directly founded." [Why not?] He added that warranty is "no more a part of the sale than the covenant of warranty in a deed is part of the conveyance." [Is it possible at the same time to convey property and undertake contractual obligations?]

**6.**  Hawkins v. Pemberton, 51 N.Y. 198 (1872).

**7.**  This practical point was emphasized in Jones v. Just, L.R. 3 Q.B. 197 (1868). Defendant sellers argued that they had relied on the selection of the goods by a supplier in Singapore; Mellor, J., replied that defendant sellers "had recourse against [the supplier] for not supplying an article reasonably merchantable."

**8.**  Unlike most of the Uniform Sales Act (USA), Section 12 was not modeled on the British Sale of Goods Act (SGA). Indeed, the USA treatment of warranties of quality departed fundamentally from the provisions on quality in the SGA. See Sales of Goods Act §§ 13 to 15, 62(1).

contracts.[9] To obliterate this approach, Section 12 of the Uniform Sales Act provided:

> Any affirmation of fact or any promise by the seller relating to the goods is an express warranty if the *natural tendency* of such affirmation or promise is to induce the buyer to purchase the goods, and if the buyer purchases the goods *relying thereon.*[10]

This language was well chosen to focus attention on the crucial question of reasonable reliance by the buyer on the seller's statements. This formulation also foreclosed difficult (and unprofitable) litigation over whether the seller's statement was a "promise" or an "affirmation of fact."

The Uniform Commercial Code in Section 2–313(1)(a) closely follows the above provision of the Uniform Sales Act. However, there is one noteworthy change: There is no reference to reliance by the buyer. Instead, an affirmation or a promise is an express warranty if it "becomes part of the basis of the bargain." The meaning of this novel phrase will be explored later.

## 2.   TYPES OF WARRANTIES

It is orthodox learning, carried forward from the Uniform Sales Act to the Uniform Commercial Code, that warranties of quality come in various "types." "Express" warranties (UCC 2–313) are to be distinguished from warranties that are "implied." Implied warranties of quality fall in two categories: "merchantable quality" (UCC 2–314), and "fitness for particular purpose" (UCC 2–315).

Consider simple examples of each of the three types of warranties. *Case 1:* B and S, a Ford automobile dealer, sign an agreement of sale for a "new Navigator." After delivery, B discovers that the car had been used as a demonstrator with the odometer disconnected. *Case 2:* A car purchased by B has a defective crankshaft that breaks two months after delivery. *Case 3:* B tells S, a paint dealer, that he wants paint for the outside of his house. S puts on the counter a can of "Lustro" which B buys. This paint is good for interior walls but is washed from exterior walls by the first rain. *Case 1* involves an express warranty (UCC 2–313), *Case 2* the warranty of merchantable quality (UCC 2–314), and *Case 3* the warranty of fitness for particular purpose (UCC 2–315).

In spite of the complexity and diversity of these statutory provisions it may help to consider whether they may be related—and possibly inspired by a common principle. For example, suppose that just before the purchase, the seller had been asked these questions: In *Case 1*, "Has anyone been driving this car before?" In *Case 2*, "Is the crankshaft sound?" In *Case 3*,

---

**9.** The Commissioners' Note to USA 12 referred to the "intent" concept and stated that "... the fundamental basis for liability on warranty is the justifiable reliance on the seller's assertions."

**10.** Emphasis added. USA 12 also included a sentence dealing with statements as to "value" or "opinion." This troublesome provision, and its overgrown offspring in UCC 2–313(2) will be considered later.

"Will the paint stand up under a rain?" Would the seller normally have given the undertakings requested by the buyer? If the seller had refused, would the buyer have purchased the goods?

Do buyers normally ask such questions? If not, why not? Because they are unimportant? Or because the answers "go without saying"?[11] As we watch the results (as contrasted with the language) of the cases it will be useful to analyze the degree of kinship between the terms of the contract (including "express" warranties) and the various "types" of "implied" warranties?[12]

These seemingly simple-minded questions have larger impact than might be evident at first glance, for the answers may be relevant not only in defining the scope of a seller's undertaking but also in determining the effectiveness of contract terms purporting to disclaim and limit implied "warranties." These questions may even be relevant to the border warfare between the "fields" of sales (contract) and tort.

## 3.   BREACH AND REMEDIES

Disputes about the quality of goods sometimes arise at the time sellers tender delivery, but warranties of quality are more likely to be invoked in disputes that arise after goods have been received by buyers and after buyers have paid all or a substantial part of the price. Enforcement of warranties of quality on goods that have been accepted and paid for is the paradigmatic remedial situation to be considered in this chapter. In later chapters, we will consider the issues presented when buyers discern non-conformities before accepting and paying for the goods.

The general remedial principle of contract law applies in warranty cases. Aggrieved buyers, like all persons aggrieved by breach of contract, are entitled to the benefit of their bargains. In simplest terms, this means that buyers' monetary recovery for breach of warranty is measured by the value of goods that would have met sellers' obligation of quality. Since buyers commonly have received goods of *some* value, that value must be taken into account in the formulation of a remedy.

---

**11.**   Are there analogous situations, outside the law of sales, where legal effect is given to understandings and expectations that are real, but normally are not fully expressed?

**12.**   Randall v. Newson, 2 Q.B.D. 102 (Court of Appeal, 1877) held a seller liable on the sale of a defective carriage pole. Lord Justice Brett, after referring to various types of warranties that had been mentioned in earlier opinions, stated: "The governing principle . . . is that the thing offered and delivered under a contract of purchase and sale must answer the description of it which is contained in words in the contract, or which would be so contained if the contract were accurately drawn out." This unified approach, however, was not sufficiently dominant in the English cases to be reflected in the drafting of the Sale of Goods Act. As a result, the different "types" of warranties, developed in the typical case-law process of distinguishing unwanted precedents, were cast into statutory form, and were carried into the Uniform Sales Act and on into the Sales article of the Code. The Code does provide, however, that "warranties whether express or implied shall be construed as consistent with each other and as cumulative. . . ." UCC 2–317.

If a buyer keeps the nonconforming goods, the value of those goods should be subtracted from the value of goods as warranted. This formula is set forth in UCC 2–714(2).[13] The market-oriented formula of UCC 2–714(2) is not an exclusive measure of buyers' damages. Buyers may seek recovery measured "in any manner which is reasonable." UCC 2–714(1). If the quality non-conformity is correctable at reasonable expense, a buyer may seek to recover the cost of repairing the defect.[14]

Buyers who accepted goods with non-conformities may not be "made whole" by monetary recovery measured only by the value of goods as warranted or by the cost of repair. The Code authorizes buyers, "in a proper case," to recover "incidental damages" in UCC 2–715(1), and "consequential damages," in UCC 2–715(2).

A buyer may prefer to return non-conforming goods to the sellers. The law allows some, but not all, aggrieved buyers to force sellers to take back "accepted" goods for quality deficiencies. The Commercial Code term for this is "revocation of acceptance." A buyer is entitled to revoke acceptance only if the non-conformity substantially impairs the value of the goods to the buyer. UCC 2–608(1).[15] A buyer that rightfully revokes acceptance of goods is entitled to monetary damages. UCC 2–711(1). The amount of a buyer's damages can be measured in two ways. The first, analogous to the market-based damages under UCC 2–714(2), allows recovery of the benefit of the bargain, i.e., the value ("market price") of conforming goods less the contract price; buyer is also entitled to get back all or any part of the price paid. The alternative measure of damages is based on buyer's cost of purchasing specific substitute goods ("cover") rather than on the general market price of conforming goods. UCC 2–712.

As we saw with remedies when buyers retain non-conforming goods, buyers who revoke acceptance may recover incidental and consequential damages. UCC 2–712(2); 2–713(1).

## 4.   COMMERCIAL AND CONSUMER BUYERS

With few exceptions, judicial decisions involving warranty law emerged historically in transactions between merchant buyers and merchant sellers,

---

**13.** "Value" in this formulation means "market value" or "market price," the amounts that informed sellers and buyers have set or would have set for goods of the different levels of quality. In active markets for goods of the kind, "market price" is a statistical compilation of many actual contract prices. Where no active market of the precise goods exists, "value" must be determined by extrapolation from other transactions. Sometimes this is done by expert appraisers.

**14.** See, e.g., Wat Henry Pontiac Co. v. Bradley, 202 Okla. 82, 210 P.2d 348 (1949) (pre-Code case). The reasonableness limitation no doubt precludes recovery of repair costs that greatly exceed the value added to a non-conforming product. Students may recall studying this as a common-law principle of damages in cases like Peevyhouse v. Garland Coal & Mining Co., 382 P.2d 109 (Okla.1962); Plante v. Jacobs, 10 Wis.2d 567, 103 N.W.2d 296 (1960).

**15.** The Code does not attempt to define "substantial impairment," but does indicate that the standard is subjective and turns on a buyer's particular circumstances. See the phrase "to him" in UCC 2–608(1) and Comment 2.

such as the "brazilletto" wood case and the "blue vitriol" case.[16] The commercial context of the early cases, in which merchants bought goods for the purpose of resale, explains the use of the rather archaic word, "merchantable," in the basic implied warranty of quality.

Transactions between business sellers and business buyers, usually corporations on both sides of the transactions, continue to be the most frequent source of warranty disputes that have been litigated to the level of appellate courts with reported opinions. In the setting of business-to-business sales, reported cases typically involve sales of equipment rather than of supplies. Ongoing commercial relationships between suppliers and business customers involve repeated sales, a "course of dealing."[17] If a relationship is valuable to both sides, any quality disputes that may arise from time to time will be adjusted amicably, without resort to litigation. The parties to equipment sales are less likely to have ongoing relationships than parties to sales of inventory or supplies. Litigation of disputes that arise in such transactions does not jeopardize a valuable relationship. Moreover, the amount at stake in a dispute over the quality of equipment is often great enough to make it practical for the parties to incur the costs of litigation.

Warranties are commonly made in sales of consumer products by retail dealers to individuals for their personal, family or household use. Reported judicial decisions involving such warranties, however, are rather rare. Part of the explanation may be that disputes are resolved within ongoing dealer-consumer relationships, but the amounts at stake in quality disputes regarding consumer products, even a consumer durable product, such as a toaster oven or a washing machine, are generally too small to make litigation practical beyond the level of small-claims courts. A few reported trial and appellate court decisions do arise out of sales of new and used automobiles. When the quality of such goods turns out to be unsatisfactory, the expense of litigation may not be a complete deterrent to a legal action.[18]

Some modern consumer product warranty law has developed by legislation. The statutory platform that existed for warranties of commercial goods was not limited to such goods. The provisions of the Uniform Sales Act and of Article 2 of the Uniform Commercial Code apply to all goods, whether bought for commercial purposes or for purposes of personal, family or household use. There are a few special consumer-protection provisions in the Article 2 provisions on quality warranties and remedies for breach of

---

**16.** The most notable exception was horse trading, perhaps one of the earliest consumer goods transactions. See K. Llewellyn, Across Sales on Horseback, 52 Harv.L.Rev. 725 (1939); K. Llewellyn, The First Struggle to Unhorse Sales, 52 Harv.L.Rev. 873 (1939).

**17.** The term is defined in the Commercial Code. See UCC 1–205(1). The Code looks to the pattern of past dealings for the purpose of interpretation of current expressions and conduct.

**18.** One means to increase the amount at stake in litigation over consumer products is to combine many individuals' claims into a single, class action. However, class actions to enforce a quality warranty are relatively rare because quality failures tend to be unique rather than common. An exception would be a condition in manufactured goods that results from the products's design.

these warranties.[19] Increasingly, warranty legislation has been enacted to protect ordinary consumers outside of Article 2. Some of that legislation has become a special part of warranty law, and we will consider some of that law in a later section of this chapter.

# SECTION 2. WARRANTIES OF QUALITY: EXPRESS AND IMPLIED

## (A) DOMESTIC UNITED STATES LAW

### 1. SUBSTANCE OF WARRANTY OBLIGATIONS AND RELATED LAW

The following cases illustrate the various types of warranties of quality, express and implied, in the context of litigated disputes. The cases also present the relationship between the warranties as defined in UCC Article 2 and common-law tort liability for misrepresentation.

## Royal Business Machines v. Lorraine Corp.

United States Court of Appeals, Seventh Circuit, 1980.
633 F.2d 34.

■ BAKER, D.J.

This is an appeal from a judgment of the district court entered after a bench trial awarding ... [Booher] $1,171,216.16 in compensatory and punitive damages against ... [Royal]. The judgment further awarded Booher attorneys' fees of $156,800.00. ... The judgment also granted Royal a set-off of $12,020.00 for an unpaid balance due on computer typewriters.

The case arose from commercial transactions extending over a period of 18 months between Royal and Booher in which Royal sold and Booher purchased 114 RBC I and 14 RBC II plain paper copying machines. [Booher bought the machines for the purpose of leasing them to its customers.] In mid-August 1976, Booher filed suit against Royal in the Indiana courts claiming breach of warranties and fraud....

The issues in the cases arise under Indiana common law and under the U.C.C. as adopted in Indiana, Ind. Code § 26–1–102 et seq. (1976). ...

### EXPRESS WARRANTIES

We first address the question whether substantial evidence on the record supports the district court's findings that Royal made and breached express warranties to Booher. The trial judge found that Royal Business Machines made and breached the following express warranties:

(1) that the RBC Model I and II machines and their component parts were of high quality;

---

**19.** See UCC 2–318, 2–719(3).

(2) that experience and testing had shown that frequency of repairs was very low on such machines and would remain so;

(3) that replacement parts were readily available;

(4) that the cost of maintenance for each RBC machine and cost of supplies was and would remain low, no more than ½ cent per copy;

(5) that the RBC machines had been extensively tested and were ready to be marketed;

(6) that experience and reasonable projections had shown that the purchase of the RBC machines by Mr. Booher and Lorraine Corporation and the leasing of the same to customers would return substantial profits to Booher and Lorraine;

(7) that the machines were safe and could not cause fires; and

(8) that service calls were and would be required for the RBC Model II machine on the average of every 7,000 to 9,000 copies, including preventive maintenance calls.

Substantial evidence supports the court's findings as to Numbers 5, 7, 8, and the maintenance aspect of Number 4, but, as a matter of law, Numbers 1, 2, 3, 6, and the cost of supplies portion of Number 4 cannot be considered express warranties.

Paraphrasing U.C.C. § 2–313 as adopted in Indiana, an express warranty is made up of the following elements: (a) an affirmation of fact or promise, (b) that relates to the goods, and (c) becomes a part of the basis of the bargain between the parties. When each of these three elements is present, a warranty is created that the goods shall conform to the affirmation of fact or to the promise.

The decisive test for whether a given representation is a warranty or merely an expression of the seller's opinion is whether the seller asserts a fact of which the buyer is ignorant or merely states an opinion or judgment on a matter of which the seller has no special knowledge and on which the buyer may be expected also to have an opinion and to exercise his judgment. . . . General statements to the effect that goods are "the best," . . . , or are "of good quality," . . . or will "last a lifetime" and be "in perfect condition," . . . are generally regarded as expressions of the seller's opinion or "the puffing of his wares" and do not create an express warranty.

No express warranty was created by Royal's affirmation that both RBC machine models and their component parts were of high quality. This was a statement of the seller's opinion, the kind of "puffing" to be expected in any sales transaction, rather than a positive averment of fact describing a product's capabilities to which an express warranty could attach. . . .

Similarly, the representations by Royal that experience and testing had shown that the frequency of repair was "very low" and would remain so lack the specificity of an affirmation of fact upon which a warranty could be predicated. These representations were statements of the seller's opinion.

The statement that replacement parts were readily available is an assertion of fact, but it is not a fact that relates to the goods sold as required by Ind.Code § 26–1–2–313(1)(a) and is not an express warranty to which the goods were to conform. Neither is the statement about the future costs of supplies being ½ cent per copy an assertion of fact that relates to the goods sold, so the statement cannot constitute the basis of an express warranty.

It was also erroneous to find that an express warranty was created by Royal's assurances to Booher that purchase of the RBC machines would bring him substantial profits. Such a representation does not describe the goods within the meaning of U.C.C. § 2–313(1)(b), nor is the representation an affirmation of fact relating to the goods under U.C.C. § 2–313(1)(a). It is merely sales talk and the expression of the seller's opinion. See Regal Motor Products v. Bender, 102 Ohio App. 447, 139 N.E.2d 463, 465 (1956) (representation that goods were "readily saleable" and that the demand for them would create a market was not a warranty). . . .

On the other hand, the assertion that the machines could not cause fires is an assertion of fact relating to the goods, and substantial evidence in the record supports the trial judge's findings that the assertion was made by Royal to Booher. The same may be said for the assertion that the machines were tested and ready to be marketed. . . .

As for findings 8 and the maintenance portion of Number 4, Royal's argument that those statements relate to predictions for the future and cannot qualify as warranties is unpersuasive. An expression of future capacity or performance can constitute an express warranty. In Teter v. Shultz, 110 Ind.App. 541, 39 N.E.2d 802, 804 (1942), the Indiana courts held that a seller's statement that dairy cows would give six gallons of milk per day was an affirmation of fact by the seller relating to the goods. It was not a statement of value nor was it merely a statement of the seller's opinion. The Indiana courts have also found that an express warranty was created by a seller's representation that a windmill was capable of furnishing power to grind 20 to 30 bushels of grain per hour in a moderate wind and with a very light wind would pump an abundance of water. Smith v. Borden, 160 Ind. 223, 66 N.E. 681 (1903). Further, in General Supply and Equipment Co. v. Phillips, supra, the Texas courts upheld the following express warranties made by a seller of roof panels: (1) that tests show no deterioration in 5 years of normal use; (2) that the roofing panels won't turn black or discolor . . . even after years of exposure; and (3) that the panels will not burn, rot, rust, or mildew. . . .

Whether a seller affirmed a fact or made a promise amounting to a warranty is a question of fact reserved for the trier of fact. General Supply and Equip. Co. v. Phillips, supra. Substantial evidence in the record supports the finding that Royal made the assertion to Booher that maintenance cost for the machine would run ½ cent per copy and that this assertion was not an estimate but an assertion of a fact of performance capability.

Finding Number 8, that service calls on the RBC II would be required every 7,000 to 9,000 copies, relates to performance capability and could constitute the basis of an express warranty. There is substantial evidence in the record to support the finding that this assertion was also made.

While substantial evidence supports the trial court's findings as to the making of those four affirmations of fact or promises, the district court failed to make the further finding that they became part of the basis of the bargain. Ind.Code § 26–1–2–313(1) (1976). While Royal may have made such affirmations to Booher, the question of his knowledge or reliance is another matter.[7]

This case is complicated by the fact that it involved a series of sales transactions between the same parties over approximately an 18–month period and concerned two different machines. The situations of the parties, their knowledge and reliance, may be expected to change in light of their experience during that time. An affirmation of fact which the buyer from his experience knows to be untrue cannot form a part of the basis of the bargain. . . . Therefore, as to each purchase, Booher's expanding knowledge of the capacities of the copying machines would have to be considered in deciding whether Royal's representations were part of the basis of the bargain. The same representations that could have constituted an express warranty early in the series of transactions might not have qualified as an express warranty in a later transaction if the buyer had acquired independent knowledge as to the fact asserted.

The trial court did not indicate that it considered whether the warranties could exist and apply to each transaction in the series. Such an analysis is crucial to a just determination. Its absence renders the district court's findings insufficient on the issue of the breach of express warranties.

Since a retrial on the questions of the breach of express warranties and the extent of damages is necessary, we offer the following observations. The court must consider whether the machines were defective upon delivery. Breach occurs only if the goods are defective upon delivery and not if the goods later become defective through abuse or neglect. . . .

In considering the promise relating to the cost of maintenance, the district court should determine at what stage Booher's own knowledge and experience prevented him from blindly relying on the representations of Royal. A similar analysis is needed in examining the representation concerning fire hazard in the RBC I machines. The court also should determine when that representation was made. If not made until February 1975,

---

**7.** The requirement that a statement be part of the basis of the bargain in order to constitute an express warranty "is essentially a reliance requirement and is inextricably intertwined with the initial determination as to whether given language may constitute an express warranty since affirmations, promises and descriptions tend to become a part of the basis of the bargain. It was the intention of the drafters of the U.C.C. not to require a strong showing of reliance. In fact, they envisioned that all statements of the seller become part of the basis of the bargain unless clear affirmative proof is shown to the contrary. See Official Comments 3 and 8 to U.C.C. § 2–313." Sessa v. Riegle, 427 F.Supp. 760, 766 (E.D.Pa.1977), aff'd without op. 568 F.2d 770 (3d Cir.1978). . . .

the representation could not have been the basis for sales made prior to that date.

## FRAUD AND MISREPRESENTATION

The district court found that beginning in April or May of 1974 and continuing throughout most of 1975, Royal, by and through its agents and employees acting in the course and scope of their employment, persuaded Booher to buy RBC I and RBC II copiers by knowingly making material oral misrepresentations which were relied upon by Booher to his injury.

Under Indiana law, the essential elements of actionable fraud are representations, falsity, scienter, deception, and injury. ... A fraud action must be predicated upon statements of existing facts, not promises to perform in the future. ... Nor do expressions of opinion qualify as fraudulent misrepresentations. The district court made no specific findings as to which of the alleged representations it relied upon in finding fraud. If the court held all eight to be fraudulent misrepresentations, the court erred as to Numbers 1, 2, and 6 because, as discussed above, these were merely expressions of the seller's opinion rather than statements of material fact upon which a fraud action could be based. Numbers 3, 4, 5, 7, and 8, on the other hand, readily qualify as material factual representations. ...

The trial court, however, is silent on the remaining question, that of deception or reasonable reliance by Booher on the representations in the various transactions. ... This issue is virtually identical to the basis of the bargain question remanded under the express warranty theory.

The district court's finding of fraud, therefore, must be set aside, and the cause remanded for retrial on the questions of the specific misrepresentations relied upon by Booher in each transaction and the reasonableness of that reliance.

With regard to rescission as a remedy for fraud, rescission would be available only for those specific sales to which fraud attached. ...

## IMPLIED WARRANTIES

The district court found that Royal breached the implied warranties of merchantability and of fitness for a particular purpose. We cannot agree that the record supports the court's findings.

A warranty of merchantability is implied by law in any sale where the seller is a merchant of the goods. To be merchantable, goods must, *inter alia*, pass without objection in the trade under the contract description, be of fair average quality, and be fit for the ordinary purposes for which such goods are used. Ind.Code § 26–1–2–314 (1976). They must "conform to ordinary standards, and ... be of the same average grade, quality and value as similar goods sold under similar circumstances." ... It was Booher's burden to prove that the copying machines were not merchantable. ... Booher failed to satisfy his burden of proof as to standards in the trade for either the RBC I or RBC II machine. No evidence supports the trial court's findings of a breach of the implied warranty of merchantability.

An implied warranty of fitness for a particular purpose arises where a seller has reason to know a particular purpose for which the goods are required and the buyer relies on the seller's skill or judgment to select or furnish suitable goods. Ind.Code § 26–1–2–315 (1976). The court found that Royal knew the particular purpose for which all the RBC machines were to be used and, in fact, that Royal had taken affirmative steps to persuade Booher to become its dealer and that occasionally its employees even accompanied Booher on calls to customers. . . .

The district court, however, failed to distinguish between implied warranties on the RBC I and on the RBC II machines. Nor did the court differentiate among the different transactions involving the two machines. On remand the district court should make further findings on Booher's actual reliance on Royal's skill or judgment in each purchase of the RBC I and RBC II machines. We view it as most unlikely that a dealer who now concedes himself to be an expert in the field of plain paper copiers did not at some point, as his experience with the machines increased, rely on his own judgment in making purchases.

\* \* \*

[Judgment reversed. Case remanded for a new trial.]

## NOTES

**(1) Express Warranties.** The trial court concluded that a set of statements made by a representative of the seller were express warranties. The Court of Appeals reversed as to all. Unpacking and critiquing the analysis of the appellate court is an excellent way to learn some of the subtle intricacies of express warranty law. The court's analysis focused on three separate aspects of the law.

*Relate to the goods.* Section 2–313(1)(a) applies only to an affirmation of fact or promise that "relates to the goods."[1] The Court of Appeals reversed the trial court on three statements because they did not relate to the goods: the affirmations that replacement parts were readily available; that the cost of supplies was and would remain low, not more than one-half cent per copy; and that the leasing business would return substantial profits. These affirmations do not describe the goods, but do you agree that the affirmations do not "relate to" the goods sold? The Comments are silent on the intended force of "relates to the goods" as a limiting concept.

Assume that the Court of Appeals was correct in holding that the three statements did not relate to the goods. Does it follow that seller is immune

---

**1.** This element is not found in UCC 2–313(1)(b) or (c). Do you understand why it is omitted there? In the taxonomy of warranties in the Uniform Sales Act, these warranties were considered to be "implied." USA §§ 14, 16. The drafters of UCC 2–313 decided to classify these warranties as "expressed." See Comments 1, 5 and 6.

for legal liability for made them? The implied premise of the appellate court's holding is that express warranties that do not relate to the goods are not actionable, that the statute precludes the possibility of common-law warranties. Is this premise justified? Recall UCC 1–103(b). Comment 2 to UCC 2–313, which deals with other aspects of warranty law, recognizes that the Code is incomplete and leaves matters beyond its scope to the courts under other law.

*Part of the basis of the bargain.* All three subsections of UCC 2–313(1) require that seller's statements or conduct be "part of the basis of the bargain." What does this term mean? Comment 3 declares that the section deals with affirmations of fact by the seller, descriptions of the goods, or exhibitions of samples "exactly as any other part of a negotiation which ends in a contract is dealt with." Common-law contract law doctrine has no analogue for the point that negotiated terms can be treated as not binding if not part of the basis of the bargain. What does the Comment mean? Is the underlying problem different from any general contract inquiry seeking to find the nature of the parties' reasonable expectations?[2]

"Part of the basis of the bargain" had no counterpart in the Uniform Sales Act. USA § 12, which dealt only with affirmations and promises relating to the goods, created warranties only "if the natural tendency of such affirmation or promise is to induce the buyer to purchase the goods, and if the buyer purchases the goods relying thereon." The "natural tendency" and "actual reliance" elements were not used in connection with warranties of description or sample. Drafters of UCC 2–313 decided not to use "natural tendency" and "actual reliance." In their place, the Code drafters inserted "part of the basis of the bargain" for all three kinds of express warranties. Comment 3 states: "no particular reliance on [affirmations of fact] need be shown in order to weave them into the fabric of the agreement. Rather, any fact which is to take such affirmations, once made, out of the agreement requires clear affirmative proof." Does the Comment suggest that, while reliance is not a part of a buyer's cause of action for breach of an express warranty, a buyer's non-reliance on a seller's affirmation could be an affirmative defense, if seller can prove that fact?

The Court of Appeals recognized that four affirmations did relate to the goods: that the machines could not cause fires; that the machines were tested and ready to be marketed; that maintenance of the machine would cost one-half cent per copy; and that service calls would be required every 7,000 to 9,000 copies. The trial court found that the affirmations had been made and the resulting warranties had been breached. The Court of Appeals reversed. It said: "While Royal may have made such affirmations to Booher, the question of his knowledge or reliance is another matter" and concluded: "An affirmation of fact which the buyer from his experience knows to be untrue cannot form part of the basis of the bargain." What experience of buyer was dispositive in the view of the court? How would you evaluate the decision to reverse the trial court on this ground?

---

2. See J. Murray, Basis of the Bargain, Transcending Classical Concepts, 66 Minn. L. Rev. 283 (1982).

*Promise or affirmation of fact; affirmation of value or seller's opinion or commendation.* Section 2–313(1) provides that express warranties are created by a promise or an affirmation of fact that relates to the goods and becomes part of the basis of the bargain, but subsection (2) provides that an affirmation "merely of the value of the goods" or a statement "purporting to be merely the seller's opinion or commendation of the goods" does not create a warranty. What is the legislative purpose for the distinction between affirmations of fact and affirmations of value? Does it derive from the concept that matters of opinion cannot be tested for truth or falsity? Comment 8 indicates that the distinction is not based on the extent to which propositions are verifiable, but rather on the psychology of ordinary buyers hearing or reading certain kinds of sellers' statements: "common experience discloses that some statements cannot fairly be viewed as entering into the bargain. Even as to false statements of value, however, the possibility is left open that a remedy may be provided by the law relating to fraud and misrepresentation." Is the Comment referring to the statutory element, "part of the basis of the bargain"? Does your experience correlate with the "common experience" recited in the Comment?[3] Sales pitches of this genre are very common; would sellers continue this practice if it did not influence buyers? Are there reasons of public policy for negating buyers' protection if sellers' affirmations or statements are not true?

Applying the value and opinion provision, the Court of Appeals held that three of seller's affirmations did not create express warranties: that the machines and component parts were of high quality; that frequency of repairs was very low and would remain so; and that the buyers would make substantial profits. The Court of Appeals introduced its analysis with a statement of the "decisive test," which is "whether the seller asserts a fact of which the buyer is ignorant or merely states an opinion or judgment on a matter of which the seller has no special knowledge and on which the buyer may be expected to have an opinion and to exercise judgment." Does the statute provide any basis for any of the elements of this "decisive test"? Why should buyer's ignorance matter? Seller's "special knowledge"?

Could the court's conclusion have been based on other reasoning? Were the affirmations too lacking in specificity to be affirmations of fact and warranties?

---

**3.** Professor Page Keeton outlined the wide variations in the impact of statements which might fall under the heading of "opinion." Quoting Learned Hand, Keeton observed that some statements are like the claims of campaign managers before election: "rather designed to allay the suspicion that would attend their absence than to be understood as having any relation to objective truth." P. Keeton, The Rights of Disappointed Purchasers, 32 Tex.L.Rev. 1, 8 (1953). In a slightly different connection, Keeton illustrated the effect of the nature of the recovery on the framing of the legal rule. A misrepresentation which is innocent ordinarily will not support an action for damages for deceit. But such a misrepresentation may more readily provide a defense to an action to enforce the agreement which it induced and even, in some cases, a basis for rescission of a completed transaction. Id. at 10. Is such shaping of the rule to the remedy feasible under current statutory structures?

The statements of the seller's representative appear to have been oral statements. There is no indication that the agreement was "reduced to writing." Oral statements tend to be more casual than statements made in writing.[4] Proof of oral statements is likely to be through testimony of individuals describing what they remember to have been said. Fact-finders often have trouble resolving different or conflicting testimony. In this case, the facts were found by a trial judge in a "bench trial" and were not subject to review by the appellate court. As a matter of the legal effect of the affirmations, however, are oral statements more likely to be a seller's opinion or commendation of the goods or part of the basis of the bargain?[5]

**(2) Implied Warranty of Merchantability.** The trial court found that seller was in breach of the implied warranty of merchantability, under UCC 2–314. The Court of Appeals reversed, holding that the buyer had failed to introduce any evidence to support the trial court's finding. The case was remanded for retrial. Can the appellate court's conclusion be reconciled with its finding (in connection with express warranties) that there was substantial evidence that the copy machines had not been tested and were not ready to be marketed, that the machines were not safe and could cause fires. How could copy machines that are not ready to be marketed "pass without objection in the trade under the contract description"? UCC 2–314(2)(a). How could copy machines that cause fires be "fit for the ordinary purposes for which such goods are used"? UCC 2–314(2)(c). The Court of Appeals said that the buyer failed to satisfy his burden of proof as to "standards in the trade." Is it conceivable that trade standards would deem copy machines with such negative qualities to pass without objection and to be fit for ordinary purposes?

**(3) Implied Warranty of Fitness for Particular Purpose.** The trial court found that seller knew the buyer's "particular purpose" in buying the copy machines and supplied machines that did not satisfy that purpose, thereby being in breach of warranty of fitness for particular purpose under UCC 2–315. The Court of Appeals reversed and remanded for new trial. Among other observations about the claim, the appellate court expressed skepticism that the buyer would be able to prove that he had relied on seller's skill or judgment to select suitable goods.

How does a fitness-for-particular-purpose warranty differ from a fitness-for-ordinary-purpose warranty? The latter, one of the meanings of merchantable quality under UCC 2–314(2), is not constrained by any statutory requirement that the buyer prove reliance on seller's skill and judgment. Is there any reason to believe that the buyer's purpose in buying the copy machines was to use them other than for their ordinary purpose?

---

**4.** Email messages, while written, appear to be more casual than other writings. What might explain that fact?

**5.** A recent case held that an oral statement made in conversation between two business executives was sufficient to create a 26–year performance warranty of a product for preventing rotting of wood used in manufacturing windows. Marvin Lumber & Cedar Co. v. PPG Industries, Inc., 223 F.3d 873 (8th Cir. 2000). See also Goodman v. PPG Industries, Inc., 849 A.2d 1239 (Pa. Super. 2004).

Should buyer's lawyer have added to the complaint a count under UCC 2–315?

**(4) Other "Fields" of Law.** As *Royal Business Machines* demonstrates, factual situations giving rise to express warranty claims are likely to give rise as well to claims of fraud or misrepresentation. The latter sound in tort. The Restatement (Second) of Torts (1977) provides:

§ 525.   Liability for Fraudulent Misrepresentation

One who fraudulently makes a misrepresentation of fact, opinion, intention or law for the purpose of inducing another to act or to refrain from action in reliance on it, is subject to liability to the other in deceit for pecuniary loss caused to him by his justifiable reliance upon the misrepresentation.

An illustration to § 525 reveals the close relationship between the tort and the law of express warranty

2.   A, in order to induce B to buy a heating device, states that it will give a stated amount of heat while consuming only a stated amount of fuel. B is justified in accepting A's statement as an assurance that the heating device is capable of giving the services that A promises.

The Restatement, § 526, defines "fraudulently" in broad terms. The Restatement adds a provision for "negligent misrepresentation," § 552, and a special provision for "innocent misrepresentation" in certain transactions, including sales or rental of goods:

§ 552C.   Misrepresentation in Sale, Rental or Exchange Transaction

(1)  One who, in a sale, rental or exchange transaction with another, makes a misrepresentation of a material fact for the purpose of inducing the other to act or to refrain from acting in reliance upon it, is subject to liability to the other for pecuniary loss caused to him by his justifiable reliance upon the misrepresentation, even though it is not made fraudulently or negligently.

"Misrepresentation," as a part of general contract law, permits a party who has been misled by a fraudulent *or* material misrepresentation in the negotiation of a contract to avoid it. Restatement (Second) of Contracts § 164 (1981). See also E. Farnsworth, Contracts §§ 4.10–4.15 (3d ed. 1999).

The trial court in *Royal Business Machines* held that the seller had knowingly made numerous oral misrepresentations which had been relied upon by the buyer. The Court of Appeals set aside the trial court's findings of fact because the judge had treated the statements, made over more than 18 months, in the aggregate and therefore had not made findings of the reasonableness of buyer's reliance as to each representation when it was made. The Court of Appeals noted that the issue, under the common-law of tort, was virtually identical to the basis of the bargain question under the Code's provision on express warranty.

Should buyer's lawyer have added to the complaint the count alleging the tort of misrepresentation?

**(5) Formation of the Contract in *Royal Business Machines.***
Underlying the many issues that were litigated in *Royal Business Machines* is the counseling question: how did the parties do such a remarkably bad job of contract formation? The facts of the warranty and misrepresentation claims involve oral statements by seller's representatives. Virtually any lawyer, looking back at this dispute, would conclude that it was a serious mistake for the seller and for the buyer to enter into this contractual relationship without a written agreement that evidenced the bargain. The manifest value of written agreements, for legal and business purposes, is so widely recognized that one rarely finds disputes in transactions involving so many goods and so much money without contractual writings. Indeed, as the amount involved in an exchange goes up, lawyer-drafted written terms will be found in the agreements. This was undoubtedly true in the case that follows.

# McDonnell Douglas Corp. v. Thiokol Corp.

United States Court of Appeals, Ninth Circuit, 1997.
124 F.3d 1173.

■ HUG, CHIEF JUDGE:

Thiokol Corporation contracted to provide Star 48 motors to McDonnell Douglas Corporation for inclusion in McDonnell Douglas' upper-stage Payload Assist Module, which is designed to propel satellites from the Space Shuttle to a geosynchronous orbit 22,000 nautical miles from Earth. In the contract, Thiokol warranted that the motors would be free of defects in material, labor, and manufacture and that the motors would comply with contract drawings and specifications. Following the failure of two satellites to reach their intended orbit, McDonnell Douglas brought this warranty action against Thiokol. The district court entered judgment against McDonnell Douglas after an eleven-day bench trial. We must decide whether Thiokol breached its warranties. We have jurisdiction, 28 U.S.C. § 1291, and we affirm.

Background

In 1976, McDonnell Douglas Corporation ("McDonnell Douglas") entered a contract with the National Aeronautics and Space Administration ("NASA") to develop and market an upper-stage Payload Assist Module ("PAM"). The PAM propels satellites from the Space Shuttle to a geosynchronous orbit some 22,000 nautical miles from Earth. It consists of several components, including: (1) a cradle that links the satellite to the Space Shuttle; (2) a mechanism that deploys the satellite from the Shuttle's cargo bay; (3) an upper-stage motor to move the satellite from the Shuttle's 160 mile parking orbit into a transfer orbit; and (4) a smaller motor to take the satellite from the apogee of the transfer orbit to its intended orbit. In 1976 there were no upper-stage motors in production that suited McDonnell Douglas' needs. To obtain such a motor, McDonnell Douglas completed Specification Control Drawing 1B98497 (the "Specification Control Drawing") on August 18, 1976, which conceptualized a motor that would meet its needs.

In response to the Specification Control Drawing, Thiokol Corporation ("Thiokol") developed a preliminary design for an upper-stage motor. Thiokol's preliminary design incorporated a carbon-carbon exit cone, rather than the more common carbon-phenolic exit cone. The use of the lighter carbon-carbon exit cone was necessary in order to comply with the weight limitations set forth in the Specification Control Drawing. Thiokol sent its preliminary design to McDonnell Douglas for its review. Because of the "young maturity" of carbon-carbon technology, Thiokol also sent a separate preliminary design of the motor's nozzle assembly, which indicated that Thiokol planned to use a carbon-carbon cone.

In 1978, Thiokol and McDonnell Douglas entered a contract for the development and qualification of an upper-stage motor. The motor became known as the Star 48 motor. The development and qualification contract was labeled the 7011 contract. This contract established a rigorous series of development and qualification tests that Thiokol's proposed design had to meet before Thiokol was allowed to begin production.

Before Thiokol could continue with development of the motor under the contract, it had to obtain McDonnell Douglas' approval of the design. The development phase thus called for a preliminary design review in which McDonnell Douglas and Thiokol engineers jointly reviewed the design of the Star 48 motor. McDonnell Douglas gave Thiokol its approval following the preliminary design review. The approval extended to the carbon-carbon exit cone.

After receiving McDonnell Douglas' approval, Thiokol conducted five engine test-firings, all of which were witnessed by McDonnell Douglas engineers. McDonnell Douglas engineers were allowed to inspect the motors following the firings and received reports analyzing the results of the tests.

After a second design review, which focused on whether the motor design complied with the requirements of the Specification Control Drawing, McDonnell Douglas again gave Thiokol its approval. Six more motors were test-fired and a qualification program review was held. The purpose of this review was to obtain McDonnell Douglas' approval of the motor, which was necessary to allow Thiokol to move into the production phase. McDonnell Douglas gave its approval, concluding that the motor met all of the performance and technical requirements of the Specification Control Drawing.

Following qualification of the motor, but before the parties agreed to a production contract, Thiokol test-fired another motor. This test resulted in a motor failure, and an investigation ensued. Although the cause of the failure was not determined with certainty, McDonnell Douglas issued a statement indicating that the most probable cause was a low density/low quality cone. The failure occurred even though the motor met all of the contract's specification and acceptance requirements.

NASA and the United States Air Force conducted and independent investigation of the test failure. Significantly, this investigation concluded, "The state of knowledge about the material properties of carbon/carbon involute exit cones is such that a meaningful margin of safety cannot be established for the Star 48 exit cone." The NASA/Air Force investigation recommended that McDonnell Douglas expand its testing procedures to detect density variations in cones that otherwise met technical and acceptance standards. McDonnell Douglas thus knew that a test firing resulted in a failure, that NASA and the Air Force believed a meaningful margin of safety could not be established, and that its acceptance testing could not detect all density variations. Despite its knowledge, McDonnell Douglas did not adopt the NASA/Air Force recommendations.

McDonnell Douglas and Thiokol entered into a production contract (the "7047 contract") in 1981. The contract required Thiokol to "maintain the system of producing hardware as established under [the 7011 contract]." The contract also incorporated Article 18 of McDonnell Douglas' Terms and Conditions Guide. That article provides:

> Seller warrants the articles delivered hereunder to be free from defects in labor, material and manufacture, and to be in compliance with any drawings or specifications incorporated or referenced herein.... All warranties shall run to [McDonnell Douglas], its successors and assigns, and to its customers and the users of its products.

On February 3, 1984, the Space Shuttle Challenger used the PAM system to deploy WESTAR–VI, a private communications satellite. The WESTAR–VI satellite failed to reach its transfer orbit. An interply density variation, which is an area of reduced density between the layers of carbonized cloth that comprise the carbon-carbon exit cone, caused the Star 48 motor to fail. Three days later, the Challenger deployed the Palapa B–2 satellite, which also failed to reach its transfer orbit because of a motor failure caused by an interply density variation.

On February 7, McDonnell Douglas convened a Failure Investigation Committee to investigate the WESTAR–VI and Palapa B–2 failures (collectively the "failures"). The Committee issued its final report in September 1984, concluding that the most probable cause of the failures were interply density variations, but that the "exact cause of these exit cone failures could not be determined." The Committee further concluded that the "materials, components, and subassemblies of the nozzle assemblies were produced to the established standards and specifications and essentially satisfied all acceptance criteria applicable to the failed motors." Additionally, the Committee found no evidence that the materials, labor, or manufacture of the WESTAR–VI and Palapa B–2 exit cones varied from contract specifications and requirements.

In March, 1985, McDonnell Douglas made a formal written warranty claim against Thiokol. It alleged that Thiokol breached the warranty provisions of the 7047 contract. McDonnell Douglas sought incidental damages of $10,926,000 (costs associated with the failure investigation) and consequential damages of $6,947,000 (the cost of replacing carbon-carbon exit cones with carbon-phenolic cones).

\* \* \*

The district court conducted an eleven-day bench trial. At the conclusion of the trial, the court issued detailed findings of fact and conclusions of law. It entered judgment against McDonnell Douglas. McDonnell Douglas filed a timely notice of appeal.

Standard of Review

We review de novo the district court's application of the principles of contract interpretation to the facts. ... Whether the seller's representations formed part of the basis of the parties' bargain is a question of fact. See Royal Business Machines Inc. v. Lorraine Corp., 633 F.2d 34, 43 (7th Cir.1980) (whether seller affirmed a fact amounting to an express warranty is a question of fact). We review the district court's factual determinations for clear error. ...

Discussion

Under California law, any affirmation of fact or promise relating to the subject matter of a contract for the sale of goods, which is made part of the basis of the parties' bargain, creates an express warranty. Cal. Com. Code § 2313 (a). California courts use a three-step approach to express warranty issues. Keith v. Buchanan, 220 Cal. Rptr. 392, 395, 173 Cal. App. 3d 13 (Ct. App. 1985). First, the court determines whether the seller's statement amounts to "an affirmation of fact or promise" relating to the goods sold. Id. Second, the court determines if the affirmation or promise was "part of the basis of the bargain." Id. Finally, if the seller made a promise relating to the goods and that promise was part of the basis of the bargain, the court must determine if the seller breached the warranty. Id.

Here, McDonnell Douglas argues that Thiokol made two separate promises, both of which constitute express warranties. McDonnell Douglas maintains that Thiokol promised to deliver goods that (1) were "free from defects in labor, material, and manufacture," and (2) complied with "any drawings or specifications incorporated [into] or referenced" by the contract. We analyze each promise separately.

### I.   Defects in Labor, Material and Manufacture

We turn first to Thiokol's promise to deliver goods free from defects in labor, material, and manufacture. There is no question that this promise relates to the goods and was made a part of the basis of the parties' bargain. It therefore constitutes an express warranty, Cal. Com. Code § 2313, and we move directly to the final step of the analysis. We must determine whether the WESTAR–VI and Palapa B–2 satellite motors suffered from defects in labor, material, or manufacture.

The district court concluded that the motor failures were caused by severe and extensive interply density variations. It further concluded such variations did not amount to a breach of Thiokol's warranty because, "where the buyer qualifies and approves product acceptance specifications, a product which satisfies all [such] specifications is not 'defective.'" The district court thus held that the interply density variations could not be considered a defect "because [they] did not [violate] the product acceptance specifications qualified and approved by [McDonnell Douglas]."

A further inquiry is necessary, however, because Thiokol did not limit its warranty to technical compliance with the specifications set forth in the contract. Thiokol made a separate promise—that the goods would be free of defects in labor, material, and manufacture. We must then make the further inquiry of whether, under the terms of the contract, the interply density variations in the motors delivered constitute a defect in labor, material or manufacture.

McDonnell Douglas offers alternative definitions of the term "defect." First, it contends that a defective product is one that "differs from the manufacturer's intended results or from other ostensibly identical units of the same product line." Barker v. Lull Engineering Co., Inc., 20 Cal. 3d 413, 429, 143 Cal. Rptr. 225, 573 P.2d 443 (1978). This argument lacks merit. While this definition of "defect" is firmly rooted in the law of products liability, McDonnell Douglas presented no evidence that the parties intended to incorporate this definition, and all of the social concerns regarding distribution of risk that it connotes, into their contract. In fact, all of the evidence is to the contrary. . . .

McDonnell Douglas advances a second definition of the phrase "defect in labor, material, and manufacture." Relying on S.M. Wilson & Co. v. Smith Int'l, Inc., 587 F.2d 1363, 1372 (9th Cir.1978), McDonnell Douglas maintains that a defect in labor, material, or manufacture is a "defect in quality." McDonnell Douglas argues that Thiokol breached its warranty by delivering motors that contained "severe and extensive interply density variations," which constituted a defect in quality.

McDonnell Douglas' definition of the critical language finds superficial support in our case law. However, a close reading of Lombard Corp. v. Quality Aluminum Products Co., 261 F.2d 336 (6th Cir.1958), the case relied on in S.W. Wilson, demonstrates that a defect in labor, material, or manufacture is a defect or flaw in the quality of the labor, material, or manufacture of the product. See Lombard 261 F.2d at 338 (holding that there was no defect in material where "the steel [used] in the tie rods was of excellent quality"). This definition of defect is compelled by the plain meaning of the terms selected by the parties because it gives meaning to the limiting language "in labor, material, or manufacture." McDonnell Douglas' definition, to the contrary, renders the limiting language superfluous.

We therefore reject McDonnell Douglas' definition of a "defect." We hold that, to prove a breach of Thiokol's warranty against defects in labor, material, or manufacture, McDonnell Douglas had to demonstrate that the WESTAR and Palapa satellite motors suffered from a flaw in the quality of the material used in their construction. See S.M. Wilson, 587 F.2d at 1372. McDonnell Douglas failed to do this.

At trial McDonnell Douglas attempted to prove that the rayon cloth provided by Union Carbide, which was used in the manufacture of Star 48 motors, was "dirty" and of substandard quality. The district court expressly found "no evidence ... that the cloth supplied by Union Carbide was defective." This conclusion is amply supported by the record and is in accord with the findings of the failure investigation committee. Additionally, there was conflicting evidence regarding the effect of "dirty" cloth. A NASA expert testified that, although NASA pursued the "dirty cloth" theory for a "number of months," it eventually concluded that the condition of the cloth at the beginning of the manufacturing process had no significant effect on the strength of the carbon-carbon exit cone.

The record is otherwise devoid of any evidence that the failures were caused by a defect in labor, material, or manufacture of the carbon-carbon exit cones. There is, rather, substantial evidence to the contrary. The failure investigation committee concluded that "changes and variations in materials or [the manufacturing] process were not a determinative cause of the failures." It also found that "equipment, work procedures, personnel and production and support systems were not proven to be contributory to the failures." Although the committee found that there was a shift in the quality of the exit cones, it concluded that "[a] single cause of density variations has not been isolated."

In light of the foregoing, we conclude that McDonnell Douglas failed to demonstrate that a flaw in labor, material, or manufacture caused the interply density variations which resulted in the failures. Accordingly, the district court properly entered judgment against McDonnell Douglas on this issue.

## II.   Failure to Comply with Drawings and Specifications

McDonnell Douglas also contends that Thiokol warranted that all Star 48 motors delivered under the contract would comply "with any drawings or specifications incorporated [into] or referenced" by the 7047 contract. The Specification Control Drawing was attached to the 7047 contract. Section 3.0 of the statement of work, which was attached to the Specification Control Drawing, stated that "all rocket motor components shall be suitable for the purpose for which they are intended." Additionally, section 3.5.4 of the statement of work stated that "the nozzle [which includes the exit cone] shall be capable of withstanding the thermal mechanical loads during motor burn without any detrimental structural failure." McDonnell Douglas argues that these provisions were incorporated into and referenced by the 7047 contract, and that Thiokol breached those provisions.

The essential inquiry is whether these statements in a drawing attached to the contract constitute additional express warranties that were understood and bargained for by the parties. These provisions would constitute performance warranties with serious financial risks involved and it would be very unusual to find the parties intended to tuck them away in drawings attached to the contract. The determinative question is whether the parties intended the warranties to be confined to those expressed in the body of the contract (products free from defects in labor, material, and manufacture) or expanded to performance warranties by drawings attached to the contract.

The district court determined that "it was the true understanding of the parties that a performance warranty ... was not part of the agreement or a basis of [McDonnell Douglas'] bargain." The facts and circumstances surrounding the making of the contract, the testimony of McDonnell Douglas agents, understandings prevalent throughout the aerospace industry, and McDonnell Douglas' own conduct all support the conclusion that McDonnell Douglas did not bargain for a performance warranty. Accordingly, we conclude that the statements in the Specification Control Drawing were not intended to be additional warranties forming a part of the bargain of the parties.

The state-of-the-art of carbon-carbon technology, which is one of the facts and circumstances surrounding the formation of the contract, indicates that a performance warranty was not technically feasible. McDonnell Douglas was aware, at the time it prepared the Specification Control Drawing, of the state-of-the-art of carbon-carbon exit cones. Additionally, McDonnell Douglas knew that the NASA/Air Force investigation of the test failures concluded that a meaningful margin of safety could not be maintained. Finally, McDonnell Douglas knew that the carbon-vapor densification process did not yield uniform density throughout the exit cone. McDonnell Douglas could not have bargained for a performance warranty because it knew that, given the state-of-the-art of carbon-carbon technology, such a promise was impossible to fulfill. See Royal Business Machines, 633 F.2d at 44 ("An affirmation of fact which the buyer from [its] experience knows to be untrue cannot form a part of the basis of the bargain.").

Moreover, juxtaposing the costs of a satellite with the costs of the Star 48 motor, indicates that a performance warranty was economically unfeasible. In an internal memorandum commenting on a NASA inquiry, a McDonnell Douglas employee stated that McDonnell Douglas "decided early on in the PAM program that the financial risks associated with performance warranties were too high considering the price of the satellite compared to the price of the PAM." McDonnell Douglas accordingly wrote its sales contracts "in terms of what the product is, not what it does" because "to prepare a contract in terms of what the hardware does would indeed be a performance warranty." McDonnell Douglas did not include the cost of a performance warranty in the price of its product. Because McDonnell Douglas knew that its profit margin was greater than Thiokol's and it knew what it paid Thiokol for the Star 48 motors, McDonnell Douglas knew that it was not being charged for a performance warranty.

The testimony of John Willacker, the McDonnell Douglas employee who drafted the specification control drawing, also supports the district court's conclusion that the parties did not bargain for a performance warranty. He testified at trial that in 1977 it was McDonnell Douglas' practice to set forth only technical requirements in specification control drawings. Willacker was asked if "it was a standard industry practice that a specification, like a specification control drawing, was not to be used to contain warranty provisions?" Willacker answered, "That's correct." More importantly, Willacker also testified that he intended only to set forth technical requirements in the document. Willacker's testimony further supports the district court's conclusion that the parties did not intend to create a performance warranty by incorporating the "drawings and specifications" of the Specification Control Drawing.

Finally, McDonnell Douglas' post-failure conduct is inconsistent with the understanding of the contract that it now advances. On February 20, 1984, D.H. Hauver, a negotiator/administrator for McDonnell Douglas, wrote to Thiokol, "Should this investigation determine that the PAM–D (STAR 48) rocket motors failed to achieve specified performance levels due to defects in their manufacture, we will expect you to comply with the warranty provisions of our subcontract." (emphasis added). Had McDonnell Douglas understood Thiokol to have provided a performance warranty, it would not have included the limiting language "due to defects in their manufacture" in the letter. This subsequent practical construction of the warranty provisions further supports the district court's conclusion that the affirmations in sections 3.0 and 3.5.4 were [not?] a basis of the parties' bargain.

In sum, McDonnell Douglas did not bargain for a warranty of performance, knew that it was not paying for such a warranty, and acted as if it understood the contract not to include such a warranty. To create a performance warranty under the circumstances of this case, the contract would have to be much more specific. Accordingly, the district court correctly concluded that statements in the Specification Control Drawings were not intended by the parties to be additional performance warranties.

Conclusion

Thiokol did not breach either of its express warranties. The judgment of the district court is

AFFIRMED.


NOTES

**(1) Warranty Against Defects in Materials or Workmanship.** One of the express warranties in this case was seller's warranty against "defect in labor, material, and manufacture." This warranty is a variant of a very common express warranty given by sellers against defects in materials and workmanship. Such express warranties are found in written agreements, drafted by counsel for sellers, who find this warranty significantly preferable to the implied warranty of merchantability. Note that, in *McDonnell Douglas*, there is no discussion of the merchantability warranty. Undoubtedly, the sales contract contained a disclaimer of that warranty.

(We will consider the law of warranty disclaimers in the next section.) For what reasons would sellers, advised by their lawyers, prefer an express warranty against defects in materials or workmanship to an implied warranty of merchantability? How do the two warranties differ?

The courts in *McDonnell Douglas* held that the seller's warranty against defects in labor, material, and manufacture was not breached. Note the difficulty of determining the meaning of "defect," a threshold problem for buyer's counsel. Two definitions were proposed by counsel, and both were rejected by the Court of Appeals. The definition adopted by the Court of Appeals required buyer to identify a specific flaw in the materials used. Evidence that the motor had failed to function properly was not sufficient to prove a breach of warranty. Would failure of goods to function as expected be sufficient evidence of a breach of a warranty of merchantability?

**(2) Warranty of Conformity to Specifications.** The goods in *McDonnell Douglas* were goods to be specially manufactured. Article 2 applies to such contracts. UCC 2–105(1). Designs for goods to be specially manufactured may be provided by sellers or buyers. The design of the goods in this case was provided by the seller in engineering drawings and specifications. Accordingly, the contract for production of the Star 48 motor had a term that required the manufacturer-seller to comply with the drawings and specifications.

**(3) Performance Warranty.** Buyer relied on two provisions that it claimed had been incorporated into the Star 48 motor contract and obligated the manufacturer of the Star 48 motor to underwrite the performance of the motor. The trial court held, and appellate court affirmed, that a performance warranty had not been incorporated by reference. Study carefully the closely-reasoned rationale of the Court of Appeals in arriving at its determination on this critical point.


# Sidco Products Marketing, Inc. v. Gulf Oil Corp.

United States Court of Appeals, Fifth Circuit, 1988.
858 F.2d 1095.

■ JONES, CIRCUIT JUDGE:

At issue here is the grant of summary judgment for the defendant [Gulf] concerning claims for breach of express and implied warranties ... in the sale [by Gulf to Sidco] of a material called "middle layer emulsion" (MLE). Texas law applies in this diversity case. Concluding essentially that Gulf did not misrepresent the nature or qualities of MLE to the ultimate purchaser Sidco, we affirm.

## I. BACKGROUND

According to Sidco, this is the story of a pig in a poke. On December 15, 1983, Gulf published a Bid Inquiry in which it invited bids from a selected group of purchasers for a product called "middle layer emulsion."

One company on the bid list was Chemwaste, Inc. Several portions of the Bid Inquiry are relevant to our discussion. First, the product was defined as Middle Layer Emulsion [MLE], "a mixture of oil, water and particulate matter." Second, paragraph 10 of the Bid Inquiry afforded any prospective purchaser the opportunity to "inspect the tanks containing MLE and . . . obtain a reasonable sample therefrom for testing." The bid price was to be gauged by the value of recoverable hydrocarbons estimated to be contained in the MLE. Third, a cautionary environmental note appeared as paragraph 14 of the Bid Inquiry:

The solids in the middle layer emulsion are listed by the United States Environmental Protection Agency in 40 CFR Part 261 as a "Hazardous Waste from Specific Sources, Slop Oil emulsion solids from the petroleum refining industry" with an EPA hazardous waste number of K049. If the solids are removed from the middle layer emulsion, then the disposal of these solids are regulated by the Federal Government as well as many state and local governments. It will be the responsibility of the successful bidder to dispose of these solids and any waste water generated in accordance with all applicable Federal, State and local rules and regulations.

Sidco became interested in purchasing MLE for processing and resale of the oil in it when its president, Dirk Stronck, obtained and read a copy of the Bid Inquiry, including paragraph 14. Because Gulf was selling the product only to authorized bidders, Stronck contacted Romero Brothers Oil Exchange, Inc., which acquired from Chemwaste the right to sell MLE. Sidco availed itself of the opportunity to examine MLE chemically and engaged E.W. Saybolt & Company, Inc. for this purpose. Upon receipt of what it believed were satisfactory test results from Saybolt, Sidco signed a contract to purchase the MLE from Romero. The Romero contract was executed for Sidco by Ron Bougere, its then vice-president.

The sale from Gulf to Chemwaste, thence to Romero and Sidco, occurred January 24, 1984. Sidco paid $394,482 for MLE estimated to yield 28,077 barrels of recoverable hydrocarbons. Sidco then entered into a processing agreement with Texas Oil and Chemical Terminal, Inc. [TOCT] for "slop oil" without showing TOCT the Bid Inquiry or advising it that the product was MLE. TOCT's attempts to process MLE encountered serious difficulty—the product first plugged a pump screen and damaged TOCT's heater and later clogged a processing tower.

After further testing, Sidco was led to inquire of the Texas Department of Water Resources whether MLE might be a "hazardous waste" regulated by federal environmental law. The department answered affirmatively. [Sidco] protested this decision, but was ordered to and did remove the MLE from the TOCT refinery, which was not licensed to process hazardous waste, and paid for repairs to TOCT's heater. Nevertheless, hydrocarbon products were eventually extracted and sold by Sidco for gross revenue exceeding $400,000.

Sidco claims to have sustained over $13 million in damages, including $60,000 out-of-pocket costs, over $360,000 in lost revenues, the loss of $5 million in financial backing for proposed slop oil activities, and foregone business opportunities exceeding $8.6 million.

Sidco's lawsuit against Gulf alleged the following causes of action:

1.  Gulf breached an express warranty regarding the nature and quality of MLE, in violation of Tex. Bus. & Com. Code Ann. § 2.313;

2.  Gulf breached the implied warranty of merchantability in that MLE was not fit for the purpose for which slop oil is ordinarily sold, violating Tex. Bus. & Com. Code Ann. § 2.314.

\* \* \*

## II.  DISCUSSION

The determination most critical to the success of Sidco's position is the nature of the misrepresentations or omissions by Gulf in its Bid Inquiry. Sidco concedes that the Bid Inquiry constitutes the only relevant communication between Gulf and Sidco's representatives prior to Sidco's purchase of MLE. Sidco charges that Gulf misrepresented three characteristics of the MLE: that it formed an unusually tight emulsion which was not susceptible to ordinary processing methods; that the product was not "ordinary slop oil," and that the product in its totality was a hazardous waste under applicable environmental regulations. Sidco alleges that all of its damages flowed from these misrepresentations. Sidco's breach of warranty claims, and its alleged breach of the DTPA founded on warranty and misrepresentation claims, depend upon the existence of these pleaded and vigorously argued misrepresentations of MLE's qualities.

Try as we may, we are unable to discern in the bare simplicity of Gulf's Bid Inquiry the false representations that Sidco asserts. The pertinent portions of the Bid Inquiry were quoted above. MLE is there described as an emulsion, which the dictionary alerts us is an "intimate mixture" of two incompletely miscible liquids, such as water and oil, or of a semisolid or solid dispersed in a liquid. Webster's Third New Int'l Dictionary. The MLE is defined to contain water, hydrocarbons and particulate matter. Prospective purchasers are offered the opportunity to sample a sufficient quantity of the MLE to determine its qualities. Finally, there is a cautionary note about the hazardous waste nature of solids contained in the MLE. There is, however, no affirmation of fact concerning the susceptibility of MLE to any particular hydrocarbon processing or refining technique. There is no representation that MLE is "ordinary slop oil." The term slop oil appears only once in the Bid Inquiry, as a descriptive term (in paragraph 14) in the title of the EPA regulation governing the nature of the solids. MLE itself is not represented in the Bid Inquiry as either environmentally hazardous or nonhazardous. The Bid Inquiry did, however, put the would-be purchaser on notice that he should sample and test the MLE in order to determine the nature and quantity of its hydrocarbon content and to calculate his bid price. To put the matter briefly, the Bid Inquiry described MLE much as would a want-ad for a "truck," in that it described the product generically and left the rest of the characteristics to be discerned by the purchaser in his test-drive or at his mechanic's shop.

A warranty is a promise or affirmation of fact concerning a product or a description of the product to which the product is represented to conform. Tex. Bus. & Com. Code Ann. §§ 2.313(a)(1) and (2). Gulf's Bid Inquiry made no promise or description of MLE with regard to its processability or its status as either "ordinary slop oil" or an EPA-regulated hazardous waste. Where there is no such representation, promise, or affirmation that becomes part of the basis of the parties' bargain, there is no express warranty to be breached. La Sara Grain Co. v. First National Bank, 673 S.W.2d 558, 565 (Tex.1984).

Sidco responds to this conclusion in two ways, which we believe are but versions of the same argument. Gulf, it says, "by its conduct" as well as by the Bid Inquiry, "acted as if" MLE was ordinary slop oil. Alternatively, the essence of Gulf's duplicitous conduct, Sidco contends, is that Gulf *omitted* to disclose that MLE could not be processed by ordinary refinery means, that it was not ordinary slop oil and that it was, irrespective of the solids it contained, a hazardous waste. Omissions, however, are not affirmative representations of any sort and thus cannot support a warranty claim, because express warranties must be explicit. . . . On the record before us, it appears that Gulf's Bid Inquiry embodied no express warranty concerning the processability of MLE or its status as "ordinary slop oil" or a non-hazardous material.

Sidco also contends that MLE was sold under an implied warranty of merchantability or fitness for the purposes for which "ordinary slop oil" is used. Gulf moved for summary judgment on this issue, asserting that slop oil is bought and sold so that it can be processed to yield valuable petroleum products. Since the MLE did eventually produce $400,000 of such products for Sidco, the implied warranty of merchantability was fulfilled. This argument suffers from the lack of record evidence demonstrating that, if MLE were to be equated to "ordinary slop oil" for implied warranty purposes, the revenue earned for its petroleum contents represented a "quality comparable to that generally acceptable in that line of trade . . ." Official Comment 2 to Tex. Bus. & Com. Code Ann. § 2.314. Alternatively, however, Gulf asserts that there can be no implied warranty of merchantability as requested by Sidco, because Gulf nowhere expressly represented MLE as "ordinary slop-oil." We find this latter rationale convincing and consistent with our previous discussion.

\* \* \*

For these reasons, the summary judgment granted by the district court is AFFIRMED.

NOTES

**(1) Merchantable Quality: Fitness for Ordinary Purposes.** Goods may be useful for more than one purpose. Flour may be useful for human consumption, but can also be used in the manufacture of ceiling tiles. Cows may be used as dairy animals, for breeding purposes, or for slaughter. What should determine the "ordinary purposes" of goods that have multiple uses? Can the answer be found in the words of the contract of the parties? Are there other sources? Once purposes are identified, how good must goods be to be deemed "fit"? What should determine the minimum standard of "fitness" of goods?

**Problem 1.** Buyer purchased a new Mustang automobile from a Ford dealer. After 30 months, during which Buyer had driven the car 75,000 miles, buyer discovered that the taillight assembly gaskets had been installed in a manner that permitted water to enter and cause severe rust damage. Did the dealer breach the warranty of merchantability? On these facts, the Wisconsin Supreme Court held that the rust problem did not render the car unfit for the purpose of driving. "When a car can provide safe, reliable transportation it is generally considered merchantable." Taterka v. Ford Motor Co., 86 Wis.2d 140, 271 N.W.2d 653 (1978). If the car had been a Mercedes, would the same ruling be appropriate?

**(2) Merchantable Quality: Pass Without Objection in the Trade.** Section 2–314(2)(a) defines merchantability by reference to trade standards. The Code provides that trade usage (UCC 1–303(c) becomes, by implication, part of the parties' bargain in fact (UCC 1–201(b)(3)) ("agreement") which results in defining their legal obligations (UCC 1–201(b)(12)) ("contract"). If goods of a certain quality are regularly accepted without objection by buyers in the trade, this provides a contractual standard against which to measure the objection of a particular buyer in the same trade. See Comment 7 to UCC 2–314. Does this suggest that the issue of sellers' responsibility should be decided as a matter of contract interpretation?

Does UCC 2–314 require that goods be "marketable"? The Court of Appeals for the Fourth Circuit found that "marketability" means that "willing buyers" exist. The court held that a warranty of "merchantability" did not include a warranty of "marketability." Pleasurecraft Marine Engine Co. v. Thermo Power Corp., 272 F.3d 654 (4th Cir. 2001).

**(3) Merchantable Quality: Fair Average Quality.** UCC 2–314(2)(b) specifies that goods must be such as "in the case of fungible goods, are of fair average quality within the description." Comment 7 implies a limited scope for this provision: " 'Fair average' is a term directly appropriate to *agricultural* bulk products ..." (emphasis added). The statute, of course, extends to non-agricultural fungible goods; "fungible" goods, as defined in UCC 1–201(17), comprise not only various bulk products (like ores) but also most manufactured goods where "any unit is, by nature or usage of trade, the equivalent of any other like unit."

Comment 7 to UCC 2–314 seeks to shed light on the standard by stating that "fair average" means "goods centering around the middle belt of quality, not the least or the worst that can be understood in the particular trade by the designation, but such as can pass 'without objection.' Of course a fair percentage of the least is permissible but the goods are not 'fair average' if they are all of the least or worst quality possible under the description."

Does the text of the statute support the implication that goods fail to be of "merchantable quality" if they are below average quality but are "within the description"? Suppose that buyers had been accepting shipments of sugar which ranged in polarization between 75 and 80, with the various shipments averaging out at 77½. Would a shipment in that case which polarized at 75 3/8 fail to meet the statutory standard? If buyers started rejecting shipments below 77½, so that the average quality of acceptable sugar rose to 79, would this in turn justify rejection of sugar below a polarization of 79? Can independent meaning be given to paragraph (b)? See 1 N.Y.L.R.C., Study of the Uniform Commercial Code 400–01 (1955). Are similar problems latent in paragraph (d)?

**Problem 2.** Manufacturer of two-way taxi radios contracted to buy 2500 microprocessors to be used as components in the radios to be delivered in installments. After 1900 had been delivered, buyer notified seller that these items were unsatisfactory. The buyer asserted that it had had 130 (some 8%) of the microprocessors tested by an independent laboratory which reported that 2.6% of those tested had failed to perform. Buyer asserted that its acceptable quality level—the number of devices which can be defective without rendering the entire shipment unacceptable—was 1%. In a suit by buyer for damages for breach of the warranty of merchantability,[6] seller's expert witness testified that a defect rate of less than 5% was sufficient to make the goods conforming. Buyer's technicians testified that, in products containing only five components, a 5% failure rate for each part would result in a probability that one in four of the products had an inadequate component. Did seller breach the warranty of merchantability? See Integrated Circuits Unlimited, Inc. v. E.F. Johnson Co., 691 F.Supp. 630 (E.D.N.Y.1988), aff'd, 875 F.2d 1040 (2d Cir.1989) (held warranty breached).

The court in *Integrated Circuits* also addressed the adequacy of evidence based upon sampling of only 8% of the microprocessors. The court noted that the tests were expensive. While the sample had not been selected randomly, the court found that selection for sampling sufficed because it had been made without bias. The court concluded that the statistical probabilities were high enough and sufficiently reliable to warrant the buyer's action.

**(4) Merchantable Quality: Contract Description.** In *Sidco*, the advocate for the MLE buyer described the contract as a purchase of "a pig in a poke." Sales in which the parties use no description of the goods are not likely to occur. When the goods are not present when contracts are made, the goods would be described verbally.[7] "Any description of the goods

---

**6.** Buyer contended it had not accepted the goods in question. Much of the legal analysis of the courts addressed the question whether buyer's rejection was rightful. On some microprocessors, the court found for the seller. As to materials rightly rejected, the buyer did not seek damages for seller's breach.

**7.** In a "present sale" (UCC 2–106(1)) words may be considerably less important than the parties' focus on the thing itself. So, too, in a sale by sample or model.

which is made part of the basis of the bargain creates an express warranty that the goods shall conform to the description." UCC 2–313(1)(b). What is added to the idea of an *express* warranty by description by the provisions in UCC 2–314(2) that define an *implied* warranty on the basis of the "contract description" (UCC 2–314(2)(a) and (b)) or "the agreement" (UCC 2–314(2)(d) and (c))? Recall the discussion in section 1 regarding the overlapping nature of the relationship of the three "types" of warranties of quality.

Section 2–314(2)(c) does not refer on its face to "contract description" or "agreement," but it declares sellers responsible for the ordinary utility of "such goods." To what antecedent could "such" refer?[8]

**(5) Merchantable Quality of Manufactured Goods: Design Standards.** Manufacturers determine their own quality-control standards. Such standards, which may be high or low, are used to decide whether the manufacturer will sell a finished product in the marketplace. (Manufacturers of some goods, e.g., glass crystal or clothing, market some products that do not meet the firms' standards as "seconds.") If a manufacturer fails to detect that a product does not conform to its own quality-control standards and, without notice of that fact, sells the product to a buyer, is the product, for that reason, unmerchantable?

**Problem 3.** A restaurant patron ordered and was served a platter that includes a portion of fish almondine. While eating, the patron choked on a fishbone, which lodged in his esophagus. The patron was rushed to a hospital where a bone, one centimeter long, was removed. Patron sued Restaurant for breach of the implied warranty of merchantability. (Note that serving food in a restaurant is a sale under UCC 2–314(1).) What result? See Morrison's Cafeteria v. Haddox, 431 So.2d 975 (Ala.1983) (jury verdict for patron reversed; as a matter of law, said the court, a one-centimeter bone in a fish fillet does not make the food unmerchantable). Sellers' liability for buyers' personal injuries that result from nonconformity of the goods is considered further later in this Chapter.

**Problem 4.** Seller, a car dealer, showed Buyer a car on display in the showroom. While Buyer was examining the car, Seller described the car as a Model XX–V. Buyer agreed to buy the car and the Seller drew up a written agreement in which the car was described as a Model XX–V. After driving the car for several weeks, Buyer learned that it was a Model XX–J. A Model XX–V has four doors and chrome trim, while a Model XX–J has two doors and no chrome trim. Otherwise the cars are the same. Has Buyer a claim for breach of warranty under UCC 2–313(1)(b)? Under UCC 2–314? See UCC 2–316(3)(b). Cf. Best Buick v. Welcome, 18 UCC Rep. 75 (Mass. Dist.Ct., App.Div.1975) (car erroneously described as "1970" model).

--------

**8.** The proposed revision of Article 2 recommends amendment of UCC 2–314(2)(c) to read "are fit for the ordinary purposes for which goods of that description are used."

## 2. REMEDIES FOR BREACH OF WARRANTY

We turn now to the remedies available to buyers for breach of warranty of quality. The Commercial Code provisions on remedies do not vary with the "type" of warranty found to be breached. The nature of the relief does depend on whether the goods are retained by a buyer or returned to the seller. If the goods are kept by buyers, damages are provided in UCC 2–714 and UCC 2–715. The materials that follow consider those provisions. Buyers may have the right to compel sellers to keep the goods or to take them back. In that situation the UCC Article 2 remedies differ. Goods that do not conform to quality warranties may have significant market value nonetheless. This is a factor in measurement of damages under UCC 2–714, but not in situations where sellers keep the goods. Remedies for that situation will be considered here and in later chapters.

# Chatlos Systems v. National Cash Register Corp.

United States Court of Appeals, Third Circuit, 1982.
670 F.2d 1304.

[Chatlos Systems, Inc. (Chatlos) designed and manufactured cable pressurization equipment for the telecommunications industry. In the spring of 1974, Chatlos decided to buy a computer system and contacted several manufacturers, including National Cash Register Corp. (NCR). NCR recommended its 399/656 disc system. NCR's representative said that the equipment would provide Chatlos with six accounting functions: accounts receivable, payroll, order entry, inventory deletion, state income tax, and cash receipts. The representative also told Chatlos that the system would solve inventory problems, result in direct savings of labor costs, and be programmed to be in full operation in six months. On July 24, 1974, Chatlos signed a written agreement in which NCR warranted the equipment "for 12 months after delivery against defects in material, workmanship and operational failure from ordinary use."

[NCR installed the equipment, but never succeeded in making it fully operational. In November 1976, Chatlos instructed NCR to remove the equipment. NCR refused.]

■ PER CURIAM

This appeal from a district court's award of damages for breach of warranty in a diversity case tried under New Jersey law presents two questions: whether the district court's computation of damages under N.J.Stat.Ann. § 12A:2–714(2) was clearly erroneous, and whether the district court abused its discretion in supplementing the damage award with pre-judgment interest. We answer both questions in the negative and, therefore, we will affirm.

Plaintiff-appellee Chatlos Systems, Inc., initiated this action in the Superior Court of New Jersey, alleging, *inter alia*, breach of warranty regarding an NCR 399/656 computer system it had acquired from defendant National Cash Register Corp. The case was removed under 28 U.S.C.

§ 1441(a) to the United States District Court for the District of New Jersey. Following a nonjury trial, the district court determined that defendant was liable for breach of warranty and awarded $57,152.76 damages for breach of warranty and consequential damages in the amount of $63,558.16. Chatlos Systems, Inc. v. National Cash Register Corp., 479 F.Supp. 738 (D.N.J.1979), aff'd in part, remanded in part, 635 F.2d 1081 (3d Cir.1980). Defendant appealed and this court affirmed the district court's findings of liability, set aside the award of consequential damages, and remanded for a recalculation of damages for breach of warranty. Chatlos Systems, Inc. v. National Cash Register Corp., 635 F.2d 1081 (3d Cir.1980). On remand, applying the "benefit of the bargain" formula of N.J.Stat.Ann. § 12A:2–714(2) (Uniform Commercial Code § 2–714(2)), the district court determined the damages to be $201,826.50, to which it added an award of pre-judgment interest. Defendant now appeals from these damage determinations, contending that the district court erred in failing to recognize the $46,020 contract price of the delivered NCR computer system as the fair market value of the goods as warranted, and that the award of damages is without support in the evidence presented. Appellant also contests the award of pre-judgment interest.

... The district court relied ... on the testimony of plaintiff-appellee's expert, Dick Brandon, who, without estimating the value of an NCR model 399/656, presented his estimate of the value of a computer system that would perform all of the functions that the NCR 399/656 had been warranted to perform. Brandon did not limit his estimate to equipment of any one manufacturer; he testified regarding manufacturers who could have made systems that would perform the functions that appellant had warranted the NCR 399/656 could perform. He acknowledged that the systems about which he testified were not in the same price range as the NCR 399/656. Appellant likens this testimony to substituting a Rolls Royce for a Ford, and concludes that the district court's recomputed damage award was therefore clearly contrary to the evidence of fair market value— which in NCR's view is the contract price itself.

Appellee did not order, nor was it promised, merely a specific NCR computer model, but an NCR computer system with specified capabilities. The correct measure of damages, under N.J.Stat.Ann. § 12A:2–714(2), is the difference between the fair market value of the goods accepted and the value they would have had if they had been as warranted. Award of that sum is not confined to instances where there has been an increase in value between date of ordering and date of delivery. It may also include the benefit of a contract price which, for whatever reason quoted, was particularly favorable for the customer. Evidence of the contract price may be relevant to the issue of fair market value, but it is not controlling. ... Appellant limited its fair market value analysis to the contract price of the computer model it actually delivered.[3] Appellee developed evidence of the

---

**3.** At oral argument, counsel for appellant responded to questions from the bench, as follows:

worth of a computer with the capabilities promised by NCR, and the trial court properly credited the evidence.[4]

Appellee was aided, moreover, by the testimony of Frank Hicks, NCR's programmer, who said that he told his company's officials that the "current software was not sufficient in order to deliver the program that the customer [Chatlos] required. They would have to be rewritten or a different system would have to be given to the customer." Appendix to Brief for Appellee at 2.68. Hicks recommended that Chatlos be given an NCR 8200 but was told, "that will not be done." Id. at 2.69. Gerald Greenstein, another NCR witness, admitted that the 8200 series was two levels above the 399 in sophistication and price. Id. at 14.30. This testimony supported Brandon's statement that the price of the hardware needed to perform Chatlos' requirements would be in the $100,000 to $150,000 range.

Essentially, then, the trial judge was confronted with the conflicting value estimates submitted by the parties. Chatlos' expert's estimates were corroborated to some extent by NCR's supporters. NCR, on the other hand, chose to rely on contract price. Credibility determinations had to be made by the district judge. Although we might have come to a different conclusion on the value of the equipment as warranted had we been sitting as trial judges, we are not free to make our own credibility and factual findings. We may reverse the district court only if its factual determinations were clearly erroneous. Krasnov v. Dinan, 465 F.2d 1298 (3d Cir. 1972).[5]

---

Judge Rosenn: Your position also is that you agree, number one, that the fair market value is the measure of damages here.

Counsel for Appellant: Yes, sir.

Judge Rosenn: The fair market value you say, in the absence of other evidence to the contrary that is relevant, is the contract price. That is the evidence of fair market value.

Counsel: That's right.

Judge Rosenn: Now seeing that had the expert or had the plaintiff been able to establish testimony that there were other machines on the market that were similar to your machine?

Counsel: Yes.

Judge Rosenn: That the fair market value of those was $50,000, that would have been relevant evidence but it had to be the same machine—same type machine.

Counsel: Well, I would say that the measure of damages as indicated by the statute requires the same machine—"the goods"—in an operable position.

**4.** We find the following analogy, rather than the Rolls Royce—Ford analogy submitted by appellant, to be on point:

Judge Weis: If you start thinking about a piece of equipment that is warranted to lift a thousand pounds and it will only lift 500 pounds, then the cost of something that will lift a thousand pounds gives you more of an idea and that may be?

Counsel for Appellee: That may be a better analogy, yes.

Judge Weis: Yes.

**5.** The dissent essentially is based on disagreement with the estimates provided by Chatlos' expert, Brandon. The record reveals that he was well qualified; the weight to be given his testimony is the responsibility of the factfinder, not an appellate court.

Upon reviewing the evidence of record, therefore, we conclude that the computation of damages for breach of warranty was not clearly erroneous. We hold also that the district court acted within its discretion in awarding pre-judgment interest, Chatlos Systems, Inc. v. National Cash Register Corp., 635 F.2d at 1088.

The judgment of the district court will be affirmed.

■ ROSENN, CIRCUIT JUDGE, dissenting.

The primary question in this appeal involves the application of Article 2 of the Uniform Commercial Code as adopted by New Jersey in N.J.S.A. 12A:2–101 et seq. (1962) to the measure of damages for breach of warranty in the sale of a computer system. I respectfully dissent because I believe there is no probative evidence to support the district court's award of damages for the breach of warranty in a sum amounting to almost five times the purchase price of the goods. The measure of damages also has been misapplied and this could have a significant effect in the marketplace, especially for the unique and burgeoning computer industry.[1]

In July 1974, National Cash Register Corporation (NCR) sold Chatlos Systems, Inc. (Chatlos), a NCR 399/656 disc computer system (NCR 399) for $46,020 (exclusive of 5 percent sales tax of $1,987.50). The price and system included:

| | |
|---|---|
| The computer (hardware) | $40,165.00 |
| Software (consisting of 6 computer programs)[2] | 5,855.00 |
| | $46,020.00 |

NCR delivered the disc computer to Chatlos in December 1974 and in March 1975 the payroll program became operational. By March of the following year, however, NCR was still unsuccessful in installing an operational order entry program and inventory deletion program. Moreover, On August 31, 1976, Chatlos experienced problems with the payroll program. On that same day and the day following NCR installed an operational state income tax program, but on September 1, 1976, Chatlos demanded termination of the lease[2] and removal of the computer.

When this case was previously before us, we upheld the district court's liability decision but remanded for a reassessment of damages, instructing the court that under the purchase contract and the law consequential

---

1.   Plaintiff's expert, Brandon, testified that generally 40 percent of all computer installations result in failures. He further testified that successful installations of computer systems require not only the computer companies' attention but also the attention of the customers' top management.

2.   Chatlos decided to lease the system rather than purchase it outright. To permit this arrangement, NCR sold the system to Mid Atlantic National Bank in July 1975 for $46,020, which leased the system to Chatlos. Chatlos made monthly payments to Mid Atlantic in amounts which would have totaled $70,162.09 over the period of the lease.

damages could not be awarded. Consequential damages, therefore, are no longer an issue here.

On remand, the district court, on the basis of the previous record made in the case, fixed the fair market value of the NCR 399 as warranted at the time of its acceptance in August 1975 at $207,826.50. It reached that figure by valuing the hardware at $131,250.00 and the software at $76,575.50, for a total of $207,826.50. The court then determined that the present value of the computer hardware, which Chatlos retained, was $6,000. Putting no value on the accepted payroll program, the court deducted the $6,000 and arrived at an award of $201,826.50 plus pre-judgment interest at the rate of 8 percent per annum from August 1975.

Chatlos contends before this court, as it had before the district court on remand, that under its benefit of the bargain theory the fair market value of the goods as warranted was several times the purchase price of $46,020. . . .

[T]he sole issue before us now is whether the district court erred in fixing the fair market value of the computer system as warranted at the time of the acceptance in August 1975 at $207,826.50.

## II.

### A.

I believe that the district court committed legal error. . . .

There are a number of major flaws in the plaintiff's attempt to prove damages in excess of the contract price. I commence with an analysis of plaintiff's basic theory. Chatlos presented its case under a theory that although, as a sophisticated purchaser, it bargained for several months before arriving at a decision on the computer system it required and the price of $46,020, it is entitled, because of the breach of warranty, to damages predicated on a considerably more expensive system. Stated another way, even if it bargained for a cheap system, i.e., one whose low cost reflects its inferior quality, because that system did not perform as bargained for, it is now entitled to damages measured by the value of a system which, although capable of performing the identical functions as the NCR 399, is of far superior quality and accordingly more expensive.

The statutory measure of damages for breach of warranty specifically provides that the measure is the difference at the time and place of acceptance between the value "of the goods accepted" and the "value they would have had if they had been as warranted." The focus of the statute is upon "the goods accepted"—not other hypothetical goods which may perform equivalent functions. "Moreover, the value to be considered is the reasonable market value of the *goods delivered*, not the value of the goods to a particular purchaser or for a particular purpose." KLPR TV, Inc. v. Visual Electronics Corp., 465 F.2d 1382, 1387 (8th Cir.1972) (emphasis added). The court, however, arrived at value on the basis of a hypothetical construction of a system as of December 1978 by the plaintiff's expert,

Brandon. The court reached its value by working backward from Brandon's figures, adjusting for inflation.

* * *

Although NCR warranted performance, the failure of its equipment to perform, absent any evidence of the value of any NCR 399 system on which to base fair market value, does not permit a market value based on systems wholly unrelated to the goods sold. Yet, instead of addressing the fair market value of the NCR 399 had it been as warranted, Brandon addressed the fair market value of another system that he concocted by drawing on elements from other major computer systems manufactured by companies such as IBM, Burroughs, and Honeywell, which he considered would perform "functions identical to those contracted for" by Chatlos. He conceded that the systems were "[p]erhaps not within the same range of dollars that the bargain was involved with" and he did not identify specific packages of software. Brandon had no difficulty in arriving at the fair market value of the inoperable NCR equipment but instead of fixing a value on the system had it been operable attempted to fashion a hypothetical system on which he placed a value. The district court, in turn, erroneously adopted that value as the fair market value for an operable NCR 399 system. NCR rightly contends that the "comparable" systems on which Brandon drew were substitute goods of greater technological power and capability and not acceptable in determining damages for breach of warranty under section 2–714. Furthermore, Brandon's hypothetical system did not exist and its valuation was largely speculation.

### B.

A review of Brandon's testimony reveals its legal inadequacy for establishing the market value of the system Chatlos purchased from NCR. Brandon never testified to the fair market value which the NCR 399 system would have had had it met the warranty at the time of acceptance. ...

Thus, the shortcomings in Brandon's testimony defy common sense and the realities of the marketplace. First, ordinarily, the best evidence of fair market value is what a willing purchaser would pay in cash to a willing seller. ... In the instant case we have clearly "not ... an unsophisticated consumer," ... who for a considerable period of time negotiated and bargained with an experienced designer and vendor of computer systems. The price they agreed upon for an operable system would ordinarily be the best evidence of its value. The testimony does not present us with the situation referred to in our previous decision, where "the value of the goods rises between the time that the contract is executed and the time of acceptance," in which event the buyer is entitled to the benefit of his bargain. ... On the contrary, Chatlos here relies on an expert who has indulged in the widest kind of speculation. Based on this testimony, Chatlos asserts in effect that a multi-national sophisticated vendor of computer equipment, despite months of negotiation, incredibly agreed to sell an operable computer system for $46,020 when, in fact, it had a fair market value of $207,000. ...

Fourth, the record contains testimony which appears undisputed that computer equipment falls into one of several tiers, depending upon the degree of sophistication. The more sophisticated equipment has the capability of performing the functions of the least sophisticated equipment, but the less sophisticated equipment cannot perform all of the functions of those in higher levels. The price of the more technologically advanced equipment is obviously greater.

It is undisputed that in September 1976 there were vendors of computer equipment of the same general size as the NCR 399/656 with disc in the price range of $35,000 to $40,000 capable of providing the same programs as those required by Chatlos, including IBM, Phillips, and Burroughs. They were the very companies who competed for the sale of the computer in 1974 in the same price range. On the other hand, Chatlos' requirements could also be satisfied by computers available at "three levels higher in price and sophistication than the 399 disc." Each level higher would mean more sophistication, greater capabilities, and more memory. Greenstein, NCR's expert, testified without contradiction that equipment of Burroughs, IBM, and other vendors in the price range of $100,000 to $150,000, capable of performing Chatlos' requirements, was not comparable to the 399 because it was three levels higher. Such equipment was more comparable to the NCR 8400 series.

\* \* \*

### III.

The purpose of the N.J.S.A. 12A:2–714 is to put the buyer in the same position he would have been in if there had been no breach. See Uniform Commercial Code 1–106(1). The remedies for a breach of warranty were intended to compensate the buyer for his loss; they were not intended to give the purchaser a windfall or treasure trove. The buyer may not receive more than it bargained for; it may not obtain the value of a superior computer system which it did not purchase even though such a system can perform all of the functions the inferior system was designed to serve. . . .

\* \* \*

### VI.

On this record, therefore, the damages to which plaintiff is entitled are $46,020 less $6,000, the fair market value at time of trial of the retained hardware, and less $1,000, the fair market value of the payroll program, or the net sum of $39,020.

Accordingly, I would reverse the judgment of the district court and direct it to enter judgment for the plaintiff in the sum of $39,020 with interest from the date of entry of the initial judgment at the rate allowed by state law.

After the decision by the panel, seller filed a petition for rehearing by the Court of Appeals *en banc*. The court declined to rehear the case. Three judges dissented from that decision. The following opinion expresses the views of the majority and minority in that determination.

## SUR PETITION FOR REHEARING

The petition for rehearing filed by appellant in the above entitled case having been submitted to the judges who participated in the decision of this court and to all the other available circuit judges of the circuit in regular active service, and no judge who concurred in the decision having asked for rehearing, and a majority of the circuit judges of the circuit in regular active service not having voted for rehearing by the court in banc, the petition for rehearing is denied. Judges Adams, Hunter and Garth would grant the petition for rehearing.

■ ADAMS, CIRCUIT JUDGE, dissents from the denial of rehearing, and makes the following statement:

Ordinarily, an interpretation of state law by this Court, sitting in diversity, is not of sufficient consequence to warrant reconsideration by the Court sitting in banc. One reason is that if a federal court misconstrues the law of a state, the courts of that state have an opportunity, at some point, to reject the federal court's interpretation. See Chuy v. Philadelphia Eagles Football Club, 595 F.2d 1265, 1286–87 (3d Cir.1979) (in banc) (Aldisert, J., dissenting). In this case, however, the majority's holding, which endorses a measure of damages that is based on what appears to be a new interpretation of New Jersey's commercial law, involves a construction of the Uniform Commercial Code as well. Rectification of any error in our interpretation is, because of the national application of the Uniform Commercial Code, significantly more difficult than it would be if New Jersey law alone were implicated. Moreover, the provision of the Uniform Commercial Code involved here is of unusual importance: the measure of damages approved by this Court may create large monetary risks and obligations in a wide range of commercial transactions, including specifically the present burgeoning computer industry. Because there would appear to be considerable force to the dissenting opinion of Judge Rosenn and because I believe that the principle articulated by the majority should be reviewed by the entire Court before it is finally adopted, I would grant the petition for rehearing in banc.

■ JAMES HUNTER, III and GARTH CIRCUIT JUDGES join in this statement.

## NOTES

**(1) Benefit of the Bargain: What Was the Bargain?** Was it reasonable for Chatlos to expect to receive goods with a market value that was five times the contract price? Should the price term be part of the "contract description" of goods sold? Consider Comment 7 to UCC 2–314: "In cases of doubt as to what quality is intended, the price at which a merchant closes a contract is an excellent index of the nature and scope of his obligation under the present section." Would it have been appropriate to probe more deeply into the probable expectations of the parties as to seller's obligation and buyer's remedy in the event that the computer system failed to perform? Should expectations as to (A) performance and (B) remedies for breach be considered in relation to each other? Are implied expectations as to the size of recovery for breach different from implied expectations as to performance, such as implied warranties of quality? Note that the court, in its earlier decision, gave full effect to an express provision in the agreement denying recovery for consequential damages. Does this shed light on the parties' allocation of the risks and benefits of the agreement?

(2) **Parol Evidence Rule.** In *Chatlos*, as in *Royal Business Machines*, sellers were charged with liability for breach of oral statements made by their representatives. When contracts of sale are reduced to writing, frequently sellers include in the document a declaration that the document contains the complete agreement of the parties and that there are no promises or representations not contained therein. These "integration" clauses are meant to invoke the parol evidence rule, which for sales contracts is codified in UCC 2–202. In addition to barring evidence that would *contradict* a writing intended as a final expression of a sales agreement, paragraph (b) bars "consistent additional terms" if the court finds "the writing to have been intended also as a complete and exclusive statement of the terms of an agreement." The parol evidence rule, and its codified sales version, are complex legal issues normally studied in the course on Contracts.

**Problem 5.** An agreement was signed for the sale of air conditioning equipment to Buyer. The written contract contained detailed specifications concerning the type of equipment, the horsepower of the motors and the tons of refrigeration to be produced. The machinery met the contract specifications, but it was not sufficiently large or powerful to cool Buyer's building. Seller refused to take back the equipment, and pointed out that Buyer received an efficiently operating unit of precisely the size called for in the contract. Buyer tells his attorney that Seller had recommended the model and size, and had assured Buyer that it would cool Buyer's building. In preparing for trial, Buyer's attorney is concerned that Buyer's testimony with respect to the foregoing statements by Seller would be excluded under the parol evidence rule. The attorney asks you to develop a line of questions that would minimize this danger.

Examine carefully the language of UCC 2–202. Note that "term" is defined (UCC 1–201(42)) as "that portion of an agreement which relates to a particular matter." Compare UCC 1–201(3) ("agreement" is defined as "the bargain of the parties in fact as found in their language or *by implication from other circumstances* ...") with UCC 1–201(11) ("contract" means "the total legal obligation which results from the parties' agreement as affected by this Act and any other applicable rules of law"). Does UCC 2–202 exclude the above evidence if offered to establish an *implied* warranty?

**(3) Lease Transactions.** The "buyer" in *Chatlos* was actually a lessee. Because Chatlos lacked sufficient credit to purchase the computer system on an installment basis, an intermediary company bought the system from NCR and leased it to Chatlos. The courts treated Chatlos as the buyer for purposes of the litigation. In 1987, Article 2A on Leases was added to the Code. Under UCC 2A–209(1), seller's warranties to a lessor extend to the lessee if the lease is a "finance lease" (UCC 2A–103(1)(g)). This provision codifies the result in *Chatlos*.

The buyer of the copying machines in *Royal Business Machines* was a "true" equipment lessor, not a financing lessor. As to its lessees, such a lessor's warranties of quality are provided in UCC 2A–210, –212, and –213. These sections parallel the warranty provisions in Article 2.

––––––––

The following case involves a dispute over the quality of goods sold, but the primary remedy sought by the buyer was to recover the purchase price. Article 2 allows certain buyers to "revoke" their acceptances of goods. UCC 2–608. A buyer may revoke acceptance only if nonconformity "substantially impairs" the value of the goods "to him." Revocation must occur, normally, within a reasonable time after a buyer discovers or should have discovered the nonconformity. A buyer that revokes acceptance properly is entitled to recover the price paid (UCC 2–711(1)), plus expectation damages (UCC 2–712, 2–713), plus incidental and consequential damages (UCC 2–715). In later chapters, we will consider more fully the mechanics of revocation of acceptance. For present purposes, the focus is on the quality standard of substantial impairment of value to the buyer and the remedies open to buyers.

## Hemmert Ag. Aviation, Inc. v. Mid–Continent Aircraft Corp.

United States District Court, District of Kansas, 1987.
663 F.Supp. 1546.

■ BROWN, J.

This is a diversity action wherein plaintiff seeks to revoke acceptance and to recover damages arising from its purchase of an agricultural spray plane from the defendant. After hearing the witnesses' testimony and counsels' arguments, examining the evidence and researching the law, the court makes the following findings of fact and conclusions of law as required by Fed.R.Civ.P. 52.

### FINDINGS OF FACT

1.   Hemmert Agricultural Aviation, Inc. ("Hemmert Ag"), is a Kansas corporation engaged in the business of agricultural spraying, primarily commercial crop dusting and fertilizer application. Hemmert Ag generally

operates within a forty mile radius of Oakley, Kansas, and its typical spray season runs from the first of May until the middle of September each year.

2.   Mark Hemmert (Hemmert) is the President and sole stockholder of Hemmert Ag. He is presently 31 years old. He has fifteen years of general flying experience and approximately ten years of agricultural spraying experience. He personally does most of the flying for Hemmert Ag, but occasionally other pilots and planes are hired on a temporary basis.

3.   Defendant, Mid–Continent Aircraft Corporation (Mid–Continent), is a Missouri corporation in Hayti, Missouri, engaged in the business of commercial crop dusting and aircraft sales. Mid–Continent is an authorized dealer of Ag–Cat spray planes. Ag–Cat spray planes were initially manufactured by Grumman, but the current manufacturer is Schweizer Aircraft Corporation.

4.   Richard Reade is the President and principal stockholder of Mid–Continent.

5.   In 1980, Hemmert purchased a 1977 used "B" model Schweizer Ag–Cat. This plane was the trade-in when the plane in issue was purchased. This 1977 "B" had a 300 gallon hopper and a larger tail and vertical fin than the Model G–164B Ag–Cat 600 Super "B" plane (Super "B"), which is the plane in issue. The Super "B" had a 400 gallon hopper and a raised upper wing. From reading advertisements and talking with Reade, Hemmert believed the raised wing on the Super "B" made it faster and more maneuverable and improved visibility. Terrell Kirk, an engineer and test pilot with Schweizer, testified the raised wing was primarily for visibility purposes.

6.   In 1984, Hemmert called Mid–Continent, as he was interested in trading in his 1977 "B" Ag Cat for a new and bigger plane, Super "B".

7.   In August 1985, Hemmert again contacted Mid–Continent, in particular Richard Reade, about purchasing the Super "B". While satisfied with the performance of his 1977 "B" Ag Cat, he had been having a good year and wanted a plane that was faster to the field, more maneuverable and more productive. Hemmert's trade-in was in good condition other than needing some routine maintenance. Hemmert purchased the Super "B" believing it would make his work easier, safer and more profitable. . . .

8.   Hemmert's belief that a Super "B" was more maneuverable than his 1977 Ag–Cat "B" was based in part on an advertisement for the 450 "B" . . . , which stated in part: "New raised wing design means more maneuverability; more visibility; more speed." The 450 "B" described in [the advertisement] differs from the Super "B" 600 hp. only in horsepower, hopper size, and length (4 inches). In fact, . . . a Schweizer advertisement brochure stamped with defendant's name and address, explains the Super "B" is powered by either a 450 or 600 horsepower engine. The 450 "B" is identical to the 600 hp. Super "B" in almost all relevant respects, except for engine size and hopper capacity.

9.   Hemmert testified that during the telephone conversation in early August 1985, Richard Reade represented the Super "B" to be faster, more

maneuverable, and having better visibility than his 1977 Ag–Cat "B". Reade denied that these representations were made and stated that he only represented the Super "B" as more productive.

10. The parties struck their bargain over the telephone on August 6, 1985. . . . The plane was sold to plaintiff for $128,000.00 total, $75,500.00 in cash plus Hemmert's trade-in. . . .

12. . . . Ed Zeeman, a ferry pilot, delivered the Super "B" to Hemmert Ag in Oakley, Kansas, on August 20, 1985. Zeeman arrived in Oakley late in the afternoon, and he was in a hurry to return that afternoon with plaintiff's trade-in.

\* \* \*

16. Prior to August 6, 1985, Hemmert had not flown the particular Super "B" he purchased nor flown any Super "B". Hemmert made no inquiries to other spray pilots who were using a Super "B". Reade acknowledged that it is not unusual for agricultural spray planes to be sold before the purchaser has actually flown them.

17. On August 20, 1985, the actual delivery date, Hemmert called Reade saying he was happy but that [certain optional equipment was] not on the aircraft. [Mid–Continent subsequently delivered these items.] Hemmert never had these options installed even though they had arrived and Mid–Continent had agreed to pay the installation cost.

18. Around August 23, 1985, Hemmert flew the Super "B" with a small load of water in an effort to calibrate the spraying system. Hemmert noticed that the shut-off valve was not developing adequate "suck back" to shut off the flow of water. After his adjustments failed to correct the situation, Hemmert called Reade and told him the valve was defective. Read said a new valve would be sent and it could be installed at Mid–Continent's expense.

19. At about the same time, Hemmert complained about the performance of the Super "B". Hemmert noted that the plane was unresponsive in pitch, rolled excessively to the right, and lost air speed in turns, giving the pilot the sensation that the aircraft was "falling out from under him". Reade suggested the performance problems could be simply due to a bad engine. Hemmert said he was not satisfied and instructed Reade not to sell his trade-in. Reade represented that the trade-in had been sold. While the sale of the trade-in was not completed until September 6, 1985, at the time of Reade's representation to plaintiff there was an outstanding offer on the plane.

20. When the second spray valve arrived within a couple of days of August 23, 1985, plaintiff and an airport mechanic installed the second valve which also proved to be defective. When Hemmert called Reade about the defective second valve, Reade said additional valves would be sent until an operative one was found.

21. Reade directed Dan Westbrook, a mechanic with Mid–Continent, to drive to Oakley, Kansas, and to replace the engine. . . . On or about

August 26, 1985, Westbrook checked over the plane and replaced the engine. Westbrook then flew the plane empty for 30–40 minutes. Westbrook detected nothing glaringly wrong with the plane's flight characteristics. He believed the plane "flew well" and that it had a "personality of its own."

22.  Still dissatisfied with the plane's flight characteristics, Hemmert contacted four other agricultural spray pilots and asked them to fly the Super "B". Each of these four spray pilots were highly experienced, but none had previously flown a Super "B". Each pilot flew the plane before Hemmert related any of his negative feelings regarding the plane. The four spray pilots were Jim Bussen of Sharon Springs, Kansas; Steven Kistler of Colby, Kansas; Kelly Henry of Augusta, Kansas; and Ken Bixeman of Colby, Kansas.

23.  Bussen owned a Grumman Ag–Cat with a small fin. He test flew the Super "B" empty and it felt heavy and like it wanted to drop out beneath him. Bussen commented the Super "B" did not turn like his old Ag–Cat. He did not feel safe in the Super "B" and expected it to fly better. The Super "B" was then loaded with 200 gallons of water and Bussen flew it. He said it felt "scary" and that it did not climb like it should have. It took him twice the radius to make the turns and any steep turns caused the feeling of an imminent stall. He said the plaintiff's Super "B" flew "too much differently" to be termed just the personal characteristics of the plane.

24.  Kistler flew the Super "B" once for 30–40 minutes with an empty hopper. Kistler's prior experience with Ag–Cats did not include the "big fin" B models. Kistler flew the plane making maneuvers similar to those in spraying a field. He never felt comfortable in the Super "B" as its power drained on right turns. The Super "B" flew seriously different from other Ag–Cats, creating the sensation that it could stall any moment in a turn. He also testified that the Super "B"'s tail configuration resembled that of the "A" models which he had flown.

25.  Bixeman and Henry experienced the same sensation of the plane's falling out from underneath them when they flew the Super "B". Henry testified that he had to make wider, easy turns with Super "B" which took extra time. At that point, Henry repeated the appropriate aphorism: "Time is money". Based upon the advertising literature that he had seen, Henry expected the Super "B" to be highly maneuverable.

26.  Mark Hemmert also talked with Charles Dykes, an experienced agricultural spray pilot from Coy, Arkansas. He has fourteen Ag–Cat models including three Super "B"'s. Dykes has never seen nor flown plaintiff's Super "B". When Dykes got his first Super "B" he grew "sick of it", as it did not respond like any other Ag–Cat spray plane that he had owned or flown. At first, Dykes was very unhappy and was scared the first couple of times. After 40–50 hours flying, he started to become accustomed to the Super "B", and after 75 hours flying, he loved his Super "B". Dykes now uses his Super "B"'s to spray fields of much smaller acreages than the

fields generally located in Western Kansas. Dykes told Hemmert to "stick with" the Super "B" and he would discover that it was a good plane.

27.    Reade next arranged for Terrill Kirk, chief test pilot for Schweizer Company, to go to Oakley, Kansas, and check out plaintiff's Super "B". Kirk has an engineering degree and has flight tested twelve different models of Ag–Cats. He did all the flight testing necessary for type certification from the Federal Aviation Administration. Kirk has no experience as a commercial agricultural spray pilot. When Kirk arrived in Oakley, he first had Hemmert explain the flying characteristics of the Super "B". Kirk then checked several measurements on the plane. Kirk next flew the plane empty, experiencing nothing unusual and finding it to be a "typical good Ag–Cat". The plane was then loaded with 270–280 gallons of water, and Kirk flew it, noting a tendency for the plane to roll into right hand turns. Kirk testified that this phenomenon could be called a stall, but that it was actually caused by pilot technique in using too much rudder. Kirk considered that technique to be a carryover from flying the big-fin "B" models like plaintiff's trade-in. Kirk thought plaintiff's Super "B" "handled good and flew well". Kirk then observed Hemmert flying the Super "B" and remarked that Hemmert made abrupt maneuvers and advised him to stop "cowboying" the plane and to try smoother turns. Kirk believed pilot technique for flying the Super "B" differs from that used on previous models.

28.    Hemmert is dissatisfied with his Super "B" and has lost his confidence in it. Each pilot that testified at trial acknowledged that a spray pilot's confidence in his aircraft is very important. Because of a spray pilot's maneuvers close to the ground, his confidence is extremely essential.

29.    In the Spring of 1986, Hemmert purchased another Ag–Cat, a 1982 600 horsepower "B" plus. This model did not have a raised wing design as found on the Super "B". Hemmert paid $78,000.00 for this plane and is still using it.

30.    Hemmert was never satisfied with the Super "B". On October 30, 1985, Hemmert's attorney sent a certified letter notifying Mid–Continent of Mr. Hemmert's intent to revoke acceptance of the Super "B" under the Uniform Commercial Code. Reade admitted the plaintiff's complaints in that letter were not new to him.

## CONCLUSIONS OF LAW

1.    The Court has jurisdiction over the parties and has subject matter jurisdiction pursuant to 28 U.S.C. Sec. 1332 by reason of diversity of citizenship and the requisite amount in controversy.

2.    The parties have stipulated that the law of Kansas is to be applied. This is a sale of goods governed by the Kansas Uniform Commercial Code, K.S.A. 84–2–102, et seq. . . .

3.    Plaintiff seeks to employ the remedy of revocation of acceptance set forth at K.S.A. 84–2–608: . . . To revoke acceptance is to refuse the delivered goods after they have been accepted and after the time for their

rejection has run. . . . While a buyer may nominally reject for any defect, acceptance cannot be revoked absent a substantial nonconformity. The purpose of this remedy is to restore the buyer to the economic status quo which would have been enjoyed if the goods had not been delivered. . . .

4.   Notice.  K.S.A. 84–2–608(2) (hereinafter 2–608) requires revocation to occur within a reasonable time after the buyer discovers or should have discovered the grounds for it. What is a reasonable time is obviously a function of circumstances. Typically, the notice of revocation will be given after the general notice of breach required under K.S.A. 84–2–607(3)(a), as the purchaser's wish to revoke is frequently the last resort after the seller's attempts to cure have failed. Because one purpose behind the notice provisions is to allow the seller the chance to cure, the outer limits of the reasonable time period should be flexible to encourage both the buyer and seller to cooperate in an effort to cure. See Murray v. Holiday Rambler, Inc., 83 Wis. 2d 406, 265 N.W.2d 513, 24 U.C.C. Rep. 52, 67–68 (1978); Official Comment 4 to 2–608. Similarly, if the seller continuously assures the buyer that the defects will be remedied, the notice period should be accordingly suspended.

Plaintiff gave notice of revocation within a reasonable time. Plaintiff properly relied on defendant's assurances that any defects would be corrected, and on defendant's subsequent efforts to cure. Hemmert promptly discovered the defects and immediately advised Reade of his complaints.

5.   Elements of Revocation Remedy. . . . As discussed more fully later in this order, the primary issue in this case is whether a substantial impairment exists when the plane's handling characteristics create fear and apprehension in the pilot for the first 50 hours of flying during the execution of maneuvers considered normal for other models of Ag–Cat planes. Substantial impairment is not defined in the Uniform Commercial Code. What constitutes a substantial impairment is considered to be a common sense determination. . . . Kansas courts have followed the interpretation of other courts and have given substantial impairment both a subjective and an objective element. [T]he Kansas Supreme Court adopted the two-step inquiry found in Jorgensen v. Pressnall, 274 Ore. 285, 545 P.2d 1382, 1384–1385 (1976), which is:

> Since ORS 72.6080(1) provides that the buyer may revoke acceptance of goods "whose nonconformity substantially impairs its value to him," the value of conforming goods to the plaintiff must first be determined. This is a subjective question in the sense that it calls for a consideration of the needs and circumstances of the plaintiff who seeks to revoke; not the needs and circumstances of an average buyer. The second inquiry is whether the nonconformity in fact substantially impairs the value of the goods to the buyer, having in mind his particular needs. This is an objective question in the sense that it calls for evidence of something more than plaintiff's assertion that the nonconformity impaired the value to him; it requires evidence from which it can be inferred that plaintiff's needs were not met because of the nonconformity. In short, the nonconformity must substantially

impair the value of the goods to the plaintiff buyer. The existence of substantial impairment depends upon the facts and circumstances in each case. (Emphasis in original.) . . .

Leading commentators have noted:

> The only element of objectivity the Jorgensen court required was evidence from which it could be inferred that the buyer's needs were not met because of the nonconformity; that evidence must be something more than the buyer's mere assertion of substantial impairment. The language of cases like Jorgensen, coupled with the subjective phrase "to him" in Section 2–608 and official Comment 2 to that section, gives an aggrieved buyer a strong argument that he has the right to revoke acceptance because of his special sensitivity to the breach of warranty, even though the defects would be considered insubstantial to the average buyer.

Clark and Smith, The Law of Product Warranties, Para. 7.03(3)(a)(1984). While the evidence in this case establishes that not just Hemmert experienced discomfort and fear from the handling characteristics of the Super "B", if Hemmert's sensitivity to the Super "B" had been unique and there had been objective evidence that his needs were not met, revocation would still be consistent with the purpose and interpretation of 2–608. In considering the subjective element, the courts have employed a term, "shaken faith." In determining whether value was substantially impaired, the courts have weighed the cost of repairs, the inconvenience resulting from the nonconformities, and the entire impact the defects had on the buyer's confidence in the goods purchased. Wallach, Buyer's Remedies, 20 Washburn L.J. 20, 34 (1980). Lost confidence has been adopted by a number of courts and labelled as the "shaken faith" doctrine. Where the buyer's confidence in the dependability of the machine is shaken because of the defects and possibly because of seller's ineffective attempts to cure, revocation appears justified. . . .

6. *Nonconformities.* A nonconformity includes breaches of warranties (implied and express) as well as any failure of the seller to perform pursuant to his contractual obligation. . . . An express warranty is created by any representation of fact or promise that relates to the goods and becomes a basis of the bargain. K.S.A. 84–2–313. . . . Advertising may form a part of an express warranty. . . . The advertisement for the 450 "B" . . . closely relates to the plane purchased by plaintiff and was relied upon by plaintiff in his decision to purchase the Super "B". Plaintiff reasonably inferred that the advertising representations for the 450 "B" were applicable to the 600 horsepower version that he purchased. The court finds an express warranty that the Super "B", because of the raised wing design, was more maneuverable and offered better visibility and more speed.

In light of that advertisement and plaintiff's reliance on the same, the court believes that Hemmert did ask Reade if the Super "B" was more maneuverable and faster and that Reade made some representations that assured Hemmert in a reasonable manner that these qualities existed.

Defendant expressly warranted that the Super "B" was more maneuverable and faster than former models of Ag–Cat spray planes.

\* \* \*

7.  Plaintiff has sustained its burden in establishing nonconformities. The handling characteristics which created fear and apprehension in plaintiff and other experienced spray pilots were directly contrary to express representations of maneuverability and speed. There being no question that Mid–Continent is a merchant as defined at K.S.A. 84–2–104(1), the Super "B" is in breach of the implied warranty of merchantability. Plaintiff has proven that the Super "B" it purchased cannot pass without objection to its handling characteristics in normal turning maneuvers in spraying fields. In a trade as hazardous as crop dusting, a pilot would not reasonably accept without objection a plane that takes some 50 hours of flight time before the pilot's unusual fears and concerns about the particular plane are allayed. This conclusion is particularly appropriate where neither the seller nor manufacturer cautions the purchaser that the particular model handles significantly different from other Ag–Cats.

\* \* \*

9.  Substantial Impairment. The relevant law regarding this question has been previously discussed. Plaintiff has proven a substantial impairment. His lost confidence in the Super "B" caused by its handling characteristics, which scare experienced pilots in making normal spraying maneuvers, amounts to a substantial impairment. A spray pilot's activities are considered dangerous in flying at very low altitudes and quickly maneuvering to apply sprays and to avoid obstacles. Undeniably, a spray pilot's confidence in his plane is absolutely crucial. Mr. Dykes' endurance of his "unhappiness" and fear for the first fifty hours of flying the Super "B" does not mean that the same fears and dissatisfaction experienced by Hemmert are not a substantial impairment of value. A pilot's confidence and willingness to undertake dangerous spraying maneuvers in a plane is reasonably destroyed when the pilot consistently experiences the sensation that the plane is about to "fall out from under him" when making normal spraying turns. Similarly, it is unreasonable to expect someone to endure his fears and otherwise operate the plane in his normal spraying business for those fifty hours. A seller's subsequent assurance that the buyer need only modify his flying technique and the sensations will no longer occur is understandably ineffective in rekindling a purchaser's confidence in a plane that he believed would be more maneuverable and faster. These nonconformities substantially impair the value of the Super "B" to plaintiff. The testimony of the four spray pilots and Dykes is evidence other than plaintiff's assertion which sustains an inference that plaintiff's needs are not met by the Super "B".

\* \* \*

11.  Remedy. When a buyer rightfully revokes his acceptance, he may recover pursuant to K.S.A. 84–2–711 a refund of the purchase price paid

and incidental and consequential damages, which may include expenses reasonably incurred in inspection, receipt, transportation and care and custody of goods and any other commercially reasonable charge or expense in effecting cover or caused by delay or other breach. The buyer is also entitled to prejudgment interest from the date that revocation is attempted.

. . .

IT IS THEREFORE ORDERED that judgment is entered in favor of plaintiff and against defendant, and defendant is herein ordered to pay plaintiff the sum of $159,314.14, which are those damages set forth in plaintiff's exhibit 10 modifying the prejudgment interest to commence on September 30, 1985. Upon payment of the entire judgment, plaintiff shall make the Super "B" available upon one week's notice for defendant to pick up the Super "B" at the plaintiff's place of business in Oakley, Kansas.

NOTES

**(1) Substantial Impairment of Value to the Buyer.** Since the right to revoke acceptance under UCC 2–608 is conditioned upon the existence of a non-conformity that substantially impairs the value of the goods to the buyer, there are three steps to the application of this section. Analysis must begin with the criteria of conforming goods. When revocation of acceptance is made on the basis of the quality of the goods, the standard of conformity may be found in express or implied warranties of quality. What warranties of quality did the court find had been breached in *Hemmert Agricultural Aviation*? Was it necessary for the court to cite more than the express warranty?

Analysis must begin with warranties, but UCC 2–608 does not allow a buyer to revoke acceptance for mere breach of warranty. The breach must be of a level of severity, indicated by the substantial impairment term. Did the court in *Hemmert Agricultural Aviation* find, correctly, that the non-conformities in the Super "B" were grave enough to cause substantial impairment of the plane's value? Do the Comments to UCC 2–608 provide any assistance to understanding the meaning of "substantially impairs its value"?

The third element in the analysis is the meaning of the statutory phrase, "to him." The phrase clearly introduces an element of subjectivity to the measurement of the impairment of value. Comment 2 suggests that the legislative intent was to give weight to a buyer's particular circumstances even though the seller did not know of them at the time of the sales contract. Cf. 2–315. How did the court in *Hemmert Agricultural Aviation* deal with the subjective-objective aspect of UCC 2–608 in the context of that case?

**(2) Buyers' Monetary Remedies After Revocation of Acceptance.** UCC 2–608(3) incorporates the "rights" applicable to rejection of goods, which include the right to seek monetary relief. UCC 2–711 allows buyers that justifiably revoke acceptance to recover "so much of the price as has been paid," plus expectation damages under UCC 2–712 or 2–713.[9] These are determined by an actual "cover" transaction or a potential market transaction whereby the buyer obtains or could obtain replacement goods. Both of those provisions allow recovery of incidental and consequential damages under UCC 2–715. Often, it appears, buyers are satisfied to get their money back and be rid of a deal that went bad. Some buyers, however, seek more than recovery of the price. The opinion of the court in *Hemmert Agricultural Aviation* does not recite the elements of buyer's claim for damages, but rather orders that seller pay a substantial sum, in excess of the sales price.

---

*Consequential Damages.* A problem of large importance in sales transactions is the scope of sellers' liability for buyers' consequential damages. The legal issue is related to general contract law growing out of *Hadley v. Baxendale.*[10] The common-law principle is codified in the Code at UCC 2–715(2).

Within the context of sales transactions, buyers may suffer many types of consequential damages resulting from non-conformity of goods purchased. However, certain categories of damages tend to arise regularly. Merchants buying inventory may suffer consequential damages in the form of lost revenues. Such a claim was advanced in *Sidco* and may explain the large amount of the compensatory damages awarded by the trial court in *Royal Business Machines.* Persons buying business equipment may incur expenses coping with the fall-out of the equipment's failure. Such a claim was advanced in *Chatlos.* Farmers buying seeds or herbicides may suffer damages in crop failures.

A quite different set of consequential losses arises when buyers suffer personal injuries as a result of defects in the goods. This branch of warranty law has become integrally related to the law of strict tort liability and other facets of product liability law.

## Carnation Company v. Olivet Egg Ranch

Court of Appeal of California, 1986. First Dist., Div. Two.
189 Cal.App.3d 809, 229 Cal.Rptr. 261.

■ Kline, J.

Olivet Egg Ranch [Olivet] . . . appeal[s] following jury trial on [its] claims of fraud and breach of various warranties arising out of [its]

---

**9.** If the buyer "covers," damages are determined by the reasonable price paid. In other cases, damages are measured by the market value of the goods.

**10.** A remarkable study of *Hadley v. Baxendale* discloses that the case, as decided, was not a contract case. See R. Danzig, *Hadley v. Baxendale*: A Study in the Industrialization of the Law, 4 J. Legal Studies 249 (1975).

purchase and use of chicken feed produced by the Albers Milling Division of the Carnation Company [Albers].

\* \* \*

[Olivet] ... controlled and managed an egg producing operation in Northern California.

For approximately five years, Olivet or its predecessors in interest purchased chickenfeed from Albers, which operated a mill in Santa Rosa. After unsuccessfully seeking payment of its bills, Carnation advised appellants they would no longer be allowed to purchase on credit. Appellants executed a note for the $606,382 balance owed to Carnation. When appellants defaulted on the note Carnation commenced this litigation. Appellants cross-complained on various theories, all premised on their assertion that the feed sold them was 'misformulated, mis-produced and nutritionally substandard' and, therefore, breached a variety of express and implied warranties made to appellants by Carnation and its employees. Appellants alleged that the feed's nutritional deficiencies had caused a decrease in Olivet's egg production revenues and sought to offset such losses against the amount due Carnation on the note.

After lengthy pretrial discovery, jury trial commenced in October 1979. Because the execution and terms of the note were uncontested, appellants proceeded as if plaintiffs and presented their case first. At the conclusion of Olivet's case Carnation successfully moved for nonsuit as to the loss of goodwill portion of Olivet's damage claim. The court granted a nonsuit on goodwill damages as to the breach of warranty causes of action only on the theory appellants had not met their burden of proving, under California Uniform Commercial Code section 2715, that they had made reasonable efforts to mitigate the damages flowing from the loss of their retail egg marketing accounts.

\* \* \*

The jury found that Carnation had breached its warranties and damaged Olivet in the amount of $225,000, but that the claim of fraudulent misrepresentation had not been established.

Separate judgments for both parties were entered and Olivet moved for a new trial on various grounds. ... The court denied the motion for new trial, granted a motion to vacate the two previously entered judgments and ordered nunc pro tunc entry of the net judgment after verdict. This appeal followed.

I.

Burden of Proof Under California Uniform Commercial Code Section 2715, subdivision (2)(a).

The nonsuit as to the $309,000 loss in goodwill appellants claimed due to their inability to service their egg marketing accounts[3] was granted upon the theory that California Uniform Commercial Code section 2715, subdivision (2)(a) places on the aggrieved party the burden of showing it took reasonable steps to mitigate its consequential damages. In granting nonsuit the court necessarily determined that, as a matter of law, Olivet failed to present evidence sufficient to meet its burden. It will be necessary to consider whether Olivet presented evidence sufficient to withstand nonsuit on this issue only if we first determine that the court's imposition of the burden on Olivet was legally correct. Olivet could not be penalized for failing to meet a burden which actually rested with Carnation. Thus, we are squarely faced with a question of first impression in California: which party bears the burden of proving the adequacy or inadequacy of efforts to mitigate consequential damages under California Uniform Commercial Code section 2715, subdivision (2)(a)?

Section 2715, subdivision (2)(a), which was adopted without change from the Uniform Commercial Code (UCC), simply declares that "[c]onsequential damages resulting from the seller's breach include ... [a]ny loss resulting from general or particular requirements and needs of which the seller at the time of contracting had reason to know and which could not reasonably be prevented by cover or otherwise."

The official comment to the parallel provision of the UCC does not shed much light on allocation of the burden of proof. Paragraph 2 of the pertinent UCC comment provides in material part that: "The 'tacit agreement' test for the recovery of consequential damages is rejected. Although the older rule at common law which made the seller liable for all consequential damages of which he had 'reason to know' in advance is followed, the liberality of that rule is modified by refusing to permit recovery unless the buyer could not reasonably have prevented the loss by cover or otherwise. Subparagraph (2) [of the statute] carries forward the provision of the prior uniform statutory provision as to consequential damages resulting from breach of warranty, but modifies the rule by requiring first that the buyer attempt to minimize his damages in good faith, either by cover or otherwise." This comment does not demonstrate, as respondent asserts, that section 2715, subdivision (2)(a) was intended to act as "a restraint on the liberality of the common law."

---

**3.** Olivet had an arrangement with several large supermarket chains pursuant to which the markets invested in the ranch partnership and purchased all of their requirements directly from the ranch at a retail price. Olivet was thereby provided with an assured outlet for its eggs and was to derive a profit for the processing and marketing, as well as the egg sale. Due to Olivet's shortfall in egg production, it ultimately was unable to keep up with the requirements of its market accounts and Olivet transferred the accounts to Olson Egg Farms. Appellants claimed the loss of the goodwill value of the retail marketing arm of its operation as an additional element of damages.

The nonsuit was granted only as to the loss of goodwill attributable to the claimed breach of warranty. Because the burden of proof on mitigation as to the fraud cause of action is on the party asserting the defense, the court ruled that the issue remained in the case as to that claim.

Paragraph 4 of the UCC comment makes specific reference to the UCC's section on the liberal administration of remedies, indicating that the right to consequential damages should be broadly, not narrowly, construed. Furthermore, while paragraph 4 states that "[t]he burden of proving the extent of loss incurred by way of consequential damage is on the buyer ..." this statement does not determine the allocation of the burden of proof on the mitigation issue. It is entirely possible for the injured party to bear the burden of proving the extent of consequential damages while the breaching party has the duty of proving those items which limit the award of consequential damages.

The UCC's failure to allocate unambiguously the burden of proving mitigation has resulted in conflicting interpretations among those jurisdictions that have considered the question. Unfortunately, these cases are of little value to us since they do not analyze the problem nor explain why the burden should rest with one party or the other. By and large the cases merely state the unembellished conclusion that one or the other party has the burden of proof on this issue.

\* \* \*

While the commentators do not unanimously support allocating the burden to the breaching party, there is substantial support among them for this position. Corbin, for example, declares that "[t]he burden of proving that losses could have been avoided by reasonable effort and expense must always be borne by the party who has broken the contract." (5 Corbin on Contracts (1964) § 1039 ...) White and Summers state that "consequential damages that the *defendant* proves the buyer could have avoided will not be allowed ..." (J. White and R. Summers, Uniform Commercial Code (2d ed. 1980) §§ 6–7, p. 250, italics added.) ...

Placing on the party who breaches the burden of showing that consequential losses could have been avoided is intuitively attractive, since proof that there has been a failure to mitigate adequately will reduce the damages awarded and, therefore, seems more in the nature of a defense than an element of the plaintiff's affirmative case. In this sense, proof of failure to mitigate is analogous to evidence showing comparative negligence in tort law, which must be alleged and proved by the defendant. ... Moreover, it is sensible to require the defendant to prove those items which go to reduce the plaintiff's recovery, as plaintiffs would have little incentive to do so.

Respondent maintains that "[i]t makes more sense to place the burden of proving efforts to mitigate on the party best able to adduce evidence of such efforts." While this argument is on its surface appealing it does not stand up to closer scrutiny. As has been noted "[v]ery often one must plead and prove matters as to which his adversary has superior access to the proof. Nearly all required allegations of the plaintiff in actions for tort or breach of contract relating to the defendant's acts or omissions describe matters peculiarly in the defendant's knowledge. Correspondingly, when the defendant is required to plead contributory negligence, he pleads facts specially known to the plaintiff.'' (McCormick on Evidence (3d ed. 1984) ch. 36, § 337 at p. 950.)

Moreover, in cases such as this defendants do not genuinely lack the ability to ascertain the pertinent facts. A carefully drafted set of interrogatories could have provided Carnation with all the information it required about Olivet's efforts to mitigate its consequential damages. Since it therefore had access to the relevant evidence we see no reason why this consideration should prevent allocation to Carnation of the burden of showing that appellants failed to adequately mitigate their consequential damages.

For the foregoing reasons, we hold that while the burden of proving the extent of loss incurred by way of consequential damages rests with the injured party, section 2715, subdivision (2)(a) imposes upon the allegedly breaching party the burden of proving the inadequacy of efforts to mitigate consequential damages. Thus, Carnation, not Olivet, properly had the burden of proof on the issue of Olivet's mitigation of the consequential damages arising from Carnation's breach. Olivet therefore had no duty to present evidence of mitigation and the granting of the nonsuit on the basis of Olivet's asserted failure to produce such evidence was error. The nonsuit removed from the jury's consideration a $309,000 damage claim. Since Carnation never presented evidence on this issue there is no way of knowing whether appellants likely would have prevailed if the court had placed the burden of proof on Carnation. Accordingly, the judgment must be reversed.

\* \* \*

■ Rouse, J., and Smith, J., concurred.

## NOTES

**(1) Loss of Revenue.** Buyers that are not end users of the goods they purchase are typically business entities that intend either to resell the goods, i.e., they are middlemen in a distribution chain, or to use the purchased goods to produce their own product or service. Quality problems with the goods may defeat the buyers' intentions, with the consequence that their revenues are less than they would have been if the goods had been of the warranted quality. Loss of revenue is a common consequential damage claimed in contracts of this kind. The opinion in this case mentions that the buyer made a claim for lost revenue, but that claim was not an issue in the appeal. How should a claim for lost revenue be valued? The question poses a counterfactual inquiry, what revenues might have been obtained by a buyer. How can this be measured? UCC 2–715(2) does not specify. Comment 4 provides that the section rejects a ''doctrine of certainty which requires almost mathematical precision in the proof of loss.'' Does the text of UCC 2–715(2) support this Comment?

Should an aggrieved buyer be entitled to the gross amount of lost revenue or to something less? What deductions or offsets should be taken into account? Any business enterprise incurs costs in generating revenues. In a situation of lost revenue, some of those costs may not be incurred. A fundamental principle of the law of contract remedies disallows recovery for harms that might have been avoided. This principle of mitigation is reflected in UCC 2–715(2)(a), which disallows recovery for a loss that could reasonably be prevented.

**(2) Loss of Goodwill.** The primary claim contested in this case was for loss of good will. What was the nature of the claim? The court refers to the buyer's loss of retail egg accounts. Would loss of these accounts result in loss of revenue? What is different if the loss is characterized as the loss as of "good will"? See footnote 3 of the court's opinion.

**(3) Mitigation of Damages; Burden of Proof.** The dispositive issue on appeal was the allocation of the burden of proving what action the buyer might have taken to mitigate the loss of good will. As the court finds, neither the text nor the comments to UCC 2–715 specify whether this is a part of the claimant's case in chief or is an affirmative defense. On what basis did the court determine how to allocate the burden in this case? Was the court's decision sound?

## (B) INTERNATIONAL SALES LAW

### 1. QUALITY OBLIGATIONS UNDER CISG

#### a. *SELLERS' OBLIGATIONS*

The Convention sets forth sellers' quality obligations in Section II of Chapter II. The primary standards, in CISG 35, resemble the warranty provisions of the UCC, but there are substantial differences. CISG does not use the term "warranty" and does not divide sellers' quality obligations into "types." CISG does not differentiate between express warranties and implied warranties. Compare carefully the provisions in CISG 35(2) with their counterparts in the various quality warranties in the UCC. Consider also the UCC provisions for which no explicit counterparts exist in CISG. What conclusions can be drawn from these comparisons? Are the quality obligations of sellers under CISG greater or less than their obligations under the UCC?

#### b. *BUYERS' REMEDIES*

Buyers' remedies under CISG are stated broadly in CISG 45, which cross refers to Articles 46 to 52 and 74 to 77. The latter set of articles deals with monetary damages recoverable for breach. Two of these, CISG 74 and 77 apply to cases in which sellers have breached the CISG 35 obligations of quality but the goods are nonetheless retained by the buyers. CISG allows some aggrieved buyers to require sellers to take back nonconforming goods. The power is termed the power to "avoid" a contract. That power is provided under CISG 49(1)(a), which deals with circumstances in which a seller's breach of contract is "fundamental." "Fundamental breach" is defined in CISG 25. Damages allowed when buyers properly avoid contracts under CISG 49(1)(a) are determined by CISG 75 to 77.

We consider first buyers' remedies when contracts are not avoided. The basic formula for measurement of damages is found in the first sentence of CISG 74. Unlike UCC Article 2 which deals separately with buyers' damages and sellers' damages, CISG 74 is a general provision that applies to both buyers' and sellers' damages. Therefore, in proceedings involving claims that sellers have breached the quality obligations of CISG 35, buyers' basic damages would be determined by CISG 74. How does this formula compare with UCC 2–714? What is the meaning of "loss ... suffered" by a buyer in the context of a claim for breach of CISG 35? Does this permit a buyer to recover damages determined by the value the goods would have had if they had been conforming, the "benefit of the bargain" principle that undergirds UCC 2–714?

"Loss suffered" is undoubtedly broad enough to include buyers' losses that common law and the UCC Article 2 characterize as consequential damages. Like the UCC, CISG limits sellers' liability for consequential damages. That limitation is found the second sentence of CISG 74. How does this limitation compare with UCC 2–715(2)? CISG has no express provision for recovery of damages characterized by common law and the UCC Article 2 as incidental damages, but, again, "loss suffered" undoubtedly broad enough to include such losses.

Buyers's damages after avoidance of sales contracts are provided by CISG 75–76. These articles deal with the possibility and the reality of buyers' entering into substitute transactions. If a buyer contracts to buy replacement goods, "cover" in UCC Article 2, buyer's basic damages are measured by the difference between the price in the substitute transaction and the contract price, CISG 75. That article adds that buyers are also entitled to any further damages recoverable under CISG 74. If a buyer has not made a purchase under CISG 75, damages are measured by the "current price" for the goods. CISG 76(1).[11] Again buyers may recover further damages under CISG 74.

UCC Article 2 lacks a general provision limiting damages for losses that aggrieved parties might have prevented from occurring, the principle of mitigation of damages. The mitigation principle is included in the Code's criteria for recovery of consequential damages, UCC 2–715(2), the section litigated in *Carnation Co. v. Olivet Egg Ranch*. The Convention has a broadly applicable rule that limits all damages that may be sought. CISG 77.

### c. OTHER "FIELDS" OF LAW

The Convention (CISG 4) "governs only" the "obligations of the seller and the buyer arising from [the international sales] contract." Does CISG displace rules of law that deal with defective goods under rubrics other than "contract"? To what extent is an international sales contract subject to law of fraud, misrepresentation or mistake, like those referred to earlier

---

**11.** "Current price" is the price prevailing at the place where delivery of the goods should have been made or, absent such price, at another place that is a reasonable substitute. CISG 76(2).

in United States law? Consider CISG 4(a). What issues are excluded from CISG as going to the "validity of the contract"? The problems regarding the relationship between the Convention and domestic law are important and difficult. See J. Honnold, Uniform Law for International Sales §§ 64–67, 238–240 (3d ed. 1999).

# Schmitz–Werke Gmbh & Co. v. Rockland Industries, Inc.

United States Court of Appeals, Fourth Circuit, 2002.
37 Fed. Appx. 687.

■ PER CURIAM.

On December 30, 1997, Plaintiff–Appellee Schmitz–Werke (Schmitz) filed a complaint in the United States District Court for the District of Maryland alleging that Defendant–Appellant Rockland International (Rockland) had breached a warranty under the United Nations Convention on the International Sale of Goods (CISG), ... by supplying defective drapery fabric. ... A bench trial took place from October 25 through 28, 1999, and on November 5, 1999, the district court found for Schmitz and orally issued on the record its findings of fact and conclusions of law. Judgment was entered in favor of Schmitz on its claim ... on December 30, 1999. ... Rockland now appeals that portion of the court's judgment in favor of Schmitz. We affirm the judgment of the district court.

## FACTS AND PROCEEDINGS BELOW

Rockland is a Maryland corporation that manufactures drapery lining fabric. In the early to mid 1990s, Rockland manufactured a type of drapery fabric called Trevira Blackout FR (Trevira). "Blackout" refers to the fabric's ability to block light completely. The fabric was manufactured to meet European flame resistance standards, and was intended for sale in European markets. Rockland no longer manufactures this fabric, and claims that this is because the product did not meet its volume requirements, while Schmitz maintains that Rockland discontinued Trevira because of numerous problems with the material.

Schmitz is a German company that manufactures, prints, and sells finished decorative fabrics in Germany and in other countries. In 1993, a Rockland representative introduced the Trevira fabric to Schmitz, and during their negotiations Rockland's representatives stated that the fabric was particularly suited to be a printing base for transfer printing. Transfer printing is a process for imprinting the base fabric with dyes of particular colors or patterns. In transfer printing, the fabric is drawn over a heated metal cylinder along with a sheet of transfer paper that contains the dye. The dye is heated by the cylinder and turns into a gas, which is picked up by the fibers in the fabric. Schmitz does not transfer print its fabrics itself. Instead, it relies on another German company, PMD, which specializes in making transfer print paper and in transfer printing fabrics.

Schmitz initially placed an order for about 200 meters of the Rockland fabric for testing. The sample was shipped to PMD, which transfer printed it. On receipt of the test results, Schmitz notified Rockland that there were several problems with the fabric but that in general they were satisfied with the material. After this test, Schmitz placed an initial order of 15,000 meters of Trevira, which was shipped via ocean freight in mid-August 1994. Schmitz noted some additional problems with this initial shipment, but decided to go ahead and print the material. After the printing, additional problems with the fabric became apparent, and a Rockland representative was offered a chance to inspect the fabric. There was conflicting testimony at trial about the results of a meeting between Schmitz and Rockland's representative that followed in October of 1994, but the district court credited Schmitz' version of events. According to Schmitz, despite some problems with the Trevira fabric, Rockland urged Schmitz to continue printing the fabric, and claimed that the lower quality portions of the Trevira fabric could successfully be transfer printed with patterns (as opposed to being printed with solid colors). In November 1994, after this meeting, Schmitz placed another order of Trevira fabric, this time for 60,000 meters.

PMD, meanwhile, was continuing to print the original shipment of the fabric. In December 1994, PMD told Schmitz about some of the problems it observed with the fabric. In February 1995, Schmitz had WKS, another German company, inspect part of the new order that Rockland had sent as part of the November 1994 order. On March 20, 1995, WKS issued its report, which indicated that it had found some problems with the Trevira fabric. By April of 1995, the post-printing percentage of fabric that was classified as "seconds" (lower-grade material) was between 15% and 20%.

On June 21, 1995, Schmitz contacted Rockland and indicated that they wanted to return approximately 8,000 meters of fabric, and eventually Schmitz shipped that amount back to Rockland. There were extended discussions between Rockland and Schmitz about how to settle this dispute, but eventually these discussions broke down and this suit followed.

After a bench trial, the district court issued its findings of fact and conclusions of law in an oral opinion on November 5, 1999. The parties agreed that the CISG governed the transaction in this case, although the correct interpretation of that treaty was (and still is) in dispute. The district court found that Rockland gave Schmitz a warranty of fitness for a particular purpose (transfer printing) under Article 35(2)(b) of the CISG. ... The court also found that the Trevira fabric sold by Rockland had latent defects which were not detectable before the fabric was transfer printed, and that Schmitz' continued printing of the fabric even after it began to discover problems was reasonable since it was at the express urging of Rockland, and was in any event the best way to mitigate its damages. ... The court specifically held that the goods did not conform to the warranty Rockland had given Schmitz, and that Schmitz had met its burden of proving that the defect existed at the time the fabric left Rockland's plant.... In making this ruling, the court held that Schmitz need not prove the exact mechanism of the defect, and that showing that the transfer printing process PMD had used on the fabric was ordinary and competent was enough to establish that the Trevira fabric was unfit for the purpose of transfer printing. . . . Rockland now appeals.

## DISCUSSION

\* \* \*

Both parties agree that this case is governed by the CISG, but there is some disagreement concerning how this Court should interpret that treaty. Case law interpreting the CISG is rather sparse. . . . When two nations are signatories to the CISG, the treaty governs contracts for the sale of goods between parties whose places of business are in those two nations, unless the contract contains a choice of law clause. . . . Courts interpreting the CISG should look to the language of the CISG and to the general principles on which the Convention is based. . . . The CISG directs that "its interpretation be informed by its 'international character and . . . the need to promote uniformity in its application and the observance of good faith in international trade.' " . . . Case law interpreting provisions of Article 2 of the Uniform Commercial Code that are similar to provisions in the CISG can also be helpful in interpreting the convention. . . .

Rockland claims that the law of Maryland also governs this case. The CISG provides that private international law is the default law to apply to a question governed by the Convention that is not settled under its own terms. . . . The parties agree that private international law would apply the choice of law rules of the forum state (Maryland), which in this case would choose to apply the law of the contracting state. . . . However, a court should only reach private international law if the CISG's text, interpreted in conformity with the general principles on which the CISG is based, does not settle the issue at hand. . . . Schmitz agrees that Maryland law applies to issues on which the CISG is silent, but notes that Maryland law should not be reached unless the CISG fails to provide a resolution of the issue.

## CAUSATION

Rockland argues that Schmitz must demonstrate both the existence and the nature of the defect in the fabric before it can recover for breach of warranty § and that to show the nature of that defect, expert testimony is required. Article 35 of the CISG governs the duty of the seller to deliver goods that conform with the contract. Article 35(2) lists various reasons goods may not conform with the contract, including goods which were expressly or impliedly warranted to be fit for a particular purpose. In response, Schmitz argues that all it need show is that the goods were unfit for the particular purpose warranted—transfer printing—and that it need not show precisely why or how the goods were unfit if it can show that the transfer printing process the goods underwent was performed competently and normally. Rockland is correct that Schmitz did not provide any evidence at trial that would establish the exact nature of the defect in the Trevira fabric. The text of the CISG is silent on this matter. . . .

Under Maryland law, Rockland is correct that a plaintiff in a products liability case must show that the product in question is defective, even if the cause of action is for breach of an express or implied warranty. ... However, Rockland's resort to Maryland law does not aid its argument—there is no support in Maryland law for Rockland's claim that the plaintiff in such a case must *always* provide expert testimony describing the exact nature of the defect. The district court in this case did not rule that expert testimony was not required to show the nature of the problem with the Trevira fabric. Instead, the district court held that since Schmitz had submitted sufficient evidence of the competence of PMD's transfer printing process, it was proper to infer that the fabric was not suited for that process, even without direct evidence of the precise nature of the fabric's unsuitability. Schmitz argues that since it did submit expert testimony regarding the transfer printing process, even if such testimony is required, Schmitz has satisfied its burden, and the district court's ruling in their favor is supported by the evidence. We agree with Schmitz.

Under either the CISG or Maryland law, Schmitz may prevail on a claim that the fabric was unfit for the purpose for which it was expressly warranted (transfer printing) by showing that when the fabric was properly used for the purpose Rockland warranted, the results were shoddy—even if Schmitz has introduced no evidence as to just *why* or how the fabric was unfit. Schmitz has shown that the fabric was defective—the fabric's defect was that it was unfit for transfer printing. Rockland attempts to counter this argument by claiming that this improperly shifts the burden of proof. Rockland's concerns are misplaced—Schmitz still must prove that the transfer printing process was ordinary and competently performed, and still must prove that the fabric was defective—it just permits Schmitz to do so without proving the exact nature of the defect.

There was significant evidence regarding PMD's transfer printing process presented at trial (including expert testimony), and the court's finding that the PMD printing process was ordinary and competent is not clearly erroneous. The district court found that Rockland warranted its fabric to be fit for transfer printing, that the fabric was transfer printed in a normal and competent way, and that the resulting printed fabric was unsatisfactory. This is enough to support the district court's factual finding in favor of Schmitz on the warranty claim—the fabric was not fit for the purpose for which it was warranted. The district court's findings as to defect in this respect are not clearly erroneous; nor did the district court err in law in regard thereto.

### RELIANCE

Rockland also argues that even if the court properly found that the Trevira fabric was not particularly well suited for transfer printing as warranted, Schmitz cannot recover on such a warranty because it did not in fact rely on Rockland's advice as required under CISG Article 35(2)(b). Rockland is correct that Article 35(2)(b) of the CISG requires that the buyer reasonably rely on the representations of the seller before liability attaches for breach of a warranty for fitness for a particular purpose. . . . The district court explicitly found that Schmitz relied on the statements of Rockland's representative that the Trevira fabric was particularly well suited for transfer printing. The court also found that Schmitz continued to print the fabric with the express consent of Rockland after it discovered and reported problems with the fabric. The district court's finding that Schmitz relied on Rockland's statements proclaiming the Trevira fabric's suitability for transfer printing is supported by the evidence and was not clearly erroneous.

* * *

CONCLUSION

Accordingly, the judgment of the district court is *AFFIRMED*.

## NOTES

**(1) Interpretation of CISG 35.** The Convention does not use the terms like "express warranty" or "implied warranty." Nonetheless, the advocates and the courts imported these UCC terms into their CISG analysis. The claim was characterized as breach of a "warranty of fitness for particular purpose." What might explain the use of terms not found anywhere in the Convention? Is this a proper way to construe CISG? See L. DiMatteo et al., The Interpretive Turn in International Sales Law: An Analysis of Fifteen Years of CISG Jurisprudence, 24 Nw. J. Int'l L. & Bus. 299 (2004) (discussing the tendency of national courts to ignore the CISG 7(1) mandate on the manner of interpreting the CISG and rather to give a domestic gloss to their readings of CISG provisions). The authors declared that the Fourth Circuit "disregarded CISG interpretive methodology and resorted to a *homeward trend* analysis. The court cited only U.S. cases and ignored other court or arbitral decisions and scholarly commentaries on the CISG." Id. at 398.

**(2) Application of CISG 35.** The decision discusses a number of specific issues that may arise in disputes over sellers' obligations of quality. The court decided the case under CISG 35(2)(b). Was that the most appropriate basis for decision on the facts? Could the case have been based entirely on CISG 35(1)? Is CISG 35(1) more than a chapeau to CISG 35(2)? Where does CISG 35 deal with obligations that arise merely from seller's affirmations of fact regarding the goods?

Without discussion, the court declared that the buyer had the burden of proving seller's breach. Does CISG 35 allocate the burden of proof? Does the formulation of CISG 35(2)(b) implicitly assign the burden of proof on the issue of buyer's reliance on the seller's skill and judgment?

Counsel for the seller contended that the buyer had not met its burden of proof because it had provided no evidence of the "nature of the defect in the fabric." Counsel for the buyer argued that it had no such burden. The court found that "the text of the CISG is silent on this matter" and resorted to domestic Maryland law. Is CISG 35 silent? Was the court's analysis of the issue of "defect" sound?

# Delchi Carrier SpA v. Rotorex Corp.

United States Court of Appeals for the Second Circuit, 1995.
71 F.3d 1024.

■ WINTER, CIRCUIT JUDGE:

Rotorex Corporation, a New York corporation, appeals from a judgment of $1,785,772.44 in damages for lost profits and other consequential damages awarded to Delchi Carrier SpA following a bench trial before Judge Munson. The basis for the award was Rotorex's delivery of nonconforming compressors to Delchi, an Italian manufacturer of air conditioners. Delchi cross-appeals from the denial of certain incidental and consequential damages. We affirm the award of damages; we reverse in part on Delchi's cross-appeal and remand for further proceedings.

## BACKGROUND

In January 1988, Rotorex agreed to sell 10,800 compressors to Delchi for use in Delchi's "Ariele" line of portable room air conditioners. The air conditioners were scheduled to go on sale in the spring and summer of 1988. Prior to executing the contract, Rotorex sent Delchi a sample compressor and accompanying written performance specifications. The compressors were scheduled to be delivered in three shipments before May 15, 1988.

Rotorex sent the first shipment by sea on March 26. Delchi paid for this shipment, which arrived at its Italian factory on April 20, by letter of credit. Rotorex sent a second shipment of compressors on or about May 9. Delchi also remitted payment for this shipment by letter of credit. While the second shipment was en route, Delchi discovered that the first lot of compressors did not conform to the sample model and accompanying specifications. On May 13, after a Rotorex representative visited the Delchi factory in Italy, Delchi informed Rotorex that 93 percent of the compressors were rejected in quality control checks because they had lower cooling capacity and consumed more power than the sample model and specifications. After several unsuccessful attempts to cure the defects in the compressors, Delchi asked Rotorex to supply new compressors conforming to the original sample and specifications. Rotorex refused, claiming that the performance specifications were "inadvertently communicated" to Delchi.

In a faxed letter dated May 23, 1988, Delchi cancelled the contract. Although it was able to expedite a previously planned order of suitable compressors from Sanyo, another supplier, Delchi was unable to obtain in a timely fashion substitute compressors from other sources and thus suffered a loss in its sales volume of Arieles during the 1988 selling season. Delchi filed the instant action under the United Nations Convention on Contracts for the International Sale of Goods ("CISG" or "the Convention") for breach of contract and failure to deliver conforming goods. On January 10,

1991, Judge Cholakis granted Delchi's motion for partial summary judgment, holding Rotorex liable for breach of contract.

After three years of discovery and a bench trial on the issue of damages, Judge Munson, to whom the case had been transferred, held Rotorex liable to Delchi for $1,248,331.87. This amount included consequential damages for: (I) lost profits resulting from a diminished sales level of Ariele units, (ii) expenses that Delchi incurred in attempting to remedy the nonconformity of the compressors, (iii) the cost of expediting shipment of previously ordered Sanyo compressors after Delchi rejected the Rotorex compressors, and (iv) costs of handling and storing the rejected compressors. The district court also awarded prejudgment interest under CISG art. 78.

The court denied Delchi's claim for damages based on other expenses, including: (I) shipping, customs, and incidentals relating to the two shipments of Rotorex compressors; (ii) the cost of obsolete insulation and tubing that Delchi purchased only for use with Rotorex compressors; (iii) the cost of obsolete tooling purchased only for production of units with Rotorex compressors; and (iv) labor costs for four days when Delchi's production line was idle because it had no compressors to install in the air conditioning units. The court denied an award for these items on the ground that it would lead to a double recovery because "those costs are accounted for in Delchi's recovery on its lost profits claim." It also denied an award for the cost of modification of electrical panels for use with substitute Sanyo compressors on the ground that the cost was not attributable to the breach. Finally, the court denied recovery on Delchi's claim of 4000 additional lost sales in Italy.

On appeal, Rotorex argues that it did not breach the agreement, that Delchi is not entitled to lost profits because it maintained inventory levels in excess of the maximum number of possible lost sales, that the calculation of the number of lost sales was improper, and that the district court improperly excluded fixed costs and depreciation from the manufacturing cost in calculating lost profits. Delchi cross-appeals, claiming that it is entitled to the additional out-of-pocket expenses and the lost profits on additional sales denied by Judge Munson.

## DISCUSSION

The district court held, and the parties agree, that the instant matter is governed by the CISG, *reprinted at* 15 U.S.C.A. Appendix (West Supp. 1995), a self-executing agreement between the United States and other signatories, including Italy.[1] Because there is virtually no caselaw under the Convention, we look to its language and to "the general principles" upon

---

**1.** Generally, the CISG governs sales contracts between parties from different signatory countries. However, the Convention makes clear that the parties may by contract choose to be bound by a source of law other than the CISG, such as the Uniform Commercial Code. See CISG art. 6 ("The parties may exclude the application of this Convention or ... derogate from or vary the effect of any of its provisions.") If, as here, the agreement is silent as to choice of law, the Convention applies if both parties are located in signatory nations. See CISG art. 1.

which it is based. *See* CISG art. 7(2). The Convention directs that its interpretation be informed by its "international character and . . . the need to promote uniformity in its application and the observance of good faith in international trade." *See* CISG art. 7(1); see generally John Honnold, Uniform Law for International Sales Under the 1980 United Nations Convention 60–62 (2d ed. 1991) (addressing principles for interpretation of CISG). Caselaw interpreting analogous provisions of Article 2 of the Uniform Commercial Code ("UCC"), may also inform a court where the language of the relevant CISG provisions tracks that of the UCC. However, UCC caselaw "is not *per se* applicable." Orbisphere Corp. v. United States, 13 C.I.T. 866, 726 F. Supp. 1344, 1355 (Ct. Int'l Trade 1989).

We first address the liability issue. We review a grant of summary judgment de novo. . . .

Under the CISG, "the seller must deliver goods which are of the quantity, quality and description required by the contract," and "the goods do not conform with the contract unless they . . . possess the qualities of goods which the seller has held out to the buyer as a sample or model." CISG art. 35. The CISG further states that "the seller is liable in accordance with the contract and this Convention for any lack of conformity." CISG art. 36.

Judge Cholakis held that "there is no question that [Rotorex's] compressors did not conform to the terms of the contract between the parties" and noted that "there are ample admissions [by Rotorex] to that effect." We agree. The agreement between Delchi and Rotorex was based upon a sample compressor supplied by Rotorex and upon written specifications regarding cooling capacity and power consumption. After the problems were discovered, Rotorex's engineering representative, Ernest Gamache, admitted in a May 13, 1988 letter that the specification sheet was "in error" and that the compressors would actually generate less cooling power and consume more energy than the specifications indicated. Gamache also testified in a deposition that at least some of the compressors were nonconforming. The president of Rotorex, John McFee, conceded in a May 17, 1988 letter to Delchi that the compressors supplied were less efficient than the sample and did not meet the specifications provided by Rotorex. Finally, in its answer to Delchi's complaint, Rotorex admitted "that some of the compressors . . . did not conform to the nominal performance information." There was thus no genuine issue of material fact regarding liability, and summary judgment was proper. . . .

Under the CISG, if the breach is "fundamental" the buyer may either require delivery of substitute goods, CISG art. 46, or declare the contract void, CISG art. 49, and seek damages. With regard to what kind of breach is fundamental, Article 25 provides:

> A breach of contract committed by one of the parties is fundamental if it results in such detriment to the other party as substantially to deprive him of what he is entitled to expect under the contract, unless the party in breach did not foresee and a reasonable person of the same kind in the same circumstances would not have foreseen such a result.

CISG art. 25. In granting summary judgment, the district court held that "there appears to be no question that [Delchi] did not substantially receive that which [it] was entitled to expect" and that "any reasonable person could foresee that shipping non-conforming goods to a buyer would result in the buyer not receiving that which he expected and was entitled to receive." Because the cooling power and energy consumption of an air conditioner compressor are important determinants of the product's value, the district court's conclusion that Rotorex was liable for a fundamental breach of contract under the Convention was proper.

We turn now to the district court's award of damages following the bench trial. A reviewing court must defer to the trial judge's findings of fact unless they are clearly erroneous. . . . However, we review questions of law, including "the measure of damages upon which the factual computation is based," de novo. . . .

The CISG provides:

> Damages for breach of contract by one party consist of a sum equal to the loss, including loss of profit, suffered by the other party as a consequence of the breach. Such damages may not exceed the loss which the party in breach foresaw or ought to have foreseen at the time of the conclusion of the contract, in the light of the facts and matters of which he then knew or ought to have known, as a possible consequence of the breach of contract.

CISG art. 74. This provision is "designed to place the aggrieved party in as good a position as if the other party had properly performed the contract." Honnold, supra, at 503.

Rotorex argues that Delchi is not entitled to lost profits because it was able to maintain inventory levels of Ariele air conditioning units in excess of the maximum number of possible lost sales. In Rotorex's view, therefore, there was no actual shortfall of Ariele units available for sale because of Rotorex's delivery of nonconforming compressors. Rotorex's argument goes as follows. The end of the air conditioner selling season is August 1. If one totals the number of units available to Delchi from March to August 1, the sum is enough to fill all sales. We may assume that the evidence in the record supports the factual premise. Nevertheless, the argument is fallacious. Because of Rotorex's breach, Delchi had to shut down its manufacturing operation for a few days in May, and the date on which particular units were available for sale was substantially delayed. For example, units available in late July could not be used to meet orders in the spring. As a result, Delchi lost sales in the spring and early summer. We therefore conclude that the district court's findings regarding lost sales are not clearly erroneous. A detailed discussion of the precise number of lost sales is unnecessary because the district court's findings were, if anything, conservative.

Rotorex contends, in the alternative, that the district court improperly awarded lost profits for unfilled orders from Delchi affiliates in Europe and from sales agents within Italy. We disagree. The CISG requires that damages be limited by the familiar principle of foreseeability established in *Hadley v. Baxendale*, 156 Eng. Rep. 145 (1854). CISG art. 74. However, it was objectively foreseeable that Delchi would take orders for Ariele sales based on the number of compressors it had ordered and expected to have ready for the season. The district court was entitled to rely upon the documents and testimony regarding these lost sales and was well within its authority in deciding which orders were proven with sufficient certainty.

Rotorex also challenges the district court's exclusion of fixed costs and depreciation from the manufacturing cost used to calculate lost profits. The trial judge calculated lost profits by subtracting the 478,783 lire "manufacturing cost"—the total variable cost—of an Ariele unit from the 654,644 lire average sale price. The CISG does not explicitly state whether only variable expenses, or both fixed and variable expenses, should be subtracted from sales revenue in calculating lost profits. However, courts generally do not include fixed costs in the calculation of lost profits. See Indu Craft, Inc. v. Bank of Baroda, 47 F.3d 490, 495 (2d Cir.1995) (only when the breach ends an ongoing business should fixed costs be subtracted along with variable costs); Adams v. Lindblad Travel, Inc., 730 F.2d 89, 92–93 (2d Cir.1984) (fixed costs should not be included in lost profits equation when the plaintiff is an ongoing business whose fixed costs are not affected by the breach). This is, of course, because the fixed costs would have been encountered whether or not the breach occurred. In the absence of a specific provision in the CISG for calculating lost profits, the district court was correct to use the standard formula employed by most American courts and to deduct only variable costs from sales revenue to arrive at a figure for lost profits.

In its cross-appeal, Delchi challenges the district court's denial of various consequential and incidental damages, including reimbursement for: (I) shipping, customs, and incidentals relating to the first and second shipments—rejected and returned—of Rotorex compressors; (ii) obsolete insulation materials and tubing purchased for use only with Rotorex compressors; (iii) obsolete tooling purchased exclusively for production of units with Rotorex compressors; and (iv) labor costs for the period of May 16–19, 1988, when the Delchi production line was idle due to a lack of compressors to install in Ariele air conditioning units. The district court denied damages for these items on the ground that they "are accounted for in Delchi's recovery on its lost profits claim," and, therefore, an award would constitute a double recovery for Delchi. We disagree.

The Convention provides that a contract plaintiff may collect damages to compensate for the full loss. This includes, but is not limited to, lost profits, subject only to the familiar limitation that the breaching party must have foreseen, or should have foreseen, the loss as a probable consequence. CISG art. 74; see *Hadley v. Baxendale*, supra.

An award for lost profits will not compensate Delchi for the expenses in question. Delchi's lost profits are determined by calculating the hypothetical revenues to be derived from unmade sales less the hypothetical variable costs that would have been, but were not, incurred. This figure, however, does not compensate for costs actually incurred that led to no sales. Thus, to award damages for costs actually incurred in no way creates a double recovery and instead furthers the purpose of giving the injured party damages "equal to the loss." CISG art. 74.

The only remaining inquiries, therefore, are whether the expenses were reasonably foreseeable and legitimate incidental or consequential damages.[2] The expenses incurred by Delchi for shipping, customs, and related matters for the two returned shipments of Rotorex compressors, including storage expenses for the second shipment at Genoa, were clearly foreseeable and recoverable incidental expenses. These are up-front expenses that had to be paid to get the goods to the manufacturing plant for inspection and were thus incurred largely before the nonconformities were detected. To deny reimbursement to Delchi for these incidental damages would effectively cut into the lost profits award. The same is true of unreimbursed tooling expenses and the cost of the useless insulation and tubing materials. These are legitimate consequential damages that in no way duplicate lost profits damages.

The labor expense incurred as a result of the production line shutdown of May 16–19, 1988 is also a reasonably foreseeable result of delivering nonconforming compressors for installation in air conditioners. However, Rotorex argues that the labor costs in question were fixed costs that would have been incurred whether or not there was a breach. The district court labeled the labor costs "fixed costs," but did not explore whether Delchi would have paid these wages regardless of how much it produced. Variable costs are generally those costs that "fluctuate with a firm's output," and typically include labor (but not management) costs. ... Whether Delchi's labor costs during this four-day period are variable or fixed costs is in large measure a fact question that we cannot answer because we lack factual findings by the district court. We therefore remand to the district court on this issue.

The district court also denied an award for the modification of electrical panels for use with substitute Sanyo compressors. It denied damages on the ground that Delchi failed to show that the modifications were not part of the regular cost of production of units with Sanyo compressors and were therefore attributable to Rotorex's breach. This appears to have been a credibility determination that was within the court's authority to make. We therefore affirm on the ground that this finding is not clearly erroneous.

Finally, Delchi cross-appeals from the denial of its claimed 4000 additional lost sales in Italy. The district court held that Delchi did not

---

**2.** The UCC defines incidental damages resulting from a seller's breach as "expenses reasonably incurred in inspection, receipt, transportation and care and custody of goods rightfully rejected, any commercially reasonable charges, expenses or commissions in connection with effecting cover and any other reasonable expense incident to the delay or other breach." U.C.C. § 2–715(1) (1990). It defines consequential damages resulting from a seller's breach to include "any loss resulting from general or particular requirements and needs of which the seller at the time of contracting had reason to know and which could not reasonably be prevented by cover or otherwise." U.C.C. § 2–715(2)(a).

prove these orders with sufficient certainty. The trial court was in the best position to evaluate the testimony of the Italian sales agents who stated that they would have ordered more Arieles if they had been available. It found the agents' claims to be too speculative, and this conclusion is not clearly erroneous.

## CONCLUSION

We affirm the award of damages. We reverse in part the denial of incidental and consequential damages. We remand for further proceedings in accord with this opinion.

## NOTES

**(1) Seller's Quality Obligation.** The trial judge concluded that "there is no question" that the goods did not conform to the terms of the contract. There was no occasion for the courts to discuss the application of CISG 35 to the evidence.

**(2) Consequential Damages.** The principal loss suffered was the profit that buyer had expected to make from sales of air conditioners. Seller contested the buyer's right to recover for this loss. The trial court allowed some of buyer's claims. The more difficult issue on appeal was the manner of trial court's calculation of this loss. By excluding fixed costs from the calculation, the courts increased the hypothetical profit. Should fixed costs have been excluded? Is this a question of interpretation of the Convention? Was the Court of Appeals reasoning on this matter a proper method of interpretation of the Convention?

The trial court disallowed recovery for expenses that had been incurred by the buyer in unsuccessful efforts to manufacture air conditioners with seller's compressors. The trial court considered these items to be included in the recovery for lost profits. The Court of Appeals disagreed. Was the appellate court correct?

**(3) Other Damages.** The trial court denied recovery for expenses incurred by the buyer in receiving and then returning the unsatisfactory compressors. The Court of Appeals reversed. Such expenses would be characterized as incidental expenses under UCC Article 2 and recoverable under UCC 2–715(1), which the court cited in a footnote. Under what language of CISG 74 are such damages recoverable? The Court of Appeals stressed that these expenses were foreseeable. Was that conclusion necessary to buyer's recovery?

**(4) Recovery of the Price Paid.** The buyer paid the full price for both shipments of compressors. The trial court found that buyer had paid almost $320,000. The compressors were returned to the seller. Was the buyer entitled to refund of the price paid under CISG? The trial court found that seller's breach was fundamental under CISG 25 and the Court of Appeals affirmed. Was this finding necessary for the courts' determination of the damages under CISG 74? If there had been no finding of fundamental breach, would the measure of damages have changed? Was a finding of fundamental breach necessary for recovery of the price? CISG 81 to 84 provide for the effects of avoidance. Under CISG 81(2), upon avoidance, a party who has performed its obligations under the contract may claim restitution of whatever was paid. Seller must pay interest on the money. CISG 84(1).

**(5) Return of the Goods.** The buyer sent the nonconforming compressors back to the seller and thereby incurred expenses that were assessed as damages. CISG determines buyers' obligations with respect to the goods after avoidance. Under CISG 81(2), buyers that avoid contracts have the duty to make restitution. They must also account for all benefits derived from the goods. CISG 84(2). Buyers ordinarily lose the right to declare contracts avoided if they cannot make restitution of the goods substantially in the condition in which they were received. CISG 82(1) and (2). Buyers are entitled to retain goods until sellers reimburse them for reasonable expenses, CISG 86(1), a right that the buyer did not insist upon in this case.

# Medical Marketing Int'l v. Internazionale Medico Scientifica

United States District Court, Eastern District of Louisiana, 1999.
1999 WL 311945.

■ DUVAL, JR., J.

Before the court is an Application for Order Conforming Arbitral Award and Entry of Judgment, filed by plaintiff, Medical Marketing International, Inc. ("MMI"). Having considered the memoranda of plaintiff, and the memorandum in opposition filed by defendant, Internazionale Medico Scientifica, S.r.l. ("IMS"), the court grants the motion.

## FACTUAL BACKGROUND

Plaintiff MMI is a Louisiana marketing corporation with its principal place of business in Baton Rouge, Louisiana. Defendant IMS is an Italian corporation that manufactures radiology materials with its principal place of business in Bologna, Italy. On January 25, 1993, MMI and IMS entered into a Business Licensing Agreement in which IMS granted exclusive sales rights for Giotto Mammography H.F. Units to MMI.

In 1996, the Food and Drug Administration ("FDA") seized the equipment for non-compliance with administrative procedures, and a dispute arose over who bore the obligation of ensuring that the Giotto equipment complied with the United states Governmental Safety Regulations, specifically the Good Manufacturing Practices (GMP) for Medical Device Regulations. MMI formally demanded mediation on October 28, 1996, pursuant to Article 13 of the agreement. Mediation was unsuccessful, and the parties entered into arbitration, also pursuant to Article 13, whereby each party chose one arbitrator and a third was agreed upon by both.

An arbitration hearing was held on July 13–15, July 28, and November 17, 1998. The hearing was formally closed on November 30, 1998. The arbitrators rendered their decision on December 21, 1998, awarding MMI damages in the amount of $357,009.00 and legal interest on that amount from October 28, 1996. The arbitration apportioned 75% of the $83,640.45 cost of arbitration to MMI, and the other 25% to IMS. IMS moved for reconsideration on December 30, 1998, and this request was denied by the arbitrators on January 7, 1999. Plaintiff now moves for an order from this court confirming the arbitral award and entering judgment in favor of the plaintiff under 9 U.S.C. § 9.

## JURISDICTION

The Federal Arbitration Act ("FAA") allows parties to an arbitration suit to apply to the "United States court in and for the district within which such award was made" for enforcement of the award. 9 U.S.C. § 9. As the arbitration in this case was held in New Orleans, Louisiana, this court has jurisdiction over petitioner's Application under 9 U.S.C. § 9. This court also has diversity jurisdiction over the case, as the amount in controversy exceeds $75,000 and the parties are a Louisiana corporation and an Italian corporation.

## ANALYSIS

The scope of this court's review of an arbitration award is "among the narrowest known to law." ... The FAA outlines specific situations in which an arbitration decision may be overruled: (1) if the award was procured by corruption, fraud or undue means; (2) if there is evidence of partiality or corruption among the arbitrators; (3) if the arbitrators were guilty of misconduct which prejudiced the rights of one of the parties; or (4) if the arbitrators exceeded their powers. Instances in which the arbitrators "exceed their powers" may include violations of public policy or awards based on a "manifest disregard of the law." ...

IMS has alleged that the arbitrators' decision violates public policy of the international global market and that the arbitrators exhibited "manifest disregard of international sales law." Specifically, IMS argues that the arbitrators misapplied the United Nations Convention on Contracts for the International Sales of Goods, commonly referred to as CISG, and that they refused to follow a German Supreme Court Case interpreting CISG.

MMI does not dispute that CISG applies to the case at hand. Under CISG, the finder of fact has a duty to regard the "international character" of the convention and to promote uniformity in its application. CISG Article 7. The Convention also provides that in an international contract for goods, goods conform to the contract if they are fit for the purpose for which goods of the same description would ordinarily be used or are fit for any particular purpose expressly or impliedly made known to the seller and relied upon by the buyer. CISG Article 35(2). To avoid a contract based on the non-conformity of goods, the buyer must allege and prove that the seller's breach was "fundamental" in nature. CISG Article 49. A breach is fundamental when it results in such detriment to the party that he or she is substantially deprived of what he or she is entitled to expect under the contract, unless the party in breach did not foresee such a result. CISG Article 25.

At the arbitration, IMS argued that MMI was not entitled to avoid its contract with IMS based on non-conformity under Article 49, because IMS's breach was not "fundamental." IMS argued that CISG did not require that it furnish MMI with equipment that complied with the United States GMP regulations. To support this proposition, IMS cited a German Supreme Court case, which held that under CISG Article 35, a seller is generally not obligated to supply goods that conform to public laws and regulations enforced at the buyer's place of business. Entscheidunger des Bundersgerichtshofs in Zivilsachen (BGHZ) 129, 75 (1995). In that case, the court held that this general rule carriers with it exceptions in three limited circumstances: (1) if the public laws and regulations of the buyer's state are identical to those enforced in the seller's state; (2) if the buyer informed the seller about those regulations; or (3) if due to "special circumstances," such as the existence of a seller's branch office in the buyer's state, the seller knew or should have known about the regulations at issue.

The arbitration panel decided that under the third exception, the general rule did not apply to this case. The arbitrators held that IMS was, or should have been, aware of the GMP regulations prior to entering into the 1993 agreement, and explained their reasoning at length. IMS now argues that the arbitration panel refused to apply CISG and the law as articulated by the German Supreme Court. It is clear from the arbitrators' written findings, however, that they carefully considered that decision and found that this case fit the exception and not the rule as articulated in that decision. The arbitrators' decision was neither contrary to public policy nor in manifest disregard of international sales law. This court therefore finds that the arbitration panel did not "exceed its powers" in violation of the FAA. Accordingly,

IT IS ORDERED that the Application for Order Conforming Arbitral Award is hereby GRANTED.

## NOTES

**(1) Commercial Arbitration and Judicial Enforcement of Awards.** Many parties to international sales contracts elect from the outset to have disputes resolved by arbitration, if any should arise. The parties to this transaction included an agreement to arbitrate in their contract. When the dispute arose they went to arbitration as agreed. The arbitrators were a panel of three, one selected by each side and a neutral third panelist. Arbitrators' decisions in favor of claimants are usually called "awards." Awards may be accepted by the losing party without further process, but awards cannot be enforced by the same means available to enforce judgments of courts. Legislation was enacted to give teeth to arbitration awards.[12] The legislation in this case, a federal statute, allows parties that prevail in arbitration to seek the assistance of federal district courts.[13] In that court proceeding, the law allows a few very limited objections to the validity of the arbitrators' decision. This procedure was followed in this case.

**(2) CISG and Commercial Arbitration.** Contracts governed by CISG are likely to have arbitration clauses for the resolution of disputes that may arise. While CISG can be enforced in national and state courts, parties to international sales contracts that choose the neutral substantive law of CISG for their transactions may also choose to refer their disputes to a neutral forum rather than to the domestic court of one of the parties. Commercial arbitration offers advantages other than neutrality, of course, which add to the incentive to include arbitration clauses in sales contracts. A principal disadvantage is that arbitrators are not judges and may not even be lawyers. Persons who seek rigorous enforcement of substantive legal norms may distrust the arbitration process to produce that result.

The seller in this case sought to persuade the district court to refuse to enforce the arbitration award for an error of law allegedly committed by the arbitrators. In most legal systems, there is no right to appeal an arbitration award comparable to the right to appeal a trial court's decision. When courts are asked to confirm an arbitration award, losing parties may try to achieve some degree of judicial review of the arbitrators' legal analysis. That of course is what seller tried to do in this case, under the rubric that the arbitrators had acted in "manifest disregard of the law." In the setting of a judicial proceeding to enforce the award, seller's effort failed.

The court does not indicate whether the arbitration in this case was conducted under the auspices of an organization for the facilitation of such dispute resolution. Several major organizations of this kind were discussed in Chapter 1.

---

**12.** International commercial law is considerably developed with regard to enforcement if the initial decision is an arbitration award. The United Nations Convention on the Recognition and Enforcement of Foreign Arbitral Awards, a multilateral treaty of 1958, commonly known as the "New York Convention," commits signatory nations to enforcement of awards. The United States, a party to the New York Convention, fulfilled its obligation by adding chapter 2 to the Federal Arbitration Act, 9 U.S.C. §§ 201–208, in 1970. The New York Convention is reprinted in the notes of United States Code Annotated at § 201.

UNCITRAL has also been active in promoting international arbitration of commercial disputes. In 1976, UNCITRAL issued Arbitration Rules that parties to international contracts can choose to incorporate into their agreements. UNCITRAL promulgated a Model Law on International Commercial Arbitration in 1985. See A. Broches in ICCA, International Handbook on Commercial Arbitration (Arb. Supp. 11, Jan. 1990); H. Holtzmann & J. Neuhaus, Guide to the UNCITRAL Model Law (1989); A. Redfern & M. Hunter, Law and Practice of International Commercial Arbitration 360–404, 416–430 (text of UNCITRAL Rules), 435–449 (text of Model Law) (1986).

**13.** The courts are authorized by the statute to enter judgments that are based upon arbitration awards. Those judgments can then be executed by public officials to compel payment, if necessary.

**(3) Application of CISG.** Although the court refused to review the merits of the arbitrators' decision, it is useful to consider the nature and strength of the seller's legal argument. If the initial decision had been that of a federal district court rather than an arbitration panel, would seller have had valid ground for appeal?

The seller's argument appeared to be that a prior decision, by the German Supreme Court, had given CISG 35 a definitive meaning that the United States courts were bound to follow. To what extent should the principle of *stare decisis* or respect for precedent apply to construction of CISG articles by national courts? Would a different legal principle apply if the original forum is an arbitration panel?

The specific issue of a seller's implicit obligation to provide goods that comply with law or regulations in the buyer's country has been litigated in a number of cases. In well-drafted agreements the buyers will include a term that explicitly deals with the issue.

The court referred to the CISG concept of "fundamental breach," which is defined in CISG 25. Under CISG 49(1)(a), a buyer may declare a contract "avoided" if the seller commits a "fundamental breach" with remedial consequences in CISG 75 and 76. This extraordinary remedy should not be confused with common (non-fundamental) breach of quality cases under CISG 35 and 36, and CISG 74 and 77.

## 2. EXAMPLES OF ARBITRAL AWARDS ON ISSUES OF QUALITY OF GOODS

The following arbitrators' awards, taken from the ICC reports, are indicative of the process in disputes involving the quality of goods delivered. Since these arose before CISG took effect, they are governed by domestic law. The arbitrators' resolution of the choice of law is also instructive. Would these disputes have been resolved differently if the governing law had been CISG?

## AWARD IN CASE NO. 3779 OF 1981
Collection of ICC Arbitral Awards 1974–85, p. 138

Arbitrator:        Prof. Jacques H. Herbots (Belgium)

Parties:           Claimant: Swiss seller
                   Respondent:  Dutch buyer

* * *

## [FACTS]

Three contracts were concluded in 1979 between the parties, all three concerning the same type of merchandise [whey powder] of which the quality was described in detail.

The merchandise, coming from a Canadian factory was to be delivered C.I.F. Rotterdam. The contracts were made in French and all contained—

except for quantities—the same conditions, including an arbitral clause referring disputes to arbitration under the Arbitration Rules of the ICC. However, only the first two contracts were signed by the parties and executed. The third contract was not signed and before shipment from Canada took place, it was cancelled by the Respondent who complained that the merchandise delivered under the first two contracts was not in accordance with the quality prescribed in the contract.

The Canadian Factory sent one of its technicians, Dr. E., to the Netherlands and samples were taken and examined in an independent laboratory. It appeared that they were in accordance with the contractual requirements when analyzed under the North American method, but not when the European analytic method was used.

Arbitration followed in which the Swiss seller claimed US $55,000 (including *inter alia* $37,500 paid to the Canadian factory) in respect of the cancellation of the third contract. The Dutch buyer introduced a counter-claim of Hfl. 181,645.—covering losses in respect of the first two contracts.

**[EXTRACT]**

## I.   Competence of Arbitrator

The clause attributing jurisdiction to the ICC occurs in two preceding and similar contracts that were signed by both parties, as well as in the third contract, that, although it was not signed, was not protested against within a reasonable delay either.

Although the contracts are independent from one another from a juridical point of view, the three contracts form a group from an economic point of view.

If, in principle, silence does not mean acceptance, this meaning is, however, attributed to it in view of the circumstances, in particular, the previous business relations of the parties.

Consequently, within the context of their juridical relation and according to their obligations of good faith, the exception of incompetence does not apply.

## II.   Law Applicable to the Contract

\* \* \*

In an international sale of goods, when the parties remain silent, the domestic law of the country in which the seller has his place of residence is to be applied (see the Hague Convention on the International Sale of Goods of June 15, 1955)....

The chosen language, the place where the contract was entered into by correspondence together with applying the theory of reception, and the way of payment, all point in the same direction.

Consequently, Swiss law is applicable to the contract in dispute.

\* \* \*

IV.  With Respect to the Merits of the Dispute

\* \* \*

3.  The misunderstanding

Both parties seem to have acted in good faith.

Actually, the Claimant had immediately declared his willingness to submit samples drawn by both parties to a test by a competent laboratory to be chosen by both parties, and to accept cancellation of the remaining contracts if this analysis proved that the Respondent's allegations had been well-founded.

The Respondent, on his part, also immediately reported the quality problems encountered, asked for an expert and sent samples to the Canadian factory. He agreed to pay for the goods that had already arrived in Rotterdam and he restricted himself to refusing to give any forwarding-instructions or to receive the goods ordered, but not yet loaded on board.

The dispute essentially arises from a misunderstanding.

The following conclusion is essential for understanding the matter: "The main conclusion of Dr. E. during his visit to the Dutch buyer was that the goods sent were not the product the Dutch buyer believed to have bought; the Dutch buyer maintains that, when the Swiss seller initially gave a description of the goods, no mention was made of a method of analysis. The Dutch buyer supposed that, since the description was given by a European firm, the European methods were to be applied ..." (quotation from document 24). To this the Claimant replies: "It goes without saying that the methods to be used should be those of the country of origin or those that are universally accepted, such as the (North American) method" (document 3).

It was only when the quality problems emerged that the Claimant announced the method of analyzing, *inter alia*, the solubility index, viz. the (North American) method that, according to him, is intentionally accepted (document 6 bis).

The Canadian factory was willing to send a technician but made the condition that first agreement should be reached on the method of analysis (document 7).

It is certain that the goods are in accordance with the contractual description, provided that the samples are analyzed according to the (North American) method.

It appears from the proceedings that, although it is not a sale on sample, a sample had been sent to the Respondent prior to the conclusion of the contracts.

The first deliveries were in accordance with this quality, the latter not, although they remained in accordance with the contractual description of the goods, which explains why it was only at a late stage that the misunderstanding came to light.

The misunderstanding is essentially about the solubility degree of the powder delivered.

The method of analysis must be carefully specified in order to be able to determine the solubility degree of the powder.

In Switzerland, methods of analysis are used that are incorporated in the Swiss Manual on Foods, of which Manual the chapter on goods like this particular powder has, unfortunately, not been published yet.

Although the North American method (actually designed for a different type of powder) is better known in the international powder industry involved than a French method, it cannot be considered, however, to be implicitly understood, at least, not on the European market.

The French method differs from the (North American) method with respect to the temperature during the dissolution and the technique of dissolution. The two methods are particularly different with respect to the method of expressing the result in a figure (the solubility index). The Canadian factory took this into account when it was too late, notably, when the Respondent complained about the quality of the goods and the question of analyzing the samples was raised.

### 4.   Shared responsibilities with respect to the origin of the misunderstanding

From a telex from the Canadian factory to the Claimant ... it appears that the factory claims to have been clear as to the description of the goods and the methodology, and that the contractual (possibly insufficient) description of the goods, given by the Claimant to his own clients, does not concern him at all, from which it can be deduced that the factory leaves the total contractual responsibility to the Claimant in the case he had not done likewise with his own principal, that is to say, the Respondent.

The Claimant should have known that there was a possibility of error on the European market with respect to the appreciation of the description of the powder.

One cannot presume that there is agreement on the (North American) method between a Swiss seller and a Dutch buyer.

The Claimant should have mentioned that the contractual description was to be interpreted according to the (North American) method, as the Canadian supplier had done in his contract with the Claimant.

The Claimant should have informed the buyer of the conditions on which he contracted (see T.G.I., Argentan, 15th October 1970, D.S., 1971, p. 718, note of M. Ghestin, quoted by Lucas de Leyssac, *L'obligation de renseignements dans les contrats*, in: *L'information en droit privé*, L.G.D., J., 1978, p. 316).

With respect to the interpretation of the contract, the (also in Swiss law) traditional rule can be applied as well: "*in dubio, contra proferentem*".

As Loysel wrote: "qui vend le pot, dit le mot".

The seller is obliged to state clearly what obligations he is undertaking.

The Respondent, on the other hand, knew very well that the goods were of Canadian origin, because he had had contact with the supplier.

Consequently, the error is equally due to his negligence, for he should have asked about the meaning of the symbols used in the contractual description of the powder, of North American origin.

The dialectics between the right of being informed, and the obligation of informing oneself is thus at the heart of the problem in the present dispute.

The error of the Respondent is due to a negligence shared with the Claimant (in Swiss law one can find the following instances of shared negligence: A and B have concluded a sale, for which the price has been fixed on the basis of a tariff, the rectification of which has been published many times. A and B conclude a contract without informing themselves about the provisions of clearing that are applicable to their deal—see ENGEL, Pierre, *Traité des obligations en droit Suisse*, Neuchatel, 1973, p. 257).

The (North American) method being more frequently used than the other methods, the negligence of the Claimant as to the information seems less than that of the Respondent.

* * *

THEREFORE:

We, Arbitrator, deciding in accordance with the provisions of the ICC Rules of Conciliation and Arbitration, within the limits of our mission, that was extended by decision of the Court of Arbitration;

> observe in the commercial relations of the parties the existence of an arbitration clause to settle the present dispute and consequently declare ourselves competent to decide and award with respect to the claim and the counterclaim;

*With respect to the claim*

> condemn the Respondent to pay to the Claimant the amount of $27,000 as indemnification for the invalidation (that is to say cancellation) of the third contract.

*With respect to the counterclaim*

> reject the claim of the Respondent for indemnification because of the non-conformity of the goods delivered under the two preceding contracts.

Order that the costs of the arbitration, including costs and fee of the arbitrator, being $8,300, will be borne by the Claimant for 2/5 and by the Respondent for 3/5.

———

AWARD MADE IN CASE NO. 2129 IN 1972, Collection of ICC Arbitral Awards 1974–1985, p. 23. A German seller contracted to deliver motor car accessories to a United States buyer. Buyer claimed relief for expenses incurred in altering the goods to make them usable on United States automobiles, which were larger than German automobiles. The arbitrator, applying the Ohio Commercial Code, found for the United States buyer:

> The defendant's equipment had to be fit for the ordinary purposes for which it was to be used. Thus, the equipment manufactured for the German market had to be modified to service the U.S. market. At the time of contracting the defendant knew the purpose for which the equipment was required and the buyer relied upon him to furnish suitable machines. ... This warranty of merchantability and fitness applies to sales for use as well as to sales for resale and can be invoked by the plaintiff as well as by his customers. The plaintiff is therefore entitled to be reimbursed for the money he spent repairing or altering the defendant's equipment pursuant to an implied warranty of merchantability and fitness.

––––––––

## AWARD OF SEPTEMBER 27, 1983, CASE NO. 3880

Arbitrators:    Dr. Werner Wenger; Prof. Lucien Simont; Prof. Marcel Storme

Parties:    Claimant: Belgian buyer A
Defendant: Belgian seller B

Published in:    110 *Journal du droit international (Clunet )* 1983, p. 897, with note Y. Derains and S. Jarvin, pp. 897–899.

### [FACTS]

On January 26, 1979, claimant A and defendant B entered into a contract whereby B undertook to supply A with 150,000 pairs of ladies' boots between April and August 1979. On the same date, B entered into an identical contract (differing only in relation to the price) with a Romanian State trading enterprise C, who was to supply the same quantity of boots to B. When the Romanian enterprise C defaulted, arbitration proceedings were commenced by A who sought damages for late delivery and defective goods. The arbitrators rejected a request by defendant B to join the claim with an arbitration it had commenced separately against its supplier, the Romanian enterprise C, based on that company's default in delivery. Claimant A was successful as to 75% of its claim.

### [EXTRACT]

[On *force majeure*:]

... [D]efendant B contends ... that to the extent that the contract obliged it to supply boots made at the factory D in Romania, the source proposed by its supplier, the Romanian enterprise C, the default of the latter constituted an insurmountable obstacle and an extraneous cause relieving it of any liability towards Claimant A.

\* \* \*

It follows that, B's obligations being in the nature of obligations of result, their non-fulfilment places B in default and involves it in liability vis-à-vis A, except for those cases where the latter company cancelled orders without justification. . . .

[On the mitigation of damages:]

B argues, however, that A could have offered its clients in sufficient time merchandise equivalent to the subject-matter of the contract between the parties, in conformity with its obligation to take all appropriate steps to limit its damage and reduce its losses.

The boots which were the subject-matter of the contract have a seasonal character and could not be sold and delivered to A's client except at the beginning of the winter season at the latest. B, on the basis of promises made by its own supplier, had led A to believe, up to August 1979 and, at least for the major part of the order, even up to the first half of September 1979, that it would be in a position to deliver the goods, admittedly late, but before the last moment. Its failure to fulfil these promises only became apparent after it was too late to obtain the merchandise elsewhere. In effect, having regard to the changing fashions to which this type of product is subject, suppliers keep very little in stock. B omits to identify the sources to which A could have turned at the end of September 1979, to obtain merchandise equivalent to that described in the Contract.

In these circumstances it is not appropriate to reduce the compensation for damages suffered by reason of a violation of the creditor to observe its obligation to mitigate its damages.

[On loss of goodwill:]

Having regard to the fact that, out of a total of about 127,000 pairs of boots ordered by A from B, a significant number, 45,509 pairs, or about 35%, were the subject of justifiable complaints about failure to meet delivery dates and defects in quality. This percentage considerably exceeds what would normally be expected to be tolerated. Having regard to the seasonal character of the merchandise, A was only able to satisfy its clients from other sources to a limited extent. One's commercial reputation would seem to be affected when a business finds itself in the position of not being able to fulfil a significant proportion of its orders.

The nature of the effect on its reputation is such as to make it impossible, in the absence of precise criteria, to determine the exact extent of the damage caused by it; that such damage cannot be evaluated. In these circumstances, it appears that for the reasons stated above, and taking all aspects of the case into consideration, particularly the net margin of A and the trading figures with the clients mentioned above from 1980–1982 in comparison with previous years, A's claim can only be deemed to be partly founded, and the sum of Bfrs. 200,000 must be allowed to it as damages for any prejudice to its commercial reputation.

## SECTION 3.   WARRANTY DISCLAIMERS AND LIMITATION OF DAMAGES CLAUSES

### (A) DOMESTIC UNITED STATES LAW

### 1.   TERMS AGREED DURING CONTRACT FORMATION

#### a.   WRITTEN TERMS

Article 2 of the Commercial Code does not require that sellers provide warranties of quality on their goods. This section considers the means by which sellers can sell goods without warranties of quality. The primary issue that recurs in this section is the nature and effectiveness of disclaimers of the implied warranty of merchantability.[1] Express warranties arise only if sellers, by their own words or conduct, take affirmative action to create them. Implied warranties of quality arise in a different manner. The warranty of merchantability arises, by implication, in every sales contract in which seller is a merchant that deals in goods of the kind. The merchantability warranty exists unless, by a clause in the sales contract, the merchant-seller has effectively disclaimed it. The Commercial Code allows sellers to disclaim implied warranties of quality if they do so in accordance with prescribed procedures.

The implied warranty provision in UCC 2–314 contains the conditioning language: "unless excluded or modified," which expressly permits the parties to agree that these warranties have been negated. As we will see, the Code further imposes certain *formal* requirements on sellers who seek to do so. UCC 2–316(2).

Article 2 does not require that the statutory remedies be available for breach of express warranties or breach of implied warranties of quality. The Commercial Code allows the parties to sales contracts to agree to remedies other than the statutory remedies. Contracts may provide remedies in addition to, or in substitution for the statutory remedies. A common contract remedy for breach of warranty is seller's undertaking, for a limited time after delivery, to repair defects in materials or workmanship that are discovered. The primary issue that we will see recurring is the nature and effectiveness of contract clauses obligating sellers to remedy defects and contract clauses excluding sellers' liability for consequential damages that result from breach of warranty.

---

1. Disclaimers of the implied warranty of fitness for particular purpose are not as significant commercially as disclaimers of the implied warranty of merchantability. Note will be taken of disclaimers of fitness-for-purpose warranties as appropriate.

The Commercial Code's treatment of clauses limiting sellers' liability for damages is found in UCC 2–719. Section 2–719(1)(a) declares that the parties "may provide for remedies in addition to or in substitution for those provided in this Article" and may agree to "limit or alter the measure of damages recoverable under this Article, as by limiting the buyer's remedies to return of the goods and repayment of the price or to repair and replacement of non-conforming goods or parts." Under UCC 2–719(3), consequential damages may be limited or excluded unless the limitation or exclusion is unconscionable.

In modern sales of most durable goods and many non-durable goods, few contracts lack a disclaimer of the implied warranty of merchantability or a damages exclusion clause, or both. In many kinds of transactions, patterns of warranty disclaimers or limitation of damages clauses have become so common that their absence in a given transaction would be remarkable. Counsel to businesses that sell goods typically advise their clients to use warranty disclaimers and damages excluders. This advice is often implemented in lawyer-drafted provisions that are included in the standard contracting forms used by sellers. In the marketplace, would clauses limiting the damages that aggrieved buyers may recover or clauses disclaiming implied warranties be equally significant in the minds of buyers? Do these clauses deal with the same or different economic risks? Which kind of clause is more likely to cause a potential buyer to forego a purchase?

## Insurance Co. of North America v. Automatic Sprinkler Corp.

Supreme Court of Ohio, 1981.
67 Ohio St.2d 91, 423 N.E.2d 151.

Appellee, Automatic Sprinkler Corporation of America ("Automatic Sprinkler"), purchased the components of a dry chemical fire protection system from appellant, The Ansul Company ("Ansul"). Both parties understood that Automatic Sprinkler would install this system in a building occupied by Youngstown Steel and Alloy Corporation ("Youngstown Steel").

A representative of Ansul signed a "Proposal," dated February 13, 1970. No one signed the proposal on behalf of Automatic Sprinkler. This document is five pages long. The front of each page includes typewritten or printed information which either describes the goods or states the price. Only the fifth and last page has printing on the back including:

"This sale is subject to the following terms and conditions:

" . . .

"9.   The Ansul extinguisher is warranted to the original purchaser for five years from date of delivery against defects in workmanship and material. The Ansul Company will replace or repair any metal parts which in its opinion are defective and have not been tampered with or subjected to misuse, abuse or exposed to highly corrosive conditions. This warranty is *in lieu of* all other warranties express or implied. The Ansul Company assumes no liability for *consequential* or other loss or *damage* whatsoever arising out of injuries to or death of persons and damages to or destruction of property in any manner caused by, incident to, or connected with the use of the equipment, and the Buyer shall *indemnify* and save harmless the Seller from and against all such claims, loss, cost or damage. In addition, unless the Ansul equipment is maintained per Ansul's recommendations, Ansul hereby disclaims all liability whatsoever, including, but not limited to, any liability otherwise attaching under the warranty provisions of this paragraph." (Emphasis added.)

There are 15 paragraphs in all—each without a heading, each without extraordinary capitalization.

Ansul delivered the goods under a "Purchase Order," dated April 14, 1970, "per Ansul Quotation 8674 signed 2–13–70."

A fire occurred on September 9, 1974, at the building occupied by Youngstown Steel. The Ansul fire extinguisher system did not discharge.

None of the aforementioned facts is disputed. Two lawsuits did result, however.

Insurance Company of North America ("INA"), subrogee to the building owner, complained against Automatic Sprinkler and Ansul (case No. 80–619). Automatic Sprinkler ultimately cross-claimed against Ansul. Youngstown Steel and its insurer sued Automatic Sprinkler (case No. 80–620) Automatic Sprinkler then filed a third-party complaint against Ansul. In both cases, the claims alleged breach of warranty and negligence.

Later, the Court of Common Pleas consolidated these cases. The trial judge granted Ansul's motion for summary judgment and dismissed Automatic Sprinkler's claims against Ansul in both cases because (1) Ansul had disclaimed all warranties on sale and limited Automatic Sprinkler's remedies to repair and replacement of defective parts and (2) Automatic Sprinkler agreed to indemnify Ansul and hold it harmless from all claims. The Court of Appeals reversed the trial court, holding that the disclaimer and exclusion of consequential damages fail because they are not conspicuous.

The Court of Appeals also held that "there is no basis for summary judgment in favor of the Ansul Company on the indemnity provision question at this stage of the case," because paragraph 9 is not conspicuous. The court reversed and remanded the cause to the trial court for further proceedings on this issue.

The cause is now before this court pursuant to the allowance of motions to certify the record.

* * *

■ LOCHER, JUSTICE.

This case presents three issues: (1) whether Ansul has effectively disclaimed all implied warranties with Automatic Sprinkler; (2) whether Ansul has effectively excluded all liability for consequential damages; and (3) whether Automatic Sprinkler must indemnify Ansul against all claims arising in this litigation. Resolving each of these issues requires an interpretation of paragraph 9.

We hold that Ansul has neither disclaimed its liability for implied warranties nor excluded its liability for consequential damages.

I.

Ansul attempted to disclaim all liability to Automatic Sprinkler for breach of implied warranties by including the following language in paragraph 9: "This warranty is in lieu of all other warranties express or implied." Automatic Sprinkler argues that this language fails as a disclaimer because it does not mention merchantability and is not conspicuous as required by [UCC 2–316(2)]. Ansul, on the other hand, suggests that the "in lieu of" language is similar to "as is" under [UCC 2–316(3)(a)]. Under Ansul's view, the disclaimer is effective regardless of whether it is conspicuous or whether it mentions merchantability.

We hold that the "in lieu of" language is not similar to "as is". . . . The effort to disclaim liability for all implied warranties fails because paragraph 9 is not conspicuous and because the disclaimer does not mention merchantability.

"As is" language describes the *quality of the goods* sold. As an example of "as is" language, [UCC 2–316(3)(a)] expressly includes "with all faults." . . . Official Comment 7 . . . further explains the intent of the drafters:

> Paragraph [(a)] deals with general items such as "as is," "as they stand," "with all faults," and the like. Such terms in ordinary commercial usage are understood to mean that the buyer takes the entire risk as to the *quality of the goods* involved. . . . (Emphasis added.)

. . .

We recognize that the courts have held that "in lieu of" language eliminates implied warranties. . . . We reject this conclusion.

Under [2–316(3)(a)] "other language which, in common understanding, calls the buyer's attention to the exclusion of warranties and makes plain that there is no implied warranty" must be language which is consistent with the intention of the drafters and the General Assembly. This language must describe the *quality* of the goods.

Accordingly, the "in lieu of" language in paragraph 9 falls outside [2–316(3)(a)].

This "in lieu of" provision does not qualify, therefore, as a disclaimer of implied warranties under [2–316(2)]. There is no mention of merchantability. In addition, we have held that paragraph 9 is inconspicuous.

[UCC 1–201(10)] defines "conspicuousness" as follows:

" 'Conspicuous': A term or clause is conspicuous when it is so written that a reasonable person against whom it is to operate ought to have noticed it. A printed heading in capitals (as: NON–NEGOTIABLE BILL OF LADING) is conspicuous. Language in the body of a form is 'conspicuous' if it is in larger or other contrasting type or color. But in a telegram any stated term is 'conspicuous.' Whether a term or clause is "conspicuous" or not is for decision by the court."

Paragraph 9 appears among 15 other paragraphs on the back of the last page of the Proposal. This is the only page with writing on the back and is unnumbered. None of these paragraphs has a heading, extraordinary capitalization or contrasting type. Furthermore, Ansul alone executed the Proposal which contained paragraph 9 approximately two months before Automatic Sprinkler submitted its purchase order. In light of all these circumstances, therefore, it is clear that paragraph 9 is inconspicuous.

Accordingly, we hold that the "in lieu of" provision in paragraph 9 does not disclaim all implied warranties.

## II.

Ansul argues that, even if the purported disclaimer fails, paragraph 9 excludes "liability for consequential or other loss or damage...." We disagree.

[UCC 2–719(3) and 2–316(4)] permit parties to exclude consequential damages without expressly requiring that the exclusion be conspicuous. Nevertheless, courts and commentators have read U.C.C. 2–719[3] and U.C.C. 2–316[4] *in pari materia*. See e.g., Avenell v. Westinghouse Electric Corp. (Cuyahoga Cty., 1974), 41 Ohio App.2d 150, 324 N.E.2d 583; Zicari v. Joseph Harris Co., Inc. (1969), 33 App.Div.2d 17, 304 N.Y.S.2d 918; Nordstrom, Law of Sales, at 276; Special Project—Article Two Warranties in Commercial Transactions, 64 Cornell L.Rev. 30, 224. Nordstrom, supra, explains why these two statutes should be read together, as follows:

> The requirement that the agreement contain the alteration of basic Code remedies brings into play those ideas discussed in the prior section of this text [dealing with disclaimers of implied warranties]. The limitation [or exclusion of remedies] must be a part of the parties' bargain in fact. If it is contained in a printed clause which was not conspicuous or brought to the buyer's attention, the seller had no reasonable expectation that the buyer understood that his remedies were being restricted to repair and replacement. As such, the clause cannot be said to be a part of the bargain (or agreement) of the parties.

Any other reading of these provisions would permit inconspicuous provisions excluding or limiting damage recovery to circumvent the protection for buyers in [2–316(2)]. ...

Paragraph 9 is inconspicuous in its entirety. The attempt to exclude liability for consequential damages, therefore, is also inconspicuous. Accordingly, Automatic Sprinkler may recover consequential damages from Ansul.

NOTES

**(1) Bargain in Fact.** Could Automatic Sprinkler Corporation of America contend persuasively that the language in the "Proposal" that disclaimed "all other warranties" was unclear to the buyer as a disclaimer of the warranty of merchantability? Could Automatic Sprinkler contend persuasively that it was reasonably unaware of the clause on Ansul's liability for consequential damages? Do you think it likely or unlikely that corporations like Automatic Sprinkler use such contractual clauses in transactions in which they are sellers?

**(2) Construction of UCC 2–316(2).** Why did the drafters of the Commercial Code include 2–316(2)? What did they intend by the requirement that a seller must "mention merchantability" to disclaim the 2–314 warranty?

The Ohio Supreme Court made no effort to resolve the controversy on the basis of the bargain in fact, but rather decided the case on the basis of Ansul's non-compliance with the "mention merchantability" clause in UCC 2–316(2) and with the court's implication of a statutory "conspicuousness" requirement in UCC 2–719. What is the public policy rationale of those *formal* requirements? Is it arguable that the legislation was designed to protect consumer buyers and not sophisticated commercial buyers like Automatic Sprinkler? Could a court properly exclude buyers who are large corporations? A federal district court held that the language denied effect in this case was sufficient to exclude the warranty of merchantability.

Section 2–316(2) treats disclaimers of merchantability and fitness-for-particular purpose rather differently. Disclaimer of merchantability may be oral, but disclaimer of fitness-for-particular-purpose must be in writing. What might explain this difference?

**(3) Legislative History.** The history of UCC 2–316 is informative. In the initial drafts of the Code, from 1940 to 1952, subsection (2) provided:

> (2) Exclusion or modification of the implied warranty of merchantability or of fitness for a particular purpose must be in specific language and if the inclusion of such language creates an ambiguity in the contract as a whole it shall be resolved against the seller; except that [the three subparagraphs now in (3) followed as exceptions].

Comments to the 1952 draft provided:

> 3.   Disclaimer of the implied warranties of merchantability and of fitness for particular purpose is permitted under subsection (2), but with the safeguard that such disclaimers must be in specific terms and that any ambiguity must be resolved against the seller.

> 4.   Implied warranties may not be excluded merely by the use of a clause disclaiming "all warranties express or implied." On the other hand, a clause such as "We assume no responsibility that the goods concerned in this contract are fit for any particular purpose for which they are being bought outside of the general purposes of goods of the

description," would normally be sufficient to satisfy the requirement that the disclaimer be in "specific terms."

5. The provision of subsection (2) that an ambiguity arising from the co-existence of words of disclaimer and evidence showing the creation of the implied warranties of merchantability or fitness for a particular purpose must be resolved against the seller is intended to pose the true issue in such cases. This section rejects that line of approach which presupposes the original existence of warranty and then attempts to deal with the question of whether it has been disclaimed by language in the agreement. ...

In 1955, the Code was revised. The language above was deleted and the current provision substituted, with the exceptions set off in a new paragraph (3). The Editorial Board, which proposed the revision, gave this brief explanation:

*Reason.* The purpose of this change is to relieve the seller from the requirement of disclaiming a warranty of fitness in specific language and yet afford the buyer an adequate warning of such disclaimer.

No explanation was given for adding the requirements (i) that a valid disclaimer must "mention merchantability," (ii) that a disclaimer of the warranty of fitness for particular purpose must be in writing and conspicuous, or (iii) that a disclaimer of warranty of merchantability, if in a writing, must be conspicuous. Comments to take account of the 1955 (and 1956) text changes were published in 1957. Comments 3, 4, and 5, in their present form, replaced the earlier comments.

Does this history shed light on the drafters' intention with regard to the necessary form of a disclaimer of the implied warranty of merchantability? What weight should a court place on such history in construing the Code as adopted by a particular legislature, such as the construction of the Ohio version of the Commercial Code in the *Insurance Company* case?

**(4) Construction of UCC 2–316(3).** The seller argued that the implied warranty of merchantability was disclaimed under UCC 2–316(3)(a) on the ground that the language in the agreement was language that "in common understanding calls the buyer's attention to the exclusion of warranties and makes plain that there is no implied warranty." Seller's argument relied on the provision in subsection (2) that it was "subject to subsection (3)," and the correlative in subsection (3) that this subsection applies "notwithstanding subsection (2)." Does subsection (3) effectively override the "must mention merchantability" provision in subsection (2)?

The Ohio Supreme Court held that subsection (3)(a) was inapplicable. Reading subsection (3) as a whole, the court concluded that the "common understanding" term had to be interpreted in light of the two terms that precede it in the sentence, "as is" and "with all faults." The court was following a common rule of statutory interpretation where terms in a sequence are deemed to be related to each other. What connotation did the court find in "as is" and "with all faults" that it applied to the "common understanding term"? What could the court have meant by its declaration, with italicized emphasis, that the first two terms describe *the quality* of the goods? The terms refer to a seller's responsibility for the quality of the goods, not the quality of the goods *vel non*.

Perhaps the court was considering the commercial situations in which sales might be made with the terms "as is" or "with all faults." Comment 6 states that there are common factual situations where these terms are used. Is it likely that these term could be appropriate in sales of goods that are present when the contracts were formed or available for inspection before the contracts were formed? Recall *Sidco Products Marketing Co. v. Gulf Oil Corp.* Cf. UCC 2–316(2)(b). Is it likely that these terms would ever be appropriate in sale of goods that are described verbally when the contracts were formed but that are to be delivered later? To put the point differently, in contracts for sale of goods to be delivered later, sellers commonly make express warranties that the goods will conform to the descriptions and combine those express warranties with clauses that disclaim the implied warranty of merchantability. As part of those contracts, sellers may make an express warranty that the goods will be "free from defects in material or workmanship. Recall *McDonnell Douglas Corp. v. Thiokol Corp.* Would it be appropriate in these contracts" for the agreements to provide that the sales are "as is" or "with all faults"? If all three terms in UCC 2–316(3)(a) are similar in meaning, a court might conclude that the "common understanding" term applies only to situation where the terms "as is" and "with all faults" might be commercially reasonable.

The Ohio Supreme Court noted that its construction of UCC 2–316(3)(a) was contrary to that of other courts. For a decision directly contrary to that of this court, see Lefebvre Intergraphics, Inc. v. Sanden Machine Ltd., 946 F.Supp. 1358 (N.D.Ill.1996) (sale of a commercial printing press).

**(5) Conspicuousness of Warranty Disclaimers.** UCC 2–316(2) does not require that a disclaimer of the implied warranty of merchantability be in writing, but adds that if a written disclaimer is made the disclaimer must be "conspicuous." Any disclaimer of the warranty of fitness for particular purpose must be in writing and must be "conspicuous." The Definitional Cross References in the Official Comment do not note that this term is defined in Article 1, UCC 1–201(b)(10). The Ohio Supreme Court declared that the paragraph 9 of the Ansul proposal was not "conspicuous," but this followed the primary conclusion that the language of that paragraph was insufficient to operate as a disclaimer. Would otherwise sufficient language be denied legal effect if a court found that the conspicuousness requirement had not been met? Consider the following:

The owner of a small business agreed to purchase a computer system (hardware and software) to increase bookkeeping efficiency. Buyer signed two separate one-sheet documents, with printing on both sides, prepared by seller. Neither document referred on its face to any warranty of quality. On the document dealing with the hardware, the last line before the place for signatures stated—in all-capital letters—that the buyer had agreed to all terms and conditions, including those on the reverse side. On the face of the software document was a provision that "THE TERMS AND CONDITIONS, INCLUDING THE WARRANTY AND LIMITATION OF LIABILITY, ON THE REVERSE SIDE ARE PART OF THIS AGREEMENT."

On the reverse side of the hardware document, in a separate numbered paragraph (one of 15), appeared the following in bold-face type:

> EXCEPT AS SPECIFICALLY PROVIDED HEREIN, THERE ARE NO OTHER WARRANTIES, EXPRESS OR IMPLIED, INCLUDING, BUT NOT LIMITED TO, ANY IMPLIED WARRANTIES OF MERCHANTABILITY OR FITNESS FOR A PARTICULAR PURPOSE.

In the software document, the same language appeared in a separately numbered paragraph (one of 14) under a heading, "WARRANTY," printed in bold face but the paragraph under the heading was not in bold type.

The computer system failed to meet the buyer's needs. Buyer sued seller. The trial court held that warranty exclusion clauses were not sufficiently conspicuous, and the United States Court of Appeals for the Ninth Circuit affirmed. Sierra Diesel Injection Service, Inc. v. Burroughs Corp., 874 F.2d 653 (9th Cir.1989)(2–1). The Court of Appeals said (pp. 658–659):

> Whether a disclaimer is conspicuous is not simply a matter of measuring the type size or looking at the placement of the disclaimer within the contract [document]. A reviewing court must ascertain that a reasonable person in the buyer's position would not have been surprised to find the warranty disclaimer in the contract [document]. ... One factor to consider is the sophistication of the parties. ... Also relevant as to whether a reasonable person would have noticed a warranty disclaimer are the circumstances of the negotiation and signing.

> The trial court found that Mr. Cathey was not familiar with computers or with contracts. Mr. Cathey read the front of the [documents], but did not notice the warranty disclaimer clauses on the back. Given Mr. Cathey's lack of sophistication in the field of contracts and the written and oral representations made by Burroughs, it is not surprising that it would require more than a collection of standardized form contracts on various subjects involved in a transaction to notify a reasonable person in Mr. Cathey's position that the [computer] came without any warranty of merchantability.

**(6) Construction of UCC 2–719.** In what sense is the *Insurance Company* decision a construction of UCC 2–719? Is it conceivable that the drafters of the Code were unaware of the differences in the formulations of UCC 2–316 and UCC 2–719? Does the court's approach trespass on the legislature's prerogative?

## Universal Drilling Co. v. Camay Drilling Co.

United States Court of Appeals, Tenth Circuit, 1984.
737 F.2d 869.

■ McKAY, CIRCUIT JUDGE.

The parties to this lawsuit are "experienced, sophisticated, intelligent business men] with vast education and experience in petroleum engineering, . . . oil and gas exploration, and . . . [the] makeup and operation of oil drilling rigs and equipment." . . . In June 1977 they entered into negotiations for the purchase and sale of two drilling rigs referred to by the parties as the Marthens Rig and Rig 10.

The negotiations resulted in a contract dated July 1, 1977, [which contained the following clauses]:

18.01  The assets being purchased and sold hereunder are being sold by [defendant] in an "as-is" condition and without any warranty of operability or fitness.

\* \* \*

26.01  This Agreement and the exhibits hereto and the agreements referred to herein set forth the entire agreement and understanding of the parties in respect of the transactions contemplated hereby and supersede all prior agreements, arrangements and understanding relating to the subject matter hereof. No representation, promise inducement or statement of intention has been made by [defendant] or [plaintiffs] which is not embodied in this Agreement or in the documents referred to herein, and neither [defendant] nor [plaintiffs] shall be bound by or liable for any alleged representation, promise, inducement or statements of intention not so set forth.\*

. . . The contract defines the property to be sold as the personal property listed in Exhibits A, B and C to the contract. Rig 10 is defined as the property in Exhibit A and the Marthens Rig is defined as the property in Exhibits B and C. [The purchase price was $2,925,000.]

Subsequent to the delivery of the property, plaintiffs complained that the property they received did not conform to the contract alleging that they were to receive two used but nevertheless operable drilling rigs. Defendant, however, relying on the contract, argued that it delivered all of the property listed in the specific exhibits. This diversity lawsuit resulted.

At trial, [t]he trial court . . . rejected plaintiffs' theory that there were breaches of express warranties based on the description of the goods contained in the contract. Plaintiffs appeal. . . .

\* \* \*

### Breach of Express Warranties by Description

Approaching this issue it must again be remembered that the parties to this suit are experienced in the field of oil and gas exploration and drilling. Furthermore, none of the parties allege that they were in an inferior bargaining position.

Plaintiffs do not dispute the trial court's finding that the contract, specifically paragraph 18.01, effectively disclaimed all implied warranties.

---

\* [The court reproduced the contract in a footnote. Eds.]

Plaintiffs do allege, however, that the description of the assets contained in the contract created an express warranty that the assets would conform to that description. In addition, plaintiffs argue that such an express warranty of description cannot be disclaimed, ... or at least was not effectively disclaimed.

Section 2–316 of the Uniform Commercial Code as adopted in Colorado provides for the modification and exclusion of warranties. Colo. Rev. Stat. § 4–2–315 (1973). In particular it provides that

> [w]ords or conduct relevant to the creation of an express warranty and words or conduct tending to negate or limit warranty shall be construed wherever reasonable as consistent with each other; but subject to the provisions of this article on parol or extrinsic evidence (section 4–2–202), negation or limitation is inoperative to the extent such construction is unreasonable.

Id. § 4–2–316(1). Accordingly, the initial inquiry must be whether express warranties were created under section 4–2–313 and if so how they are affected by section 18.01 of the contract.

Plaintiff argues that this case is controlled by Section 4–2–313(b) which provides that "[a]ny description of the goods which is made part of the basis of the bargain creates an express warranty that the goods shall conform to the description." Colo. Rev. Stat. § 4–2–313(b). The principles underlying section 4–2–313 are set out in comment four to that section:

> 4. In view of the principle that the whole purpose of the law of warranty is to determine what it is that the seller has in essence agreed to sell, the policy is adopted of those cases which refuse except in unusual circumstances to recognize a material deletion of the seller's obligation. Thus, a contract is normally a contract for a sale of something describable and described. A clause generally disclaiming "all warranties, express or implied" cannot reduce the seller's obligation with respect to such description and therefore cannot be given literal effect under Section 2–316.
>
> This is not intended to mean that the parties, if they consciously desire, cannot make their own bargain as they wish. But in determining what they have agreed upon in good faith is a factor and consideration should be given to the fact that the probability is small that a real price is intended to be exchanged for a pseudo-obligation.

Id. § 4–2–313 comment 4.

Similarly, Professors White and Summers argue that a seller should not be able to disclaim a warranty created by description.

> We hope courts will reach similar conclusions and strike down attempted disclaimers in cases in which the seller includes a description of the article which amounts to a warranty and then attempts to disclaim all express warranties. To illustrate further: assume that the sales contract describes machinery to be sold as a "haybaler" and then attempts to disclaim all express warranties. If the machine failed to

bale hay and the buyer sued, we would argue that the disclaimer is ineffective. In our judgment, the description of the machine as a "haybaler" is a warranty that the machine will bale hay and, in the words of 2–316, a negation or limitation ought to be "inoperative" since it is inconsistent with the warranty.

J. White & R. Summers, Handbook of the Law Under the Uniform Commercial Code § 12–3 at 433 (2d ed. 1980).

Plaintiff relies principally on two cases that follow this rationale. Century Dodge Inc. v. Mobley, 155 Ga. App. 712, 272 S.E. 2d 502, 504 (1980) (cert. denied); Blankenship v. Northtown Ford, Inc., 95 Ill. App. 3d 303, 420 N.E. 2d 167, 170–71 (1981). In both cases automobile dealers had sold "new" cars which for various reasons did not meet the description of a "new" car. Consequently the courts held that the boilerplate disclaimer provisions of the consumer sales contracts did not relieve the dealers of their responsibility to deliver a "new" car.

We do not question the rationale of the above authorities. Nonetheless, we find them not controlling the instant case. If in this case we were dealing with a consumer transaction, as in the cases just cited, we would be more inclined to follow those authorities. However, as noted in subsequent cases, "the courts are less reluctant to hold educated businessmen to the terms of contracts to which they have entered than consumers dealing with skilled corporate sellers." . . .

Furthermore, both sections 4–2–313 and 4–2–316 express the policy of the statutory scheme to allow parties to make any bargain they wish. Comment four to section 4–2–313 states that if parties consciously desire they can disclaim whatever warranties they wish. Colo. Rev. Stat. § 4–2–313 comment 4 (1973). In addition, comment one to section 4–2–316 explains that its purpose is to "protect a buyer from unexpected and unbargained language of disclaimer." Id. § 4–2–316 comment 1. Consequently, we will not rewrite the contract in this case. The exhibits to the contract which described the goods must be read in conjunction with the contract itself. The contract states that the goods are used and there is no guarantee that they are fit or even *operable*.

If we were to hold the contract in the instant case created undisclaimable express warranties by description, we cannot think of alternative language that would memorialize the intent of the parties—to purchase and sell used "as is" equipment which has value but which may need repairs or additional parts to be fit and operable.

Our holding on this issue does not leave plaintiffs in general without remedy in similar contexts or the plaintiffs in this case with an "empty bargain." If the goods delivered do not meet the description in the contract there is a breach of the contract. In short, if no mast were delivered or if what was delivered was junk metal which in no way resembled a mast, plaintiffs would have a cause of action for breach of the contract.

Finally, plaintiffs did not receive an empty bargain. An appraisal which plaintiffs commissioned valued the goods received at an amount in excess of $3,000,000. . . . The purchase price for the assets was $2,925,000.

The trial court did not err in excluding plaintiffs' evidence regarding breach of warranty.

* * *

AFFIRMED.

NOTES

**(1) "As Is"; "With All Faults."** UCC 2–316(3)(a) declares that "all implied warranties are excluded by expressions like 'as is' [or] 'with all faults.'" This subsection begins with a qualifier: "unless the circumstances indicate otherwise." What the meaning of the introductory phrase?

**Problem 1.** In negotiations that led to the purchase of a mobile home, the seller showed a model mobile home to the buyer. The contract stated in capital letters that the sale was "AS IS." The buyer asserts that the mobile home delivered to him was not like the model. What result? See UCC 2–313(1)(c), 2–316(1); Consolidated Data Terminals v. Applied Digital Data Systems, 708 F.2d 385 (9th Cir.1983).

**(2) Construction of UCC 2–316(1).** Buyer's attorney apparently argued, under UCC 2–316(1), that the words of negation of warranty in ¶ 18.01 were "inoperative" in light of the words of description. Could buyer's attorney have made the essential point differently? Suppose counsel had argued that the "operability" language in ¶ 18.01 referred to future performance of the rigs, but was not intended to declare that the rigs were presently not in operating condition. Would that have been a persuasive argument?

**(3) Commercial Sophistication of Buyers.** On the surface of the UCC Article 2 provisions defining sellers' responsibility for quality, the Code does not differentiate among buyers who are seasoned veterans in buying goods of the kind, buyers who are commercially naive, and buyers in between.[2] Nor does the Code's provision on exclusion or modification of warranties. What, then, explains the emphasis that the *Universal Drilling* court put on the experience and sophistication of the parties? The buyer relied principally on two decisions involving consumer retail sales of new automobiles. The Tenth Circuit expressed no question about the rationale of those decisions, but found them not controlling. Does the Code permit such different treatment for consumer retail sales and sales of business equipment?[3]

---

**2.** The Code does differentiate among sellers on the basis of commercial experience in UCC 2–314. Only a seller who is "a merchant with respect to [the] goods" sold makes an implied warranty of merchantability. "Merchant" is defined in UCC 2–104(1).

**3.** Elsewhere the Commercial Code is sensitive to market levels in sales transactions. The Code provision on contractual limitation or exclusion of consequential damages sets forth

# Western Industries, Inc. v. Newcor Canada Limited

United States Court of Appeals, Seventh Circuit, 1984.
739 F.2d 1198.

■ POSNER, CIRCUIT JUDGE.

Western Industries purchased several custom-built welding machines from Newcor Canada for use in manufacturing microwave oven cavities. The machines did not work right and Western brought this breach of contract action against Newcor, basing federal jurisdiction on diversity of citizenship. Newcor counterclaimed for the unpaid portion of the purchase price of the machines. The jury awarded Western damages of $1.3 million dollars and Newcor about half that (the full unpaid balance of the purchase price of the machines) on its counterclaim. Separate judgments were entered on the two claims and both parties have appealed. The appeals raise a variety of interesting substantive and procedural issues, the former being controlled (the parties agree) by the law of Wisconsin, including the Uniform Commercial Code, which Wisconsin has adopted.

The contract between Western and Newcor grew out of Western's contract with a Japanese manufacturer of microwave ovens, Sharp, to supply Sharp with cavities for microwave ovens. Sharp wanted Western to weld the cavities by a process known as projection welding, because that is how microwave oven cavities are made in Japan; and Western agreed. The projection method is not used in the United States to weld thin metal, such as the cavities of microwave ovens are made of; spot welding is the method used here. So when Western went to Newcor, a leading manufacturer of specialty welding machines, to explore the possibility of buying machines for use in fulfilling its contract with Sharp, it had to ask Newcor to design and build a type of welding machine that Newcor was unfamiliar with. Newcor agreed to do this, however, and after further discussions Western's director of engineering placed a purchase order by phone for eight machines with Newcor's sales engineer on May 17, 1979. According to the memoranda that both men made of the conversation, no specific terms other than the date of delivery were discussed; price was not discussed, for example. On May 23 Newcor delivered to Western a formal written quotation of terms for the sale. On the back of one page a number of standard contract terms were printed, including one disclaiming all liability for consequential damages. Western did not reply immediately, but in mid July it sent Newcor a formal purchase order, mysteriously pre-dated to May 15, that included on the back a set of printed terms one of which stated that the buyer (Western) was entitled to general as well as special damages in the event of a breach of the seller's warranties. On July 20 Newcor sent Western an acknowledgment form stating, "In conformity with our conditions of sale appearing in [the written quotation ...] furnished to you by us, this approves and accepts your order." Western did not respond. The parties never discussed any of the printed terms contained in the contract

---

two standards, one for "injury to the person in the case of consumer goods" and another for "loss [that] is commercial." UCC 2–719(3).

forms that they had exchanged. Three machines were bought later through a similar exchange of forms. The parties treat the sale of all 11 machines as one contract, as shall we.

The machines were built and delivered but turned out to be unusable for making microwave oven cavities. Newcor took the machines back and rebuilt them as spot welding machines, redelivering them to Western a year after the delivery date called for in the contract. As a result of the delay in getting machines that it could use, Western incurred unforeseen expenses in fulfilling its commitment to Sharp; for example, it had to manufacture cavities manually at much higher cost than it would have incurred if it has had proper machines. These expenses are the basis of its damage claim against Newcor.

Newcor's first ground of appeal is that the district judge improperly excluded evidence that the custom of the specialty welding machine trade is not to give a disappointed buyer his consequential damages but just to allow him either to return the machines and get his money back or (for example if the breach consists in delivering them late) keep the machines and get the purchase price reduced to compensate for the costs of delay. . . . Newcor contends that it is not liable for any damages above the purchase price, however those damages are described; and if this is right, then even if Newcor had a contract with Western that it broke it is not liable for any of the damages that Western was awarded.

Although trade custom or usage is a question of fact, see UCC 1–205(2) and Official Comments 4 and 9; . . . the district judge refused to allow Newcor's three principal witnesses on the existence of the alleged trade custom to testify, on the ground that they were incompetent to give such testimony; and having done this the judge later instructed the jury that there was no issue of trade custom in the case. Two of the three witnesses whom Newcor wanted to call were experienced executives of companies that manufacture specialty welding machines (one of them was also the president of those manufacturers' trade association), and between them the two had almost 75 years of experience in selling such machines. The third witness was a former executive of Western and had long experience in buying such machines. These witnesses were prepared to testify that consequential damages were unheard of in their trade. When a machine did not work the manufacturer would spend his own money to fix it or would take it back and refund the purchase price to the buyer, but he would not compensate the buyer for the disruption to the buyer's business caused by the defect.

\* \* \*

Although we are in no position to determine whether the custom alleged by Newcor actually exists, we think it relevant to note that the hypothesis that it exists is certainly not so incredible that testimony on the subject could be excluded by analogy to the principle that excludes testimony in contradiction of the laws of nature. The relevant trade is the manufacture of a particular kind of custom-built machinery. A custom-built machine is quite likely either not to be delivered on time or not to work (not at first, anyway) when it is delivered; anyone who has ever had a house built for him knows the perils of custom design. If a custom-built machine is delivered late, or does not work as the buyer had hoped and expected it would, the buyer's business is quite likely to suffer, and may even be ruined; and as the buyers of these welding machines are substantial manufacturers to whose businesses the machines are essential, the potential costs of defective design or late delivery are astronomical.

. . . [A]ll we need find in order to conclude that Newcor's evidence of trade custom was admissible is that a rational jury could have concluded that, yes, it was the custom for manufacturers of specialty welding machines not to be liable for consequential damages. That contractual liability for such damages (in the absence of special notice) is of relatively recent vintage, that many breaches of contract are (as here) involuntary, that only the sky would be the limit to the amount of consequential damages that manufacturers of machinery indispensable to their customers' businesses might run up, that those manufacturers not only have a better idea of what the potential injury to them might be but also might be able to avert it more easily than their supplier—all these things make it not at all incredible that a custom might have evolved in this industry against a buyer's getting consequential damages in the event of a breach.

If there was such a custom, it would not take the manufacturers of specialty welding machines off the financial hook completely. When they have to take back and resell custom-built machines they face the prospect of a heavy loss. A machine custom-designed to one manufacturer's specifications may not fit any other's. That is no doubt why Newcor spent hundreds of thousands of dollars to rebuild these machines as spot-welding machines that Western could use. That is also why we reject Newcor's argument that Western should be estopped to claim damages because it induced Newcor to rebuild the machines. Newcor rebuilt them in its own interest, to mitigate the loss it would have incurred if it had had to take back the machines and refund the purchase price; if it had taken back the machines it would have had to rebuild them in order to be able to resell them.

But a disclaimer of liability for consequential damages would place some limit on the exposure of the manufacturers of specialty welding machines. It would also give buyers incentives to take their own precautions, which might be efficacious, against the disasters that might befall them if the machines did not work. . . . There was much evidence that Western made a serious mistake in agreeing with Sharp (rather casually as it appears) to build microwave oven cavities by projection welding, a process which, it turned out, American safety standards made infeasible. Western would have been less likely to make such mistakes if it had known with certainty that it would not be able to get consequential damages if the machines didn't work.

* * *

Newcor has a second ground of appeal. It wanted to put before the jury not only the theory that trade custom had supplied a silent contractual term excluding liability for consequential damages, but also the theory that the explicit terms of the contract excluded such liability....

\* \* \*

As a practical matter, however, Newcor's alternative theory is not very different from its main theory—that the custom of the trade excluded liability for consequential damages. Given an exchange of inconsistent forms, Newcor would have to present a reason why its form disclaiming liability for consequential damages should be accepted over Western's form asserting such liability; and the reason would have to be the custom of the trade, as that is the only substantial ground that Newcor has for claiming precedence for its disclaimer....

\* \* \*

The parties raise some other issues, which we have considered but find to have no merit. The judgment in favor of Western on its claim and the judgment in favor of Newcor on its counterclaim are reversed and the case is remanded for a new trial on both claims, with no costs in this court.

REVERSED AND REMANDED.

NOTES

**(1) Battle of the Forms.** The facts in *Western Industries* illustrate a familiar process in which the representatives of the two contracting firms communicate with each other by inserting the details of the particular deal on their firm's printed standard forms. Who writes the terms that are printed on such forms? How can the drafters design terms that will fit the unknown particular agreements in which the forms may be used?

The portion of the court's opinion addressed to the battle of the forms has been omitted. We reviewed the matter in Chapter 2.

**(2) Implied Warranty Disclaimers or Implied Limitations of Damages.** The Commercial Code expressly declares that implied warranties can be excluded or modified by course of dealing, course of performance, or usage of trade. UCC 2–316(3)(c). Recall the decision in *Royal Business Machines*, Section 2, supra. No similar provision is found in UCC 2–719. Is the omission significant?

# Kunststoffwerk Alfred Huber v. R.J. Dick, Inc.

United States Court of Appeals, Third Circuit, 1980.
621 F.2d 560.

■ WEIS, CIRCUIT JUDGE.

In this diversity case, the district court concluded that under the Uniform Commercial Code the buyer has the burden of establishing that the seller agreed to pay consequential damages when goods proved defective. We hold that to avoid such liability the seller must prove an agreement that limits damages, and, in this instance, the course of dealing between the parties was not adequate to demonstrate such an understanding. Accordingly, we modify a judgment in favor of the plaintiff-seller for goods sold to allow credits for losses on resale incurred by the defendant-buyer.

The plaintiff brought suit in the United States District Court for the Eastern District of Pennsylvania to recover the cost of nylon industrial belting it sold to the defendant. Counterclaims asserted that some of the belting had been defective. After a bench trial, the district court entered judgment for the plaintiff, deducting from the requested damages portions of the amounts sought by two of the defendant's counterclaims.

The defendant, R.J. Dick, Inc., distributes nylon cord belting throughout the United States. Its principal place of business is in Iowa, and it maintains a warehouse in King of Prussia, Pennsylvania. The plaintiff is a sole proprietorship that manufactures nylon cord belting in Offenburg, West Germany under the trade name "Vis."

In September 1967 plaintiff's export manager, Alfred Ziegler, sent a letter to the defendant's president, quoting prices on belting and enclosing terms for delivery and payment. Included in the correspondence was a form entitled "General Terms of Sales II." One paragraph in the form limited the plaintiff's liability for defective merchandise to replacement or price reduction and excluded damages of any kind:

> [Reclamations must be made within 10 days after receipt of merchandise and prior to processing or use. Our guaranty is limited to replacement or price reduction and excludes damages of any kind. Also, we do not give a guaranty for specific utilization. Minor deviations do not provide grounds for reclamations.]*

In the following month, Ziegler and Vis's owner, Alfred Huber, visited King of Prussia and arranged for sale of their product to the Dick Company. At no time were the Vis general terms of sale discussed, and, consequently, Dick did not agree to be bound by the provisions of the form, including the limitation on damages recoverable for defective merchandise.

During the period from 1967 to 1974 there were occasions when the plaintiff's product did not meet the defendant's standards, either on initial inspection or after a period of use by defendant's customers. When the defendant issued a credit to a customer for belting that had manufacturing defects, a claim was made to the plaintiff for replacement or credit. If a difference arose between the parties over whether the defect was attributable to the manufacturer, the claim would be compromised.

---

* [The court reproduced the contract clause in a footnote. Eds.]

In late 1973, Dick's problems with the belting increased, the most frequent being delamination, which made the product unusable. Beginning at that time and continuing through 1974, Ziegler complained about Dick's delay in payments. This suit followed the parties' inability to resolve these difficulties.

At trial, the plaintiff asserted that after making allowances for various credits to which it was agreeable, the defendant owed $30,910.29. Against this figure, however, the defendant asserted four counterclaims.

\* \* \*

The court did allow partial recovery on the third and fourth counterclaims. The defendant contended in the third claim that it was entitled to $7,300.69, the amount it had credited its customers for defective material supplied by the plaintiff in 1974. The Court, however, awarded $3,398.25, a sum representing the price the defendant paid plaintiff. ... The fourth claim was for defective belting that one of Dick's distributors sold to a company called Wesco. Dick issued a credit of $7,092.80 on that transaction, but again the court allowed only the amount the defendant had paid plaintiff for the goods, $3,301.95. ... The defendant appeals.

\* \* \*

The issue underlying the remaining two claims is straightforward: Was the defendant entitled to recover the credits granted customers when the product proved defective? In other words, was the defendant entitled to the profits it would have made on those sales? The parties agree that Pennsylvania law applies, particularly Article 2 of the Uniform Commercial Code.

\* \* \*

There is no dispute that plaintiff was aware of the nature of defendant's business, i.e., that the goods were to be resold. In these circumstances, we conclude that under § 2–715(2)(a) the credits that defendant was obliged to extend to customers are proper consequential damages. ...

The plaintiff does not dispute this proposition but argues that the parties agreed to exclude recovery of such damages under U.C.C. § 2–719(1)(a). That section provides that the agreement between the parties may provide for limiting the measure of damages, as by restricting the buyer's remedy to return of the goods and repayment of the price or to repair and replacement nonconforming goods. Pa. Stat. Ann. tit. 12A, § 2–719(1)(a) (Purdon 1970).

There is insufficient evidence in the record to establish an express agreement to limit damages. The trial judge found that the only communication between the parties bearing on the subject was the form sent by plaintiff to defendant in September 1967. He stated that "Dick never expressly consented to the Huber contract" and therefore could not be held subject to it. Nevertheless, the trial judge reasoned that the form had put the defendant on notice that Huber did not intend to assume liability for consequential damages and that Dick therefore had the burden, which it failed to carry, of informing plaintiff that such damages might be demanded.

\* \* \*

The plaintiff argues ... that there was a "course of performance" under U.C.C. § 2–208(1) which established an agreement to forgo consequential damages. Since there was no single contract between the parties, but rather a series of separate sales, we believe it more accurate to characterize the conduct as a "course of dealing," defined in U.C.C. § 1–205(1). The plaintiff's argument is not weakened by adopting the course of dealing route because the Code specifically permits a course of dealing or a usage of trade, unlike a course of performance, to "give particular meaning to and supplement or qualify terms of an agreement." U.C.C. § 1–205(3), Pa. Stat. Ann. tit. 12A, § 1–205(3) (Purdon 1970) (emphasis added).[6] In *Posttape Associates v. Eastman Kodak Co.*, 537 F.2d 751 (3d Cir.1976), we concluded that a limitation of damages could be imposed by a trade usage; it follows that a course of dealing is a circumstance that may establish this term as part of the bargain of the parties in fact. U.C.C. § 1–201(3), Pa. Stat. Ann. tit. 12A, § 1–201(3) (Purdon 1970).

The inquiry then is whether the record establishes the course of dealing the plaintiff suggests. Initially we observe that the burden is on the plaintiff to prove the limitation agreement, ... especially where it is to be found in a course of dealing.[7]

In its findings the district court did not set out facts that would constitute a course of dealing establishing defendant's agreement to forgo consequential damages. On appeal, the plaintiff does not point to specific parts of the record where such facts may be found, nor has our independent review disclosed such evidence. It is not enough that the defendant accepted replacement or credits for the purchase price in many instances. Obviously, if the defects were detected before resale and supplies of belting were available to fill outstanding orders, the defendant might not have had a claim for lost profits. In other instances it may well be that even after resale, the defendant's customers were content to accept replacement rather than demand a refund. Moreover, the record does show that the parties compromised many of the claims for defects in workmanship.

---

**6.** By its own terms, a course of performance goes no further than being "relevant to determine the meaning of the agreement." U.C.C. § 2–208(1), Pa. Stat. Ann. tit. 12A, § 2–208(1) (Purdon 1970). Nevertheless, courts have generally allowed a course of performance to supplement and qualify the terms of an agreement as well. J. White & R. Summers, Uniform Commercial Code § 3–3 (1972).

**7.** In discussing terms supplied by a course of dealing, a usage of trade, and a course of performance, Professors White and Summers observed:

"Who has the burden of proof? The Code does not say. Yet courts are likely to impose the burden of proof on the party who seeks to benefit from evidence of course of dealing, trade usage, or course of performance."

J. White & R. Summers, Uniform Commercial Code § 3–3, at 88 (1972) (footnote omitted).

We find no instances in which the defendant had made a claim for loss of profits on resale transactions other than those underlying the counterclaims. If such claims had been made and then been denied by the plaintiff without protest from the defendant, the argument that a course of dealing established such a limitation might have some force. Cf. U.C.C. § 2–208(1), Pa. Stat. Ann. tit. 12A, § 2–208(1) (Purdon 1970) ("any course of performance accepted or acquiesced in without objection shall be relevant to determine the meaning of the agreement").... Absent such circumstances, however, we cannot say that the plaintiff has met the burden of proving a limitation agreement. Accordingly, the defendant is entitled to recover on the two counterclaims for loss of profits on actual sales.

The total of the two counterclaims is $14,393.49. The parties agree that the increases sought by the defendant and contained in this figure accurately reflect the loss on sales. That total will therefore be deducted from the amount which plaintiff claimed to be due? $30,910.29—thus resulting in an award to the plaintiff of $16,516.80. The case will be remanded to the district court so that it may modify its judgment accordingly.

NOTES

**(1) Choice of Forum.** The German seller in *Kunststoffwerk* was the plaintiff in this suit, which it brought in a foreign court, the "home" court of the United States buyer. What led to this choice of forum? In counseling German or other non-United States sellers or buyers dealing with United States firms, would you recommend structuring transactions to obtain a more familiar or at least a neutral forum? How could this be done?

**(2) Seller's Express Exclusion of Damages.** The German seller's standard form would have excluded liability for consequential damages. Why did the court not give effect to this form? What should seller have done to make this provision part of the agreement?

**(3) Damages Exclusion by Course of Dealing.** Seller's counsel argued that an agreement to exclude liability for consequential damages could be proved by course of performance. The court first corrected counsel's argument, which should have been characterized as based on course of dealing. Should an advocate in the Court of Appeals be expected to know the difference? The appellate court, having recast the argument, rejected it. Was the court's reasoning sound? Was there any conduct inconsistent with the alleged course of dealing? Why is that not sufficient to show agreement?

*b.  ORAL EXPRESS WARRANTIES AND WRITTEN NEGATIONS*

The Commercial Code allows disclaimers only of implied warranties of quality. Purported negation of an express warranty is addressed in UCC 2–316(1). That section directs courts to attempt to give effect to words or conduct that negate express warranties if that construction is consistent, but if consistent construction fails, words or conduct that negate or limit the express warranty are inoperative.

The UCC 2–316(1) rule that protects express warranties against negation is expressly subject to the parol evidence rule in UCC 2–202. Transactions frequently occur in which buyers and sellers execute contract documents that contain a clause negating the existence of any express warranties that are not contained in the documents. Buyers often contend later that, before the documents were brought out for signatures, the sellers had made oral affirmations or promises that would constitute express warranties under UCC 2–313. Efforts to introduce that testimony are contested under a claim that the terms in the documents were intended to be complete and exclusive statements of the terms of the agreement and are therefore excluded by UCC 2–202(b). The words of negation in such documents cannot be construed reasonably as consistent with the words allegedly spoken. The UCC 2–316(1) rule would make the words of negation inoperative, but UCC 2–202 reverses that outcome. Terms in a writing that the parties intended as a final expression of their agreement may not be contradicted by evidence of any prior agreement or of a contemporaneous oral agreement.

Absent a clause in a document that negates express warranties that are not incorporated therein, testimonial evidence that seller made oral affirmations and promises could be offered as additional evidence that supplements the document. While UCC 2–202(a) allows other kinds of parol evidence to be admitted to prove consistent additional terms, the section is silent on admission of testimonial evidence of oral express warranties. Should courts admit such evidence?

Sellers' standard documents often have a clause declaring that the writing is a complete and exclusive statement of the terms of the agreement. These clauses are sometimes referred to as "merger clauses," signifying that all the terms that had been negotiated and agreed to have been merged into the terms of the document. Buyers effort to show, by testimony, that sellers made oral warranties of quality might be challenged as inadmissible under UCC 2–202 on two grounds: (1) that the additional evidence contradicts the merger clause and (2) that document on its face declares that it is intended to be a complete and exclusive statement of the terms of the agreement.

## 2. TERMS ADDED DURING OF AFTER PERFORMANCE

### a. *TERMS IN SELLERS' INVOICES*

In many sales transactions, sellers create and send documents to buyers together with the goods or after delivery. If a transaction involves seller's granting credit, the seller will commonly attach to the goods or send to the buyer an invoice stating the amount due. Sellers sometimes include contract terms in their invoices. If buyers subsequently pay the stated price, do the terms on the invoice become part of the contracts? If the documents have clauses that purport to disclaim implied warranties or exclude statutory damages, are those terms enforceable?

In *Hemmert Agricultural Aviation, Inc. v. Mid–Continent Aircraft Corp.*, part of which we considered in Section 2, there was another issue involving seller's disclaimer of the implied warranty of merchantability. Recall that the parties struck their bargain for sale of a crop duster plane over the telephone. A ferry pilot, Zeeman, delivered the plane to Hemmert two weeks later. Zeeman was in a hurry to return that afternoon with buyer's trade-in. Zeeman asked Hemmert to sign a Purchase Order and Delivery Receipt. Hemmert glanced at the documents and then signed them. Immediately above Hemmert's signature the following printed language appears:

> The undersigned PURCHASER agrees that he has read and that he understands the provisions set out on the reverse side and that the same are included in and are a part of this Aircraft Purchase Order all as if fully set forth on the face hereof.

On the backside of the Purchase Order, there was a disclaimer of the implied warranties of merchantability and fitness for particular purpose. The court refused to enforce the disclaimer.[4]

> The parties did not intend the purchase order to be the final expression of their agreement. The plaintiff's order was taken over the telephone, and the parties never signed a negotiated document. This form purchase order is easily susceptible to interpretation as a billing statement rather than a fully integrated contract, the printed language toward the top providing: "The undersigned agrees to complete the contract and accept delivery as stated in the terms, conditions, warranty and limitations of liability printed on the reverse side of this order." This document creates the impression that it serves as acknowledgment of receipt and that the terms of the contract can be found elsewhere. This case is one where unexpected and unbargained for disclaimers appear in a printed form prepared by the seller. . . .

In several recent cases, the issue was the enforceability of pre-judgment interest provisions that were stated for the first time in sellers' invoices. The courts held that the terms were enforceable. Vulcan Automotive Eqpt. Ltd. v. Global Marine Engine & Parts, Inc., 240 F. Supp. 2d 156 (D.R.I. 2003); Mid–State Contracting, Inc. v. Superior Floor Co., 258 Wis.2d 139, 655 N.W.2d 142 (Wis. App. 2002); Advance Concrete Forms, Inc. v. McCann Construction Specialities Co., 916 F.2d 412 (7th Cir. 1990). The courts held that the governing law was UCC 2–207(2), but reached this remarkable conclusion without determining whether an invoice falls within subsection (1). It is highly questionable that a post-performance invoice could be properly characterized as either an "expression of acceptance" or

---

**4.** The court cited Transamerica Oil Corp. v. Lynes, Inc., 723 F.2d at 762–63; Christopher & Son v. Kansas Paint & Color Co., 215 Kan. 185, 523 P.2d 709, modified on other grounds, 215 Kan. 510, 525 P.2d 626 (1974); Van Den Broeke v. Bellanca Aircraft Corp., 576 F.2d 582 (5th Cir.1978).

a "confirmation." Both kinds of documents are exchanged before the performance stage of contracts.[5]

In another recent case, a clause requiring disputes to be submitted to arbitration was stated for the first time in seller's invoice. The court held that the arbitration clause was not part of the contract. Sibcoimtrex, Inc. v. American Foods Group., Inc., 241 F. Supp. 2d 104 (D. Mass. 2003). Like the other courts, this court held that the controlling law was UCC 2–207(2). The court determined that the term for arbitration was a material alteration of the agreement.[6]

## b. *SHRINKWRAP, CLICKWRAP AND OTHER FORMS OF ELECTRONIC CONTRACTING*

Internet, telephone and mail-order contracting sometimes involves addition of terms to contracts after agreements to purchase have been reached and, indeed, after buyers have paid the purchase price. The following case is one of continuing and intense controversy. It centers on a provision for arbitration in material in the box containing a computer that buyer had purchased and paid for by telephone.

# Hill v. Gateway 2000, Inc.

United States Court of Appeals, Seventh Circuit, 1997.
105 F.3d 1147.

■ EASTERBROOK, CIRCUIT JUDGE.

A customer picks up the phone, orders a computer, and gives a credit card number. Presently a box arrives, containing the computer and a list of terms, said to govern unless the customer returns the computer within 30 days. Are these terms effective as the parties' contract, or is the contract term-free because the order-taker did not read any terms over the phone and elicit the customer's assent?

One of the terms in the box containing a Gateway 2000 system was an arbitration clause. Rich and Enza Hill, the customers, kept the computer more than 30 days before complaining about its components and performance. They filed suit in federal court. . . . Gateway asked the district court to enforce the arbitration clause; the judge refused, writing that "the present record is insufficient to support a finding of a valid arbitration agreement between the parties or that the plaintiffs were given adequate notice of the arbitration clause." Gateway took an immediate appeal, as is its right. 9 U.S.C. § 16(a)(1)(A).

---

**5.** See Comment 1. In a true "battle of forms" case, Comment 5 to UCC 2–207 declares that "a clause providing for interest on overdue invoices" is not a material alteration under UCC 2–207(2). The Comment does not say that this clause can appear for the first time in an invoice.

**6.** In a "battle of forms" case, a federal court of appeals held that an arbitration clause was not a material alteration. In that case, however, the court took into account testimony that there was a trade usage for arbitration of disputes in contracts of that kind. Aceros v. TradeArbed, Inc., 282 F.3d 92 (2d Cir. 2002).

The Hills say that the arbitration clause did not stand out: they concede noticing the statement of terms but deny reading it closely enough to discover the agreement to arbitrate, and they ask us to conclude that they therefore may go to court. Yet an agreement to arbitrate must be enforced "save upon such grounds as exist at law or in equity for the revocation of any contract." 9 U.S.C. § 2. . . . A contract need not be read to be effective; people who accept take the risk that the unread terms may in retrospect prove unwelcome. . . . Terms inside Gateway's box stand or fall together. If they constitute the parties' contract because the Hills had an opportunity to return the computer after reading them, then all must be enforced.

ProCD, Inc. v. Zeidenberg, 86 F.3d 1447 (7th Cir.1996), holds that terms inside a box of software bind consumers who use the software after an opportunity to read the terms and to reject them by returning the product. Likewise, Carnival Cruise Lines, Inc. v. Shute, 499 U.S. 585, 113 L. Ed. 2d 622, 111 S. Ct. 1522 (1991), enforces a forum-selection clause that was included among three pages of terms attached to a cruise ship ticket. ProCD and Carnival Cruise Lines exemplify the many commercial transactions in which people pay for products with terms to follow; ProCD discusses others. 86 F.3d at 1451–52. The district court concluded in ProCD that the contract is formed when the consumer pays for the software; as a result, the court held, only terms known to the consumer at that moment are part of the contract, and provisos inside the box do not count. Although this is one way a contract could be formed, it is not the only way: "A vendor, as master of the offer, may invite acceptance by conduct, and may propose limitations on the kind of conduct that constitutes acceptance. A buyer may accept by performing the acts the vendor proposes to treat as acceptance." Id. at 1452. Gateway shipped computers with the same sort of accept-or-return offer ProCD made to users of its software. ProCD relied on the Uniform Commercial Code rather than any peculiarities of Wisconsin law; both Illinois and South Dakota, the two states whose law might govern relations between Gateway and the Hills, have adopted the UCC; neither side has pointed us to any atypical doctrines in those states that might be pertinent; ProCD therefore applies to this dispute.

Plaintiffs ask us to limit ProCD to software, but where's the sense in that? ProCD is about the law of contract, not the law of software. Payment preceding the revelation of full terms is common for air transportation, insurance, and many other endeavors. Practical considerations support allowing vendors to enclose the full legal terms with their products. Cashiers cannot be expected to read legal documents to customers before ringing up sales. If the staff at the other end of the phone for direct-sales operations such as Gateway's had to read the four-page statement of terms before taking the buyer's credit card number, the droning voice would anesthetize rather than enlighten many potential buyers. Others would hang up in a rage over the waste of their time. And oral recitation would not avoid customers' assertions (whether true or feigned) that the clerk did not read term X to them, or that they did not remember or understand it. Writing provides benefits for both sides of commercial transactions. Customers as a group are better off when vendors skip costly and ineffectual steps such as telephonic recitation, and use instead a simple approve-or-return device. Competent adults are bound by such documents, read or unread. For what little it is worth, we add that the box from Gateway was crammed with software. The computer came with an operating system, without which it was useful only as a boat anchor. ... Gateway also included many application programs. So the Hills' effort to limit ProCD to software would not avail them factually, even if it were sound legally—which it is not.

For their second sally, the Hills contend that ProCD should be limited to executory contracts (to licenses in particular), and therefore does not apply because both parties' performance of this contract was complete when the box arrived at their home. This is legally and factually wrong: legally because the question at hand concerns the formation of the contract rather than its performance, and factually because both contracts were incompletely performed. ProCD did not depend on the fact that the seller characterized the transaction as a license rather than as a contract; we treated it as a contract for the sale of goods and reserved the question whether for other purposes a "license" characterization might be preferable. 86 F.3d at 1450. All debates about characterization to one side, the transaction in ProCD was no more executory than the one here: Zeidenberg paid for the software and walked out of the store with a box under his arm, so if arrival of the box with the product ends the time for revelation of contractual terms, then the time ended in ProCD before Zeidenberg opened the box. But of course ProCD had not completed performance with delivery of the box, and neither had Gateway. One element of the transaction was the warranty, which obliges sellers to fix defects in their products. The Hills have invoked Gateway's warranty and are not satisfied with its response, so they are not well positioned to say that Gateway's obligations were fulfilled when the motor carrier unloaded the box. What is more, both ProCD and Gateway promised to help customers to use their products. Long-term service and information obligations are common in the computer business, on both hardware and software sides. Gateway offers "lifetime service" and has a round-the-clock telephone hotline to fulfil this promise. Some vendors spend more money helping customers use their products than on developing and manufacturing them. The document in Gateway's box includes promises of future performance that some consumers value highly; these promises bind Gateway just as the arbitration clause binds the Hills.

Next the Hills insist that ProCD is irrelevant because Zeidenberg was a "merchant" and they are not. Section 2–207(2) of the UCC, the infamous battle-of-the-forms section, states that "additional terms [following acceptance of an offer] are to be construed as proposals for addition to a contract. Between merchants such terms become part of the contract unless...." Plaintiffs tell us that ProCD came out as it did only because Zeidenberg was a "merchant" and the terms inside ProCD's box were not excluded by the "unless" clause. This argument pays scant attention to the opinion in ProCD, which concluded that, when there is only one form,

"§ 2–207 is irrelevant." 86 F.3d at 1452. The question in ProCD was not whether terms were added to a contract after its formation, but how and when the contract was formed—in particular, whether a vendor may propose that a contract of sale be formed, not in the store (or over the phone) with the payment of money or a general "send me the product," but after the customer has had a chance to inspect both the item and the terms. ProCD answers "yes," for merchants and consumers alike. Yet again, for what little it is worth we observe that the Hills misunderstand the setting of ProCD. A "merchant" under the UCC "means a person who deals in goods of the kind or otherwise by his occupation holds himself out as having knowledge or skill peculiar to the practices or goods involved in the transaction", § 2–104(1). Zeidenberg bought the product at a retail store, an uncommon place for merchants to acquire inventory. His corporation put ProCD's database on the Internet for anyone to browse, which led to the litigation but did not make Zeidenberg a software merchant.

At oral argument the Hills propounded still another distinction: the box containing ProCD's software displayed a notice that additional terms were within, while the box containing Gateway's computer did not. The difference is functional, not legal. Consumers browsing the aisles of a store can look at the box, and if they are unwilling to deal with the prospect of additional terms can leave the box alone, avoiding the transactions costs of returning the package after reviewing its contents. Gateway's box, by contrast, is just a shipping carton; it is not on display anywhere. Its function is to protect the product during transit, and the information on its sides is for the use of handlers ("Fragile!" "This Side Up!") rather than would-be purchasers.

Perhaps the Hills would have had a better argument if they were first alerted to the bundling of hardware and legal-ware after opening the box and wanted to return the computer in order to avoid disagreeable terms, but were dissuaded by the expense of shipping. What the remedy would be in such a case—could it exceed the shipping charges—is an interesting question, but one that need not detain us because the Hills knew before they ordered the computer that the carton would include some important terms, and they did not seek to discover these in advance. Gateway's ads state that their products come with limited warranties and lifetime support. How limited was the warranty—30 days, with service contingent on shipping the computer back, or five years, with free onsite service? What sort of support was offered? Shoppers have three principal ways to discover these things. First, they can ask the vendor to send a copy before deciding whether to buy. The Magnuson–Moss Warranty Act requires firms to distribute their warranty terms on request, 15 U.S.C. § 2302(b)(1)(A); the Hills do not contend that Gateway would have refused to enclose the remaining terms too. Concealment would be bad for business, scaring some customers away and leading to excess returns from others. Second, shoppers can consult public sources (computer magazines, the Web sites of vendors) that may contain this information. Third, they may inspect the documents after the product's delivery. Like Zeidenberg, the Hills took the third option. By keeping the computer beyond 30 days, the Hills accepted Gateway's offer, including the arbitration clause.

* * *

... The decision of the district court is vacated, and this case is remanded with instructions to compel the Hills to submit their dispute to arbitration.

## NOTES

**(1) Rolling Contracts.** This case is one of the most controversial commercial law decisions of recent years. It has spawned the phrase "rolling contract" to describe a theory of contract formation that makes the point of closure of the bargain later than would otherwise have been found under the formation rules of UCC Article 2.

*UCC 2–204 and 2–206.* The Court of Appeals declared that the critical question was "how and where the contract was formed." The court concluded that the contract was still being formed when the buyers received the goods and that their retention of the goods for more than 30 days bound them to the arbitration clause that was in a document in the box. The court did not refer to UCC 2–204 or UCC 2–206, the primary provisions on formation of sales contracts.[7] If UCC 2–204 had been applied to the facts set forth in the first paragraph of the opinion, was a contract formed by the end of the telephone call? UCC 2–206(1)(b) provides that an offer to buy goods for prompt shipment shall be construed as inviting acceptance either by a prompt promise to ship or by prompt shipment. If those provisions had been applied, when was buyer's offer accepted?

The Court of Appeals justified deferral of the time of contract formation on two quite different grounds: (i) The court found that the Hills were aware that "some important terms" would be found in the box containing goods purchased. (ii) The court found that, in some negotiation settings, practical considerations preclude sellers from making full disclosures of their contract terms. Are either of these grounds persuasive?

The warranty-in-the-box ground refers to a familiar commercial situation in which buyers contract with retail dealers to buy goods that are delivered with warranties. Often the warranties are not those of the sellers, but are rather manufacturers' warranties. Sometimes, as here, manufacturers sell directly to the end-users. Are warranty obligations that are undertaken after a contract has been formed enforceable or unenforceable under UCC Article 2? Such obligations enlarge the legal rights of buyers, whose

---

**7.** The court relied extensively on an earlier Seventh Circuit decision that did refer to UCC 2–204 and 2–206. ProCD, Inc. v. Zeidenberg, 86 F.3d 1447 (7th Cir. 1996). ProCD did not involve a sale of goods. The issue in that case was the nature of a software license. Nonetheless, the court applied Article 2 in that dispute.

tacit assent to that result can be taken for granted and whose subsequent conduct may reflect actual reliance on the warranty terms. The warrantors' obligations do not require buyers to pay more for the goods, but modification agreements are enforceable without the need for consideration under UCC 2–209(1). Could merchant sellers renege of the warranties and be acting in good faith? Does it follow that buyers' power to enforce post-sale warranties depends on buyers' willingness to be bound by post-sale terms that reduce their contract rights or impair their ability to enforce those rights?

The "practical considerations" rationale for allowing sellers to incorporate contract terms into the boxes is dubious. First, sellers' terms that reduce buyers' contract rights or impair their ability to enforce those rights are not complex. It takes only a moment to say "Disputes under this agreement must be submitted to arbitration." There is no practical problem in disclosing, or at least outlining, rights-negating terms at the point of sale in any contracting situation, whether by telephone, email, or in-store. The verbose terms to which the court appears to refer are the terms of the sellers' express warranties and related promises, which add to the buyers' contract rights, in ways that the buyers generally expect in transactions of that kind. Second, even if non-disclosure is impractical in an immediate negotiation, is it impractical for sellers to communicate, in full text, all of their required terms before they ship the goods? Before they cash credit card vouchers?

*UCC 2–207.* The buyers tried to escape from the arbitration clause by argument based on UCC 2–207(2), which binds only merchants. It is not clear whether they also argued that the clause was a material alteration. The court held that UCC 2–207 was inapplicable.

The basic transactional pattern in *Hill* has been litigated repeatedly in a line of cases, many involving the same seller.[8]

BROWER v. GATEWAY 2000, INC., 676 N.Y.S.2d 569, 246 App. Div. 2d 246 (App. Div. 1998). The facts are similar to *Hill*. The complaint alleged, *inter alia*, that Gateway was in breach of an express warranty.

---

**8.** This line of cases includes a number disputes that involve software license agreements rather than sales of tangible goods. Many people consider the first case in the line to be *ProCD v. Zeidenberg*, a software license case. Software license cases have spawned colorful new jargon to describe various transactional events, such as "shrinkwrap" and "clickwrap." In these license cases, some courts tend to apply UCC Article 2 as the governing law, but that choice of law remains a disputed question. Recall that the Proposed Revision of Article 2, with no change in the text, contains a comment stating that "this article does not directly apply to an electronic transfer of information, such as the transaction involved in *Specht v. Netscape*, 150 F. Supp. 2d 585 (S.D.N.Y. 2001), *aff'd*, 306 F.3d 17 (2d Cir. 2002)." R2–103, Comment 7. The Court of Appeals in that case found it unnecessary to decide whether the matter was governed by common law or UCC Article 2. The new Comment arguably applies to the current text of Article 2. Whether this or other reasoning will change the pattern of courts' referring to Article 2 in license software cases is yet to be determined.

Gateway moved to compel enforcement of the arbitration clause. The court adopted the analysis of the Seventh Circuit, declared that the transaction was outside the scope of UCC 2–207, and held that the buyer had agreed to the arbitration clause contained in the document that was in the box by retention of the equipment beyond 30 days. The court held, further, that the arbitration clause was unconscionable because, under the method of arbitration specified (International Chamber of Commerce), a claimant had to pay up front a filing fee of $4,000.00, half of which was non-refundable whatever the outcome. The amount of the filing fee was in excess of the price of the computer equipment. Gateway proposed change to the American Arbitration Association. The appellate court remanded the case to the trial court for determination of the burden of the AAA system on a consumer buyer.[9]

KLOCEK v. GATEWAY, INC., 104 F. Supp. 2d 1332 (D. Kan. 2000). This case is similar to *Hill.* The complaint alleged, *inter alia,* that Gateway was in breach of an express warranty of quality. At the procedural stage of the decision, on motion to dismiss the complaint, the parties were in disagreement as to the facts. Buyer asserted that he bought and paid for a computer at a Gateway retail store and took it home with him. Seller asserted that the computer had been shipped to the buyer from the factory. Inside the box was a document that contained an arbitration clause. Unlike the 30–day provision in *Hill,* the document in Klocek's box declared: "by keeping your Gateway 2000 computer system beyond five (5) days after the date of delivery, you accept these Terms and Conditions." The court rejected the analysis of the *Hill* court, held that the case was governed by UCC 2–207, and declined to enforce the arbitration clause on the ground that Klocek, a non-merchant, had not agreed to Gateway's proposed addition to the contract.[10]

**(2) Post–Sale Disclaimers or Damages Excluders.** Warranty, disclaimer of implied warranty and damages exclusion were involved only obliquely in *Hill* and the line of sales cases that followed. The issue before the courts was the enforceability of an arbitration clause.[11] The court's decision does not turn on how much buyers may have lost in warranty protection or remedial rights. Were *Hemmert* and the invoice cases relevant to the problem in *Hill* and the later cases?

---

**9.** The New York court was persuaded in part by the action of a federal district court, in a similar case involving the same Gateway arbitration clause. That court had ordered that arbitration be conducted under the AAA rules. Filias v. Gateway 2000, Inc., 1997 WL 33814599 (E.D. Mich. 1997).

**10.** The court declared, without any analysis, that the document in the box was either an "expression of acceptance" or a "confirmation," and therefore was within UCC 2–207(1).

**11.** Gateway's arbitration clause was held to be unconscionable in Brower v. Gateway 2000, Inc., 246 App.Div.2d 246, 676 N.Y.S.2d 569 (App.Div.1998). The New York court

### c. WARRANTIES AND REMEDIAL PROMISES "IN THE BOX"

Not all terms added during performance are inimical to the interests of buyers. Commonly the terms of express warranties of quality or remedial promises are detailed for the first time when goods are delivered to buyers. There may have been allusions to these commitments during pre-purchase negotiations, but often the exact terms are not negotiated or discussed at that stage. Sellers who assume responsibility for the quality of the goods in these post-purchase commitments do not contest their enforceability, even though, under contract doctrines of agreement and consideration, it might be difficult to find grounds for enforcement.[12]

Packaging warranties and remedial promises with the goods may be done by the immediate seller, but this form of merchandising is more commonly used by manufacturers who have no contractual relationship with retail buyers. We will consider commitments by manufacturers in the next chapter.

## (B) INTERNATIONAL SALES LAW

The Convention on Contracts for the International Sale of Goods does not contain regulatory provisions comparable to UCC 2–316 and 2–719. Under CISG 6, the parties may "derogate from or vary the effect of" any of the Convention's provisions. Article 6 therefore permits parties to agree to disclaimers of a quality warranty, that would otherwise arise under CISG 35(2),[13] or to clauses limiting damages otherwise provided by the Convention, particularly by CISG 74. On the surface, therefore, it appears that the regulatory provisions of domestic law, like those of UCC Article 2, would not apply to international sales contracts.

However, the Convention does not purport to exclude application of all domestic laws to international sales contracts. Thus, CISG 4(a) declares that the Convention is not concerned with "the validity of the contract or any of its provisions." Should CISG 4 be construed to permit challenge of

---

followed the Seventh Circuit analysis in *Hill* with respect to contract formation. After striking down the Gateway clause, the appellate court remanded the case to allow the trial court to fashion an arbitration clause that was not unconscionable.

**12.** Reported cases involving sellers' resisting enforcement of remedial promises have not been found, but there are a few reported cases in which manufacturers contended that their "in the box" promises or warranties were not enforceable on the ground that these promises or warranties were not "part of the basis of the bargain" under UCC 2–313. Two courts accepted the dubious contention that UCC 2–313 was the governing law and held that delivery of the "in the box" documents had occurred soon enough after the sale to satisfy the requirement of that section of Article 2. Fire Insurance Exchange v. Electrolux Home Products, 2006 WL 2925286, 61 U.C.C. Rep. Serv. 2d 181 (E.D. Mich. 2006); Murphy v. Mallard Coach Co., 179 A.D.2d 187, 582 N.Y.S.2d 528 (1992).

**13.** CISG 35(2) also contains a provision that the parties may agree otherwise.

warranty disclaimers or clauses limiting damages in international sales contracts as "invalid" under United States or another nation's domestic law?[14]

"The answer should be No. ... It would be awkward to require [an international sales] contract to 'mention merchantability' in order to disclaim an implied obligation under [CISG] 35(2) that ... does not itself refer to 'merchantability.' ...

"The argument [that CISG 4(a) incorporates UCC 2–316(2) and (3)] proves too much for it leads to the conclusion that any domestic rule that denied full literal effect to a contract provision on the ground that it does not accurately represent the parties' understanding would constitute a rule of "validity." The reference to domestic rules of "validity" in Article 4(a) cannot be carried this far without intruding on the Convention's rules for interpreting international sales contracts. More specifically, Article 8 addresses a basic question of interpretation in a manner somewhat similar to the rules of domestic law in UCC 2–316. ... The point is not, of course, that Article 8 of the Convention and UCC 2–316 are identical but rather that both address the same issue. It follows that the reference to "validity" in Article 4(a) of the Convention may not be read so broadly as to import domestic rules that would supplant articles of the Convention such as Article 8." J. Honnold, Uniform Law for International Sales §§ 233–234 (2d ed. 1991). *Contra*: Note, 53 Fordham L. Rev. 863 (1985).

Whether or not CISG 4(a) incorporates regulatory provisions of the Uniform Commercial Code, counsel for sellers engaged in international sales transactions to which United States law may apply would be prudent to advise their clients to contract in accordance with the disclosure requirements of the UCC. However, an international sales contract drafter should not rely on the UCC rules that a disclaimer clause is sufficient if it uses the phrases "as is" or "with all faults." To a non-U.S. buyer, the full import of these provisions may not have been clear.

———

**Problem 2.** The parties in *Western Industries* were a United States buyer and a Canadian seller. The transaction occurred before the CISG took effect. If the CISG had applied, would the outcome have changed?

**Problem 3.** The parties in *Kunststoffwerk* were a United States buyer and a German seller. The transaction occurred before the CISG took effect. If the CISG had applied, would the outcome have changed?

---

**14.** CISG 7(2) refers to the rules of private international law for choice of law on questions not settled by the Convention. Since questions of "validity" are expressly not governed by the Convention, the law governing such questions would be found by application of the choice of law rules under private international law. In an appropriate case, United States domestic law might be chosen as the governing law.

---

## SECTION 4.   REMEDIAL PROMISES: OBLIGATION TO REPAIR OR REPLACE GOODS

### (A) DOMESTIC UNITED STATES LAW

#### 1.   INTRODUCTION

Remedial promises have been part of sales contracts for some time. There is a relationship between sellers' remedial promises and sellers' warranties of quality. Understanding that relationship requires close legal analysis. Remedial promises are also related to statutory remedies for breach of warranties of quality. The nature of these relationships has been confusing to many lawyers and judges. The core of the analytic difficulties lies in the difference between a contractual obligation, which may or may not be met, and the legal remedy for breach of another contractual obligation. Consider the following contract scenarios:

*Case 1.* A contract for sale of a printing press is formed without any express warranties of quality and includes effective disclaimers of all implied warranties. The contract has the following clause: "If the printing press is found to be defective in materials or workmanship within one year after it has been delivered to the buyer, seller will, at its option, repair or replace the printing press."

*Case 2.* A contract for sale of a printing press is formed with effective disclaimer of all implied warranties of quality but including the following express warranty and remedy clauses: "Seller warrants that the printing press is free of defects in materials or workmanship if, and only if, any such defect is brought to seller's attention within one year after delivery. In the event of breach of this warranty, seller's liability shall be limited to the repair or replacement, at seller's option, of the printing press. This is buyer's exclusive remedy. Seller assumes no liability for incidental or consequential damages."

Functionally, the two contracts are quite similar. Both involve manufactured goods, which have substantial market value and which are expected to have a relatively long useful life. These are the kinds of transactions in which the repair or replace arrangement is likely to be found. Buyers that discover defects in materials or workmanship within the prescribed time have the right to call on the sellers to repair the defects or replace the equipment. From a buyer's perspective, either outcome gives buyer equipment that works as expected, although perhaps not at the date expected, without need to use any legal process. From a seller's perspective, the bargain provides the opportunity to fulfill a contractual obligation by using its own personnel and resources to make post-delivery repair to the original equipment, and, if necessary, to replace the original equipment with another of its products. The cost to seller of repairing or replacing defective goods is likely to be less than the amount of the damages that would be at risk in a legal proceeding for breach of warranty. The contracts have many of the positive aspects of a win-win arrangement.

The win-win outcome does not occur, however, if the seller does not repair defective equipment or replace it with non-defective goods. Seller and buyer now have a legal dispute in which the buyer is the aggrieved party. Neither type of contract has an agreed remedy for this dispute. If the parties do not settle the matter, the dispute will be referred to a court of law. Legally, however, the two cases will be quite dissimilar.

The aggrieved buyer in *Case 1* has a cause of action for seller's breach of a contractual promise,[1] but no claim for breach of warranty. There are no warranties of quality in *Case 1*.[2]

Although the controversy arises out of a sales contract, no provisions in Article 2 are germane.[3] Therefore, under UCC 1–103(b), the matter would be determined by the underlying principles of law and equity. Under those principles, the aggrieved buyer in *Case 1* is entitled to damages that are measured by the value of the seller's promise to repair or replace, together with incidental and consequential damages for that breach.

There is an express warranty of quality in *Case 2* and that warranty has been breached, but the contract excluded all statutory remedies for that breach of warranty and substituted seller's obligation to repair or replace defective goods. The buyer still has an unsatisfied grievance for breach of the express warranty. Does the buyer have a claim for damages? An answer might be found by interpretation of the sales contract: Did the buyer and seller intend that, if seller failed to repair or replace defective goods, buyer should be left without any redress? Or did the parties agree, implicitly, that the clause excluding all statutory remedies would become inoperative if seller failed to repair or replace and buyer could seek damages provided by the Commercial Code?

Although the issue might be resolved as a matter of interpretation of the parties' agreement in fact, Article 2 appears to provide an answer as a matter of law. UCC 2–719(1)(a) lists repair or replacement of nonconforming goods as an example of a contract "remedy." UCC 2–719(2) provides: "Where circumstances cause an exclusive or limited remedy to fail of its essential purpose, remedy may be had as provided in this Act."[4] The

---

**1.**  Seller may have contract defenses to a claim of breach. If, for example, buyer refused to allow seller to have access to the goods, seller would not be in breach. Other contract defenses may exist.

**2.**  To underscore this conclusion, assume that the clause in *Case 1* was not in the sales contract, but was rather in a contract with a third party. Such arrangements between buyers and non-sellers, sometimes called something like "extended warranties," are often found in the marketplace. The non-sellers have no warranty obligations, but they do have whatever obligations they undertake in their contracts.

**3.**  The proposed revision of Article 2 would adds a set of provisions on remedial promises made by sellers in contracts of sale.

**4.**  The quality of the drafting of this subsection can be criticized on multiple levels. Efforts to interpret the subsection by close attention to its words and syntax are frustratingly difficult. The use of the passive voice is one source of difficulty of obscurity. To what does

statutory remedy for breach of warranty is damages, which are ordinarily measured by UCC 2–714. If buyer has the goods repaired by a third party, the cost of repair might be claimed as damages under UCC 2–714(1). Alternatively, the buyer is entitled, under UCC 2–714(2), to damages measured by the difference between the market value of conforming goods and the market value of the delivered goods.

But the buyer may have other legal rights. Consider again the meaning of the sales contract in *Case 2*. Did the buyer and seller intend that seller could repair or replace, if it wished to do so, but could decide to refuse to repair or replace and not thereby incur liability? In simplest terms, did the seller in *Case 2* have a contractual obligation comparable to the seller in *Case 1*? The answer appears to be affirmative. If the sales contract in *Case 2* obligates the seller to repair or replace the goods, that contractual obligation has not been performed.[5] The remedies for breach of that obligation are not the same as the remedies for breach of a warranty of the quality of the goods. The aggrieved buyer in *Case 2*, if enforcing the promise to repair or replace, has the same rights and remedies as the buyer in *Case 1*. An aggrieved buyer in *Case 2* cannot recover damages for breach or warranty and damages for breach of the remedial promise to the extent that the remedies overlap. Courts should and do deny double recovery.

Breach of warranty and breach of remedial promise differ on matters other than remedies. One of these differences involves the statute of limitations. The date on which the period of limitations begins to run for breach of warranty is different from the date for breach of a remedial promise. Section 2–725(1) has a 4–year limitations period that applies to claims for breach of warranty. Claims for breach of remedial promises may or may not be governed by the statute of limitations in Article 2. These claims may be subject to the general contract limitations period, which is longer than four years in most jurisdictions, commonly six years.

In the cases and materials that follow, buyers are aggrieved by the failure or refusal of sellers to do what they said they would do and are seeking to recover statutory remedies for breach of warranty. The cases are of a kind that resembles *Case 2*. Subsection 2–719(2) is in play. The remedy that the buyers seek, however, is not only damages measured by UCC 2–714. The most contested question is whether buyers can recover consequential damages notwithstanding provisions in the sales contracts that excluded liability for consequential damages.

---

"circumstances" refer? Does "circumstances" extend to anything other than the seller's action or inaction? A remedy cannot have a "purpose." The persons that place an exclusive remedy clause in a sales contract have purposes, but the purpose of the buyer and the purpose of the seller are probably not the same. Whose purpose is "essential"?

Comment 1 states: "... where an apparently fair and reasonable clause because of circumstances fails of its purpose or operates to deprive either party of the substantial value of the bargain, it must give way to the general remedy provisions of this Article." Does the Comment help to give meaning to the text? Does the Comment have substantive provisions that have no textual basis?

**5.** Failure to repair or replace may not be a breach of contract if the seller has a contract defense.

## 2. SUBSTANCE OF SELLERS' OBLIGATION

# Milgard Tempering, Inc. v. Selas Corp.

United States Court of Appeals, Ninth Circuit, 1990.
902 F.2d 703.

■ HALL, CIRCUIT JUDGE:

This appeal marks the end of nearly seven years of litigation over a "sure fire" glass tempering furnace purchased over ten years ago. The seller, Selas Corporation of America ("Selas") appeals the judgment of the district court awarding the buyer, Milgard Tempering, Inc. ("Milgard"), damages resulting from its failure to repair serious defects in the furnace. ... We have jurisdiction under 28 U.S.C. § 1291 (1988) and affirm.

I

... On June 11, 1979, [Milgard] entered into a carefully-negotiated contract with appellant/cross-appellee Selas to purchase a horizontal batch tempering furnace. ... Under the contract, Selas agreed to design and manufacture the furnace for $1.45 million. Its design was complex, and in Selas' eyes, experimental. However, Selas marketed it as a working piece of equipment. The contract provided a $50,000 bonus if Selas delivered all the major components before January 31, 1980. It also provided a penalty of $5,000 per week (not to exceed a total of $25,000) for every week of late delivery after March 31, 1980. Selas failed to meet either deadline, having completed delivery of major components in November, 1982.

Selas agreed to assemble the furnace at Milgard's plant and to assist in a "debugging period" that both parties expected would end June or July 1980. The contract also required Selas, in a series of preacceptance tests, to demonstrate that the furnace was capable of achieving designated yield and cycle rates. Section 28.5 of the contract limited Selas' liability for breach of warranty to repair or replacement of the furnace and barred liability for consequential damages. The parties modified the contract and agreed to forego the preacceptance tests and instead place the furnace in commercial production in July, 1980, thus making glass available for the "debugging" process.

By January 1982, Selas continued work on the furnace, but failed to achieve yield and cycle rates that substantially conformed with the contract specifications. Milgard then filed suit against Selas for breach of contract. In March 1982, the parties, without counsel, attempted to enter into a contractual agreement to settle the dispute. Under the proposed agreement, Selas would take over the tempering operation for 60 days to demonstrate the furnace's ability to achieve a 90 yield rate. It would also pay any operating losses Milgard incurred during that period. Then, if Milgard operated the furnace for six months without incident, Selas would "finetune" the furnace to achieve a 95 rate. Selas did the work and paid Milgard's operating losses. Milgard dismissed the suit without prejudice.

However, during the six-month period, the furnace failed to perform to the specifications of either the contract or the attempted settlement agreement.

Milgard initiated a second lawsuit on March 4, 1983, alleging breach of contract and breach of warranty. On June 29, 1984, Judge Tanner in the district court granted summary judgment in favor of Selas. . . . This court, in *Milgard Tempering, Inc. v. Selas Corp. of America*, 761 F.2d 553 (9th Cir.1985) [hereinafter Milgard I], reversed and remanded for trial. . . .

On remand, after a five-week bench trial, Judge Bryan in the district court found that the furnace had never lived up to the specifications in the contract. He held that the limited repair remedy failed of its essential purpose and that Selas' default was sufficiently severe to expunge the cap on consequential damages. He awarded Milgard $1,076,268 in net damages. . . .

Selas appeals the judgment and denial of its motion for new trial. . . . We affirm.

## II

Selas . . . argues that the district court erred in ruling that the limited repair remedy failed of its "essential purpose" and that such failure lifted the contractual cap on consequential damages.

### A

Section 28.5 of the contract limited Milgard's remedies in the event of breach of warranty to repair or replacement of the defective equipment.

[In the event of a breach of any warranty, express, implied or statutory, or in the event the equipment is found to be defective in workmanship or material or fails to conform to the specifications thereof, *[Selas'] liability shall be limited to the repair or replacement of such equipment as is found to be defective or non-conforming,* provided that written notice of any such defect or non-conformity must be given to Selas within 1 year from the date of acceptance, or 15 months from completion of shipment, whichever first occurs. In the event that acceptance is delayed through the fault of Selas, then the Selas 1 year warranty shall be applicable and not begin until the date of acceptance. *Selas assumes no liability for no [sic] consequential or incidental damages of any kind (including fire or explosion in the starting, testing, or subsequent operation of the equipment), and the Purchaser assumes all liability for the consequences of its use or misuse by the Purchaser or his employees. In no event will Selas be liable for damages resulting from the non-operation of Purchaser's plant, loss of product, raw materials or production as a result of the use, misuse or inability to use the equipment covered by this proposal* or from injury to any person or property alleged to be caused by or resulting from the use of the product produced with the equipment to be supplied to Purchaser by Selas pursuant to this proposal whether the customer or Purchaser is mediate or immediate. Purchaser hereby releases [Selas] of and from and indemnifies [it] against, all liability not specifically assumed by [it] hereunder. (Emphasis added).]*

Such limitations on a party's remedies are permitted by Washington's version of the U.C.C., Wash.Rev.Code § 62A.2–719(1)(a) (West Supp. 1989).

An exclusive or limited remedy ... must be viewed against the background of § 62A.2–719(2).... This section requires a court to examine the contract in general and the remedy provision in particular to determine what the remedy's essential purpose is and whether it has failed.

A limited repair remedy serves two main purposes. First, it serves to shield the seller from liability during her attempt to make the goods conform. Second, it ensures that the buyer will receive goods conforming to the contract specifications within a reasonable period of time....

A contractual provision limiting the remedy to repair or replacement of defective parts fails of its essential purpose within the meaning of § 62A.2–719(2) if the breaching manufacturer or seller is unable to make the repairs within a reasonable time period. ... It is not necessary to show negligence or bad faith on the part of the seller, for the detriment to the buyer is the same whether the seller's unsuccessful efforts were diligent, dilatory, or negligent. ...

The district court in this case found that the furnace had never lived up to the specifications of the contract. ... Moreover, the court found that the few successful improvements were not made within a reasonable period of time, taking over two and one-half years. We agree that under these circumstances, the unreasonable delay and ultimate failure in repair made the repair remedy ineffective; thus, the remedy failed of its essential purpose.

Although the contract did not guarantee a specific time for completion of debugging, the court found that the writing was not completely integrated.... Looking at the commercial context, the court found that both parties implicitly agreed that the complete period for start up and "debugging" would take about eight weeks....

### B

Washington courts have not addressed the issue of whether failure of a limited repair remedy may serve to invalidate a consequential damages exclusion. Therefore, it is our responsibility to determine how the state's supreme court would resolve it. In undertaking this task, we may draw upon recognized legal sources including statutes, treatises, restatements, and published opinions.... We may also look to "well-reasoned decisions from other jurisdictions." ...

### 1

We begin our analysis with Fiorito Bros., Inc. v. Fruehauf Corp., 747 F.2d 1309, 1314–15 (9th Cir.1984). In that case, we held that under

---

* [The court reproduced the contract in a footnote. Eds.]

Washington law, the failure of a repair remedy does not automatically remove a cap on consequential damages. We predicted that Washington courts would take a case-by-case approach and examine the contract provisions to determine whether the exclusive remedy and damage exclusions are either "separable elements of risk allocation" or "inseparable parts of a unitary package of risk-allocation." Id. at 1315 (quoting district court).

If the exclusions are inseparable, we reasoned, a court's analysis should track the Official Washington Comments to § 62A.2–719(2) [hereinafter Washington Comments], which explain that the subsection "relates to contractual arrangements which become oppressive by change of circumstances...." 747 F.2d at 1315. We then affirmed the district court's ruling that the seller's arbitrary and unreasonable refusal to live up to the limited repair clause "rendered the damages limitation clause oppressive and invalid." Id.

Fiorito relied heavily on this circuit's analysis of Cal. Com. Code § 2719(2) (West 1964) in [S.M. Wilson & Co. v. Smith Int'l, Inc.,], 587 F.2d 1363. Wilson involved a contract between commercially sophisticated parties for a tunnel boring machine. The contract contained both a limited repair clause and a cap on consequential damages. After concluding that the repair remedy failed of its essential purpose within § 2719(2), this court held that the bar to consequential damages remained enforceable. We explained:

> Parties of relatively equal bargaining power negotiated an allocation of their risks of loss. Consequential damages were assigned to the buyer, Wilson. The machine was a complex piece of equipment designed for the buyer's purposes. The seller Smith did not ignore his obligation to repair; he simply was unable to perform it. This is not enough to require that the seller absorb losses the buyer plainly agreed to bear. Risk shifting is socially expensive and should not be undertaken in the absence of a good reason. An even better reason is required when to so shift is contrary to a contract freely negotiated. *The default of the seller is not so total and fundamental as to require that its consequential damage limitation be expunged from the contract.*

Id. at 1375 (emphasis added). However this court in Wilson quickly pointed out that its holding was limited to the facts and was in no way intended to state that consequential damages caps always survive failure of limited repair remedies. Id. at 1375–76.

### 2

The district court in the instant case found Selas' default "fundamental, but not total." Nonetheless, it found the breach sufficiently fundamental to remove the cap on consequential damages. Selas claims that the court misunderstood the legal standard and that consequential damages may be allowed only when the seller's breach is both total and fundamental.

We agree that the district court's characterization of the case law was flawed. However, the analysis it employed was not. This court has found nothing magical about the phrase "total and fundamental" default in relation to U.C.C. 2–719(2). In Fiorito we eschewed such wooden analysis, leaving "[e]ach case [to] stand on its own facts." Id., 747 F.2d at 1314 (quoting Wilson, 587 F.2d at 1376). We further expressed our distaste for talismanic analysis in Milgard I, finding the "oppressive circumstances" analysis utilized by Fiorito and the Washington Comments and the "total and fundamental" default analysis in Wilson in accord with each other. 761 F.2d at 556.

The task before the district court was to examine the remedy provisions and determine whether Selas' default caused a loss which was not part of the bargained-for allocation of risk.... This was the analysis that the district court actually employed.

We agree with the district court's decision to lift the cap on consequential damages. Milgard did not agree to pay $1.45 million in order to participate in a science experiment. It agreed to purchase what Selas represented as a cutting-edge glass furnace that would accommodate its needs after two months of debugging. Selas' inability to effect repair despite 2.5 years of intense, albeit injudicious,[9] effort caused Milgard losses not part of the bargained-for allocation of risk. Therefore, the cap on consequential damages is unenforceable.

### III

Next, Selas challenges the district court's determination of damages. The court had found that for 21 months (April 1, 1980 to December 31, 1982), the furnace was incapable of reaching any of the yield rates outlined in the contract. Thereafter, the furnace could reach a few with some regularity. Accordingly, the district court calculated damages for two time periods. First, it calculated Milgard's lost profits during the 21–month "damage" period. Second, it calculated losses Milgard did and would incur after December 31, 1982.

\* \* \*

All three tests for loss of profits have been met in this case. First, the district judge made the factual finding that the parties contemplated the possibility of lost profits. Because § 28.5 of the contract refers to such profits, this finding is not clearly erroneous.

Second, the district court found that the failure of the machine to conform to the contract specifications proximately caused Milgard to lose profits. Selas does not challenge this finding and we do not disturb it.

---

**9.** Selas exacerbated the repair problem by not providing a qualified process engineer during the initial debugging period and stubbornly refusing to replace the unproven ircon transfer system with more reliable methods that were available. We therefore agree with the district court's conclusion that "Selas did not make a completely open and honest effort to bring the furnace into compliance with the contract requirements." ... However, as noted earlier, the question of Selas' good faith is not dispositive of this appeal.

Third, the district court had a sufficient factual basis upon which to make its computation of lost profits. As forecast by Larsen and its progeny, Milgard's sole source of evidence in this area was its expert witness, Dr. Finch. Although the district judge found some of Dr. Finch's figures difficult to swallow, he pointed out that that did not negate them. . . . [T]he court discounted the damage award in accordance with the weight of Finch's testimony. Therefore, we find no error.

\* \* \*

## VIII

For these reasons, the judgment of the district court is AFFIRMED.

NOTES

**(1) The Case–By–Case Approach.** The Ninth Circuit Court of Appeals, in this and the earlier *Fiorito* and *S.M. Wilson* cases, decided to make each case turn on its facts rather than to fashion a general rule by construction of UCC 2–719(2). These were diversity-of-citizenship cases, and the court therefore attributed its decision to the laws of Washington and California, but there were no definitive judgments of the courts of those states. When a seller's repair/replace obligation has not been performed, what kinds of fact issues should determine whether a particular buyer can recover consequential damages for breach of warranty?

In *Milgard*, what facts were determinative? The court declared that buyer "did not agree to pay $1.45 million in order to participate in a science experiment," and that seller had represented the furnace as "a cutting-edge furnace that would accommodate [buyer's] needs after two months of debugging." The court also noted that the degree of certainty of the workability of the design of the furnace in seller's sales talk was not consistent with its private view that the design was experimental. Do such facts have any relevance to the contractual allocation of the risk of consequential damages in the event that the furnace was not as warranted? The court also noted that the seller was unable to effect repair "despite 2.5 years of intense, albeit injudicious effort," which a footnote explained included failure for a time to provide a qualified process engineer and stubborn refusal to replace an unproven system with a more reliable one. The footnote concluded that seller's failure to make "a completely open and honest effort to bring the furnace into compliance" was not "dispositive." Were these facts important, even if not dispositive?

The *Milgard* opinion said nothing about the facts in *Fiorito* and little about the facts that might have been determinative in *S.M. Wilson*. *Fiorito* arose out of a sale of thirteen dump truck bodies to a construction company buyer for use in carrying wet concrete. Before the agreement, seller assured buyer that the bodies were suitable for this purpose. None was able to handle wet concrete. Seller declared that the problems were not covered by its warranty and that they were the result of buyer's misuse. Seller never attempted to repair the truck bodies, much less replace them. The Court of

Appeals declared: "It cannot be maintained that it was the parties inten-tion that Defendant be enabled to avoid all consequential liability for breach by first agreeing to an alternative remedy provision designed to avoid consequential harms, and then scuttling that alternative through its recalcitrance in honoring the agreement." Were these facts sufficient to be dispositive? Do you agree with the premise that clauses for repair or replacement are designed to avoid consequential harms?

The *Milgard* court noted a few facts from the *S.M. Wilson* decision, that the product was a tunnel boring machine, and quoted a passage from its opinion in that case: "The seller ... did not ignore his obligation to repair; he simply was unable to perform it." From the full opinion in *S.M. Wilson*, it appears that the seller did repair the tunnel boring machine after failing, for some considerable time, to diagnose the cause of the machine's malfunctioning. The consequential damages sought were losses of revenue incurred during the down time of the machine. Were these facts sufficient to be dispositive?

**(2) State Comments to the Commercial Code.** The Ninth Circuit in *Milgard* and in *Fiorito* declared that its analysis should track the Official Washington Comments. When the Uniform Commercial Code is promulgat-ed by the Uniform State Laws Conference and the American Law Institute for adoption by state legislatures, some states have studies conducted before the legislatures act. Commonly, committees of state bar associations take on this task. In some instances, the studies also produce local com-ments, like the Official Washington Comments. To the extent that the local comments differ from the Official Comments, they compromise the national goal of uniformity. The Official Washington Comment cited by the court "explains" that UCC 2–719 "relates to contractual arrangements which become oppressive by change of circumstances." Does anything in the text UCC 2–719 suggest that it applies to arrangements that "become oppres-sive"? Should that concept be general approach to the question whether to abrogate clauses that exclude liability for consequential damages in re-pair/replace contracts? Was it a factor in the Ninth Circuit's decisions?

# Smith v. Navistar International Transportation Corp.

United States Court of Appeals, Seventh Circuit, 1992.
957 F.2d 1439.

■ COFFEY, CIRCUIT JUDGE.

Plaintiff-appellant Jeary Smith appeals the district court's grant of partial summary judgment in favor of the defendants after determining that Smith was not entitled to consequential or incidental damages result-ing from a defective truck purchased from the defendants. Smith also appeals the district court's judgment in his favor for the purchase price of the truck. We affirm.

## I.

Plaintiff-appellant Jeary Smith brought this action charging the Navis-tar International Transportation Corporation ("Navistar"), Navistar Financial Corporation ("Navistar Financial") and J. Merle Jones & Sons, Inc. ("Jones"), a truck dealer, located in Ottawa, Illinois, with breach of warranty on the purchase of a truck. In 1984, Smith, an independent owner-operator of long distance trucks, decided to purchase a new truck, and Smith requested a list of sixteen options and/or components on the truck. After discussing the proposed purchase with several dealers, Smith decided to buy the Navistar semi-tractor truck Model 9370 as specified, from Jones (a Navistar authorized dealership), on November 7, 1984. Smith signed a Retail Order at the time of purchase which included the following warranty:

> International Harvester Company's [now Navistar] Promise to You. We promise to you, the first user purchaser, that we will replace or repair any part or parts of your new International motor vehicle which are defective in material or workmanship without charge for either parts or labor during the first year or 12,000 miles of operation, whichever occurs first.

* * *

> THIS WARRANTY IS IN LIEU OF ALL OTHER WARRANTIES, EXPRESSED OR IMPLIED, INCLUDING WITHOUT LIMITATION, WARRANTIES OF MERCHANTABILITY AND FITNESS FOR PARTICULAR PURPOSE, ALL OTHER REPRESENTATIONS TO THE FIRST USER PURCHASER, AND ALL OTHER OBLIGATIONS OR LIABILITIES, INCLUDING LIABILITY FOR INCIDENTAL AND CONSEQUENTIAL DAMAGES ON THE PART OF THE COMPANY OR THE SELLER.

(Capitalization in original).[2] . . .

Upon delivery of the truck Smith received an Owner's Limited Warranty booklet which in pertinent part read:

> International Harvester [now Navistar] will repair or replace any part of this vehicle which proves defective in material and/or workmanship in normal use and service, with new or ReNewed parts, for the first twelve months from new vehicle delivery date or for 50,000 miles (90,000 Km), whichever occurs first, except as specified under "What is Not Covered."

On the second page of the Owner's Limited Warranty booklet are additional warranty disclaimers:

NOTE: DISCLAIMER!

THERE ARE NO WARRANTIES WHICH EXTEND BEYOND THE DESCRIPTION ON THE FACE HEREOF. THIS WARRANTY IS IN LIEU OF ALL OTHER WARRANTIES, EXPRESSED OR IMPLIED. THE COMPANY SPECIFICALLY DISCLAIMS WARRANTIES OF MERCHANTABILITY AND FITNESS FOR A PARTICULAR PUR-

---

**2.** Smith later purchased an extended warranty for the Cummins engine in the Navistar truck. Smith's purchase of additional warranty protection implies that he had read and understood the terms of the Retail Order warranty.

POSE, ALL OTHER REPRESENTATIONS TO THE FIRST USER/PURCHASER, AND ALL OTHER OBLIGATIONS OR LIABILITIES. THE COMPANY FURTHER EXCLUDES LIABILITY FOR INCIDENTAL AND CONSEQUENTIAL DAMAGES, ON THE PART OF THE COMPANY OR THE SELLER. No person is authorized to give any other warranties or to assume any liabilities on the Company's behalf unless made or assumed in writing by the seller. (emphasis in original).

These disclaimers are similar to those disclaimers set forth in the Retail Order that Smith signed when executing the bill of sale.

Some nine days after Smith's purchase of the truck, he experienced problems with the truck's braking system. On no fewer than ten separate occasions between November 7, 1984 and April 1985, Smith brought the truck to authorized Navistar dealers for repairs. Thus, the truck was out of service for a period of forty-five days.[3] Smith alleges that throughout the period of repair, the defendants were aware that he had a contract with one firm that he relied upon for his business and that if he was unable to operate his truck he would lose the contract. Notwithstanding Smith's dissatisfaction with the number and frequency of the alleged defects, Smith continued to use the truck during the problem time period and eventually ran up some 48,488 miles on it. On June 6, 1985, Smith sent a letter to the . . . defendants expressing his intention to revoke his contract based upon his dissatisfaction with the final repair effort. . . .

Almost two years later, on May 4, 1987, Smith brought suit against the defendants Navistar and Jones for their alleged breach of express and implied warranties, and breach of contract in the truck purchase. . . . After extensive discovery, the defendants moved for summary judgment, and on January 27, 1989, the district court denied defendants' motion for summary judgment on the issue of liability, but granted defendants' motion as to damages in an opinion reported at 714 F. Supp. 303 (N.D.Ill.1989). The practical effect of this order was to limit the amount of damages a jury could award to $19,527.70, the amount Smith had paid for the truck prior to the revocation of his acceptance. After repeated attempts by the defendants to pay Smith the full amount of damages Smith was entitled to under the district court ruling, the defendants presented a motion . . . offering to have judgment entered against them in the amount of $19,527.70. Over the plaintiff's objection the court granted the defendants' motion for judgment and entered a judgment against the defendants on February 28, 1989. . . . Smith appeals.

\* \* \*

## III.   DISCUSSION

### A.   Consequential Damages

Illinois law applies in this diversity action, and the transaction is governed under Article 2 of the Uniform Commercial Code. The plaintiff

---

**3.** Neither Navistar nor any of its dealers ever refused to work on Smith's truck, and Smith was never charged for any of the repairs undertaken.

Smith argues that, because this is a diversity action, the district court was required to determine the applicable law of the State of Illinois when determining whether the plaintiff was entitled to consequential damages. The plaintiff contends that because, "the Illinois Supreme Court has not addressed the issue in question, the district court was required to use the predictive approach and in applying this approach, the district court disregarded the sole Illinois appellate decision on point and chose a resolution having no basis in Illinois law."

Our review of the district court's grant of partial summary judgment in favor of the defendants is de novo. . . . In its denial of partial summary judgment, the district court cited two conflicting cases which dealt with the issue of whether consequential damages could be awarded when a limited warranty failed to provide the protection the buyer expected. The first of these cases was a decision of an intermediate appellate court, Adams v. J.I. Case Co., 125 Ill. App. 2d 388, 261 N.E.2d 1 (4th Dist. 1970). The second was a decision of this court, AES Technology Systems, Inc. v. Coherent Radiation, 583 F.2d 933 (7th Cir.1978). Smith in essence argues that the district court erred in granting partial summary judgment because it chose to follow AES rather than Adams. However, federal courts are not bound by the decision of a lower state court unless the state's highest court in the jurisdiction whose law governs the diversity action has ruled on the matter. . . .

Smith's signature on the Retail Order would ordinarily constitute an effective waiver of any right to recover incidental and consequential damages arising from the loss of his single employment contract. However, the U.C.C. provides that "where circumstances cause an exclusive or limited remedy to fail of its essential purpose, remedy may be had as provided in this Act." Ill. Rev. Stat. ch. 26, § 2–719(2). In Adams, the Illinois Appellate Court adopted a categorical approach and held that the seller's breach of a limited warranty to repair or replace defective tractor parts automatically exposes the seller to liability for the buyer's consequential damages despite an otherwise enforceable disclaimer:

> The limitations of remedy and of liability are not separable from the obligations of the warranty. Repudiation of the obligations of the warranty destroyed its benefits. . . . It should be obvious that they cannot at once repudiate their obligation under the warranty and assert its provisions beneficial to them.

Adams, 261 N.E.2d at 7–8.

However, in AES, this court rejected the categorical approach enunciated in Adams, and refused to automatically sever a consequential damage disclaimer from a contract merely on the failure of a limited warranty to provide the benefits that the parties bargained for:

> [s]ome courts have awarded consequential damages, when a remedy failed of its essential purpose, in the face of prohibitions in the contract against consequential damages. . . . However, we reject the contention that failure of the essential purpose of the limited remedy automatical-

ly means that a damage award will include consequential damages. An analysis to determine whether consequential damages are warranted must carefully examine the individual factual situation including the type of goods involved, the parties and the precise nature and purpose of the contract. The purpose of the courts in contractual disputes is not to re-write contracts by ignoring parties' intent; rather, it is *to interpret the existing contract as fairly as possible when all events did not occur as planned.*

AES, 583 F.2d at 941 (footnote omitted) (emphasis added).

Other courts have similarly adopted this case-by-case approach. In Chatlos Systems v. National Cash Register Corp., 635 F.2d 1081 (3d Cir.1980), the court held that the failure of the essential purpose of a limited remedy does not automatically mean that a damage award will include consequential damages:

> New Jersey has not taken a position on this question, so in this diversity case we must predict which view the New Jersey Supreme Court would adopt if the question were presented to it.
>
> It appears to us that the better reasoned approach is to treat the consequential damage disclaimer as an independent provision, valid unless unconscionable. This poses no logical difficulties. A contract may well contain no limitation on breach of warranty damages but specifically exclude consequential damages. Conversely, it is quite conceivable that some limitation might be placed on a breach of warranty award, but consequential damages would expressly be permitted.
>
> The limited remedy of repair and a consequential damages exclusion are two discrete ways of attempting to limit recovery for breach of warranty. The Code, moreover, tests each by a different standard. The former survives unless it fails of its essential purpose, while the latter is valid unless it is unconscionable. We therefore see no reason to hold, as a general proposition, that the failure of the limited remedy provided in the contract, without more, invalidates a wholly distinct term in the agreement excluding consequential damages. The two are not mutually exclusive.

Id. at 1086 (footnotes and citations omitted).

Similarly, in S.M. Wilson & Co. v. Smith International, Inc., 587 F.2d 1363 (9th Cir.1978) (California law), the court determined that consequential damages were not warranted even though the limited repair warranty failed to achieve its essential purpose:

> The issue remains whether the failure of the limited repair remedy to serve its purpose requires permitting the recovery of consequential damages.... We hold it does not. In reaching this conclusion we are influenced heavily by the characteristics of the contract between [seller] and [buyer].....Parties of relatively equal bargaining power negotiated an allocation of their risks of loss. Consequential damages were assigned to the buyer, Wilson. The machine was a complex piece of

equipment designed for the buyer's purposes. The seller Smith did not ignore his obligation to repair; he simply was unable to perform it. This is not enough to require that the seller absorb losses the buyer plainly agreed to bear. Risk shifting is socially expensive and should not be undertaken in the absence of a good reason. An even better reason is required when to so shift is contrary to a contract freely negotiated. The default of the seller is not so total and fundamental as to require that its consequential damages limitation be expunged from the contract.

Id. at 1375.

We believe the district court's reliance on AES rather than Adams was correct. The case-by-case approach adopted by AES and the other decisions allows some measure of certainty in that parties of relatively equal bargaining power can allocate all of the risks that may accompany a breach of warranty, and prevents the court from upsetting that allocation upon a breach of contractual duties. Moreover, in those situations where the limited warranty fails to provide the benefits that the buyer expected (i.e., to repair or replace defective parts) and the parties are clearly on unequal terms with respect to relative bargaining power, the case-by-case approach enunciated in AES enables the courts to examine "the intent of the parties, as gleaned from the express provisions of the contract and the factual background" to determine whether consequential damages are warranted, rather than automatically exposing the seller to liability for consequential damages despite an otherwise valid disclaimer. AES, 583 F.2d at 941. Thus, we agree with the district court that the rationale underlying AES and the other decisions adopting the case-by-case approach is more compelling than the categorical approach enunciated in Adams.

Smith also argues that "even if the district court was correct in the approach that it chose, the case-by-case approach, it misapplied that approach." Smith contends that the district court failed to analyze "all of the attendant objective facts and circumstances, including the language of the agreement, the relative bargaining power of the parties and the commercial context of the transaction" in order to determine which party should bear the risk of consequential damages. In our opinion, this argument is without merit as the district court noted that Smith failed to present any evidence in opposition to the damages awarded in the summary judgment motion. Moreover, our review of the record reveals that at the time Smith purchased the truck he was an experienced operator of long-distance trucks and had visited at least six different truck dealers in Indiana and Illinois, and had drawn up a list of sixteen specifications for the truck that he felt met his specific need. Having refused to accept any truck that did not meet his list of sixteen requirements, Smith presented the necessary components and options to defendant Jones, who offered the plaintiff-appellant the Navistar truck that met his specifications. At the time of purchase, Smith signed a Retail Order specifically excluding liability on the part of the seller for incidental and consequential damages:

THIS WARRANTY IS IN LIEU OF ALL OTHER WARRANTIES, EXPRESSED OR IMPLIED, INCLUDING WITHOUT LIMITATION, WARRANTIES OF MERCHANTABILITY AND FITNESS FOR PARTICULAR PURPOSE, ALL OTHER REPRESENTATIONS TO THE FIRST USER PURCHASER, AND ALL OTHER OBLIGATIONS OR LIABILITIES, INCLUDING LIABILITY FOR INCIDENTAL AND CONSEQUENTIAL DAMAGES ON THE PART OF THE COMPANY OR THE SELLER.

Moreover, Smith accepted a warranty which also clearly excluded seller liability for incidental and consequential damages in a section set off with the words, "NOTE: DISCLAIMER!". Smith read the terms and conditions of the warranty and failed to ask any questions regarding the terms of the Retail Order or warranty before signing the same. We have failed to discover evidence in the record that the parties intended that the defendants bear the risk of consequential damages or that the parties' relative bargaining power was so unequal that the disclaimer was unconscionable and we refuse to re-write the contract including the Retail Order's clear exclusion of consequential damages.

* * *

IV.  CONCLUSION

The decision of the district court is AFFIRMED.

## NOTES

**(1) Case–By–Case Approach.** The Seventh Circuit purports to accept the case-by-case approach to the question of enforcement of clauses excluding liability for consequential damages. Is the approach of the Seventh Circuit (applying Illinois law) the same as that of the Ninth Circuit (applying California and Washington law)? Note that the Seventh Circuit opinion does not cite either *Fiorito* or *Milgard*, but does refer to *S.M. Wilson*.

What facts are apparently dispositive in the Seventh Circuit's case? The opinion has long quotes of the terms of the contract (some more than once). It emphasized that the buyer was "an experienced operator of long-distance trucks," had shopped extensively before agreeing to buy the Navistar truck, and "accepted a warranty which ... clearly excluded seller liability for incidental and consequential damages.... [Buyer] read the terms and conditions of the warranty and failed to ask any questions regarding the Retail Order or warranty before signing the same. We have failed to discover any evidence ... that the parties' relative bargaining position was so unequal that the disclaimer was unconscionable and we refuse to re-write the contract...." How did this approach compare with that of the Ninth Circuit?

Although not stressed by the Seventh Circuit, its opinion referred to the seller's—and buyer's—conduct when the buyer experienced problems with the truck. The court noted that seller made numerous attempts to repair the truck and never charged buyer for any of the repairs undertaken. Even though buyer said that he was revoking his acceptance, he continued to use the truck and logged over 48,000 miles of travel. After two and a half years, when buyer sued seller, seller tried to give the buyer the entire purchase price, but buyer refused to accept the money. What weight should these facts have in the court's decision?

ARABIAN AGRICULTURE SERVICES CO. v. CHIEF INDUSTRIES, INC., 309 F.3d 479 (8th Cir. 2002). The contract was to design and construct 16 large hopper-bottom silos for buyer's facility in the port of Damman, Saudi Arabia. During contract negotiations, buyer learned that some of seller's silos had collapsed in Korea. Seller agreed to a seven-year warranty against defects in materials, workmanship or design. The contract provided that the sole and exclusive remedy for breach was repair or replacement of the silos by the seller. The contract further declared that seller was not responsible for any consequential damages. Two years after the silos were completed, 15 of the 16 collapsed. The collapsing silos crushed a nearby building. Buyer requested seller to repair or replace the silos. After investigation, seller determined that the cause of the silos collapse was the length of time in which buyer had stored corn in them and therefore declined to take any remedial action. Buyer sued for and recovered damages of $1,466,507, of which $88,000 was for consequential damages. The trial court found that seller's excuse for not performing was not valid. On appeal, seller contended that its refusal, even if wrong, had been made in good faith. The Court of Appeals affirmed. The court declared that, given seller's failure to perform its warranty obligations, the limited remedy failed of its essential purpose and buyer was entitled to all remedies under UCC Article 2, including consequential damages.

**(2) Unconscionability.** In the concluding paragraph of the Seventh Circuit opinion, the court found that the clause excluding liability for consequential damages (the court called the clause a "disclaimer") was not unconscionable. Unconscionability appeared in the body of the opinion in the court's reference to the Third Circuit's opinion in the *Chatlos* case.[6] How does the Commercial Code provision on unconscionability become part of the analysis? Does reference to unconscionability indicate the facts that determine whether buyers are entitled to consequential damages when sellers fail to repair or replace defective goods? Recall that unconscionability, under UCC 2–302, is determined entirely by facts that exist at the time of contract formation. Events that occur during performance of contracts are not material. Is UCC 2–302 the appropriate source of the law to be applied in these cases?

Unconscionability has been the ground for striking out clauses excluding consequential damages in a number of cases arising out of sales of equipment and supplies to farmers. See, e.g., Mullis v. Speight Seed Farms, Inc., 234 Ga.App. 27, 505 S.E.2d 818 (1998); Lutz Farms v. Asgrow Seed

---

6.   We studied a later opinion in the *Chatlos* controversy in Section 2.

Co., 948 F.2d 638 (10th Cir. 1991); Martin v. Joseph Harris Co., 767 F.2d 296 (6th Cir. 1985); A & M Produce Co. v. FMC Corp., 135 Cal.App.3d 473, 186 Cal.Rptr. 114 (1982); Durham v. Ciba–Geigy Corp., 315 N.W.2d 696 (S. D. 1982).

## 3. DAMAGES FOR BREACH OF REMEDIAL PROMISES

The core issue in the cases above was the right of buyers to recover consequential damages, despite clauses in the contracts that excluded such recovery, in circumstances where remedial promises were said to have failed of their essential purpose. It is conceivable, of course, that promissees of remedial promises may seek to recover for breach of those promises.

*Breach.* What constitutes breach of a remedial promise to repair or replace? If the promissor refuses to take any action the answer is relatively clear. If the promissor acts but the results are unsatisfactory, does the promissee have a cause of action. An Illinois court held that a promissor must succeed in repairing a new car after a "reasonable number of attempts." Pearson v. DaimlerChrysler Corp., 349 Ill.App.3d 688, 286 Ill.Dec. 173, 813 N.E.2d 230 (2004).

*Ordinary damages.* How should ordinary expectation damages be determined? Nothing in the current Commercial Code addresses the question? At common law, one can measure the damages by the cost that the aggrieved party reasonably incurs in obtaining performance from someone else or by determining the value of the promised performance offset by the value, if any, of performance made.

*Consequential damages.* Under common law, a party aggrieved by breach of contract is entitled to recover consequential damages under the doctrine of *Hadley v. Baxendale.* In many circumstances, the makers of repair/replace promises would know what losses are likely to be incurred by aggrieved buyers. As we have seen, sellers that make remedial promises commonly also obtain agreement from buyers to exclude consequential damages. These agreements are in sales contracts. These damage exclusion clauses apply to sellers' obligation as sellers. Would these clause also apply to the sellers as makers of remedial promises?

*Refund of Price.* Many sales contracts are formed with explicit or implicit promises by sellers to take back the goods and refund the price. Most of these involve sales of non-durable goods that have relatively low market value compared with commercial equipment and durable consumer goods. In some instances, price refund is available on request; buyers dissatisfied with the goods for any reason are allowed to get their money back. The commercial explanation for this widespread practice is the good will that sellers generate with repeat customers.

In other sales contracts, price return is an agreed remedy for breach of a warranty of quality. UCC 2–719(1)(a) mentions repayment of the price in its illustrative list of remedies that may be agreed to in place of the Commercial Code's remedies. Price-return agreements are often made without clauses excluding consequential damages for breach of warranty.

The nature of goods involved in small-ticket sales does not generally create a risk of significant consequential damages. An important exception is in sales of seeds, fertilizer and herbicide to farmers. Crop losses of considerable magnitude can result from nonconforming seeds, fertilizers and herbicides. We will see that problem in the forthcoming section on manufacturers' warranties.[7]

## (B) International Sales Law

The Convention on Contracts for International Sales of Goods has no provisions regarding remedial promises.

---

## Section 5.   Personal Injuries and Warranty Law

### (A) Domestic United States Law

In cases decided in the late 19th century and early 20th century, courts implied warranties of quality in ordinary retail sales,[1] even in transactional settings where the goods were canned or packaged and the retail sellers did not know, and had no practical way of finding out the quality of the goods.[2]

---

**7.** Remedial promises to refund the price are distinct from the remedy of price recovery for seller's breach in UCC 2–711(1). The right to recover the price depends upon the severity of a nonconformity complained of. Promises to refund the price are typically available more generally, and sometimes without a requirement that a buyer show the existence of any nonconformity.

**1.** The British Sale of Goods Act and its United States counterpart, the Uniform Sales Act, posed a problem for buyers: the basic warranty of quality, merchantability, was not "implied" in ordinary retail sales of food or other goods. Caselaw codified by these statutes had found the warranty of merchantability arising in situations where sellers had contracted to supply goods that would fit contract descriptions; Mackensie Chalmers "restated" the cases by limiting merchantability to sales "by description." Protection had to be found under the rubric of fitness for particular purpose.

The change is well illustrated by developments in Massachusetts. Farrell v. Manhattan Market Co., 198 Mass. 271, 84 N.E. 481 (1908) (buyer suffered ptomaine poisoning from a fowl: buyer denied relief); Ward v. Great Atlantic & Pacific Tea Co., 231 Mass. 90, 120 N.E. 225 (1918) (buyer broke a tooth on a stone in a can of baked beans: buyer recovered); Flynn v. Bedell Co., 242 Mass. 450, 136 N.E. 252 (1922) (buyer contracted skin disease from dyed fur collar of coat: verdict for buyer upheld).

Consumers injured by unwholesome food or beverages served by a restaurant or hotel faced an additional legal hazard. At common law, some courts considered such transactions a service ("uttering") rather than a sale and, therefore, not transactions in which a warranty of quality applied. Compare Friend v. Childs Dining Hall Co., 231 Mass. 65, 120 N.E. 407 (1918), with Nisky v. Childs, 103 N.J.L. 464, 135 A. 805 (1927). The Commercial Code declares that such transactions are sales under Article 2. UCC 2–314(1).

**2.** Compare Julian v. Laubenberger, 16 Misc. 646, 38 N.Y.S. 1052 (Sup. Ct. 1896) (sale of can of salmon: since both parties knew that seller had not prepared the food, had not inspected it, and was entirely ignorant of the contents of the can, it would be unreasonable to say that the buyer had relied upon the superior knowledge of the seller), with Ward v. Great Atlantic & Pacific Tea Co., 231 Mass. 90, 120 N.E. 225 (1918) (sale of can of baked beans and pork: even though seller is not the manufacturer, seller is in a better position to ascertain the

The list of such goods was confined initially to food, beverages, and other items of "intimate bodily use." Once courts found that a warranty had been breached, they had no difficulty in broadening the losses compensable as consequential damages to personal injuries and property damage.

The move toward protection of the lives and health of consumers did not end with recognition of retailers' liability. In 1960, in *Henningsen v. Bloomfield Motors*,[3] the New Jersey Supreme Court held that the owner of an automobile, injured when the steering failed, had a warranty claim against the manufacturer.

Shortly after the *Henningsen* decision, courts of many states recognized a new common-law tort, originally known as strict tort liability.[4] The new tort became the principal claim advanced by counsel for buyers who had suffered personal injuries that were caused by "defective" products. Warranty claims continued to be made by personal injury lawyers, but these claims were not their preferred cause of action.[5] The law of the tort of strict liability was revised in the 1997 Restatement of the Law of Torts, Third: Products Liability.

---

reliability of the manufacturer; the principle of retailers' liability may work apparent hardship in some instances, but that is no reason to change it).

**3.** 32 N.J. 358, 161 A.2d 69 (1960).

**4.** Two years after *Henningsen*, the California Supreme Court recognized a new tort to protect the consumer-owner of a lathe injured when a piece of wood was ejected from the equipment. Greenman v. Yuba Power Products, Inc., 59 Cal.2d 57, 27 Cal.Rptr. 697, 377 P.2d 897 (1963). At this time, the American Law Institute was preparing a second edition of the Restatement of Torts. The new tort was inserted into the revision as § 402A, Special Liability of Seller of Product for Physical Harm to User or Consumer. Reception of § 402A as new common law was rapid and widespread. Only a small number of state supreme courts have rejected strict tort liability. E.g., Cline v. Prowler Industries of Md., Inc., 418 A.2d 968 (Del.Supr.1980); Swartz v. General Motors Corp., 375 Mass. 628, 378 N.E.2d 61 (1978); Prentis v. Yale Manufacturing Co., 421 Mich. 670, 365 N.W.2d 176 (1984). In New York, the Court of Appeals initially rejected the new tort. Mendel v. Pittsburgh Plate Glass Co., 25 N.Y.2d 888, 304 N.Y.S.2d 4, 251 N.E.2d 143 (1969). However, the New York court quickly joined the majority of states. Codling v. Paglia, 32 N.Y.2d 330, 345 N.Y.S.2d 461, 298 N.E.2d 622 (1973).

**5.** A major difference in the two theories lies in the measure of recovery. Plaintiffs proceeding in a tort theory ordinarily are permitted to recover damages for pain and suffering and, in extraordinary cases, may be permitted to recover punitive damages. Proof of a defendant's liability on a strict tort theory is therefore less difficult than the proof under a warranty theory. The strict tort theory is also more protective of consumers with regard to contractual disclaimers or clauses limiting damages. Comment *m* to § 402A states that the "consumer's" cause of action "is not affected by any disclaimer or other agreement."

Moreover, a consumer who suffers an injury some considerable time after the good was sold may be unable to proceed successfully on a warranty theory while the strict tort theory is still available. The warranty statute of limitations begins to run at the time of delivery of the goods. UCC 2–725(1). If an injury occurs more than four years after delivery, the tort statute may be more favorable to plaintiffs. The tort statute of limitations does not begin to run until the injury.

The warranty statute of limitations may be more favorable to a plaintiff who suffers injury shortly after goods have been delivered but fails to institute legal proceedings within the one-or two-year limitation period generally provided for tort claims. Even though the tort claim is time-barred, the warranty period may not have expired on the date of filing suit.

Judicial acknowledgment of the new tort did not displace consumers' warranty claims arising out of the same facts. What has emerged, therefore, is that consumer buyers in most states have substantially overlapping theories of possible recovery for personal injuries. Full consideration of the law of products liability is beyond the scope of these materials. However, certain issues that arise in warranty claims for personal injuries should be considered.

## Castro v. QVC Network, Inc.

United States Court of Appeals for the Second Circuit, 1998.
139 F.3d 114.

■ Calabresi, Circuit Judge:

In this diversity products liability action, plaintiffs-appellants alleged, in separate causes of action for strict liability and for breach of warranty, that defendants-appellees manufactured and sold a defective roasting pan that injured one of the appellants. The United States District Court for the Eastern District of New York (Leonard D. Wexler, Judge) rejected appellants' request to charge the jury separately on each cause of action and, instead, instructed the jury only on the strict liability charge. The jury found for appellees and the court denied appellants' motion for a new trial. This appeal followed. We hold that, under New York law, the jury should have been instructed separately on each charge, and, accordingly, reverse and remand for a new trial on the breach of warranty claim.

### I.   BACKGROUND

In early November 1993, appellee QVC Network, Inc. ("QVC"), operator of a cable television home-shopping channel, advertised, as part of a one-day Thanksgiving promotion, the "T–Fal Jumbo Resistal Roaster." The roaster, manufactured by U.S.A. T–Fal Corp. ("T–Fal"), was described as suitable for, among other things, cooking a twenty-five pound turkey. Appellant Loyda Castro bought the roasting pan by mail and used it to prepare a twenty-pound turkey on Thanksgiving Day, 1993.

Mrs. Castro was injured when she attempted to remove the turkey and roasting pan from the oven. Using insulated mittens, she gripped the pan's handles with the first two fingers on each hand (the maximum grip allowed by the small size of the handles) and took the pan out of the oven. As the turkey tipped toward her, she lost control of the pan, spilling the hot drippings and fat that had accumulated in it during the cooking and basting process. As a result, she suffered second and third degree burns to her foot and ankle, which, over time, has led to scarring, intermittent paresthesia, and ankle swelling.

It is uncontested that in their complaint appellants alleged that the pan was defective and that its defects gave rise to separate causes of action for strict liability and for breach of warranty. Moreover, in the pre-charge conference, appellants' counsel repeatedly requested separate jury charges on strict liability and for breach of warranty. The district court, nevertheless, denied the request for a separate charge on breach of warranty. Judge Wexler stated that "you can't collect twice for the same thing," and deemed the warranty charge unnecessary and "duplicative." The court, therefore, only gave the jury the New York pattern strict products liability charge.

The jury returned a verdict for appellees QVC and T–Fal. Judgment was entered on September 14, 1995. Appellants subsequently moved, pursuant to Federal Rule of Civil Procedure 59, that the jury verdict be set aside and a new trial be ordered for various reasons including that the court had failed to charge the jury on appellants' claim for breach of warranty. By order dated July 10, 1996, the district court denied appellants' Rule 59 motion, reasoning that the breach of warranty and strict products liability claims were "virtually the same." This appeal followed.

## II.  DISCUSSION

We review a district court's denial of a new-trial motion for abuse of discretion. . . .

### A.  Two Definitions of "Defective" Product Design

Products liability law has long been bedeviled by the search for an appropriate definition of "defective" product design. Over the years, both in the cases and in the literature, two approaches have come to predominate. The first is the risk/utility theory, which focuses on whether the benefits of a product outweigh the dangers of its design. The second is the consumer expectations theory, which focuses on what a buyer/user of a product would properly expect that the product would be suited for.

Not all states accept both of these approaches. Some define design defect only according to the risk/utility approach. . . . Others define design defect solely in terms of the consumer expectations theory.

One of the first states to accept both approaches was California, which in Barker v. Lull Engineering Co., 20 Cal. 3d 413, 573 P.2d 443, 143 Cal. Rptr. 225 (Cal. 1978), held that "a product may be found defective in design, so as to subject a manufacturer to strict liability for resulting injuries, under either of two alternative tests"—consumer expectations and risk/utility. 573 P.2d at 455–56. Several states have followed suit and have adopted both theories. . . .

Prior to the recent case of Denny v. Ford Motor Co., 87 N.Y.2d 248, 662 N.E.2d 730, 639 N.Y.S.2d 250 (1995), it was not clear whether New York recognized both tests. In Denny, the plaintiff was injured when her Ford Bronco II sports utility vehicle rolled over when she slammed on the brakes to avoid hitting a deer in the vehicle's path. See Denny v. Ford Motor Co., 42 F.3d 106, 108 (2d Cir.1994), certifying questions to Denny, 87 N.Y.2d 248, 662 N.E.2d 730, 639 N.Y.S.2d 250. The plaintiff asserted claims for strict products liability and for breach of implied warranty, and the district judge—over the objection of defendant Ford—submitted both causes of action to the jury. The jury ruled in favor of Ford on the strict liability claim, but found for the plaintiff on the implied warranty claim. On appeal, Ford argued that the jury's verdicts on the strict products liability claim and the breach of warranty claim were inconsistent because the causes of action were identical.

This court certified the Denny case to the New York Court of Appeals to answer the following questions: (1) "whether, under New York law, the strict products liability and implied warranty claims are identical"; and (2) "whether, if the claims are different, the strict products liability claim is broader than the implied warranty claim and encompasses the latter."

In response to the certified questions, the Court of Appeals held that in a products liability case a cause of action for strict liability is not identical to a claim for breach of warranty. Moreover, the court held that a strict liability claim is not per se broader than a breach of warranty claim such that the former encompasses the latter. Thus, while claims of strict products liability and breach of warranty are often used interchangeably, under New York law the two causes of action are definitively different. The imposition of strict liability for an alleged design "defect" is determined by a risk-utility standard.... The notion of "defect" in a U.C.C.-based breach of warranty claim focuses, instead, on consumer expectations. ...

B.   When Should a Jury be Charged on Both Strict Liability and Warranty Causes of Action?

Since Denny, then, it has been settled that the risk/utility and consumer expectations theories of design defect can, in New York, be the bases of distinct causes of action: one for strict products liability and one for breach of warranty. This fact, however, does not settle the question of when a jury must be charged separately on each cause of action and when, instead, the two causes are, on the facts of the specific case, sufficiently similar to each other so that one charge to the jury is enough.

While eminent jurists have at times been troubled by this issue, the New York Court of Appeals in Denny was quite clear on when the two causes of action might meld and when, instead, they are to be treated as separate. It did this by adding its own twist to the distinction—namely, what can aptly be called the "dual purpose" requirement. Thus in Denny, the Court of Appeals pointed out that the fact that a product's overall benefits might outweigh its overall risks does not preclude the possibility that consumers may have been misled into using the product in a context in which it was dangerously unsafe. And this, the New York court emphasized, could be so even though the benefits in other uses might make the product sufficiently reasonable so that it passed the risk/utility test.

In Denny, the Ford Bronco II was not designed as a conventional passenger automobile. Instead, it was designed as an off-road, dual purpose vehicle. But in its marketing of the Bronco II, Ford stressed its suitability for commuting and for suburban and city driving. Under the circumstances, the Court of Appeals explained that a rational factfinder could conclude that the Bronco's utility as an off-road vehicle outweighed the risk of injury resulting from roll-over accidents (thus passing the risk/utility test), but at the same time find that the vehicle was not safe for the "ordinary purpose" of daily driving for which it was also marketed and sold (thus flunking the consumer expectations test).

That is precisely the situation before us. The jury had before it evidence that the product was designed, marketed, and sold as a multiple-use product. The pan was originally manufactured and sold in France as an all-purpose cooking dish without handles. And at trial, the jury saw a videotape of a QVC representative demonstrating to the television audience that the pan, in addition to serving as a suitable roaster for a twenty-five pound turkey, could also be used to cook casseroles, cutlets, cookies, and other low-volume foods. The court charged the jury that "[a] product is defective if it is not reasonably safe[,] that is, if the product is so likely to be harmful to persons that a reasonable person who had actual knowledge of its potential for producing injury would conclude that it should not have been marketed in that condition." And, so instructed, the jury presumably found that the pan, because it had many advantages in a variety of uses, did not fail the risk/utility test.

But it was also the case that the pan was advertised as suitable for a particular use—cooking a twenty-five pound turkey. Indeed, T–Fal added handles to the pan in order to fill QVC's request for a roasting pan that it could use in its Thanksgiving promotion. The product was, therefore, sold as appropriately used for roasting a twenty-five pound turkey. And it was in that use that allegedly the product failed and injured the appellant.

In such circumstances, New York law is clear that a general charge on strict products liability based on the risk/utility approach does not suffice. The jury could have found that the roasting pan's overall utility for cooking low-volume foods outweighed the risk of injury when cooking heavier foods, but that the product was nonetheless unsafe for the purpose for which it was marketed and sold—roasting a twenty-five pound turkey—and, as such, was defective under the consumer expectations test. That being so, the appellants were entitled to a separate breach of warranty charge.

### III. CONCLUSION

In light of the evidence presented by appellants of the multi-purpose nature of the product at issue, the district court, applying New York law, should have granted appellants' request for a separate jury charge on the breach of warranty claim in addition to the charge on the strict liability claim. Accordingly, we reverse the order of the district court denying the motion for a new trial, and remand the case for a new trial on the breach of warranty claim, consistent with this opinion.

### NOTES

**(1) Nature of the Warranty Allegedly Breached.** The court's references to the warranty do not indicate, for the most part, whether the warranty on which the plaintiff relies is the implied warranty of merchantability or an express warranty of quality. The question certified to the New York Court of Appeals in the *Denny* case referred only to an implied warranty. How would you characterize the warranty in *Denny*? The warranty in this case? Does it matter whether the warranty in issue is an express warranty or an implied warranty?

**(2) Goods Not Fit for Ordinary Purposes and Defective Goods.** The trial court held that the warranty claim and the products liability claim amounted to the "same thing." If the warranty in question is a warranty that the goods are fit for their ordinary purposes, does it not follow that defective goods which cause personal injuries are not fit for such purposes? The logical force of that proposition is the basis for the conclusion that the two claims are the same thing. But logic does not support the inverse. Goods that are not fit for their ordinary purposes may or may not have a defect sufficient to be actionable under the doctrine of products liability. The reason is that the level of a reasonable buyer's expectation of quality, the warranty obligation, is derivative from the seller's description of the goods. A seller's description can be the basis of a claim under UCC 2–314 or UCC 2–313. The descriptions in *Castro* and *Denny* were of the goods being used in certain particular ways, the kind of descriptions that are appropriately express warranties.

**(3) Preclusive Effect.** Although the procedural postures of the cases differ, the core legal issue in *Castro* and *Denny* was the effect on plaintiff's warranty claim of a verdict in favor of the seller in her tort claim. In *Castro*, plaintiff's counsel alleged claims in tort and contract, but the trial court submitted only the tort claim to the jury. In post-trial proceedings, the plaintiff contended that she was entitled to separate trials of each claim. The trial court determined that the warranty claim was barred by the judgment on the tort claim. The Second Circuit reversed. In *Denny*, both claims were tried but the jury returned a verdict for the defendant on the tort claim and a verdict for the plaintiff on the warranty claim. The New York Court of Appeals determined that the verdict for the plaintiff on the warranty claim was not undermined. In what way(s) did the warranty claims differ from the tort claims?

**(4) Persons Protected: Horizontal Privity.** The principal plaintiff in *Castro* was the individual who purchased the roasting pan. In many circumstances, however, the person who suffers personal injuries is in the same person who bought the goods. It would be remarkable if the class of persons protected by implied warranty were limited to the individuals who were parties to sales contracts. Product liability law does not limit tort recovery to buyers. In contract law, the question of the scope of protected persons is commonly referred to as the matter of horizontal privity. If claimants are not parties in the chain of distribution of the goods, but are related in some way to the buyers in the last retail sales of the goods, may they recover.

Article 2 of the Commercial Code provides that some non-buyers may recover in breach of warranty actions against sellers of goods. The caption of the section, UCC 2–318, refers to the extended class of potential claimants as third party beneficiaries. General contract law allows contracting parties to agree that the contractual obligations of one contracting party may be enforced by someone other than the other contracting party. A classic example is the contract of life insurance, in which the terms of the policy make the insurer's obligation to pay enforceable by a person designated by the owner of the policy as the beneficiary.

In UCC Article 2 today, UCC 2–318 appears with three alternatives. In the original (1962) Code, however, Alternative A was the only provision. Alternatives B and C were put forward by the sponsors of the Commercial Code in 1966.[6] The sponsors were willing, in this matter, to surrender any effort to make the law uniform across the states. Most states had already adopted the Code before Alternatives B and C were promulgated and did not revisit the question. A few states adopted Alternative B or Alternative C. Several states have chosen non-uniform variations of UCC 2–318 or omitted the section altogether.[7]

Alternative A is the most narrow of the choices. The class of protected beneficiaries extends only to individuals ("natural persons") who are in the family or household of the buyer or are guests in the buyer's home, provided that sellers reasonably expect that these individuals may use, consume or be affected by the goods.[8] Beneficiaries under this provision cannot recover for diminution in the value of the goods or for consequential economic loss. The only harms covered are injury to person or property.[9]

Alternative B extends to all natural persons whom sellers may reasonably expect to use, consume, or be affected by the goods. This Alternative eliminates the family/guest limitation, but retains the restriction to personal injuries. Indeed, the phrase "affected by" may extend protection to individuals, wholly unrelated to buyers, who happened to be in the vicinity of goods that caused their injuries, such as an exploding bottle of soda.

Alternative C broadens the protection in two ways. Injury is not limited to personal injury or property damage and protected persons include business entities as well as individuals.

A class of individuals who sometimes suffer personal injury caused by failure of goods to conform to quality warranties are employees of firms that purchased warranted equipment. Clearly these individuals are outside

---

6.  See Comments 2 and 3.

7.  The Uniform Reporting Service provides a useful state-by-state comparison of the state enactments.

8.  An early UCC case involved a young child who was killed when a vaporizer-humidifier malfunctioned. The product had been purchased by the child's aunt, who lived next door. The Pennsylvania Supreme Court held that the child was not in the "family" of the buyer for purposes of UCC 2–318. Miller v. Preitz, 422 Pa. 383, 221 A.2d 320 (1966).

9.  In some circumstances, a person other than a buyer of goods may be aggrieved by the loss in value of the goods resulting from breach of a warranty of quality or a remedial promise. Such a case arose in Pennsylvania. The buyer of a new automobile died months after the purchase and his widow inherited it. When the automobile was three years old, it began to exhibit signs of a defective transmission. The widow sued the manufacturer for breach of express and implied warranties of quality. The manufacturer argued, under UCC Article 2, that the widow was not the "buyer" of the automobile and, under UCC 2–318, had no standing to sue because her claim was not for injury to the person. The defense was upheld. Johnson v. General Motors Corp., 349 Pa.Super. 147, 502 A.2d 1317 (1986).

the scope of Alternative A, but would be protected under Alternatives B or C.

## (B) INTERNATIONAL SALES LAW

The Convention on Contracts for the International Sale of Goods does not apply to goods bought for personal, family or household use, pursuant to CISG 2(a), and does not apply to the liability of sellers for death or personal injury caused by the goods to any person, pursuant to CISG 5. Professor Honnold commented:[10]

> In UNCITRAL attention was drawn to the development of national legislation and case law designed to protect consumers; it was agreed that the Convention should not supersede these rules. Consideration was given to a provision that the Convention would not override any domestic rule that was "mandatory" or that implemented "public policy" (*ordre public*) but it was found that these concepts carried different meanings in various legal systems; the clearest and safest solution was specifically to exclude consumer purchases from the Convention. . . .

> The strong protection that the Convention gives to the international sales contract made it necessary to limit the Convention's scope lest the Convention collide with the special protection that some domestic rules provide for the noncommercial consumer. . . . A similar purpose underlies [CISG 5].

## SECTION 6. LEGAL BARS TO ACTIONS FOR BREACH OF WARRANTY

### (A) DOMESTIC UNITED STATES LAW

In this section we consider two legal issues that may bar buyers from recovery for breach of warranties of quality even if the buyers were able to prove their claims on the merits. Both of the issues are time-related. One deals with a requirement that buyers give sellers prompt notice of non-conformities. The other deals with a requirement that an aggrieved buyer commence litigation within a period of time, commonly called the period of limitations. Recall that we considered both of these potential bars to recovery in the Chapter on Warranty of Title. The application of these provisions in suits for breach of warranties of quality differ somewhat from the application in suits for breach of the warranty of title.

UCC Article 2 provides that a buyer may be barred from proceeding with litigation of the merits of a warranty claim against a seller if the buyer had failed to give the seller timely notice of the seller's breach. The notice-to-seller requirement is found in UCC 2–607(3)(a). The language of the second part of this subsection ("barred from any remedy") could be

---

**10.** J. Honnold, Uniform Law for International Sales §§ 50, 71 (3d ed. 1999).

construed to make absence of notice an affirmative defense, i.e., an issue that arises only if a defendant asserts it. However, courts have generally construed the statute to make it part of a plaintiff's burden to plead and prove that a required notice was given.

Even if a buyer's notice was timely, the buyer may be barred from relief in an action against the seller if the buyer has not commenced its law suit within the period of limitations prescribed by Article 2. The statute of limitations for transactions in goods is UCC 2–725. The statute of limitations is an affirmative defense. In most states, a general statute of limitations applies to actions for breach of contract. The period of limitations in those general provisions is typically longer than the period of limitations in the Article 2, commonly six years. Litigation about the statute of limitations generally arises by a defense pretrial motion to dismiss a complaint or for summary judgment.

## 1.   NOTICE OF BREACH

Lawyers representing sellers in warranty litigation are drawn to the "slam dunk" provision that results in buyers' being "barred from any remedy." UCC 2–607(3)(a). A buyer is subject to this catastrophic result if, after acceptance of goods, the buyer fails to notify seller of breach within a reasonable time after the buyer discovered or should have discovered the breach. This is one of the most frequently litigated issues under Article 2.[1]

## M.K. Associates v. Stowell Products, Inc.

United States District Court for the District of Maine, 1988.
697 F.Supp. 20.

■ CARTER, DISTRICT JUDGE.

### I.   Introduction

M.K. Associates, a seller of wood products, has brought an action to recover the remainder of the purchase price due from a sale of ash dowels to the defendant Stowell Products, Inc. The defendant claims that the plaintiff breached the contract because the dowels were defective. The defendant argues that it is entitled to set off the remaining amount due as damages caused by the defective goods.

The case was tried before the court on September 19, 1988. For the reasons set forth below, the court finds for the plaintiff. The findings of fact and conclusions of law follow.

### II.   Findings of Fact

From December, 1986 through February, 1987, Stowell Products, through its purchasing manager, Wayne Curley, made a series of offers for ash dowels from M.K. Associates. The dowels were delivered during the

---

**1.**   See Annot., Sufficiency and Timeliness of Buyer's Notice Under UCC § 2–607(3)(a) of Seller's Breach of Warranty, 89 A.L.R.5th 319 (2003).

period from December, 1986 to March, 1987. Stowell Products intended to use the dowels to manufacture products to fill a contract with another company, Mirro/Foley Corp., due in late August, 1987. Although Stowell Products made periodic payments to M.K. Associates on these orders up through the fall of 1987, it was substantially in arrears as early as March, 1987. The parties have stipulated that the amount still due for the purchase and delivery of the ash dowels is $10,518.40.

The employee who received the orders from M.K. Associates noticed that some of the dowels were defective because they were "out of round," and he reported this defect to Wayne Curley, the purchasing manager. The factory foreperson, Virginia Johnson, found she was unable to use the dowels because of the defects. From June to September, 1987, Johnson ran the dowels through a "seavey" machine in order to correct the defects. This corrective process enabled Stowell Products to use the dowels for the Mirro/Foley order, although the order was not shipped until September 25, 1987, about a month late.

In the spring of 1987, Wayne Curley, purchasing manager of Stowell Products, and Doug Bucy, general manager, had a series of conversations with M.K. Associates. These conversations discussed the fact that Stowell Products was behind on its payments for the order. Only one conversation, however, made any mention of problems with the dowels. This conversation occurred between Curley and Marshall Kates, owner of M.K. Associates, in March, 1987. At this time, Curley asked Kates if one of the orders could be cancelled because of problems in running the dowels through the production process. Kates answered that he couldn't cancel. They did not discuss the issue further.

Stowell Products made no other attempts to raise the issue of defects in the dowels to M.K. Associates. On September 2, 1987, M.K. Associates filed a complaint in this court for the remainder due from Stowell Products on the dowel order.

## III.   Conclusions of Law

The issue in this case is whether Stowell Products is entitled to deduct damages for defects in the dowels purchased from M.K. Associates against the amount owed for the orders. The defendant does not dispute that Stowell Products accepted the dowels from M.K. Associates, and that it did not revoke this acceptance. Instead, the defendant decided to keep the dowels and use them in its business. . . .

Nonetheless, accepting defective goods does not preclude a buyer from pursuing remedies for breach of contract due to defects in goods. 11 M.R.S.A. § 2–607(2). "The buyer on notifying the seller of his intention so to do may deduct all or any part of the damages resulting from any breach of the contract from any part of the price still due under the same contract." 11 M.R.S.A. § 2–717. A buyer claiming a breach of contract after accepting goods must, however, notify the seller of the breach within a reasonable time after discovery of the breach, or the buyer will be barred from any breach of contract remedy. 11 M.R.S.A. § 2–607(3)(a).

The critical question in this case, therefore, is whether the defendant gave timely notice of the breach of contract claim. What constitutes reasonable time depends on the particular circumstances of a case. 11 M.R.S.A. § 1–204. The policies underlying the requirement of timely notice are first, to enable the seller to cure or replace, second, to give the seller an opportunity to prepare for negotiation and litigation, and third, to ensure finality. J. White & R. Summers, Uniform Commercial Code 421–22 (2d ed. 1980). ... To further these purposes, "reasonable time" for notice is interpreted strictly for commercial buyers. See 11 M.R.S.A. § 2–607, Uniform Commercial Code (U.C.C.) Comment 4.

The defendant argues that notice of the breach was given by Wayne Curley, purchasing manager for Stowell Products, to Marshall Kates, owner of M.K. Associates, in their conversation in March, 1987. In this conversation, Curley told Kates that defects in some dowels were causing production problems, and Kates said he could not cancel the order. The defendant argues that Curley's conversation with Kates was sufficient notice. It is true that "no formality of notice is required." 11 M.R.S.A. § 2–717, U.C.C. Comment 2. "The content of the notification need merely be sufficient to let the seller know that the transaction is still troublesome and must be watched." 11 M.R.S.A. § 2–607, U.C.C. Comment 4. Nevertheless, after Kates responded that he would not be able to cancel the order, Curley let the matter rest and gave Kates no indication that Stowell Products pursued it further. Therefore, the defendant did not give adequate notice that the transaction was still troublesome.

Moreover, the U.C.C. Comments emphasize that notice of a claim of breach is crucial. "The notification which saves the buyer's rights under this Article need only be such as informs the seller that the transaction is claimed to involve a breach, and thus opens the way for normal settlement through negotiation." 11 M.R.S.A. § 2–607, U.C.C. Comment 4. Even if the seller knows of defects in the goods, the buyer must notify the seller of the buyer's claim that the defects constitute a breach. ... The requirement that a commercial buyer's notice must include an indication that the buyer considers the contract breached is consistent with the policies behind the notice requirement, which include ensuring finality for transactions and allowing the seller to prepare for negotiation and settlement. In the conversation with Kates, however, Curley did not clearly let Kates know that Stowell Products considered the contract breached.

Finally, U.C.C. Comment 2 to 11 M.R.S.A. § 2–717 states that "any language which reasonably indicates the buyer's reason for holding up his payment is sufficient." Despite repeated conversations concerning late payments, no one from Stowell Products suggested to M.K. Associates that payments were being withheld to cover the costs of defects in the dowels.

Therefore, Stowell Products' only notice of the breach was in its answer to the plaintiff's complaint, filed on October 13, 1987, more than five months after the dowels were received and more than three months after the dowels were received and more than three months after the defendant began processing the dowels. The defendant argues that it was reasonable to wait until the Mirro/Foley order was completed in order to determine the total amount of damages.

The U.C.C. does not require, however, that the buyer give notice of the exact amount of damages that will be incurred. . . . At least by June, 1987, the defendant knew of significant costs that would be incurred by correcting the defective dowels. The defendant has given no reason to justify letting several months go by while it used the defective goods for its own business purposes before warning M.K. Associates that it considered the contract breached.

The defendant also claims that the delay was reasonable in light of the purposes of the notice requirement, since ample time for settlement remained after the plaintiff began this litigation. Courts have held, however, that waiting until the seller sues for the purchase price to claim a breach of contract fails to satisfy the requirement of timely notice. . . .

### IV.   Conclusion

The defendant accepted and used the dowels from M.K. Associates despite any defects it found. The defendant failed to notify the plaintiff of any claim of a breach of contract until the plaintiff began this litigation. This delay was unreasonable, and therefore the defendant is barred from deducting damages for breach of contract.

Accordingly, the Court hereby ORDERS that judgment in this action be entered for the plaintiff in the amount of Ten Thousand Five Hundred Eighteen Dollars and Forty Cents ($10,518.40), plus interest and costs as provided by law.

NOTES

(1) **Understanding the Buyer's Delay.** Can you think of a possible explanation for the almost complete failure of the buyer's purchasing manager to mention the problem that the factory was experiencing with the dowels in his series of conversations with the seller's general manager? For his polite inquiry about cancellation rather than complaint about nonconformity? At what point in this transaction does it appear that buyer came to the conclusion that seller was in breach of warranty?[2] Do you think this occurred before seller obtained legal representation?

(2) **UCC 2–607(3): Rationale and History.** Comment 4 states that "the rule of requiring notification is designed to defeat commercial bad faith. . . ." The court in *M.K. Associates* gives three quite different policies said to underlie the requirement. Does the *text* of 2–607(3)(a) support the positions in the comment or the opinion? What purpose could be important enough to justify totally barring a buyer's claim without regard to the degree of injury, if any, to the interest of the seller? Comment 4 declares that the necessary content of a buyer's notice is minimal: "merely suffi-

---

**2.** Recall the effect in the court's reasoning of buyer's continuing to accept further deliveries of copy machines in *Royal Business Machines*, section 2, supra.

cient to let the seller know that the transaction is still troublesome and must be watched ..., [not] a clear statement of all the objections that will be relied upon by the buyer ..., and [not] a claim for damages or of any threatened litigation or other resort to a remedy."[3] Can the extreme consequence be reconciled with that minimal information requirement?

As indicated in the comment (Prior Uniform Statutory Provision), 2–607(3) has an antecedent in § 49 of the Uniform Sales Act, which also barred buyers who failed to give sellers timely notice of breach. USA 49 had no counterpart in the British Sale of Goods Act. What policy reason might have motivated the drafters of the United States statute add this element? See S. Williston, The Law Governing Sales of Goods at Common Law and Under the Uniform Sales Act § 488 (1909).[4]

Some civil law jurisdictions also impose a requirement of buyer's prompt notice of default. Some nations provide very short periods within which notices must be given to sellers. G. Treitel, Remedies for Breach of Contract: A Comparative Account 141 (1988). Under the German Commercial Code, §§ 377–378, commercial buyers are required to examine goods promptly after delivery and to give notice of any discernible lack of conformity discovered; if a buyer fails to give such notice, goods are deemed to be in conformity with the contract. Id.

Could UCC 2–607(3)(a), in its present form, be construed to provide relief only if a seller can show that buyer's delay has prejudiced the seller and limiting the bar to recovery to the extent necessary to overcome the prejudice shown? One commentator argues for an affirmative answer:[5]

> Many courts have in effect interpreted the "reasonable time" standard of the rule to reflect a rough balance of the interests of the buyer in obtaining a remedy against the interests [of the seller] served by the notice rule. Because the legislatures have not provided any guidance on the policy goals underlying the notice rule, the courts are free to construe them as broadly or narrowly as they think proper. ...

> The prejudice least likely to justify barring all of the buyer's claim is loss of opportunity to cure [the nonconformity]. When the seller demonstrates such a loss, the court might use the mitigation principle to justify barring only the costs that the seller could have avoided.

> [For the prejudice resulting from seller's loss of the opportunity to gather evidence of the goods conformity, courts should employ an evidentiary presumption in seller's favor.] Traditionally. courts place the burden of production of evidence on the party with the best access to the relevant evidence. Courts should also be free to employ presumptions to prevent the careless or deliberate behavior of one litigant from prejudicing the opposing litigant's defense or prosecution.

---

**3.** Would a notice be sufficient if it stated in entirety: "Your delivery was nonconforming"?

**4.** See also John C. Reitz, Against Notice: A Proposal to Restrict the Notice of Claims Rule in UCC § 2–607(a)(3), 73 Cornell L. Rev. 534, 540–541 (1988).

**5.** John C. Reitz, note 4 supra, at 588–589.

Do you agree with this analysis?

## 2.  STATUTE OF LIMITATIONS

The UCC shortened the period of limitations for actions for breach of warranty or any other breach of a contract of sale. In most states, the period of limitations for breach of contract is six years. Before the adoption of UCC Article 2, the general contract statute of limitations applied to sales contracts. Section 2–725(1) provides a four-year period for breaches of warranties of quality.[6] The period begins to run when a buyer's cause of action accrues, defined for most transactions as the date of tender of delivery.[7] UCC 2–725(2). Buyer's knowledge or lack of knowledge of the breach is not material.

### a.  *IMPLIED WARRANTIES*

When does the period of limitations begin to run on seller's breach of implied warranty of merchantability? Of fitness for particular purpose? As might be expected, UCC 2–725(2) provides that a cause of action accrues when "breach occurs," but the section adds that breach of warranty occurs when tender of delivery is made unless there is a warranty that "explicitly extends to future performance of the goods." Explicit extension of warranties can occur only by expression, not by implication. Breach of an implied warranty of quality always occurs, therefore, at tender of delivery of the goods.

Could the limitations period expire before a buyer has learned of the breach of an implied warranty? Again UCC 2–725(2) is clear: A cause of action accrues "regardless of the aggrieved party's knowledge of the breach." If the limitations period begins to run before a buyer finds out that there was a breach of warranty, the period could expire while the buyer is still in the dark. What is the policy rationale for a rule that will lead, in some cases, to warranty claims being time-barred before buyers are aware that there are any non-conformities in the goods? The Comment to the section provides no explanation. Nor can an answer be found in the Uniform Sales Act, which had no statute of limitations. Prior to adoption of the Commercial Code, the statute of limitations for claims of breach of warranty was the general statute for all contract actions.[8]

---

**6.**  UCC 2–725(1) permits parties to a contract of sale to reduce the limitations period (with a one-year minimum) but not to extend it.

**7.**  Application of UCC 2–725 to sales contracts that obligate sellers not only to deliver goods to buyers, but also to install and test the goods after delivery, has proven to be controversial. See Flagg Energy Development Corp. v. General Motors Corp., 244 Conn. 126, 709 A.2d 1075 (1998); Washington Freightliner, Inc. v. Shantytown Pier, Inc., 351 Md. 616, 719 A.2d 541 (1998); Baker v. DEC International, 458 Mich. 247, 580 N.W.2d 894 (1998). These cases are discussed in J. Wladis, R. Hakes, M. Kotler, R. Meadows & P. Tauchert, Uniform Commercial Code Survey: Sales, 54 Bus. Law. 1831, 1844–1846 (1999).

**8.**  A New York case involved a claim for severe injuries suffered by a child when she ran into a glass door that broke. The injury occurred more than four years after the door had been purchased. Shortly after the accident, the claim made was that the glass door did not conform to the implied warranty of merchantability and that this caused the child's injuries. (New York

### b.  *EXPRESS WARRANTIES*

Under UCC 2–725(2), the period of limitations begins to run on seller's breach of an express warranty of quality at the date of tender of delivery of the goods unless the warranty "explicitly extends to future performance of the goods and discovery of the breach must await the time of performance." For ordinary express warranties that derive from affirmations of fact that relate to the goods under UCC 2–313, the four-year period of limitations begins to run on the day when tender of delivery is made. As with implied warranties, running of the limitations period occurs without regard to the buyer's knowledge of a breach.

*Future performance warranties.* If a warranty extends to future performance of the goods, the four-year period commences when the breach is or should have been discovered. Whether a warranty extends to future performance has posed a most difficult task for lawyers and judges. The issue arises in transactions for durable goods, goods that are expected to have an extended useful life. In such transactions, buyers sometimes want sellers' assurance that the goods will "hold up," i.e., will continue to function for some time. Sellers, on the other hand, have no control of the manner of buyers' use or of the buyers' maintenance practices. They tend to be loathe to make performance warranties that run for the entire expected useful life of durable goods, even for goods that have very long life expectancies.

CONTROLLED ENVIRONMENTS CONSTRUCTION, INC. v. KEY INDUSTRIAL REFRIGERATION CO., 266 Neb. 927, 670 N.W.2d 771 (2003). In sale of refrigeration equipment, the agreement provided a separate warranty on the compressor: "Four year extended compressor warranty." The court held that the warranty did not extend to future performance of the compressor.

MOORMAN MANUFACTURING CO. v. NATIONAL TANK CO., 91 Ill.2d 69, 61 Ill.Dec. 746, 435 N.E.2d 443 (1982). In 1966 Moorman purchased a large grain-storage tank from National. The contract of sale contained the following provision: "Tank designed to withstand 60 lbs. per bushel grain and 100 m.p.h. winds." Winds of that velocity are not regular occurrences. In 1976 a crack developed in the tank. Moorman brought suit against National in 1977. One count of the complaint, based on the quoted language, alleged breach of express warranty. National contended that the claim was barred by the statute of limitations. The trial court, relying on the exception in 2–725(2), held that Moorman's claim was not time-barred. The Illinois Supreme Court reversed. The court relied on the decision in Binkley Co. v. Teledyne Mid–America Corp., 333 F.Supp. 1183 (E.D.Mo. 1971), aff'd 460 F.2d 276 (8th Cir.1972), where the seller of a welding machine had expressly warranted that a welder would weld at a rate of

---

courts did not recognize the tort of strict liability at the time of this case.) The child's claim was held to be time-barred under UCC 2–725. Mendel v. Pittsburgh Plate Glass Co., 25 N.Y.2d 888, 304 N.Y.S.2d 4, 251 N.E.2d 143 (1969). Within a few years, New York joined the large number of states that allowed tort recovery in cases of this kind. Codling v. Paglia, 32 N.Y.2d 330, 345 N.Y.S.2d 461, 298 N.E.2d 622 (1973).

1,000 feet per 50–minute hour, which it never did. The court defined
"explicit" under 2–725(2) as "[n]ot implied merely, or conveyed by implication; distinctly stated; plain in language; clear; not ambiguous; express;
unequivocal." Although the warranty expressly stated that the welder
would weld at 1,000 feet per hour, the court found that the statute had
lapsed because there was no reference to future time in the warranty and,
thus, no explicit warranty of future performance. In response to the buyer's
argument that he was unable to test the product until after delivery the
court pointed to the clear language of section 2–725(2) which provides that
the breach occurs at the time of delivery "regardless of the aggrieved
party's lack of knowledge." We agree with the decision in that case as well
as the appellate decisions in this State adhering to the clear language of the
statute.

## (B) International Sales Law

### 1. NOTICE OF BREACH

Assume that *M.K. Associates* had been an international sales transaction governed by CISG. Would the result have been the same or different?
See CISG 39(1). The answer seems reasonably clear. Like the UCC, CISG
imposes a notice requirement with comparable elements of "reasonable
time" and buyer's discovery. Instead of "barred from any remedy" CISG
uses "loses the right to rely on a lack of conformity." Is there a different
meaning?

A perceptive reader of CISG 39(1), familiar with the UCC, would
observe that the CISG demands more in the content of a buyer's notice
than "of breach." How much factual detail must buyers include to "specify
. . . the nature of the lack of conformity"? If multiple non-conformities are
discovered, must each be detailed? When a second non-conformity surfaces
after a notice has been given, must another notice be sent?

Having worked through the CISG provision and made comparison to
UCC Article 2, one might stop the legal analysis. To do so would be to
commit a grave error. See CISG 44, which significantly modifies CISG
39(1).[9]

The danger continues beyond noticing that CISG 44 modifies CISG
39(1). On the face of CISG 44, a reader might conclude that relief from loss
of the right to rely on a lack of conformity is available only if a buyer has
not yet paid the full price. "[T]he buyer may reduce the price in accordance

---

**9.** Professor Honnold explained the reason for such closely related provisions appearing
in different Articles of CISG. In the last days of the diplomatic conference that produced the
Convention, there was still major inter-regional disagreement regarding the notice requirement in CISG 39. Developing countries wanted to relax the notice requirement, but their
proposals were not adopted. Dissatisfied proponents of modifying CISG 39 were sufficiently
numerous that the necessary two-thirds vote in favor of the Convention was in jeopardy. A
compromise solution was proposed and became CISG 44. It was made a separate article so that
the added provision would apply also to the notice requirements of CISG 43(1). J. Honnold,
Uniform Law for International Sales § 261 (3d ed. 1999).

with article 50....'' When one turns to CISG 50, however, one learns that a buyer can "reduce" a price "whether or not the price has already been paid." In short, a buyer who is excused under CISG 44 has not only the right to set off damages against the unpaid price, but also has an affirmative right to recover some or all of the price paid.

The CISG imposes an outside limit on the time for a buyer's notice to the seller specifying the nature of the lack of non-conformity. Buyers must give notice within two years from the date the goods were "actually handed over" to them, whether or not the buyers discovered or ought to have discovered the non-conformities ("in any event"). CISG 39(2). An exception exists if this time limit is "inconsistent with a contractual period of guarantee." Note that the CISG 44 excuse provision is not available against the CISG 39(2) time bar.

The UCC has no provision comparable to CISG 39(2).

## FINAL AWARD IN CASE NO. 5713 OF 1989
ICC 15 Y.B. Comm. Arb. 70 (1990)

| Parties: | Claimant/counterdefendant: Seller |
| | Defendant/counterclaimant: Buyer |

Place of
Arbitration: Paris, France

### Facts

In 1979, the parties concluded three contracts for the sale of a product according to certain contract specifications. The buyer paid 90% of the price payable under each of the contracts upon presentation of the shipping documents, as contractually agreed.

The product delivered pursuant to the first and third contracts met the contract specifications. The conformity of the second consignment was disputed prior to its shipment. When the product was again inspected upon arrival, it was found that it did not meet the contract specifications. The product was eventually sold by the buyer to third parties at considerable loss, after having undergone a certain treatment to make it more saleable.

The seller initiated arbitration proceedings to recover the 10% balance remaining due under the contracts. The buyer filed a counterclaim alleging that the seller's claim should be set off against the amounts which the buyer estimates to be payable to the buyer by the seller, i.e., the direct losses, financing costs, lost profits and interest.

### Excerpt

I.  Applicable Law

The contract contains no provisions regarding the substantive law. Accordingly that law has to be determined by the Arbitrators in accordance with Art. 13(3) of the ICC rules.[11] Under that article, the Arbitrators will "apply the law designated as the proper law by the rule of conflicts which they deem appropriate".

The contract is between a Seller and a Buyer [of different nationalities] for delivery [in a third country]. The sale was f.o.b. so that the transfer of risks to the Buyer took place in [the country of the Seller]. [The country of the Seller] accordingly appears as being the jurisdiction to which the sale is most closely related.

The Hague Convention on the law applicable to international sales of goods dated 15 June 1955 (Art. 3) regarding sales contracts, refers as governing law to the law of the Seller's current residence.... [12] [The country of the Buyer] has adhered to the Hague Convention, not [the country of the Seller]. However, the general trend in conflicts of law is to apply the domestic law of the current residence of the debtor of the essential undertaking arising under the contract. That debtor in a sales contract is the Seller. Based on those combined findings, [the law of the country of the Seller] appears to be the proper law governing the Contract between the Seller and the Buyer.

As regards the applicable rules of [the law of the country of the Seller], the Arbitrators have relied on the Parties' respective statements on the subject and on the information obtained by the Arbitrators from an independent consultant.... The Arbitrators, in accordance with the last paragraph of Art. 13 of the ICC rules, will also take into account the "relevant trade usages".

## II.   Admissibility of the Counterclaim

(a) Under [the law of the country of the Seller]

\* \* \*

(b) Under the international trade usages prevailing in the international sale of goods

The Tribunal finds that there is no better source to determine the prevailing trade usages than the terms of the United Nations Convention

---

**11.** Art. 13 of the ICC Rules of 1975 (Not amended by the 1988 amendments) reads in relevant part:

"3.   The parties shall be free to determine the law to be applied by the arbitrator to the merits of the dispute. In the absence of any indication by the parties as to the applicable law, the arbitrator shall apply the law designated as the proper law by the rule of conflict which he deems appropriate.

(....)

5.   In all cases the arbitrator shall take account of the provisions of the contract and the relevant trade usages."

**12.** Art. 3 of the Hague Convention on the Law Applicable to the International Sales of Goods reads in pertinent part:

"In default of a law declared applicable by the parties under the conditions provided in the preceding article, a sale shall be governed by the domestic law of the country in which the vendor has his habitual residence at the time when he received the order...."

on the International Sale of Goods of 11 April 1980, usually called "the Vienna Convention". This is so even though neither [the country of the Buyer] nor [the country of the Seller] are parties to that Convention. If they were, the Convention might be applicable to this case as a matter of law and not only as reflecting the trade usage.

The Vienna Convention, which has been given effect to in 17 countries, may be fairly taken to reflect the generally recognized usages regarding the matter of the non-conformity of goods in international sales. Art. 38(1) of the Convention puts the onus on the Buyer to "examine the goods or cause them to be examined promptly". The Buyer should then notify the Seller of the non-conformity of the goods within a reasonable period as of the moment he noticed or should have noticed the defect; otherwise he forfeits his right to raise a claim based on the said non-conformity. Art. 39(1) specifies in this respect that:

> In any event the buyer shall lose the right to rely on a lack of conformity of the goods if he has not given notice thereof to the seller within a period of two years from the date on which the goods were handed over, unless the lack of conformity constituted a breach of a guarantee covering a longer period.

In the circumstances, the Buyer had the shipment examined within a reasonable time-span since [an expert] was requested to inspect the shipment even before the goods had arrived. The Buyer should also be deemed to have given notice of the defects within a reasonable period, that is eight days after the expert's report had been published.

Tribunal finds that, in the circumstances of the case, the Buyer has complied with the above-mentioned requirements of the Vienna Convention. These requirements are considerably more flexible than those provided under [the law of the country of the Seller]. This law, by imposing extremely short and specific time requirements in respect of the giving of the notices of defects by the Buyer to the Seller appears to be an exception on this point to the generally accepted trade usages.

In any case, the Seller should be regarded as having forfeited its right to invoke any non-compliance with the requirements of Arts. 38 and 39 of the Vienna Convention since Art. 40 states that the Seller cannot rely on Arts. 38 and 39, "if the lack of conformity relates to facts of which he knew, or of which he could not have been unaware, and which he did not disclose". Indeed, this appears to be the case, since it clearly transpires from the file and the evidence that the Seller knew and could not be unaware [of the non-conformity of the consignment to] contract specifications.

NOTES

**(1) The Choice of Law.** Although the Final Award says very little about the parties to the transaction or the nature of the product, the award does report that the seller and buyer are from different countries and that neither country had ratified CISG at the time of this sale. As we saw in Chapter 2, the Convention declares its scope of application in CISG 1(a).

For international sales outside the scope of the Convention, private international law provides an international set of rules to determine which national law governs. The 1955 Hague Convention on the Law Applicable to International Sales of Goods is one possible source of private international law rules.[10] In Part I of the Award, the arbitrators declared that the convention applied even though the seller's country had not ratified it. The result was to make the domestic law of seller's country the applicable law.

In Part II of the Award, the arbitrators applied CISG rather than the law of the seller's country to determine whether buyer's notice was timely. The arbitrators noted that the CISG provisions were "considerably more flexible" than the domestic law of seller's country. which has "extremely short and specific time requirements in respect of giving notice of defects." How did the arbitrators justify using CISG? Was that reasoning sound?

**(2) Application of CISG 39.** The buyer gave the seller notice of non-conformities eight days after an expert inspector published its report on the quality of the goods. The Award is not clear as to the time and place of the expert's inspection other than noting that it took place before the goods arrived. In this transaction the goods were shipped by a carrier and the buyer paid most of the contract price when the documents signifying the carriage arrangement were presented. Commonly, in transactions of this kind, buyers retain the services of experts at the place of shipment to examine the goods as they are loaded. That appears to be what was done in this transaction. When and how the expert "published" its report is unknown.

In later chapters, we will consider transactions like this in greater detail. As we will see, sales contracts that contemplate payment against documents before arrival of the goods sometimes require that the sellers present to buyers the reports of the independent inspectors as one of the documents necessary to trigger the buyers' duty to pay the price. That method of transacting was apparently not followed in this case.

**(3) Application of CISG 40.** An alternative holding of the arbitrators applied CISG 40, which absolves buyers of the duty to give sellers notice of any nonconformities. The Award does not provide the factual basis for the conclusion that the seller "knew and could not be unaware" of the nonconformity in this case.

Does UCC Article 2 have an analogous provision that dispenses with the requirement of notice in UCC 2–607(3)(a)? Should it? Cf. UCC 2–206(1)(b) (shipment of nonconforming goods by seller in response to an order is not an acceptance if the seller seasonably notifies the buyer that the shipment is offered only as an accommodation to the buyer).

## UNCITRAL CLOUT Abstract No. 285

Oberlandesgericht, Koblenz, Germany, 1998.

A Moroccan buyer, plaintiff, purchased raw material for manufacturing plastic PVC tubes (dryblend) from a German seller, defendant. When the

---

10.   Only seven nations have ratified this convention as of 2010. All are in Europe.

buyer discovered that the dryblend was not suitable for use in its manufacturing facilities, the buyer claimed lack of quality and sued for damages.

The court dismissed the claim. It held that the buyer had lost its right to rely on the lack of conformity according to CISG 39(1). Giving notice to the seller three weeks after delivery was held as being too late. The court said that, if trial processing was necessary to examine the quality of the goods, a period of one week for examination and another week for giving notice would have been reasonable. As to the buyer's argument that it had been unable to examine the goods any earlier because the manufacturing facilities were still under construction, the court held that this did not constitute a reasonable excuse (article 44 CISG). Such an excuse demanded that the buyer acted with reasonable care in providing for prompt examination of the goods, which included the timely supply of machinery necessary for trial processing. The buyer failed to provide particulars that it had acted with such due care. Moreover, disorganisation on the part of the buyer was not an aspect to be considered in determining the period practicable in the circumstances (article 38(1) CISG).

Since the seller was found not to have been aware of the fact that the dryblend was not suitable for producing plastic tubes in the buyer's manufacturing facilities, as the buyer had failed to inform the seller of the kind of equipment in use, the seller did not lose its right to rely on late notification (article 40 CISG). The court said that, although there would be a loss of the right to rely on late notification if the seller had had a duty to warn the buyer or provide additional information about the goods delivered, in this case there had been no such obligation.

NOTES

(1) **Application of CISG 39(1).** The transaction in this case involved a product "raw material" that the buyer purchased to use in manufacturing plastic PVC tubes. It appears that the buyer discovered the nonconformity in the course of manufacturing and gave prompt notice after that discovery. The court held that the buyer should have done "trial processing" of the raw material before the normal manufacturing process occurred and measured the reasonable of the time for CISG 39(1) notice from the time that "trial processing" should have been completed. Was the court's holding a proper application of CISG 39(1)?

(2) **Frequency of Litigation Involving CISG 39 and 44.** Collections of CISG decisions contain a considerable number of cases in which CISG 39 and 44 have been applied. Courts and arbitrators have been rigorous in narrow interpretations of "reasonable time" under CISG 39(1). See the UNCITRAL Digest of case law under the CISG at www.uncitral. org/CLOUT, and the Pace University Law School data base at www.cisg. law.pace.edu. Many of the cases were litigated in German courts, which would be familiar with the strict notice requirements of the German Commercial Code.

(3) **Waiver by Seller.** A court may find that a seller has waived the right to rely on CISG 39. An Austrian buyer sued a German seller for

damages caused by surface-protective film that left residues of glue on polished high-grade steel products. After buyer gave seller notice of the nonconformity of the film, seller and buyer entered into negotiations as to the amount of damages and the manner in which the damages should be paid. Negotiations continued over 15 months but failed to settle the dispute. In the suit, seller contended that buyer had not given timely notice under CISG 39. The court held that seller had waived the defense. UNCITRAL abstract no. 270, Bundesgerichtshof, Germany, 1998.

**(4) Contract Terms: Time and Form of Notice.** CISG does not prohibit parties from providing in their contracts for the time or the form of notices of non-conformities. CISG 6. In some transactions, the parties agree that written notice is required and that notice must be given within a specific number of days. A clause of that kind was included in the seller's standard form in MCC–Marble Ceramic Center, Inc. v. Ceramica Nuova d'Agostino, S.P.A., which we considered in Chapter 2. Buyer did not comply with these requirements and seller sought to have the claim dismissed on this ground. The court allowed parol evidence to prove that the clause was not part of the contract.

## 2.   PERIOD OF LIMITATIONS

CISG contains no period of limitations. That subject is found in an entirely separate convention, the United Nations Convention on the Limitation Period of the International Sale of Goods. A convention was required to replace the greatly diverse limitation ("prescription") periods among various nations' domestic laws. A sufficient number of nations had ratified this Convention for it to take effect in 1988. The United States is a party to the Convention, which is in force in 23 nations.[11]

Like UCC 2–725, the Convention sets a four-year limitation period.

Article 11 of the Limitation Period Convention contains a provision on extended warranties that differs from the analogous UCC provision:

> If the seller has given an express undertaking relating to the goods which is stated to have effect for a certain period of time, whether expressed in terms of a specific period of time or otherwise, the limitation period in respect of any claim arising from the undertaking shall commence on the date on which the buyer notifies the seller of the fact on which the claim is based, but not later than on the date of the expiration of the period of the undertaking.

Is the Convention provision better than that in the Commercial Code?

## SECTION 7.   ALTERNATIVE TO WARRANTY LAW AS A MEANS OF ASSURING QUALITY OF GOODS

The law of quality warranties and their enforcement are a kind of *ex post* response to market failures. The question we wish to raise in this

---

**11.**   See J. Honnold, Uniform Law for International Sales § 261.1 (3d ed. 1999).

section is whether society would be better served by other mechanisms for assuring the "optimal" quality of goods. Alternatives may include legal mechanisms for quality assurance that are *ex ante*, i.e., that address quality assurance in the production and marketing of goods.

Warranties of quality are enforced after buyers discover that the goods delivered or tendered by sellers are deficient in some respect. Commonly, buyers make this discovery after the goods have been put to use, if the buyer is a consumer or processor, or resold, if the buyer is a dealer in goods of that kind. Certain economic efficiency is attained in that only qualitatively poor goods are subject to warranty enforcement. Buyers have the risk of discovery of any defects in purchased goods and the burden of seeking compensation for their losses. To the extent that aggrieved buyers seek and obtain damages, the costs of marketing suboptimal quality goods is transferred back to sellers; the prospect of this occurring may induce sellers to avoid or minimize these costs by use of better designs or better methods of quality control so that defective goods do not enter the market.

Not all aggrieved buyers will seek and obtain relief for breach of warranties of quality. Various practical reasons for this exist. Moreover, transaction costs of such *ex post* quality assurance, for buyers and sellers, are high. The harm suffered may be so small in relation to transaction costs that the aggrieved party has no incentive to pursue a contractual or legal remedy. The harm suffered may be so great that a seller lacks the financial resources to pay. The question to be considered is whether there are means, better than warranty law, for reaching the desired outcome of optimal quality in good sold. Can the law induce an *ex ante* response by sellers to improve the quality of their goods?

The market already creates powerful *ex ante* economic incentives for sellers to generate higher product quality. To the extent that buyers are informed about aspects of quality and are capable of appreciating their significance, better quality products will command a premium. In theory, sellers will be induced to supply goods of a quality at which the marginal cost for further improvement begins to exceed the marginal benefits to buyers, and the market equilibrium will be efficient.

This economic theory fails if buyers are not adequately informed about aspects of quality or lack ability to appreciate their significance *before purchase*. Economists refer to this as a problem of imperfect information. If buyers cannot cheaply assess the quality of goods for sale, willingness to buy and pay will not adjust to improvements in quality, and the economic incentive to raise quality will be diminished. Because better quality is generally costly to produce, poorer-quality products can outcompete higher-quality products, and the market equilibrium may result in production of suboptimal low-quality products exclusively.

To some extent, markets respond to the problem of imperfect information without the intervention of regulatory law. The development of marketing reputation through word-of-mouth and through investment in brand-name capital is one way that some manufacturers have gained a stake in setting and maintaining quality. Sellers may transmit useful quality related information to potential buyers through advertising, if it is deemed credible. Independent agencies, such as Consumer Reports or Good Housekeeping or Underwriter's Laboratories, may supply useful information as to the quality of goods in the marketplace. For products that are repeatedly purchased, buyers may reward sellers of products perceived—in past used to be higher in quality. Even sellers' quality warranties may be part of an *ex ante* market response, if prospective buyers perceive the seller's willingness to issue a warranty as a signal of the product's quality.

These market responses, separately or collectively, do not fully solve the problem of imperfect information. One alternative solution would be to create a system for close evaluation o manufacturers' production facilities and processes under standards developed, promulgated, and administered by third-party organizations of unquestioned independence and integrity. Certification of a manufacturer would depend upon finding that its quality-assurance system meets prescribed standards and provides buyers objective evidence on which to base their choice of suppliers. Establishment of such a system probably requires the participation of a government, or set of governments, to assure that it is independent of the manufacturers or sellers and capable of designing and administering quality-assurance standards.

### ISO 9000 Standard Series

An example of such an organization is the International Organization for Standardization (ISO), an international body consisting of the representatives of all nations who wish to participate. The impetus for establishment of the ISO in 1947 came from the United Nations. More than 90 countries are represented in ISO. Each nation delegates its own representative to the ISO; the United States is represented by a private entity, the American National Standards Institute, assisted by the American Society for Testing Methods and the American Society for Quality Control. In recent years, after abandoning its earlier practice of requiring unanimity for the creation of standards, the ISO has undertaken a major initiative in quality assurance. The ISO 9000/10011 standard requires the management of a company seeking ISO certification to document formally its policy on quality, to ensure that this policy is understood by all concerned with the company, and to take appropriate steps to see that the policy is fully implemented.

ISO 9000 takes the mystery out of quality. It defines quality chapter by chapter, verse by verse, thereby providing a clearly defined path to set up a world-class quality assurance system that is elemental in its logic and application.

The standards do not apply to products. Instead, they provide assurance § primarily through a system of internal and external audits—that a certified company has a quality system in place that will enable it to meet its published quality standards. . . .

A key characteristic of ISO certification is that it requires third-party registration. The third party in this case is an authorized assessor or registrar who conducts an independent audit of an organization's quality system.... If it passes the audit, the system is registered and certified. Regular maintenance audits are conducted to ensure that the system doesn't degrade.[15]

SGS (Société Générale de Surveillance) is the world's leading certification company. With 39,000 employees, SGS operates a network of 1,000 offices and laboratories around the world. More than 40,000 companies have chosen SGS as the certifying body that performs the audit of their Quality Management Systems against the ISO 9000 standards.

ISO 9000 certification is not a requirement for selling goods in the private sector. Buyers are free to purchase goods from uncertified sources. However, if several suppliers are trying to land a contract, the one with ISO 9000 certification is likely to have a substantial competitive advantage. The situation is different in sales of goods to governments and public agencies; ISO certification may be mandatory.

A set of ISO standards is being used by the United States Department of Defense and by the NATO. More importantly, the European Union adopted ISO standards to provide a universal framework for quality assurance within that 25—nation economic area. Firms seeking to sell products to government-controlled industries in Europe typically have to establish quality systems that meet ISO standards.

Conforming to the standards of ISO 9000 has become a condition of doing business in many parts of the world.

### QS 9000

The International Automotive Sector Group (IASG) is an international ad hoc working group consisting of automotive-OEM representatives, accreditation bodies, and suppliers. The IASG oversees implementation of the standards of ISO 9000 and QS 9000 that are followed by General Motors, Ford, Chrysler, Toyota, and other manufacturers.

---

15. Hockman, The Last Barrier to the European Market, Wall Street Journal, Oct. 7, 1991.

# CHAPTER 5

# MANUFACTURERS' WARRANTIES AND REMEDIAL PROMISES TO DOWNSTREAM BUYERS

## SECTION 1. INTRODUCTION

This chapter addresses warranties and remedial promises of manufacturers that run to downstream buyers. The fact situation for these warranties and promises arise from the system for distribution of new goods through intermediaries that are commonly called distributors, wholesalers, and retailers.

The commercial context for manufacturers warranting their goods to remote buyers and undertaking to remedy defects in those goods has roots in the middle of the 19th century, but the practice flowered in the 20th century. Several economic and legal developments contributed to this. One was the creation of assembly lines which had the capacity to mass produce large quantities of standardized goods.[1] Another was the development of trade marks and brand names, which are legally protected forms of intellectual property and which became powerful tools for marketing of mass-produced goods.[2] Corporations that owned the production facilities, the trade marks, and the brand names became large national enterprises, many of which have grown into huge transnational enterprises. Manufacturers of brand-named goods spend large sums to advertise their products to potential downstream buyers in order to increase demand in retail markets. Commercial television, most national magazines, and the advertising industry depend heavily on these expenditures.

---

1. References to "manufacturers" in this section include businesses that assemble components made by others into final products that carry the brand name of the assemblers, such as some makers of computers, as well as businesses that process primary goods into brand named final products, such as oil companies.

2. Some large retail business enterprises, using the marketing power of known brand names, sell goods with brand names owned by the retailers, so-called "store-brands." Store-brand goods are not manufactured by the retailers, but are made for them by manufacturers, usually manufacturers that make and sell similar goods under the manufacturers' own brand names. Sears Roebuck Co. sells many goods of this kind under its brand names, Kenmore and Craftsman. Buyers of store-brand goods are normally unaware of the identity of the manufacturers of the goods. Warranties associated with store-brand goods are warranties of the retailers and not of the manufacturers. These warranties arise within sales contracts and are not warranties to remote buyers.

Perhaps the earliest product produced and marketed in this way in the United States was the Singer sewing machine. Isaac Singer did not invent the sewing machine, but he found a way to sell his name-branded machines to families all over the country.[3] Today, most durable consumer goods are sold under the manufacturers' brand names through retail outlets.

The automobile sector of the economy is a prominent example of marketing durable goods through franchised dealerships. In this economic sector, manufacturers control the distribution chain, which is made up of independent businesses that are "authorized" dealers or distributors. The dealers and distributors are in long-term contractual relationships with the manufacturers. In other economic sectors, goods move through independent wholesalers and distributors that are not affiliated with the manufacturers.

Communication of warranties and remedial promises from manufacturers to end users can take various routes, but two methods have become predominant. One route is to package the warranties or remedial promises with the goods; the warranties and promises become one of the "things" delivered to user/buyers. Manufacturers of computers and printers, major appliances, consumer electronic products, cameras, and many other durable goods that are delivered in boxes use the technique of packing warranty materials in the boxes. Another route is to place advertisements in media or publish catalogues or brochures which they can be read by individuals who are prospective buyers.

This commercial pattern is made possible by a set of contracts. Two are contracts for the sale of goods, one at the wholesale level and one at the retail level. Manufacturers and dealers enter into contracts of sale, whereby dealers obtain their inventory from manufacturers. Dealers and their customers enter into retail sales contracts. These are contracts of the type we considered in earlier chapters. One important aspect of the retail sales contracts is that the dealers routinely make no express warranties of quality and disclaim all implied warranties of quality, particularly the implied warranty of merchantability. The retailers tell their customers, sometimes as an explicit term of a written contract of sale, that buyers will receive the benefit of the manufacturers' warranties and remedial promises and that these are their only protection.[4]

The legal issues addressed in this chapter are, for the most part, matters of domestic United States law. The major legal problem is charac-

---

**3.** The sewing machine was the first major item of home equipment to be used by women. One of Singer's marketing challenges was to persuade men, who tended to control family finances, to spend a substantial amount of money on a labor-saving device for their wives. Among his many innovations was the invention of retail instalment purchasing and franchised dealerships.

**4.** Occasionally a retail seller will fail to comply with the UCC 2–316 requirements for effective disclaimer of implied warranties, or fail to eliminate from the contract a salesman's oral express warranty by a merger clause that is effective under UCC 2–202, or otherwise stumble into assuming responsibility for the quality of the goods. Such aberrations are exceedingly rare, however. Dealers tend to use standard contract forms that have been carefully drafted by lawyers to achieve the desired immunity from liability.

terization of the relationship between a manufacturer and a downstream buyer and determination of the governing law. If the relationship is characterized as contractual, a solution must be found for the fact that the parties are not parties to a contract of sale and are not in privity with each other. As we will see, domestic United States law deals with this in a variety of ways. International sales law, particularly the Convention on Contracts for International Sale of Goods, provides no basis for dealing with a manufacturer's warranty or remedial promise to a downstream buyer unless the manufacturer is party to the contract of sale to that buyer.

## SECTION 2.   MANUFACTURERS' EXPRESS WARRANTIES

### (A) DOMESTIC UNITED STATES LAW

Many manufacturers make affirmations of fact regarding their products. These are commonly made in advertisements and promotional literature. They resemble the express warranties that we considered in Section 2 of Chapter 4, but they do not arise within contracts of sale. It seems obvious that such warranties should be legally enforceable by the beneficiaries to whom the warranties were addressed. The challenge is to find an appropriate legal platform. The most likely choice is contract law, but there are doctrinal challenges to applying traditional common-law contract doctrine, which is based on concepts of offer and acceptance, consideration, and contractual privity.

In some commercial scenarios, a manufacturer might authorize a retailer to transmit the manufacturer's express warranty to a retail buyer in conjunction with the retailer's contract of sale with the buyer. The manufacturer does not become a party to the sales contract, but only to the whatever is the obligation of the manufacturer's warranty. The manufacturer would be the principal in making the warranty, and the retailer would be the manufacturer's agent. If agency theory can be sustained, a direct relationship between the manufacturer and the retail buyer can be found. This might satisfy the requirement of contractual privity, but that still leaves unresolved how the transaction satisfies the other doctrinal prerequisites of contract law. If the warranty is construed to be an offer, what constitutes acceptance by the downstream buyer? What is the consideration for the manufacturer's promise?

The consideration problem arose in a well-known late 19th century British case, which arose out of a manufacturer's promise made in newspaper advertisements.[1] The manufacturer was marketing a product (a "smoke ball") that would protect users against an array of illnesses. The advertising gimmick was the manufacturer's promise to pay a substantial "reward" to anyone who became ill after using the smoke ball. In an action to collect the reward, the manufacturer contended that there was no consideration to

---

**1.** Carlill v. Carbolic Smoke Ball Co., [1893] 1 Q.B. 256 (C.A. 1892).

support the promise. The British court held that the retail buyer had given consideration when it bought the smoke ball from a dealer. Prior British cases had said that consideration must "move to" the promissor. This decision liberalized the common-law doctrine.

The smoke ball case was decided before Mackensie Chalmers drafted the British Sale of Goods Act and before the Uniform Sales Act was promulgated in the United States. Neither statute contained any provision regarding manufacturers' warranties to downstream buyers.

A 1960s New York case arose from a claim by a garment manufacturer against a chemical company, manufacturer of a resin that it claimed would make fabrics shrink-proof.[2] The manufacturer made its claim in trade journal advertising and on labels that it provided to fabric suppliers for attachment to fabric treated with the resin. The garment manufacturer bought resin-treated fabric bearing the labels. The fabric was not shrink-proof. The chemical company's defense was lack of privity of contract. The garment manufacturer' suit was allowed. The controversy went to the state's highest court, the Court of Appeals, which decided the case as a matter of common law. At the end of its opinion, the court noted that the Uniform Sales Act, which New York had adopted, defined express warranties, but added that the uniform act was silent on the question of privity. The court said nothing about UCC Article 2, which was in late stages of preparation.[3]

Some courts apply UCC Article 2 to claims by downstream buyers based on breach of manufacturers' express warranties. Sometimes the cases involve suits against both the dealer and the manufacturer. Action against a dealer would be governed by UCC 2–313. Even though the language of that section makes it inapplicable to a manufacturer's warranty to a downstream buyer, some courts bracket both defendants as UCC 2–313 warrantors.

The consequences of this choice are profound. In part this stems from the provisions of UCC 2–313 itself, principally the requirement that a warranty is not actionable unless it is "part of the basis of the bargain." There is no "bargain" between a downstream buyer and a manufacturer. Other parts of UCC Article 2 bar recovery for breach of warranty are problematic in relation to manufacturers' warranties. Does the notice requirement, UCC 2–607(3)(a), apply? Is the limitations period four years under UCC 2–725 or six years, as in contract law generally?

The following case is an example of overlapping express warranty obligations of an immediate seller and a remote supplier. The warranty issues that arise with respect to the immediate seller are a reprise of

---

**2.** Randy Knitwear v. American Cyanamid Co., 11 N.Y. 5, 181 N.E.2d 399, 226 N.Y.S.2d 363 (1962).

**3.** A similar decision from the same time period involved suit by the buyer of a new car against the manufacturer on the basis of the manufacturer's warranty. Inglis v. American Motors Corp., 3 Ohio St.2d 132, 209 N.E.2d 583 (1965). The opinion of the court did not mention the Uniform Sales Act.

materials that we considered in Chapter 4. Our main focus is on the express warranty issues that arise with respect to the remote supplier. The court's solution to those issues is instructive. In a later section, we will consider the court's treatment of the claim of breach of an implied warranty made by the manufacturer.

## Martin Rispens & Son v. Hall Farms, Inc.

Supreme Court of Indiana, 1993.
621 N.E.2d 1078.

■ KRAHULIK, J.

We grant transfer to address whether defendants, Martin Rispens & Son, and Petoseed Company, Inc. are entitled to summary judgment on certain warranty, negligence and strict liability in tort claims filed by Hall Farms, Inc. Martin Rispens & Son v. Hall Farms, Inc. (1992), Ind. App., 601 N.E.2d 429.

Facts

The facts pertinent to Hall Farms' petition are as set forth in the opinion of the Court of Appeals:

Hall Farms, Inc., farms about 1,400 acres of mostly rented land in Knox County, Indiana. It produces grain, row crops, hay, watermelons, and cantaloupes and raises a few hogs and cows. In 1989, Hall Farms employed between 116 and 170 people; that year's watermelon and cantaloupe crop generated some $440,000 in gross revenues, despite the fruit blotch. Much of Hall Farms' past success in the melon market is attributable to the Prince Charles variety watermelon seed, known for its high yield and resistance to disease. Hall Farms had used the variety since 1982 or 1983.

In August of 1988, Hall Farms ordered 40 pounds of Prince Charles seeds from Rispens at a cost of $85.40 per pound. As requested, Rispens delivered the seeds, packaged in sealed one pound cans, in February 1989. Hall Farms stored the unopened cans until early April, at which time the watermelon seeds were germinated in two greenhouses.

On April 25th Mark Hall noted that about 15 seedlings were spotted with small yellow lesions. Suspecting gummy stem blight, a seed borne disease, Hall contacted a neighbor who, in turn, contacted Dr. Richard Latin, a plant pathologist from Purdue University. After transporting samples to the Purdue laboratory, Dr. Latin concluded the problem was neither gummy stem blight nor any fungus.

The lesions did not affect the plants' growth, however, and no plants died. The asymptomatic seedlings were transplanted to the fields between May 8th and 10th. Mark Hall monitored the plants every three or four days for the next several weeks, as was his custom. Although some looked a little "funny," they were nevertheless "growing like mad."... On July 5th or 6th, Hall spotted a watermelon blemished by a small purple blotch. By July 15th, the blotch was "spreading like wildfire." ... By harvest time ten days later, a significant portion of the watermelon crop had been ruined.

Hall Farms left most of the blotched Prince Charles watermelons in the fields. They were eventually plowed under in early September in preparation for the planting of oats and then soybeans. Volunteer plants appeared the next summer, but Mark Hall killed them with Blazer, a herbicide, before Dr. Latin could examine them. Hall Farms suffered no watermelon blotch in 1990, even in fields that were infected the year before. During its investigation, Hall Farms learned the Prince Charles variety seeds it planted came from Petoseed's Lot Nos. 1018 and 5024. Lot 1018 was grown in China; lot 5024 was grown in Mexico.

Based on his discussions with Dr. Latin, who was of the opinion the bacteria causing the fruit blotch were introduced into Indiana through the Prince Charles seeds, Hall reasoned the Chinese or Mexican fields must have had the fruit blotch because his plants had it. Petoseed, a part of Hall Farms' argument goes, was therefore culpable to the extent it knew or should have known the fields were infected and yet harvested the seeds of the infected watermelons for resale to businesses like his.

Rispens, 601 N.E.2d at 432–3 (footnote omitted).

Hall Farms sued Rispens (the seed retailer) and Petoseed (the seed grower) seeking a recovery on theories of ... breach of express and implied warranties. After the trial court denied defendants' motions for summary judgment, defendants brought an interlocutory appeal. For Petoseed, the Court of Appeals ordered the trial court to enter summary judgment on the ... breach of warranty claims. ... For Rispens, the Court of Appeals ordered the trial court to enter summary judgment on ... all but one of the warranty counts. Summary judgment was denied with respect to one express warranty claim. Additionally, the Court held that Rispens and Petoseed had effectively limited their liability to the cost of the seed....

Plaintiff Hall Farms seeks reinstatement of the trial court's denial of summary judgment on all issues. ...

## I. Warranty Claims

### A. Express Warranties

Hall Farms argues that the Court of Appeals erred (1) in deciding the non-existence of certain express warranties as a matter of law, and (2) in holding that certain language on the Petoseed can and the Rispens order form did not create express warranties.

Where an agreement is entirely in writing, the question of whether express warranties were made is one for the court.... Here, all the representations upon which Hall Farms relies were in writing. Therefore, the Court of Appeals correctly determined the existence of express warranties as a matter of law.

Hall Farms' warranty claims arise out of the sale of goods and, thus, those claims are governed by Article 2 of the Uniform Commercial Code ("UCC"), Ind. Code Ann. § 26–1–2–101 through § 26–1–2–725 (West 1980 & Supp. 1992). The UCC provides for the creation of express warranties. Ind. Code § 26–1–2–313.

An express warranty requires some representation, term or statement as to how the product is warranted. Candlelight Homes, Inc. v. Zornes (1981), Ind. App., 414 N.E.2d 980, 983. Stated another way, an express warranty may be created if the seller asserts a fact of which the buyer is ignorant, but not if the seller merely states an opinion on a matter on which the seller has no special knowledge and on which the buyer may be expected also to have an opinion and to exercise his judgment. Royal Business Machines, Inc. v. Lorraine Corp., 633 F.2d 34, 41 (7th Cir.1980). Thus, a seller's factual statement that a machine had a new engine constituted an express warranty. Perfection Cut, Inc. v. Olsen (1984), Ind. App., 470 N.E.2d 94, 95. Assurances by a seller that carpet would be replaced if any defects surfaced within one year of purchase was sufficient to create an express warranty. Carpetland U.S.A. v. Payne (1989), Ind. App., 536 N.E.2d 306, 308.

By contrast, statements of the seller's opinion, not made as a representation of fact, do not create an express warranty. Thompson Farms, Inc. v. Corno Feed Products (1977), 173 Ind. App. 682, 708, 366 N.E.2d 3, 18; James J. White & Robert S. Summers, 1 Uniform Commercial Code § 9–4, at 445 (3d ed. 1988) (hereafter "White & Summers"). The statement that a product "is the best" is simply puffing which does not create an express warranty. Thompson Farms, 173 Ind. App. at 708, 366 N.E.2d at 18.

Petoseed. The label on the Petoseed cans of Prince Charles watermelon seeds states that they are "top quality seeds with high vitality, vigor and germination." This printed label is the sole basis for Hall Farms' express warranty claims against Petoseed.

Hall Farms equates the phrase "top quality seeds" with the statement that the goods were "in good order, condition and repair," found to be an express warranty in Continental Sand & Gravel, Inc. v. K & K Sand & Gravel, Inc., 755 F.2d 87, 90–91 (7th Cir.1985), and with the statement that a truck was "road ready," held to be an express warranty in Wiseman v. Wolfe's Terre Haute Auto Auction, Inc. (1984), Ind. App., 459 N.E.2d 736, 737. We do not agree. The phrase contains no definitive statement as to how the product is warranted or any assertion of fact concerning the product, but is merely the opinion of Petoseed that the seeds are "top quality." The Court of Appeals correctly concluded that the statement "top quality seeds" is a "classic example of puffery." 601 N.E.2d at 435.

Hall Farms also argues that the Court of Appeals erred in holding that, although the phrase "with high vitality, vigor and germination" constituted an express warranty, Petoseed did not breach this warranty because the growth of the seeds conformed to the affirmation on the label. 601 N.E.2d at 435. This phrase is a promise that the seeds will perform in a certain manner; it is not simply the opinion of the seller. However, we are not able to determine as a matter of law whether this express warranty was breached. On the one hand, Petoseed asserts that the promise made was only that the seeds would germinate and grow, which according to Mark Hall, they did. On the other hand, Hall Farms asserts that the presence of the disease inhibited the vitality and vigor with which the plants grew. We agree with Hall Farms that the issue of whether the seeds which carried the watermelon fruit blotch had the capacity for natural growth and survival is one for the finder of fact. Thus, summary judgment is not appropriate on this express warranty claim.

Rispens. Rispens' purchase order, the sole basis for Hall Farm's express warranty claim against Rispens, stated in pertinent part:

> The seller agrees to deliver such seeds in good merchantable condition as hereinafter defined and of good germination for the crop of the current year. The phrase "in good merchantable condition" is defined as seeds properly fitted for seeding purposes, by thorough screening, and where necessary by hand picking; approximately free from foreign seeds distinguishable by their appearance.

The parties agree that the language "properly fitted for seeding purposes," created an express warranty, but they assign different meanings to it. Rispens asserts that the warranty is merely that the can contains Prince Charles watermelon seeds and not some other type of seed. Hall Farms asserts that the warranty contains a quality component promising that the seeds would be free of a latent bacteria such as watermelon fruit blight. Although courts decide as a matter of law the existence of express warranties when the representations are in writing, if the writing is ambiguous, then its interpretation is one of fact.... Questions of fact exist as to the meaning of the express warranty and, thus, the Court of Appeals correctly held that Rispens is not entitled to summary judgment on whether this express warranty was breached....

Hall Farms also argues that the phrase, "strictly high grade seeds," which appeared at the top of the purchase order, created an express warranty. The Court of Appeals held that this language may have constituted an express warranty, but Hall Farms failed to meet its burden of proof by presenting evidence about the meaning of this phrase, so Rispens was entitled to summary judgment.... Whether Rispens gave an express warranty which was breached encompasses a question of fact: in the seed industry, does "high grade" connote some promise that the seeds will be free from disease or is it mere puffing. However, it is Rispens' burden, as the movant, to show the absence of material fact. Having failed to do so, Rispens is not entitled to summary judgment on the express warranty claim.

### B.  Implied Warranties

Hall Farms alleged that both Petoseed and Rispens breached certain implied warranties. The Court of Appeals held that the language on the

Petoseed seed can had effectively excluded any implied warranty. . . . Hall Farms does not seek transfer [to this court] on that holding.[2]

With respect to Rispens, the Court of Appeals held that, although the language on Rispens' purchase order did not effectively exclude the implied warranty of merchantability, Rispens established such exclusion by usage of trade. . . . On transfer [to this court], Hall Farms argues that the Court of Appeals erred in deciding usage of trade as a matter of law. We agree.

Unless excluded or modified, a warranty that goods shall be merchantable is implied in a contract for their sale if the seller is a merchant with respect to goods of that kind. Ind. Code § 26–1–2–314; Travel Craft v. Wilhelm Mende (1990), Ind., 552 N.E.2d 443, 444. Disclaimers of implied warranties are not favored and are strictly construed against the seller for reasons of public policy. Woodruff v. Clark County, 153 Ind. App. at 45, 286 N.E.2d at 196.

Effective disclaimers of implied warranties must be conspicuous; whether a term or clause is conspicuous is a question of law for the court. Jones v. Abriani (1976), 169 Ind. App. 556, 571, 350 N.E.2d 635, 645. Where a purported exclusion of implied warranties was located at the bottom of the reverse page of a contract, which page did not contemplate the signature of the buyer, the court could properly find that the purported disclaimer was not sufficiently conspicuous. Jerry Alderman Ford Sales, Inc. v. Bailey (1973), 154 Ind. App. 632, 645, 294 N.E.2d 617, 619. Usually, to exclude the implied warranty of merchantability, the disclaimer must contain the word "merchantability." Travel Craft, 552 N.E.2d at 444.

Here, the attempted disclaimer (1) did not mention the word merchantability, (2) appeared on the reverse side of the purchase order which did not require a signature, and (3) was not conspicuous. Jerry Alderman, 154 Ind. App. at 645, 294 N.E.2d at 619.

Notwithstanding, Rispens argues that even if the content of the disclaimer did not conform to certain requirements, the warranties were effectively disclaimed by usage of trade. An implied warranty may be excluded or modified by usage of trade. Ind. Code § 26–1–2–316(3)(c). A usage of trade is "any practice or method of dealing having such regularity of observance in a place, vocation or trade as to justify an expectation that it will be observed with respect to the transaction in question." Ind. Code § 26–1–1–205(2). Commercial acceptance of a usage of trade "makes out a prima facie case that the usage is reasonable, and the burden is no longer on the usage to establish itself as being reasonable." Ind. Code § 26–1–1–205, cmt. 6. A buyer need not have actual knowledge of the usage of trade. See Western Industries, Inc. v. Newcor Canada Ltd., 739 F.2d 1198, 1203 (7th Cir. 1984); White & Summers, § 3–3. It is sufficient either that the

---

**2.** In addition, we note that the lack of privity between Hall Farms and Petoseed would also defeat any action by Hall Farms against Petoseed for breach of an implied warranty. In Indiana, privity between the seller and the buyer is required to maintain a cause of action on the implied warranties of merchantability, Ind. Code § 26–1–2–315. Prairie Prod., Inc. v. Agchem Div.–Pennwalt Corp. (1987), Ind. App., 514 N.E.2d 1299, 1301; Candlelight Homes, Inc. v. Zornes (1981), Ind. App., 414 N.E.2d 980, 982.

usage of trade is used in the vocation or trade in which the contracting parties are engaged or that the usage is one of which the parties are or should be aware. Ind. Code § 26–1–1–205(3).

Rispens and Hall Farms are not in the same trade; Rispens is in the business of selling seeds while Hall Farms is in the business of planting seeds and producing crops. Thus, Rispens can effectively negate the implied warranty of merchantability only by establishing that Hall Farms was or should have been aware of the asserted usage of trade. To do so, Rispens submitted affidavits from, among others, the Executive Vice–President of the American Seed Trade Association, which stated that the implied warranty of merchantability is uniformly disclaimed by seed merchants. Hall Farms submitted no evidence suggesting otherwise. To show that Hall Farms should be charged with this knowledge, Rispens submitted purchase orders used by another seed company with whom Hall Farms had dealt in the past which also disclaimed the implied warranty of merchantability. In response, Hall Farms submitted testimony of Mark Hall to the effect that he had never read such disclaimers on the purchase orders. With these conflicting facts, we cannot conclude, as a matter of law, that Hall Farms is charged with the knowledge that seed distributors routinely disclaim implied warranties of merchantability. Therefore, whether the implied warranty of merchantability was disclaimed by usage of trade is a question of fact which must be resolved at trial. Summary judgment on the implied warranty of merchantability is not appropriate for Rispens.

## II. Limitation of Liability on Warranty Claims

We next address the validity of the attempts by Petoseed and Rispens to limit the amount recoverable under the warranties that accompanied the sale of the seeds. Petoseed and Rispens assert that they effectively limited Hall Farms' remedy, if any, to the purchase price of the seed. Hall Farms responds that these limitations are unenforceable because they fail in their essential purpose and are unconscionable. We hold that, although such limitations are enforceable generally, there remains a question of fact as to their applicability here.

Buyers and sellers may agree on a limitation of remedy. Ind. Code § 26–1–2–719. A "limitation of remedy" acknowledges the quality commitment of a warranty, but restricts the type or amount of remedy available once a breach has been established. Hahn v. Ford Motor Co. (1982), Ind. App., 434 N.E.2d 943, 952–3. Limitations of remedy are not favored in Indiana and are strictly construed against the seller on the basis of public policy. Id. at 948.

### A. Failure of Essential Purpose.

Hall Farms argues that limiting recovery to the cost of the seed fails of its essential purpose because: (1) the presence of the bacteria was a novel circumstance not contemplated by the parties; and (2) Hall Farms bargained for seed which would produce a money crop, it will be deprived of the substantial value of its bargain if the limitation is enforced. We hold that limitation on the measure of damages does not fail of its essential purpose.

Commentators have suggested that § 2–719, as it relates to failure of essential purpose, is not concerned with arrangements which were oppressive at the inception which is a question of unconscionability, but with the application of an agreement to "novel circumstances not contemplated by the parties." White & Summers, § 10–12. In addition, they have suggested that this provision should be triggered when the remedy fails of its essential purpose, not the essential purpose of the UCC, contract law, or of equity. Id. One author suggests that the method used to decide whether a particular limitation fails of its essential purpose is to identify the purpose underlying the provision and determine whether application of the remedy in the particular circumstances will further that purpose. If not, then, and only then, is there a failure of essential purpose. Jonathan A. Eddy, On The "Essential" Purposes of Limited Remedies: The Metaphysics of UCC § 2–719(2), 65 Cal. L. Rev. 28, 36–40 (1978). Thus, for example, where the sale of a car was accompanied by the exclusive remedy of repair and replacement of defective parts but attempted repairs were ineffective in correcting the problems, the purchaser was entitled to recover an amount in excess of the cost of repairs. Riley v. Ford Motor Co., 442 F. 2d 670 (5th Cir.1971). The exclusive remedy of repair and replacement of defective parts failed of its essential purpose because the car could not be repaired so as to operate free of defects as promised in the express warranty. Id.

Petoseed. Here, the label on the Petoseed can stated in pertinent part:

2. LIMITATION OF LIABILITY: Purchaser's exclusive compensation for loss or damage arising from purchase or use of seed from Petoseed Co., Inc., shall be limited to an amount equal to the purchase price of the seed. There shall not be included any amount for incidental or consequential damages, nor for amounts expended in using or growing such seed, nor for harvesting the produce of such seed. This limitation of liability shall be applicable to any claims presented to Petoseed, regardless of the legal theory forming the basis of such claim, and whether such theory involves negligence, contractual liability, or otherwise.

This provision clearly states that liability is limited to the purchase price of the seed, and does not allow any amount for incidental or consequential damages such as Hall Farms' lost profits. Obviously, the purpose of the limitation was to limit contract liability to the purchase price of the seed. The contract term has not failed of its essential purpose; rather, enforcement of the limitation will serve precisely the purpose intended.

Rispens. Rispens' contract conditions on the reverse side of the invoice provided:

Paragraph 10. . . . In [any] event, however, the seller shall not be liable to the purchaser for any loss or damages in a sum greater than the invoice price of the individual lot of seed which is the cause of the complaint, arbitration or action at law.

Paragraph 11. ... Our liability, in all instances, is limited to the purchase price of the seed.

The intent of this limitation of liability is also clear. Limiting any warranty recovery to the price of the seed serves the intended purpose of the limitation.

We do not accept Hall Farms' assertion that the presence of the watermelon fruit blotch was a novel circumstance not contemplated by the parties because the fact that the seeds might not conform to the warranties is a possibility that should occur to both buyer and seller.

As to the benefit of the bargain argument, Hall Farms bargained for seed, not, as its argument suggests, for a full-grown crop of watermelons. If Hall Farms deemed recovery of the purchase price inadequate, then it was free to bargain for a more comprehensive remedy. Therefore, the terms limiting Hall Farms' remedy against Petoseed to the purchase price of the seeds have not failed of their essential purpose.

B.   Unconscionability

Hall Farms also argues that the limitation of liability is substantively unconscionable because farmers will be denied a minimum adequate remedy while giving seed manufacturers and distributors effective immunity from liability in a situation where the defect in the seed was latent. Ind. Code § 26–1–2–719(3) provides that consequential damages may be limited or excluded unless the limitation or exclusion is unconscionable. Unconscionability is a question of law determined on the basis of circumstances existing at the time the contract was made. Ind. Code § 26–1–2–302(1). The party raising the issue bears the burden of proof. Hahn v. Ford Motor, 434 N.E.2d at 950.

"Substantive unconscionability" refers to oppressively one-sided or harsh terms of a contract, and generally involves cases where courts have determined the price to be unduly excessive or where the terms of the contract unduly limit a buyer's remedies. Hahn, 434 N.E.2d at 951. A substantively unconscionable contract is one that no sensible man would make and such as no honest and fair man would accept. Weaver v. American Oil Co. (1972), 257 Ind. 458, 462, 276 N.E.2d 144, 146. Often there are circumstances which show that there was unequal bargaining power at the time the contract was executed which led the party with lesser power to enter it unwillingly or without knowledge of its terms. Dan Purvis Drugs, Inc. v. Aetna Life Ins. (1981), Ind. App., 412 N.E.2d 129, 131; see also Sho–Pro of Indiana, Inc. v. Brown (1992), Ind. App., 585 N.E.2d 1357, 1360.

In keeping with this standard, Indiana courts have rejected claims that contractual limitations of remedy are substantively unconscionable. Carr v. Hoosier Photo Supplies, Inc. (1982), Ind., 441 N.E.2d 450, 454 (film processor's receipt issued to knowledgeable consumer); Hahn, 434 N.E.2d at 952 (automobile warranty issued to consumer); General Bargain Center v. American Alarm Co. (1982), Ind. App., 430 N.E.2d 407, 411 (alarm system contract).

Hall Farms argues that the limitation of remedy was substantively unconscionable because the defect in the seed was latent, not being discoverable until the plants began growing. Once discovered, the growing season was too far along for Hall Farms to replant. Thus, Hall Farms asserts that for the loss occasioned by the infected seeds to fall only upon Hall Farms would be unconscionable. Hall Farms cites Martin v. Joseph Harris Co., Inc., 767 F.2d 296 (6th Cir.1985), and Lutz Farms v. Asgrow Seed Co., 948 F.2d 638, 646 (10th Cir.1991), as examples of latent defects rendering a limitation of remedy unconscionable. There are also cases holding that such limitations are not unconscionable. See, e.g., Estate of Arena v. Abbott & Cobb, Inc. (1990), 158 A.D.2d 926, 551 N.Y.S.2d 715 (remedy limited to the purchase price of seed); and Southland Farms, Inc. v. Ciba–Geigy Corp. (1991), Ala., 575 So. 2d 1077, 1079–81 (consequential damages limited for agricultural chemical).

We are not persuaded that the limitation is unconscionable simply because the defect is latent. Although a seller may not limit liability for a defect which he knows to be nonconforming to warranties without disclosing that knowledge, the evidence is not conclusive that either Petoseed or Rispens was aware that the seeds carried disease. The possibility that a latent defect may exist is one of the risks present at the time the contract is formed. Had the parties contemplated this possibility, Indiana law would have left them free to allocate that risk as they saw fit. It is not unconscionable for the seed producer and distributor to redistribute such risks.

Left unanswered, however, is whether the parties in fact agreed to redistribute the risk of a latent defect in the seed. The question is whether there was mutual assent to the limitation of liability contained on the Petoseed can and the Rispens purchase order. Contract formation requires mutual assent on all essential contract terms. Carr v. Hoosier Photo, 441 N.E.2d at 455. Without mutual assent, the limitations are ineffective as a matter of law. Hahn, 434 N.E.2d at 948. Assent to a limitation of liability may be assumed where a knowledgeable party enters into the contract, aware of the limitation and its legal effect, without indicating non-acquiescence to those terms. . . . However, the intention of the parties to include a particular term in a contract is usually a factual question determined from all of the circumstances. . . .

Therefore, we must determine if there is a genuine issue of fact about whether Hall Farms assented to the limitation of liability.

Petoseed. Petoseed's limitation appeared in the printed material on the label affixed to the side of the seed cans. Mark Hall testified that, although he read the printed material on the top of the can which Hall Farms asserts gave an express warranty, he did not read the material on the side of the can relating to the limitation of liability. Thus, whether there was mutual assent to the limitation of liability is a question of fact precluding summary judgment.

Rispens. Rispens' limitation appeared on the reverse side of the purchase order for the seeds. This side of the purchase order did not require Hall's signature and he testified that he did not read it. Therefore, there is a question of fact about whether Hall Farms intended to accept the limitation of liability from Rispens.

\* \* \*

Conclusion

In summary, we grant transfer, vacate the opinion of the Court of Appeals, and remand this case to the trial court with directions to enter summary judgment against Hall Farms on all claims except those of breach of express warranties as to both defendants and breach of the implied warranty of merchantability as to Rispens and to proceed in a manner consistent with this opinion.

NOTES

**(1) Law Governing the Manufacturers' Express Warranties.** The Indiana Supreme Court declared, without any discussion, that the law governing the downstream buyer's claim of breach by the manufacturer of its express warranty is Article 2 of the Commercial Code, and in particular UCC 2–313. Although the court cited a number of cases in its introduction of the law, it fails to note whether any of those cases involved a manufacturer's warranty to a downstream buyer. The alternative characterization of the warranties as matters governed by common law was not considered.

**(2) Nature of the Manufacturer's Express Warranty; Part of the Basis of the Bargain.** The manufacturer's only express warranties in this case were affirmations printed on the label of the cans containing the seeds. If UCC 2–313 governs, on what theory would these affirmations be "part of the basis of the bargain" between Hill Farms and Petoseed? The issue before the Indiana Supreme Court was whether to affirm or reverse the summary judgment for the manufacturer in the trial court. On remand, would Supreme Court's characterization of plaintiff's claim require the plaintiff to show that the terms on the can were part of the basis of the bargain?

CIPOLLONE v. LIGGETT GROUP, INC., 893 F.2d 541 (3d Cir.1990).[4] Suit by a smoker against a cigarette manufacturer that had made affirmations about the safety of its product in advertisements over many years. Smoker contended that the affirmations were express warranties that had been breached. The Court of Appeals for the Third Circuit assumed that the claim was governed by UCC 2–313 and declared:

> Ordinarily a guarantee or promise in an advertisement or other description of the goods becomes part of the basis of the bargain if it would naturally induce the purchase of the product and no particular

---

4. Reviewed on other grounds, 505 U.S. 504, 112 S.Ct. 2608, 120 L.Ed.2d 407 (1992).

reliance by the buyer on such statement needs to be shown. However, if the evidence establishes that the claimed statement cannot fairly be viewed as entering into the bargain, that is, that the statement would not naturally induce the purchase of a product, then no express warranty has been created.

. . . We hold that once the buyer has become aware of the affirmation of fact or promise, the statements are presumed to be part of the "basis of the bargain" unless the defendant, by "clear affirmative proof," shows that the buyer knew that the affirmation of fact or promise was untrue. . . .

Applying our interpretation of section 2–313 to the case at bar, we conclude that the district court's jury instructions were erroneous for two reasons. First, they did not require the plaintiff to prove that Mrs. Cipollone had read, seen, or heard the advertisements at issue. Second, they did not permit the defendant to prove that although Mrs. Cipollone had read, seen, or heard the advertisements, she did not believe the safety assurances contained therein. We must therefore reverse and remand for a new trial on this issue.

PPG INDUSTRIES v. JMB/HOUSTON CENTERS PARTNERS LTD. PARTNERSHIP, 146 S.W.3d 79 (Tex.2004). Suit by the owner of One Houston Center, a 46–story skyscraper, against PPG, the manufacturer of 12,000 Twindows, a dual-pane glass window installed in the Center. Prior to the contract for construction, PPG had published an advertisement in a major trade publication often relied upon by architects:

Twindows units are warranted for twenty (20) years . . . from the date of manufacture against failure of the hermetic seal due to faulty manufacturing of the unit by PPG. Pursuant to this limited warranty, PPG will only supply a new unit, and no labor, installation or special or consequential damages are included. This limited warranty is effective if the unit is property installed, and is not effective if the unit is installed in sloped glazing. PPG makes no other warranty.

The documents in the construction contract for the Center provided that the glazing would be Twindows and that PPG would install them. The documents made no reference to a warranty on the heremetic seals. The documents did provide for the following five-year warranty by PPG:

PPG . . . warrants all material furnished and work performed is in accordance with the plans and specifications as amended by changes thereto by the owner or his authorized representative, and further warrants material furnished and labor performed to be free from defects and watertight for five years from April 1, 1978 [the date the building was completed]. Should such a defect occur within this warranty, PPG . . . shall, upon receipt of written notice, repair and/or replace the defective product.

By July 1982, the owner discovered serious problems with the Twindows. Between 1982 and 1985, PPG replaced more than 3,000 Twindows. In 1989, PPG refused to repair or replace any more Twindows. Extensive

Twindows problems appeared in 1991. The law suit, filed that years, alleged breach of the twenty-year warranty and the five-year warranty. The Texas Supreme Court held that the claim on the five-year warranty was barred by the statute of limitations. The court held further that the advertisement may have created a twenty-year warranty. On this warranty, in a jury trial, the trial court entered judgment against PPG as a matter of law that did not require consideration by the jury. The Supreme Court reversed and remanded. Citing UCC 2–313(a), the Supreme Court said:

> Before any extra-contractual statement becomes a warranty, it must become "part of the basis of the bargain." Thus, for example, a statement cannot be the basis of the bargain if one of the parties does not know about it. . . . Here, there was conflicting evidence whether a twenty-year warranty was a basis of the parties' bargain. There was no evidence the contracting parties ever mentioned the Sweets ad in their negotiations, bid documents, or contracts. There is no evidence anyone other than the Houston Center's lead architect . . . ever saw it. While the architect testified he relied on the Sweets warranty, jurors would not have been required to credit his testimony, as he did not explain why he omitted it when he drew up the bid specifications that included numerous shorter warranties. PPG's witnesses testified the parties' bargain was only what they included in their contract documents, not the unmentioned advertisement. . . . A jury might find the parties' bargain here included a twenty-year warranty in an advertisement in a trade magazine, even though they never discussed it and omitted it from the extensive contract documents. But they would not have to; they might find that the parties' bargain was no more than they stated.

Three dissenting justices concluded that the trial court had not abused its discretion in refusing to submit the "basis of the bargain" issue to the jury and would have affirmed. The dissenters did not disagree with the view that the warranty issue was governed by UCC 2–313(a).

FIRE INSURANCE EXCHANGE v. ELECTROLUX HOME PRODUCTS, 2006 WL 2925286, 61 U.C.C. Rep. Serv. 2d 181 (E.D. Mich. 2006). Suit by insurance company, subrogee of buyer, against manufacturer of a home clothes dryer. Home owner had purchased the dryer from Best Buy in 1997. Printed material, provided by the manufacturer, declared that "with regular use and care the dryer will provide a long life of service and will provide quick and efficient drying of laundered items." This document was inside the box when buyer received the dryer. Seven years later, a fire resulted in severe damage to buyer's house. Plaintiff contended that the cause of the fire was a defect in the dryer, in breach of manufacturer's express warranty. Manufacturer argued that the claim failed because there was no evidence that buyer had read or relied on the document. The district court denied manufacturer's summary judgment motion. The court found that the law governing the manufacturer's alleged express warranty was UCC 2–313 and found, further, that the claim met the terms of the statute because there was no requirement under that section that the buyer had read the document since the express warranty was consistent with the buyer's general expectations.[5]

**(3) Affirmation of Fact or Opinion.** UCC 2–313(3) allows sellers latitude to make statements of opinion or value without incurring liability. Should that rule be applied to manufacturers? The Indiana Supreme Court, applying UCC 2–313(3), held that manufacturer's affirmation that the seeds were "top quality" was a "classic example of puffery" and therefore not a warranty, but remanded for trial the "high vitality, vigor and germination" affirmation. Would the analysis be different under common law?

**Problem 1.** M, a manufacturer of building materials, markets its products through independent distributors. However, M sends sales engineers to construction companies to explain the uses of M's products and promote their purchase. Following such a visit by one of M's sales engineers, the B construction company buys M's roofing material from distributor, D. B claims that the roofing material does not have the qualities described by M's sales engineer, and sues M for breach of express warranty. What result? See M. Ruud, Manufacturers' Liability for Representations made by their Sales Engineers to Subpurchasers, 8 U.C.L.A. L. Rev. 251 (1961).

**Problem 2.** Manufacturer of wood preservative sold the product to a manufacturer of windows. The preservative seller expressly warranted that its product would be effective to prevent wood rot for 26 years. The window manufacturer used the product but did not communicate any information about the 26–year warranty to any of the buyers of its windows. In selling windows, the window manufacturer provided a one-year warranty on the windows. Many of the windows suffered wood rot. Buyers of those windows learned of the preservative manufacturer's warranty before it expired but after the window manufacturer's one-year warranty had lapsed. The window buyers sued the preservative manufacturer for breach of its express warranty. What result? In most express warranty disputes, the upstream manufacturers take action to communicate their affirmations or promises in a way that the downstream buyers are aware of them at the time of their contracts with their immediate sellers. The manufacturers' commercial objective is to increase the sales of their goods in the downstream market. Publicity is essential to achieving that purpose. If that were not done, should manufacturers be accountable?[6]

---

**5.** There was no indication that the manufacturer raised the defense that the suit was barred by the statute of limitations.

**6.** See Goodman v. PPG Industries, Inc., 2004 Pa. Super. 151, 849 A.2d 1239 (2004). The Superior Court held that the governing law was Article 2 and that the window buyers had no UCC 2–313 claim against the preservative manufacturer because express warranties rest on the "dickered" aspects of bargains between the immediate parties to sales contracts, elements missing in this case where the parties were contractually unknown to each other. The court also considered whether the window buyers could enforce the UCC 2–313 warranty that was made to the window manufacturer and held against the buyers. The Superior Court held that a manufacturer that is willing to make a specific and ambitious warranty to its immediate buyer must be able to retain some measure of control over the class of people to whom it is

**(4) Remedies.** Since the case was decided on the basis of the pleadings, the court had no occasion to consider in full the questions of the remedies available for breach of a manufacturer's express warranty to a downstream buyer. However, the court did discuss the effectiveness of the manufacturer's attempt to displace the monetary remedies otherwise available as a matter of law with the promise to refund the price. Buyer's counsel contended that the limitation of remedy should be struck down as violative of UCC 2–719. The remedies issues posed by these cases are complex and difficult.

*Price refund.* Paragraph 2 of the label on the container contained an implied obligation by the manufacturer to refund "an amount equal to the purchase price" of the watermelon seeds together with a clause excluding liability for consequential or incidental damages. The price-refund clause applies whenever there is "loss or damage arising from purchase or use of seed." The clause can be read, by implication, to obligate the manufacturer to pay the stated amount, but the buyer plainly had no interest in enforcing the obligation. Relative to the harm suffered from loss of the crop, recovery of the price would be insignificant. If, however, buyer sought to collect the price from the manufacturer, what law would govern? Could the manufacturer contend successfully that its implied promise was unenforceable?

*Limitation of remedies.* The clause that matters greatly to both the buyer and the manufacturer is the clause that excludes recovery for consequential damages, including specifically amounts expended in using the seed. The exclusion-of-consequential-damages sentence refers to any theory of legal liability that a buyer's lawyer might rely upon. There is no specific mention of a breach of warranty claim. The drafter of this clause, undoubtedly a lawyer, seemed to be working from this premise: We have not undertaken any express warranty obligation to end users of our seeds and we don't believe that we have any implied warranty obligation to such end users, but if it turns out that we're wrong about any of that, our liability is limited. If you were counsel to the seed manufacturer, could you do a better job of counseling your client?

The buyer attacked the clause that excluded consequential damages. Apparently buyer's counsel invoked UCC 2–719. Without discussing the relevance of UCC Article 2 to this dispute, the court rejected buyer's contention that the clause failed under UCC 2–719(2) and (3). If you were counsel to the buyer, could you have done a better job of representing your client?

*Failure of essential purpose: UCC 2–719(2).* Buyer's counsel apparently argued that the price-refund remedy failed of its essential purpose and, therefore, buyer was entitled to all of its UCC Article 2 remedies including consequential damages. The court never got to the second part of the

---

willing to extend the warranty and the precise parameters of the warranty it may be obliged to honor. The court added that it would be "incongruous" to allow third parties to benefit from an express warranty that they were not aware of. The case is pending in the Supreme Court of Pennsylvania. The Pennsylvania Supreme Court affirmed in 2005 without an opinion. 584 Pa. 537, 885 A.2d 982.

contention. Rather it concluded that the purpose of the price-refund remedy was to protect the manufacturer. Turning UCC 2–719(2) on its head, the court construed the "purpose" of the price-refund clause to be to protect the manufacturer from greater contract liability. The clause excluding consequential damages was, certainly, a clause intended to protect the manufacturer, but that can hardly have been the purpose of the price-refund clause. As we learned in Chapter 4, in transactions where repair/replace remedial promises were coupled with clauses excluding consequential damages, courts sometimes found that the repair/replace promise failed of its essential purpose (to correct nonconformities) and refused to give effect to the damage exclusion clause. In other transactions, courts enforced the damage exclusion clause even though a remedial promise failed of its essential purpose. The Indiana court did not make the two-step analysis. Had it treated the price-refund as intended to protect the seed buyer, would that remedy have failed of its essential purpose? If so, what would have been the effect on the clause excluding consequential damages? If the court had recognized that UCC 2–719(2) does not apply to these facts, how would a common-law court look at the combination of a price refund promise and exclusion-of-consequential-damages provision?

*Unconscionability: UCC 2–719(3).* Buyer's counsel apparently argued that the clause excluding consequential damages was unconscionable under UCC 2–719(3). The Indiana Supreme Court rejected the remote buyer's argument that the manufacturer's limitation of remedy was substantively unconscionable. In the court's view, if the parties here knew that there were latent risks in the quality of seed, the law of Indiana would have left them free to allocate the risk as they saw fit. The court implied that the ruling would have been otherwise if there had been conclusive evidence that the manufacturer had been aware that the seeds carried disease. If the court had recognized that UCC 2–719(3) does not apply to these facts, how would a common-law court look at the combination of a price refund promise and exclusion-of-consequential-damages provision?

Other courts have found manufacturers' limitations of damages clause unconscionable in suits brought by downstream buyers. See, e.g., Mullin v. Speight Seed Farms, Inc., 234 Ga.App. 27, 505 S.E.2d 818, 37 U.C.C. Rep. Serv. 2d 88 (1998); Durham v. Ciba–Geigy Corp., 315 N.W.2d 696 (S.D. 1982). Similar holdings have been made in transactions where manufacturers sold directly to farm users. E.g., Lutz Farms v. Asgrow Seed Co., 948 F.2d 638 (10th Cir. 1991) (Colorado law): Martin v. Joseph Harris Co., 767 F.2d 296 (6th Cir. 1985) (Michigan law).

*Buyer's assent to the damages exclusion clause.* In the closing paragraphs of the Indiana Supreme Court's opinion, the court held that there was an open question of fact whether there had been "mutual assent to the limitation of liability" in the printed material on the seed containers and remanded the case for trial of this issue. Although phrased as a question of "mutual assent," the question, in the court's view, was only whether the downstream buyer had assented to the manufacturer's terms. The court observed that an agent of the buyer testified that, during the retail sale, he had read some of the terms in the label but had not read the entire label. The Indiana court did not identify any legal authority under which the remote buyer's assent or lack of assent to the limitation of liability terms would be a pertinent issue of fact. Was the court implicitly invoking common law?

## (B)  INTERNATIONAL SALES LAW

The Convention on International Sales of Goods is drafted to deal with the rights and remedies of the immediate parties to sales contracts.

The CISG has no specific provisions regarding privity of contract or the liability of remote manufacturers. With regard to vertical privity, CISG provisions on the responsibilities of sellers and rights of buyers are drafted in terms of "the seller" and "the buyer" and "the contract," language which strongly implies a requirement of contractual privity.

Suppose, however, that a manufacturer participates actively in marketing its products by providing dealers with the manufacturer's written "warranty" for delivery to buyers from those dealers. Even if it were held that the "warranty" created a contractual obligation to the ultimate buyers, should the rules of the Convention apply to that contractual relationship?

Professor Honnold provided this commentary to CISG:[7]

In recent decades some legal systems have established contractual rights for buyers against manufacturers for damage or loss caused by defects in goods which the buyer purchased from a retail dealer or other distributor. At the outset this development responded to the plight of consumers who suffer personal injury from dangerous products—an area that lies outside the Convention because of the general exclusion of consumer purchases ... and the further exclusion ... of the liability of "the seller for the death or personal injury caused by the goods to any person:" However, in some legal systems this development has made manufacturers liable, without regard to negligence, for economic loss caused by defective products purchased from a dealer or other distributor.

The first edition of this work concluded that this development under the Convention was barred by the language of Article 4 that the Convention "governs only the formation of the contract of sale and the obligations of the seller and the buyer arising from such a contract:" See, e.g., B sued manufacturer (M) for defects in a machine B purchased from S. B's suit was dismissed because B had not contracted with M. GER LG Dusseldorf, 31–0–231/94, 23–06–'94. UNILEX D. 1994–16. (For US domestic cases rejecting this approach, see, e.g., Reitz, 75 Wash.U.L.Rev. 357 at 361 (1997).)

Further reflection calls for reexamination in some commercial settings. For example, some manufacturers (and similar mass distribu-

---

7.  J. Honnold, Uniform Law for International Sales § 63 (3d ed. 1999).

tors such as importers) provide dealers with a written "guarantee" or "warranty" by the manufacturer and instruct dealers to give buyers the manufacturer's "guarantee" in connection with the sale. One purpose is to encourage sales because of the confidence that prospective buyers have in a guarantee to them by a well-known manufacturer. A second, less evident, purpose is to limit their responsibility (*e.g.*) to the replacement of defective parts for a specified limited period and thereby to bar claims for consequential damages caused by defects in the goods.

The difficult problem is whether the manufacturer is a "seller" within the language of Article 4 in view of the fact that the dealer executed the contract with the buyer, delivered the goods and received the price.

Some tribunals applying the Convention, like some tribunals applying domestic laws governing the "sale of goods", may be impressed by the fact that the delivery of a "guarantee" through a local dealer was part of a larger setting in which the manufacturer played a dominant role in the sale—by franchise agreements controlling aspects of the dealer's performance and by mass-media advertising addressed to prospective buyers. Indeed, advertising appeals are typically designed to say or imply: "Go to our dealers and buy our product. If you do you will get a good product." This in substance is an offer of a unilateral contract: "If you will do X you will get Y."

Of course these facts alone do not make the manufacturer a "seller"—a contract of sale depends on the buyer's completing a transaction with a dealer. But some tribunals may conclude that when such a transaction is completed the manufacturer, although not *"the* seller", has participated with the dealer in a "contract of sale" with the buyer.

The supplier's participation may be more evident—as when a representative of the manufacturer personally contacts the buyer and persuades him to purchase the manufacturer's goods from a local dealer. In many cases participation by the manufacturer is more tenuous, confined to advertising and possibly control of aspects of the dealer's business such as promotion methods, volume, stocking of repair parts, training of mechanics and, in some cases, the price to be charged.

When (as in the usual case) the buyer and dealer are in the same State the Convention would not apply to a claim against the dealer. . . . Similarly, the Convention would not apply to a claim against even a foreign supplier if the supplier's place of business applicable to this transaction . . . is in the same State as the buyer. In any event, when domestic law is favorable and the dealer is financially responsible it usually will be more convenient to confine one's claim to a local action against the dealer. The same may be true even when the claim might jeopardize the dealer's resources since the dealer may be able to bring in the manufacturer to defend the action and to satisfy any judgment.

Thus, attempts to extend the Convention to foreign suppliers may be confined to special situations such as financial failure of the local dealer. Even here the rules on jurisdiction, private international law and domestic sales law in the buyer's jurisdiction may meet the buyer's needs.

On the other hand, it seems hasty to conclude that the "buyer-seller" language of Article 4 will be an impassable barrier in cases where the supplier has participated substantially (although not formally) in the sale to the buyer. Domestic experience suggests that legal relations with foreign suppliers may be a field for gradual development.

# Caterpillar, Inc. v. Usinor Industeel

United States District Court, N.D. Illinois, 2005.
393 F.Supp.2d 659.

■ PALLMEYER, J.

Plaintiffs Caterpillar, Inc. ("Caterpillar") and Caterpillar Mexico, S.A. ("CMSA") filed this action against three defendants: Usinor Industeel ("Usinor"), a French steel manufacturer; Usinor Industeel (USA), Inc. ("UsinorUSA"), Usinor's U.S. subsidiary; and Leeco Steel Products, Inc. ("Leeco"), Usinor's North American distributor. At issue is a transaction involving a specialized type of steel called Creusabro 8000 that Usinor manufactured and sold to CMSA through Leeco. CMSA used the steel to fabricate heavy-duty dump truck bodies for Caterpillar which, in turn, sold the trucks to its customers for use in mining operations. Caterpillar alleges that most of the truck beds made with Creusabro 8000 cracked and became unusable, forcing Caterpillar to replace the trucks at great cost to itself and its reputation.

In their eleven-count Complaint, Plaintiffs assert individual claims against each Defendant. Specifically, Plaintiffs charge Usinor with breach of express and implied warranties and failure to deliver conforming goods in violation of the United Nations Convention on Contracts for the International Sale of Goods . . . and the Illinois version of the Uniform Commercial Code (Counts II and V); promissory estoppel (Counts III and VIII); and violation of French law (Count XI). Plaintiffs charge Usinor USA with promissory estoppel (Counts IV and X) and breach of express and implied warranties in violation of the UCC (Count VII). Finally, Plaintiffs charge Leeco with breach of express and implied warranties and failure to deliver conforming goods in violation of the CISG and the UCC (Counts I and VI), and promissory estoppel (Count IX). Usinor and Usinor USA together move to dismiss all eight counts asserted against them (Counts II–V, VII, VIII, X, and XI) pursuant to Fed. R. Civ. P. 12(b)(6). . . . For the following reasons, Defendants' motions are granted in part and denied in part.

FACTUAL BACKGROUND

The facts are drawn from Plaintiffs' Complaint. . . .

## A.  The Parties

Plaintiff Caterpillar is an Illinois corporation with its principal place of business in Peoria, Illinois. Caterpillar specializes in the manufacture and distribution of heavy equipment, including heavy-duty dump trucks used in mining operations. Caterpillar maintains a plant in Decatur, Illinois, which specializes in manufacturing such trucks. Plaintiffs assert that Caterpillar is well known for its high-quality dump trucks and derives significant competitive advantage from this reputation in the industry.

Plaintiff CMSA, a Mexican corporation with its principal place of business in Monterrey, Mexico, is a subsidiary of Caterpillar. CMSA manufactures truck bodies for Caterpillar at its facilities in Mexico. Plaintiffs assert that CMSA was experienced at manufacturing truck bodies for Caterpillar and had a proven track record of producing high-quality truck bodies.

Defendant Usinor, a steel manufacturer, is a French corporation with its principal place of business in Cedex, France. Defendant Usinor USA is a Delaware corporation with its principal place of business in Pennsylvania. Plaintiffs assert that Usinor USA was a wholly owned subsidiary and alter ego of Usinor, and that Usinor USA acted as Usinor's actual agent, at all times relevant to this dispute.

Defendant Leeco is an Illinois corporation with its principal place of business in Darien, Illinois. Plaintiffs assert that Leeco is Usinor's exclusive North American distributor, and that Leeco was Usinor's agent at all times relevant to this dispute.

## B.  Creusabro 8000 Steel

In 1998, Usinor and Usinor USA (collectively "the Usinor Defendants") requested a meeting with Caterpillar to present what Caterpillar characterizes as a "sales pitch" for a new type of steel called Creusabro 8000 ("Creusabro"). At a meeting on April 20, 1998 in Decatur, Illinois, and at a similar meeting in Joliet, Illinois, the Usinor Defendants claimed that Creusabro was the "next generation" of steel because it was harder, had a higher yield strength, had better welding characteristics, and could be processed more inexpensively than regular steel. Specifically, the Usinor Defendants told Caterpillar that Creusabro steel did not require preheating for welded joints which were less than 50 mm, or two inches, thick. This was a significant improvement over the steel Caterpillar was then using, which required preheating for joints thicker than 40 mm. The Usinor Defendants also claimed that any of four industry-accepted welding processes would work with Creusabro.

Upon Caterpillar's request following the April 1998 meeting, the Usinor Defendants provided samples of Creusabro, which Caterpillar then tested and determined would perform as the Usinor Defendants had claimed. Plaintiffs assert that the Usinor Defendants promised that the sample was representative of steel they could provide on a high volume basis and that all Creusabro would perform as well as the sample.

In the spring of 2000, representatives of the Usinor Defendants met with Caterpillar at Caterpillar's dump-truck plant in Decatur, Illinois. This time, representatives from Leeco, the Usinor Defendants' exclusive North American distributor, attended as well. All Defendants made another presentation about the benefits of Creusabro and promised, both orally and in writing, that Creusabro could be welded without preheating in thicknesses up to 50 mm. Caterpillar informed Defendants that it intended to use Creusabro for truck bodies, and gave the Usinor Defendants and Leeco design specifications for the truck bodies that would be manufactured using Creusabro steel. The Complaint does not provide any details regarding the written representations that Creusabro could be welded without preheating.

Caterpillar submitted proposals to its dump truck customers for lighter weight truck bodies that would result from using Creusabro steel. While it planned ultimately to sell the truck bodies, Caterpillar did not plan to manufacture all the truck bodies itself. Some would be fabricated by CMSA, its Mexican subsidiary, and some by Western Technology Services International, Inc. ("Westech"), a Wyoming company unrelated to Caterpillar. Representatives of Leeco and of the Usinor Defendants inspected CMSA's plant in Mexico and assured CMSA that its facilities were appropriate for fabricating truck bodies with Creusabro. Having previously visited Westech's plant as well in May 1999, Leeco and the Usinor Defendants informed Caterpillar that the facilities and processes in place at both CMSA and Westech were appropriate for fabricating truck bodies with Creusabro.

After entering into contracts with its customers to sell the lighter weight truck bodies, Caterpillar issued purchase orders to CMSA and Westech for completed truck bodies. CMSA and Westech then issued purchase orders to Leeco for Creusabro steel to be used in fabricating the truck bodies. Plaintiffs assert that the Usinor Defendants instructed CMSA and Westech to buy the Creusabro from Leeco.

C.   Problems with the Creusabro Steel

CMSA and Westech received their first shipments of Creusabro in 2000. Using steel from the first shipment of Creusabro, Westech fabricated eight truck bodies and delivered them to the Bald Mountain mine in Nevada in June 2000. No problems were reported with these trucks. Beginning with the next shipment of Creusabro steel, however, Plaintiffs assert that "serious problems with the steel began to occur." Seven truck bodies manufactured by Westech for delivery to the Centralia Mine in Washington in June and July 2000 displayed "hydrogen-induced cracking" in their floors during manufacture and along the side walls once in use. In July 2000, four more Westech-made trucks had to be taken out of service from the Chino Mine in New Mexico due to cracks throughout their bodies. The customer at the Chino Mine demanded that Caterpillar provide replacement truck bodies using a different kind of steel; Caterpillar did so. In September 2000, a Westech-made truck body delivered to Tyrone Mine in

New Mexico also displayed cracking, forcing Westech to add horizontal and vertical ribs to reduce flexing and cracking.

* * *

Truck bodies manufactured by CMSA fared no better. When CMSA delivered nineteen truck bodies to Bagdad Mine in Arizona, hydrogen-induced cracking was present where the shipping brackets were placed, even though CMSA had implemented additional processing measures during fabrication, including preheating throughout the welding process. Hydrogen-induced cracking was so severe in the beds of seven CMSA-made truck bodies delivered to the Syncrude Mine in Alberta, Canada beginning in October 2000 that none of the truck bodies was assembled or put in service; all seven truck beds were scrapped.

Three truck bodies delivered to Bingham Canyon Mine in Utah between August 2000 and March 2001 showed hydrogen-induced cracking in hundreds of places, and one could not even be assembled at the mine. Of the three, Westech made one and CMSA made the other two. Plaintiffs assert that additional truck bodies delivered to other customers had similar problems, and that hydrogen-induced cracking rendered inoperable the vast majority of truck bodies that Caterpillar sent to its customers.

In addition to the cracking, Plaintiffs allege that much of the Creusabro steel provided to CMSA was of low quality, with surface slag left over from the manufacturing process, grind marks, and gouges. These problems made the steel harder to work with and "dramatically" increased costs. Plaintiffs further assert that chemical analysis of Creusabro from CMSA and Westech confirmed that the steel "failed to comply with the chemical specifications that had originally been provided," and that the steel in no way resembled the quality of the sample that the Usinor Defendants had provided to Caterpillar. . . .

D.  Defendants' Responses

In response to these difficulties with the Creusabro steel, Caterpillar, CMSA, and Westech contacted Leeco and the Usinor Defendants. In addition to "many telephone calls and e-mails," meetings took place in Wyoming, Mexico, and Illinois to discuss the problems. Plaintiffs assert that during these discussions, the Usinor Defendants modified their suggested procedures for welding the Creusabro steel. In November 2000, the Usinor Defendants suggested preheating the steel to 212 degrees Fahrenheit for all crack repairs, and using only a welding process known as "GMAW." Plaintiffs assert that these suggestions were contrary to the Usinor Defendants' earlier assurances that no preheating was necessary, and that four different welding processes could be used.

In January 2001, after Caterpillar and CMSA notified Leeco and the Usinor Defendants of continued problems with hydrogen-induced cracking, the Usinor Defendants suggested preheating all welds to 300 degrees, "permitting a soak time to three inches," and grinding and cleaning all metal parts. Plaintiffs allege that all of these suggestions were being presented for the first time, and that all increased the costs of working with the steel. After further review and testing, Caterpillar determined that Creusabro steel could not be welded without preheating, and that in light of the specifications for truck bodies that it had provided to the Usinor Defendants and to Leeco, the steel was not fit for use in manufacturing truck beds.

Caterpillar asserts that it was forced to repair all the cracked truck bodies pursuant to warranty, at a cost of over $1.8 million, and that it suffered injury to its reputation. CMSA alleges that it incurred over $1 million in extra costs for processing the steel, resulting in a net loss of over $1 million. Defendants rejected Plaintiffs' attempts to return their excess inventory of Creusabro steel, which Plaintiffs sold for scrap in an effort to mitigate damages. Plaintiffs seek damages in an amount to be proven at trial.

E.  Plaintiffs' Lawsuit

On April 6, 2004, Caterpillar and CMSA filed an eleven-count Complaint against Leeco, Usinor USA, and Usinor. Both Plaintiffs claim that Defendants are liable to them under theories of breach of express and implied warranties (Counts I, II, V–VII), failure to deliver conforming goods (Counts I and II), and promissory estoppel (Counts III, IV, VIII–X). Plaintiffs bring these claims under both Illinois law and the CISG. Plaintiffs also assert an additional claim against Usinor under French law (Count XI).

Of the eleven counts in the Complaint, CMSA brings four (Counts I–IV), Caterpillar brings six (Counts V–X), and CMSA and Caterpillar jointly assert the French law claim (Count XI). Plaintiffs base their claims against Usinor on the theory that Leeco and Usinor USA were Usinor's agents. Accordingly, with the exception of Count I, Plaintiffs' claims against Leeco and Usinor USA (Counts IV, VI, VII, IX, and X) are alleged only in the alternative, in the event the court finds that either Leeco or Usinor USA was not Usinor's agent. Plaintiffs assert Count I against Leeco directly.

On July 28, 2004, the Usinor Defendants filed a motion to dismiss all eight counts against them under Fed. R. Civ. P. 12(b)(6). The Usinor Defendants argue that Leeco and Usinor USA were not Usinor's agents, and that any claims that rely on these agency relationships should be dismissed. The Usinor Defendants further contend that all of Plaintiffs' state law claims are preempted by the CISG. Even absent preemption, the Usinor Defendants argue, Caterpillar's state law claims for breach of warranty fail for lack of privity or reliance, and the promissory estoppel claims fail to allege the necessary elements and are barred by the statute of frauds in any event. Finally, the Usinor Defendants argue that in Count XI, Plaintiffs fail to state a claim under the terms of Article 1109 of the French Civil Code. Alternatively, Defendants move for a more definite statement as to Count XI under Fed. R. Civ. P. 12(e).

\* \* \*

DISCUSSION

## I. Standard of Review

On a motion to dismiss pursuant to Fed. R. Civ. P. 12(b)(6), the court accepts all well-pleaded allegations in the complaint as true and draws all reasonable inferences in favor of the plaintiffs. . . . The court must accept a pleading's factual allegations because "a motion to dismiss tests the legal sufficiency of a pleading." . . . Dismissal under Rule 12(b)(6) is appropriate only if "it appears beyond doubt that the plaintiff can prove no set of facts in support of his claim which would entitle him to relief." . . .

## II. French Law Claim (Count XI)

As noted, Plaintiffs bring their claims under the CISG, Illinois law, and French law. Plaintiffs assert Count XI, the French law claim, only in the alternative in the event the court determines that any of their claims against Usinor are governed by French law. Plaintiffs assert claims under French Civil Code, Article 1109, for breach of contract, breach of express and implied warranties, failure to provide goods that conformed to the sample provided, breaches of the express promises made regarding Creusabro steel, and error on the very substance of the goods. Because the court finds that French law does not apply in this case, the court dismisses Count XI without prejudice.

A federal district court with jurisdiction over a state law claim applies the choice of law rules of the state in which it sits. . . . Under Illinois law, choice of law in contract-based claims involves selecting the jurisdiction with the most significant contacts with the transaction and the parties. . . . The court considers factors such as the place of contracting, the place of the negotiation, the place of performance, the location of the subject matter of the contract and the domicile and nationality of the parties, according to these factors' relative importance with respect to the particular issue at stake in the litigation.

Applying Illinois choice of law rules, it is clear that none of Plaintiffs' claims are governed by French law. The only connection with France is that Usinor has its principal place of business there. Leeco and the Usinor Defendants met with Caterpillar in Illinois to make their sales presentations in 1998 and 2000, and met with CMSA in Mexico to evaluate the manufacturing facilities. Defendants shipped Creusabro steel to Mexico and Wyoming for use in the truck bodies, which in turn were delivered to mines throughout North America. The complaint is devoid of any allegations that negotiation or performance of the contract took place anywhere but Illinois, Wyoming, or Mexico. In fact, the bulk of the contracting activity occurred in Illinois. Accordingly, Illinois law, not French law, applies to Plaintiffs' state law claims. The court thus grants the Usinor Defendants' motion to dismiss Count XI, without prejudice, and denies Defendants' alternative Rule 12(e) motion for a more definite statement.

III. Agency Allegations

Plaintiffs assert that Leeco and Usinor USA were agents of Usinor. They thus bring Counts IV, VI, VII, IX, and X only in the alternative, in the event the court finds that either Leeco or Usinor USA was not Usinor's agent. The Usinor Defendants argue that any claims that rely on agency should be dismissed because Plaintiffs have not adequately established any agency relationships. Accordingly, the court first examines whether Plaintiffs have sufficiently pleaded an agency relationship between Usinor and either Leeco or Usinor USA.

Under Illinois law, the test for agency is whether the alleged principal has the right to control the manner in which work is carried out by the alleged agent, and whether the alleged agent can affect the legal relationships of the principal. . . . Agency can arise when an agent has either "actual" or "apparent" authority to act on the principal's behalf. . . . The agent has actual authority when the principal's words or actions would lead a reasonable person in the agent's position to believe that he or she was so authorized. An agent has apparent authority to act on the principal's behalf in relation to a third party when the words or conduct of the principal would lead a reasonable person in the third party's position to believe that the principal had so authorized the agent. . . . Where an agent with such authority contracts with a third party on behalf of a disclosed principal, the agent does not become a party to the contract and is not liable upon it. . . . The principal, not the agent, is liable in such a situation. . . .

\* \* \*

An agent's apparent authority is determined in light of the principal's conduct towards a third party; the principal must do something to lead the third party to believe that the agent is authorized to act on the principal's behalf. . . . In other words, there must be "some form of communication, direct or indirect," by which the principal instills such a reasonable belief in the mind of the third party. . . . Plaintiffs here have asserted that Usinor and Usinor USA instructed CMSA and Westech to buy the Creusabro from Leeco. This fact alone is sufficient, at this stage of the proceedings, to establish that Leeco was an apparent agent of Usinor and of Usinor USA. . . .

The Usinor Defendants argue that Leeco cannot be an agent because it was merely a distributor, and a distributor is not considered an agent of a manufacturer as a matter of law. Defendants are only partially correct. It is true that Leeco's status as Usinor's distributor does not, in itself, make Leeco an agent of Usinor. . . . Plaintiffs, however, have not based their assertion that Leeco was Usinor's agent merely on the fact that Leeco was Usinor's distributor; as noted above, Plaintiffs also allege that Usinor instructed CMSA to buy the steel from Leeco. Furthermore, Plaintiffs have alleged more activity on Leeco's part than simply buying steel from Usinor and re-selling it to CMSA and Westech. Leeco joined Usinor and Usinor USA in their sales presentation to Caterpillar in Illinois in 2000, and in their visits to Westech and CMSA to evaluate the manufacturing facilities.

Thus, especially in light of the low threshold of federal notice-pleading, Plaintiffs have sufficiently alleged that Leeco was the agent of both Usinor and Usinor USA.

Plaintiffs' allegations of agency regarding Usinor USA are also sufficient. Plaintiffs have asserted that Usinor and Usinor USA together requested and attended both the 1998 and the 2000 sales presentations in Illinois; together provided the samples of Creusabro; together visited Westech and CMSA; together made the alleged promises and representations regarding the steel; and together were involved in discussions with Plaintiffs after problems emerged with Creusabro. Plaintiffs also allege, on information and belief, that Usinor USA was a wholly owned subsidiary and "alter ego" of Usinor. In light of these assertions, Plaintiffs would be entitled to a reasonable belief that Usinor USA was under the control of Usinor. Under the federal notice-pleading standard, this is sufficient to establish that Usinor USA was Usinor's agent for purposes of a motion to dismiss. . . .

In light of the court's determination that Plaintiffs have adequately alleged an agency relationship between Usinor and Leeco and Usinor USA, Counts IV, VI, VII, IX, and X, which Plaintiffs asserted as alternative claims in the event the court found that agency was lacking, are dismissed without prejudice. . . .

Of the remaining claims (Counts I, II, III, V, and VIII), all are asserted against Usinor save Count I, which is a CISG claim asserted by CMSA against Leeco. The court will not dismiss Count I at this time because Leeco has not moved to dismiss it, and because unlike the other claims against Leeco, it was not brought as an alternative claim. The court will continue with its analysis of Counts II, III, V, and VIII.

IV.   Preemption by the CISG

The Usinor Defendants argue that Plaintiffs' state law UCC and promissory estoppel claims are preempted by the CISG. The CISG is an international treaty, ratified by the United States in 1986, that "sets out substantive provisions of law to govern the formation of international sales contracts and the rights and obligations of the buyer and seller." Usinor Industeel v. Leeco Steel Products, Inc., 209 F.Supp.2d 880, 884 (N.D.Ill. 2002). The CISG applies to international sales contracts between parties that are located in signatory countries, and who have not opted out of CISG coverage at the time of contracting.

As a treaty to which the United States is a signatory, the CISG is federal law; thus, under the Supremacy Clause, it preempts inconsistent provisions of Illinois law where it applies. Usinor Industeel, 209 F.Supp.2d at 884–85 (citing U.S. CONST., art VI, cl. 2). The issue is one of scope. State law causes of action that fall within the scope of federal law are preempted. . . . Conversely, state law causes of action that fall outside the scope of federal law will not be preempted. . . . Thus, the CISG preempts Plaintiffs' UCC and promissory estoppel claims only if such claims fall within the scope of the CISG. . . .

The Usinor Defendants interpret the CISG as having a "broad scope." Defendants argue that the purpose of the CISG is the adoption of uniform rules to govern international contracts, and that the application of state law here would frustrate that purpose. Plaintiffs argue that the CISG applies only to claims between a buyer and a seller. Thus, Plaintiffs argue, the CISG applies to, and can preempt, only those claims involving CMSA as the buyer of the steel, and not any claims brought by Caterpillar.

Case law interpreting the preemptive effect of the CISG is sparse. Usinor Industeel, 209 F.Supp.2d at 884 (noting the dearth of federal cases interpreting the CISG). Under general principles of preemption, however, courts must be reluctant in finding federal preemption of a subject "traditionally governed by state law." . . . Preemption cannot occur absent "the clear and manifest purpose of Congress," the best evidence of which is found in the plain text of the statute. Thus the court must "focus on the plain wording. . . . which necessarily contains the best evidence of Congress' preemptive intent." . . . Accordingly, the court begins by looking at the text of the CISG.

Article 4 of the CISG states that the CISG governs only the formation of the contract of sale and the rights and obligations of the seller and the buyer arising from such a contract. In particular, except as otherwise expressly provided in this Convention, it is not concerned with: (a) the validity of the contract or of any of its provisions or of any usage; (b) the effect which the contract may have on the property in the goods sold. The plain text of the CISG limits its application to claims between buyers and sellers. As the Usinor Defendants correctly note, Caterpillar did not directly buy Creusabro steel from anyone; Caterpillar bought completed truck bodies from CMSA and Westech.

CMSA, not Caterpillar, bought the steel from Leeco, Usinor's agent. As such, only CMSA can assert claims under the CISG, and it has (in Counts I and II).

In support of their respective positions, both sides cite to Usinor Industeel, 209 F.Supp.2d 880, an action between two of the defendants in this case, Usinor and Leeco. Usinor Industeel, as it happens, involved shipments of the very Creusabro steel which Leeco bought from Usinor and intended to sell to Caterpillar. Under the terms of the contract between Leeco and Usinor, Usinor remained the owner of the steel until Leeco paid Usinor in full, which Leeco was obligated to do within 60 days following receipt of the steel. Id. Leeco, however, bought the steel on a line of credit from LaSalle Bank, giving LaSalle a security interest in the steel. After Caterpillar stopped using Creusabro, Leeco was left with a large amount of steel for which it owed Usinor nearly a million dollars. Usinor filed a diversity action for replevin in federal court.

LaSalle intervened, arguing that under the UCC, its security interest in the steel gave it superior title, thus precluding Usinor's ability to replevin the steel. According to Usinor, however, any interest that LaSalle had in the steel could have arisen only from the contract between Leeco and Usinor, which Usinor claimed was governed by the CISG. Usinor argued that the CISG preempted the UCC, thus voiding any interest LaSalle might have had under the UCC and allowing Usinor to replevin the steel. The court disagreed with Usinor. While noting that the CISG would preempt the UCC if it applied, the court held that the CISG did not apply when a third party had an interest in the goods, and that the UCC should govern. Under the UCC, Usinor had merely an unperfected reservation of a security interest in the steel, which was inferior to LaSalle's interest and, thus, insufficient to maintain an action for replevin.

In this case, the Usinor Defendants argue that the holding of Usinor Industeel should be limited to situations where the third party's interest is in title to the goods, thus preserving a broader concept of preemption. As this court reads that decision, however, it suggests a narrower interpretation of the CISG's preemptive force. Noting Article 4's limitation of the application of the CISG to the rights and obligations of the buyer and the seller, the Usinor Industeel court quoted commentators who suggested that the CISG simply does not apply to third parties who are not parties to the contract. . . . 209 F.Supp.2d at 885 (quoting Richard Speidel, The Revision of UCC Article 2, Sales in Light of the United Nations Convention on Contracts for the International Sale of Goods, 16 NW. J. INT'L L. & BUS. 165, 173 (1995) ("CISG is not concerned with . . . the rights of third persons who are not parties to the contract . . . CISG is limited to two-party commercial contracts for sale. . . .")); see John Honnold, Uniform Law for International Sales § 444.1 (3d ed. 1999) ("[T]he [CISG's] rules are limited to the rights 'of the seller and the buyer' and yield to the rights of third persons such as creditors *and purchasers*." ) (emphasis added).

\* \* \*

Defendants also argue that the CISG preempts Plaintiffs' promissory estoppel claims (Count III, by CMSA, and Count VIII, by Caterpillar). They cite no authority in support of this position. . . . In fact, the court can find no reported decision which holds that the CISG preempts promissory estoppel claims. . . . In light of the need for reluctance in finding preemption in areas traditionally governed by state law, . . . the court declines to extend the preemptive force of the CISG to state law claims for promissory estoppel.

In sum, the court finds that the CISG does not preempt Count V, Caterpillar's UCC claim against Usinor, because Caterpillar is not a party to the contract. Nor does the CISG preempt Counts III or VIII, Plaintiffs' promissory estoppel claims against Usinor. Accordingly, the court will determine the validity of those claims under Illinois law; the CISG will govern only Counts I and II.

V. The CISG Claim (Count II)

CMSA brings Count II against Usinor under the CISG for breach of express and implied warranties, including an implied warranty of fitness for a particular purpose and failure to deliver conforming goods. CMSA alleges that the purchase orders issued by CMSA to Leeco specified that the

CISG would govern terms and conditions, and that Usinor is liable on the purchase orders as Leeco's principal. Usinor argues that Leeco was not its agent, and that, as CMSA issued purchase orders only to Leeco and not to Usinor, there was no privity between CMSA and Usinor. This argument need not detain the court. As noted above, Plaintiffs have adequately alleged that Leeco was Usinor's agent. Under agency law, a disclosed principal is a party to a contract made by the principal's agent if the agent acted within its authority. ... Usinor is therefore alleged to be a party to the purchase orders issued by CMSA to Leeco, and Count II cannot be dismissed for lack of privity.

As for the substantive allegations, Article 35 of the CISG provides that the seller must deliver goods which are of the quality and description required by the contract; the goods do not conform with the contract unless they possess the qualities of goods held out to the buyer as a sample. Article 36 establishes the seller's liability for any lack of conformity. CMSA has asserted that Usinor did not provide goods of the quality and description required by the purchase orders, and has detailed numerous problems with the Creusabro steel, including hydrogen-induced cracking and other quality issues. CMSA has also asserted that the steel did not possess the qualities held out by Usinor as a sample. CMSA has thus sufficiently stated a claim under the CISG.

## VI.   The UCC Claim (Count V)

Caterpillar brings Count V against Usinor for breach of express and implied warranties under Illinois's codification of the UCC, 810 ILCS 5/2–313 and 810 ILCS 5/2–315. Caterpillar alleges that Usinor, through its agents Leeco and Usinor USA, made numerous unambiguous promises about Creusabro steel; that these promises were in writing, including in brochures and marketing materials; that these promises were breached when the steel did not perform as promised; that the steel did not possess the qualities of goods held out as a sample; that Usinor knew that the steel was being purchased for a particular purpose; and that Usinor knew that Caterpillar was relying on Usinor's skill and judgment in selecting and furnishing the steel.

Usinor argues that both the express and implied warranty claims fail for lack of vertical privity. Usinor notes that Caterpillar only bought truck bodies from CMSA, and never directly bought Creusabro steel from anyone. Usinor further argues that even if the required privity were present, Caterpillar cannot state a claim for breach of implied warranty under 810 ILCS 5/2–315 because Caterpillar has not shown that it relied on Usinor's skill and judgment.

### A.   Breach of Express Warranty

To state a claim for breach of express warranty in Illinois, a plaintiff must show a breach of an affirmation of fact or promise that was made a part of the basis of the bargain. 810 ILCS 5/2–313 ... The seller may be liable if the goods sold fail to conform to the affirmations, promises, or descriptions of the goods. . . . A sample of the goods which is made part of the basis of the bargain creates an express warranty that the whole of the goods shall conform to the sample. 810 ILCS 5/2–313. To enforce an express warranty under Illinois law, however, a party without a warranty assignment alleging purely economic loss must be in privity of contract. . . .

Here, Caterpillar was not in privity of contract with Usinor. Caterpillar issued purchase orders to CMSA for truck bodies; it was CMSA who bought the steel from Leeco, Usinor's agent. Caterpillar may have established the existence of an express warranty by alleging that Usinor made numerous promises regarding the performance of the Creusabro steel; that the steel failed to conform to those promises; and that the steel failed to measure up to the sample. Only CMSA was in privity with Usinor, however, and Plaintiffs have made no assertion that CMSA assigned warranty rights to Caterpillar. Thus, Caterpillar cannot enforce the express warranty and its claim of breach against Usinor cannot be sustained.

B.  Breach of Implied Warranty

To state a claim for breach of implied warranty, a plaintiff must show that before the sale, the seller had reason to know the particular purpose for which the plaintiff bought the goods; that the plaintiff was relying on the seller's skill or judgment to select goods suitable for that purpose; and that the goods were not suitable for that particular purpose. 810 ILCS 5/2–315. . . . Once again, however, "privity of contract is a prerequisite to recover economic damages for breach of implied warranty" under Illinois law. At least with respect to purely economic loss, implied warranties "give a buyer of goods a potential cause of action only against his immediate seller." . . .

As noted above, Caterpillar was not in privity of contract with Usinor. Caterpillar nonetheless argues that an exception to the vertical privity rule exists in Illinois. Caterpillar cites to a line of cases which held that privity is not required where a manufacturer knows the identity, purpose, and requirements of its distributor's customer and manufactures goods specifically to meet those requirements. . . . Caterpillar argues that the exception applies here because Caterpillar gave Usinor specifications for its truck bodies, and because Usinor was well aware of Caterpillar's uses and requirements for the Creusabro steel. The court disagrees.

To begin with, it is far from certain that Illinois permits any exception to the vertical privity requirement for breach of implied warranty in light of the decisions of the Illinois Supreme Court. . . . Even if the exception still exists in Illinois, the cases cited by Caterpillar are distinguishable. . . .

Caterpillar's claim for breach of implied warranty thus fails for lack of privity. Having reached this conclusion, the court need not address Defendants' argument that Caterpillar has not shown the requisite reliance. The Usinor Defendants' motion to dismiss Count V for failure to state a claim is granted.

VII.  Promissory Estoppel (Counts III and VIII)

CMSA brings Count III, and Caterpillar brings Count VIII, against Usinor for promissory estoppel. To state a claim for promissory estoppel in Illinois, a plaintiff must allege: (1) an unambiguous promise; (2) reasonable and justifiable reliance by the party to whom the promise was made; (3) the reliance was expected and foreseeable by the promisor; and (4) the promisee relied upon the promise to her detriment. . . . Plaintiffs allege that Usinor, through its agents Usinor USA and Leeco, made clear and definite oral and written promises about Creusabro steel that Plaintiffs relied upon to their detriment, and that such reliance was reasonable and foreseeable to Usinor. Usinor argues that Plaintiffs have not established the necessary elements of a promissory estoppel claim because they fail to allege either a promise or reasonable reliance. . . .

A.  The Alleged Promises

Plaintiffs contend that Usinor made several clear promises in this case: that the Creusabro steel was harder, had a higher yield strength, and could be processed more cheaply than regular steel ; that Creusabro did not require preheating for joints less than 50 mm thick; that all the Creusabro would perform as well as the sample; and that CMSA's and Westech's facilities were appropriate for making truck bodies with Creusabro. Usinor argues that these were mere descriptions of the qualities of Creusabro or opinions of the facilities at CMSA and Westech, none of which constitutes a "promise."

Promissory estoppel is usually based on a promise of future action, not a representation of fact. . . . A promise for purposes of promissory estoppel typically involves "a declaration that one will do or refrain from doing something specified." . . . A statement that refers to "a past or existing condition rather than committing to some future action is thus more precisely described as a warranty than as a promise." . . .

As Usinor urges, none of the statements referred to by Plaintiffs as "promises" constitute a declaration that Usinor or its agents will do or refrain from doing any future action. They are, instead, arguably mere representations of fact and opinion regarding the inherent qualities and likely performance of Creusabro steel, as well as the appropriateness of CMSA's facilities for fabricating truck bodies with that steel. The court is not persuaded, however, that a seller's representations regarding the qualities of goods can never constitute a promise in the context of a promissory estoppel claim. . . .

. . . Usinor's representations of opinion and fact regarding Creusabro essentially constitute a warranty, the breach of which Caterpillar cannot allege because of the vertical privity rule. Accordingly, the court finds that Usinor's representations regarding the properties and performance of Creusabro, the promise that the steel would perform like the sample, and the statements regarding the appropriateness of CMSA's facilities for using the steel, constitute promises for purposes of Caterpillar's promissory estoppel claim (Count VIII).

In contrast, CMSA's relationship with Usinor is governed by an express contract—the purchase orders issued to Leeco. CMSA could use Usinor's promises to establish a claim for breach of warranty under that contract and, in fact, CMSA has alleged precisely that claim under the CISG in Count II. There is no reason to allow CMSA to proceed with a state law claim for promissory estoppel that essentially duplicates its breach of warranty claim under the CISG. "Promissory estoppel is not a doctrine designed to give a party . . . a second bite at the apple in the event it fails to prove a breach of contract." . . . The court thus grants the Usinor Defendants' motion to dismiss Count III for failure to state a claim.

### B.  Caterpillar's Reliance

Even if Usinor's representations constitute a promise for purposes of Caterpillar's promissory estoppel claim (Count VIII), Usinor further argues that Plaintiffs have not alleged the requisite reliance. To state a claim for promissory estoppel, a plaintiff must allege that it reasonably and justifiably relied on the defendant's promise. . . . Usinor contends that Caterpillar could not have reasonably relied on Usinor's representations because Caterpillar obtained and tested a sample of Creusabro long before even informing Usinor of its proposed use.

Usinor's argument fails because Caterpillar has alleged promises that have nothing to do with Caterpillar's testing of the sample. For instance, Caterpillar alleges that Usinor promised that the sample of Creusabro was representative of the steel that Usinor would provide, and that all the Creusabro would perform as well as the sample. Indeed, the first shipment of Creusabro showed no problems; the problems began with the second shipment. After the problems developed, chemical analysis from CMSA and Westech showed that the later shipments of Creusabro steel failed to comply with the chemical specifications originally provided; the later shipments of steel were not of the same quality as the sample. Thus, while Caterpillar, by testing the sample, had initially and partially relied on its own expertise in selecting Creusabro, it was further relying on Usinor's promise to provide steel which would perform as well as that sample.

Caterpillar has also alleged that it relied on Usinor's promise that the facilities at CMSA and Westech were appropriate for fabricating truck bodies using Creusabro steel. This promise, too, has nothing to do with Caterpillar's testing of the sample. Indeed, the mere fact that Caterpillar tested the sample does not serve to absolve Usinor of responsibility for the variety of promises and representations that Caterpillar has alleged Usinor made. In fact, Usinor has cited no authority in support of the notion that a buyer's testing of a sample provides such blanket immunity to the seller. Finally, Caterpillar has alleged that it relied on all of Usinor's representations, not just those it could have verified by testing the sample, in submitting proposals for lighter-weight truck bodies to its customers. Caterpillar has sufficiently alleged reliance on Usinor's promises, and has thus stated a claim for promissory estoppel.

\* \* \*

The court thus grants the Usinor Defendants' motion to dismiss CMSA's promissory estoppel claim (Count III), but denies the motion to dismiss Caterpillar's claim (Count VIII).

* * *

## CONCLUSION

For the foregoing reasons, the Usinor Defendants' motion to dismiss is granted as to Counts III, IV, V, VII, X, and XI, but denied as to Counts II and VIII. . . . [T]he court further dismissed Count IX.

## NOTES

**(1) The Business Structure on the Supply Side.** Usinor Industeel, a major steel manufacturer, is a French corporation with its principal facilities in France but with customers around the world. For purposes of marketing steel in the United States, Usinor set up a subsidiary corporation, organized under Delaware law and wholly owned by the French parent corporation. This is a common pattern of organization for transnational enterprises and is adopted by TNEs for many legal purposes, such as laws regarding corporate governance and accounting, income tax liability, etc. In form, when goods are marketed, sales contracts are formed and performed between the parent and subsidiary corporations as buyer and seller.[8] Usinor's business structure had another layer within the United States, an independent corporation that acted as a distributor of Usinor's products. Usinor's U.S. subsidiary, in form, sells Usinor products to the distributor. Commonly, in distributorship contracts, the distributor retains an agreed percentage of the prices of sales to ultimate buyer/users and remits the balance. There are many business reasons for manufacturers, foreign or domestic, to use the services of distributors for marketing their products.

As a result of this business structure, the Creusabro steel in this case was sold through a chain of three contracts: from the Usinor parent to the Usinor subsidiary, from the Usinor subsidiary to the distributor, and from the distributor to Mexican corporation (CMSA) that was a subsidiary of Caterpillar, an Illinois corporation.

**(2) The Steel Buyer's Litigation Strategy and Its Consequences.** When dispute arose regarding the quality of the steel, counsel for the ultimate buyer of the steel, CMSA, was not content to sue its immediate seller, the distributor. What legal or business reasons might have led to the strategic decision of counsel for this plaintiff to sue the remote sellers, the Usinor subsidiary and Usinor itself, as well as the distributor? In making this decision, counsel took on the difficult legal burden of prosecut-

---

**8.** Contract terms are, obviously, not negotiated at arms length when the subsidiary is wholly owned by the parent. The prices fixed in these contracts are sometimes referred to as "administered prices."

ing a claim for breach of a sales contract against two upstream parties that were not, in form, parties to the buyer's contract of sale.

What law determines whether this downstream buyer can sue the remote sellers? The buyer's claim against the distributor was clearly governed by the CISG. Mexico and the United States are CISG contracting parties. Does the CISG or some body of domestic law determine whether the remote sellers can be sued as well? The court never questioned the determination that CISG 35 governed the substance of CMSA's claim. In concluding that the CISG claim ran against the Usinor subsidiary and Usinor parent corporations, however, the court applied the domestic law of Illinois. Was the court's analysis sound?[9]

The choice of Illinois law brought to bear the established jurisprudence of that state that bars suits for economic loss against upstream sellers for lack of vertical privity. Plaintiff's counsel was able to overcome that body of law by persuading the court that the three "sellers" were all parties to the ultimate sales contract on the theory that the distributor and the Usinor subsidiary were merely agents acting on behalf of a principal, the Usinor parent. For this purpose, the court applied the domestic law of Illinois. In United States legal parlance, decisions like this are sometimes described as "piercing the corporate veil." This complex body of United States domestic law lies outside the scope of these materials.

Could the "agency" question have been decided under the CISG without reference to the domestic law of the United States? CISG applies by its terms to "contracts of sale" between parties that are referred to a "buyers" and "sellers," but none of these terms is defined by the Convention. The agency theory used by the court resulted in the conclusion that the Usinor parent was the seller, acting through agents. Could the same analysis have been founded in the CISG? Is CISG 4 relevant? CISG 7(a)? CISG 7(b)?

**(3) The Business Structure on the Demand Side.** Caterpillar, an Illinois corporation, elected to use other corporations to fabricate the trucks that it sold under its brand name. One of these was a Mexican subsidiary of Caterpillar, CMSA; the other was an independent entity, Westech. As a result of this structure, the steel needed for building the trucks was bought by CMSA and Westech. The completed trucks were then sold by CMSA and Westech to Caterpillar, which sold them to various customers. The business and legal reasons for Caterpillar to set up this structure are not known. Its use of a Mexican subsidiary may be an example of the practice of "out sourcing" of production activities from a developed to a developing country.

**(4) The Truck Buyer's Legal Strategy and Its Consequences.** Plaintiffs' counsel elected not to use the strategy of collapsing the linked

---

**9.** Part of the question here is the possible effect on the application of the CISG when the "real" seller is determined to be different that the nominal seller. In this case the Usinor parent corporation has its place of business in France, which is a CISG contracting party. Whether the distributor or the Usinor parent is the seller for purposes of CISG 1(a), the parties have their places of business in different states. Suppose, however, the parent had been incorporated in the United Kingdom or Japan, which are not contracting parties.

entities on the demand side that they employed in characterizing the linked entities on the supply side. Counsel framed the case as two separate and distinct plaintiffs, the Caterpillar parent corporation and CMSA. Westech was not a party to the case. What strategic purposes might have been served by counsel's putting the case in this form? Would it have been useful for defense counsel to contend that the CMSA and Westech were merely agents of Caterpillar in this transaction?

A legal consequence of the plaintiff's strategy was that the claim of CMSA and the claim of Caterpillar were deemed to be based on different legal grounds. The CMSA claim was a straightforward claim of a buyer for breach of a contract of sale. The Caterpillar complaint alleged breach of express and implied warranty, claims that emanate from contracts of sale, but the court granted the defendants' motion to dismiss those claims because Caterpillar was not a party to the contract to sell the steel. Could counsel for Caterpillar have avoided this result?

The only Caterpillar claim that survived the motion to dismiss was a claim that was described by the court as a "promissory estoppel claim." This description was a short-hand way of describing a claim for breach of a contract that was not the contract of sale for the steel. Under the plaintiffs' theory, the parties to this other contract were the Usinor parent and Caterpillar and the substance of the contract were promises regarding the quality of the steel that Usinor made directly to Caterpillar. The role of promissory estoppel in this scenario was to provide a legal basis for enforcement of those promises in the absence of "consideration," a requirement of domestic United States law for enforcement of promises. "Consideration" exists in ordinary sales contracts as a result of the mutual promises of an exchange: goods for money. The alleged Usinor–Caterpillar contract was not perceived as an exchange transaction. If Caterpillar promised nothing to Usinor, Usinor's promise would not be "supported by consideration." In classic common-law analysis, that promise would be unenforceable. Common-law courts developed a exception to the requirement that promises unsupported by consideration are unenforceable. That exception, articulated as domestic United States law in Section 90 of the Restatements of Contracts, allows a promissee of a certain kind of promises to enforce it if the promissee changes position, i.e., detrimentally "relies" on the promise. The court in this case concluded, at the pleading stage, that Caterpillar had stated a claim of breach of a promise enforceable under the rubric of promissory estoppel.

Anterior to this analysis is the fundamental issue of choice of law. In Count XI, counsel for plaintiffs alleged all of their claims, presumably including breach of the Usinor–Caterpillar promise, under French domestic law as an alternative to Illinois law. Why did the court conclude that the Caterpillar claim for breach of Usinor's promise was governed by domestic United States law? Defense contended, apparently, that the governing law was the CISG. What was the purpose for that? Apparently defense counsel did not contend that French law governed this claim. Should they? The court concluded that the alleged Usinor–Caterpillar promise was not within the scope of the CISG, which deals only with sales contracts, and applied domestic United States law, the law of Illinois.

## SECTION 3.   MANUFACTURERS' REMEDIAL PROMISES TO REPAIR OR REPLACE GOODS

### (A) DOMESTIC UNITED STATES LAW

The materials that follow consider manufacturers' promises, made to downstream buyers, to repair or replace goods. In transactions of this kind, the value of the goods tends to be the dominant concern, although these transactions may also involve losses in the form of consequential damages.

For these cases, the legal platform becomes more complex. In addition to the common law and UCC Article 2, there is a federal statute of significance. The Magnuson–Moss Warranty Act (MMWA)[1] was designed primarily for the situation of manufacturers' warranties to the ultimate consumer/users of goods. The MMWA applies only to marketing of consumer products, but these constitute most of the transactions in which manufacturers' repair/replace promises are made to downstream buyers.

The Magnuson–Moss Warranty Act applies to any transaction in which a manufacturer undertakes "to refund, repair, replace, or take other remedial action" with respect to a consumer product in the event that the product fails to meet the specifications in the undertaking. Such undertakings, called "written warranties" in the MMWA,[2] are the primary grist for the application of the federal act.[3] The MMWA applies to any "supplier" of a consumer product that provides a "written warranty." "Supplier" refers primarily to manufacturers,[4] but the term would include a retailer if the retailer provided a "written warranty."

A major impetus to this legislation was the view that manufacturers, particularly manufacturers of automobiles, were not making adequate remedial promises and were not living up to the promises that they had made. Through 1960, all United States automobile manufacturers, using virtually identical language, undertook to repair new cars for only 90 days or 4,000 miles of use, whichever came first. In that year, the New Jersey Supreme Court declared that the common remedial promise was inimical to

---

**1.** 15 U.S.C. §§ 2301–2312. The MMWA has been interpreted and supplemented by regulations promulgated by the Federal Trade Commission. 16 CFR Parts 700–703.

**2.** MMWA 101(6)(B). References to the MMWA in these materials use the section numbers of the Act rather than the section numbers of the U.S. Code. Statutory supplements for law students contain the MMWA with the Act's section.

**3.** The MMWA has a second definition of a "written warranty." A warranty that a consumer product is defect free or will meet a specified level of performance over a period of time is also a "written warranty." MMWA 101(6)(A). Such written warranties are rare.

**4.** "Supplier" means "any person engaged in the business of making a consumer product directly or indirectly available" to consumers. MMWA 101(4).

the public good and invalid.[5] Automobile manufacturers began to offer express warranties that differed in terms and duration and that had different remedial promises, but consumer organizations lobbied strongly for stronger legal protection. One result was the 1975 Magnuson–Moss Warranty Act.

The MMWA is in part a regulatory statute and in part a statute that tries to influence the practices of manufacturers. One of the Act's objectives was to induce manufacturers to provide remedial promises of greater value to consumers. Most of the Act was focused on this primary goal. A second objective was to enhance the ability of aggrieved consumers to enforce remedial promises that were not performed. The Act contains a number of provisions intended to help consumers and their lawyers to obtain judicial relief. The regulatory provisions of the MMWA are built on the underlying state warranty and contract law.

The strategy of the MMWA was not to require manufacturers to provide remedial promises but was, rather, to create legal and market conditions that would induce manufacturers to improve consumer protection. One piece of this strategy was to define the minimum elements of what Congress deemed to be a satisfactory remedial promise.[6] Any manufacturer that elects to use the congressionally-approved terms is permitted to tout its undertaking as a FULL WARRANTY in its advertising and promotional materials.[7] Other manufacturers are required to give consumers a conspicuous signal that they are offering lesser protection. They must label their repair/replace promises as only a LIMITED WARRANTY.[8] Coupled with the requirement of this signal to consumers, the MMWA required manufacturers to make all of the warranty terms available to prospective buyers, at the point of retail sales, before shoppers commit to become buyers.[9] Congress apparently believed that competition for customers among manufacturers would lead to widespread use of FULL WAR-

---

**5.** Henningsen v. Bloomfield Motors, Inc., 32 N.J. 358, 404, 161 A.2d 69, 75–76 (1960): "The disclaimer of the implied warranty and exclusion of all obligations except those specifically assumed by the express warranty signify a studied effort to frustrate that protection. True, the Sales Act authorizes agreements between buyer and seller qualifying the warranty obligations. But quite obviously the Legislature contemplated lawful stipulations (which are determined by the circumstances of a particular case) arrived at freely by parties of relatively equal bargaining strength. The lawmakers did not authorize the automobile manufacturer to use its grossly disproportionate bargaining power to relieve itself from liability and to impose on the ordinary buyer, who in effect has no real freedom of choice, the grave danger of injury to himself and others that attends the sale of such a dangerous instrumentality as a defectively made automobile. In the framework of this case, illuminated as it is by the facts and the many decisions noted, we are of the opinion that Chrysler's attempted disclaimer of an implied warranty of merchantability and of the obligations arising therefrom is so inimical to the public good as to compel an adjudication of its invalidity."

**6.**   MMWA 104.

**7.**   MMWA 103(a)(1).

**8.**   MMWA 103(a)(2).

**9.**   MMWA 102. The Act relies extensively on Federal Trade Commission regulations to implement this requirement.

RANTIES and that knowledgeable consumers would examine the different terms of manufacturers and buy goods that came with the more attractive remedial promises. The hope that most manufacturers of consumer durable goods would offer FULL WARRANTIES has proven to be unfounded.[10]

The MMWA sought, in several ways, to improve enforcement of manufacturers' remedial promises. These provisions have had little practical effect. The Act created a federal forum for warranty litigation,[11] authorized a special kind of federal class action,[12] and provided that successful claimants could recover attorneys' fees and costs.[13] The Act also provides the consumers may seek relief in state courts.[14] In a state-court action that is "brought" under the federal Act, claimants who prevail are entitled to seek recovery of attorneys' fees and costs.[15] The MMWA also encouraged creation and use of alternative dispute resolution mechanisms for warranty disputes.[16] None of these provisions has been more than marginally successful.

Although the W in MMWA refers to warranties, the Act has no application to ordinary express warranties of quality like those created under common law or UCC 2–313. This results from the Act's extremely precise and narrow definition of "written warranty." The Act's use of the word "warranty" is quite misleading. "Written warranty," in practical terms, means a remedial promise. An ordinary manufacturer's express warranty of the quality of the goods is outside the scope of the Act.

SKELTON v. GENERAL MOTORS CORP., 660 F.2d 311 (7th Cir. 1981). Shortly after the MMWA was enacted, a class action was brought against General Motors on behalf of individuals who had purchased new cars advertised by GM as having particular transmissions that would give superior performance. The complaint alleged that GM used inferior transmissions in cars manufactured between 1976 through 1979. The court dismissed the complaint because the representations of the quality of the transmissions in GM promotional literature did not constitute a MMWA "written warranty."

---

**10.** A notable exception was American Motors, Co., which offered FULL WARRANTIES on its automobiles in the late 1970s. The manufacturer did not survive.

FULL WARRANTIES are more prevalent in marketing of relatively low-priced consumer products, transactions in which manufacturers are willing to replace the goods or refund the retail price of defective goods.

**11.** MMWA 110(d)(1)(A).

**12.** MMWA 110(d)(3)(C) and (e).

**13.** MMWA 110(d)(2).

**14.** MMWA 110(d)(1)(A).

**15.** State trial courts have general jurisdiction over such cases without reference to the MMWA. Whether a case is brought under that general jurisdiction or under the MMWA can be difficult to determine. See C. Reitz, Consumer Product Warranties Under Federal and State Laws 134–143 (2d ed. 1987).

**16.** MMWA 110(a); FTC Reg. 703.

## SECTION 4.   MANUFACTURERS' IMPLIED WARRANTIES OF QUALITY

### (A) DOMESTIC UNITED STATES LAW

### 1.   CONSUMER GOODS

This section is divided between consumer goods and commercial goods. Consumer goods are conventionally defined as goods purchased for personal, family, or household use. The law of sales evolved to permit consumers to recover from manufacturers for personal injuries caused by defective products. The legal doctrine used by the courts was to hold manufacturers liable for breach of implied warranties of quality. Over time, consumers sought to recover for economic losses as well. In order to understand the current situation it is necessary to go back into history.

#### a.   *LAW PRIOR TO THE COMMERCIAL CODE*

For several decades before 1960, when products caused death or personal injuries, courts allowed downstream buyers—and other individuals—to recover for their injuries on the basis of manufacturers' breach of implied warranties of quality. The accepted substantive law principle was that products that were harmful were not merchantable. This was the era when it could be said, with plausibility, that the implied warranty was implied by law rather than by contractual agreement. The products that gave rise to these decisions were largely products that consumers ate or drank or applied to their bodies. There was not much concern for explaining the substantive content of implied warranties on food, beverages, or cosmetics. Human life and safety were the standard.

A more difficult legal question derived from lack of privity of contract between the manufacturers and the injured consumers that were downstream from those manufacturers. A modern doctrine of general contract law allows enforcement of a contract only by the parties to the contract and those in privity with them.[1] Courts determined that this common-law rule should be reformed to allow an exception in these limited circumstances.

---

**1.** "The modern doctrine of privity, ... a set of rules whereby a contract cannot confer rights or impose liabilities on third parties, was not really known as such until very late in the nineteenth century. ... There is a sense in which the new doctrine of privity was an important development in the law at a time of increasing complexity in multilateral commercial relationships. The appearance of middlemen in all sorts of commercial situations served to separate the parties at either end of the transaction, and it was generally accepted that no privity existed between them. Economically, this may have served a useful purpose, in that it encouraged the development of a more market-based concept of enterprise liability. But on some occasions the results were not only economically dubious but socially disastrous." P. Atiyah, The Rise and Fall of Freedom of Contract 413–414 (1979).

United States courts never applied the common-law requirement of privity-of-contract with the rigor of British courts. Restatements of contract law in this country did not even use "privity" in their black-letter formulations of the law. See, e.g., Restatement, Contracts

During this period, sales law was codified by some states in the Uniform Sales Act. Courts continued to find a basis for buyers and other injured parties to recover. Commonly, the courts found that the warranty provisions in the Sales Act provided a substantive standard of quality.[2] On the question of privity, the Act was silent and common law was used.

In 1960, Professor William Prosser wrote an extraordinarily influential law review article about the body of cases in which manufacturers had been held accountable for breach of implied warranties of quality.[3] Prosser's literary trope was fall of the citadel of privity, but his real purpose was to recharacterize the substance of warranty cases involving personal injuries as cases that *really* sounded in tort. Court acceptance of Prosser's thesis came quickly.[4] The new tort was added at the last minute to the Restatement (Second) of Torts.[5] Since that time, most state courts have recognized the tort as part of their jurisprudence. Some states have codified the tort in statutory form.

Judicial recognition of the new tort did not end the legal history of recoveries for personal injury in warranty. Indeed, that history was moving forward at about the same time as the new tort was being developed. Drafting and enactment of the Commercial Code occurred in the 1950s and 1960s. Article 2 included a number of provisions that relate expressly to

---

(1933); Restatement (Second), Contracts (1981). Rather, United States contract doctrine defines the persons that had the power to enforce contracts which they had no role in forming. Two recognized classes of such persons are assignees and third party beneficiaries.

In U.S. tort law, privity was once a requirement in negligence claims. That requirement was abrogated in a famous opinion of Judge Cardozo, MacPherson v. Buick, 217 N.Y. 382, 111 N.E. 1050 (1916).

**2.**  A technical problem in the law of merchantability arose. Under the Sales Act, this warranty arose only in contracts for sale of goods "by description." Where buyers bought goods from the retailer's inventory, they did not buy "by description." To overcome this, courts turned to the warranty of fitness for particular purpose, which had no such limitation.

**3.**  W. Prosser, The Assault Upon the Citadel (Strict Liability to the Consumer), 69 Yale L.J. 1099 (1960).

**4.**  In the year that Prosser's article appeared, the New Jersey Supreme Court expanded the category of implied warranty situations in which privity would not be required to include automobiles. Henningsen v. Bloomfield Motors, Inc., 32 N.J. 358, 161 A.2d 69 (1960). Two years later, the California Supreme Court announced the strict tort liability. Greenman v. Yuba Power Products, Inc., 59 Cal.2d 57, 27 Cal.Rptr. 697, 377 P.2d 897 (1963). A curious factual coincidence links the New Jersey decision in *Henningsen* and the California decision in *Greenman*. In both cases, the product that caused injury was purchased as a gift and the person injured was the donee. Fundamental to the new tort was the explicit omission of any requirement that the injured consumer or user have had a contract with the seller or manufacturer.

**5.**  Restatement (Second) of Torts § 402A(2)(b). The numbering system for the Restatement had gelled before the new tort was recognized. To avoid renumbering, the "A" suffix was used to position the new in the Restatement. The drafters of § 402A were explicit in declaring that downstream buyers had a cause of action against manufacturers, but they issued a caveat on the horizontal privity question whether bystanders or others who were neither users nor consumers should be permitted to recover.

For the most recent Restatement articulation of this tort, see Restatement of the Law, Torts: Products Liability § 1 (1996).

products liability. Although nothing explicit about risk of personal injury was included in the formulation of the implied warranties of quality,[6] any seller's' limitation of consequential damages for injury to the person in sales of consumer goods was declared to be prima facie unconscionable. UCC 2–719(3). The matter of privity was addressed in the original version of UCC 2–318 (now Alternative A of that section). That section allowed individuals who were in a buyer's family or household and who were "injured in person" to recover against "the seller." The original version of UCC 2–318 was silent on anyone's right to recover for personal injuries against remote manufacturers.[7]

Our immediate concern here is whether downstream consumer buyers can recover from manufacturers for economic losses on the basis of implied warranties of quality. In economic loss cases, courts have generally held that the tort of strict liability (as well as the tort of negligence) is not available.[8] Courts refer to this as "the economic loss doctrine." As a result, economic loss claims were pressed as contract claims.

Before states enacted the Commercial Code, state courts divided over whether to allow implied warranty of merchantability claims by ordinary consumers (or by commercial buyers)for economic losses to succeed against remote manufacturers. New Jersey allowed recovery, but the state supreme court declared that a simpler theory of recovery would have been the newly recognized strict tort.[9] Not many courts followed the New Jersey precedent.[10]

The Commercial Code was enacted across the country in the 1960s and 1970s. Is Article 2 of the Commercial Code relevant to the situation of economic loss claims presented as manufacturers' breach of implied warranties? The substantive provision most likely to apply is the provision on the implied warranty of merchantability, UCC 2–314(2)(c) provides that goods are merchantable if they are "fit for the ordinary purposes for which

---

**6.** Safety was recognized implicitly in the UCC 2–314(1). which declared that serving food or drink for value is a sale, thus rejecting judicial decisions to the contrary where restaurant patrons had been denied recovery for personal injuries in warranty cases. See Comment 5.

**7.** A Comment declared that "the section . . . is neutral and is not intended to enlarge or restrict the developing case law on whether the seller's warranties, given to his buyer who resells, extend to the other persons in the distribution chain." See current Comment 3.

**8.** Leading case is East River Steamship Corp. v. Transamerica Delaval, Inc., 476 U.S. 858, 106 S.Ct. 2295, 90 L.Ed.2d 865 (1986); Seely v. White Motor Co., 63 Cal.2d 9, 45 Cal.Rptr. 17, 403 P.2d 145 (1965). See also Hutton v. Deere & Co., 210 F.3d 389 (10th Cir. 2000); Daanen & Janssen, Inc. v. Cedarapids, Inc., 216 Wis.2d 395, 573 N.W.2d 842 (1998). And see Note, Manufacturers' Liability to Remote Purchasers for "Economic Loss"—Tort or Contract?, 114 U. Pa. L. Rev. 539 (1966).

**9.** Santor v. A & M Karagheusian, Inc., 44 N.J. 52, 207 A.2d 305 (1965).

**10.** Contemporaneously with the decision in *Santor*, the California Supreme Court held that the new strict tort was not available in claims for economic loss. Seely v. White Motor Co., 63 Cal.2d 9, 45 Cal.Rptr. 17, 403 P.2d 145 (1965). *Seely* upheld a commercial truck buyer's recovery from the manufacturer for breach of the manufacturer's express warranty. The court had no occasion to rule on the right to recover under an implied warranty theory.

such goods are used.''. Unquestionably, this warranty is pertinent to economic losses of consumer buyers. This is also manifest in the principal Article 2 remedies for breach of warranty, UCC 2–714 and 2–715.

While the Code deals with economic losses caused by breach of warranty, the text of the implied warranty section is plainly based on a contract for sale of goods. The warranty is made by ''the seller'' and derives its primary meaning from the contract description of the goods. UCC 2–314(2)(c). By its terms, UCC 2–314 does not recognize a manufacturers' warranty that extends to downstream buyers. The related provisions in UCC 2–316 that deal with disclaimers of implied warranties of quality presuppose that a disclaiming seller and the person potentially protected by a warranty are in a contract relationship. Section 2–719 of the Code allows sellers and buyers to agree on the measure of damages recoverable for breach of warranty and, in particular, to agree to exclude consequential damages for economic losses. Again, the presupposition is that the parties negotiated and came to an agreement.

### b.  UCC 2–318; THREE VERSIONS

UCC Article 2 addresses privity in UCC 2–318. Does UCC 2–318 allow a downstream buyer to bring an action against a remote manufacturer to recover for economic loss caused by the manufacturer's breach of an implied warranty of quality? To answer, one needs to recall that UCC 2–318 is not uniform as promulgated. In states that adopted Alternative A or B, privity exists only with respect to personal injury claims. In the very few states that adopted Alternative C, an economic claim can be pursued be pursued by a person other than the buyer against the ''seller'' if the third party is a person who may reasonably be expected to use, consume or be affected by the goods. Although the text does not refer to a downstream buyer, such a buyer would meet the criteria of one reasonably expected to use or consume the goods. Thus, Alternative C could be construed to allow a downstream buyer to sue manufacturer for economic loss. Note that UCC 2–318 deals only with privity. It does not deal with the manufacturer's implied warranty obligations as a seller, which are covered by UCC 2–314 and 2–315. See Comment 2.

Although the text of UCC 2–318 is silent on whether it deals with recovery by downstream buyers, the Comments to the section are not. Comment 3 to UCC 2–318 states that the section ''is neutral and is not intended to enlarge or restrict the developing case law on whether the seller's warranties, given to his buyer who resells, extend to other persons in the distribution chain.'' A downstream buyer is a person in the distribution chain. The Comment leaves to courts further liberalization of the requirement of privity. The Supreme Court of Alaska took up that invitation is the case noted below.

MORROW v. NEW MOON HOMES, 548 P.2d 279 (Alaska 1976). Buyers purchased a mobile home from a retailer. A plaque on the side indicated that the mobile home had been manufactured by New Moon Homes, Inc. Numerous problems developed. Buyers sued the dealer and the manufacturer for breach of the implied warranty of merchantability. A default judgment was entered against the dealer, which appeared to have gone out of business. The trial court dismissed the claim against the manufacturer for want of privity; the buyers appealed. The Supreme Court of Alaska reversed. The court decided that the manufacturer, as a seller, was governed by UCC 2–314 and 2–315 when it sold the mobile home. (That buyer may not have been the retailer that sold the mobile home to the plaintiffs.) The opinion noted that UCC 2–318 was silent on the matter of vertical privity and cited Comment 3. The court held the requirement of vertical privity was abolished in Alaska.[11] In the court's view, this meant that the downstream consumer buyers could enforce implied warranties in the upstream first sale of the mobile home, if any warranties had been made. The court added that manufacturers "may possibly" disclaim implied warranties under UCC 2–316 or limit liability for damages under UCC 2–719. In a footnote, the court said its abolition of the vertical privity requirement was limited to claims of diminished value of the goods only, and did not go to recovery of consequential economic loss.

*Morrow* was a reversal of the trial court's dismissal of the case on the pleadings and remand for trial. The *Morrow* court could not know the warranty terms in the sales contract between the manufacturer and its buyer, nor whether the contract had implied warranty disclaimer or a clause limiting liability for damages. All that remained to be proven in the trial court on remand.

*c.  NON–UNIFORM VERSIONS OF UCC2–318*

Several states have enacted their own idiosyncratic versions of UCC 2–318. One of these states is Texas. In the case noted below, the Supreme Court of Texas relied on its version of UCC 2–318 to uphold a judgment for a downstream buyer against the manufacturer for breach of the implied warranty of merchantability.

NOBILITY HOMES OF TEXAS, INC. v. SHIVERS, 557 S.W.2d 77 (Tex.1977). Buyer purchased a mobile home from a retail dealer. When deficiencies appeared, the buyer sued the manufacturer. (The dealer had since gone out of business). The trial court held that the manufacturer had breached the implied warranty of merchantability. The court found that the value of the mobile home was $8,750 less than the retail price and awarded that amount in damages. The Texas Supreme Court affirmed. The court held that manufacturers are governed by UCC 2–314 and 2–315. With respect to privity, the court quoted the Texas version of UCC 2–318:

> This chapter does not provide whether anyone other than a buyer may take advantage of an express or implied warranty of quality made to the buyer and whether the buyer or anyone entitled to take advantage of a warranty made to the buyer may sue a third party other than the

---

**11.** The court relied on an earlier Pennsylvania case which had come to the same conclusion eight years earlier in a case involving commercial goods. Kassab v. Central Soya, 432 Pa. 217, 246 A.2d 848 (1968).

immediate seller for deficiencies in the quality of the goods. These matters are left to the courts for their determination.

The Texas court noted division among the courts of other states, without considering that none of them had the Texas version of UCC 2–318. The court elected to place Texas among the states whose courts had abolished the requirement of vertical privity.

### d.  MAGNUSON–MOSS WARRANTY ACT

In a previous section, we considered the MMWA rules for labeling manufacturers' remedial promises as FULL or LIMITED WARRANTIES. The MMWA provisions on remedial promises also deal with manufacturers' implied warranties of quality. Indeed, the most significant effect of the MMWA may be in its provisions on implied warranties. Three aspects are important to understanding the Act:

First, there is no federal definition of "implied warranty" in the MMWA. The Act defines "implied warranty" as an implied warranty arising under state law.[12] The substance of any manufacturers' obligation must be found in state law. In referring to state law, the MMWA does not distinguish between common law and legislation. The MMWA makes no reference to UCC Article 2.

The main MMWA provision on implied warranties deals with disclaimers. The Act bans disclaimer of implied warranties of quality by any manufacturer that offers a FULL or LIMITED WARRANTY on its product. MMWA 108(a) declares in pertinent part:

> No supplier may disclaim or modify any implied warranty to a consumer with respect to [a] consumer product if . . . such supplier makes any written warranty to the consumer with respect to such consumer product.

Section 108(a) does not state that implied warranties exist. The Act provides only that, if an implied warranty exists under relevant state law, a manufacturer may not disclaim or modify it if the manufacturer makes a "written warranty."

Third, the MMWA has a series of provisions that were intended to increase the ability of consumers to pursue claims of MMWA protected rights against manufacturers,[13] Consumers were provided with access to federal district courts for individual or class action suits, but those provisions have been largely ineffective. Suits by consumers against manufacturers are brought in state courts. If a consumer prevails on the merits of an MMWA claim, the Act allows recovery of attorneys' fees and litigation costs.[14]

---

**12.** MMWA 101(7). The MMWA allows manufacturers to limit the "duration" of implied warranties to the duration of their remedial promises. MMWA 108(b). We will postpone examination of this peculiar provision later.

**13.** MMWA 110(d).

**14.** MMWA 110(d)(2). To be entitled to this added recovery, a consumer plaintiff must "bring suit" under the MMWA. The Act does not make clear how a suit is characterized as

The following case reflects the effect of the MMWA in an implied warranty case brought by a consumer in the state courts of Indiana. These were the courts that held against a commercial buyer's implied warranty claim in *Martin Rispen & Son*.

# Hyundai Motor America, Inc. v. Goodin

Supreme Court of Indiana, 2005.
822 N.E.2d 947.

■ BOEHM, JUSTICE.

We hold that a consumer may sue a manufacturer for economic loss based on breach of the implied warranty of merchantability even if the consumer purchased the product from an intermediary in the distribution chain. There is no requirement of "vertical" privity for such a claim.

### Facts and Procedural Background

On November 18, 2000, Sandra Goodin test drove a Hyundai Sonata at AutoChoice Hyundai in Evansville, Indiana. The car was represented as new and showed nineteen miles on the odometer. Goodin testified that when she applied the brakes in the course of the test drive she experienced a "shimmy, shake, pulsating type feel." The AutoChoice salesperson told her that this was caused by flat spots on the tires from extended inactivity and offered to have the tires rotated and inspected. After this explanation, Goodin purchased the Sonata for $22,710.00.

The manufacturer, Hyundai, provided three limited warranties: 1 year/12,000.miles on "wear items;" 5 years/60,000 miles "bumper to bumper;" and 10.years/100,000 miles on the power train.[1] Hyundai concedes that brake rotors, brake calipers, and brake caliper slides were subject to the 5.year/60,000 mile warranty covering "[repair or replacement of any component originally manufactured or installed by [Hyundai] that is found to be defective in material or workmanship under normal use and maintenance." To claim under this warranty, a vehicle must be serviced by an authorized Hyundai dealer who is then reimbursed by Hyundai for any necessary parts or labor.

---

being under the MMWA, but it appears to be sufficient for the complaint to refer explicitly, in some manner, to the MMWA.

**1.** On the "Buyers Order," AutoChoice Hyundai included the following preprinted language in capital letters:

ALL WARRANTIES, IF ANY, BY A MANUFACTURER OR SUPPLIER OTHER THAN DEALER RE THEIRS, NOT DEALER'S, AND ONLY SUCH MANUFACTURER OR OTHER SUPPLIER SHALL BE LIABLE FOR PERFORMANCE UNDER SUCH WARRANTIES, UNLESS DEALER FURNISHES BUYER WITH A SEPARATE WRITTEN WARRANTY MADE BY DEALER ON ITS OWN BEHALF. DEALER HEREBY DISCLAIMS ALL WARRANTIES, EXPRESS OR IMPLIED, INCLUDING ANY IMPLIED WARRANTIES OF MERCHANTABILITY OR FITNESS FOR A PARTICULAR PURPOSE, ON ALL GOODS AND SERVICES SOLD BY DEALER . . .

Three days after the car was purchased, Goodin's husband, Steven Hicks, took it back to AutoChoice for the promised tire work. Goodin testified that she continued to feel the shimmy but did nothing further for a month. On December 22, she took the car to a different Hyundai dealer, Bales Auto Mall, in Jeffersonville, Indiana, for an unrelated problem and also made an appointment six days later for Bales to inspect the brakes. Bales serviced the brake rotors for warping, but on May 1, 2001, Goodin returned to Bales complaining that the vehicle continued to vibrate when the brakes were applied. Bales found the rotors to be out of tolerance and machined them. Eighteen days later Goodin again returned to Bales, reporting that she still felt vibrations and for the first time also heard a "popping" noise. Goodin told the service advisor at Bales that she thought there may be a problem with the suspension, and Bales changed and lubed the strut assembly. Eleven days later Goodin once more brought the car to Bales reporting continued shimmy and also a "bed spring type" noise originating from the brakes. The Bales mechanic was unable to duplicate the brake problem, but balanced and rotated the tires as Goodin had requested. One week later Goodin returned to Bales where she and Jerry Hawes, Bales's Service Manager, test drove the Sonata. The brake problem did not occur during the test drive, but Hawes identified a noise from the direction of the left front tire and repaired the rubber mounting bracket.

Goodin told Hawes that the brake problem had occurred about seventy percent of the time. The problem was worse when it was wet or cool, was consistently occurring when she drove down a steep hill near her home, and was less frequent when a passenger's weight was added. Goodin made arrangements to leave the car with Hawes at Bales, but, according to Hawes, over a several day period he could not duplicate the symptoms Goodin reported.

On August 24, 2001, Goodin took her car back to her original dealer, AutoChoice, reporting that the brakes "squeak and grind when applied." Goodin left the car with AutoChoice where the left front rotor was machined and loose bolts on the front upper control arm were tightened. Goodin testified that after this five-day procedure the brakes began to make the same noises and vibrations even before she arrived home.

In October 2001 Goodin hired an attorney who faxed a letter to Hyundai Motor America giving notice of her complaint and requesting a refund of the purchase price. On November 13, 2001, Goodin filed a complaint against Hyundai Motor America, Inc. alleging claims under the Magnuson–Moss Warranty Act, 15 U.S.C. §§ 2301–2312, for breach of express warranty, breach of implied warranty, and revocation of acceptance. On April 23, 2002, in anticipation of litigation, Goodin hired William Jones to inspect her car. Jones noted that the odometer read 57,918 miles and the car was still under warranty. Jones drove the car approximately five miles and found "severe brake pulsation on normal stops" which "was worse on high speed stops." Although he did not remove the tires to inspect the brake rotors, Jones opined that the rotors were warped and defective or there was "a root cause that has not been discovered and corrected by the repair facilities." His ultimate conclusion was that the "vehicle was defective and unmerchantable at the time of manufacture and unfit for operation on public roadways." Three weeks later, after the 5 year/60,000 mile warranty had expired, Goodin's husband, Hicks, replaced the rotors with new rotors from a NAPA distributor.[2] After this repair, according to Hicks, the pulsation went from "very bad" to "mild" and "less frequent."

Steven Heiss, District Parts and Service Manager for Hyundai Motor America served as the liaison between Hyundai and the dealers and provided warranty training. If a dealer is not performing repairs correctly, Hyundai, through its liaisons, addresses the problem. Heiss inspected Goodin's Sonata on October 21, 2002. At that point the Sonata had been driven 77,600 miles. He testified that during his twenty-three mile test drive he neither heard the noise described by Goodin nor felt any vibration from the brakes. However, Heiss did hear a "droning noise" which he later concluded was due to a failed left rear wheel bearing. He regarded this as a serious problem and not one caused by abuse or misuse of the vehicle. The wheel bearing would have been covered by the 5 year/60,000 mile warranty. Before his inspection, Heiss had been told that the rotors had been changed by Hicks five months earlier, and when Heiss measured the rotors he found that they were out of standard. Heiss testified a miscast from the factory was one of a number of possible reasons for damaged rotors.

At the conclusion of a two day trial, the jury was instructed on all claims. Over defendants' objection, the instructions on implied warranties made no reference to a privity requirement. The jury returned a verdict for Hyundai on Goodin's breach of express warranty claim, but found in favor of Goodin on her claim for breach of implied warranty of merchantability. Damages of $3,000.00 were assessed and Goodin's counsel was later awarded attorneys' fees of $19,237.50 pursuant to the fee shifting provisions of the Magnuson–Moss Warranty Act.

Hyundai orally moved to set aside the verdict as contrary to law on the ground that Goodin purchased the car from AutoChoice and therefore did not enjoy vertical privity with Hyundai. The court initially denied that motion, but the following day set aside the verdict, holding lack of privity between Goodin and Hyundai precluded a cause of action for breach of implied warranty. Goodin then moved to reinstate the verdict, and, after briefing and oral argument, the trial court granted that motion on the ground that Hyundai was estopped from asserting lack of privity.

Hyundai appealed, asserting: (1) it was not estopped from asserting a defense of lack of privity;.and (2) lack of vertical privity barred Goodin's recovery for breach of implied warranty of merchantability. The Court of Appeals agreed on both points, holding that Hyundai was not estopped from asserting that privity was an element of Goodin's prima facia case, and, because privity was lacking, Goodin did not prove her case. *Hyundai Motor Am., Inc. v. Goodin*, 804 N.E.2d 775, 781 (Ind.Ct.App.2004). The

---

**2.** Hicks is an A.C. Certified Master Engine Machinist and Diesel Fuel Technician who had been trained in brakes during his certification process

Magnuson–Moss Warranty Act looks to state law for the contours of implied warranties. The Court of Appeals was "not unsympathetic" to Goodin's claims but regarded itself as bound by a footnote in Martin Rispens & Son v. Hall Farms, Inc., 621 N.E.2d 1078, 1084 n. 2 (Ind.1993), where this Court stated: "In Indiana, privity between the seller and the buyer is required to maintain a cause of action on the implied warranties of merchantability." Id. at 784. . . .

Vertical Privity

A.   The Relationship Between Federal and State Law in Claims Based on Implied Warranty of Merchantability

This case is brought under a federal statute. The Magnuson–Moss Warranty Act . . . provides a federal right of action for consumers to enforce written or implied warranties where they claim to be damaged by the failure of a supplier, warrantor, or service contractor to comply with any obligation under that statute or under a written warranty, implied warranty, or service contract. The Act also limits the extent to which manufacturers who give express warranties may disclaim or modify implied warranties, but looks to state law as the source of any express or implied warranty. . . . As the Seventh Circuit recently put it: "Because §§ 2308 and 2304(a) do not modify, or discuss in any way, a state's ability to establish a privity requirement, whether privity is a prerequisite to a claim for breach of implied warranty under the Magnuson–Moss Act therefore hinges entirely on the applicable state law." Voelker v. Porsche Cars N. Am., Inc., 353 F.3d 516, 525 (7th Cir.2003).

Goodin's claim is for breach of the implied warranty of merchantability, not for violation of any substantive provision of the federal statute. Accordingly, her claim lives or dies on the resolution of an issue of state law, specifically whether Indiana requires privity between buyer and manufacturer for a claim of breach of implied warranty.

* * *

C.   Origins of Privity

Indiana has adopted the Uniform Commercial Code, notably its provision that: "A warranty that the goods shall be merchantable is implied in a contract for their sale if the seller is a merchant with respect to goods of that kind." Ind.Code § 26–1–2–314(1) (2004). Hyundai asserts, and the Court of Appeals found, Indiana law requires vertical privity between manufacturer and consumer when economic damages are sought. . . . Goodin argues that traditional privity of contract between the consumer and manufacturer is not required for a claim against a manufacturer for breach of the implied warranty of merchantability, especially if the manufacturer provides a Magnuson–Moss express warranty with the product.

Privity originated as a doctrine limiting tort relief for breach of warranties. The lack of privity defense was first recognized in Winterbottom v. Wright, 10 M. & W. 109, 152 Eng Rep 402 (Ex. 1842). . . . In that case, the court sustained a demurrer to a suit by an injured coachman for breach of warranty by a third party who contracted with the owner to maintain the coach. In this century, however, MacPherson v. Buick Motor Co., 217 N.Y. 382, 111 N.E. 1050 (1916), and Henningsen v. Bloomfield Motors, Inc., 32 N.J. 358, 161 A.2d 69 (1960), established that lack of privity between an automobile manufacturer and a consumer would not preclude the consumer's action for personal injuries and property damage caused by the negligent manufacture of an automobile.

"Vertical" privity typically becomes an issue when a purchaser files a breach of warranty action against a vendor in the purchaser's distribution chain who is not the purchaser's immediate seller.... Simply put, vertical privity exists only between immediate links in a distribution chain. ... A buyer in the same chain who did not purchase directly from a seller is "remote" as to that seller.

"Horizontal" privity, in contrast, refers to claims by nonpurchasers, typically someone who did not purchase the product but who was injured while using it. ... Goodin purchased her car from a dealership and is thus remote from the manufacturer and lacks "vertical" privity with Hyundai.

"Although warranty liability originated as a tort doctrine, it was assimilated by the law of contracts and ultimately became part of the law of sales." ... But "privity is more than an accident of history. It permitted manufacturers and distributors to control in some measure their risks of doing business.".Richard W. Duesenberg, The Manufacturer's Last Stand:.The Disclaimer, 20 Bus. Law 159, 161 (1964). Because vertical privity involves a claim by a purchaser who voluntarily acquired the goods, it enjoys a stronger claim to justification on the basis of freedom of contract or consensual relationship. It nevertheless has come under criticism in recent years, and this is the first opportunity for this Court to give full consideration to this issue.

D.   Indiana Case Law

Although this Court did not address the issue, even before the Products Liability Act, both the Court of Appeals and federal courts applying Indiana law held that a claimant was not required to prove privity to succeed in a personal injury action in tort based on breach of implied warranties. ... Three federal court decisions drew on these decisions to conclude that privity of contract is not required in Indiana to maintain a cause of action for personal injury based on breach of an implied warranty.
. . .

However, several Court of Appeals decisions subsequently held that recovery of economic loss for alleged failure of the expected benefit of the bargain based on breach of implied warranty under the UCC required a buyer to be in privity of contract with the seller. ...

This Court has mentioned the common law privity requirement in the context of actions sounding in contract only once, and that in a footnote. Martin Rispens & Son v. Hall Farms, Inc., 621 N.E.2d 1078 (Ind.1993), addressed negligence and express and implied warranty claims by a farmer against both the direct seller and the grower of seed that allegedly damaged the farmer's crops. The footnote cited to the UCC and two Court of Appeals decisions and other courts have taken the footnote as settled Indiana law on this issue. As the Court of Appeals put it in its decision in this case: [T]he [footnote] indicates our supreme court's unequivocal acceptance that privity between a consumer and a manufacturer is required in order to maintain a cause of action for breach of an implied warranty of merchantability. . . . Any change in the law removing the privity requirement in implied warranty actions should be left to that court. . . . To the extent Goodin argues that this result is inequitable, we are not entirely unsympathetic. Whether the cons of the vertical privity rule outweigh the pros is something for either our supreme court or the General Assembly to address. . . . In Martin Rispens, the implied warranty claims were rejected based on an effective disclaimer of implied warranty, under Indiana Code section 26–1–2–316(2) which permits parties to agree to exclude or modify implied warranties if done in a particular manner. The farmer did not present privity as an issue on transfer to this Court and neither party briefed it. It was not necessary to the decision. Accordingly, the language in Martin Rispens, though often cited, is dicta and we accept the invitation from the Court of Appeal to reconsider it.

\* \* \*

E.  Statutory Developments in Indiana

The Product Liability Act, Indiana Code § 34–20–2–1 et seq. (1999), does not require a personal injury plaintiff to prove vertical privity in order to assert a products liability claim against the manufacturer. . . . Even before the Product Liability Act in 1978, the requirement of privity of contract in warranty actions in Indiana began to erode in 1963 with the passage of the Uniform Commercial Code under section 2–318: . . . Section 2–318 was taken verbatim from the UCC as originally prepared by the Uniform Code Committee Draftsmen in 1952. It eliminated "horizontal" privity as a requirement for warranty actions. However, that version of 2–318 took no position on the requirement of vertical privity. . . .

The majority of states, including Indiana, retained or adopted the 1952 version of section 2–318, which now appears in the Uniform Commercial Code as "Alternative A." . . . Because Alternatives A and B of 2–318 are limited to cases where the plaintiff is "injured in person," they do not authorize recovery for such loss. But neither do they bar a non-privity plaintiff from recovery against such a remote manufacturer for direct economic loss. . . . Thus, Alternatives A and B of 2–318 do not prevent a court from abolishing the vertical privity requirement even when a non-privity buyer seeks recovery for direct economic loss. . . .

Alternative C is the most expansive in eliminating the lack-of-privity defense. . . . Alternative C expands the class of plaintiffs to include other nonpurchasers such as the buyer's employees and invites, and bystanders. . . . Alternative C also eliminates the vertical privity requirement, but is not restricted to "personal" injury. Because Alternative C refers simply to "injury," plaintiffs sustaining only property damage or economic loss in some states have been held to have standing to sue under this language. . . . This is consistent with the stated objective of the drafters that the third alternative follow "the trend of modern decisions as indicated by Restatement of Torts 2d § 402A (Tentative Draft No. 10, 1965) in extending the rule beyond injuries to the person." . . . But see Nebraska Innkeepers, Inc. v. Pittsburgh–Des Moines Corp., 345 N.W.2d 124, 129 (Iowa 1984) (holding Alternative C did not permit non-privity plaintiffs to seek recovery solely for economic loss).

The commentaries to the UCC were careful to explain that these alternatives were not to be taken as excluding the development of the common law on the issue of vertical privity: [Alternative A] expressly includes as beneficiaries within its provisions the family, household and guests of the purchaser. Beyond this, the section in this form is neutral and is not intended to enlarge or restrict the developing case law on whether the seller's warranties, given to his buyer who resells, extend to other persons in the distributive chain. UCC § 2–318, CMT. n. 3.

F.   Privity as an Obsolete Requirement as Applied to Consumer Goods

There is a split of authority in other jurisdictions with similar or identical versions of section 2–318 on the availability of implied warranty claims by remote purchasers, particularly if only economic loss is claimed, as in the present case. Courts of other jurisdictions that have retained or adopted Alternative A note that the statute speaks only to horizontal privity, and is silent as to vertical privity. See, e.g., Morrow v. New Moon Homes, Inc., 548 P.2d 279, 287 (Alaska 1976); Kassab v. Central Soya, 432 Pa. 217, 246 A.2d 848, 855 (1968), overruled on other grounds, AM/PM Franchise Ass'n v. Atlantic Richfield Co., 526 Pa. 110, 584 A.2d 915, 926 (1990). As the Pennsylvania Supreme Court put it: "Merely to read the language [of § 2–318] is to demonstrate that the code simply fails to treat this problem. There thus is nothing to prevent this court from joining in the growing number of jurisdictions which, although bound by the code, have nevertheless abolished vertical privity in breach of warranty cases." Kassab, 246 A.2d at 856 (emphasis in original). Indiana has not legislated on this issue since 1966 when the UCC adopted these three alternatives. . . . In short, the General Assembly in keeping Alternative A left to this Court the issue of to what extent vertical privity of contract will be required.

Courts that have abolished vertical privity have cited a variety of reasons. Principal among these is the view that, in today's economy, manufactured products typically reach the consuming public through one or more intermediaries. As a result, any loss from an unmerchantable product is likely to be identified only after the product is attempted to be used or consumed. . . . Others have cited the concern that privity encourages thinly capitalized manufacturers by insulating them from responsibility for inferior products. . . . Yet others have focused on the point that if implied warranties are effective against remote sellers it produces a chain of lawsuits or crossclaims against those up the distribution chain. . . . And some focus on the reality in today's world that manufacturers focus on the consumer in communications promoting the product. . . .

Finally, some jurisdictions have abolished privity in warranty actions where only economic losses were sought based on the notion that there is "no reason to distinguish between recovery for personal and property injury, on the one hand, and economic loss on the other." . . . A variance on this theme is the view that abolishing privity "simply recognizes that economic loss is potentially devastating to the buyer of an unmerchantable product and that it is unjust to preclude any recovery from the manufacturer for such loss because of a lack of privity, when the slightest physical injury can give rise to strict liability under the same circumstances." . . . One court preserving the privity requirement expressed the view that "there may be cases where the plaintiff may be unfairly prejudiced by the operation of the economic loss rule in combination with the privity requirement." Ramerth v. Hart, 133 Idaho 194, 983 P.2d 848, 852 (1999).

In Indiana, the economic loss rule applies to bar recovery in tort "where a negligence claim is based upon the failure of a product to perform as expected and the plaintiff suffers only economic damages." Martin Rispens, 621 N.E.2d at 1089. Possibly because of the economic loss rule, Goodin did not raise a negligence claim here. Furthermore, at oral argument Goodin's attorney pointed to the warranty disclaimer in the Buyer's Order as a bar to Goodin's ability to sue her direct seller, AutoChoice, which could then have sued Hyundai for reimbursement. This disclaimer, Goodin contends, precluded a chain of claims ultimately reaching the manufacturer. Therefore, Goodin claims that if this Court does not abolish the vertical privity requirement she will be left without a remedy for Hyundai's breach of its implied warranty of merchantability, and Hyundai's implied warranty becomes nonexistent in practical terms.

The basis for the privity requirement in a contract claim is essentially the idea that the parties to a sale of goods are free to bargain for themselves and thus allocation of risk of failure of a product is best left to the private sector. Otherwise stated, the law should not impose a contract the parties do not wish to make. . . .

Generally privity extends to the parties to the contract of sale. It relates to the bargained for expectations of the buyer and seller. Accordingly, when the cause of action arises out of economic loss related to the loss of the bargain or profits and consequential damages related thereto, the bargained for expectations of buyer and seller are relevant and privity between them is still required.

Implied warranties of merchantability and fitness for a particular use, as they relate to economic loss from the bargain, cannot then ordinarily be sustained between the buyer and a remote manufacturer. . . . We think that this rationale has eroded to the point of invisibility as applied to many types of consumer goods in today's economy. The UCC recognizes an implied warranty of merchantability if "goods" are sold to "consumers" by one who ordinarily deals in this product. Warranties are often explicitly promoted as marketing tools, as was true in this case of the Hyundai warranties. Consumer expectations are framed by these legal developments to the point where technically advanced consumer goods are virtually always sold under express warranties, which, as a matter of federal law run to the consumer without regard to privity. 15 U.S.C. § 2310. Magnuson–Moss precludes a disclaimer of the implied warranty of merchantability as to consumer goods where an express warranty is given. 15 U.S.C. § 2308. Given this framework, we think ordinary consumers are entitled to, and do, expect that a consumer product sold under a warranty is merchantable, at least at the modest level of merchantability set by UCC section 2–314, where hazards common to the type of product do not render the product unfit for normal use. . . .

Even if one party to the contract—the manufacturer—intends to extend an implied warranty only to the immediate purchaser, in a consumer setting, doing away with the privity requirement for a product subject to the Magnuson–Moss Warranty Act, rather than rewriting the deal, simply gives the consumer the contract the consumer expected. The manufacturer, on the other hand is encouraged to build quality into its products. To the extent there is a cost of adding uniform or standard quality in all products, the risk of a lemon is passed to all buyers in the form of pricing and not randomly distributed among those unfortunate enough to have acquired one of the lemons. Moreover, elimination of privity requirement gives consumers such as Goodin the value of their expected bargain, but will rarely do more than duplicate the Products Liability Act as to other consequential damages. The remedy for breach of implied warranty of merchantability is in most cases, including this one, the difference between "the value of the goods accepted and the value they would have had if they had been as warranted." I.C. § 26–1–2–714(2). This gives the buyer the benefit of the bargain. In most cases, however, if any additional damages are available under the UCC as the result of abolishing privity, Indiana law would award the same damages under the Products Liability Act as personal injury or damage to "other property" from a "defective" product. . . .

For the reasons given above we conclude that Indiana law does not require vertical privity between a consumer and a manufacturer as a condition to a claim by the consumer against the manufacturer for breach of the manufacturer's implied warranty of merchantability.

### Conclusion

The judgment of the trial court is affirmed.

NOTES

**(1) Vertical Privity.** Why did the Indiana Supreme Court abolish the requirement of privity in an implied merchantability warranty claim brought by a consumer buyer of goods against a remote manufacturer? The court declared that "warranties are often explicitly promoted as marketing tools, as was true in the case of the Hyundai warranties. Consumer expectations are framed by these legal developments to the point where technically advanced consumer goods are virtually always sold under express warranties which, as a matter of federal law run to the consumer without regard to privity." Is that relevant to an implied warranty of merchantability?

**(2) Manufacturer's Express Quality Obligation.** Buyer claimed breach by Hyundai of an express warranty. The "express warranty" was apparently Hyundai's remedial promise to repair defects in materials and workmanship during specified warranty periods. The court noted that plaintiff's brake problems were covered by Hyundai's 5–year limited warranty and that various attempts to address the problem had been made. The jury found that Hyundai was not in breach of express warranty. Since the problem persisted, what did the verdict signify? What constitutes breach of a manufacturer's repair/replace promise? Does repetitive failure to succeed in making a repair constitute a breach if the manufacturer continues to try to fix the product?

**(3) Manufacturer's Implied Quality Obligation.** The jury found for the buyer on an implied warranty of merchantability claim. The only defense to this claim referred to by the court was lack of privity. (Since Hyundai gave a MMWA warranty, it was precluded from disclaiming the implied warranty.) What did the court mean by the statement that "we think ordinary consumers are entitled to, and do, expect that a consumer product sold under a warranty is merchantable, at least at the modest level of merchantability set by UCC section 2–314 where hazards common to the type of product do not render the product unfit for normal use"? On what date was the implied warranty breached?

**(4) Buyer's Remedies.** The jury verdict in this case awarded the buyer damages and the court awarded attorneys' fees.

*Damages.* The damages were assessed at $3,000.00. The Indiana Supreme Court sustained the award by reference to UCC 2–714(2): the difference between the value of the goods accepted and the value they would have had if they had been as warranted. Section 2–714 is drafted to express buyers' damages for breach in regard to accepted goods. Subsection (1) refers to "the buyer" and "the seller." Those parties in this case were Sandra Goodin and AutoChoice Hyundai. "The seller" was not Hyundai Motor America, Inc. Subsection (2) is a common formula for implementation of subsection (1). Was the court correct to apply UCC 2–714 to the claim against the upstream manufacturer? Does it matter whether the matter is governed by UCC 2–714 or common law? If market values determine the amount of a plaintiff's recovery, the relevant market must be determined. A manufacturer and a consumer function in different market levels. Wholesale market values are considerably lower than retail market values. Is a consumer entitled to the benefit of retail market values in an action against a manufacturer that does not sell in that market? The Indiana court did not indicate whether it was referring to values in the wholesale or retail markets for new automobiles when it upheld the $3,000.00 award.

*Attorneys' fees.* The attorneys' fees awarded were $19,237.50, six times more than the damage award. The award was based on MMWA 110(d)(2). That section allows an award only if the costs were "reasonably incurred." Was it reasonable to incur costs of this amount in light of the damages award?

*Consequential economic losses.* In warranty actions by consumers buyers against remote manufacturers, can damages be recovered for buyers' consequential economic losses? The Indiana court dealt with this question in an interesting dictum referring to the law of product liability, which was codified in Indiana. The only losses covered by this tort are personal injuries and property damage. Consequential damages in commercial law may include other kinds of harm, such as lost profits. How should these be treated in actions against manufacturers for breach of warranty?

SZAJNA v. GENERAL MOTORS CORP., 115 Ill.2d 294, 104 Ill.Dec. 898, 503 N.E.2d 760 (1986). Buyer purchased a 1979 Pontiac Ventura from a retail dealer. The dealer delivered the vehicle together with the LIMITED WARRANTY made by the manufacturer, General Motors (GM). Subsequently, the buyer discovered that the transmission in the Pontiac Ventura was one that GM had designed for a smaller and less expensive automobile, the Chevette. Buyer instituted a law suit against GM on behalf of all buyers of Pontiac Venturas that were equipped with Chevette transmissions. Count 1 of the complaint, relying on UCC 2–314, alleged *inter alia* that these Pontiacs were not merchantable because they would not pass without objection in the trade under the contract description. Count 1 declared that the complaint was brought under MMWA 110(d). The trial court dismissed the complaint on the ground that there was no privity between GM and the buyers.[15] The Supreme Court of Illinois reversed and remanded the case for trial on Count 1. The court declined to abolish the requirement of privity that existed under state law, but the court held that where a manufacturer makes a MMWA "written warranty" to a downstream "consumer," that person should be permitted to maintain an action on an implied warranty of quality against the MMWA "warrantor" in the state courts of Illinois. The court did not discuss whether the use of Chevette transmissions was a breach of an implied warranty of quality, nor whether UCC 2–314 applied to General Motors.[16]

---

**15.** The class action in this case was brought in an Illinois state court under state procedural law. The class action authorized by the MMWA requires that the number of named plaintiffs be at least 100. Efforts by plaintiffs counsel to gather that number of named plaintiffs for a federal MMWA class action have been, in the main, futile. Illinois law, like the law of most states, did not require 100 named plaintiffs for a class action in state court. However, the trial court had not yet certified a class when the complaint was dismissed.

**16.** Count 2 of the complaint alleged that GM was in breach of a UCC 2–313 express warranty The Illinois Supreme Court held that the manufacturer's labeling the car as a Pontiac did not encompass a description of the transmission.

## 2.  COMMERCIAL GOODS

It is now time to consider manufacturers' implied warranties of quality in transactions with downstream commercial buyers. The history from the period before 1960 when individuals were allowed to recover from manufacturers for death of bodily injuries is irrelevant to the claims of commercial buyers' claims for economic losses. The development, after 1975, of readings of the Magnuson–Moss Warranty Act that enable consumer buyers to recover from manufacturers for economic losses is likewise irrelevant. The MMWA does not apply to transactions in commercial goods. Since 1960, and without any help from the MMWA, some state courts have allowed buyers of commercial goods to pursue implied warranty claims against remote manufacturers. The relevant law therefore is either common law or UCC Article 2.

As you consider the cases, it is also useful to contemplate the kinds of transactions in commercial goods that might give rise to implied warranty claims against remote manufacturers. Buyers of commercial goods are, in general, more commercially sophisticated than are ordinary consumers. They bargain for and obtain express warranties on the particular qualities of goods that are most important to them rather than rely on the general criteria of implied warranties. On the other side, manufacturers of commercial goods are likely to disclaim implied warranties or to limit the available remedies. Whether disclaimers and limitations are effective against downstream buyers presents a legal question. It is a fair assumption, however, that the kinds of transactions in which downstream buyers might press implied warranty claims against remote manufacturers will be somewhat unusual.

The courts in *Hyundai Motor v. Goodin* and *Skajna v. General Motors* explicitly limited the decisions relaxing the requirement of vertical privity to claims brought by ordinary consumers. It is a reasonable inference that commercial buyers claims against manufacturers in Indiana and Illinois would remain barred by the vertical privity requirement.

Other states differ from Indiana and Illinois. In some of the states that take a different view, the requirement of vertical privity was abolished by the highest state courts. An example of a case decided in the early years of the Commercial Code is Kassab v. Central Soya, 432 Pa. 217, 246 A.2d 848 (1968). The Pennsylvania Supreme Court determined that the Pennsylvania version of UCC 2–318, Alternative A, was silent on vertical privity and permitted the court to determine the law on this issue. *Kassab* was decided in the early years of judicial recognition of manufacturers' strict tort liability, and the court was influenced by that development in deciding to abolish the requirement of privity in implied warranty cases brought against manufacturers on economic loss claim. Another leading case is Spring Motors Distributors, Inc. v. Ford Motor Co., 98 N.J. 555, 489 A.2d 660 (1985).

Some states have abolished the vertical privity requirement through legislative enactments, often by enacting non-uniform versions of UCC 2–318. The Virginia statute provides:

Lack of privity between plaintiff and defendant shall be no defense in any action brought against the manufacturer or seller of goods to recover damages for breach of warranty, express or implied, or for negligence, although the plaintiff did not purchase the goods from the defendant, if the plaintiff was a person whom the manufacturer or seller might reasonably have expected to use, consume, or be affected by the goods. . . .

The Virginia statute is based in part on Alternative C, but in contrast to the Alternative, refers explicitly to claims against remote manufacturers.[17]

If the privity requirement is relaxed, does the common law or UCC Article 2 govern the substantive issues arising from implied warranty claims? As we learned earlier, with respect to express warranties, most courts tend to apply UCC 2–313 to manufacturers' warranties. The same result is found in implied warranty cases, whether brought by consumer buyers or commercial buyers. The courts in *Morrow, Hyndai Motor* and *Skajna* applied UCC 2–314 to determine the nature of the manufacturers' implied warranty obligation. *Kassab* and *Spring Motors* did so as well. Courts tend to rely on the provision in UCC 2–314(2)(c) that defines merchantable goods as goods that a fit for the ordinary purposes of such goods. If these courts had ruled instead that the governing law was common law rather than Article 2 of the Commercial Code, it is not likely that there would have been different determinations regarding the quality of the goods.

That is not true on legal issues on which the common law and Article 2 of the Code are significantly different. Consider the following case from the Fourth Circuit applying the law of Virginia.

## Beard Plumbing and Heating, Inc. v. Thompson Plastics, Inc.

United States Court of Appeals for the Fourth Circuit, 1998.
152 F.3d 313.

■ ERVIN, CIRCUIT JUDGE:

In this diversity action, Beard Plumbing and Heating, Inc., (Beard), appeals from a grant of summary judgment to Thompson Plastics, Incorporated (Thompson), and NIBCO, Incorporated (NIBCO) on Beard's claims of negligence and breach of warranty. For the reasons which follow, we affirm the decision of the district court.

\* \* \*

### II.

Beard is a Virginia corporation engaged in providing materials and labor related to plumbing and heating. Thompson, an Alabama corporation,

---

**17.** The Virginia statute abolishes vertical privity for claims based on negligence. The law of negligence is not codified in Article 2 of the Commercial Code.

and NIBCO, an Indiana corporation, manufacture postchlorinated polyvinyl chloride (CPVC) plumbing components.

In 1992, Beard, engaged as the plumbing subcontractor in a condominium development in Woodbridge, Virginia, installed CPVC plumbing fittings manufactured by Thompson or NIBCO. Beard purchased these fittings from two third-party suppliers, Thomas Somerville Co., which was originally named as a defendant in the case but later non-suited after Thompson and NIBCO were granted summary judgment, and National Plumbing Store, which was never named as a party. There were no contracts between Beard and either manufacturer. When the fittings cracked and subsequently leaked after hot water was used in the system, the general contractor required Beard to replace the fittings and repair the damage sustained by the homes and then dismissed Beard from the job. The general contractor proceeded to sue Beard, which settled for $165,878.93. In addition to that loss, Beard claims it was denied compensation for performing change orders on the site, was denied compensation for the cost of repairs to the damaged buildings, was denied the remainder of its contract price, incurred legal fees, and lost revenue due to damage to its business reputation. . . .

To recover these losses, Beard filed the instant diversity action on June 8, 1995, alleging both breach of warranty and negligence. Beard contends that the CPVC fittings manufactured by Thompson and NIBCO were defective and that certain adapters failed when they attempted to shrink around thermally-expanded metal fittings during cool-down. On November 1, 1995, NIBCO filed for summary judgment, and Thompson followed on November 7, on the ground that Beard could not recover economic losses in these circumstances. The district court . . . granted both motions for summary judgment on Beard's contract and tort claims. . . . This appeal followed.

### III.

Beard seeks to assert three causes of action: a negligence claim sounding in tort, and two warranty claims sounding in contract, one for breach of the warranty of fitness for a particular purpose under Va. Code § 8.2–315 and the other for breach of the implied warranty of merchantability under Va. Code § 8.2–314. The first two claims are barred by Virginia law in these circumstances and will be dealt with first. The final claim of breach of the implied warranty of merchantability is a more difficult question and will be treated last.

\* \* \*

### B.

Beard's claim for breach of the warranty of fitness for a particular purpose must also fail. Va. Code § 8.2–315 provides:

> Where the seller at the time of contracting has reason to know any particular purpose for which the goods are required and that the buyer is relying on the seller's skill or judgment to select or furnish suitable

goods, there is unless excluded or modified under the next section . . . , an implied warranty that the goods shall be fit for such purpose.

The Supreme Court of Virginia has interpreted this section to require the buyer to prove three elements: (1) the seller had reason to know the particular purpose for which the buyer required the goods, (2) the seller had reason to know the buyer was relying on the seller's skill or judgment to furnish appropriate goods, and (3) the buyer in fact relied upon the seller's skill or judgment. Medcom, Inc. v. C. Arthur Weaver Co., 232 Va. 80, 348 S.E.2d 243, 246 (Va. 1986).

Beard has not satisfied the third element, nor can it. . . . Beard contends that an implied warranty arises because the "suppliers of the resin used in the manufacture of the CPVC fittings published catalogs which expressly warranted that the female and male adapters were intended for, and could be used in, hot and cold water systems." This statement clearly demonstrates that Beard did not rely upon Thompson or NIBCO's skill or judgment but rather upon some representation made by a more remote merchant. Whether that representation can pass through Thompson and NIBCO and hold that remote merchant liable on its warranty (whether express or implied) is not at issue here. Because there was never any communication between Beard and Thompson or NIBCO, there can be no genuine dispute that Beard did not, in fact, rely upon Thompson or NIBCO's skill or judgment in furnishing goods suitable for a particular purpose. Beard's reliance on § 8.2–318's abrogation of the privity requirement is misplaced, for that section only provides that lack of privity shall be no defense in certain circumstances. Before even reaching possible defenses, Beard . . . must prove as an element of its claim that it in fact relied on Thompson and NIBCO's skill or judgment. Because Beard cannot make a sufficient showing on this essential element, its claim must fail. . . . Therefore, summary judgment on this claim was appropriate and the district court's judgment hereon is affirmed.

## C.

Beard's final claim of breach of the implied warranty of merchantability is a much more difficult problem. The district court's ruling did not even address this claim. Moreover, the record before this court does not contain the parties' memoranda concerning the summary judgment motion nor other sufficient evidence to fully determine that there is not a genuine dispute as to a material fact. Thus, the grant of summary judgment on this claim can only be upheld if Beard's claim is barred as a matter of law since this court reviews that grant de novo. . . .

\* \* \*

. . . Thompson and NIBCO claim that because Beard suffered only economic losses it cannot recover under Virginia's Commercial Code, in effect, because of lack of privity. In support of this claim, Thompson and NIBCO argue that the Code's damages provisions in §§ 8.2–714 & –715, even read together with § 8.2–318, which apparently abrogates the privity requirement, will not permit economic losses to be recovered for breach of warranty absent privity. However, Thompson and NIBCO cite no case law in support of their argument because there is none.

Beard, on the other hand, claims that § 8.2–318, by its own terms, clearly abolishes the privity requirement.... Indeed, ... it would be odd if economic losses, which result from the frustration of bargained-for expectations, could not be recovered for breach of warranty, notwithstanding the lack of privity, given the especially broad reach of Virginia's § 8.2–318. ...

Having determined that this issue was undecided under Virginia law and having found no case in any jurisdiction jointly construing UCC provisions § 2–318 and § 2–715 with regards to economic loss, we certified the question to the Supreme Court of Virginia on January 17, 1997.

Our question to that court was phrased as follows:

> Is privity required to recover economic loss under Va. Code § 8.2–715(2) due to the breach of the implied warranty of merchantability, notwithstanding the language of Va. Code § 8.2–318?

On September 12, 1997, the Virginia Supreme Court answered our question in the affirmative, holding in part:

> To answer this question, we must first determine whether § 8.2–715(2) requires the existence of a contract for the recovery of economic loss damages in breach of warranty cases. ...

> This section does not address economic loss damages. However, because the Court of Appeals directed its inquiry specifically to this section, we assume that the Court of Appeals concluded that the economic loss damages claimed by Beard were consequential damages rather than direct damages. We also limit our discussion to subparagraph (a), since injury to persons or property is not involved in this case.

> Section 8.2–715(2)(a) is part of the UCC, a comprehensive statutory scheme affecting commercial transactions. Although the UCC is based on a uniform act now adopted by virtually every state, we found no case interpreting the language of § 8.2–715(2)(a) as it relates to the requirement of a contractual relationship between the parties.

> Nevertheless, the language of the section itself contains a presumption that there is a contract between the parties. The phrase "at the time of the contracting" in subparagraph (a) conveys the understanding of a contract between two parties. To assert, as Beard did at oral argument, that the purpose of the phrase is only to establish the historical moment for judging the seller's foreseeability, does not eliminate the connotation of the existence of a contract inherent in the phrase. Beard's interpretation would require substituting the word "sale" for the word "contracting," and we decline the invitation to rewrite the statute. Therefore, we conclude that § 8.2–715(2)(a) requires a contract between the parties for the recovery of consequential

economic loss damages incurred as a result of a breach of warranty by the seller.

The second part of the certified question asks us to determine whether the provisions of § 8.2–318 supersede the contract requirement of § 8.2–715(2)(a). Section 8.2–318 provides in pertinent part:

> Lack of privity between plaintiff and defendant shall be no defense in any action brought against the manufacturer or seller of goods to recover damages for breach of warranty, express or implied, or for negligence, although the plaintiff did not purchase the goods from the defendant, if the plaintiff was a person whom the manufacturer or seller might reasonably have expected to use, consume, or be affected by the goods[.]

The provisions of this section appear to conflict with § 8.2–715(2)(a) regarding the requirement of a contract for the recovery of consequential damages in a breach of warranty action. Rules of statutory construction, however, resolve the apparent conflict. In construing conflicting statutes, if one section addresses a subject in a general way and the other section speaks to part of the same subject in a more specific manner, the latter prevails. . . . Applying this rule, we conclude that, to the extent the two statutes conflict, § 8.2–715(2)(a) prevails.

The general subject of § 8.2–318 is the ability to raise the common law requirement of privity as a defense. We have not previously construed § 8.2–318; however, we have referred to it as modifying the common law privity rule. . . .

The contract requirement of § 8.2–715(2)(a), however, is not a privity requirement imposed by the common law. Part 7 of Title 8.2 of the UCC imposes a number of limitations and conditions on the recovery of damages in a breach of warranty claim. See, e.g., § 8.2–714 (defining measure of damages), § 715(1) (identifying recoverable incidental damages), and § 719(b)(3) (ability to exclude consequential damages). The contract requirement of § 8.2–715(2)(a) is one of those limitations. Section 8.2–715(2)(a) does not address the general subject of the common law privity requirement's effect on the ability of a litigant to maintain an action for breach of warranty. It is limited to that part of the litigation dealing with the damages which may be recovered and imposes a contract requirement only where recovery of con sequential damages is sought. Applying the rule of statutory construction recited above, the limited contract requirement of § 8.2–715(2)(a) prevails over the general provisions relating to common law privity in § 8.2–318.

Accordingly, because § 8.2–715(2)(a) requires a contract between the parties for recovery of consequential economic loss damages in a claim for breach of the implied warranty of merchantability, we answer the certified question in the affirmative.

Based upon the reasoning of the Virginia Supreme Court, we affirm the grant of summary judgment in favor of Thompson and NIBCO on Beard's claim for breach of implied warranty of merchantability.

### IV.

The judgment of the district court is in all respects affirmed.

### NOTES

(1) **State Law in Federal Courts.** In most diversity cases, federal judges seek to find the relevant state law in decisions of state courts, particularly decisions of the highest state court. Federal civil procedure provides an alternative means for ascertaining state law, certified questions. That procedure was invoked by the Court of Appeals in this case. The federal appellate court submitted questions to the Supreme Court of Virginia and relied on that court's replies. Note that the procedure does not transfer the whole case from federal to state court. The inter-court exchange is limited to the specific questions asked and answered.

(2) **Privity.** The Court of Appeals, before framing its question to the Virginia Supreme Court, concluded that the privity requirement had been clearly abolished by the legislation. The manufacturers could not defend on that ground. Of what value was this holding to the buyer?

(3) **Manufacturer's Obligation.** The opinion states that plaintiff's counsel, in the complaint, claimed that the manufacturer was in breach of the implied warranty of fitness for particular purpose under UCC 2–315 and of the implied warranty of merchantability under UCC 2–314.

The Court of Appeals held against the plaintiff on the UCC 2–315 claim. Was this correct? Could a downstream buyer satisfy any of the elements of UCC 2–315? On these facts, could plaintiff have asserted plausibly that the manufacturer had made and breached an express warranty? Would the result have differed if counsel had based the case on common law warranties of quality?

The Court of Appeals assumed *arguendo* that there was a claim for breach of the implied warranty of merchantability. It did not need to determine whether there was a valid claim under UCC 2–314.

(4) **Remedies; Consequential Damages.** The question certified by the Court of Appeals asked only about the application of UCC 2–715 in claims by downstream buyers against manufacturers. That is section that allows an aggrieved buyer to recover for consequential damages. The expense of having to remove and replace the pipes was Beard's primary injury. The Virginia legislature had adopted the uniform version of UCC 2–715. The Virginia court declared that UCC 2–715 has an implicit requirement of privity that derives from the phrase "at the time of contracting," but the focus of the court's concern was the element of foreseen harm as a condition for allowing recovery of consequential damages under that section of the Code. The Virginia version of UCC 2–318 generally abrogates

the privity requirement, but that section did not speak to the specific issue of consequential damages. Using a principle of statutory interpretation that gives effect to the more specific provision, the Supreme Court stated that a claim for consequential damages resulting from breach of warranty was not permitted in an action by a remote buyer against manufacturers. Was the Virginia Supreme Court's answer a correct interpretation of UCC 2–715? Would plaintiff have a better case under common-law doctrine pertaining to consequential damages?

## SECTION 5.   DOWNSTREAM BUYERS' ACTIONS UNDER LAW OTHER THAN UCC ARTICLE 2

Remote buyers seeking relief from manufacturers are not limited to claims grounded in the law of warranty. Some buyers may have claims arising under tort law, a branch of common law. Some consumer buyers may have claims under non-uniform consumer protection legislation.

*Strict tort liability.* In actions against manufacturers for goods of unsatisfactory quality, counsel for buyers often seek relief on both tort and warranty theories. The principal tort theory on which they rely, strict tort liability, has come to be known as product liability.[1] The law of product liability has aspects that are valuable to some buyers: First, the tort has a substantive standard of manufacturers' conduct. The standard is independent of the terms of any contract. The standard is an implementation of a public policy enunciated by courts as a matter of common law. Second, the law of product liability has no privity requirement. Actions against manufacturers can be brought by individuals who suffered certain kinds of injury, whether those individuals were downstream buyers or mere by-standers.

Product liability is not useful to buyers aggrieved by disappointment in the diminished value of the goods resulting from nonconformity with their sales contracts. Product liability is concerned only with harms done by products that injure or kill persons or damage other property. This body of tort law is not concerned with goods that are qualitatively disappointing. A fundamental precept of tort law is that tort liability does not extend to "economic losses." For a comprehensive history of buyers' efforts to use the theory of product liability to recover damages based upon the expected value of goods purchased, see East River S.S. Corp. v. Transamerica Delaval, Inc., 476 U.S. 858, 106 S.Ct. 2295, 90 L.Ed.2d 865 (1986) (failures of turbines in supertankers not ground for action under strict tort liability).

*Deceptive Acts and Practices Acts.* Many states have enacted laws to protect consumers against deceptive acts and practices.[2] As indicated by the

---

1.  Counsel often add counts in negligence, a claim that can be sustained only if there is evidence of fault on the part of manufacturers.

2.  Although these acts are sometimes referred to as "uniform," they are not a product of the National Conference of Commissioners on Uniform State Laws.

title, the statutes deal with wrongdoing in the marketplace. An action under one of these statutes by the buyer of a new BMW automobile became a case of wide national interest because of the size of the initial award of punitive damages.[3]

Dr. Ira Gore purchased a BMW sports sedan for $40,750 from a dealer in Birmingham, Alabama. Shortly after receiving the car, Dr. Gore discovered that the car had been repainted after manufacture. Dr. Gore sued the United States distributor of BMW automobiles for failure to disclose the repainting in violation of Ala. Code § 6–5–102 (1993). The BMW distributor acknowledged it had a policy concerning cars damaged in the course of manufacture or transportation: where cost of repair was less than 3% of the suggested retail price, repairs were made by the distributor without informing retail dealers and such cars were sold as new. The cost of repainting the car later sold to Dr. Gore had been about 1.5% of suggested retail price and the dealer had not been informed. An Alabama jury returned a verdict for compensatory damages of $4,000 and punitive damages of $4,000,000.

The Alabama Supreme Court affirmed the trial court's judgment but reduced the punitive damages to $2,000,000.[4] The Supreme Court of the United States held that the reduced award was still grossly excessive in light of three guideposts on punitive damages: the degree of reprehensibility of the non-disclosure, the disparity between the harm or potential harm suffered by Dr. Gore and the punitive damages award, and the difference between this punitive damages remedy and civil penalties authorized or imposed pursuant to statutes in comparable cases.[5] On remand, the Alabama Supreme Court awarded Dr. Gore punitive damages in the amount of $50,000.[6]

*"Lemon laws."* A large number of states have enacted "lemon laws" that give special protection, including the right to revoke acceptance, when defects in motor vehicles are not corrected within a reasonable time. While non-uniform in their language, these statutes tend to allow consumers to demand that manufacturers either refund the retail purchase price or replace the car. Commonly a buyer's right to relief matures when the "same defect" continues to exist after four unsuccessful attempts to repair it during a statutory time period or the car was out of service for 30 days during the statutory period. See C. Reitz, Consumer Product Warranties Under Federal and State Laws, ch. 14 (2d ed. 1987).

---

**3.** Section 908(2) of the Restatement, Second, of Torts provides that such damages may be awarded "for conduct that is outrageous, because of the defendant's evil motive or his reckless indifference to the rights of others." In recent years, large punitive damages awards have created concern that there may need to be a limiting principle to define when such awards are excessive.

**4.** BMW of North America v. Gore, 646 So.2d 619 (Ala.1994).

**5.** BMW of North America, Inc. v. Gore, 517 U.S. 559, 116 S.Ct. 1589, 134 L.Ed.2d 809 (1996).

**6.** BMW of North America, Inc. v. Gore, 701 So.2d 507 (Ala.1997).

## SECTION 6.   LEGAL BARS TO RECOVERY

## (A) DOMESTIC UNITED STATES LAW

### 1.   NOTICE

Does the notice-to-seller provision in UCC 2–607(3)(a) bar a buyer/user of goods from recovering damages from an upstream manufacturer for breach of a warranty of quality or breach of a remedial promise if the buyer fails to give prompt notice to the manufacturer? The question could be answered in two ways: First, one could conclude that UCC Article 2 does not govern the relationship between a manufacturer and a downstream buyer because that relationship is not a contract of sale. Common law rather than UCC Article 2 would apply. There is no common-law provision that conditions a party's right to relief on giving of prompt notice. Second, even if UCC Article 2 applies to the relationship between a manufacturer and a downstream buyer, UCC 2–607(3)(a) is not applicable. That section, by its explicit terms, applies to the parties of sales contracts, *the* buyer and *the* seller. It applies when a "tender [of delivery of the goods] has been accepted." Tender of delivery and acceptance are reciprocal steps in the performance of bilateral sales contracts. See UCC 2–503, 2–606. Upstream manufacturers do not tender delivery of goods to downstream buyers, and buyers' acceptances are relevant only with respect to their immediate sellers. Therefore, one could conclude that a downstream buyer's action against a manufacturer cannot be barred by UCC 2–607(3)(a). Alternatively, one could conclude that notice requirement applies notwithstanding the language of UCC 2–607(3)(a).

Often, in litigation where the defense of lack of notice has been raised, buyers elected to sue both their immediate sellers and the remote manufacturers. Counsel for plaintiffs framed the complaints against both defendants under UCC Article 2 and, apparently did not consider the alternative of suit against the immediate seller under the Commercial Code and suit against the manufacturer under common law.

## Cooley v. Big Horn Harvestore Systems, Inc.

Supreme Court of Colorado, 1991.
813 P.2d 736.

■ KIRSHBAUM, J.

\* \* \*

I

In July 1980, plaintiffs Robert Cooley and Rita Cooley executed two agreements with defendant Big Horn Harvestore Systems, Inc. (hereinafter Big Horn), in connection with their purchase of a Harvestore automated grain storage and distribution system for use in their dairy operation. Big Horn is an independent distributor of Harvestore systems pursuant to agreements with defendant A.O. Smith Harvestore Products, Inc. (hereinafter AOSHPI), the manufacturer of the Harvestore system. The Cooleys purchased the Harvestore system to improve the efficiency and productivity of their dairy. . . .

The Harvestore system is designed to enhance the nutritional quality of cattle feed by means of an in-silo fermentation process. An essential feature of the system is its asserted ability to limit oxygen contact with the feed, thus facilitating long-term storage of grain. The Harvestore silo itself is composed of glass-fused-to-steel panels. The silo also features breather bags which expand or contract to equalize the pressure inside and outside the silo no matter how frequently outside temperature patterns might vary. Because the oxygen exchange takes place completely within the breather bags, damaging oxygen contact with the feed is limited. During the two years prior to the sale, Big Horn provided the Cooleys with numerous promotional materials prepared by AOSHPI, including films, videotapes, pamphlets, and a book explaining the Harvestore system.

[The purchase agreement contains the following provisions:

[WARRANTY OF MANUFACTURER AND SELLER

[If within the time limits specified below, any product sold under this purchase order, or any part thereof, shall prove to be defective in material or workmanship upon examination by the Manufacturer, the Manufacturer will supply an identical or substantially similar replacement part f.o.b. the Manufacturer's factory, or the Manufacturer, at its option, will repair or allow credit for such part . . .

[SECOND DISCLAIMER

[NO OTHER WARRANTY, EITHER EXPRESS OR IMPLIED AND INCLUDING A WARRANTY OF MERCHANTABILITY AND FITNESS FOR A PARTICULAR PURPOSE HAS BEEN OR WILL BE MADE BY OR IN BEHALF OF THE MANUFACTURER OR THE SELLER OR BY OPERATION OF LAW WITH RESPECT TO THE EQUIPMENT AND ACCESSORIES OR THEIR INSTALLATION, USE, OPERATION, REPLACEMENT OR REPAIR. NEITHER THE MANUFACTURER NOR THE SELLER SHALL BE LIABLE BY VIRTUE OF THIS WARRANTY, OR OTHERWISE, FOR ANY SPECIAL OR CONSEQUENTIAL LOSS OR DAMAGE (INCLUDING BUT NOT LIMITED TO THOSE RESULTING FROM THE CONDITION OR QUALITY OF ANY CROP OR MATERIAL STORED IN THE STRUCTURE) RESULTING FROM THE USE OR LOSS OF THE USE OF EQUIPMENT AND ACCESSORIES. THE MANUFACTURER MAKES NO WARRANTY WITH RESPECT TO THE ERECTION OR INSTAL-

LATION OF THE EQUIPMENT, ACCESSORIES, OR RELATED EQUIPMENT BY THE HARVESTORE DEALER, WHO IS AN INDEPENDENT CONTRACTOR, OR ANY OTHER INDEPENDENT CONTRACTOR. IRRESPECTIVE OF ANY STATUTE, THE BUYER RECOGNIZES THAT THE EXPRESS WARRANTY SET FORTH ABOVE, IS THE EXCLUSIVE REMEDY TO WHICH HE IS ENTITLED AND HE WAIVES ALL OTHER REMEDIES, STATUTORY OR OTHERWISE.]

In early 1981, the Cooleys began to feed their herd with grain stored in the Harvestore system. Shortly thereafter, the health of the herd began to deteriorate and milk production substantially declined. The Cooleys informed Big Horn of these developments, and over the succeeding eighteen months Big Horn representatives made repairs to the structure, gave advice to the Cooleys concerning feed ratios, and assured the Cooleys that the system was functioning properly.

The health of the cows continued to deteriorate. Some died, and the Cooleys ultimately sold the remainder of the herd in 1983. The plaintiffs then filed this action against Big Horn and AOSHPI seeking damages based on claims of breach of implied warranties of merchantability and fitness for a particular purpose, breach of express warranties, breach of contract because of the failure of essential purpose of a limited remedy of suit for breach of warranty to repair or replace any defective part thereof (hereinafter referred to as the "failure of essential purpose" claim), negligence, deceit, and revocation of acceptance.

Prior to the commencement of trial, the trial court entered summary judgment in favor of the defendants and against the plaintiffs on all claims of breach of implied warranties and breach of express warranties. The claims alleging revocation of acceptance and deceit were also dismissed by the trial court. The jury was instructed solely on the claim against AOSHPI and Big Horn for failure of essential purpose of the warranty and on a claim against Big Horn for negligence in recommending improper nutritional programs.

The jury returned a verdict in favor of the plaintiffs and against Big Horn on the negligence claim in the total amount of $87,723.77. The jury also returned a verdict in favor of the plaintiffs and against both Big Horn and AOSHPI in the amount of $245,077.26 on the failure of essential purpose claim. In special verdict forms, the jury assigned seventy-five percent liability to Big Horn and twenty-five percent liability to AOSHPI on the failure of essential purpose claim. ... The trial court also determined that the award of damages returned by the jury on the negligence claim duplicated a portion of the award of damages returned on the failure of essential purpose claim. The trial court ultimately entered judgment for the plaintiffs and against Big Horn and AOSHPI in the amount of $245,077.26.

On appeal, the Court of Appeals affirmed the negligence verdict against Big Horn but reversed the failure of essential purpose verdict against AOSHPI and Big Horn. The court held that the plaintiffs were barred from asserting their failure of essential purpose claim because AOSHPI was entitled to receive timely notice of the claim pursuant to section 4–2–607(3)(a), 2 C.R.S. (1973), of the Colorado Commercial Code (hereinafter the Code) and the plaintiffs did not give such notice to AOSHPI. The court reversed the failure of essential purpose verdict against Big Horn on the ground that the purchase agreement limited Big Horn's responsibility to proper installation of the Harvestore system and the evidence did not establish any failure of installation. Observing that it could not determine what factors were considered by the jury in its calculations of damages on the negligence claim, and determining that the plaintiffs were entitled to recover damages for economic loss on their negligence claim, the Court of Appeals remanded the case for a new trial on the issue of the amount of damages attributable to Big Horn's negligence.

We granted the plaintiffs' petition for certiorari and the defendants' cross-petitions for certiorari to consider the following issues: whether section 4–2–607(3)(a), 2 C.R.S. (1973), requires notice to a remote manufacturer as a condition precedent to the initiation of a breach of contract claim based on the failure of essential purpose doctrine; whether evidence of specific defects in material or workmanship is essential to a failure of essential purpose claim; whether a contractual disclaimer of consequential damages is rendered invalid by the establishment of a failure of essential purpose claim; whether an exculpatory clause was sufficient to disclaim negligence in providing nutritional advice; whether the record contains sufficient evidence to establish the plaintiffs' claim of negligent nutritional advice; and whether the case should be remanded for retrial on the issue of damages.

## II

The Court of Appeals held that a commercial buyer seeking recovery from a manufacturer for a breach of contract claim resulting in property damage alone must, pursuant to the provisions of section 4–2–607(3)(a), 2 C.R.S. (1973), give the manufacturer timely notice of the claimed breach as a condition precedent to any recovery. The plaintiffs contend that they complied with the notice provisions of the statute by giving timely notice of their failure of essential purpose claim to Big Horn. We agree with the plaintiffs' contention.

Section 4–2–607(3)(a), 2 C.R.S. (1973), provides that "where a tender has been accepted: (a) the buyer must within a reasonable time after he discovers or should have discovered any breach, notify the seller of breach or be barred from any remedy...." This provision serves as a condition precedent to a buyer's right to recover for breach of contract under the statute. Palmer v. A.H. Robins Co., 684 P.2d 187, 206 (Colo. 1984). The question of what constitutes a reasonable time is dependent on the circumstances of each case. White v. Mississippi Order Buyers, Inc., 648 P.2d 682 (Colo. App. 1982). The parties agree that the plaintiffs gave timely notice to Big Horn of their claim but did not directly notify AOSHPI of such claim.

The notice provision of section 4–2–607(3)(a) serves three primary purposes. It provides the seller with an opportunity to correct defects, gives the seller time to undertake negotiations and prepare for litigation, and protects the seller from the difficulties of attempting to defend stale claims. Palmer v. A.H. Robins Co.; Prutch v. Ford Motor Co., 618 P.2d 657 (Colo. 1980). See generally White and Summers, Uniform Commercial Code § 11–10 at 481 (3d ed. 1980). The Code defines 'seller' as "a person who sells or contracts to sell goods." § 4–2–103(1)(d), 2 C.R.S. (1973). The official comment to the Code states in pertinent part that "the rule of requiring notification is designed to defeat commercial bad faith, not to deprive a good faith consumer of his remedy." § 4–2–607, 2 C.R.S. comment 4 (1973).

In Palmer v. A.H. Robins Co., 684 P.2d 187, this court construed the statute's notice provision in the context of a product liability action. In Palmer, a consumer injured through use of a defective intrauterine device sought recovery for damages against the manufacturer of the product, A.H. Robins Co. Although the plaintiff, prior to initiating litigation, notified the immediate seller, her doctor, of the fact that she allegedly sustained injuries as a result of defects in the product, she did not so notify Robins. Robins argued that the plaintiff's claims against it should be dismissed for failure to comply with section 4–2–607(3)(a).

We rejected that argument. We construed the term "seller" as used in section 4–2–607(3)(a) to "refer only to the immediate seller who tendered the goods to the buyer." Palmer at 206. We explained that "under this construction, as long as the buyer has given notice of the defect to his or her immediate seller, no further notification to those distributors beyond the immediate seller is required." Id. We also observed that a relaxed notification requirement was especially appropriate in Palmer because the plaintiff was a lay consumer who "would not ordinarily know of the notice requirement." Id. at 207 n.3.

The Court of Appeals concluded that the plaintiffs here were commercial purchasers who suffered only economic loss, as distinguished from the lay consumer who sought relief in Palmer. Assuming, arguendo, that the plaintiffs here were commercial purchasers, it must be observed that our decision in Palmer required construction of a statute adopted by the General Assembly for application in all commercial contexts. The language of section 4–2–607(3)(a) is unambiguous: it requires a buyer to give notice of a defective product only to the "seller." See 2 Anderson, Uniform Commercial Code § 2.607:24. The General Assembly has not elected to require advance notice to a manufacturer of litigation for breach of the manufacturer's warranty of a product, and we find no compelling reason to create such a condition precedent judicially in the context of commercial litigation. The filing of a lawsuit is sufficient notice to encourage settlement of claims, and applicable statutes of limitation protect manufacturers from the difficulties of defending against stale claims. . . .

Several courts considering whether a purchaser seeking recovery under a manufacturer's warranty must give notice to the manufacturer as well as to the seller of the product under statutory provisions similar to section 4–

2–607(3)(a) have reached a similar result. . . . Some courts have reached contrary results. . . . Many such courts have recognized that in most nationwide product distribution systems, the seller/representative dealer may be presumed to actually inform the manufacturer of any major product defects. . . . This presumption forms the basis of the principle that a remote manufacturer may raise as its own defense the buyer's failure to give timely notice to the immediate seller. . . . In view of the unambiguous language of section 4–2–607(3)(a), we conclude that a purchaser injured by a product is not required to give notice of such injury to a remote manufacturer prior to initiating litigation against such manufacturer.

AOSHPI urges us to adopt the rationale expressed in Carson v. Chevron Chemical Co., 6 Kan. App. 2d 776, 635 P.2d 1248 (1981). In that case three farmers brought suit against a herbicide manufacturer and dealer to recover damages for breach of warranties. Observing that in ordinary buyer-seller relationships the Kansas Commercial Code equivalent of section 4–2–607(3)(a) requires that notice of an alleged breach need only be given to the buyer's immediate seller, Carson at 1256, the Kansas Court of Appeals concluded that the plaintiffs were required to notify the manufacturer under the particular circumstances of that case. The court explained its holding as follows:

> In those instances, however, where the buyer and the other parties to the manufacture, distribution and sale of the product are closely related, or where the other parties actively participate in the consummation of the actual sale of the product, the reasons for the exclusion of such other parties from the K.S.A. 84–2–607(3)(a) notice provision cease to exist.

Id.

In our view, the rationale of Carson supports the result we reach. The Kansas Court of Appeals emphasized that under the circumstances disclosed by the evidence the defendant was in effect a direct seller to the plaintiffs. Here, AOSHPI, the manufacturer, was isolated and insulated from the plaintiffs. The contract specified that Big Horn was the seller. AOSHPI, if a seller, was a seller to Big Horn, not to the plaintiffs. As far as the plaintiffs were concerned, the only direct relationship established by the contract and by the conduct of the parties was their relationship with Big Horn. Under these circumstances, to require the plaintiffs to give statutory notice to AOSHPI when not specifically required to do so by statute would unreasonably promote commercial bad faith and inequitably deprive good faith consumers of a remedy, contrary to the purpose of the statute. We reject such a construction.

### III

AOSHPI contends that to recover on their failure of essential purpose claim, the plaintiffs were required to establish the existence of some specific defect in materials or workmanship, which they failed to do. AOSHPI alternatively asserts that the purchase contract itself prohibits recovery of consequential damages by the plaintiffs. We disagree with these arguments.

### A

Section 4–2–719, 2 C.R.S. (1973), contains the following pertinent provisions respecting the abilities of contracting parties to limit the remedies which are available to a purchaser in the event a seller breaches an agreement: . . . These provisions allow great flexibility in negotiations for the provision of goods. Section 4–2–719(2), however, reflects a legislative determination that in limited circumstances enforcement of an agreement to restrict a buyer's potential remedies would produce unconscionable results. See generally, Eddy, On the Essential Purpose of Limited Remedies: The Metaphysics of UCC Section 2–719(2), 65 Calif. L. Rev. 28 (1977).

The plaintiffs' failure of essential purpose claim is premised on the language of section 4–2–719(2). The plaintiffs acknowledge that the purchase agreement contains an express warranty of repair or replacement and a disclaimer clause limiting their remedy to a suit for breach of that warranty. They argued at trial that because this remedy failed of its essential purpose, the language of the agreement purporting to limit their available remedies was not enforceable. The failure of essential purpose claim was tried on this theory, and the jury instructions stated that to return a verdict for the plaintiffs against AOSHPI, the jury must first determine that the plaintiffs had established the necessary factual predicate for application of the failure of essential purpose doctrine. . . .

AOSHPI initially asserts that there was insufficient evidence for the jury to find a failure of essential purpose because there was no evidence of any specific defect in material or workmanship and because AOSHPI was not given an opportunity to repair or replace such defect.

The policy behind the statutory provision establishing the failure of essential purpose doctrine is discussed in the official comments to the Code, as follows:

> It is of the very essence of a sales contract that at least minimum adequate remedies be available. If the parties intend to conclude a contract for sale within this Article they must accept the legal consequence that there be at least a fair quantum of remedy for breach of the obligations or duties outlined in the contract. . . . Under subsection (2), where an apparently fair and reasonable clause because of circumstances fails in its purpose or operates to deprive either party of the substantial value of the bargain, it must give way to the general remedy provisions of this Article.

§ 4–2–719, 2 C.R.S. comment 1 (1973). The comment makes clear that determination of the applicability of the failure of essential purpose doctrine requires a two-tiered evaluation: first, identification of the essential purpose of the limited remedy, and second, whether the remedy in fact failed to accomplish such purpose. Milgard Tempering, Inc. v. Selas Corp., 902 F.2d 703 (9th Cir. 1990); Chatlos Systems, Inc. v. National Cash

Register Corp., 635 F.2d 1081 (3d Cir. 1980). From a buyer's standpoint, a promise to repair or replace defective parts supplies assurance that within a reasonable period of time defective goods will be put into the condition they were warranted to be in at the time they were purchased. Milgard; Chatlos; Clark v. International Harvester Co., 99 Idaho 326, 581 P.2d 784 (1978); Beal v. General Motors Corp., 354 F. Supp. 423 (D. Del. 1973). See C. Smith & B. Clark, The Law of Product Warranties, 8.04[2] at 8–52 (1984). The plaintiffs introduced sufficient evidence to establish that the Harvestore system was never functional, thus permitting the jury to conclude that the limited remedy of a suit for breach of the warranty to repair or replace failed of its essential purpose.

AOSHPI suggests that its warranty protecting against a defect in material and workmanship is limited solely to protection against flaws resulting from the manufacturing process and did not encompass general product design defects. From this premise, AOSHPI concludes that lack of evidence of some specific defect in some specific manufactured part is fatal to the failure of essential purpose claim. This view of the transaction is not supported by the evidence.

The product advertised, purchased, and warranted was a functioning system for storage and distribution of grain. The Cooleys purchased this system. They did not purchase a combination of component parts. . . . A remedy fails of its essential purpose if it operates to deprive a party of the substantial value of the contract. § 4-2-719(2), 2 C.R.S. comment 1 (1973). Fair application of warranty principles require a determination of what the seller has agreed to sell and what the buyer has agreed to pay for. See § 4-2-313, 2 C.R.S. comment 4 (1973). . . . The Cooleys' purchase had value only to the extent the Harvestore system functioned, as advertised, as an entire unit to increase the productivity of their dairy herd. Additionally, AOSHPI's warranty promised repair or replacement of any defective product or part thereof. The evidence established that the product was defective and was not repaired or replaced with a non-defective product. In these circumstances, the Cooleys were entitled to argue to the jury that the limited remedy of repair or replacement failed to guarantee them the value of the system they purchased. . . . The record clearly supports the jury's conclusion that the system as a whole was defective.

AOSHPI's argument that it was not given an opportunity to repair or replace the Harvestore system is not persuasive. The purchase agreement does not specify the means by which the Cooleys were to provide AOSHPI with the opportunity to repair or replace defects. The agreement does provide that "no product or part shall be returned to the Seller without written authorization and shipping instructions first having been obtained from the Seller." This provision in essence directs the Cooleys to address any questions concerning the Harvestore system to Big Horn. The evidence fully supports the conclusion that, as the Cooleys alleged, the agreement was intended to assure the Cooleys that Big Horn would assume any role assigned by the purchase agreements to AOSHPI to repair defects in the system; to determine what parts, if any, to replace; and to inform the

Cooleys how the provisions of the remedy to repair or replace were to be effectuated.

B

AOSHPI also argues that the purchase agreement prohibits the plaintiffs from recovering any consequential damages on their failure of essential purpose claim. We disagree.

The jury returned a verdict in the amount of $245,077.26, against AOSHPI and Big Horn on the plaintiffs' failure of essential purpose claim, which sum included consequential damages for injuries to the plaintiffs' herds and for loss of milk profits. The verdict form did not require the jury to itemize its damage award. However, the evidence with regard to damages was presented in three distinct categories, as follows: the value of the Harvestore system ($88,636.00), damage to the dairy herds ($87,723.77), and loss of milk profits ($68,717.49).

The purchase agreement contains the following pertinent provision:

NEITHER THE MANUFACTURER NOR THE SELLER SHALL BE LIABLE BY VIRTUE OF THIS WARRANTY, OR OTHERWISE, FOR ANY SPECIAL OR CONSEQUENTIAL LOSS OR DAMAGE (INCLUDING BUT NOT LIMITED TO THOSE RESULTING FROM THE CONDITION OR QUALITY OF ANY CROP OR MATERIAL STORED IN THE STRUCTURE) RESULTING FROM THE USE OR LOSS OF THE USE OF EQUIPMENT AND ACCESSORIES.

The trial court concluded that this provision did not bar the plaintiff from recovering consequential damages in view of the language of section 4–2–719(2), 2 C.R.S. (1973). AOSHPI argues that section 4–2–719(3), 2 C.R.S. (1973), which permits buyers to waive their rights to recover consequential damages, controls. We agree with the trial court.

We have determined that the evidence supports the jury's verdict that the limited remedy of replacement or repair of defective parts failed of its essential purpose. Section 4–2–719(2) states that when a seller is found liable to a buyer on the basis of the failure of essential purpose doctrine, "remedy may be had as provided in this title." Section 4–2–714(3) of the Code expressly provides that a purchaser may recover consequential damages resulting from a seller's breach of contract. Thus the Code clearly establishes consequential damages as a remedy available to buyers of goods.

Section 4–2–719(3) of the Code states as follows:

Consequential damages may be limited or excluded unless the limitation or exclusion is unconscionable. Limitation of consequential damages for injury to the person in the case of consumer goods is prima facie unconscionable, but limitation of damages where the loss is commercial is not.

§ 4–2–719(3), 2 C.R.S. (1973). AOSHPI argues that section 4–2–719(3) establishes the right of contracting parties to limit the general availability of consequential damages established by section 4–2–714 and that the Cooleys did so limit their rights here.

Courts that have considered the relationship of these two provisions as they appear in other state commercial codes have reached divergent results. Many courts have concluded that the broad sweep of the literal language of provisions identical to section 4–2–719(2) represents a legislative decision to permit a buyer who suffers loss because of the failure of essential purpose of a limited remedy of repair or replacement to recover all damages resulting from such failure. See, e.g., Milgard, Tempering Inc. v. Selas Corp., 902 F.2d 703 (9th Cir. 1990) (applying Washington law); Fiorito Bros. v. Fruehauf Corp., 747 F.2d 1309 (9th Cir. 1984); Soo Line R.R. v. Fruehauf Corp., 547 F.2d 1365 (8th Cir. 1977); Beal v. General Motors Corp., 354 F. Supp. 423 (D. Del. 1973); Jones & McKnight Corp. v. Birdsboro Corp., 320 F. Supp. 39 (N.D. Ill. 1970); Clark v. International Harvester Co., 99 Idaho 326, 581 P.2d 784 (1978). . . .

It has been observed that the decision of contracting parties to limit potential remedies to the single remedy to repair or replace defective parts is based on a number of assumptions which, if unfounded, fundamentally change the parties' intended allocation of risk. Clark v. International Harvester Co., 99 Idaho 326, 581 P.2d 784 (1978). These include the assumptions that the seller will diligently and in good faith attempt to repair, that the seller will be able to effect repairs within a reasonable time period, and that any consequential loss sustained during the period of repair will be minimal. Waters v. Massey–Ferguson, Inc., 775 F.2d 587 (4th Cir. 1985); S. M. Wilson & Co. v. Smith International, 587 F.2d 1363 (9th Cir. 1978); AES Technology Sys., Inc. v. Coherent Radiation, 583 F.2d 933 (7th Cir. 1978). See generally, Eddy, On the Essential Purpose of Limited Remedies: The Metaphysics of UCC Section 2–719(2), 65 Calif. L. Rev. 28 (1977). Under the rationale of these cases, a loss that is itself caused by the failure of the remedy of suit for breach of a warranty to repair or replace defective parts could not be within the contemplation of the parties, and therefore should not be prohibited when such bargained-for remedy fails of its essential purpose. A buyer reasonably expecting to avoid significant consequential loss through the effective use of such remedy should not be required to absorb such loss when the remedy fails of its essential purpose. See Waters v. Massey–Ferguson, Inc., 775 F.2d 587, 591–92 (4th Cir. 1985); Kearney & Trecker v. Master Engraving, 107 N.J. 584, 527 A.2d 429 (1987).

A few courts have determined that the adequacy of the buyer's remedy in the absence of the ability to recover consequential damages should govern the applicability of the two provisions. Kelynack v. Yamaha Motor Corp., U.S.A., 152 Mich. App. 105, 394 N.W.2d 17 (1986) (where the bulk of the damages were consequential, remedy without consequential damages was no remedy at all); see also Earl M. Jorgensen Co. v. Mark Constr. Inc., 56 Haw. 466, 540 P.2d 978 (1975); Oldham's Farm Sausage Co. v. Salco, Inc., 633 S.W.2d 177 (Mo. App. 1982). These courts give great weight to language in their statutes that mirrors the language of section 4–2–719 of the Code. This approach requires determination on a case-by-case basis of whether a particular limitation is conscionable under all applicable circumstances.

Finally, some courts, emphasizing language of commercial code provisions adopted in their jurisdictions that parallel the language of section 4–2–719(3), have concluded that the two sections constitute distinct clauses applicable to different circumstances. Under this view, section 4–2–719(3) is a particular provision modifying the availability of consequential damages established generally by section 4–2–714(3). See Kaplan v. RCA Corp., 783 F.2d 463, 467 (4th Cir. 1986); Lewis Refrigeration Co. v. Sawyer Fruit, Vegetable and Cold Storage Co., 709 F.2d 427, 434–35 (6th Cir. 1983); Chatlos Systems, Inc. v. National Cash Register Corp., 635 F.2d 1081, 1086 (3d Cir. 1980); S.M. Wilson & Co. v. Smith Int'l, Inc., 587 F.2d 1363, 1375 (9th Cir. 1978); Johnson v. John Deere Co., 306 N.W.2d 231, 238 (S.D. 1981); Envirotech Corp. v. Halco Eng'r, Inc., 234 Va. 583, 364 S.E.2d 215, 220 (1988). See also J. White & R. Summers, Uniform Commercial Code § 12–10 (3d ed. 1980); B. Clark & C. Smith, The Law of Product Warranties § 8.04[2][c] (1984 & 1990 Supp.). This approach suggests that the failure of essential purposes doctrine articulated in section 4–2–719(2) requires application of a substantial value of the bargain standard, while the question of the viability of a contractual waiver of the availability of the remedy of consequential damages contained in section 4–2–719(3) is measured by a conscionability standard. Thus, a remedy may fail in its essential purpose because it deprives a party of the substantial value of a bargained-for benefit, but a clearly expressed exclusion of consequential damages as a remedy available to such party in that circumstance is enforceable if not unconscionable.

In construing statutory provisions, we must give effect to the language and intent of the General Assembly and seek to harmonize apparently contrasting provisions. ... The Code itself provides some guidance in resolving the issue here presented. It is designed to enhance freedom of contract and innovation in commercial practices while establishing good faith, diligence and reasonableness as limits upon such freedom of contract. § 4–1–102, 2 C.R.S. (1973). It also provides that the remedies provided thereunder are to be liberally administered to further those ends. § 4–1–106, 2 C.R.S. (1973). In view of these guidelines, we find persuasive those authorities which suggest that the two subsections in question must be construed together to effectuate their purposes.

In adopting section 4–2–719(2), the General Assembly recognized that while contracting parties may generally limit the remedies available in the event of foreseeable and bargained-for contingencies, when a limited remedy fails of its essential purpose any contractual limitation directly related to the assumption that the limited remedy constituted a sufficient remedy must also fail. In effect, this provision protects contracting parties from unforeseen and unbargained-for contingencies. In adopting section 4–2–719(3), the General Assembly recognized that in most situations contracting parties may agree to limit or exclude the availability of the remedy of consequential damages, subject to a conscionability standard. Neither section grants absolute rights to contracting parties.

It is neither possible nor desirable to suggest absolute guidelines for the reconciliation of these two provisions in all cases. In this case, however, the applicability of the statutory scheme is not difficult. The purchase agreement purports to exclude all warranties other than the promise to repair or replace defective parts while simultaneously excluding all remedies for the recovery of economic loss sustained as a breach of that limited warranty. The language excluding consequential damages and the language limiting remedies appears in the same sentence of the purchase agreement. That sentence commences with the following phrase: "Neither the manufacturer nor the seller shall be liable by virtue of this warranty, or otherwise, for any special or consequential loss or damage...."

In construing the terms of a contract, courts must give full effect to the intent of the parties as expressed by the language of the agreement. In re May v. United States, 756 P.2d 362 (Colo. 1988). The above-quoted sentence of the purchase agreement refers to the exclusion of the remedy of consequential damages resulting from liability "by virtue of this warranty, or otherwise." The remedy of suit for breach of warranty having failed in its essential purpose, the plaintiffs' remedy of consequential damages here does not arise by virtue of that warranty. The phrase "or otherwise" does not, in our view, evidence an intent to render consequential damages unavailable when the only remedy provided by the purchase agreement fails of its essential purpose and therefore is no remedy at all.

While in other circumstances parties may, pursuant to section 4–2–719(3), by clear and unambiguous language, unequivocally state in a separate provision that the remedy of consequential damages shall not be available in the event the remedy of a suit for breach of a limited warranty to repair or replace fails of its essential purpose, no such intent may be gleaned from the language of this purchase agreement. To the extent the parties here agreed to limit the availability of consequential damages as a remedy, they did so on the assumption that the limited warranty to repair or replace would suffice to protect the plaintiffs from substantial consequential damage losses. The total inadequacy of that warranty was neither foreseen nor bargained for. ...

When a purchase agreement establishing that the only warranty provided is a warranty to repair or replace defective parts contains no separate provision unambiguously recording the intent of parties to prohibit a buyer's recovery of consequential damages even when such sole remedy fails of its essential purpose, the buyer is entitled by virtue of section 4–2–719(2) to the statutory remedy of consequential damages notwithstanding a general contractual disclaimer to the contrary. The purchase agreement here contains no such provision; thus the trial court properly concluded that the plaintiffs were not foreclosed from recovering consequential damages.

\* \* \*

## VI

For the foregoing reasons, we reverse those portions of the judgment of the Court of Appeals vacating the trial court judgment entered in favor of the plaintiffs on their failure of essential purpose claim against AOSHPI. The judgment of the Court of Appeals is otherwise affirmed, and the case is remanded to that court with directions to reinstate the judgment entered by the trial court in favor of the plaintiffs and against AOSHPI on the failure of essential purpose claim and in favor of the plaintiffs and against Big Horn on the negligence claim.

## NOTES

(1) **Contract Architecture.** An unusual nature of this transaction was that the product sold by the manufacturer to the dealer was a set of components which the dealer sold to the plaintiff under a contract that required the dealer to assemble the components into the final product. The upstream and downstream contracts were not for the same thing.[1] One consequence was the manner of communicating the manufacturer's obligation to the end user, which was to authorize the dealer to include the manufacturer's obligation and its disclaimers in the retail contract. Note that the manufacturer did not warrant affirmatively that the goods were free of defect in materials and workmanship. Existence of such a defect was an expressed condition on the obligation to repair or replace. The manufacturer did not specify how or by whom the remedial promise would be performed.(Since the silo was not a consumer product, the manufacturer was not precluded by the Magnuson–Moss Warranty Act from disclaiming implied warranties, and the manufacturer did so.)

If you were counseling the manufacturer is transactions like this, how would you advise structuring the transaction?

(2) **Contract Breach.** Plaintiff's complaint alleged many causes of action against the dealer and the manufacturer, but the only claim against the manufacturer that was submitted to the jury was described by the court as "breach of contract because of failure of essential purpose of a limited remedy." What was the "breach of contract"? Did the manufacturer fail or refuse to "supply an identical or substantially similar replacement part"?

The court's opinion stated: "The product advertised, purchased, and warranted was a functioning system for storage and distribution of grain. The Cooleys purchased this system. They did not purchase a combination of component parts." The court was referring in this passage only to the manufacturer, not to the dealer. Was the court's characterization an accurate account of the manufacturer's obligation? Does it conform to the

---

**1.** It is conceivable that the assembled and installed silo would be so affixed to real estate as not to be "goods" as defined in UCC 2–105(1). This issue was not discussed by the court. This may explain, in part, why the principal claim against the dealer was framed in terms of negligence.

fact that the trial court dismissed all claims of breach of express warranty and implied warranty of quality by the manufacturer?

The quoted language is found in a section of the opinion responding to an argument by manufacturer's counsel that the plaintiff had not introduced evidence of a defect in materials or workmanship. If you had been representing the manufacturer, would you have made that argument?

The court determined that the manufacturer had authorized the dealer to perform the manufacturer's remedial promise or to be the manufacturer's representative in having that done. In support of this conclusion, the court quoted a provision in the retail sales contract regarding how the buyer might return materials to the dealer. Is there any indication that the quoted language was made by or authorized by the manufacturer or that it refers to the manufacturer's remedial promise?

This segment of the court's opinion responded to the manufacturer's argument that it was never given the opportunity to perform its remedial promise. In essence, this was an argument that the manufacturer was not in breach of its contract obligation to the plaintiff. Was this a credible argument?

**(3) Notice of Breach to the Manufacturer.** The court took up the notice issue before it considered the nature of the manufacturer's breach. (This may have reflected the order of issues presented in the manufacturer's brief.) Would the analysis of UCC 2–607(3)(a) have changed if the issues had been addressed in a different order? There is no indication that plaintiff's counsel argued that the manufacturer's obligation arose outside UCC Article 2 and that there is no common-law notice requirement.

**(4) Benefit-of-the-Bargain Damages.** In general contract law and under the Commercial Code, the primary remedy for breach of contract is to put the aggrieved party in the position it would have been in if the promise had been performed. See UCC 1–305(a), 2–714(1) and (2). If the manufacturer was in breach of a repair/replace promise a silo, how would such monetary damages be determined? If the manufacturer was in breach of an obligation to provide the plaintiff with a functioning system for storage and distribution of grain, how would such monetary damages be determined? Does it matter how one characterizes the manufacturer's obligation? What is the relevance of UCC 2–719(2) to this question?

**(5) Consequential Damages.** A major part of plaintiff's claim was for consequential losses. Standing in the way of recovery was the no-liability clause in the purchase agreement. Plaintiff relied on UCC 2–719(3) to overcome this impediment. Many of the cases cited by the court in support of this position arose from disputes between buyers and sellers within two-party sales contracts, which we considered in Chapter 4. Was that analysis pertinent in a claim for consequential damages against an upstream manufacturer?[2]

---

2. Courts are more likely to hold that notice to manufacturers is not required where the claim is for personal injuries. E.g., Connick v. Suzuki Motor Co., 174 Ill.2d 482, 221 Ill.Dec. 389, 675 N.E.2d 584 (1996).

# U.S. Tire–Tech, Inc. v. Boeran, B.V.

Court of Appeals of Texas, First District, Houston, 2003.
110 S.W.3d 194.

■ RADACK, J.

A jury awarded Boeran damages and attorneys' fees in its suit against U.S. Tire–Tech, Inc. . . . Tire–Tech, in four issues, contends that the trial court erred when it rendered judgment on a Texas Deceptive Trade Practices–Consumer Protection Act (DTPA) breach of express warranty claim and awarded damages. . . . .

## Background

Tire–Tech manufactures a tire-liner product that is designed to seal punctures in tires. Jerry Vickery, doing business as Marketing Ventures, Inc. (MVI), marketed Tire–Tech's product under the label name "Tire Seal." Boeran, a Dutch corporation, initially purchased a sample of Tire Seal from MVI. After Boeran tested the sample and was satisfied with it, Boeran became a wholesale distributor for MVI in the Netherlands and purchased a large, commercial quantity of Tire Seal in June or July of 1994. Boeran did not have any contact with Tire–Tech during this transaction and assumed MVI was the manufacturer of Tire Seal.

A few months later, Boeran began receiving complaints from its customers about the performance of Tire Seal. The product was separating into liquid and solid parts in its container and was causing tires to become unbalanced after it was applied. In 1995, Boeran began informing MVI through faxes and letters that it was experiencing problems with Tire Seal. MVI later informed Tire–Tech by fax that there was a problem with the product in the Netherlands, but did not identify Boeran as the customer. There was no direct contact between Boeran and Tire–Tech until this lawsuit was initiated.

When Boeran requested its money back, MVI replied that Boeran was contractually limited to replacement of the product. Boeran refused to accept that remedy. Boeran sued Tire–Tech and MVI under numerous theories of recovery. The jury charge contained questions on breach of implied warranty, breach of express warranty, DTPA violations, and revocation of acceptance. A jury found that both Tire–Tech and MVI had breached an implied warranty of merchantability and an express warranty. MVI was found liable under other theories as well, but MVI did not appeal. The jury awarded Boeran $64,946.28 in damages and $45,996.00 in attorneys' fees. The court then rendered judgment against Tire–Tech and MVI, jointly and severally, for the full amount of damages and attorneys' fees found by the jury.

## TIRE–TECH'S APPEAL

However, while the court rendered judgment against MVI under all theories of recovery found by the jury, the judgment stated that Tire–Tech was liable under the DTPA only for breach of an *express* warranty, not for breach of an implied warranty as also found by the jury. Tire–Tech filed a post-judgment motion requesting modification of the judgment or, in the alternative, a new trial. The motion was denied and this appeal then ensued.

### Privity of Contract in Breach of Express Warranty Claims

In its first issue for review, Tire–Tech contends the trial court erred in granting judgment on the DTPA based on breach of an express warranty because there was no privity of contract between Tire–Tech and Boeran. Boeran contends an express warranty was created through representations made by Tire–Tech to MVI and passed on to Boeran. Boeran acknowledges a lack of privity because it contracted exclusively with MVI, but contends that privity of contract is not required to maintain an action for breach of an express warranty.

The question before us is whether privity of contract is required in order to recover under the DTPA for breach of an express warranty when purely economic loss is involved. Generally, in order to recover for breach of an express warranty under the DTPA, a plaintiff must prove (1) he or she is a consumer, (2) a warranty was made, (3) the warranty was breached, and (4) as a result of the breach, an injury resulted. . . . Privity is not required in order to be a consumer under the DTPA. . . . Yet, the DTPA does not define or create any warranties. . . . Warranties actionable under the DTPA, both express and implied, must first be recognized by common law or created by statute. . . . . Thus, even in a case where damages are recovered under the DTPA, we must look outside the DTPA to the existing law of warranties to determine if privity is required for express-warranty claims.

Express warranties on goods are defined by the Uniform Commercial Code (UCC). *See* TEX. BUS. & COM. CODE ANN. § 2.313 (Vernon 1994). However, the Texas version of the UCC is neutral regarding any privity requirement. *Nobility Homes of Tex., Inc. v. Shivers*, 557 S.W.2d 77, 81, 21 Tex. Sup. Ct. J. 5 (Tex. 1977). In fact, the code specifically "does not provide . . . whether the buyer or anyone entitled to take advantage of a warranty made to the buyer may sue a third party other than the immediate seller for deficiencies in the quality of the goods." TEX. BUS. & COM. CODE ANN. § 2.318 (Vernon 1994). Instead, the code states, "These matters are left to the courts for their determination." *Id*.

The Texas Supreme Court held in 1977 that privity of contract is not required in order to recover purely economic losses from the breach of an implied warranty of merchantability. *Nobility Homes*, 557 S.W.2d at 81. . . . The supreme court, however, has not clearly stated whether privity of contract is required in order to recover purely economic losses for breach of an *express* warranty, and the courts of appeals are divided on the issue.

In the 1970s, several courts held that privity of contract was required in cases involving purely economic losses and express warranties, and these courts have not addressed the issue since that time. . . . The more recent trend among courts of appeals, however, has been to find that privity of contract is not required in this situation. . . .

We agree with the reasoning of the more recent cases and hold that privity of contract is not required in order to sustain a breach of express-warranty claim for purely economic losses. To hold otherwise could allow unscrupulous manufacturers who make public representations about their product's performance to remain insulated from express-warranty liability if consumers did not purchase the product directly from them. . . .

We overrule Tire–Tech's first issue.

## Notice of Breach

In its second issue for review, Tire–Tech contends the trial court erred in rendering judgment against it because Boeran failed to provide Tire–Tech with notice of the alleged breach of express warranty. The Texas UCC states that, after a tender has been accepted, "the buyer must within a reasonable time after he discovers or should have discovered any breach notify the seller of breach or be barred from any remedy." TEX. BUS. & COM. CODE ANN. § 2.607(c)(1) (Vernon 1994). In 1986, the supreme court acknowledged that there was a split among the courts of appeals regarding whether a buyer is required to give notice of an alleged breach of warranty to a remote seller-manufacturer. *Wilcox v. Hillcrest Mem'l Park of Dallas*, 701 S.W.2d 842, 843, 29 Tex. Sup. Ct. J. 136 (Tex. 1986) (refusing writ of error). While the supreme court expressly reserved judgment on the issue in *Wilcox*, it has not since decided the issue. *See id.*

In *Wilcox*, the Dallas Court of Appeals held that section 2.607(c)(1) required a buyer to notify a remote manufacturer or be barred from recovery. *Wilcox v. Hillcrest Mem'l Park of Dallas*, 696 S.W.2d 423, 424–25 (Tex. App.—Dallas 1985), *writ ref'd n.r.e. per curiam*, 701 S.W.2d 842, 29 Tex. Sup. Ct. J. 136 (Tex. 1986). *Wilcox* expressly disagreed with the El Paso Court of Civil Appeals, which held that "the notice requirement of Section 2.607 applies only as between a buyer and his immediate seller." *Vintage Homes, Inc. v. Coldiron*, 585 S.W.2d 886, 888 (Tex. Civ. App.—El Paso 1979, no writ).

We note the supreme court has clearly rejected the notion that the Texas UCC was drafted "only with the intention of governing relations between immediate buyers and sellers." *Garcia*, 610 S.W.2d at 465; *see Nobility Homes*, 557 S.W.2d at 80. It is difficult to conceive how the term "seller" could be read broadly to include a remote manufacturer when rejecting a privity requirement, as in *Nobility Homes*, but then read narrowly under section 2.607 so as to require that a buyer give notice only to an immediate seller. The drafters of the UCC did not read section 2.607 as referring solely to the relationship between a buyer and an immediate seller. *See* TEX. BUS. & COM. CODE ANN. § 2.607 cmt. 5 (Vernon 1994) (commenting that injured non-buyer beneficiary also required to notify seller). Professors White and Summers, explaining their endorsement of a notice requirement for remote manufacturers, state, "If the manufacturer is to be held responsible for the buyer's losses, it needs the protection of timely notice at least as much as the buyer's immediate seller." JAMES J. WHITE & ROBERT S. SUMMERS, UNIFORM COMMERCIAL CODE § 11–10 (4th ed. 1995). We concur in that assessment and hold that, under section 2.607(c)(1), a buyer is required to give notice of an alleged breach of warranty to a remote manufacturer. *Wilcox*, 696 S.W.2d at 424–25; *see Melody Home Mfg. Co. v. Morrison*, 502 S.W.2d 196, 203 (Tex. Civ. App.— Houston [1st Dist.] 1973, writ ref'd n.r.e.). However, we do note that the "reasonable time" to give notice may be extended in light of the level of difficulty required in identifying the remote manufacturer. TEX. BUS. & COM. CODE ANN. § 2.607(c)(1); *cf.* TEX. BUS. & COM. CODE ANN. § 2.607 cmt. 4, 5 (Vernon 1994) (extending "reasonable time" for lay consumers and beneficiaries).

\* \* \*

Boeran presented no evidence that it directly gave Tire–Tech notice prior to filing suit. Boeran notified MVI, and MVI later informed Tire–Tech of a problem in the Netherlands without identifying Boeran. This notice to MVI, however, does not satisfy Boeran's notice requirement toward Tire–Tech. *See Connick v. Suzuki Motor Co.*, 174 Ill. 2d 482, 675 N.E.2d 584, 590, 221 Ill. Dec. 389 (Ill. 1996) (holding manufacturer's generalized knowledge of concerns insufficient to meet UCC notice requirement). The manufacturer must be made aware of a problem with a particular product purchased by a particular buyer. *Id.* Neither did the commencement of litigation satisfy this notice requirement. *See Wilcox*, 696 S.W.2d at 424–26; *see also Draper*, 89 A.L.R.5th 319, at § 10[b] (noting cases with this holding). Thus, we must conclude that the trial court erred in rendering judgment in favor of Boeran based on the breach of an express warranty because no evidence was presented showing that Boeran gave Tire–Tech proper notice of the alleged breach of warranty as required by section 2.607(c)(1).

We sustain Tire–Tech's second issue.

\* \* \*

## CONCLUSION

Having sustained Tire–Tech's second issue for review . . ., we reverse the judgment and render judgment that Boeran take nothing against Tire–Tech.

## NOTES

**(1) Manufacturer's Warranty.** The opinion of the court did not describe the evidence on which the jury found that the manufacturer had made an express warranty other than a brief reference to statements published by the manufacturer. The opinion referred to UCC 2–313 as the legal basis for express warranties, but did not discuss how the manufacturer's representations would become actionable warranties under that Code provision. The apparent explanation is that the manufacturer did not include this issue in its appeal.

**(2) Privity.** The manufacturer's first issue on appeal was absence of privity with the downstream purchaser. The court applied Texas law. As we learned earlier in this Chapter, and restated here, the Texas version of UCC Article 2–318 is a non-uniform provision that leaves the privity question to the courts. The Texas Supreme Court had held previously, in *Nobility Homes*, that lack of privity was not a defense to an implied warranty of merchantability claim by a downstream consumer/buyer against a mobile home manufacturer. Was that precedent distinguishable?

**(3) Notice to the Manufacturer.** The court held that the downstream buyer's claim against the manufacturer was barred for lack of prompt notice under UCC 2–607(3)(a). The court relied on two sources, Comment 5 to UCC 2–607 and a treatise. Comment 5 deals with personal injury claims by individuals who were not buyers but are considered third-party beneficiaries of sales contracts(UCC 2–318). Is the Comment relevant to claims against manufacturers by downstream buyers for economic losses? The treatise contains the authors' statement that a manufacturer "needs the protection of timely notice at least as much as the buyer's immediate seller."[3] Is this policy statement germane to the construction of the language UCC 2–607(3)(a)? Would it support imposing a timely notice requirement as a matter of common law?

## 2. STATUTE OF LIMITATIONS

Two issues arise in every application of a statute of limitations: what is the limitations period and when does it start to run. In claims by downstream buyers against manufacturers, there are two possible statutes of limitations that might apply, UCC 2–725 or the general contract statute of limitations. Depending on which is applicable, the limitations period will be four years or, in most states, six years. The limitations period begins to run, under UCC 2–725(2), when breach occurs; a breach of warranty occurs when tender of delivery is made unless the warranty extends to future performance of the goods. Under a general contract law statute of limitations, the period begins to run when a cause of action accrues. Determining which statute of limitations to apply to law suits by downstream buyers against manufacturers can make a major difference in the outcomes. If UCC Article 2 is applied, the period will be shorter and may begin to run earlier.

There has been considerable litigation regarding durable consumer goods which were sold by dealers and which came with manufacturers' remedial promises in the form of Magnuson–Moss Act limited warranties. The following two cases are part of that body of case law.

---

**3.** The quoted language appears in the most recent edition of the treatise at J. WHITE & R. SUMMERS, UNIFORM COMMERCIAL CODE § 12.10 (6th ed. 2010)

# Tittle v. Steel City Oldsmobile GMC Truck, Inc.

Supreme Court of Alabama, 1989.
544 So.2d 883.

■ Shores, Justice.

The plaintiff, Rodney K. Tittle, appeals a summary judgment entered in favor of defendants, Steel City Oldsmobile GMC Truck, Inc. (hereinafter "Steel City"), and General Motors Corporation (hereinafter "General Motors").

Tittle purchased a 1981 Oldsmobile automobile from Steel City on October 9, 1981, and accepted delivery of it the same day. With the purchase of his automobile, General Motors provided Tittle with a document entitled "1981 Oldsmobile New Car Warranty." This writing provided that Steel City, as Tittle's Oldsmobile dealer, would repair and adjust defects in material or workmanship that occurred during the first 12 months or first 12,000 miles in which the car was in use. The document provided, further, that the warranty period would begin on the date the car was first delivered or placed in service. In addition to this warranty, Tittle purchased from General Motors Acceptance Corporation (hereinafter "GMAC"), the company with whom he financed the purchase of the car, a supplemental warranty that extended coverage of the original warranty to 36 months or 36,000 miles.

After Tittle accepted the automobile, he discovered numerous defects in it and repeatedly asked Steel City and GMAC to cure the problems. When Steel City proved unable, after a number of attempts, to repair the vehicle, Tittle met with the zone representative for GMAC, Don Ackerman. Tittle alleges that Mr. Ackerman, as agent for GMAC, offered to extend the existing warranty on the vehicle for an additional 12 months or 12,000 miles if Tittle would allow Steel City another opportunity to repair the defects in the vehicle. Tittle agreed, but following several unsuccessful attempts to repair the vehicle, Tittle returned the car to Steel City.

Tittle sued on January 29, 1986, in Jefferson County Circuit Court, alleging that Steel City, GMAC, and General Motors had breached their respective express warranties as well as implied warranties of merchantability and fitness. Tittle founded his claims upon the federal Consumer Product Warranty Act, known commonly as the Magnuson–Moss Act, 15 U.S.C. § 2301 et seq., and upon Alabama's version of the Uniform Commercial Code (hereinafter "U.C.C."), § 7–1–101 et seq., Ala. Code (1975). In their answers to the plaintiff's complaint, both Steel City and General Motors specifically pleaded the statute of limitations as an affirmative defense.

Steel City and General Motors filed motions for summary judgment based upon the statute of limitations defense. During the hearing on the motions, the trial judge asked the parties to present the court with additional authorities supporting their respective positions. The court requested that the parties submit these authorities on or before April 1, 1988. General Motors responded to the trial court's request by providing it with four cases. Tittle, however, filed both a supplemental brief opposing the defendants' motion for summary judgment and an affidavit containing facts not alleged at the time the court heard the summary judgment motions.

On April 4, 1988, the trial court entered summary judgment in favor of Steel City and General Motors. The court found that Tittle's claims were barred by the statute of limitations at the time his complaint was filed. The trial court specifically noted that the plaintiff's case remained pending as to defendant GMAC, but made its order final with respect to Steel City and General Motors. See, Ala. R. Civ. P. 54(b). It is from this summary judgment that the plaintiff appeals. Apparently anticipating Tittle's argument on appeal, General Motors filed a motion to strike the plaintiff's affidavit from the record, on June 20, 1988.

The issue presented this Court for review is whether the trial court erred in entering summary judgment for these two defendants on the ground that Tittle's claim for breach of an express warranty was barred by the statute of limitations. In arguing this issue, the parties raise five questions this Court must address: first, what statute of limitations applies in cases brought under the Magnuson–Moss Act or the breach of warranty claims brought under Alabama's version of the U.C.C.2; second, does Ala. Code (1975), § 8–20–12, toll the statute of limitations for breach of warranty in consumer cases until the breach is discovered?; third, does the warranty issued by General Motors explicitly extend to the future performance of the vehicle?; fourth, is a repair and replacement warranty breached upon tender of the car or upon refusal or failure to repair an alleged defect?; and fifth, was Mr. Tittle's affidavit properly submitted to the trial court and included in the record on appeal, and, if so, did the affidavit present a genuine issue of material fact precluding the trial court's summary judgment?

## I.

The Magnuson–Moss Act authorizes civil actions by consumers in state or federal court when suppliers, warrantors, or service contractors violate its provisions. 15 U.S.C. § 23l0(d)(1). The Act, however, does not provide a statute of limitations for claims that arise under this legislation. Where a federal statute grants a cause of action, but does not include a statute of limitations governing the scope of that statute's application, federal common law requires that the court apply the state statute of limitations governing the state action most closely analogous to the federal claim. . . . The state law action most analogous to Tittle's Magnuson–Moss warranty claim is an action for breach of warranty in a contract for sale. Thus, the statute of limitations that appropriately applies to Tittle's state breach of warranty action is the same statute of limitations that appropriately applies to his federal Magnuson–Moss claim. Under Alabama's version of the U.C.C., the statute of limitations that applies to an action for breach of any contract for sale is found in § 7–2–725, Ala. Code (1975).

\* \* \*

III.

Under § 7–2–725(2), a cause of action for breach of warranty accrues when the seller tenders to the buyer the goods made the basis of the warranty. Once the cause of action accrues, the statute provides a four-year limitations period in which the buyer may file suit, subject to two exceptions. First, a cause of action will not accrue, in the case of consumer goods, on a claim for damages for injury to the person until the injury occurs. And, second, where the seller of consumer goods gives the buyer an express warranty that extends to the future performance of the goods, a cause of action will not accrue until the buyer discovers or should have discovered the defect in the goods.

Tittle argues that the trial court erred in entering summary judgment in this case even if the limitations period contained in § 7–2–725 is the one that appropriately applies to his cause of action, because, he says, the warranties given him by Steel City and General Motors explicitly extended to the future performance of his automobile. Consequently, Tittle claims that his cause of action did not accrue until he discovered or should have discovered the breach of the Steel City and General Motors warranties.

While Tittle's argument has been addressed in other jurisdictions, the question of whether a so-called "repair and replacement" warranty extends to the future performance of goods, so as to fall within the limited exception set out in § 7–2–725(2), is a case of first impression for this Court. Therefore, a brief analysis of the case law interpreting this section is appropriate. Before we analyze case law, however, it is critical that we consider exactly what the warranties given Tittle purport to guarantee.

Page 2 of Tittle's warranty is entitled, "1981 Oldsmobile New Car Limited Warranty." This document provides that "Oldsmobile Division, General Motors Corporation, warrants each new 1981 car," that "this warranty covers any repairs and needed adjustments to correct defects in material or workmanship," and that "the warranty period begins on the date the car is first delivered or put in use." The warranty further provides, "your Oldsmobile dealer will make the repairs or adjustments, using new or remanufactured parts." The warranty stipulates on page 3 that "it is our intent to repair under the warranty, without charge, anything that goes wrong during the warranty period that is our fault." The warranty then distinguishes the term "defects," which "are covered [under the warranty] because we, the manufacturer, are responsible," from the term "damages," which are not covered by the warranty because the manufacturer has "no control over damage caused by such things as collision, misuse and lack of maintenance which occurs after the car is delivered." . . .

In 1976, in the leading case of Voth v. Chrysler Motor Corp., 218 Kan. 644, 545 P.2d 371 (1976), the Supreme Court of Kansas spoke to Tittle's argument. The warranty in Voth read in pertinent part:

Chrysler Corporation warrants this vehicle to the first registered owner only against defects in material and workmanship in normal use as follows: (1) the entire vehicle (except tires) for 12 months or 12,000 miles of operation after the vehicle is first placed in service, whichever occurs first, from the date of sale or delivery thereto; and (2) the engine block, head and all internal engine parts, water pump, intake manifold, transmission case and all internal transmission parts, torque converter (if so equipped), drive shaft universal joints, rear axle and differential, and rear wheel bearings for 5 years or 50,000 miles of operation after the vehicle is first placed in service, whichever occurs first, from the date of such sale or delivery. Any part of this vehicle found defective under the conditions of this warranty will be repaired or replaced, at Chrysler's option, without charge at an authorized Imperial, Chrysler, Plymouth, or Dodge dealership.

Voth, 218 Kan. at 647, 545 P.2d at 374–75 (quoting Chrysler's warranty from the record).

This warranty is similar to the warranty issued by General Motors in this case. The Kansas Supreme Court held that the Chrysler warranty did not explicitly extend to the future performance of the vehicle. Moreover, the court found that the warranty did not guarantee performance without malfunction during the term of the warranty, but warranted only that the manufacturer would repair or replace defective parts in the event the car malfunctioned. Voth, 218 Kan. at 648, 545 P.2d at 375. The Kansas court explains its rationale through a quotation from Owens v. Patent Scaffolding Co., 77 Misc.2d 992, 354 N.Y.S.2d 778 (Sup. Ct. 1974), rev'd on other grounds, 50 A.D.2d 866, 376 N.Y.S.2d 948 (1975), in which an argument similar to Tittle's was rejected:

In this case the warranty does not go to performance of the equipment. To warrant to make needed repairs to leased equipment is not a warranty extending to its future performance. All that the supplier promises is that if the equipment needs repairs he will make them. It does not promise that in the future the goods will not fall into disrepair or malfunction, but only that if it does, the supplier will repair it. [Underlying] the warranty to make needed repairs is the assumption that the goods may fall into disrepair or otherwise malfunction. No warranty that the goods will not, is to be inferred from the warranty to make needed repairs.

Voth, 218 Kan. at 651, 545 P.2d at 378 (quoting Owens, supra, 77 Misc.2d at 999, 354 N.Y.S.2d at 785).

In articulating the distinction between a warranty to repair and a warranty extending to future performance, the court in Owens said:

A promise to repair is an express warranty that the promise to repair will be honored [citations omitted]. The seller's warranty ... that ... [goods] "will give satisfactory service at all times" is distinguishable from the supplier's warranty to "make modifications, alterations or repairs to the component parts of the equipment" when necessary. [The words in the former warranty] go to the performance of the goods; that it "will give satisfactory service at all times." When the

time came that the [goods] did not give satisfactory service, the
warranty was breached. [The former warranty] explicitly extended to
future performance of the goods, and its breach could only be discovered at the time of such performance.

77 Misc.2d at 998, 354 N.Y.S.2d at 784.

In Ontario Hydro v. Zallea Systems, Inc. 569 F.Supp. 1261 (D.Del.
1983), Chief Judge Latchum expressed the distinction between these two
types of warranties in this manner:

[T]he key distinction between these two kinds of warranties is that a
repair or replacement warranty merely provides a *remedy* if the product becomes defective, while a warranty for future performance *guar-*
*antees the performance* of the product itself for a stated period of time.
In the former case, the buyer is relying upon the warranty merely as a
method by which a defective product can be remedied which has no
effect upon his ability to discover his breach. In the latter instance, the
buyer is relying upon the warranty as a guarantee of future performance and therefore has no opportunity to discover the breach until the
future performance has been tested. (Emphasis in original.)

Ontario Hydro, at 1266.

Other courts and authorities support the same conclusion: a promise to
repair is not necessarily a promise of future performance. . . . See also, W.
D. Hawkland, Uniform Commercial Code Service, § 2–725:02 at 480 (the
hardship to the buyer that may sometimes be created by the four-year
limitations period as measured from tender of delivery is thought to be
outweighed by the commercial benefit derived from an established limitations period).

Tittle, in response to the foregoing cases, proffers two cases that he
suggests represent substantial authority from other jurisdictions directly
contrary to Voth and similar cases. In the first case, Standard Alliance
Industries, Inc. v. Black Clawson Co., 587 F.2d 813 (6th Cir.1978), cert.
denied, 441 U.S.923, 99 S.Ct. 2032, 60 L.Ed.2d 396 (1979), the seller of a
forging machine, in addition to warranting specific performance levels for
the operation of the machine, warranted that "the equipment manufactured by it would be *free from defects* in workmanship and material" for a
period of one year. 587 F.2d at 816–17 (emphasis added). When the
manufacturer failed, after numerous attempts, to repair the defective
machinery, the buyer brought an action against the seller alleging breach of
his express warranty. The Standard Alliance court held that the warranty
at issue in the case extended to the future performance of the machine for
a period of one year and that the buyer's cause of action accrued when the
purchaser discovered or should have discovered that the machine was
defective. Id., at 817.

In the second case, R. W. Murray Co. v. Shatterproof Glass Corp., 697
F.2d 818 (8th Cir.1983), the manufacturer's warranty provided:

Vision and spandrel glass shall be guaranteed by the glass manufacturer for a period of ten (10) years from the date of acceptance of the

project to furnish and replace any unit which develops material destruction of vision between the interglass surfaces. This guarantee is for material and labor costs for replacing.

697 F.2d at 821–22 n. 2.

Shatterproof Glass Corporation warrants its insulating glass units for a period of twenty (20) years from the date of manufacture against defects in material or workmanship that result in moisture accumulation, film formation or dust collection between the interior surfaces, resulting from failure of the hermetic seal. Purchaser's exclusive remedy and Shatterproof's "total" liability under this warranty shall be limited to the replacement of any lite failing to meet the terms of this warranty. Such replacement will be made F.O.B. Detroit to the shipping point nearest the installation.

697 F.2d 822 n. 3. The court construed these warranties as extending to the future performance of the goods for periods of 10 years and 20 years, respectively, and held that the purchaser's cause of action for breach of warranty accrued when the breach was, or should have been, discovered.

Despite the language used in the Shatterproof Glass warranties, guaranteeing for a specified period of time that a product is "free" from defects, as in Standard Alliance, seems to us altogether different from guaranteeing that product "against" defects, as in Voth. In the first instance, the manufacturer guarantees that the product possesses no defect whatsoever, while in the second instance the manufacturer guarantees that where defects emerge, he will remedy them, generally by repairing or replacing the defective part. While Shatterproof Glass used the term "against" in its warranty, we reconcile the holding in that case with Voth and Standard Alliance by noting the explicit nature of the remaining language in the warranty. Had the Shatterproof Glass court held that the warranties fell outside the U.C.C. § 2–725(2) "extends to future performance" exception, then despite the 10—and 20–year periods set out in the warranties, § 2–725(1) would have terminated the plaintiff's right of action four years after tender of the goods. (Section 2–725(1) provides in pertinent part, "By the original agreement the parties may reduce the period of limitation to not less than one year but may not extend it [beyond four years from the date of tender].")

In the present case, the warranty under which Tittle pursued his claim is even more free of ambiguity than that found in Voth and the other cases. The activating language of that warranty provides: "This warranty covers any repairs and needed adjustments to correct defects in material or workmanship." This language clearly does not guarantee that the car will perform free of defects for the term of the agreement. In fact, as the court in Voth recognized, the language of the guarantee anticipates that defects will occur. We, therefore, hold that the warranty provided Tittle upon the purchase of his car did not extend to the car's future performance.

We recognize that, under the analysis adopted by this Court, one might reasonably suggest that the language of the "Emission Components Defect

Warranty" places it within our definition of a warranty that extends to future performance, at least within the limited scope of that separate provision. The emissions warranty provides: "Oldsmobile . . . warrants . . . that the car . . . is free from defects in material and workmanship which cause the car to fail to conform with applicable Federal Environmental Protection Agency regulations for a period of use of 50,000 miles or 5 years, whichever comes first." We note, however, that although he enumerates an exhaustive list of defects, Tittle never alleged in his complaint or elsewhere that his vehicle failed to conform to EPA emissions standards. Hence, this provision is not applicable to the case before us.

## IV.

Tittle next contends that even if the General Motors and Steel City warranties do not extend to the future performance of the vehicle, the cause of action does not accrue until there is a refusal or failure to repair. This contention, however, directly contradicts the plain meaning of the language in § 7–2–725, which states that a cause of action for breach of any contract for sale accrues when the breach occurs and that the breach occurs upon tender of delivery, regardless of the buyer's knowledge of the breach, unless the warranty explicitly extends to future performance. We have earlier determined that Tittle's warranty does not extend to the future performance of his car. The trial court, therefore, correctly determined that Tittle's cause of action, by statute and by the express terms of his warranty, accrued at the time Steel City delivered the vehicle to him.

## V.

Finally, Tittle argues that even if we affirm the lower court's rulings regarding interpretation of § 7–2–725, the trial court still erred in granting summary judgment because, he says, a material issue of fact exists as to whether the defendants are estopped to assert the statute of limitations based upon their agent's representations.

\* \* \*

. . . General Motors and Steel City argue that they should not be estopped from raising the statute of limitations defense because, they say, no evidence exists that the misrepresentations made by Mr. Ackerman were intentional or fraudulent, or that Tittle, relying on these representations, was induced not to file a lawsuit. . . .

Tittle states in his affidavit that in 1984 a General Motors representative, Mr. Don Ackerman, represented that Steel City would repair the defects in his vehicle; that Mr. Ackerman indicated that if Tittle would allow Steel City another opportunity to repair the car, then Ackerman would extend the warranty 12 months or 12,000 miles; and that based on Mr. Ackerman's representations, he continued to attempt to have the car repaired rather than returning the car to the appellees. We find that a jury might conceivably construe Mr. Ackerman's statements as a promise to make repairs in return for a promise not to sue.

In reviewing a disposition of a motion for summary judgment, we use the same standard as that of the trial court in determining whether the evidence before the court made out a genuine issue of material fact. . . . We do not here decide whether these defendants are estopped as a matter of law from asserting the statute of limitations as a defense; rather, we hold that a fact issue exists as to whether Ackerman acted as an agent for General Motors and Steel City and made a statement that Tittle reasonably relied on in delaying the filing of this lawsuit.

We, therefore, reverse the summary judgment in favor of General Motors and Steel City.

REVERSED AND REMANDED

NOTES

**(1) UCC 2–725 or General Contract Law.** There is no indication that buyer's counsel contended that the relevant statute of limitations was the statute for contracts generally. It appears that counsel tried to rely first on the Magnuson–Moss Warranty Act, which does not have a limitations provision, and, second, on the UCC 2–725 exception for warranties that extend to future performance of the goods. Would buyer have been able to avoid summary judgment if the general contract statute had been applied?

Counsel for the buyer framed the complaint as a suit for breach of express warranty and of implied warranties of merchantability and fitness for purpose and joined three defendants, the manufacturer (General Motors), the retail dealer (Steel City Oldsmobile GMC Truck), and the provider of a "supplemental warranty" (General Motors Acceptance). Did these choices lead to the court's use of UCC 2–725?

**(2) Magnuson–Moss Warranty Act.** The buyer based his claim in part on the Magnuson–Moss Warranty Act. Nothing in that Act deals with the statute of limitations. The Alabama court found, properly, that state law provided the limitations period for the federal cause of action.

**(3) Application of UCC 2–725(2).** Counsel for buyer argued that the remedial promise in the New Car Limited Warranty brought it within the exception for warranties that extend to future performance. After extensive review of precedents, the court concluded that the language of the Limited Warranty "does not guarantee that the car will perform free of defects for the term of the agreement," and therefore buyer's warranty claims are time-barred under the four-year statute of limitations. Was the court's analysis correct?

In some sales contracts, sellers warrant that the goods are free of defect in materials and workmanship, but that the exclusive remedy for breach of that warranty is a remedial repair promise. The New Car Limited Warranty had only the remedial promise. Is there a substantive difference between the two forms? Should a seller's explicit promise to repair defects, if defects arise within a stated period of time, be construed as implying that the goods would be free of defects for that time? Notice the importance of the legal sophistication of the lawyers who draft warranty documents for their clients.

**(4) Commencement of the Limitations Period.** Counsel for buyer argued that breach of the remedial promise would not occur until that had been refusal or failure to repair. The court found that this contradicted the plain language of UCC 2–725(2). Was there any way to construe UCC 2–725 to reach a different result? Buyer's argument as to accrual of a cause of action on the remedial promise would have been quite appropriate to application of the general contract statute of limitations.

The "supplemental warranty" obligor was not in the case on appeal, but that "warranty" was described by the Alabama court as a repair promise that became operative after the expiration of the12 months or 12.000 mile period of the promise in the manufacturer's New Car Limited Warranty and extended protection to 36 months or 36.000 miles of usage. When would the statute of limitations begin to run on a claim of breach of the "supplemental warranty"? How could the Alabama Supreme Court distinguish the repair promise in "supplemental warranty" from the repair promise in the New Car Limited Warranty for statute of limitations purposes?

**(5) Warranties of Quality; Remedies.** The case was remanded by the Alabama Supreme Court to consider whether the defendants were estopped from relying on the statute of limitations. Assume that the claim is found not to be time-barred. On the basis of your understanding of transactions of this kind, how would you evaluate the likely success of plaintiff on the various warranty counts? Against the dealer? Against the manufacturer? Against the provider of the "supplemental warranty"? What remedies would be available if the claims are upheld?

## Nationwide Insurance Co. v. General Motors Corp.

Supreme Court of Pennsylvania, 1993.
533 Pa. 423, 625 A.2d 1172.

■ CAPPY, JUSTICE.

This appeal presents the issue of whether an express, 12 month/12,000 mile "New Car Limited Warranty" promising "repairs and needed adjustments" to correct manufacturing defects is a warranty that "explicitly extends to future performance of the goods" for purposes of determining when a cause of action for breach of that warranty accrues under the statute of limitations provision of the Uniform Commercial Code—Sales, 13 Pa.C.S. § 2725. We are also asked to determine whether the implied warranties of merchantability and fitness for a particular purpose so extend. For the following reasons, we hold that the express warranty does explicitly extend to future performance of the goods but that the implied warranties do not. We now reverse in part and affirm in part the decision of the Superior Court.

The essential facts are undisputed. On June 20, 1986, the Appellant, Nationwide Insurance Company, instituted this action against Appellee General Motors Corporation/Chevrolet Motor Division.... According to the Complaint ..., Appellant is the insurance carrier for Michael Joseph Villi, who on January 5, 1982, purchased and accepted delivery of a 1982 Chevrolet Corvette manufactured by Appellee. On November 22, 1982, the car "malfunctioned and/or exhibited a defect, caught fire and was destroyed." Appellant paid Mr. Villi $18,473.00 for damage to the vehicle. The Complaint alleged that Appellee was liable for this amount because it had breached: (1) a written 12 month/12,000 mile warranty (Count One); (2) an implied warranty of merchantability (Count Two); and (3) an express or implied warranty of fitness for a particular purpose (Count Three).

Appellee filed a motion for summary judgment, which the Court of Common Pleas of Allegheny County initially denied. Upon reargument, however, the court granted the motion on the basis that the action was barred by the four-year statute of limitations at 13 Pa.C.S. § 2725: Although the action had been filed within four years of the date the car allegedly malfunctioned or displayed a defect, it had not been filed within four years of the date of tender of delivery. The trial court deemed the cause of action to have accrued upon tender of delivery because the court specifically found that the express, 12 month/12,000 mile warranty did not "explicitly extend to future performance of the goods" and therefore that the "discovery rule" exception of § 2725 did not apply. The Superior Court affirmed in an unpublished opinion, with Judge Brosky dissenting. 396 Pa.Super. 662, 570 A.2d 1093.[3] This Court granted Appellant's Petition for Allowance of Appeal.

... In this case, the question is whether the warranties explicitly extended to future performance of the vehicle so that the cause of action accrued when the breach was discovered (allegedly November 2, 1982),[4] in which case the action was timely filed, or whether the general rule regarding breach of warranty applies and the cause of action accrued upon tender of delivery (January 5, 1982), so that the action was untimely filed.

In the ordinary case, a breach of warranty action accrues on, and suit must be filed within four years of, the date the seller tenders delivery of the goods, even if the breach is not apparent until after delivery has been tendered. Section 2725 sets tender of delivery as the point at which the cause of action accrues because the section "presumes that all warranties, express or implied, relate only to the condition of the goods at the time of sale." Max E. Klinger, The Concept of Warranty Duration: A Tangled Web, 89 Dick.L.Rev. 935, 939 (1985) (hereinafter, "A Tangled Web"). Such

---

**3.** The lower courts did not address Appellee's argument that it was entitled to summary judgment because the express warranty promised only the repair or replacement of defective parts and specifically excluded liability for consequential damages, and that issue is not before us.

**4.** This point fell within the warranty period because it was less than 12 months from the date the car was "first delivered or put in use" ..., and the car had been driven less than 12,000 miles.

warranties are breached, if at all, when the goods are delivered but do not meet that standard. Of course, the deficiency contained in the goods may not be discovered by the buyer within four years of delivery. However,

> [i]n the usual circumstances, . . . defects are apt to surface within that time period, and the few odd situations where this is not the case, resulting in hardship to the buyer, are thought to be outweighed by the commercial benefit derived by allowing the parties to destroy records with reasonable promptness.

William D. Hawkland, Uniform Commercial Code Series § 2–725:02, at 480 (1984). See 13 Pa.C.S. § 2725, Uniform Commercial Code Comment (four year period "is most appropriate to modern business practice" because it "is within the normal commercial record keeping period"). Thus, in breach of warranty cases the four-year statute of limitations is essentially a statute of repose.

Section 2725 contains an exception, however, for warranties that "explicitly extend to future performance of the goods" where discovery of the breach must await the time of future performance. Where such a warranty is involved, the cause of action does not accrue until "the breach is or should have been discovered." This exception has caused confusion among courts, lawyers, and commentators for years. See generally, e.g., James J. White & Robert S. Summers, Uniform Commercial Code § 11–9 (3d ed. 1988); Klinger, A Tangled Web, 89 Dick.L.Rev. at 937–950 (discussing conflicting cases). Professors White and Summers have noted that "[a]lthough the time of accrual under [§ 2725] is ordinarily clear—'when tender of delivery is made'—the exception to this general rule poses interpretive difficulties." White & Summers, Uniform Commercial Code § 11–9, at 477. They go on to cite the very type of express warranty at issue here as an agreement that "leaves one in considerable doubt about its true meaning" and that could be interpreted either as a warranty that "explicitly extends to future performance" or as simply an agreement to repair.[5] Id. at 479.

Despite its ambiguity, one thing the plain language of § 2725(b) makes clear is that our analysis of whether the written warranty "explicitly" extends to future performance must focus on the express language of that warranty. It is entitled "1982 Chevrolet New Car Limited Warranty" and provides, in part:

## WHAT IS COVERED

CHEVROLET Chevrolet Motor Division, General Motors Corporation, warrants each new 1982 car.

DEFECTS This exclusive warranty covers any repairs and needed adjustments to correct defects in material or workmanship.

---

**5.** The example cited is an agreement in which "the manufacturer promises to repair any defect in a car's drivetrain that occurs within two years or 24,000 miles, whichever occurs first."

REPAIRS Your Chevrolet dealer will make the repairs or adjustments, using new or remanufactured parts.

WHICHEVER COMES FIRST This warranty is for 12 months or 12,000 miles, whichever comes first.

WARRANTY BEGINS The warranty period begins on the date the car is first delivered or put in use.

NO CHARGE Warranty repairs and adjustments (parts and/or labor) will be made at no charge. A reasonable time must be allowed after taking the car to the dealer.

WARRANTY APPLIES This warranty is for Chevrolets registered and normally operated in the United States or Canada.[6]

Appellant argues that the express warranty explicitly extends to future performance of the goods because the warranty is for a specific duration, "12 months or 12,000 miles, whichever comes first." According to Appellant, such a warranty must contemplate the vehicle's future performance, at least for the stated period following delivery. Appellee, on the other hand, argues that the warranty does not explicitly extend to future performance of the goods because it does not promise that the goods will perform in a particular way in the future.[7]

---

**6.** The document also states: "ANY IMPLIED WARRANTY OF MERCHANTABILITY OR FITNESS FOR A PARTICULAR PURPOSE APPLICABLE TO THIS CAR IS LIMITED IN DURATION TO THE DURATION OF THIS WRITTEN WARRANTY. CHEVROLET SHALL NOT BE LIABLE FOR CONSEQUENTIAL OR INCIDENTAL DAMAGES RESULTING FROM BREACH OF THIS WRITTEN WARRANTY."

Under "WHAT IS NOT COVERED," the warranty excludes tires; damage due to accidents, misuse, or alterations; damage from the environment; and damage due to lack of maintenance or use of the wrong fuel, oil or lubes. It also states that normal maintenance is the owner's responsibility and that "extra expenses" relating to the loss of use of the car during repairs are not covered.

**7.** This position has been taken by courts in other states that have considered similar automobile warranties. See, e.g., Tittle v. Steel City Oldsmobile GMC Truck, Inc., 544 So.2d 883 (Ala.1989); Voth v. Chrysler Motor Corp., 218 Kan. 644, 545 P.2d 371 (1976); Stoltzner v. American Motors Jeep Corp., 127 Ill.App.3d 816, 82 Ill.Dec. 909, 469 N.E.2d 443 (1984) (also holding that express disclaimer of implied warranties "for any period beyond the express warranty" did not amount to explicit extension), appeal denied; Poppenheimer v. Bluff City Motor Homes, 658 S.W.2d 106 (Tenn.Ct.App.1983); Muss v. Mercedes–Benz of North America, Inc., 734 S.W.2d 155 (Tex.Ct.App.1987). n construing the same General Motors warranty language that is at issue in this case, the Supreme Court of Alabama stated:

> This language clearly does not guarantee that the car will perform free of defects for the term of the agreement. In fact, as the court in Voth [v. Chrysler Motor Corp., 218 Kan. 644, 545 P.2d 371 (1976)] recognized, the language of the guarantee anticipates that defects will occur. We, therefore, hold that the warranty provided Tittle upon the purchase of his car did not extend to the car's future performance.

Tittle, 544 So.2d at 891.

Decisions of the courts of other states on this issue are influential, given the purposes of the UCC. One of the explicit purposes of the Code in general is "[t]o make uniform the law among the various jurisdictions." 13 Pa.C.S. § 1103(b)(3). Section 2725 is intended specifically to "introduce a uniform statute of limitations for sales contracts." 13 Pa.C.S. § 2725, Uniform Commercial Code Comment. It would, therefore, be both acceptable and tempting simply to

We cannot accept Appellee's position for a number of reasons. First, we do not read the words "explicitly extends to future performance of the vehicle" to require that the warranty make an explicit promise regarding how the goods will perform in the future. We believe that the focus of § 2725 is not on what is promised, but on the duration of the promise—i.e., the period to which the promise extends. Cf. Safeway Stores, Inc. v. Certainteed Corp., 710 S.W.2d 544, 549 (Tex. 1986) (Robertson, J., concurring) (pointing out that "explicitly" modifies the words "extends," and not the word "warranty"; therefore, it is the extension that must be explicit). Therefore, we agree with Appellant that the phrase "explicitly extends to future performance" can be interpreted to include a promise that, by its terms, comes into play upon, or is contingent upon, the future performance of the goods. There can be little doubt that an explicit extension has been given where the warranty itself plainly states that it "is for 12 months or 12,000 miles" and that "[t]he warranty periods begins on the date the car is first delivered or put in use." (emphasis added). Logically, a promise to repair or adjust defective parts within the first 12 months or 12,000 miles after delivery cannot be breached until the vehicle requires repair or adjustment, and "discovery of the breach must await the time of [future] performance."

Second, the essence of Appellee's position is that the document here is not a warranty, but a promise to repair or replace defective parts.[9] To be sure, the agreement here is not a model of clear draftsmanship. It could plausibly be interpreted any one of three ways: as creating a warranty that extends for 12 months or 12,000 miles, with a limited remedy of repair or adjustment for breach of the warranty; as creating not a warranty, but a repair agreement that extends 12 months or 12,000 miles; or as creating an "un-extended" warranty with a limited remedy of repair or adjustment if a breach is reported within 12 months or 12,000 miles. However, any difficulty interpreting the agreement must be resolved in favor of the non-drafting party. ... It was the Appellee who drafted the document here, labeled it a "warranty," and included statements such as: "Chevrolet Motor Division, General Motors Corporation, warrants each new 1982 car"

---

follow the lead of other courts. However, we decline to do so because we believe that the other courts' reasoning is flawed and would lead to absurd results if extended to its logical conclusion. For example, carrying through with the analysis described above would lead to a situation where a consumer who purchases a vehicle with a 7 year/70,000 mile warranty would have no cause of action for breach of that warranty if the breach were to occur in the fifth year following the date of delivery. Further, with the exception of the General Motors warranty at issue in Tittle, the warranties involved in the cited cases were worded differently from the warranty in the case sub judice, and some are distinguishable on that basis. The warranties in Stoltzner, Poppenheimer, and Muss, in particular, were more clearly promises to repair or replace defective parts for the stated "warranty" period.

**9.** Appellee never explicitly argues that the document is not a warranty. Indeed, having drafted the document and labeled it a warranty, Appellee would be hard-pressed to so argue. Instead, Appellee argues, somewhat disingenuously, that this is not a "performance warranty," but a "repair warranty." Section 2725 draws no such distinction. In addition, although Appellee argues that the document makes no promise regarding the condition or performance of the vehicle, its statement that it "warrants each new 1982 car" could be read to provide otherwise.

and "This warranty is for 12 months or 12,000 miles, whichever comes first." (emphasis added). If the drafter did not intend the document to operate as a warranty—and, more importantly for our purposes, if it did not intend the warranty to "[be] for 12 months or 12,000 miles,"—then it should have stated so more clearly.

Moreover, Appellee's attempt to argue, in essence, that this is not really a warranty reveals the internal inconsistency, and hence the weakness, in its position. On the one hand, Appellee's position depends upon calling the document a warranty, because only then can it argue that the cause of action accrued upon tender of delivery. On the other hand, Appellee argues that the "warranty" promises nothing about the condition or performance of the car, but is simply a promise to repair or replace defective parts. If that were the case, then the cause of action would not accrue until the promise to repair were breached.

We recognize that the document does not create a classic warranty that fits neatly within the UCC view of warranties. Although it is a "promise made by the seller to the buyer which relates to the goods," 13 Pa.C.S. § 2313(a)(1), . . . it does not "express[ly] warran[t] that the goods shall conform to the . . . promise." (emphasis added). However, even if "repair or replace" warranties are viewed as remedies rather than as warranties, they do not fit strictly into the conceptual framework established by the provisions of the UCC, and a conceptually satisfactory resolution cannot be achieved. See generally Klinger, A Tangled Web, 89 Dick.L.Rev. at 943–950 (pointing out difficulty in distinguishing between limited warranty and limited remedy and in applying warranty and remedy provisions of UCC to "repair or replace" warranties). We also note that, although "repair or replace" warranties are not traditional warranties, they do fit within the modern concept of warranty. For example, the federal Magnuson–Moss Warranty Act includes in its definition of "warranty"

> any undertaking in writing in connection with the sale by a supplier of a consumer product to refund, repair, replace, or take other remedial action with respect to such product in the event that such product fails to meet the specifications set forth in the undertaking . . .

15 U.S.C. § 2301(6)(B).

Furthermore, we will not permit Appellee and other sellers who draft similar documents to escape the consequences of presenting them to the consumer as "extended warranties." There can be little question that the consumer will consider the length of any warranty offered in determining whether to purchase a particular vehicle: The consumer naturally would believe that the longer the warranty, the greater the protection, and hence, the better the value, he or she is receiving. If Appellee's position were to prevail, the protection afforded the buyer during the latter part of a warranty approaching four years would be largely illusory, as the buyer would have a very short period of time in which to bring a cause of action for breach. Moreover, the longer-term protection afforded by a warranty extending beyond four years would be completely illusory.

Finally, reading the express warranty as one that "explicitly extends to future performance of the goods" will do no violence to the purposes of § 2725. Sellers will still be able to determine the time period for which they should maintain their records, simply by adding the limitation period to the warranty period. In addition, nothing in our analysis would prevent the parties from reducing the period of limitation in accordance with § 2725(a), which provides that "[b]y the original agreement the parties may reduce the period of limitation to not less than one year but may not extend it," provided, of course, that the period is reduced in a way that is not unconscionable.

Because we find that the express warranty "explicitly extends to future performance of the goods" for purposes of applying 13 Pa.C.S. § 2725, we find that the cause of action alleging breach of that warranty was timely filed and reverse the decision of the Superior Court with respect to Count One of the Complaint. We express no opinion, however, as to whether a cause of action has been stated or as to the appropriate remedy for breach of the express warranty.

Although we find the express warranty to explicitly extend to future performance of the goods, we cannot find that the implied warranties of merchantability and fitness for a particular purpose so extend. The warranty contains the following language: "ANY IMPLIED WARRANTY OF MERCHANTABILITY OR FITNESS FOR A PARTICULAR PURPOSE APPLICABLE TO THIS CAR IS LIMITED IN DURATION TO THE DURATION OF THIS WRITTEN WARRANTY." We do not read this language as explicitly extending the terms of any implied warranties, because the document states that any implied warranties are of a duration no longer than that of the express warranty and not that they are of a duration equal to that of the express warranty. The quoted language does not create implied warranties, because such warranties are created not by contract language but by operation of law in certain circumstances. See 13 Pa.C.S. §§ 2314 and 2315. The legal effect of the quoted language is merely to limit the protection that the law might otherwise impose. Therefore, it cannot be read as the type of language that "explicitly extends to future performance" for purposes of § 2725(b). In addition, the great weight of authority takes the position that an implied warranty, by nature, cannot "explicitly" extend to future performance. . . . Anno., What Constitutes Warranty Explicitly Extending to "Future Performance" for Purposes of UCC § 2-725(2), 93 A.L.R.3d 690, § 2 (collecting cases).

Because the implied warranties do not explicitly extend to future performance of the car, we conclude that Counts Two and Three of the complaint, alleging breach of implied warranties, were filed too late.

Accordingly, we reverse the decision of the Superior Court as to Count One and affirm as to Counts Two and Three. The case is remanded to the Court of Common Pleas of Allegheny County for further proceedings consistent with this opinion.

■ LARSEN, JUSTICE, dissenting.

I dissent. I would hold that the implied warranties of merchantability and fitness for a particular purpose also extend to the future performance of the vehicle because these implied warranties are expressly linked temporally to the express warranty by the following language contained in the express warranty at issue: "ANY IMPLIED WARRANTY OF MERCHANTABILITY OR FITNESS FOR A PARTICULAR PURPOSE APPLICABLE TO THIS CAR IS LIMITED IN DURATION TO THE DURATION OF THIS WRITTEN WARRANTY." . . .

■ ZAPPALA, JUSTICE, dissenting.

I am compelled to dissent from the opinion of the Court because I believe a number of serious flaws in the reasoning lead the Court to an incorrect result.

First, the majority finds that the warranty in this case, by specifying a 12 month/12,000 mile duration, "explicitly extends to future performance of the goods." I do not follow the logic. Granted, a warranty that explicitly extends to future performance of goods will by definition in most cases specify a certain time period. It does not follow, however, that because a certain time period is specified a warranty necessarily applies to future performance of the goods. The scope of the warranty—what is promised—may be something other than a representation about how the goods will perform and yet still contain a specified time period.

Here, the promise is to repair or adjust defective parts for 12 months or 12,000 miles. This is not the same as a promise that the car and its parts will remain free of defects for 12 months or 12,000 miles. The latter promise "explicitly extends to future performance of the goods;" the former promise does not.

The majority applies a faulty grammatical analysis of the phrase "where a warranty explicitly extends to future performance of the goods" to expand the reach of 13 Pa.C.S. § 2725(b). It is true that the adverb "explicitly" modifies the verb "extends" and not the noun "warranty," and thus it is the extension that must be explicit. In this context, however, the verb "extend" does not merely describe temporal duration, as the majority suggests. Rather, it describes scope or application. The conceptual difficulty with this case is that the Appellant characterized the warranty as a representation "that said vehicle would be free from defects in material and workmanship, for at least 12 months or 12,000 miles," in order to bring this action within the exception of 13 Pa.C.S. § 2725(b), when in fact the warranty was not so worded.

Second, the majority, states that "the essence of Appellee's position is that the document here is not a warranty, but a promise to repair or replace defective parts." In doing so, it sets up a straw man, mis-characterizing the Appellee's position in order to more easily refute it. The essence of the Appellee's argument is not that the document is not a warranty, but that it is not a warranty within the definition of 13 Pa.C.S. § 2313.[1]

---

1. The majority also errs in perceiving an internal inconsistency in the appellee's argument based on its erroneous characterization of the argument. The appellee argues that if

In the Uniform Commercial Code, the term "warranty" is given a very specific definition. "Any affirmation of fact or promise made by the seller to the buyer which relates to the goods and becomes a basis of the bargain creates an express warranty that the goods shall conform to the affirmation or promise." 13 Pa.C.S. § 2313(a)(1) (emphasis added). Likewise, "[a]ny description of the goods which is made a part of the bargain creates an express warranty that the goods shall conform to the description," 13 Pa.C.S. § 2313(a)(2), and "[a]ny sample or model which is made part of the basis of the bargain creates an express warranty that the whole of the goods shall conform to the sample or model." 13 Pa.C.S. § 2313(a)(3).

A warranty, in this sense, establishes as a term of the agreement certain qualities of the goods being sold. If the goods actually delivered do not possess such qualities, the buyer has remedies for breach of warranty. It is thus entirely sensible that in setting out when a cause of action accrues, the Code states that "[a] breach of warranty occurs when tender of delivery is made, except that where a warranty explicitly extends to future performance of the goods and discovery of the breach must await the time of such performance the cause of action accrues when the breach is or should have been discovered." 13 Pa.C.S. § 2725(b). Since a warranty as defined by the Code is a promise as to qualities of the goods, if the goods, when tendered, possess the qualities promised, the warranty has been satisfied; if the goods, when tendered, do not possess the promised qualities, the warranty has been breached. In the limited case where the promise is that the goods will have certain qualities, or will perform in a certain way, at a time beyond when the goods are delivered, it cannot be determined at the time of delivery whether the goods possess the promised qualities. Because the promise endures over a period of time, whether a breach has occurred can only be determined when the specified time has passed.

Here, in the document captioned "1982 Chevrolet New Car Limited Warranty", the seller did not promise that the car would perform without defect for twelve months or 12,000 miles; in fact, the "Limited Warranty" contained no specific promise or affirmation of fact relating to the car. The only promise was that any repairs and adjustments to correct defects in materials or workmanship would be made free of charge during the specified period. This promise related to the seller's obligations under the contract, not to the quality of the goods. Although this document is a warranty in the general sense in that it guarantees or promises something, it is not a warranty as to the quality of the car or as to its performance.

Indeed, as the majority notes, "although 'repair and replace' warranties are not traditional warranties, they do fit within the modern concept of

---

the warranty is construed as a promise about the quality or condition of the car, it does not "explicitly extend to future performance," therefore an action under that theory had to be commenced within four years of the date of delivery. If, however, the warranty is construed as a promise to repair, I believe the Appellee would concede that the four year limitation would not have commenced until this promise had been breached, if the complaint had alleged this as the basis for the action.

warranty," and a document such as the one involved here fits within the definition of "warranty" under the federal Magnuson–Moss Warranty Act, 15 U.S.C. § 2301(6)(b). This, I believe, is the ultimate source of the difficulty in this case. General Motors, selling its product in a national market, produces a standard document that includes a promise to repair or adjust defective parts. Under federal law, such a promise is properly captioned a warranty. Unfortunately, it does not "fit[ ] neatly within the UCC view of warranties." When an action is later brought under the UCC, GM suffers the consequence of having the "difficulty interpreting the agreement" be resolved against it, the drafter.

I think it entirely unjust to apply this rule of construction in these circumstances. As noted above, the Appellant mischaracterized the nature of the warranty in order to bring it within the exception to the limitations period under § 2725(b) of the UCC. To my mind, the Appellant is as much responsible for the "difficulty interpreting the agreement" as the Appellee. Had the action been brought under the Magnuson–Moss Warranty Act, 15 U.S.C. § 2310(d)(1)(A), the "difficulty" would not have arisen. The warranty could then have been analyzed as a promise as to the Appellee's conduct and a determination made whether the failure, or practical inability, to repair the vehicle constituted a breach of that promise.

This analysis also avoids the "problem" identified by the majority with respect to warranties of duration longer than four years. Because such warranties set forth promises as to the seller's conduct during a specified period of time, any breach of such promise will occur, and therefore any cause of action for breach of such promise will accrue, only after the lapse of time. Thus, for example, under a seven year/seventy thousand mile "repair and adjust" warranty, if a defect appeared in the fifth year, there would no longer be an action for breach of warranty to claim that the car was not of the quality bargained for, but the seller would still be obligated by the terms of the contract to make the necessary repairs or adjustments. Refusal to do so would be actionable as a breach, the cause of action accruing at the time of the breach and the limitation period extending four years from that point.

In the case presently before the Court, if the defect was such that the car delivered was not in fact possessed of a quality that had been bargained for, a breach of warranty action pursuant to the UCC could have been maintained. Such claim, however, would have to have been brought within four years of the date of delivery. Because this action was not commenced within four years of delivery, the Appellant could no longer make such a claim. Instead, the Appellant attempted to make the seller's promise into something that it plainly is not—a guarantee of the future performance of the car—in order to bring the action within the exception of the statutory limitation period.

Had the Appellant alleged that the seller breached the promise that it had made, the action would have been timely and the grant of summary judgment would have been improper. The Appellant made no such allegation. It was not alleged that the seller refused to make repairs or needed adjustments to correct defects in material or workmanship; nor was it alleged that any such refusal was the cause of the Appellant's damages.

By obligingly adopting the Appellant's transmogrification of this action in order to secure a remedy, the majority has, I fear, thrown the entire law of warranty under the Code in Pennsylvania into confusion.

I dissent and would affirm the grant of summary judgment.

NOTES

**(1) UCC 2–725 or General Contract Law.** The difference between the analyses in the majority opinion and the dissenting opinion of Justice Zappala is largely difference in characterization of the claim. The majority concluded that the claim, which should have survived the defense motion for summary judgment under UCC 2–725, was a claim for breach of the manufacturer's express warranty that extended to future performance of the goods. The dissent decided that the manufacturer's obligation was not a warranty that extended to future performance of the goods and, therefore, that a claim for breach of such a warranty was time-barred under UCC 2–725. This part of both opinions accepts without any discussion or analysis that the law governing the timeliness of plaintiff's claim was UCC 2–725. It appears that the opinions reflect the positions advocated by counsel for both sides.

Justice Zappala went on to say that the manufacturer had made a remedial promise, which was not time-barred, but that the plaintiff had not alleged breach of that promise. To what statute of limitations might Justice Zappala have been alluding: UCC 2–725 or general contract law?

**(2) Remedy.** The plaintiff was a not the buyer of the Corvette. The plaintiff was a casualty insurance company who had paid the buyer for the loss of his car and was subrogated by law to the buyer's rights against third parties. What remedy did plaintiff seek in this case? Could that remedy be granted on the basis of the manufacturer's promise to repair? Could that remedy be granted on the basis of a warranty that extended to future performance of the goods?

**(3) Rejection of Precedent.** A footnote in the majority, after reviewing prior decisions of several courts, including the Alabama Supreme Court's decision in *Tittle*, declared that the court would decline to follow the lead of other courts because "we believe that the other courts' reasoning is flawed and would lead to absurd results if extended to its logical conclusion." Was it necessary for the majority to declare its opposition to decisions like *Tittle*? Could those cases be distinguished from *Nationwide Insurance*?

**(4) Duration of Implied Warranties.** Justice Larsen's brief dissent, based on the mysterious provision in § 108(b) of the Magnuson–Moss Warranty Act, concluded that a term in the manufacturer's Limited Warranty had the legal effect of postponing, for a year, commencement of the remote buyer's cause of action for breach of implied warranties of quality. The Limited Warranty provided:

> ANY IMPLIED WARRANTY OF MERCHANTABILITY OR FITNESS FOR A PARTICULAR PURPOSE APPLICABLE TO THIS CAR IS LIMITED IN DURATION TO THE DURATION OF THIS WRITTEN WARRANTY.

This sentence, which clearly refers to implied warranties of quality, does not mention the period of limitations. It purports only to limit the "duration" of implied warranties.

The language in the Limited Warranty closely tracks the language in MMWA § 108(b). In most, if not all, limited warranties that have been provided by manufacturers since 1975, the same term has appeared. All of the lawyers who have drafted standard warranty forms for manufacturer clients have decided, it appears, that the term, which is permitted but not required by the MMWA, must have some value to their clients. By now, the term has appeared in untold numbers of limited warranties. What did all those lawyers think that the term means? If they had an inkling that the term might mean that their clients were exposed to more than the four-year limitations period, would they have incorporated the term in the limited warranty forms?[4]

What are the possible meanings of the mysterious concept of duration of an implied warranty? Some years ago, one of the editors of this casebook offered the following analysis:[5]

> The notion of limiting duration connotes the shortening of a period of time. Implied warranties of quality do not have any period of existence. An implied warranty is breached or is not breached in the scintilla of time that marks tender of delivery of the goods. A time period begins to run from that moment, the period of the statute of limitations. But plainly an implied warranty is not some kind of continuing promise.
>
> At least five possible meanings might be ascribed to contract terms limiting the duration of implied warranties of quality:
>
>      1.   Shortening of the statute of limitations period to the contract period, if shorter than the statutory period.
>
>      2.   Lengthening the statute of limitations period to the contract period, if longer than the statutory period.
>
>      3.   Defining the time within which a buyer must give notice of breach or be barred from any remedy under UCC 2–607(3) or a contractually imposed notice requirement.

---

**4.** Drafters of manufacturers' limited warranties were evidently aware that their clients were not obligated to remote buyers for implied warranties of quality. We considered this issue in section 4. The drafters of the standard forms tried to avoid language that would clearly acknowledge that implied warranties of quality existed. The duration-limitation term applies to "*any* implied warranty," a verbal formulation that left room for the argument that none existed, but, if any implied warranty were found, it had a limited duration.

**5.** C. Reitz, Consumer Product Warranties Under Federal and State Laws 82, 86, 95 (2d ed. 1987).

4.   Defining a point in time after which a buyer cannot complain of non-conformities that later come to light even though they could not reasonably have been discovered earlier.

5.   Defining a time during which buyer is entitled to seek seller's repair or other promised post-delivery relief for breach of an implied warranty of quality.

None of the suggested meanings is entirely satisfactory as a matter of statutory construction. The fifth meaning comes closest to the spirit of the Act. It also makes some sense in the marketplace.

What are your views of the meaning of MMWA 108(b)?

# Joswick v. Chesapeake Mobile Homes, Inc.

Court of Appeals of Maryland, 2001.
362 Md. 261, 765 A.2d 90.

■ WILNER, JUDGE.

The issue before us is whether an action filed by petitioners in 1997 for breach of an express that accompanied their purchase of a mobile home in 1988 is barred by the statute of limitations set forth in the Maryland Uniform Commercial Code ... The Circuit Court for Harford County and the Court of Special Appeals, for different reasons, held that the action was barred. We agree with the reasoning of the Circuit Court and, on that basis, shall affirm the judgment of the Court of Special Appeals.

## BACKGROUND

Petitioners purchased the mobile home in March, 1988, from Chesapeake Mobile Homes, Inc. In February, 1995, they noticed, for the first time, that the roof was and had been leaking, due, apparently, to the fact that the shingles at the eaves had been improperly installed and did not sufficiently overhang in order to allow rain water to drip off the roof. That, according to their experts, caused water to back into the facia area and rot out facia boards and plywood. Correction of the problem would cost $4,275. It is undisputed that the alleged defect was present when the mobile home was delivered to petitioners in 1988.

The mobile home was sold with an express limited warranty by the manufacturer, Brigadier Homes of North Carolina, Inc. (Brigadier). In relevant part, Brigadier warranted the mobile home "when purchased new, to be free from substantial defects of material and workmanship under normal use and service for a period of twelve (12) months from the date of delivery to the first retail purchaser." The warranty expressly stated, however, that "[t]he exclusive remedy for any such defect is the Manufacturer's obligation to repair or replace, at its option without cost to the purchaser ... at the site of the mobile home, any defective part or parts within the scope of this limited warranty, provided that written notice of the defect is received from the purchaser ... by the Manufacturer or dealer ... within one (1) year and ten (10) days from the date of delivery to the first retail purchaser." The warranty was stated to be in lieu of all other express and implied warranties and provided that the manufacturer assumed no responsibility for any consequential or incidental damages incurred as a result of any defect in the mobile home.

In June, 1997, petitioners filed suit in the District Court against Brigadier, Chesapeake, and Sterling Bank and Trust Co., which financed the purchase of the home, for breach of the warranty. The suit sought not only the $4,275 cost of repair but also $15,681 for damage to the interior of the mobile home allegedly caused by the leakage from the roof.[1] Upon Brigadier's demand for jury trial, the case was transferred to the Circuit Court for Harford County which, after some discovery and in three separate orders, entered summary judgment in favor of the three defendants on the ground that the action was barred by limitations. Petitioners appealed all three judgments to the Court of Special Appeals but later dismissed their appeals with respect to Chesapeake and Sterling, leaving Brigadier as the only defendant. The Court of Special Appeals affirmed. Joswick v. Chesapeake Mobile Homes, Inc., 130 Md.App. 493, 747 A.2d 214 (2000).

## DISCUSSION

Mobile homes are considered to be "goods" under the Maryland Uniform Commercial Code (U.C.C.). ... Accordingly, the sale of such a home is governed by the Maryland U.C.C., which, in § 2–725, contains its own statute of limitations governing actions for breach of contract and warranty. ...

As is evident from a reading of the two provisions [of the statute], the general rule is that a breach of warranty occurs when tender of delivery is made, and an action for breach of that warranty must be filed within four years after that event, even if the buyer is unaware of the breach. If the warranty explicitly extends to future performance of the goods, however, and discovery of the breach must await the time of that performance, the cause of action accrues not upon tender of delivery but when the breach is or should have been discovered, and the buyer has four years after that time within which to file suit. The threshold question in this case is

---

**1.** The validity of the two provisions that would exclude consequential damages is not before us. The warranty stated, in that regard, that "some States do not allow the exclusion or limitation of incidental or consequential damages, so the above limitation or exclusion may not apply to you." Section 2–714(3) of the Maryland U.C.C., dealing with a buyer's damages for breach in regard to accepted goods, states that "[i]n a proper case any incidental and consequential damages under the next section may also be recovered." Section 2–715 defines consequential damages resulting from a seller's breach to include "[i]njury to person or property proximately resulting from any breach of warranty." Section 2–719(3), however, provides that "consequential damages may be limited or excluded unless the limitation or exclusion is unconscionable." The section goes on to state that a limitation of consequential damages for injury to the person in the case of consumer goods is prima facie unconscionable "but limitation of damages where the loss is commercial is not." ... See also § 2–316.1(3).... If the contractual exclusion of consequential damages is valid and enforceable, petitioners would presumably be precluded from recovering the $15,681 they sought for damage to the interior of the home. Because the action was dismissed on limitations grounds, that issue was not addressed by either the Circuit Court or the Court of Special Appeals.

whether the warranty by Brigadier "explicitly extends to future performance" of the mobile home and discovery of any breach must await the time of that performance. If not, the breach occurred in March, 1988, when the mobile home was delivered to petitioners, and their lawsuit, filed nine years later, is barred. If so, there is the additional question of whether the discovery rule is limited by the one-year period of the warranty.

The Circuit Court construed the warranty language as "naming a twelve month period in which the buyer can expect the product to be free from substantial defects" and found from that that the warranty did extend to future performance and that the breach therefore occurred when petitioners discovered or should have discovered the defect. It concluded, however, that, as the warranty period was twelve months, the extended period of limitations was applicable only to the extent that the defect was discovered within that twelve-month period. In effect, it construed § 2–725(2), in light of the warranty period, as requiring an action to be brought within four years after expiration of the twelve-month warranty—a total of five years after delivery. The summary judgment for Brigadier stemmed from the undisputed fact that the action was not filed within that five-year period. The Court of Special Appeals, as noted, affirmed, but on a different basis. That court seemed to accept that there was a warranty that the mobile home was to be free of substantial defects for twelve months but determined that Brigadier's only commitment with respect to that warranty was its promise to repair or replace any defective parts. Accordingly, it concluded that "because the only remedy available to [petitioners] was repair and replacement, the warranty was a promise to cure defects, and not an 'explicit reference to future performance.'" Joswick v. Chesapeake Mobile Homes, Inc., supra, 130 Md.App. at 504, 747 A.2d at 220.

There have been dozens—perhaps hundreds—of cases throughout the country construing § 2–725(2) with respect to whether a warranty, limited or not limited by a promise to repair or replace, constitutes a warranty explicitly extending to future performance and thus invokes the discovery rule set forth in that subsection. The language of the warranty under consideration often differs from case to case, which may explain some of the variations in result, but a number of the cases do go in different directions and cannot easily be reconciled.

One thing that does seem clear is that a commitment to repair or replace defective parts (1) is not, itself, a warranty explicitly extending to future performance, and (2) does not serve either to convert a separate warranty that does not otherwise explicitly extend to future performance into one that does so or, conversely, convert a warranty that does extend to future performance into one that does not do so. The predominance of this view in the case law has led one learned commentator to make the flat statement that "[a] warranty to repair or replace is not a warranty as to the future performance of the goods." Ronald Anderson, Uniform Commercial Code, § 2–725:129 at 293 (3d ed.1994 rev.). . . .

On the other hand, a repair or replacement warranty does not warrant how the goods will perform in the future. Rather, such a warranty simply provides that if a product fails or becomes defective, the seller will replace or repair within a stated period. Thus, the key distinction between these two kinds of warranties is that a repair or replacement warranty merely provides a remedy if the product becomes defective, while a warranty for future performance guarantees the performance of the product itself for a stated period of time. . . .

The commitment to repair or replace is an enforceable undertaking, but it is not a warranty of future performance that falls within the exception stated in § 2–275(2). The repair and replacement commitment in this case required that the seller be given written notice of the defect within one year and ten days after the date of delivery. Obviously, that did not happen. The issue as to any failure to repair or replace, therefore, is not one of limitations, but of no breach. The seller was not asked, within the applicable period, to make any repairs or replacement, and thus it cannot be held to have violated that undertaking.

The question, then, is whether the warranty that the mobile home would be "free from substantial defects of material and workmanship under normal use and service for a period of twelve (12) months from the date of delivery to the first retail purchaser" constitutes, on its own, a warranty that explicitly extends to future performance and, if so, whether petitioners filed their action within the limitations period allowed by § 2–725(2).

This has been one of the more troublesome issues arising under § 2–725; the issue, indeed, pre-dated the Uniform Commercial Code and existed under the antecedent Uniform Sales Act. See Michael Schmitt and Kenneth Hanko, For Whom the Bell Tolls—An Interpretation of the UCC's Exception as to Accrual of a Cause of Action for Future Performance Warranties, 28 Ark. L. Rev. 311 (1974). Most of the cases and commentators note generally that the discovery rule exception provided in § 2–725(2) was intended to be a narrow one, strictly construed. See Anderson, Uniform Commercial Code, supra, § 2–725:123; William D. Hawkland, Uniform Commercial Code Series, § 2–725:2. To some extent, that view proceeds from the fact that the exception is just that, an exception to what was intended to be a fixed, uniform limitations period, as well as from the manner in which it is phrased, that the warranty must "explicitly" extend to future performance.

Thus, citing cases from five States, Anderson concludes that "[a] provision will not be interpreted as applying to future performance unless it very clearly does so" and that "[i]f there is any ambiguity it must be interpreted against the existence of such a warranty." Anderson, supra, § 2–725:123 at 285. Hawkland adds that the exception "seems limited to a single situation, namely, where the seller expressly gives a warranty for a period of time, such as guaranteeing a roof for 20 years." Hawkland, supra, § 2–725:2. . . .

There is no problem when the warranty simply states that the goods have a certain positive quality or are free from all or certain defects but states no time period during which the goods will continue to have that quality. That kind of warranty does not reference or extend to any future performance. If the goods do not have the warranted quality or are defective, the warranty is breached upon tender of delivery, and the buyer has four years from that date in which to file suit, even if the breach is not, in fact, discovered within that period. . . .

The matter is equally clear at the other end of the spectrum—where the warranty is that the goods will perform in a certain manner for a certain period of time or until a certain date. In that situation, not only does the warranty clearly and explicitly extend to future performance, but, unless the breach somehow manifests itself earlier, the buyer will be unable to determine whether the warranty is breached until the time stated for the performance arrives or, if the warranty is a continuing one, expires. That kind of warranty will fall within the § 2–725(2) exception, and, upon the discovery of non-performance at the stated time, or at any point short of the stated time, the buyer will have four years from that date within which to file suit.

The problem arises where, as in this case, the warranty is that the goods will have a certain quality or be free from defects for a certain period of time. There is no explicit reference to a particular kind or level of performance, but the quality of the goods, which underlies an expected performance, is warranted for a certain period of time and, absent a sooner manifestation, the buyer will not know whether there has been a breach until that time has expired. A number of courts have treated that kind of warranty as extending to future performance and have therefore applied the discovery rule stated in § 2–725(2). . . .

We believe that to be the correct view, one that is in accord with the nature of an express warranty. Section 2–313(1)(a) of the Maryland U.C.C. provides that "[a]ny affirmation of fact or promise made by the seller to the buyer which relates to the goods and becomes part of the basis of the bargain creates an express warranty that the goods shall conform to the affirmation or promise." If the seller affirms that the goods will have a certain quality or be free from defects for a stated period of time, that constitutes a warranty that the goods will conform to that affirmation and have that quality throughout the stated period, and thus explicitly extends to the future. Moreover, the quality of the goods, either by positive attribute or by negation of defects, necessarily relates to their performance. If the goods do not have the stated quality or develop a defect warranted against, they likely will not perform in the manner of goods that conform to the promise and thus in the manner that is reasonably anticipated by the parties. A warranty that goods will have a certain quality or be free from defects for a stated time thus, in our view, explicitly extends to future performance and is subject to the exception stated in § 2–725(2).

That does not, however, assist petitioners in this case. The stated period of the warranty was one year from delivery. No representations were made with respect to defects discovered after the expiration of that period. We reject as unsound petitioners' notion that the discovery period allowed by § 2–725(2) is unlimited. . . . Statutes must be read reasonably, to conform to their purpose and not to create absurdities. It cannot have been the legislative expectation that, when a seller provides a warranty of future performance limited to a stated period, it remains subject to liability forever or for an indefinite time. Such a view is wholly inconsistent with the paramount intent expressed in the Official Comment to the section of providing certainty in the statute of limitations. Once the stated period expires, the warranty does as well, and, unless the breach was, or reasonably should have been, discovered sooner, any action based on the warranty must be brought within four years after that expiration. Petitioners in this case thus had a maximum of five years from delivery to file their action. They failed to do so, and, for that reason, the action was properly dismissed.

Judgment of Court of Special Appeals affirmed, with costs.

NOTES

**(1) The Nature of the Manufacturer's Legal Undertaking.** Unlike the automobile manufacturers in *Tittle* and *Nationwide Insurance*, the manufacturer of the motor home provided to the ultimate buyer/consumer the manufacturer's Limited Warranty that the product would be free from substantial defects in materials and workmanship for a period of time. Like the automobile manufacturers, the motor home manufacturer provided a remedial repair/replace promise for a period of time. What did the drafter of the motor home Limited Warranty intend to be the relationship between the free-from-defects clause and the repair/replace clause? What did the court hold was the relationship between these clauses? Assuming that the motor home manufacturer was advised by counsel in drafting its contract document, how would you evaluate the quality of the lawyers' work?

**(2) Warranty Extending to Future Performance: Free from Defects.** The grammar of the free-from-defects clause used the phrase "to be free" with a one-year period of time. As we have considered previously, some manufacturers and sellers prefer to use a free-from-defects clause rather than the to be held to the fitness-for-ordinary-purpose implication of the warranty of merchantability. The facts relevant to a free-from-defects clause are facts that occur before delivery of the goods. That is when the materials are used and the work performed.

What was the meaning of the free-from-defects clause that ran for one year beyond delivery of the motor home? Did the clause contemplate that the manufacturer would do more work or use more materials within that year? Was the clause intended to define a period of time for the buyer to discover a latent defect that existed at delivery of the motor home? What meaning did the court give to the clause? What did the free-from-defects clause warrant as to the "future performance" of the motor home?

**(3) Construction of UCC 2–725 and of Time–Limited Warranties that Extend to Future Performance.** The exception clause in UCC 2–725(2) provides that a four-year period of limitations begins to run on a warranty that extends to future performance when "the breach is or should have been discovered." The statute says nothing about the period of time specified by the warrantor. Warranties that extend to future performance are almost always drafted to be limited to a stated time period. These warranties generally say nothing about the time for buyers' discovery of breach or about the onset of the period of limitations. How can the contractual terms and the statute be reconciled?

There are two possible scenarios: a breach is discovered before the end of the warranty period, or a breach is discovered after the warranty period ended. Under the first scenario, the statute and the warranty can be read together to provide that the period of limitations begins to run at the time the breach was discovered or should have been discovered, not from the end of the warranty period. What reading is appropriate if a breach occurs during the warranty period but is not, and should not have been, discovered before the end of the warranty period?

How was the issue presented in this case? Was the court's reasoning sound? Did the court find that the buyer had discovered or should have discovered the defect within one year from delivery? If the court had determined that the buyer's claim against the manufacturer was not "an action for breach of [a] contract for sale," should the court have held that UCC 2–725(1) was not the applicable law for determining the period of limitations? If the general contract period of limitations in Maryland is six years and begins to run when a cause of action accrues, would plaintiff's claim have been time-barred under that law?

**(4) Manufacturer's Remedial Promise.** The Maryland court held that the motor home manufacturer's repair/replace promise was an enforceable obligation, separate from the manufacturer's warranty of quality.

The court held that the plaintiff had not established that there had been any breach of that promise. The court reached that conclusion by interpreting the time term in the promise. Was the court's interpretation sound?

The time term in the promise was ten days longer than the time term in the warranty. What might have led the drafter of the manufacturer's Limited Warranty to do that?

On the Maryland court's analysis, what period of limitations would apply to a claim of breach of the remedial promise? When would a cause of action accrue? In a footnote (not reprinted above), the court cited the November 2000 draft of the proposed revision of UCC Article 2 for the proposition that "a promise by a seller to take remedial action 'is not a warranty at all and therefore is not subject to either the time-of-tender or discovery rule [of UCC 2–725(2)].' "The court did not discuss whether the four-year provision of UCC 2–725(1) or the general contract statute of limitations would apply.

HIGHWAY SALES, INC. v. BLUE BIRD CORP., 559 F.3d 782 (8th Cir. 2009). On July 31, 2003, Donald Oren purchased a Blue Bird Wanderlodge recreational vehicle (RV) from Shorewood RV, a Blue Bird authorized dealer. Oren paid the purchase price, $337,244, in full. Shorewood RV delivered the RV and a Blue Bird "limited warranty" as follows:

### LIMITED WARRANTY

1. Blue Bird Wanderlodge (Wanderlodge) warrants each Wanderlodge to the original purchaser to be free from defects in material and workmanship under normal use and service within the limits described below: For a period of two years from the date of delivery to the original purchaser warrants all components installed by Blue Bird and Wanderlodge, except diesel engines, automatic transmissions, tires and batteries, which are warranted by their manufacturers.

2. Wanderlodge's obligation covered in this Limited Warranty is limited to the repair or replacement of such parts as shall, under normal use and service, appear to have been defective in workmanship or material.

**ANY IMPLIED WARRANTIES, INCLUDING THOSE OF MERCHANTABILITY OR FITNESS, ARE LIMITED TO THE WARRANTY PERIOD OF THIS WRITTEN WARRANTY. WANDERLODGE SHALL NOT BE LIABLE FOR INCIDENTAL OR CONSEQUENTIAL DAMAGES RESULTING FROM BREACH OF THIS WRITTEN WARRANTY OR ANY IMPLIED WARRANTY. NO PERSON, INCLUDING SALESPEOPLE, DEALERS, SERVICE CENTERS, OR FACTORY REPRESENTATIVES OF WANDERLODGE, IS AUTHORIZED TO MAKE ANY REPRESENTATION OR WARRANTY CONCERNING WANDERLODGE PRODUCTS EXCEPT TO REFER TO THIS LIMITED WARRANTY.**

3. Defects shall be repaired promptly after discovery of the defect and within the warranty period as stated herein. All claims for warranty adjustments must be received by Wanderlodge not later than 30 days after the repair date, and shall be channeled through an authorized Wanderlodge dealer or factory representative. Any suit alleging a breach of this limited warranty or any other alleged warranty must be filed within one year of breach.

Following the sale, Oren discovered failures of the vehicle's electrical system, batteries, seals, slides, gauges, compressor, monitor, and lighting. Oren returned the RV to Shorewood RV for repairs on a number of occasions. Despite Shorewood RV's efforts, Oren continued experiencing problems with the vehicle.

On July 2, 2004, Oren delivered the RV to Shorewood RV. Oren informed Anthony Santarsiero, a Shorewood RV employee, that Oren was returning the vehicle as of that day. Santarsiero gave Oren the name of Blue Bird's CEO and told Oren to call or write the CEO a letter to try to resolve the problem. On July 8, 2004, Oren wrote a letter to Blue Bird's CEO asking him to authorize repurchase of the vehicle at its original cost. The letter stated, in part:

... After almost a year of continued problems with this motor home, I have run out of patience, confidence, and trust that the problems can be fixed in a reasonable time, and I request that you return my purchase price. I'm not interested in further retrofits, patches, or excuses. I will never take this coach back.

On July 31, 2004, a Blue Bird technician came to Shorewood RV and performed a major electrical retrofit on the vehicle. The batteries failed again on August 12, 2004. Additional repairs were made by the Blue Bird technician on August 19, 2004.

On September 7, 2004, Blue Bird rejected Oren's request for a refund, asserting:

[y]our electrical issue on your motor home has been repaired.... We do not refund purchases or buy units back. We are committed to working with our Dealers and Customers to resolve any service needs that may occur. I know you have had some battery issues with your unit, but I am confident that these issues have been resolved. You have a reliable unit that should give you the service and performance it is designed for.

On September 14, 2004, Oren signed an agreement authorizing Shorewood RV to sell the RV on behalf of Oren. Oren agreed to pay Shorewood RV a percentage of the proceeds. A Shorewood RV mechanic made additional repairs to the vehicle on September 28, 2004, and October 4, 2004 and Shorewood RV displayed the vehicle for sale on the lot with other used RVs.

On October 27, 2004, Oren again wrote to Blue Bird, demanding refund of the purchase price. On November 5, 2004, Blue Bird replied. Blue Bird refused to provide a refund, declaring "Blue Bird stands behind this motor home which is a reliable unit and will give you the service and performance for which it is designed." Blue Bird then apologized for any inconvenience Oren incurred while the vehicle was being repaired and offered to "send a Wanderlodge factory representative to Shorewood to provide additional owner training and a systems check" of the vehicle.

On November 17, 2004, Oren went to the Shorewood RV lot where he found the batteries were dead.

On November 29, 2004, Oren replied to Blue Bird, enclosing a spreadsheet detailing the problems he had experienced with the vehicle and stating

My purpose in sending along this information is to document the fact that neither Blue Bird, nor its authorized representative, Shorewood R.V. Center, has succeeded in meeting its obligations to conform the vehicle to the applicable express warranties. As the record clearly demonstrates, even after a reasonable number of attempts to repair the electrical and other problems that have haunted this unit, it remains unfit for the purpose it was intended; therefore, I reiterate my demand that Blue Bird make a full refund of the purchase price of the unit.

On July 15, 2005, Oren filed suit against Blue Bird. The complaint asserted breach of express warranty and implied warranty of merchantability under UCC Article 2. Blue Bird agreed that the Limited Warranty constituted an express warranty of future performance under UCC 2–725(2), but asserted that all warranty claims were time-barred by lapse of the one year period of limitations in the Limited Warranty. Blue Bird moved for summary judgment. In the trial court, the motion was considered first by a federal magistrate, who found that implied warranty was time-barred, but not the express warranty. The District Judge ruled that all warranty claims were barred.

The Court of Appeals stated that breach of the express warranty would occur when the manufacturer refused or was unable to make the warranted repair. The court held that Blue Bird had not stopped trying to remedy the defects, but that breach would occur at the time Oren subjectively concluded that Blue Bird was unable to remedy the defects. The court held that there was a genuine issue of material fact as to when Oren made such a determination. The summary judgment in favor of Blue Bird was reversed.

The Court of Appeals stated that breach of an implied warranty of merchantability occurs on the date of delivery. A majority of the court held that one-year period in the Limited Warranty had elapsed well before the suit was filed. A dissenting judge would have found that the one-year provision was not sufficiently conspicuous and too ambiguous to be enforced and, further, that the manufacturer's attempts to repair tolled the period. Oren did not argue that the Limited Warranty's Magnuson–Moss term referring to the "duration" of the implied warranty had any effect on fixing date of breach of that warranty and the majority did not discuss that issue. Characterizing the Limited Warranty as an obligation to make the RV merchantable (rather than free from defects in material or workmanship) for a two-year period after delivery, the dissent found it against public policy for the merchantability warranty to expire before that period ended.

Counsel for Oren did not contend that the remedial promise failed of its essential purpose, per UCC 2–719(2), and that the buyer was therefore entitled to UCC Article 2 remedies.

There is no indication that counsel or the courts considered common contract law instead of UCC Article 2 as the law governing the manufacturer's Limited Warranty obligation.

CHAPTER 6

# EXECUTION OF SALES CONTRACTS: MANNER, TIME AND PLACE OF SELLERS' AND BUYERS' PERFORMANCES

Previous chapters were concerned with the "what" (title and quality) and the "who" (privity) of sales transactions. This chapter considers "when," "where," and "how" the parties execute the promises made in contracts of sale. Buyers and sellers may fix the terms of time, place and manner of performance by agreement. Terms may be set by express agreement or by implication from trade usage, course of dealing, or course of performance.

It is not uncommon for agreements to confer on one party discretion to determine certain matters regarding particulars of performance, perhaps within limits. Thus, an agreement may require seller to ship goods in March, the exact date to be determined by the seller. Under domestic United States law, when an agreement "leaves particulars of performance to be specified by one of the parties, . . . specification must be made in good faith and within limits set by commercial reasonableness." UCC 2–311(1).

Buyers and sellers often fail to agree, even by implication, on time, place and manner of each party's performance. Such buyers and sellers look to the law to fill the gaps. One of the functions of modern commercial law is to provide a set of gap-fillers.

---

## SECTION 1. LOCAL SALES TRANSACTIONS

### (A) DOMESTIC UNITED STATES LAW

Performance of sales contracts is relatively simple when the places of business or the residences of the buyers and sellers are in the same local area. Sellers' obligation is to hand over the goods and buyers' obligation is to pay the purchase price. When the parties are close enough that it is practical for them to meet, their contract obligations can be performed in face-to-face meetings where goods and money are exchanged. In the absence of agreement, the law determines where and when those meetings occur and what actions the parties are required to take there. Rules supplied by law are commonly referred to as "default rules."

Contractual terms on when, where and how sales contracts are to be executed are enforceable obligations. A party who fails, without excuse, to meet an obligation when due is in breach of contract, and the aggrieved party will have one or more legal remedies. The terms of parties' agreements or the law's default rules provide the normative standards against which to measure whether sellers' or buyers' acts or omissions were in breach of their obligation to execute sales contracts.

Basic performance obligations and related default rules are stated by UCC Article 2. The Code provisions are found largely in Parts 3 and 5 of that Article. You should read those parts of the Code to get a general sense of the matters that are covered.

Section 2–301 of the Code states the general obligation of both parties:

The obligation of the seller is to transfer and deliver and that of the buyer is to accept and pay in accordance with the contract.

"Transfer" refers to title to the goods and "deliver" refers to the physical goods themselves. On the buyers' side, the general obligation to "pay" is coupled with the obligation to "accept" the goods. This purport of the obligation to "accept" is, on the surface, strange;[1] if sellers are paid, would they care whether buyers "accept" the goods? We will defer further consideration of that matter until the next chapter.

The parties' UCC 2–301 obligations are elaborated in the operational standards of *tender of delivery* and *tender of payment*. Tender connotes performance by the tendering party that satisfies its obligation and puts the other party in default if it fails to execute its obligation. See UCC 2–507(1) and 2–511(1). The default rules on time, place and manner of the parties' performance obligations use the concept of tender.

*Sellers' Tender of Delivery of Goods.* "Tender of delivery requires that the seller put and hold conforming goods at the buyer's disposition and give the buyer any notification reasonably necessary to enable him to take delivery." UCC 2–503(1). The "put and hold" formulation, which by implication excludes "let go," is the essence of the concept of tender of goods. Tender must be at a "reasonable hour" and tendered goods must be kept available for "the period reasonably necessary to enable the buyer to take possession." UCC 2–503(1)(a). "Tender" begins delivery, but effecting completed delivery usually requires a buyer's response.

*Place of Sellers' Tender.* If the agreement is silent, the default rule establishes the place of delivery at a merchant seller's place of business.

---

**1.** Students should be cautious to avoid confusing "acceptance of goods" with the concepts of offer and acceptance familiar from general contract law and found in UCC Article 2 in UCC 2–206 and 2–207. "Acceptance of an offer" is a way of describing formation of contracts. "Acceptance of goods" is a concept used in connection with buyers' performance of sales contracts. Referring to "acceptance" without indicating whether one is referring to acceptance of an offer or of goods can be confusing, but context usually indicates which type of acceptance is meant. See, e.g., UCC 2–310.

UCC 2–308(a). In this circumstance, a seller tenders by holding the goods at its place of business and notifying buyer that the goods are available.[2] Sellers may agree to take the goods to their buyers; in such transactions, the Code provides that buyers must furnish facilities reasonably suited to receipt of the goods.[3] UCC 2–503(1)(b).

*Time of Sellers' Tender.* Section 2–503(1)(a) provides that sellers' tender must be made at a reasonable hour and for a reasonable duration, but does not have a default rule for the date on which a seller is required to have the goods ready. The Code's answer is a "reasonable time" standard. UCC 2–309(1). Under this provision, a seller has some leeway before failure to tender delivery becomes a breach of contract. The outside limits of that period of time will be difficult to fix as an exact date in most transactions. In some circumstances, however, the time of sellers' performances can be critical to the buyers' ability to realize the expected value of the goods purchased.[4]

*Time of Payment.* Sales contracts are more likely to have express or implied terms regarding buyers' time payment than sellers' tender of delivery. In certain transactions, the contract requires buyers to pay part of the price before seller tenders delivery of the goods. Such payments are often called "down payments." Parties to sales contracts often agree to a payment term that involves sellers' extending credit to the buyers. Sellers willing to extend credit deliver the goods before buyers pay the price. Sometimes the credit period is relatively short, e.g., 10 days after invoice or at the end of the month after delivery. In other transactions, the credit period is quite long. Long-term credit arrangements are often part of secured transactions or other arrangements that reduce the risk of buyers' failure to pay. In contracts that are silent on the time that payment is due, the default rules fill that gap and provide further for other incidents of buyers' performance.

*Tender of Payment.* UCC Article 2 refers to "tender of payment" in UCC 2–511, but does not define what constitutes such a tender. By analogy to tender of delivery, tender of payment occurs when a buyer "puts and holds" money or other instrument or payment device at the disposition of a seller. If a buyer tenders a personal bank check,[5] seller may insist on legal tender but must give buyer any additional time needed to procure it. UCC 2–511(2). Many sellers now accept payment in the form of a bank-issued

---

**2.** The Commercial Code has no provision declaring that buyers are contractually obligated to take possession of tendered goods. When sellers put and hold goods at buyers' disposition, in the overwhelming majority of transactions the buyers will dispose of them. They want to have possession of the goods they agreed to buy. That may explain why the Code is silent on the matter.

**3.** This provision on buyers' obligation is oddly located in a section defining the manner of sellers' tender of delivery. Comment 4 to 2–503 states that this obligation of the buyer is no part of the seller's tender.

**4.** One of the circumstances is sale of perishable commodities.

**5.** Personal checks would likely be considered a means of payment "current in the ordinary course of business." UCC 2–511(2). A buyer's personal check is an order by the buyer to a designated bank to pay money to a designated payee on demand. See UCC 3–104.

credit card, but sellers are not required to take payment in this form. Another form of payment, the debit card, authorizes buyer's bank to make an immediate transfer funds from buyer's bank account to seller's bank account. This mode of payment is quite satisfactory to sellers that have the requisite telecommunication connections.

*Place and Time of Buyers' Tender.* A buyer's payment is due "at the time and place at which the buyer is to receive the goods...." UCC 2–310(a). If the place of delivery is the merchant seller's place of business, the default rule of UCC 2–308(a), then that is the place of payment as well. If the parties agreed that the goods would be delivered elsewhere, then the place of payment changes accordingly.

When the default rules are applicable, performances by seller and buyer are required to occur simultaneously. UCC 2–511(1) declares that "tender of payment is a condition to the seller's duty to tender and complete any delivery," while UCC 2–507(1) declares that "tender of delivery is a condition to the buyer's ... duty to pay...."

*Buyers' Right to Inspect Before Payment.* Before paying, a buyer has the right to inspect the goods. UCC 2–513(1) provides that "where goods are tendered or delivered or identified to the contract of sale, the buyer has a right before payment ... to inspect them ... in any reasonable manner." The Code does not define "inspect." The word could have many different meanings, including simple visual examination, scientific chemical or physical analysis, and trial use. The drafting of UCC 2–513 is a source of further confusion. It ties the right to inspect to three events, stated in the alternative. For present purposes, the difference between "tender" and "delivery" are pertinent.[6] "Tender" means put-and-hold, but not let-go. Tendered goods are still in the seller's control. "Delivery" implies transfer of possession to the buyer. The nature of a possible inspection of goods that are in the buyer's possession is quite different from the nature of an inspection of goods that are in the seller's possession. The problem with UCC 2–513(1) is that it does not provide whether the right to inspect is triggered by the first or the last of the listed events. The use of 'or' suggests that passage of any of them will be sufficient.

*Tender of Delivery in "Lots."* Ordinarily, sellers must tender at one time all the goods sold, but the Code has an exception for partial deliveries.[7] If a seller properly delivers goods in installments, in the absence of

---

**6.** Seller's identification of goods to a sales contract is an event that precedes tender. Identification of goods is not an incident of performance. The goods may be identified at the time of contracting if the goods exist then. For "future goods" other than certain agricultural products, identification is done by sellers, unilaterally. See UCC 2–501(1). After goods have been identified to a sales contract, the buyer has an insurable interest in the goods. Id. Identification also gives a pre-paying buyer the right to recover the goods from an insolvent seller. UCC 2–502.

**7.** When a single article has been sold, delivery or tender of that article is the only performance possible. However, sometimes the goods sold are physically divisible into "lots." UCC 2–105(5). Under what circumstances may a seller make a proper delivery or tender of less than all of the goods? The agreement may provide for multiple deliveries. In the absence of express agreement, the circumstances may indicate that this is not only proper but

agreement otherwise, a buyer must pay for each delivery if the contract price can be apportioned; otherwise the buyer can withhold all payment until all the goods have been tendered. UCC 2–307.

**Problem 1.** Wire Manufacturer ordered a quantity of certain copper from Copper Trading Co., which agreed to supply it. The sales agreement specified no delivery date. Manufacturer knew that Trading Co. would have to find a source of copper that met Manufacturer's needs, but assumed that no shortage of such copper existed. Trading Co. also assumed that it would have little difficulty locating the needed copper at a favorable price. Trading Co. discovered that the copper market is "tight" and spot prices are high. Trading Co. extended its search for copper to look for a relatively low price in the current market or, if necessary, to wait out what it hopes is a temporary peak in market prices.

(a) Manufacturer, whose inventory of copper is running low, demands that Trading Co. make immediate delivery. Trading Co. responds that it will deliver soon but gives no specific date.

(i) As counsel for Manufacturer, advise it on when Trading Co. was or will be in default.

(ii) As counsel for Trading Co., advise it as to the outside limit of its time for performance without breach.

(b) Manufacturer declares Trading Co. in default and institutes legal action. Which party has the burden of proving that a reasonable time had elapsed before Manufacturer's decision?

**Problem 2.** Plastics agreed to manufacture and deliver 40,000 pounds of special high-impact polystyrene pellets at 19 cents a pound for Industries. Industries agreed to accept delivery at the rate of 1000 pounds per day as the pellets were produced. Two weeks after the June 30 agreement, Plastics notified Industries that it was ready to deliver. Industries telephoned to say that labor difficulties and vacation schedules made it impossible to receive any pellets immediately; in that conversation Plastics replied that it would complete production and that it hoped that Industries would start taking delivery soon.

(a) On August 18, Plastics wrote to Industries: "We produced 40,000 pounds of high-impact pellets to your special order. You indicated that you would be using 1,000 lbs. per day. We have warehoused these products for more than forty days. However, we cannot keep these products indefinitely and request that you begin taking delivery. We have done everything that we agreed to do." After another month, Industries has not taken any pellets. Plastics consults you for legal assistance. What advice would you give? Is UCC 2–610 applicable? Compare Multiplastics v. Arch Industries, 166 Conn. 280, 348 A.2d 618 (1974).

---

necessary. For example, the buyer of a large quantity of bricks needed to construct a large building may lack space at the site to store all the bricks if delivered at one time; when both seller and buyer are aware of this, multiple deliveries are proper. The default rule, however, is that all the goods must be delivered or tendered in a single lot. UCC 2–307.

(b) Suppose Plastics had consulted you before sending its August 18 letter. Would you have advised changes in the letter? Would you have set a specific date as a deadline for Industries to take delivery? Is UCC 2–311 helpful? Would you advise sending a written demand pursuant to UCC 2–609(1)?

**Problem 3.** Consumer and Car Dealer entered into a sales agreement for a new automobile. Three weeks after the agreement, Car Dealer notified Consumer that the specified car had arrived. Consumer went to Car Dealer's place of business, looked at and sat in the car, kicked the tires, lifted the hood and peered at the engine. Consumer asked for the keys in order to "take it for a spin" to see if the car performed satisfactorily. Car Dealer responded that Consumer could have the keys only after he had paid the price. Has Consumer had a reasonable opportunity to inspect? The Code declares that "tender of payment is a condition of the seller's duty to . . . complete any delivery." UCC 2–507(1). Does this support Car Dealer's contention that Consumer's right to inspect includes only what Consumer can learn from examination of the goods while still in the Car Dealer's possession?

**Problem 4.** Builder, constructing a new house, ordered appliances from Dealer. The sales contract required Dealer to deliver the appliances to the construction site on February 1. Builder agreed to pay 30 days after delivery. When Dealer's truck arrived, after 5 p.m., Builder's employees had gone home for the night. Dealer's truck driver put the appliances into the garage and locked it. Were Dealer's actions in conformity with the requirements of UCC 2–503? See Ron Mead T.V. & Appliance v. Legendary Homes, 746 P.2d 1163 (Okla. App. 1987).

## (B)   INTERNATIONAL SALES LAW

The Convention on Contracts for International Sale of Goods states the general obligation of buyers and sellers. Article 30 provides:

> The seller must deliver the goods, hand over any documents relating to them and transfer the property in the goods, as required by the contract and this Convention.

Article 53 is the reciprocal provision for buyers:

> The buyer must pay the price for the goods and take delivery of them as required by the contract and this Convention.

The Convention does not use the concept of *tender* for either party's performance.

Because of its scope, CISG is more concerned with sales transactions in which the parties are in different nations and are therefore likely to be at considerable distance from each other. However, the Convention does provide default rules of performance of contracts that do not involve use of the services of a carrier to transport the goods. The default rules apply only to the extent that the agreement of the parties is silent.

*Time and Place of Seller's Delivery.* Seller's obligation to deliver consists of "placing the goods at the buyer's disposal at the place where the seller had his place of business at the time of the conclusion of the contract," CISG 31(c), unless the parties knew from the circumstances of the contract that the goods would be placed at buyer's disposal at another location. CISG 31(b).

*Time and Place of Buyers' Payment.* Unless otherwise agreed, "a buyer must pay when the seller places either the goods or documents controlling their disposition at the buyer's disposal in accordance with the contract and this Convention." CISG 58(1). If payment is to be made against the handing over of goods or of documents, a buyer must pay "at the place where the handing over takes place." CISG 57(1)(b). Otherwise, payment must be made "at the seller's place of business." CISG 57(1)(a).

*Inspection of Goods Before Payment.* Absent agreement to the contrary, buyers are not bound to pay the price until they have had opportunity to examine the goods. CISG 58(3).

## SECTION 2. CONTRACTS PERFORMED VIA CARRIERS

### (A) DOMESTIC UNITED STATES LAW

We turn now to transactions in which sales contracts are performed through an intermediary, a carrier, and the necessary adaptation of agreements and the law governing performance of those contracts. Goods move to their markets on trucks, railroads, airplanes, and ships whose owners are transportation companies that sell a commercial service. Some carriers hold themselves out as available to the public; they are deemed "common carriers" and are regulated by federal and state laws. Others, known as "contract carriers," do not offer their services to the general public.[1]

Sales agreements determine whether sellers are required or authorized to ship the goods to buyers via carriers. The most elementary type of agreement involves simply that, a requirement or authorization to ship. In many circumstances, even though agreements are silent on the matter of shipment, the distance between sellers and buyers makes it evident that the default rules for local transactions are not appropriate and that the shipment of the goods is the implicitly expected method of delivery. Once an agreement authorizes or requires the seller to ship the goods, absent further agreement on the manner and time of shipment, all other elements of performance of the sales contract could be supplied by law.

Domestic United States law recognizes two standard variants of sales transactions in which carriers are used to transport goods from sellers to buyers. The difference between the two variants depends upon the place of

---

**1.** There is a large body of commercial practice and commercial law that deals with contracts for transport of goods. These materials refer to those practices and law only to the extent necessary to understand their effect on sales contracts

a seller's performance that conforms to the sales contract. The more common variant provides that a seller performs its duties under the sales contract when it turns over the goods to the carrier. Sales contracts of this kind are referred to as "shipment contracts." The alternative place of a seller's performance is at the termination of the transportation, where the carrier turns over the goods to the buyer. These sales contracts are referred to as "destination contracts." Significant legal issues regarding the time and manner of sellers' and buyers' performance depend upon whether their sales contracts are shipment contracts or destination contracts.[2]

## 1.   SHIPMENT CONTRACTS

When a sales contract is a shipment contract, the default rules for the seller's performance are found in UCC 2–503(2) and UCC 2–504. Section 2–504(a) and (c) states two basic requirements. A seller must:

> (a) put the goods in the possession of the carrier and make a contract for their transportation as may be reasonable having regard to the nature of the goods and other circumstances,[3] and . . .

> (c) promptly notify the buyer of the shipment.

Comment 1 to UCC 2–504 declares that the general principles of the section cover the cases of "F.O.B. [free on board] point of shipment contracts." This Comment refers to a common trade term that sellers and buyers may use in their sales agreements when they contemplate that the goods will be shipped by railroad.[4] To make commercial sense, an F.O.B. term must refer to a place where the goods are to be "free on board." The Comment refers to the place as the "point of shipment," i.e., the place where a seller puts the goods in the possession of a carrier. Often sales contracts that use an F.O.B. point-of-shipment term will identify the point of shipment merely by reference to the city where sellers have their places of business, e.g., "F.O.B. Sellersville."

Shipment contracts are often performed through use of transportation modes other than rail. Goods may be sent by various ground, air or water transportation carriers. The provisions of sales contracts for such means of shipment will vary with the nature of the services used, but are not likely to be expressed in an F.O.B. term.

*Manner of Sellers' Tender of Delivery of the Goods.* Designation of the seller's city in the F.O.B. term of a sales contract or use of any other term that authorizes or requires a seller to ship the goods to the buyer has the

---

**2.** Sellers and buyers who are located at a distance from each other may make arrangements for transporting the goods that do not entail the use of carriers. Sellers or buyers may have their own vehicles that they use to send or pick up the goods. Sales contracts that contemplate use of these vehicles are not shipment or destination contracts. The applicable default rules of law are those that apply to local transactions.

**3.** Specifications and arrangements relating to shipment are at the seller's option unless otherwise agreed. UCC 2–311(2) . . .

**4.** The meaning of the F.O.B. term, when used in sales contracts, is defined in UCC 2–319(1).

important legal effect of defining the seller's obligations with respect to tender of the goods.[5] Section 2–503(2) provides that "tender requires that the seller comply with [UCC 2–504]." The Code does not elaborate on the criteria for determining the mode of transport or the nature of the "reasonable contract" that a seller must make with a transportation company.[6] The Code does indicate that the criteria may vary with the nature of the goods. Use of the term F.O.B. place-of-shipment has the added meaning, under UCC 2–319(1)(a) that the seller must "bear the expense and risk of putting the goods into the possession of the carrier."[7]

*Time of Sellers' Tender of Delivery.* When sellers are authorized or required to ship goods to buyers via carriers, the matter of time of performance can be broken down into multiple questions: when must seller deliver to carrier, when must seller give notice of shipment to buyer, and when must carrier deliver to buyer? If the sales contract is a "place of shipment" contract, it may provide that seller must ship within a stated time, but in the absence of agreement the reasonable-time standard would apply. UCC 2–309(1). A contract may have a term that requires seller to use the fastest means, such as overnight deliver or air transport, but land and water transportation companies do not generally guarantee dates of arrival. Once a shipment is begun, seller's notification to buyer must be made "promptly." UCC 2–504(c).

*Time, Place and Manner of Buyers' Payment.* In shipment contracts, sellers complete their performance obligations substantially before buyers physically receive the goods. The simultaneous exchange of performances that occur in local transactions is not feasible. The tender rules, for both sellers and buyers, must accommodate to that fact. The Commercial Code contains default rules for the time, place and manner of buyers' payment when goods are delivered by carrier pursuant to an elementary shipment contract.

Unless otherwise agreed, payment is due at the time and place at which the buyer is to receive the goods. UCC 2–310(a). This rule applies even though the place of shipment is the place of delivery. Buyers ordinarily receive shipped goods at the termination of the carriage. Sellers may

---

**5.** The Code describes an F.O.B. term as a "delivery term," UCC 2–319(1), and not "merely a price term." Comment 1.

**6.** The basis of the controversy in *Hadley v. Baxendale* was the decision of transportation company to use water transport rather than rail to carry a piece of broken manufacturing equipment to the place where it could be repaired. Water transport was slower (and perhaps less expensive) than transport by rail. The delay caused the mill to be shut down longer than it would have been. The mill owner sought consequential damages for loss of revenue from the mill during the extended down-time. See R. Danzig, *Hadley v. Baxendale*: A Study in the Industrialization of the Law, 4 J. Legal Studies 249 (1975).

**7.** When, according to the sales contract, the buyer bears the cost of freight, as in an F.O.B. Sellersville contract, the seller may pay the carrier and add the freight charge to the invoice for the contract price. When, according to the sales contract, the seller bears the cost of freight, as in an F.O.B. Sellersville contract, the price of the goods will likely be high enough to cover all of the seller's costs, including the costs of freight. Freight costs initially allocated to sellers are likely to be passed through to their buyers.

designate an agent to receive payment at that time and place. Some carriers offer this as an additional service. In the absence of someone authorized to receive payment being there when the goods arrive, buyers must send the price to sellers. This can be done by mailing checks but, if the agreements require faster transmittal of the funds, by "wire transfers" or other electronic forms of payment.

*Inspection of the Goods.* The rule, in UCC 2–513(1), that a buyer has the right to inspect the goods before payment applies to shipment contracts. That subsection declares: "When the seller is required or authorized to send the goods to the buyer, the inspection may be after their arrival." In these elementary shipment contracts, carriers deliver the goods to buyers on arrival. Buyers are thus in possession of the goods to be inspected.

## 2.   DESTINATION CONTRACTS

The default performance rules that apply to destination contracts are different from the default rules that apply to shipment contracts. If a seller is required to deliver the goods *at a particular destination*, the tender rules applicable to local transactions apply, but the locale for performance of both parties is at the place where the carrier holds the goods for delivery to the buyer. UCC 2–503(3).

If the parties use an F.O.B. term in a sales contract and designate "the place of destination," UCC Article 2 characterizes this as a contract in which seller is required to deliver *at* a particular destination. A seller must, at its own expense, transport the goods to "*the* place of destination" and *there* tender delivery of the goods to the buyer. UCC 2–319(1)(b). The tender rules are otherwise comparable to rules for sellers' tender in local transactions, UCC 2–503(3), except the place of tender is at the destination of the transportation. Seller must tender at that place within the time permitted by the sales contract. In all likelihood, the seller will not be "there" in person to put and hold the goods at buyer's disposition. This is often effected by the carrier acting pursuant to seller's instructions.

In destination contracts, absent further agreement, the put-and-hold manner of seller's tender of delivery of the goods would apply if seller has an agent at the place of destination that is able to make tender in that manner. Under the default rules of the Commercial Code, seller would not be obligated to hand over the goods until buyer tendered any payment due and buyer's right to inspect may have to be exercised before the goods are handed over.

In destination contracts, the required time for sellers to deliver is more complicated than in local transactions. Sellers typically cannot control the speed of service by rail, truck, or water carriers.[8] Contracts of sale that contemplate use of independent carriers rarely provide a firm date for

---

**8.**   Some transportation services will guarantee delivery within a specified time, e.g., overnight or second-day delivery, but these carriers tend to place severe restrictions on their liability for defaults.

delivery. However the reasonable-time default rule of UCC 2–309(1) is likely to apply. Consider the following case.

# Mendelson–Zeller Co. v. Joseph Wedner & Son Co.

U.S. Department of Agriculture, 1970.
29 Agriculture Decisions 476.

■ Flavin, Judicial Officer.

## PRELIMINARY STATEMENT

This is a reparation proceeding under the Perishable Agricultural Commodities Act, 1930, as amended (7 U.S.C. 499a et seq.) A timely complaint was filed in which complainant seeks reparation against respondent in the amount of $2,480.73 in connection with a shipment of cantaloupes and lettuce in interstate commerce.

A copy of the formal complaint and of the Department's report of investigation were served upon the respondent, and respondent filed an answer denying liability. The answer included a counterclaim for $2,892.73. Complainant did not file a reply to the counterclaim and therefore it is deemed to be denied pursuant to section 47.9(a) of the rules of practice (7 CFR 47.9(a)).

An oral hearing at the request of respondent was held at Pittsburgh, Pennsylvania, on July 30, 1969. Respondent was represented by counsel at the hearing. One witness appeared for respondent. Complainant filed a brief.

## FINDINGS OF FACT

1. Complainant, Mendelson–Zeller Co., Inc., is a corporation whose address is 450 Sansome Street, San Francisco, California. At the time of the transaction involved herein, complainant was licensed under the act.

2. Respondent, Joseph Wedner & Son Co., is a corporation whose address is 2018 Smallman Street, Pittsburgh, Pennsylvania. At the time of the transaction involved herein, respondent was licensed under the act.

3. On or about March 7, 1968, in the course of interstate commerce, complainant contracted orally to sell to respondent, a mixed truckload of produce consisting of 25 cartons of cantaloupes Jumbo size 45 at $17.75 per carton, 85 cartons of cantaloupes Jumbo size 56 at $15.25 per carton, and 574 cartons of lettuce size 24 at $3.45 per carton, delivered Pittsburgh, Pennsylvania. The total delivered price for the truckload, including $15.00 for top ice, was $4,116.55. It was agreed that shipment would begin on March 8. The parties estimated that delivery would be in time for the market of Tuesday morning, March 12, 1968.

4. Complainant shipped the lettuce at 9:40 a.m. March 8, 1968, from El Centro, California, and the cantaloupes were shipped at 10:00 p.m. the same day from Nogales, Arizona, in a truck operated by Arkansas Traffic Service, Inc., of Redfield, Arkansas. At 12:00 a.m. March 12, the truck

driver called respondent stating that the truck would arrive about 3:00 or 3:30 p.m. and requesting that respondent's men wait to unload the truck. Respondent checked with its men, who said they would not wait, and then told the truck driver to arrive at 3:00 a.m. the morning of March 13th.

5.  The truckload of produce arrived at respondent's place of business at 5:00 a.m., March 13, 1968, approximately 103 hours after leaving Nogales, Arizona.

6.  Respondent unloaded and sold the commodities and remitted the net proceeds in the amount of $1,635.82 to complainant.

7.  The formal complaint was filed on August 1, 1968, which was within 9 months after accrual of the cause of action.

## CONCLUSIONS

Complainant seeks to recover the full delivered price for the truckload of produce sold to respondent and respondent contends that it was justified in remitting only the net proceeds resulting from its resale of the produce. The only material factual dispute relates to whether a delivery time of 3:00 a.m. March 12, 1968, was specified as a condition of the delivered sale contract. Complainant contends that such time was not specified as a contract condition but was merely the estimated time of arrival assuming normal condition, and that a 48 hour leeway is allowable by custom in such cases.

On March 13, 1968, the day the truck actually arrived, respondent's Manager, Norman Wedner, wrote to complainant's Sales Manager, Mr. E. A. Melia, Jr., in part as follows:

> The truck of mixed lettuce and cantaloupes was due for the market of Tuesday morning at 3:00 AM March 12, 1968.
>
> The truck driver called us at noon Tuesday and said he would be in at 3:00 or 3:30 PM Tuesday afternoon, and asked us to have the men wait to unload him. We held him on the phone and our warehouse men said they could not wait for him. We then told him to be at the warehouse at 3:00 AM Wednesday morning. He said fine, he would be there.
>
> He didn't arrive until 5:00 AM Wednesday Mar. 13, 1968. The lettuce wasn't available for delivery until 6:30 AM, causing us to miss a large chain store order.

Complainant's Traffic Manager, John Monk testified by deposition and referred to an exhibit which he said was a correct copy of his notes concerning instructions for the shipment of the produce. The exhibit is entitled "Loading and Delivery instructions," and in part gives the following information: "Delivery Date *Tues* Time *3:30 AM.*" Mr. Monk stated that this exhibit reflected the estimated time of arrival and that he "was given no specific instructions as to actual time of delivery other than the delivery was to be planned so that if at all possible it would arrive in Pittsburgh on Tuesday morning." Complainant's Salesman, Irving Raznikov, stated that he was the actual recipient of the telephone order from Mr.

Wedner. Although he stated that "Wedner requested a Tuesday a.m. arrival and I indicated to him that under normal circumstances there would be no problem with said delivery schedule," he also stated that he "stressed with Mr. Wedner that we could not and would not guarantee any specific arrival."

Respondent as the party alleging that a specified arrival time was a part of the contract of sale had the burden of proving by a preponderance of the evidence that its allegation was true. In view of the foregoing discussion we conclude that respondent has not met its burden of proof.

Section 2–309(1) of the Uniform Commercial Code provides that the time for delivery in the absence of an agreed time shall be a reasonable time. The load was tendered and accepted at 5:00 a.m. March 13, about 103 hours after the truck left Nogales, Arizona. Under the circumstances, we are unable to say the delivery was not within a reasonable time.

The failure of respondent to pay to complainant the full purchase price of $4,116.55 for the lettuce was in violation of section 2 of the act. Respondent has already paid net proceeds of $1,635.82 to complainant. Reparation should therefore be awarded to complainant for the balance of the purchase price of $2,480.73, with interest. In the absence of any breach of contract on the part of complainant, respondent's counterclaim should be dismissed.

## ORDER

Within 30 days from the date of this order, respondent shall pay to complainant, as reparation, $2,480.73, with interest thereon at the rate of 6 percent per annum from April 1, 1968, until paid.

The counterclaim should be dismissed.

## NOTES

**(1) Delay in Buyer's Receipt of the Goods.** This case illustrates how much economic significance can attach to time of performance in certain kinds of sales transactions. Buyer resold lettuce and cantaloupes after 5:00 a.m. for $1,635.82, less than half of the original contract price. Moreover, buyer claimed damages of nearly $2,900.00, presumably profit that buyer allegedly would have made on resale to the large chain store. Assuming that the resale was reasonable[9] and the amount claimed as damages was not exaggerated, goods delivered at 3:00 a.m. were worth $5,000 more than goods delivered at 5:00 a.m.

**(2) Contract Interpretation.** Buyer's counsel apparently contended that the delivery term in the "Loading and Delivery instructions" was binding upon the seller. Was this document part of the contract of sale? On what theory might it reflect on the sales contract?[10]

---

**9.** The opinion does not suggest that the buyer "dumped" the goods for less than their market value at the time of resale.

**10.** A different legal question is whether the terms of the document were part of the contract of carriage and binding on the carrier. Although the buyer was not a named party to

**(3) Time of Seller's Tender of Delivery.** The judicial officer concluded that the sales contract did not provide either the day and the hour for seller's delivery of the goods. The question whether the seller made timely tender of delivery depended upon characterization of the shipping term contract. If the sales contract is a shipment contract, the timeliness of seller's tender of delivery is determined under UCC 2–504(a). The issue refers to the day and hour when the seller put the goods into the carrier's possession in El Centro, California, and Nogales, Arizona. If the sales contract is a destination contract, the timeliness of seller's tender of delivery is determined under UCC 2–309(1). The issue refers to the day and hour that the seller tendered the goods to the buyer at its place of business in Pittsburgh.

Was this sales contract a shipment contract or a destination contract? What was the judicial officer's characterization of the contract? There is no reference in the sales contract to an F.O.B. term or any other trade term in common usage. The opinion noted that the contract price was a "delivered price," i.e., the lump sum included the cost of freight and top ice. Was this relevant? Determinative? Would there have been an issue of the timeliness of seller's tender of delivery if this were a shipment contract?[11]

**(4) Construction of UCC 2–309.** Accepting for the purpose of further analysis that this sales contract was a destination contract, the seller's performance obligation on time of tender of delivery was found in the default rule of UCC 2–309. Do you agree with the judicial officer's application of that provision to the facts of this case? Note the judicial officer's odd double negative conclusion: "we are unable to say the delivery was not within a reasonable time." Was this equivalent to a conclusion that delivery *was made* within a reasonable time?

The truck driver could have delivered on the afternoon of March 12. Was it not reasonable to require the goods to be delivered at 3:00 a.m. the next morning, in time to make the prime market for that day?

The goods were not delivered on March 12 because the buyer did not have employees who were willing to wait until the truck was expected to arrive, in mid-afternoon. Was the inability of the buyer to take delivery on March 12 pertinent to its claim that the delivery on March 13 was in violation of the seller's obligation? Consider the application of the require-

---

the contract of carriage, the buyer might be able to seek a remedy from the carrier for its breach of that contract. Cf. UCC 2–722. In the principal case, of course, the carrier was not a party to the litigation.

**11.** The law governing the *Mendelson–Zeller* case is UCC Article 2 supplemented by a federal statute, the Perishable Agricultural Commodities Act. 7 U.S.C. §§ 499a–499s. The act and regulations issued under it determine the obligations of parties to sales contracts. Many trade terms used in sales agreements for perishable agricultural commodities are specially defined in 7 C.F.R. § 46.43. Nothing in the case turned on provisions of the federal statute.

Under the federal act, when parties use certain trade terms, buyers are precluded from rejecting goods on arrival. Among them are "f.o.b. acceptance final," "rolling acceptance," and "purchase after inspection." See, e.g., L. Gillarde Co. v. Joseph Martinelli & Co., 169 F.2d 60 (1st Cir.), cert. denied, 335 U.S. 885, 69 S.Ct. 237, 93 L.Ed. 424 (1948).

ments of UCC 2–503(1)(a) and (b): Tender must be at a reasonable hour and buyer must furnish facilities reasonably suited to the receipt of the goods.

### 3.   DISTINGUISHING BETWEEN SHIPMENT AND DESTINATION CONTRACTS

As *Mendelson–Zeller* illustrates, if sellers and buyers do not use a commonly recognized trade term that indicates their intent that the sales contracts are either a shipment contract or a destination contract, interpretation of the sales contracts on this point can be difficult. Other contract terms might be used as a guide. Pre–Code law provided that a sales contract was a destination contract if the contract contemplated that the seller would pay the cost of transportation. Comment 5 to UCC 2–503 declares that the Code intentionally omitted this rule. The Comment declares that "under this Article the 'shipment' contract is regarded as the normal one and the 'destination' contract as the variant type." The Comment continues:

> The seller is not obligated to deliver at a named destination . . . unless he has specifically agreed so to deliver or the commercial understanding of the terms used by the parties contemplates such delivery.

*Quare:* Does the Comment go beyond the text of the Code? Does it provide a reasonable interpretation of the text?

**Problem 1.** Buyer telephoned Catalogue Seller and ordered a compact disc player. In the conversation, Buyer said: "Please send the CD player by parcel post." Seller accepted the order without more being said about the price or the delivery term. Is the contract a place-of-shipment or at-a-particular-destination contract? Which party must pay the parcel post charges? See Pestana v. Karinol Corp., 367 So.2d 1096 (Fla.App.1979).

**Problem 2.** National Heater Co., located in St. Paul, Minnesota, offered to sell heating units to Corrigan Co. to be used by the buyer in construction of an automobile plant in Fenton, Missouri. National Heater's written proposal of the terms of sale stated the price as $275,640, "F.O.B. St. Paul, Minn. with freight allowed." Corrigan then submitted a purchase order with the following: "Price $275,640—Delivered." National Heater sent an acknowledgment which included: "$275,640 Total Delivered to Rail Siding." Is the contract a place-of-shipment or at-a-particular-destination contract? See National Heater Co. v. Corrigan Co., 482 F.2d 87 (8th Cir.1973).

## (B)  INTERNATIONAL SALES LAW

As noted in section 1, the primary duties of sellers and buyers under the Convention on Contracts for International Sale of Goods are stated in CISG 30 and CISG 53. Sellers must deliver the goods and transfer the property as in the goods "as required by the contract and this Convention," and buyers must pay the price and take delivery of the goods "as required by the contract and this Convention."

*Manner and Place of Delivery.* Sales contracts governed by CISG are between parties from different nations and are, therefore, highly likely to require use of the services of carriers. Absent agreement on the nature of sellers' performance, the Convention provides that sellers' obligation has the following steps: Seller "must make such contracts as are necessary for carriage to the place fixed [by agreement] by means of transportation appropriate in the circumstances and according to the usual terms for such transportation." CISG 32(2). Seller must "hand ... the goods over to the first carrier for transmission to the buyer." CISG 31(a). If the goods are not clearly identified to the sales contract, by markings on the goods or by documents or otherwise, when handed over to the carrier, seller must give buyer notice of the consignment, CISG 32(1); the Convention does not require sellers to give notice of shipment in all transactions.[12]

Unlike the Commercial Code the Convention does not distinguish between place-of-shipment and at-a-particular-destination contracts. The latter are not contemplated, no doubt in light of prevailing mercantile practice.

> [E]ven when the seller undertakes to pay freight costs to destination under "C.I.F." and "C. & F." ... quotations, it has long been settled that the seller ... completes his delivery duties ... when the goods are (at the latest) loaded on the carrier.

J. Honnold, Uniform Law for International Sales § 209(1) (3d ed. 1999). Moreover, the Convention, unlike the Code, contains no provisions regarding the meaning of shipment terms.

In their contracts, parties to international sales transactions often refer to a set of trade terms which are known as **Incoterms.** Incoterms are prepared and promulgated by the International Chamber of Commerce (ICC).[13] Incoterms, last revised in 2010, categorize shipping or delivery terms into four principal categories: main carriage paid by seller (e.g., Cost and Freight, CFR, or CIF), main carriage paid by buyer (e.g., FAS, FOB vessel), departure terms (Ex Works), and arrival terms (e.g., Delivered Ex Ship or Delivered Ex Quay). Incoterms 2010 do not use the FOB term other than at the port of shipment. Departure terms do not oblige sellers to contract for carriage. The arrival term requires a seller to place the goods at the disposal of the buyer on board the vessel at the usual unloading point or on the quay in the named port of destination.[14]

---

**12.** As we will see in the next section, international sales transactions may be documentary transactions in which seller "must ... hand over [to the buyer] any documents relating to [the goods]." CISG 30.

**13.** The ICC is a non-governmental organization with members from most countries of the world. From its wide membership base, the ICC is able to compile information on business practices and to develop expertise in the needs of the marketplace for various shipment terms. Parties to particular contracts can incorporate Incoterms in their agreements as they deem appropriate.

The ICC also sponsors the International Court of Arbitration, which we considered in earlier chapters.

**14.** During the drafting of the Convention, consideration was given to inclusion of a term that would have had the effect of incorporating trade terms in common usage, like

The ICC noted a growing practice of use of shipment terms in international sales transactions that authorize carriers to deliver the goods to designated consignees, transactions that have been referred to here as elementary shipment transactions.

*Time of Delivery.* The Convention looks to the parties' contract of sale as the primary source of the time term. CISG 33(a). Often, international sales contracts specify a period of time within which delivery is to occur. The agreement may provide further how an exact date will be set by one or both of the parties. If a period of time is stated without more, CISG 33(b) states a default rule that permits the seller to choose to perform "at any time within that period unless circumstances indicate that the buyer is to choose a date." When the contract is silent on time, CISG 33(c) requires a seller to perform "within a reasonable time after the conclusion of the contract."

*Buyers' Payment.* The Convention does not have any provisions on the manner of buyers' payment beyond the requirement in CISG 54 that a buyer's obligation includes "taking such steps and complying with such formalities as may be required under the contract or any laws and regulations to enable payment to be made."

*Time and Place of Buyers' Payment.* Unless otherwise agreed, "a buyer must pay when the seller places either the goods . . . at the buyer's disposal in accordance with the contract and this Convention." CISG 58(1). If payment is to be made against the handing over of goods, a buyer must pay "at the place where the handing over takes place." CISG 57(1)(b). Otherwise, payment must be made "at the seller's place of business." CISG 57(1)(a).

*Inspection of Goods Before Payment.* Absent agreement to the contrary, buyers are not bound to pay the price until they have had opportunity to examine the goods. CISG 58(3). If the contract involves carriage of goods, a seller may contract with the carrier of the goods that the goods will not be handed over to the buyer except against payment of the price. CISG 58(2). Since some forms of examination of goods can occur while goods are in the possession of carriers, CISG 58(2) does not override CISG 58(3).[15]

*Sellers' Duty to Deliver When Buyers' Provide Vessels.* In some international transactions that involve transport of large quantities of goods by sea, the parties agree that the buyer will contract to provide a vessel onto which the seller loads the goods at a designated port. Seller cannot deliver until the vessel is in the port, but it is usually important that the goods be available to be loaded as soon as the vessel arrives.

---

*Incoterms,* into all international sales contracts. This proposal was opposed, in part because it would impose trade terms on a party, perhaps one from a developing country, whether or not it knew or ought to have known of them. The Convention's general provision on trade usage would direct tribunals to consider *Incoterms* if both parties knew or ought to have known of them. CISG 9(2). See J. Honnold, Uniform Law for International Sales § 118 and n. 5 (3d ed. 1999).

**15.**   See J. Honnold, Uniform Law for International Sales § 338 (3d ed. 1999).

A transaction of this kind gave rise to a controversy that was litigated in a U.K. court under British law. Seller and Buyer contracted for sale of 12,000 tons of sugar to be delivered at the port of Dunkirk in May or June 1986 on board one or more ships provided by Buyer. The contract required Buyer to give Seller not less than 14 days' notice of the vessels' readiness to load. The contract also incorporated by reference the Rules of the London Refined Sugar Association (LRSA). One LRSA Rule stated: "the seller shall have the sugar ready to be delivered at any time within the contract period." Another LRSA Rule provided: "the buyer, having given reasonable notice, shall be entitled to call for delivery of the sugar between the first and the last working days inclusive of the contract period." A third LRSA Rule stated that the buyer was responsible for costs incurred by the seller if the nominated vessel did not present herself within five days of the date specified in the buyer's notice. On May 15, Buyer gave notice calling on Seller to load the sugar on board the *Naxos*, estimated to arrive in Dunkirk between May 29 and 31. The *Naxos* was at the dock in Dunkirk and ready to load on May 29. Seller informed Buyer that the sugar would be available on June 3.The House of Lords held that seller was bound to have the sugar ready for loading immediately upon the ship's arrival. Seller contended that the contract permitted commencement of loading within a reasonable time after the ship had arrived. The House of Lords construed the notice provision of the agreement and the Rules to require the seller to have the sugar at the dock, ready to be loaded, when the ship arrived. See Compagnie Commerciale Sucres et Denrees v. C. Czarnikow Ltd. (*The Naxos*), [1990] 1 W.L.R. 1337 (H.L.), reversing [1989] 2 Lloyd's Rep. 462 (C.A.).

If the governing law had been the CISG, how should the case have been decided?

---

## SECTION 3.   DOCUMENTARY SALES

## (A) DOMESTIC UNITED STATES LAW

### 1.  BASIC COMPONENTS

Elementary shipment or destination contracts are satisfactory for sales transactions in which sellers are willing to extend short-term credit to buyers, or vice versa. Such contracts are not satisfactory to sellers that are unwilling to allow the buyers to take control of goods without paying for them. Simultaneous tenders of delivery and of payment eliminate credit risk. In simultaneous exchange transactions, sellers extend no credit to buyers and buyers extend no credit to sellers. Such exchanges are paradigmatic in local sales transactions. They can be replicated, in a more complex legal way, even when sellers and buyers are not in the same locales. Documents of title, negotiable instruments, and the laws that undergird them, are the means to this end.

*a. DOCUMENTS OF TITLE*

A negotiable document of title is a document that effectively controls the rights to ownership and possession of goods *vis-à-vis* the issuer of the document. Documents of title are pieces of paper that, with the proper legal platform, are themselves important items of property. One can "own" a document of title and thereby own the underlying rights in the goods. The person entitled to the rights represented by a document of title is referred to as the "holder" of the document. A holder can transfer a document of title to another holder. Transfer of a document of title, in a certain manner, transfers those key rights to goods.

*Order bills of lading.* A classic example of a document of title is a negotiable or "order" bill of lading. A bill of lading (originally a bill of "loading") is a document that a carrier (e.g., railroad, ship owner, air freight carrier) issues when goods are delivered to it for shipment. Carriers that issue bills of lading may issue either of two kinds of bills of lading, the "order bill of lading" and the "straight bill of lading." Under an "order" bill of lading, a carrier agrees to deliver the goods *to the order of* a stated person, e.g., to "the order of Seller & Co." An "order" bill of lading typically provides:

> The surrender of this Original Bill of Lading properly indorsed shall be required before the delivery of the property.

A standard form order bill of lading begins:

> RECEIVED, subject to the classifications and tariffs in effect on the date of issue of this Bill of Lading, the property described below, in apparent good order, except as noted (contents and conditions of contents of packages unknown) marked, consigned and designated as indicated below, which [carrier] agrees to carry to its usual place of delivery at said destination. . . .

The bill of lading has boxes on its face in which the carrier enters the "number of packages", the carrier's "description of the articles, special marks and exceptions," and the weight of the goods.

*Straight bills of lading.* A straight bill is a document of title but it does not control the rights to ownership or possession of the goods. Straight bills can be used in elementary shipment or destination contracts of the kind that were considered in section 2. Under a "straight" bill, a carrier undertakes to deliver goods at a stated destination to a stated person, e.g., "to Buyer & Co." Order bills are documents of title and have the added dimension that makes a simultaneous exchange feasible even though a seller and a buyer are unable to meet in the same place. The simultaneous exchange involves the money and the document.

A bill of lading, in part, embodies the contract between the carrier and the shipper, who is often termed the *consignor*. A number of terms are printed on the front of printed bills of lading where data describing specific shipments are filled in; the back contains more standard contract terms, often densely packed in small print. The bill of lading identifies the carrier receiving the goods, the shipper or consignor, the goods, the intended destination, the *consignee*, and possibly other terms.[1]

When parties to sales contracts elect to enter into "documentary transitions," they commonly enlist the aid of banks to accomplish the result. Banks are linked together globally to provide a communications network that allows funds to be transferred, but the banking system also serves to transport documents of title. Using the mix of transportation services provided by carriers and financial services provided by banks, a seller and a buyer are able to effect simultaneous exchange of a document of title to goods in exchange for payment of the price. The payment side of the exchange is facilitated by the use of a common negotiable instrument, a bill of exchange, the negotiable draft.

### b. *NEGOTIABLE INSTRUMENTS*

A "draft" is a negotiable instrument in which one party, the seller (the *drawer*) orders another party, the buyer (the *drawee*), to pay a specified amount of money at a specified time. In a documentary transaction, a draft is drawn *by* a seller *on* a buyer for the amount of money due to the seller under a sales contract.

*Sight drafts*. Typically, the seller's draft will order buyer to pay the price when the draft is presented to buyer ("at sight"); drafts payable on demand are called "sight drafts." A sight draft looks very much like an ordinary bank check, which is a sight draft drawn on a bank. A sight draft used in a documentary transaction is a draft drawn on the buyer.

*Time drafts*. An alternative transaction involves use of a "time draft," which contains an order to the buyer to pay the amount of the draft at the end a specified period of time after the draft has been presented to the buyer.

We will consider first a sales contract that provides for a "documentary transaction" that contemplates simultaneous performances by seller and buyer. The basic form of such a transaction involves use of a sight draft and an order bill of lading. The commercial purpose of time drafts in documentary transactions will be considered later.

### c. *CARRIERS' AND BANKS' SERVICES*

The sequence of steps in performance of a typical documentary transaction utilizes the services of carriers and banks.

Seller first delivers the goods to a carrier and obtains an "order bill of lading" from the carrier. In a "consigned to" box, after the printed words ORDER OF the carrier enters the name of the consignee provided by the seller. In a documentary sale, a seller typically designates itself as the consignee. In a "destination" box the carrier notes the city to which the goods are to be carried. Below that, in a "notify" box, is the name of the

---

1. In these materials, we are concerned with only those aspects of carriage contracts that are significant to the performance of sales transactions.

person to be notified by the carrier when goods have arrived. The person listed is the buyer.

Seller then prepares a "sight draft" directing the buyer to pay the price due under the sales contract.

Seller then indorses the order bill of lading,[2] attaches the indorsed bill of lading to the sight draft, and delivers both documents to its local bank for transmission to the buyer through banking channels.

Seller's bank forwards the documents through the network of bank-to-bank relationships that exists for this (and many other) purpose.

In due course, the draft and order bill of lading arrive at a specified bank in buyer's city, typically the bank with which the buyer has an ongoing banking relationship. It is the function of that bank to effect the exchange of goods for money by turning over the order bill of lading when buyer pays the amount of the sight draft.

After payment is made to the "presenting bank," the funds are transferred back to seller's bank and eventually to seller, again through banking channels.

Once a document of title has been transferred to a buyer, it can surrender the document to the carrier for the goods or it can sell the document of title to a third party.

Performance of documentary transactions is quite different from performance of sales contracts that require sellers to tender delivery of goods without the aid of carriers and require buyers to tender payment in exchange for tender of delivery of the goods. In documentary transactions, sellers tender delivery of documents of title and buyers are required to make payment in exchange for the documents. The shorthand expression for this exchange is "payment against documents." Goods are not present when a documentary exchange takes place. Indeed the goods are probably still en route to their destination.

### d. C.O.D. CONTRACTS

A transaction type equivalent in some respects to a documentary transaction is possible if a carrier agrees not only to transport the goods but also to collect payment from the buyer before handing over the goods. Some carriers offer this added service (for an added fee, of course). Transactions of this kind, referred to as collect-on-delivery or C.O.D. transactions, are usually sales in which the price of the goods is relatively small, as in retail sales of consumer goods.

### 2. CONTRACTING FOR DOCUMENTARY TRANSACTIONS

Payment against documents is required only if the parties to a sales contract have agreed to this manner of performance. The Commercial

---

**2.** Sellers' indorsements are usually "in blank," i.e., the indorsement authorizes any one in possession of the document to negotiate it further without indorsement. Blank indorsements facilitate forwarding of the documents through banking channels.

Code, together with federal law, assists sellers and buyers to perform their obligations under documentary transactions, but those obligations can arise only if the parties have agreed to this transaction type in their sales contracts. It is important to know the nature of the contract terms that have the effect of requiring payment against documents. A common term used for this purpose in sales contracts is: "Sight draft against order bill of lading."

Sales contracts may use certain shipment terms which, by law, have the effect of requiring buyers to pay against documents. The shipment terms that have this effect are terms commonly associated with transport of goods on deep water ships. UCC Article 2 refers to four such terms: C.I.F., C. & F., F.A.S. vessel, and F.O.B. vessel. The term C.I.F. means that the contract price includes, in a single sum, the price of the goods plus cost of insurance and freight to a named destination.[3] C. & F. is similar, but omits insurance.[4] F.A.S. vessel means "free alongside" a ship at a named port.[5] F.O.B. vessel means on board a named vessel.[6] UCC Article 2 declares that, when these terms are used in sales contracts, sellers must obtain negotiable bills of lading,[7] and unless otherwise agreed, the buyers must make payment against tender of the required documents. Sellers may not tender nor buyers demand delivery of the goods in substitution for the documents.[8]

*Time, Place and Manner of Sellers' Tender of Documents Under UCC Article 2.* When a seller, in conformity with a contract of sale, ships goods under an "order" bill of lading, UCC 2–504(b) adds a third requirement to seller's manner of execution of a shipment contract. Seller must tender the bill of lading, properly indorsed so that the buyer is empowered to obtain possession of the goods from the carrier. Tender of any documents needed to obtain possession of goods must be made "promptly" under UCC 2–504(b). UCC 2–503(5)(b) provides that "tender [of such documents] through customary banking channels is sufficient." Through "banking channels" or otherwise, a seller can transmit documents to a buyer. "Properly indorsed" means that the seller must act so that the buyer becomes the holder of the bill of lading, the person entitled to obtain the goods from the carrier.

The default provisions in UCC Article 2 are complemented by other bodies of law: the Federal Bill of Lading Act and Articles 3 and 4 of the Commercial Code.

---

**3.** UCC 2–320(1).

**4.** Id.

**5.** UCC 2–319(2).

**6.** UCC 2–319(1)(c).

**7.** UCC 2–320(2)(a), 2–323(1). The requirement in UCC 2–323(1) is limited to sales contracts that contemplate "overseas shipment" of the goods, defined in UCC 2–323(3) to mean any contract that by agreement or trade usage is subject to the commercial, financial or shipping practices of international deep water commerce.

**8.** UCC 2–319(4); 2–320(4).

*Federal Bill of Lading Act.* The primary law that undergirds negotiable bills of lading and proper indorsement thereof is federal law, the Federal Bill of Lading Act.[9] This Act sets out the criteria for making a bill of lading negotiable and for negotiating such a bill once it has been issued.[10] The provisions most pertinent to the carriers' role in the execution of documentary transactions are the sections on carrier's duty to deliver goods to the holder of a negotiable bill of lading, carrier's liability for delivery of the goods to a person not entitled thereto,[11] and carrier's liability for nonreceipt of the goods described in a bill of lading or misdescription of the goods.[12]

*UCC Articles 3 and 4.* The legal platform for the banks' role in execution of documentary transactions is found in Articles 3 and 4 of the Uniform Commercial Code. These articles refer to a draft that is accompanied by a bill of lading as a "documentary draft."[13] A bank taking a documentary draft and an order bill of lading from a seller is authorized to present the draft to buyer or to send it via another bank or banks to buyer.[14] Each bank that handles a seller's draft becomes a "collecting bank"[15] with the duties to send forward or to present the draft and accompanying documents.[16] The last bank in the chain of banks is the "presenting bank."[17] Unless otherwise instructed, the bank presenting a "sight draft" is authorized to send buyer a written notice that it holds a draft for payment.[18] A buyer to whom a notice is sent has three banking days from the date the notice was sent to make payment.[19] The bank must deliver the bill of lading accompanying the draft to the buyer "only on payment."[20] Upon receipt of payment, the presenting bank remits the funds to the seller.[21]

---

**9.** 49 U.S.C. §§ 80101–80116. The federal act applies to bills of lading issued by common carriers for interstate transportation or export of goods. Id. § 80102. The law governing bills of lading for intrastate transportation of goods is found in Article 7 of the Uniform Commercial Code.

**10.** Id. §§ 80103(a), 80104. UCC criteria for making bills of lading negotiable are found in UCC 7–104. Negotiation requirements are set forth in UCC 7–501.

**11.** Id. §§ 80110, 80113. For carriers' obligation to deliver goods under UCC Article 7, see UCC 7–403, 7–404.

**12.** Id. § 80113. The comparable provision in the Commercial Code is UCC 7–301.

**13.** UCC 4–104(a)(6).

**14.** Banks who handle the paper are agents and subagents of sellers. UCC 4–201(a).

**15.** UCC 4–105(5).

**16.** UCC 4–501.

**17.** UCC 4–105(6).

**18.** UCC 4–212(a).

**19.** UCC 4–212(b). See also UCC 3–502(c).

**20.** UCC 4–503(1).

**21.** The speed of carriage of goods by air required adaptation of the method of issuing and transmitting bills of lading. Taking a bill of lading at the point of shipment and forwarding it through banking channels to the destination to be exchanged for the price would be too slow. A solution was found by using electronic communications. The Commercial Code

*Negotiation; Rights of Holders.* Both the order bill of lading and the negotiable draft move through these steps by the process of *negotiation*, not by mere *transfer*.[22] "Holders" of negotiable documents of title or of negotiable instruments may receive greater legal protection than mere transferees. In Chapter 3, we noted that the concept of good faith purchase has developed in a wider setting than purchase of goods. Commercial law offers very significant legal protection to holders in due course of negotiable instruments,[23] and to holders of negotiable documents of title to whom the documents have been duly negotiated.[24] These protections are often significant to buyers and sellers as well as to the banks whose services they use in carrying out documentary transactions.

*Inspection of the Goods and of the Documents.* Buyers' agreement to documentary sales has severe consequences on their right to inspect the goods before payment. The default rule of UCC 2–513(3)(b) provides that a buyer is not entitled to inspect the goods before payment of the price "when the contract provides for payment against documents of title. . . ."[25]

If the parties to a sales contract agree, inspection of the goods can be made before or at the time the goods are turned over to the carrier. Buyers are not likely to be at that location, but they are often able to hire inspectors to examine the goods. Alternatively, sales contracts can provide that sellers must arrange for inspection of the goods by independent inspectors. In either event, the sales contracts may provide that the inspectors' certificates must be tendered along with the bills of lading and drafts.

The inspection provisions of UCC 2–513 are concerned only with inspection of the goods, but, in documentary transactions, buyers will inspect the documents tendered to them when drafts are presented for payment. The right to inspect an instrument upon presentment is stated in UCC 3–501(b)(2).

*Time, Place, and Manner of Buyer's Tender of Payment.* In documentary transactions, the time, place, and manner of buyer's tender of payment are determined by the rules on the proper presentment of sight drafts. Under UCC 2–507(1), "tender of delivery" is a condition of buyer's duty to pay. The section does not specify tender of delivery *of goods* and could be read to mean tender of delivery *of documents*. This alternative reading is

---

permits a carrier, at the request of a consignor, to issue a bill of lading at the point of destination, UCC 7–305(a) and to deliver it to a local bank. Meanwhile, seller (or seller's bank) wires a draft on the buyer to the bank holding the bill. Within hours, the bank notifies buyer who pays the draft and obtains the bill.

**22.** 49 U.S.C. § 80104, UCC 3–201, 7–501.

**23.** UCC 3–303 to 3–305.

**24.** 49 U.S.C. § 80105; UCC 7–502.

**25.** This is a default rule that is explicitly subject to agreement otherwise. The subsection refers to an exception for transactions in which an agreement provides that payment is due only after the goods are to become available for inspection. See Comment 5.

explicit in UCC 2–507(2), which refers to payment that is due either on delivery of the goods or documents of title.[26]

*Dishonor.* If a buyer, presented with a documentary sight draft, fails or refuses to make payment when due, the presenting and collecting banks have further duties. Buyer's failure or refusal is referred to as "dishonor."[27] Upon dishonor, the presenting bank must use diligence and good faith to ascertain the reason for dishonor, must notify its transferor of the dishonor and of the results of its effort to ascertain the reasons therefor, and must request instructions.[28] The bank is under no obligation with respect to the goods represented by the documents of title except to follow reasonable instructions received.[29] Upon learning that the draft has not been paid in due course, each collecting bank must seasonably notify its customer of that fact.[30]

*Time, Place, and Manner of Seller's Delivery of the Goods.* A sales contract, in the form of a documentary transaction, is not completely executed when a presenting bank delivers a document of title to a buyer and buyer pays the amount of a sight draft. Seller's underlying obligation to tender delivery of the goods is not satisfied by the delivery and acceptance of the document of title. In all likelihood the sales contract in a documentary transaction is a shipment contract with respect to the goods.[31] Seller's obligation under UCC 2–504(b) to tender promptly a document of title is in addition to its obligations under UCC 2–503(a) to put the goods in the possession of a carrier and contract for their transportation. The time, place, and manner of seller's compliance with the requirements of UCC 2–504(a) and (c) were considered in the previous section.

### a.   *THE SITUATION OF BUYERS*

Documentary transactions in the basic form just described reduce the credit risk for buyer and sellers in many ways, but they leave buyers in a precarious position in a number of respects. The following problems are intended to develop your understanding of the mechanics of documentary transactions and to examine the situation of buyers who are expected to pay the purchase price in exchange for a negotiable bill of lading.

**Problem 1.** Seller & Co. of Sellersville, N.Y., agreed to sell a large quantity of paper bags to Buyer & Co., of Buyersville, California, who

---

**26.**  The default provision on seller's duty to tender, UCC 2–511(1), is similarly drafted so that delivery could refer either to goods or documents. See also Comment 1: "in the case of specific transactions such as . . . agreements providing for payment against documents, the provisions of this subsection must be considered in conjunction with the special sections of the Article dealing with such terms."

**27.**  UCC 3–502(b)(2), 3–502(c).

**28.**  UCC 4–503(2).

**29.**  UCC 4–503.

**30.**  UCC 4–501.

**31.**  Contracts that require seller to tender goods after they arrive at their destination are not likely to be used in documentary transactions. After a buyer has receive an indorsed negotiable bill of lading, only the buyer can obtain the goods from the carrier.

agreed to pay $10,000.00, F.O.B. Sellersville. The parties agreed to a payment term: "sight draft against order bill of lading." Seller & Co. turned over the goods to Railroad and received a negotiable bill of lading made out to the order of Seller & Co. Seller & Co. prepared a draft for the purchase price, indorsed the bill of lading "in blank,"[32] and forwarded the draft and bill through Sellersville Bank to Buyer & Co.

(a) Before the goods have arrived in Buyersville, Buyersville Bank received the draft and bill of lading. Buyersville Bank promptly notified Buyer & Co. that it had a draft and bill of lading. Buyer & Co. refused to pay the draft on the ground that it had not had an opportunity to inspect the goods. Is Buyer & Co. permitted to refuse to pay pending arrival of the goods and inspection of them? See UCC 2–513(3)(b); see also 2–310(b).

(b) Assume that Buyer & Co. paid when the sight draft was presented and obtained the bill of lading. Subsequently, the railroad car containing the 50 cartons of paper bags arrived in Buyersville and Railroad so notified Buyer & Co.[33] Buyer & Co. surrendered the bill of lading to Railroad and took possession of the goods. Upon opening the boxes, Buyer & Co. discovered that a large percentage of the paper bags had been improperly glued. Is Seller & Co. in breach? What are the remedies of Buyer & Co.? See UCC 2–512(2). To what extent are buyer's rights affected by the fact that it has already paid the price?

(c) Assume that Buyer & Co. paid when the sight draft was presented and obtained the bill of lading. The goods did not arrive within the expected time. When Buyer & Co. asked Railroad for information, Railroad disclosed that the car containing the goods had been attached to the wrong train in St. Louis and had to be rerouted. The goods arrived in California three weeks later than anticipated. Is Seller & Co. in breach? If the sales contract had provided that the goods be shipped F.O.B. Buyersville, would Seller & Co. be in breach?

(d) On the facts of the previous question, does Buyer & Co. have a cause of action against Railroad for delivering goods that do not conform to the sales contract? If the description of the goods in the bill of lading was "Bags, paper," would that create a basis for carrier liability for the quality of the goods? See 49 U.S.C. § 80113; UCC 7–301(1).

Carriers have some duties regarding the quality and quantity of goods not in packages or sealed containers. Thus a carrier must ascertain the kind and quantity of bulk freight, and may be liable for misdescription or

---

**32.** A negotiable document of title running to the order of a named person can be negotiated by indorsement and delivery. An indorsement "in blank" permits further negotiation by delivery alone. 49 U.S.C. § 80104(a); UCC 7–501(1). Negotiation of documents of title within banking channels is facilitated by "in blank" indorsements. This permits a document to move forward without the necessity that each bank sign it and identify the next bank in the chain.

**33.** Order bills of lading usually indicate the person to be notified upon arrival of the goods at their destination. The "notify" provision does not authorize the carrier to deliver goods to the party listed without surrender of the bill of lading.

nonreceipt of the goods.[34] To protect themselves against claims that goods were damaged en route, carriers may add notes on bills of lading about the condition of the goods or packages.

### b.  *THE SITUATION OF SELLERS*

Sellers who engage in documentary exchange transactions incur certain risks of transaction failure. *Vis-à-vis* buyers, risk exists that buyers will not make payment against tender of documents. Sellers may want to stop transport of the goods, then en route to buyers' locations, and either get the goods back or divert them to other destinations. Carriers permit consignors to modify the routing of goods, but sellers lose time and incur expenses in making these changes.

Sellers are dependent upon banks and carriers to carry out their respective services. If they should fail to do so, sellers might be deprived of their goods without having received the promised payments.

**Problem 2.** Buyer and Seller agreed on sale of a lathe No. 3X from Seller's current catalogue with payment to be made against documents. The next day, Seller delivered a No. 3X lathe to the railroad, obtained a bill of lading that calls for delivery to "order of Seller," indorsed the bill in blank, and gave it along with a sight draft drawn on Buyer to its local bank for transmittal to Buyer. The documents were forwarded to a bank in Buyer's city, which sent a notice to Buyer that it held these documents for Buyer's payment.

(a) Buyer ignored the notice. What is the nature of the bank's obligation?

(b) Has Buyer dishonored the draft by not responding to the bank's notice? See UCC 3–502(c)?

(c) Is the presenting bank obliged to do more than inform seller of buyer's dishonor? See UCC 4–503(2). What might be the reason for these obligations?

**Problem 3.** Assume the facts as above, except that the presenting bank gave Buyer the bill of lading in exchange for the Buyer's uncertified check in the amount of the draft. Before the Buyer's check was paid, Buyer obtained the lathe from the railroad and stopped payment on its check.[35]

(a) What are Seller's rights?

(b) Does Seller have a claim against Railroad? See 49 U.S.C. § 80110; UCC 7–404.

(c) Does Seller have a claim against the presenting bank? See UCC 4–202(1), 4–211(1), 4–103(5). And see Bunge v. First National Bank of Mount Holly Springs, 118 F.2d 427 (3d Cir.1941).

(d) Does Seller have a claim against its local bank for the actions of the presenting bank? See UCC 4–202(3) and Comment 4.

---

**34.**  49 U.S.C. § 80113; UCC 7–301(2).

**35.**  See UCC 4–403(a).

(e) Does Seller have a claim against Buyer? See UCC 2–301, 2–507. Of what practical value to Seller is 2–507(2)?

**Problem 4.** Assume the same facts as in preceding problem, except that Buyer, without paying the draft or obtaining the bill of lading, gets possession of the lathe from Railroad.

(a) What are Seller's rights?

(b) Does Seller have a claim against Railroad? See 49 U.S.C. §§ 80110, 80111; UCC 7–403(1). What would be the proper measure of damages? See Alderman Bros. Co. v. New York, etc. R. Co., 102 Conn. 461, 129 A. 47 (1925).

(c) Does Seller have a claim against any bank?

(d) Does Seller have a claim against Buyer?

## 3.   SELLERS' USE OF DRAFTS TO OBTAIN CREDIT

Sellers engaging in documentary transactions sometimes seek to speed up the inflow of cash by getting the monetary amount of the drafts, less a discount, from the banks who take them for collection and presentment. The context of documentary transactions gives banks reasonable assurance that credit extended to sellers will be repaid promptly from proceeds of the drafts. Moreover, the drafts are negotiable instruments on which the sellers are liable as drawers.[36] The banks are holders of indorsed bills of lading and therefore have security for repayment in their control of the goods. Not uncommonly, therefore, banks taking drafts for collection will "discount" them.

Sellers may also "discount" drafts to anticipate payment when underlying documentary transactions require buyers to accept "time drafts" upon presentment rather than make immediate payment. Drafts may be discounted before their presentment. The banks' legal rights in the period before presentment are similar to their rights in discount of sight drafts. The situation changes when buyers "accept" time drafts.[37] Acceptance of a draft establishes a new obligation on a drawee/acceptor.[38] This obligation is independent of the payment obligation in the sales contract and can be enforced by subsequent holders of the instrument without regard to the buyer's rights under the sales contract. The drawer is also obligated to pay the amount of the draft to a subsequent holder of the instrument. The drawer's liability is secondary to that of the acceptor.[39] Accepted time drafts arising from documentary transactions are referred to as "trade acceptances." Trade acceptances are very negotiable instruments.

---

**36.**   UCC 3–414(b).

**37.**   "Acceptance" means the drawee's signed agreement to pay a draft as presented. UCC 3–409(a).

**38.**   UCC 3–413(a).

**39.**   UCC 3–414(b) and (d); but see UCC 3–414(e) (drafts drawn "without recourse").

## (B) INTERNATIONAL SALES LAW

Documentary transactions of the kind described in this section are used less in international sales than in domestic United States sales. Part of the explanation, no doubt, is the absence of an international legal platform comparable to the domestic United States laws on negotiable instruments and negotiable documents of title. Given the choice of law rules of private international law, no nation's domestic laws are likely to have sufficient scope of application to provide an adequate legal platform for the execution of documentary transactions in international sales.

Even without such a platform, parties engaged in international trade often understand and accept the reliability of the commitment of ocean carriers, which issue negotiable bills of lading, that goods will be delivered only upon surrender of a properly indorsed bill of lading. International sales contracts that incorporate certain shipping terms are understood to require sellers to obtain and deliver negotiable bills of lading. In the oil business, crude oil in holds of supertankers steaming across oceans is often bought and sold many times while the ships are en route.

If international sales contracts involve negotiable documents of title, the Convention has a brief provision regarding sellers' duty to deliver the documents. Sellers are bound to hand over documents relating to the goods "at the time and place and in the form required by the contract." CISG 34. The Convention has no default rule for when or where this is to occur.

Payment by buyers against documents of title, the essence of domestic documentary transactions is not mentioned by CISG.[40] In international transactions, payment arrangements typically involve bank letters of credit. Letter of credit transactions are taken up in the next section.

---

## SECTION 4.   PAYMENT BY LETTER OF CREDIT

## (A) DOMESTIC UNITED STATES LAW

Documentary transaction arrangements are useful in producing a kind of simultaneous exchange, but such arrangements do not assure sellers that buyers will make payment against sight drafts or accept time drafts upon presentment. Dishonor is a risk whenever a buyer decides not to fulfill its obligation under the sales contract or the buyer, for some reason, is unable to pay (or accept) the draft. If a buyer dishonors a draft, the seller has not lost ultimate control of the goods, but, when dishonor occurs, the goods are en route to their original destination and must be brought back or diverted.

---

**40.** Common-law courts have long held that an obligation to pay against documents is implicit in certain international sales contracts. The leading case is Biddell Bros. v. E. Clemens Horst Co., [1912] A.C. 18 (H.L.) (sale of hops shipped from San Francisco C.I.F to London, Liverpool, or Hull). This common-law rule was incorporated into the Uniform Commercial Code, which provides that contractual use of terms associated with water transport (C.I.F., C. & F., F.A.S., F.O.B. vessel) creates a duty on buyers to pay against documents. UCC 2–319(4), 2–320(4), 2–321(3).

To avoid the risk of dishonor by a buyer on presentment of documents, parties to sales contracts can contract for a payment arrangement whereby a draft and a negotiable document of title, and perhaps other documents, are presented to a bank that is independently obligated to pay (or accept) the draft. Banks commonly undertake such obligations when they issue commercial letters of credit.[1]

## 1. CONTRACTING FOR PAYMENT BY LETTER OF CREDIT

A buyer's obligation to make payment though a letter of credit must be bargained for in the sales contract. Use of a letter of credit is not a default obligation. Terms of sales contracts that call for payment by letter of credit provide not only that a letter of credit may be used, but also provide whether the credit is for immediate payment or for acceptance of a time draft and specify in detail the exact documents that will be sufficient to trigger payment by the bank that issued the credit. Banks issue letters of credit of two kinds: revocable or irrevocable. Sellers normally negotiate for buyers to obtain irrevocable letters of credit. Sellers typically require buyers to open letters of credit for an amount in excess of the contract price so that sellers can recover incidental expenses incurred on buyers' behalf. If the date of shipment is uncertain at the time of the sales contract, the parties negotiate for the length of time during which a letter must remain open.

Counsel for buyers should be especially careful in negotiating the letter of credit terms of sales contracts, because their clients will have almost no control of the banks' conduct when demand for payment is made. Conversely counsel for sellers negotiating these terms should be careful to identify the bank or class of banks that is acceptable as issuer of a letter of credit and specify only documents that the sellers can prepare or obtain.

Once a sales contract calling for payment by letter of credit is concluded, two other independent contracts must be formed. First, the buyer must negotiate with a bank for the bank to issue a letter of credit and the terms to be included in the credit. Critical to this negotiation from the bank's standpoint, is the method for the bank to be reimbursed. Also to be agreed between the bank and the buyer is the bank's fee for its participation. The second contract, which is not a negotiated contract, is the contract between the bank and the seller that arises when the bank issues its letter of credit to the seller (beneficiary of the credit). If a bank issues an irrevocable letter of credit, the bank must pay (or accept) the seller's drafts that satisfy the conditions specified in the letter.

Each of the three contracts: the underlying sales contract, the buyer-bank contract, and the bank-beneficiary contract is legally independent of the others. Obligations to perform the promises in each contract are not conditional on performances or events under the other contracts. Thus, a

---

**1.** Bank letters of credit are extraordinarily important payment devices in international sales transactions, but such letters of credit are often used in domestic sales transactions within the United States.

seller's breach of its obligation under the underlying sales contract or a buyer's breach of its obligation to reimburse the issuing bank is not a defense to the bank's obligation to pay (or accept) under its letter of credit. This is often referred to as the *independence principle* among the set of contracts that are involved in letter of credit transactions.

Buyers obligated under sales contracts to *open* letters of credit are likely to want to go to the banks with which they have ongoing banking relationships. Sellers, on the other hand, are likely to want to have letters of credit from banks that are conveniently located for presentment. Letter of credit practice developed two solutions for this situation. In one scenario, sellers are authorized by letters of credit to present their drafts and documents to local banks which forward the paper to the issuing banks. This scenario resembles the arrangement in documentary transactions, but presentment in a letter of credit transaction is to the issuing bank rather than to the buyer.

In an alternative scenario, parties to sales contracts arrange for seller's bank to issue its letter of credit on the strength of a letter of credit issued by buyer's bank. In banking and commercial practice, the bank issuing the second letter is said to *confirm* the first letter of credit. Sellers who want a local bank's commitment must negotiate buyers' obligation to obtain a letter of credit from an issuing bank that will, in turn, secure a confirming bank.[2] If a seller does not negotiate for the commitment of a local bank as a confirming bank, enforcement of the issuing bank's obligation may require litigation in a foreign country.[3] The conditions on payment in the two letters of credit are identical. When a confirming bank pays under its letter of credit, it is entitled to reimbursement from the original bank.

*UCC Article 2.* UCC Article 2 has one section on the use of letter of credit payments in sales contracts. The section deals in part with interpretation of payment terms in sales contracts and in part with performance of buyers' obligations to furnish letters of credit.

Section 2–325(3) is pertinent to interpretation of some terms used in sale contract. It provides that contractual reference to "letter of credit" or "banker's credit" obligates a buyer to obtain an irrevocable letter of credit. Moreover, the issuing bank must be a "financing agency of good repute" and, where shipment is to an overseas buyer, the issuing bank must be "of good international repute." A sales contract's reference to a "confirmed credit" means that the credit must carry the direct obligation of a bank that does business in the seller's financial market.

---

**2.** In making its commitment to the beneficiary of a confirmed credit, the confirming bank is relying entirely on the credit of the issuing bank. This works better when the banks have a continuing relationship. "It is customary that the issuing bank requests a bank of its choice to advise and, as the case may be, to confirm its credit to the beneficiary." ICC, Case Studies on Documentary Credits, Case 26, p. 39 (J. Dekker 1989).

**3.** See Pacific Reliant Industries, Inc. v. Amerika Samoa Bank, 901 F.2d 735 (9th Cir.1990) (Oregon seller of building materials to Samoa buyer agreed to letter of credit issued by Samoan bank; seller's suit to enforce the credit in Oregon federal district court dismissed for lack of personal jurisdiction over the bank).

Sales contracts may provide explicitly the time for buyers to furnish sellers with letters of credit that conform to sales contracts. UCC 2–325(1) implies that a letter of credit must be furnished "seasonably," but does not otherwise elaborate on the time, place or manner of a buyer's performance. Banks that issue letters of credit customarily send them directly to the named beneficiaries as soon as they have accepted buyers' applications.[4]

UCC 2–325(1) declares that failure of the buyer seasonably to furnish an agreed letter of credit is a breach of the sales contract.

## 2.   THE LAW UNDERLYING ENFORCEMENT OF LETTERS OF CREDIT

*UCC Article 5.* Article 5 of the Uniform Commercial Code contains domestic United States law on enforcement of letters of credit. This Article provides a broad legal platform that undergirds letter of credit transactions in sales contracts. Article 5 refers to parties only by their roles in a letter of transaction, principally applicant, issuer, confirmer, beneficiary.[5] The independence principle is stated in UCC 5–103(d). For sales contracts that contemplate payment by letter of credit, Article 5 serves the same purpose as UCC Articles 3 and 4 serve in domestic documentary transactions.

*Uniform Customs and Practices for Documentary Credits.* Contracting for payment by letter of credit is greatly aided by the availability of the Uniform Customs and Practices for Documentary Credits (UCP). The UCP are a product of the International Chamber of Commerce (ICC). Banks commonly incorporate the UCP in letters of credit, whether the underlying transaction is domestic or international. Bankers from throughout the world have established, within the ICC, a Commission on Banking Technique and Practice. The UCP, adhered to by banks in over 145 nations, are practically universal in the scope of their application. The UCP originated in the 1930s and have been revised a number of times. The most recent revision, known as UCP 600, was promulgated in 2007.

The ICC project goes beyond promulgation of the UCP. The Commission on Banking Technique and Practice issues opinions on interpretation of UCP provisions from time to time. The Commission also has a group of experts, the International Centre for Expertise, who respond to queries about the application of the UCP to particular circumstances.[6]

UCP provisions are not law. They constitute an elaborate body of standard contract terms which parties to contracts may elect to incorporate in their agreements. When buyers and sellers specify payment by letter of

---

**4.** Delivery of a proper letter of credit creates a bank's obligation to honor the credit and suspends buyer's obligation to pay the contract price. UCC 2–325(2). If a letter of credit is dishonored, seller may proceed against the bank or, on seasonable notification, against the buyer. Id.

**5.** All of these are defined terms under UCC 5–102(a).

**6.** Opinions of the Banking Commission are published regularly by the ICC. See ICC Publications 371, 399, 434 and 469. For responses to recent queries, see Case Studies on Documentary Credits: Problems, Queries, Answers (C. del Busto, 1995).

credit, they commonly add that they intend letters of credit under the UCP. When banks issue or confirm letters of credit, the letters specify that they are subject to the UCP. Contract provisions incorporating the UCP are enforceable to the extent that the domestic laws otherwise governing the transactions give effect to the terms of the contracts.

Although UCP provisions are not law, many of the provisions address matters that are covered by Article 5 of the Uniform Commercial Code, which is a statute. The 1960s version of UCC Article 5 clashed with the UCP of that period.[7] The recent revision of Article 5 is quite compatible with the UCP. Comment 8 to UCC 5–108 refers to the UCP as a valid source of customs governing letters of credit. "Clearly, the Article 5 drafters intended that their rules parallel the UCP rules."[8]

*Revocable Letters of Credit.* Banking practice developed two types of letters of credit, revocable and irrevocable. Issuing banks and their customers choose whether the customers have power to revoke without the consent of the beneficiaries of the credits. Normally issuing banks are careful to state explicitly whether a letter of credit is revocable or irrevocable. If, however, a bank fails to do so, in a credit subject to the UCP, UCP 600 provides that the credit is irrevocable. (Note that the UCP provision deals only interpretation of letters of credit and has no application to interpretation of sales contracts when those contracts lack specification as to the revocability or irrevocability of required letters of credit.)

## (B) INTERNATIONAL SALES LAW

Although terms requiring letter of credit payment are ubiquitous in international sales transactions, the Convention on Contracts for International Sale of Goods is silent on these terms. CISG 54 provides only that a buyer's obligation "includes taking such steps ... as may be required under the contract...." There is no body of international commercial law on letters of credit used as means of payment of the price in sales contracts.[9] In international sales transactions, parties commonly incorporate the Uniform Customs and Practices into letters of credit. The legal platform for enforcement of the UCP provisions is the general contract of

---

**7.** Four states, including New York, adopted Article 5 with non-uniform amendments providing that the statute would not apply to letters of credit that were issued subject to the UCP. The New York action was particularly significant, since banks in New York City were prominent among United States banks that issued letters of credit. See J. Dolan, Letter of Credit: A Comparison of UCP 500 and the New U.S. Article 5, [1999] J. Bus. L. 521.

**8.** J. Dolan, Letter of Credit: A Comparison of UCP 500 and the New U.S. Article 5, [1999] J. Bus. L. 521, 523. Professor Dolan concluded, however, that the efforts of the drafters of Article 5 were not entirely successful. He found two areas in which there is some measure of dissonance.

**9.** UNCITRAL concluded a proposed United Nations Convention on Independent Guarantees and Stand–By Letters of Credit in 1995. A guarantees or stand-by letter of credit is a contractual device for obtaining the obligation of a third party that can be called upon if the primary obligor defaults. They differ significantly in commercial purpose and context from payment letters of credit.

the jurisdiction whose law governs pursuant to the choice-of-law principles of private international law.

**Problem 1.** A contract for the sale of 3000 tons of Brazilian ground-nuts called for shipment from Brazil to Genoa between February 1 and April 30, at the option of the sellers. The contract further provided: "Payment: By opening of a confirmed, irrevocable, divisible, transmissible and transferable credit opened in favour of the sellers and utilisable by them against delivery of the following documents." The buyer established the letter of credit on April 22. The seller had already resold the goods on the ground that the credit was established too late in the light of the seller's privilege to ship in February or March. Seller sued the buyer for damages. What result under CISG? What evidence of custom and what arguments concerning seller's need for the letter of credit would be relevant?[10]

**Problem 2.** If a buyer has the obligation to arrange for shipping and has the privilege of selecting the date for shipment within a designated period, may the buyer delay establishing the letter of credit until the end of the period? What would be the effect of a showing by seller that it was customary in this trade to use the letter of credit in order to raise funds to pay the seller's supplier?[11]

**Problem 3.** If a sales contract requires only that buyer furnish a letter of credit, does buyer meet that obligation by obtaining a revocable letter of credit? Domestic United States law, the Commercial Code, declares that buyer must provide an irrevocable letter of credit. UCC 2–325(3). Would the same result follow under CISG?[12]

---

# Section 5.   Transactions in Goods Not to be Moved

## (A) Domestic United States Law

In some circumstances, owners of goods, having put them into storage, decide to sell the goods to buyers who want to keep the goods where they are. The persons with custody of the goods, often warehouse operators, are characterized legally as bailees. Performance of sellers obligations in sales contracts that concern goods that are not to be moved require, in effect, that the sellers transfer to the buyers the bailees' obligation to surrender the goods.[1]

---

**10.**   See Pavia & Co. v. Thurmann–Nielsen, [1952] 1 All Eng.L.R. 492 (C.A.).

**11.**   See Ian Stach, Ltd. v. Baker Bosly, Ltd., [1958] 1 All E.R. 542 (interesting and instructive opinion by Diplock, J., on the practical problems presented by using the ultimate buyer's letter of credit to finance "a string of merchants' contracts between the manufacturer or stockist and the ultimate user"); 108 L.J. 388 (1958).

**12.**   A similar, but quite different question arises of interpreting a letter of credit that does not declare whether or not it is revocable.

**1.**   The situation of a sale of goods in possession of bailee is analogous to the situation of a sale of goods in possession of a carrier. The carrier with custody of the goods is not generally characterized as a bailee.

An example of a market situation in which goods may be sold without intent to move them at the time of sale occurs in sales of propane and natural gas, which are held in huge underground storage facilities. Sellers and buyers perform contracts for sale of the goods by transfer to buyers of commitments to deliver by operators of the storage facilities. See., e.g., Commonwealth Petroleum Co. v. Petrosol International, Inc., 901 F.2d 1314 (6th Cir.1990).

Performance rules for such contracts are provided in UCC 2–503(4) for transactions in which the parties have not specifically described the manner of sellers' performance.

*Manner of Sellers' Tender.* Some bailees in possession of goods issue negotiable documents of title, similar to negotiable bills of lading issued by carriers, that control the right to obtain possession of the goods.[2] Such documents are called negotiable warehouse receipts. If goods are covered by such a document, a seller performs its obligation under the sales contract by tendering the document in a form that makes the buyer the holder of the document. UCC 2–503(4)(a). Alternatively, a seller performs by procuring the bailee's acknowledgment of the buyer's right to possession of the goods.

Section 2–503(4) goes on to qualify the tender rules of subsection (a). When goods are stored with a bailee that has not issued a negotiable document of title, tender occurs when a seller tenders a non-negotiable document of title or a written direction to the bailee to deliver the goods to the buyer, unless the buyer objects to tender in this manner. If a buyer does object, seller's tender obligation is met provisionally upon the bailee's receipt of notification of the buyer's rights, but that tender is defeated if the bailee refuses to obey the direction. UCC 2–503(4)(b).

*Manner of Buyers' Tender; Inspection.* The Commercial Code does not have a default rule for buyers' inspection of the goods or tender of payment of the price in transactions where goods are to be delivered without being moved. Therefore, a buyer has the right to inspect the goods before payment is due under UCC 2–513(1). Seller's tender entitles the seller to payment according to the contract under UCC 2–507(1).

The Commercial Code contains no default rules on the time and place for sellers' tender under UCC 2–503(4) or buyers' tender under UCC 2–507.

## (B) INTERNATIONAL SALES LAW

The Convention on Contracts for International Sale of Goods has no provisions on performance of contracts for sales of goods in storage.

---

**2.** The governing law is Article 7 of the Commercial Code. The prototypical document of title issued by a bailee is a warehouse receipt. UCC 1–201(b)(42), 7–202.

# CHAPTER 7

# PERFORMANCE STAGE CONTROVERSIES

## SECTION 1. INTRODUCTION

The performance stage of sales contracts is a time in which diverse controversies can arise. That is not often the case in sales contracts where the parties and the goods being sold are present at the time the contracts are formed. If performance occurs immediately after formation, the likelihood of performance stage controversy is slight.[1] As the period between contract formation and performance lengthens, the probability of performance-stage controversy increases. A number of reasons exist: A gap between contract formation and performance usually results because the goods contracted for are "future goods."[2] In such transactions, sellers may not be able to make or buy goods that conform completely to contract descriptions. n such transactions, buyers opportunity to see and examine the goods arises when the goods are tendered or delivered. Inspection of the goods may reveal qualities that are not satisfactory to the buyers. Any problems in the manner, time or place of performance become manifest in the performance stage of sales of future goods.

An added factor that causes instability in the performance stage of many sales contracts is the possibility of reduced commitment to the deal on the part of one of the parties. The values of the exchange anticipated by a buyer and a seller at the time of contract formation may not exist at the time of performance. The simplest reason for this would be change in the market value of goods sold for a fixed price. In a market with falling prices for available goods, a buyer may regret its agreement to pay the higher-than-market contract price. Other changes in the situations of buyers, such as their planned use of the goods, may also result in reduced commitment to the contracts. If regrets or changed circumstances lead a buyer to want to escape from its contract obligation without liability for breach, a buyer may become extremely finicky about every aspect of the seller's performance. If the contract conditions on a buyer's duty to pay are not fulfilled, the buyer can walk away without liability. Analogous incentives may exist on the sellers' side of contracts, but the contract conditions on a seller's duty to deliver goods are different.

---

**1.** Non-conformities may exist in present goods, such as breach of a warranty of quality or title, but these non-conformities are likely to be latent and not detected by buyers until performances have been completed. When latent non-conformities are discovered by buyers, their remedies in the post-performance stage were considered in Chapters 3 and 4.

**2.** See UCC 2–105(2).

Strategic behavior of the kind just discussed is unlikely to occur when the parties have an ongoing and mutually valued commercial relationship.[3] If continuation of a relationship has a sufficient value to both of the parties, neither is likely to raise performance-stage issues in an effort to escape from one unfavorable deal. Indeed, when market breaks occur or circumstances change otherwise, both sides may have commercial incentives to modify terms of contracts not yet executed to take account of the changes that have occurred.

As you consider cases and problems in which performance-stage controversies arise, be aware of the contract relationships between the parties and the extent to which one of the parties may be seeking to escape from a deal that it no longer considers favorable. Also consider the role of counsel in advising sellers or buyers in the performance stage of contracts that may be prone to have controversy.

Prominent among performance-stage controversies are controversies that arise when sellers' performances do not conform to their contractual obligations or are perceived by buyers not to conform. The next two sections of this chapter considers the performance options available to buyers when, in fact, sellers have tendered or delivered non-conforming goods or non-conforming documents or otherwise failed to satisfy their contract obligations, the performance options available to sellers when buyers decide not to accept goods, and the legal remedies that flow from the parties' exercise of their options. Section 4 examines performance stage controversies that arise in connection with letters of credit.

Another set of controversies stems from some casualty to the goods, e.g., loss or damage, during the performance stage of sales contracts. The loss of value in goods identified to sales contracts is a major risk, which parties may address in their sales contracts. Default rules on "risk-of-loss" are an important part of any body of sales law. These are considered in Section 5.

Section 6 takes up the law governing disputes when there has been no performance. Included is the law dealing with repudiation or breach that occurs before the contract date for performance.

## SECTION 2. NONCONFORMING PERFORMANCE BY SELLERS: BUYERS' ACCEPTANCE OR REJECTION, AND SELLERS' CURE

### (A) DOMESTIC UNITED STATES LAW

#### 1. ACCEPTANCE

*Buyers' Duty to Accept Goods.* UCC 2–301 declares that buyers are obligated to "accept" goods delivered by sellers, and UCC 2–507(1) states

---

**3.** If one of the parties to a long-term contractual relationship determines that the relationship is no longer sufficiently valuable to it, it may seek legal grounds for termination of the long-term contract. See, e.g., Advent Systems, Ltd. v. Unisys Corp., Chapter 2 supra.

that: "tender entitles the seller to [buyer's] acceptance of the goods...." Although not clearly stated, these provisions cannot be read reasonably to impose on buyers the obligation to accept non-conforming goods or goods tendered in a manner, time or place that does not conform to sellers' obligation. Implicit in buyers' obligation is the condition that the tender and the tendered goods conform to the contract.

The opposite of acceptance is rejection. Buyers may reject non-conforming goods or documents and may reject goods or documents tendered other than in conformity with the contract. The basic provisions on rejection are found in UCC 2–601 and UCC 2–612(2).

*Manner of Buyers' Acceptance of Goods.* UCC Article 2 has a three-pronged definition of how a buyer can accept goods: (1) an overt statement of acceptance to the seller, (2) estoppel resulting from a buyer's handling of the goods, and (3) lapse of time after delivery or tender of delivery. UCC 2–606(1).

In most ordinary commercial and consumer transactions, acceptance is the result of mere lapse of time. Sometimes a buyer may "[signify] to the seller that the goods are conforming or that he will take them or retain them in spite of their non-conformity," UCC 2–606(1)(a), but, more likely, buyers receive goods and simply say nothing to the seller about conformity or non-conformity.[1] Continued silence becomes "failure to make an effective rejection," UCC 2–606(1)(b), because "rejection of goods must be within a reasonable time after their delivery or tender." UCC 2–602(1).[2]

*Time of Acceptance: Inspection of Goods Before Acceptance.* Acceptance by signification or by lapse of time cannot occur until buyers have had "a reasonable opportunity to inspect" the goods. UCC 2–606(1)(a) and (b), 2–513(1). In Chapter 6 we considered buyers' right to inspect before the obligation to pay matured. The same provisions of the Code condition both the obligation to accept and the obligation to pay with buyers' right to inspect. The Code declares that buyers may inspect goods "in any reasonable manner," UCC 2–513(1), but offers no criteria for determining what inspection methods are reasonable.

ZABRISKIE CHEVROLET, INC. v. SMITH, 99 N.J.Super. 441, 240 A.2d 195 (1968). Buyer purchased a new car from Dealer. Buyer gave the Dealer his personal check for the price and took possession of the car. After driving 7/10 of a mile from Dealer's showroom, Buyer discovered a nonconformity. Buyer stopped payment on his check. Dealer sued for the purchase price under UCC 2–709(1)(a). Dealer contended that buyer had accepted the car. The court found that Buyer had not accepted. In so deciding, the court concluded that Buyer had not completed his inspection

---

**1.** Businesses courting good will sometimes inquire about customer satisfaction with the goods received. This may produce express responses, but thank-you notes or equivalent are not commonplace occurrences in market transactions.

**2.** The third prong, "does any act inconsistent with the seller's ownership," UCC 2–606(1)(c), is based on buyers' conduct. Common acts that may fit this prong are buyers' consumption of the goods or transfer of them to a sub-purchaser.

of it when he paid and drove it away: "To the layman, the complicated mechanisms of today's automobiles are a complete mystery. To have the automobile inspected [in the showroom] by someone with sufficient expertise to disassemble the vehicle in order to discover latent defects ... is assuredly impossible and highly impractical. ... Consequently, the first few miles of driving become even more significant to the excited new car buyer. This is the buyer's first reasonable opportunity ... to see if it conforms to what it was represented to be.... How long the buyer may drive the new car under the guise of inspection is not an issue in the present case."

*Significance of Acceptance.* Acceptance of goods is a significant legal watershed: at that moment the legal positions of a buyer and a seller change substantially. Acceptance precludes rejection. UCC 2–607(2). The buyer must pay at the contract rate for any goods accepted. UCC 2–607(1).

Acceptance of goods does not foreclose buyers from relief if the goods do not conform to the contract. As we learned in Chapters 3 and 4, buyers may have claims for breach of warranties of title or quality.[3] In such litigation, the burden is on the buyers to establish any breach with respect to accepted goods. UCC 2–607(4). Unless time-barred under UCC 2–725 or barred for lack of notice under UCC 2–607(3)(a), aggrieved buyers may recover damages under UCC 2–714 and 2–715. As you recall, monetary relief under UCC 2–714 and 2–715 is not the sole remedy for aggrieved buyers. Some buyers are empowered to revoke their acceptances under UCC 2–608 and are entitled to recover the contract price as well as damages.

## 2.  REJECTION

*Buyers' Right to Reject Goods or Documents.* The antithesis of acceptance is rejection. The right of buyers to reject goods or documents is set forth in UCC 2–601 for single-delivery sales contracts and in UCC 2–612 for sales contracts in which sellers' performances are divided into installments.

*Grounds for Rejection.* Grounds for rejection of goods of documents may be non-conformities of any kind.

*Quality or title.* The rounds for rejection of goods include, of course, failure of the goods to conform to warranties of quality or title. We considered these warranties in Chapters 3 and 4, primarily in the context of disputes that arose after the goods had been accepted. If non-conformities as to quality or title are manifest when tender of delivery is made, buyers have the power to reject or to accept the goods. The right to inspect goods before acceptance is instrumental in permitting buyers to discern non-conformities in that period and to exercise the option of acceptance or rejection.

*Quantity or timeliness.* Non-conformities of goods with respect to the quantity term or the time term of sales contracts are likely to be discernible

---

**3.** Nearly all the breach of warranty of quality cases and problems in Chapter 4 and breach of the warranty of title cases and problems in Chapter 3 involved buyers who had accepted goods

at the time of tender of delivery. Disputes as to these matters are less likely to arise in the period after acceptance of the goods.

*Rejection of Documents.* Grounds for rejection of documents derive from the terms in the sales contract that specify the nature of the documents that may be tendered. In Chapter 6, the section on documentary sales transactions emphasized the importance to the parties of clarity and specificity of the description of the documents in sales contracts. One critical document is the bill of lading, issued by a carrier. It is vital for a buyer to be able to rely upon that document as assurance that conforming goods have been shipped when the sales contract requires the buyer to pay the contract price in exchange for that document. The earliest cases in the common-law history of the perfect tender rule involved the power to reject documents of title for discrepancies apparent on the face of those documents.

*Significance of Rejection.* Rejection of goods, if rightful, means that a seller has failed to meet its obligation to make due tender of conforming goods. Buyer is released from obligation to pay the contract price, UCC 2–507(1), and, absent cure of the deficiencies in seller's performance, is entitled to monetary remedies, which are catalogued in UCC 2–711. In addition to recovering any part of the contract price paid, UCC 2–711(1), buyer is entitled to damages measured by the cost of purchasing substitute goods ("cover") from another source, UCC 2–712, or by the differential between market price and contract price, UCC 2–713, together with incidental or consequential damages under UCC 2–715. Responsibility for disposition of rejected goods is on sellers, although some buyers have the right or duty to act on sellers' behalf in disposing of them.

*Rightful and Wrongful Rejection.* The decision to reject tendered goods or documents is made unilaterally by the buyer. That decision may be rightful, that is, justified by the law, or wrongful, that is without legal justification. The basic standard that differentiates rightful from wrongful rejection is UCC 2–601.[4] In transactions that involve a single delivery of goods, a buyer is permitted to reject "if the goods or the tender of delivery fail in any respect to conform to the contract." Common legal usage refers to this standard as the "perfect tender rule."[5] Goods or the tender of delivery may fail to conform to the contract in many respects, but four tend to predominate: clouds on title, defects in quality, deficiencies or excesses in quantity, and late deliveries.

Historians identify a mid–19th century British decision as the origin of the perfect tender rule. Bowes v. Shand, [1876] 1 Q.B.D. 470, [1877] 2 Q.B.D. 112, [1877] 2 App. Cas. 455. Professor Grant Gilmore said that the perfect tender rule in the United States dates from October 26, 1885, when the Supreme Court decided Norrington v. Wright, 115 U.S. 188, 6 S.Ct. 12,

---

**4.**   Buyers are permitted, of course, to accept goods known to be non-conforming. See UCC 2–607(2). There is no concept of wrongful acceptance.

**5.**   Comment 2 to UCC 2–106(2) (definition of "conforming") states: "It is in general intended to continue the policy of exact performance by the seller of his obligations as a condition to his right to require acceptance."

29 L.Ed. 366 (1885), and Filley v. Pope, 115 U.S. 213, 6 S.Ct. 19, 29 L.Ed. 372 (1885). See E. Peters, Commercial Transactions 33 (1971). A high (or low) water mark cited by Professor (later Connecticut Supreme Court Chief Justice) Peters was Frankel v. Foreman & Clark, 33 F.2d 83 (2d Cir.1929) (permitting rejection of a shipment of coats for trivial and inconsequential non-conformities in less than 2% of the coats). Id. at 34. The perfect tender rule was not stated explicitly in either the Sale of Goods Act or the Uniform Sales Act.[6] For a comprehensive review of court decisions applying the perfect tender rule prior to the Commercial Code, see J. Honnold, Buyer's Right of Rejection, 97 U. Pa. L. Rev. 457 (1949).

The perfect tender rule was codified in early versions of the Uniform Commercial Code. After the Code had been promulgated for adoption by the states, a major study was conducted under the aegis of the Law Revision Commission of the State of New York. That Commission recommended that "the right of rejection as stated in Section 2–601 be limited to material breach." The Editorial Board responsible for revising the Code following the New York study did not accept this recommendation. That Board relied on two grounds: "first, . . . the buyer should not be required to guess at his peril whether a breach is material; second, . . . proof of materiality would sometimes require disclosure of the buyer's private affairs such as secret formulas or processes." R. Braucher & E. Sutherland, Commercial Transactions 56 (1964). Other considerations, noted by Professor Honnold in Buyer's Right of Rejection, supra, at 466–72, were: (1) the hazard for buyers of securing redress when full cash payment is demanded on tender of the goods; (2) the difficulty in many cases of measuring, without controversy, the extent of the deficiency in sellers' performances. Are these reasons persuasive?[7] Do the rules of the Code fit these underlying interests as well as is feasible?[8]

The perfect-tender rule does not apply to sellers' tenders of goods in installment contracts. Section 2–601 is "subject to the provisions of this Article on breach in installment contracts." The substance of the governing provision, UCC 2–612, is closer to the common-law standard for contract performance that entitles those rendering performance to the contract price.[9] However, the text of UCC 2–612 is detailed and complex. We take up its provisions later in this section.

---

**6.** See the Prior Uniform Statutory Provision segment of the Comment to UCC 2–601.

**7.** See W. Lawrence, Appropriate Standards for a Buyer's Refusal to Keep Goods Tendered by a Seller, 35 Wm. & Mary L. Rev. 1635 (1994); J. Sebert, Rejection, Revocation, and Cure Under Article 2 of the Uniform Commercial Code: Some Modest Proposals, 84 Nw. U. L. Rev. 375 (1990); W. Lawrence, The Prematurely Reported Demise of the Perfect Tender Rule, 35 Kan. L. Rev. 557 (1987).

**8.** See E. Peters, Remedies for Breach of Contracts Relating to the Sale of Goods Under the UCC, 73 Yale L.J. 199, 206–27 (1963); G. Priest, Breach and Remedy for the Tender of Nonconforming Goods: An Economic Approach, 91 Harv.L.Rev. 960 (1978); Schmitt & Frisch, 13 Toledo L.Rev. 1375 (1982).

**9.** See E. Farnsworth, Contracts § 8.16 (3d ed. 1999); Restatement, Second, Contracts §§ 237, 241 (1981).

*Manner and Time of Buyers' Rejection of Goods.* Rejection of goods must be made before lapse of a reasonable time after tender or delivery, UCC 2–602(1). The only way for a buyer to reject effectively is to notify the seller seasonably. UCC 2–602(1). The Code does not prescribe the minimum content of an effective rejection notice, but does provide that certain buyers' failure to describe particular defects will preclude them from later relying on unstated defects to justify their rejection or to establish sellers' breach. UCC 2–605.[10]

*Cure.* Rejection of goods or documents opens another performance option for sellers. UCC 2–508 sometimes gives sellers a second chance to perform.[11]

*Responsibility for Rejected Goods.* Goods rejected by buyers are not necessarily worthless. Although goods may not conform to the terms of a sales contract, the goods may be useful and marketable under accurate contract descriptions. When a buyer's rejection occurs at or before the seller's tender of delivery, the seller is not likely to complete delivery and the goods remain in the seller's control. The seller can make an alternative disposition of the goods. In sales contracts that involve carriers' transport of the goods, but that require buyers' inspection of the goods before carriers hand them over to the buyers, rejected goods are in the possession of the carriers and can be rerouted or returned on instructions from the sellers.[12]

The situation is more complicated, commercially and legally, when rejection decisions are made and communicated after the goods have been received by the buyers. If a non-merchant buyer has taken possession of goods before rejecting them, that buyer must hold the goods with reasonable care for a time sufficient to permit the seller to remove them, UCC 2–602(2)(b), but has no further obligations with regard to the goods. UCC 2–602(2)(c). A merchant buyer in possession of rejected goods must follow seller's reasonable instructions. UCC 2–603(1). A merchant buyer in possession of perishable goods or goods whose market value may decline speedily, in the absence of seller's instructions, must make reasonable efforts to sell

---

**10.** Compare the necessary content of buyers' notices to sellers with regard to nonconformity of accepted goods. UCC 2–607(3)(a) and Comment 4.

**11.** There is a common-law doctrine on the right to cure defective performances. The common-law rule was influenced by UCC 2–508. See E. Farnsworth, Contracts § 8.17 (3d ed. 1999)

**12.** In at-a-particular-destination contracts, when sellers tender goods through carriers *at* the stated place, buyers accept or reject in response to such tenders in the same way as they perform the acceptance obligation in transactions performed without carriers. Within a reasonable time after tender, they must elect to accept or reject the goods. UCC 2–606(1)(b). In-the-place-of-shipment contracts, tender may be completed before arrival of the goods, but the time period for a buyer to accept or reject does not begin to run until buyer has had an opportunity to inspect the goods. UCC 2–606(1)(b). Unless the agreement designates a different time and place, the inspection opportunity begins when the goods have arrived. UCC 2–513(1). Thus, within a reasonable time after arrival of the goods, buyers must elect to accept or reject the goods. UCC 2–606(1)(b).

the goods for the seller's account. Id.[13] If sellers give no instructions within a reasonable time after notification of rejection, buyers may store the goods, ship them back to sellers, or sell them for the sellers' accounts. UCC 2–604.

KELLER v. INLAND METALS ALL WEATHER CONDITIONING, INC., 139 Idaho 233, 76 P.3d 977 (2003). Owner of athletic club purchased a new 7½ ton dehumidifier to replace an unsatisfactory smaller unit in the swimming pool area. Seller installed the dehumidifier in June 1997. Four days later, buyer informed the seller that the unit was not working properly. Over several months, seller tried to improve the performance of the unit. In October 1977, buyer filed a suit for breach of warranty. As part of the complaint, buyer formally notified seller that it was rejecting the dehumidifier. Seller did not remove the unit, which buyer continued to use. The Supreme Court of Idaho held that the rejection was timely and, further, that buyer's continued use of the dehumidifier was appropriate conduct to mitigate the damages.

*Litigation After Rejection.* Buyers must decide to reject goods or documents unilaterally. If in doubt about the rightfulness of their actions, a buyer that is contemplating rejection can seek advice of counsel, but there is no practical way to obtain a judicial ruling that a rejection is legally rightful. Buyers therefore act at some considerable peril that, if sellers sue, courts may decide that the buyers' actions were wrongful.

There are practical considerations that may influence buyers' decisions. If a buyer has paid all or most of the price and the buyer rejects, the buyer must consider how it will recover the amount paid. If a buyer has taken possession or control of the goods, the buyer has a security interest for the payments it made. UCC 2–711(3).[14] Other buyers face the problem of compelling recalcitrant sellers to return the money. Another practical consideration is the relationship between the contract price and the market value of the goods at the time of the acceptance/rejection choice. If the market has gone down since the contract was formed, a buyer may be able to make a current purchase of the goods for less than the contract price. Conversely, if the market has gone up, the rejecting buyer may have to pay more than the contract price. Not surprisingly, buyers are more prone to reject goods when market prices have fallen since the contracts were formed.

Litigation after rejection may be initiated by buyers, perhaps to recover the price paid, but also to recover for expectation damages. If a buyer's rejection is found to have been rightful, the remedial provisions are outlined in UCC 2–711.

---

**13.**  Resales of goods before rejection would normally constitute acceptances of the goods under the provision that an act inconsistent with sellers' ownership constitutes acceptance. UCC 2–606(1)(c). However, resale of rightfully rejected goods in conformity with the Code is neither acceptance nor conversion of them. UCC 2–603(3), 2–604.

**14.**  A security interest allows a buyer to sell the goods and retain the proceeds to the extent needed to satisfy its interest.

Litigation after rejection often takes the form of a price action by unpaid sellers who take the position that buyers' rejections were wrongful. UCC 2–709 allows some aggrieved sellers to recover the full contract price of goods that buyers have wrongfully rejected. However. aggrieved sellers have an alternative causes of action for damages that are more likely to be legally available. The Code provisions on sellers' damages for wrongful rejection are found in UCC 2–703, 2–706, and 2–708. The cases in this Section are cases in which sellers sought to recover (or to retain) the price from buyers that based their defenses on the right to reject. In the next section, we will consider cases involve sellers' claims for damages.

# Moulton Cavity & Mold v. Lyn–Flex Industries

Supreme Judicial Court of Maine, 1979.
396 A.2d 1024.

■ DELAHANTY, JUSTICE.

Defendant, Lyn–Flex Industries, Inc., appeals from a judgment entered after a jury trial by the Superior Court, York County, in favor of plaintiff, Moulton Cavity & Mold, Inc. The case concerns itself with an oral contract for the sale of goods which, as both parties agree, is governed by Article 2 of the Uniform Commercial Code, 11 M.R.S.A. §§ 2–101 et seq. For the reasons set forth below, we agree with defendant that the presiding Justice committed reversible error by instructing the jury that the doctrine of substantial performance applied to a contract for the sale of goods. We do not agree, however, that based on the evidence introduced at trial defendant is entitled to judgment in its favor as a matter of law. The appeal is therefore sustained and the case remanded for a new trial.

An examination of the record discloses the following sequence of events: On March 19, 1975, Lynwood Moulton, president of plaintiff, and Ernest Sturman, president of defendant, orally agreed that plaintiff would produce, and defendant purchase, twenty-six innersole molds capable of producing saleable innersoles. The price was fixed at $600.00 per mold. Whether or not a time for delivery had been established was open to question. In his testimony at trial, Mr. Moulton admitted that he was fully aware that defendant was in immediate need of the molds, and he stated that he had estimated that he could provide suitable molds in about five weeks' time. Mr. Sturman testified that "I conveyed the urgency to [Mr. Moulton] and he said 'within three weeks I will begin showing you molds and by the end of five weeks you will have [the entire order].' "

In apparent conformity with standard practice in the industry, plaintiff set about constructing a sample mold and began a lengthy series of tests. These tests consisted of bringing the sample mold to defendant's plant, fitting the mold to one of defendant's plastic-injecting machines, and checking the innersole thus derived from the plaintiff's mold to determine if it met the specifications imposed by defendant. After about thirty such tests over a ten-week period, several problems remained unsolved, the most significant of which was "flashing," that is, a seepage of plastic along the seam where the two halves of the mold meet. Although characterized by plaintiff as a minor defect, Mr. Moulton admitted that a flashing mold could not produce a saleable innersole.

It was plaintiff's contention at trial, supported by credible evidence, that at one point during the testing period officials of defendant signified that in their judgment plaintiff's sample mold was turning out innersoles correctly configured so as to fit the model last supplied by defendant's customer. Allegedly relying on this approval, plaintiff went ahead and constructed the full run of twenty-six molds.

For its part, defendant introduced credible evidence to rebut the assertion that it had approved the fit of the molds. It also noted that Moulton's allegation of approval extended only to the fit of the mold; as Moulton conceded, defendant had never given full approval since it considered the flashing problem, among others, unacceptable.

On May 29, some ten weeks after the date of the oral agreement and five weeks after the estimated completion date, Mr. Sturman met with plaintiff's foreman at the Moulton plant. A dispute exists regarding the substance of the ensuing conversation. Plaintiff introduced evidence tending to show that at that time, Mr. Sturman revoked defendant's prior approval of the fit of the sample mold and demanded that plaintiff redesign the molds to fit the last. Testimony introduced by defendant tended to show that it had never approved the fit of the molds to begin with and that on the date in question, May 29, plaintiff's foreman indicated that plaintiff simply would not invest any more time in conforming the molds to the contract. Mr. Sturman met the next day with Mr. Moulton, and Moulton ratified the position taken by his foreman. Thereupon, Mr. Sturman immediately departed for Italy and arranged to have the molds produced by the Plastak Corporation, an Italian mold-making concern, at a cost of $650.00 per mold. Plaintiff later billed defendant for the contract price of the molds, deducting an allowance for "flashing and shut-off adjustments." Upon defendant's refusal to pay, plaintiff brought this action for the price less adjustments. Defendant counterclaimed for its costs in obtaining conforming goods to the extent that they exceeded the contract price.

At trial, plaintiff's basic theory of recovery was that it had received approval with regard to the fit of the sample mold, that in reliance on that approval it had constructed a full run of twenty-six molds, and that defendant had, in effect, committed an anticipatory breach of contract within the meaning of Section 2–610 by demanding that the fit of the molds be completely redesigned. On its counterclaim, and in response to plaintiff's position, defendant advanced the theory that plaintiff had breached the contract by failing to tender conforming goods within the five-week period mentioned by both parties.

After the presiding Justice had charged the jury, counsel for plaintiff requested at side bar that the jury be instructed on the doctrine of substantial performance. Counsel for defendant entered a timely objection to the proposed charge which objection was overruled. The court then supplemented its charge as follows:

The only point of clarification that I'll make, ladies and gentlemen, is that I've referred a couple of times to performance of a contract and you, obviously, have to determine no matter which way you view the contract to be, and there might even be a possible third way that I haven't even considered, whether the contract whatever it is has been performed and there is a doctrine that you should be aware of in considering that. That is the doctrine of substantial performance.

It is not required that performance be in any case one hundred percent complete in order to entitle a party to enforcement of their contractual rights. That is not to say within the confines of this case that the existence of flashing would be excused or not be excused. It is just a recognition on the part of the law when we talk about performance, probably if we took any contract you could always find something of no substance that was not completed one hundred percent. It is for you to determine that whether it has been substantially performed or not and what in fact constitutes substantial performance.

In your consideration, and as I say in this case, that's not to intimate that something like flashing is to be disregarded or to be considered. It's up to you based upon facts.

The jury returned a verdict in favor of plaintiff in the amount of $14,480.82.

I

In Smith, Fitzmaurice Co. v. Harris, 126 Me. 308, 138 A. 389 (1927), a case decided under the common law, we recognized the then-settled rule that with respect to contracts for the sale of goods the buyer has the right to reject the seller's tender if in any way it fails to conform to the specifications of the contract. We held that "[t]he vendor has the duty to comply with his order in kind, quality and amount." Id. at 312, 138 A. at 391. Thus, in *Smith*, we ruled that a buyer who had contracted to purchase twelve dozen union suits could lawfully refuse a tender of sixteen dozen union suits. Various provisions of the Uniform Sales Act, enacted in Maine in 1923, codified the common-law approach. R.S. (1954) ch. 185, §§ 11, 44. The so-called "perfect tender" rule came under considerable fire around the time the Uniform Commercial Code was drafted. No less an authority than Karl Llewellyn, recognized as the primum mobile of the Code's tender provisions (see, e.g., W. Twining, Karl Llewellyn and the Realist Movement 270–301 (1973); Carroll, Harpooning Whales, of Which Karl N. Llewellyn is the Hero of the Piece; or Searching for More Expansion Joints in Karl's Crumbling Cathedral, 12 B.C.Indus. & Comm.L.Rev. 139, 142 (1970)), attacked the rule principally on the ground that it allowed a dishonest buyer to avoid an unfavorable contract on the basis of an insubstantial defect in the seller's tender. Llewellyn, On Warranty of Quality and Society, 37 Colum.L.Rev. 341, 389 (1937). Although Llewellyn's views are represented in many Code sections governing tender,[6] the basic tender

---

**6.** See, e.g., §§ 2–508 (seller's limited right to cure defects in tender), 2–608 (buyer's limited right to revoke acceptance), and 2–612 (buyer's limited right to reject nonconforming tender under installment contract).

provision, Section 2–601, represents a rejection of Llewellyn's approach and a continuation of the perfect tender policy developed by the common law and carried forward by the draftsmen of the Uniform Sales Act. See Official Comment, § 2–106; Priest, Breach and Remedy for the Tender of Nonconforming Goods Under the Uniform Commercial Code: An Economic Approach, 91 Harv.L.Rev. 960, 971 (1978). Thus, Section 2–601 states that, with certain exceptions not here applicable, the buyer has the right to reject "if the goods or the tender of delivery fail *in any respect* to conform to the contract...." (emphasis supplied). Those few courts that have considered the question agree that the perfect tender rule has survived the enactment of the Code. Ingle v. Marked Tree Equipment Co., 244 Ark. 1166, 428 S.W.2d 286 (1968); Maas v. Scoboda, 188 Neb. 189, 195 N.W.2d 491 (1972); Bowen v. Young, 507 S.W.2d 600 (Tex.Civ.App.1974). We, too, are convinced of the soundness of this position.

In light of the foregoing discussion, it is clear that the presiding Justice's charge was erroneous and, under the circumstances, reversibly so. The jury was informed that "[i]t is not required that performance be in any case one hundred percent complete in order to entitle a party to enforcement of their contractual rights." Under this instruction, the jury was free to find that although plaintiff had not tendered perfectly conforming molds within the agreed period (assuming the jury found that the parties had in fact agreed on a specific time period for completion) it had nevertheless substantially performed the contract within the agreed time frame and was merely making minor adjustments when defendant backed out of the deal. Had the jury been instructed that plaintiff was required to tender perfectly conforming goods—not just substantially conforming goods—within the period allegedly agreed to and had they been instructed that, under Section 2–711, the buyer has the absolute right to cancel the contract if the seller "fails to make delivery," a different verdict might have resulted. Indeed, the supplemental instruction tended to encourage the jury to resolve the question by deciding whether "flashing" was or was not a substantial defect:

> It is not required that performance be in any case one hundred percent complete in order to entitle a party to enforcement of their contractual rights. That is not to say within the confines of this case that the existence of flashing would be excused or not be excused. ... It is for you to determine ... whether [the contract] has been substantially performed or not and what in fact constitutes substantial performance.

We find unpersuasive plaintiff's argument that the presiding Justice's instruction merely informed the jury that if it found that defendant had committed an anticipatory breach of the contract then plaintiff was not thereafter required to complete its performance as a condition precedent to recovery under the contract. Such an instruction might well have been appropriate and would certainly have been supportable under the applicable law. Dehahn v. Innes, Me., 356 A.2d 711, 719 (1976) ("When the other party has already repudiated the agreement, a tender would be a futile act and is not required by law."); §§ 2–610, 2–704. However, an examination of the passage of the charge in question leads us to reject plaintiff's interpretation. Without informing the jury that it must first find that defendant had committed an anticipatory repudiation, the presiding Justice, without qualification, stated that "performance [need not] be ... one hundred percent complete in order to entitle a party to enforcement of their contractual rights." Furthermore, the court drew a distinction between substantial and insubstantial defects, a distinction which, on these facts and under plaintiff's interpretation of the charge, would have been completely irrelevant. Finally, both the presiding Justice and counsel for plaintiff referred to the instruction at side bar as an explanation of the "substantial performance" doctrine. In legal parlance, that doctrine requires a buyer, under certain circumstances, to accept something less than a perfectly conforming tender. See, e.g., Rockland Poultry Co. v. Anderson, 148 Me. 211, 216, 91 A.2d 478, 480 (1952) (construction contract); Jacob & Youngs, Inc. v. Kent, 230 N.Y. 239, 129 N.E. 889 (1921) (Cardozo, J.) (construction contract). As such, it has no application to a contract for the sale of goods, and the jury should not have been permitted to consider it.

## II

In his testimony at trial, Mr. Moulton indicated that he was aware that to defendant time was a critical factor. He also stated that he had given defendant an estimated delivery date of five weeks from the date the contract was formed. On appeal, defendant takes the position that the parties agreed on a five-week time period for delivery and that plaintiff's failure to tender conforming goods after ten weeks constitutes a breach as a matter of law and precludes plaintiff from recovering under the contract.

We disagree. While on the one hand Mr. Sturman testified that Mr. Moulton had told him that the goods would be delivered in five weeks, on the other hand Mr. Moulton testified that it was clear that he was merely making an estimate. The testimony thus left the jury at liberty to decide the factual question of whether the five-week time period was an agreed delivery date and thus a term of the contract or merely an estimate. While the interpretation of unambiguous language in a written contract falls within the province of the court, Blue Rock Industries v. Raymond International, Inc., Me., 325 A.2d 66 (1974), questions of fact concerning the terms of an oral agreement are left to the trier of fact, Carter v. Beck, Me., 366 A.2d 520 (1976).

The entry is: Appeal sustained. New trial ordered.

## NOTES

**(1) Substantial Performance.** Most students will recall from general contract law that a party is entitled to the full contract price if it has substantially performed its contractual obligations. To the extent that less than exact performance has been rendered, the other party is entitled to recoupment in the amount of any damages. A leading contracts case is Judge Cardozo's opinion in Jacob & Youngs v. Kent, 230 N.Y. 239, 129 N.E.

889 (1921) (the Reading pipe case), cited by the Maine court. See also Restatement (Second) of Contracts §§ 237, 241, which puts the same performance standard in terms of material failure. On request of seller's counsel, the trial court in *Moulton Cavity & Mold* framed the jury charge on the substantial performance standard. What argument could be made in support of the trial court's decision?

**(2) Manner and Time of Buyer's Rejection.** The manner and time of buyer's rejection in *Moulton Cavity & Mold* is unclear. Any legal question of the sufficiency of buyer's actions was masked by the overriding issue of the legal standard for rejection. However, the court's opinion contains a factual account of the behavior of the buyer and the seller as the controversy emerged. Does this account show a clear-cut rejection decision by the buyer and communication of that decision to the seller?

**(3) Seller's Price Action.** The law suit in *Moulton Cavity & Mold* was brought by the seller for the contract price. This is a common litigation position in cases that involve buyers' rejection of goods. Buyers that have paid the purchase price are far less likely to reject goods. Can you articulate practical reasons for buyers' behavior in this respect? What lessons does this teach in counseling sellers and buyers with respect to terms of sales contracts on the timing of the parties' respective performances?

**Problem 1.** Grain Supply and Miller made a contract for the sale to Miller of 1,000 bushels of wheat at $5.00 per bushel. The contract specified that the wheat would be delivered on June 1, and would be of No. 1 milling quality, free of weevil; Miller was to pay the price of $5,000 within 60 days after delivery. On delivery of the wheat, Miller inspected the wheat and found that it was "crawling" with weevils and was totally unfit for milling; he instructed his manager to sell the wheat for chicken feed. The manager suggested that they get in touch with Supply and work out some adjustment. Miller, thoroughly disgusted with Supply's performance, said: "I'm not having anything more to do with that outfit. Just let them try to collect for this rotten stuff." The wheat, sold for chicken feed, brought only $2,000—a fair price under the circumstances. Three months later, Supply called Miller and reminded him that the bill was overdue. Miller said "You should know that I won't pay for such a rotten shipment," and hung up.

Supply brought an action to recover the contract price for the wheat. Miller counterclaimed on grounds of breach of express and implied warranty and demanded damages resulting from the necessity of purchasing the No. 1 wheat elsewhere at $6.00 per bushel.

(a) What result in Supply's action to recover the contract price? UCC 2–709, 2–606.

(b) What result in Miller's counterclaim for damages? UCC 2–607(3)(a).[15]

**Problem 2.** Assume that in Problem 1, when the wheat arrived on June 1, Miller wired Grain Supply, "Wheat defective. Holding you responsi-

---

15.  See Economy Forms Corp. v. Kandy, 391 F.Supp. 944 (N.D.Ga.1974).

ble." Supply did not respond. Miller stored the wheat in his warehouse, and two months later (on August 1) Miller wired Supply, "What do you want done with your weevily wheat?" Supply wired back, "You bought the wheat, and I expect you to pay your bill," and brought suit. Miller interposed all available defenses and counterclaims.

By the time of trial, the wheat, which at delivery had been worth $2,000 for chicken feed, had been further damaged by the weevils; and in the meantime the price level for feed grains had dropped so that the shipment was worth only $300.

(a) May Miller defeat the claim for payment of the price on the ground that he has made an effective rejection of the goods? See UCC 2–607(1), 2–606(1)(b), 2–602(1).

(b) Assume that the court finds that Miller's rejection was not effective. What judgment should be entered? Was Miller's brief wire of June 1 adequate to meet the requirements of UCC 2–607(3)(a)? See Comment 4. Who bears the deterioration and price decline that occurred after delivery? See UCC 2–510(1), UCC 2–606(1)(b), UCC 2–714.

# Plateq Corp. v. Machlett Laboratories

Supreme Court of Connecticut, 1983.
189 Conn. 433, 456 A.2d 786.

■ ELLEN PETERS, JUDGE.

In this action by a seller of specially manufactured goods to recover their purchase price from a commercial buyer, the principal issue is whether the buyer accepted the goods before it attempted to cancel the contract of sale. The plaintiff, Plateq Corporation of North Haven, sued the defendant, The Machlett Laboratories, Inc., to recover damages, measured by the contract price and incidental damages, arising out of the defendant's allegedly wrongful cancellation of a written contract for the manufacture and sale of two leadcovered steel tanks and appurtenant stands. The defendant denied liability and counterclaimed for damages. After a full hearing, the trial court found for the plaintiff both on its complaint and on the defendant's counterclaim. The defendant has appealed.

The trial court, in its memorandum of decision, found the following facts. On July 9, 1976, the defendant ordered from the plaintiff two leadcovered steel tanks to be constructed by the plaintiff according to specifications supplied by the defendant. The parties understood that the tanks were designed for the special purpose of testing x-ray tubes and were required to be radiation-proof within certain federal standards. Accordingly, the contract provided that the tanks would be tested for radiation leaks after their installation on the defendant's premises. The plaintiff undertook to correct, at its own cost, any deficiencies that this post-installation test might uncover. The plaintiff had not previously constructed such tanks, nor had the defendant previously designed tanks for this purpose. The contract was amended on August 9, 1976, to add construction of two metal stands to hold the tanks. All the goods were to be delivered to the defendant at the plaintiff's place of business.

Although the plaintiff encountered difficulties both in performing according to the contract specifications and in completing performance within the time required, the defendant did no more than call these deficiencies to the plaintiff's attention during various inspections in September and early October, 1976. By October 11, 1976, performance was belatedly but substantially completed. On that date, Albert Yannello, the defendant's engineer, noted some remaining deficiencies which the plaintiff promised to remedy by the next day, so that the goods would then be ready for delivery. Yannello gave no indication to the plaintiff that this arrangement was in any way unsatisfactory to the defendant. Not only did Yannello communicate general acquiescence in the plaintiff's proposed tender but he specifically led the plaintiff to believe that the defendant's truck would pick up the tanks and the stands within a day or two. Instead of sending its truck, the defendant sent a notice of total cancellation which the plaintiff received on October 14, 1976. That notice failed to particularize the grounds upon which cancellation was based.[3]

On this factual basis, the trial court, having concluded that the transaction was a contract for the sale of goods falling within the Uniform Commercial Code, General Statutes §§ 42a-2-101 et seq., considered whether the defendant had accepted the goods. The court determined that the defendant had accepted the tanks, primarily by signifying its willingness to take them despite their nonconformities, in accordance with General Statutes § 42a-2-606(1)(a), and secondarily by failing to make an effective rejection, in accordance with General Statutes § 42a-2-606(1)(b). Once the tanks had been accepted, the defendant could rightfully revoke its acceptance under General Statutes § 42a-2-608 only by showing substantial impairment of their value to the defendant. In part because the defendant's conduct had foreclosed any post-installation inspection, the court concluded that such impairment had not been proved. Since the tanks were not readily resalable on the open market, the plaintiff was entitled, upon the defendant's wrongful revocation of acceptance, to recover their contract price, minus salvage value, plus interest. General Statutes §§ 42a-2-703; 42a-2-709(1)(b). Accordingly, the trial court awarded the plaintiff damages in the amount of $14,837.92.

\* \* \*

Upon analysis, all of the defendant's claims of error are variations upon one central theme. The defendant claims that on October 11, when its engineer Yannello conducted the last examination on the plaintiff's premises, the tanks were so incomplete and unsatisfactory that the defendant was rightfully entitled to conclude that the plaintiff would never make a

---

**3.** The defendant sent the plaintiff a telegram stating: "This order is hereby terminated for your breach, in that you have continuously failed to perform according to your commitment in spite of additional time given you to cure your delinquency. We will hold you liable for all damages incurred [sic] by Machlett including excess cost of reprocurement."

conforming tender. From this scenario, the defendant argues that it was justified in cancelling the contract of sale. It denies that the seller's conduct was sufficient to warrant a finding of tender, or its own conduct sufficient to warrant a finding of acceptance. The difficulty with this argument is that it is inconsistent with the underlying facts found by the trial court. Although the testimony was in dispute, there was evidence of record to support the trial court's findings to the contrary. ... There is simply no fit between the defendant's claims and the trial court's finding that, by October 11, 1976, performance was in substantial compliance with the terms of the contract. The trial court further found that on that day the defendant was notified that the goods would be ready for tender the following day and that the defendant responded to this notification by promising to send its truck to pick up the tanks in accordance with the contract.

On the trial court's finding of facts, it was warranted in concluding, on two independent grounds, that the defendant had accepted the goods it had ordered from the plaintiff. Under the provisions of the Uniform Commercial Code, General Statutes § 42a–2–606(1) "[a]cceptance of goods occurs when the buyer (a) after a reasonable opportunity to inspect the goods signifies to the seller ... that he will take ... them in spite of their nonconformity; or (b) fails to make an effective rejection."

In concluding that the defendant had "signified" to the plaintiff its willingness to "take" the tanks despite possible remaining minor defects, the trial court necessarily found that the defendant had had a reasonable opportunity to inspect the goods. The defendant does not maintain that its engineer, or the other inspectors on previous visits, had inadequate access to the tanks, or inadequate experience to conduct a reasonable examination. It recognizes that inspection of goods when the buyer undertakes to pick up the goods is ordinarily at the seller's place of tender. See General Statutes §§ 42a–2–503, 42a–2–507, 42a–2–513; see also White & Summers, Uniform Commercial Code § 3–5 (2d ed. 1980). The defendant argues, however, that its contract, in providing for inspection for radiation leaks after installation of the tanks at its premises, necessarily postponed its inspection rights to that time. The trial court considered this argument and rejected it, and so do we. It was reasonable, in the context of this contract for the special manufacture of goods with which neither party had had prior experience, to limit this clause to adjustments to take place after tender and acceptance. After acceptance, a buyer may still, in appropriate cases, revoke its acceptance, General Statutes § 42a–2–608, or recover damages for breach of warranty, General Statutes § 42a–2–714. The trial court reasonably concluded that a post-installation test was intended to safeguard these rights of the defendant as well as to afford the plaintiff a final opportunity to make needed adjustments. The court was therefore justified in concluding that there had been an acceptance within § 42a–2–606(1)(a). A buyer may be found to have accepted goods despite their known nonconformity ... and despite the absence of actual delivery to the buyer. ...

\* \* \*

Once the conclusion is reached that the defendant accepted the tanks, its further rights of cancellation under the contract are limited by the governing provisions of the Uniform Commercial Code. "The buyer's acceptance of goods, despite their alleged nonconformity, is a watershed. After acceptance, the buyer must pay for the goods at the contract rate; General Statutes § 42a–2–607(1); and bears the burden of establishing their nonconformity. General Statutes § 42a–2–607(4)." . . . After acceptance, the buyer may only avoid liability for the contract price by invoking the provision which permits revocation of acceptance. That provision, General Statutes § 42a–2–608(1), requires proof that the "nonconformity [of the goods] substantially impairs [their] value to him." . . . On this question, . . . the trial court again found against the defendant. Since the defendant has provided no basis for any argument that the trial court was clearly erroneous in finding that the defendant had not met its burden of proof to show that the goods were substantially nonconforming, we can find no error in the conclusion that the defendant's cancellation constituted an unauthorized and hence wrongful revocation of acceptance.

Finally, the defendant in its brief, although not in its statement of the issues presented, challenges the trial court's conclusion about the remedial consequences of its earlier determinations. Although the trial court might have found the plaintiff entitled to recover the contract price because of the defendant's acceptance of the goods; General Statutes §§ 42a–2–703(e) and 42a–2–709(1)(a); the court chose instead to rely on General Statutes § 42a–2–709(1)(b), which permits a price action for contract goods that cannot, after reasonable effort, be resold at a reasonable price.[19] Since the contract goods in this case were concededly specially manufactured for the defendant, the defendant cannot and does not contest the trial court's finding that any effort to resell them on the open market would have been unavailing. In the light of this finding, the defendant can only reiterate its argument, which we have already rejected, that the primary default was that of the plaintiff rather than that of the defendant. The trial court's conclusion to the contrary supports both its award to the plaintiff and its denial of the defendant's counterclaim.

There is no error.

## NOTES

**(1) Seller's Price Action.** This is an action by the seller for the contract price of the goods, two steel tanks and appurtenant stands. UCC

---

**19.** . . . It should be noted that § 42a–2–709(1)(b) is not premised on a buyer's acceptance. Instead, it requires a showing that the goods were, before the buyer's cancellation, "identified to the contract." In the circumstances of this case, that precondition was presumably met by their special manufacture and by the defendant's acquiescence in their imminent tender. See White & Summers, Uniform Commercial Code, § 7–5 (2d ed. 1980). The defendant has not, on this appeal, argued the absence of identification.

It should further be noted that § 42a–2–709(1)(b), because it is not premised on acceptance, would have afforded the seller the right to recover the contract price even if the trial court had found the conduct of the buyer to be a wrongful rejection (because of the failure to give the seller an opportunity to cure) rather than a wrongful revocation of acceptance.

2–709 authorizes sellers' recovery of the price in limited circumstances. The trial court held for the seller under UCC 2–709(1)(b), which allows recovery of the price of goods identified to the contract if the seller is unable to resell them at a reasonable price. The steel tanks had been specially manufactured according to buyer's specifications. The trial court found, no doubt, that any reasonable effort by seller to resell these tanks would be unavailing. On appeal, the Supreme Court affirmed, but did so on a totally different legal analysis. Judge Peters found for the seller under the "goods accepted" clause of UCC 2–709(1)(a), which entailed her extensive analysis of the question whether the buyer had accepted the steel tanks. Why did the Supreme Court decline to affirm the trial court on that court's legal theory?

UCC Article 2 does not well integrate its provisions on the performance options of the parties to sales contracts, accept or reject, with its remedial provisions. The provisions on rejection are keyed to sellers' conforming or not conforming to their contract obligations. UCC 2–601 allows a buyer to reject for nonconformity in any respect. The price remedy provision is silent on the issue of conformity of sellers' performance. Does UCC 2–709(1)(b) allow a seller to recover the price of unsaleable goods if the goods did not conform to the contract? Does the "goods accepted" provision of UCC 2–709(1)(a) allow a seller to recover the price of goods that did not conform to the contract? You should now understand why Judge Peters did not affirm on the trial court's legal analysis.

**(2) Buyer's Acceptance.** UCC 2–606(1) gives three different scenarios that constitute a buyers's acceptance of goods. Which of the three was the basis of the decision of the Connecticut Supreme Court?

The trial court found ("secondarily" according to Judge Peters) that buyer had failed to make an effective rejection under UCC 2–602(1). Failure to make an effective rejection occurs under UCC 2–602(1) when a buyer fails to act within a reasonable time after delivery or tender of delivery of the goods. A buyer is not obligated to choose between acceptance and rejection before the seller has at least tendered delivery. Did the seller tender delivery of the steel tanks?

Can a buyer accept non-conforming goods under UCC 2–606(1)(a)? Can a buyer accept non-conforming goods before seller tenders delivery under UCC 2–606(1)(a)? Judge Peters analysis is built on the premise that the answer to these questions is "yes" and that the buyer in this case not only could accept non-conforming goods before tender but that it did so. The trial court also found such an acceptance. Was this decision sound as a matter of statutory construction?

# T.W. Oil, Inc. v. Consolidated Edison Co.

Court of Appeals of New York, 1982.
57 N.Y.2d 574, 457 N.Y.S.2d 458, 443 N.E.2d 932.

■ Fuchsberg, Judge.

In the first case to wend its way through our appellate courts on this question, we are asked, in the main, to decide whether a seller who, acting in good faith and without knowledge of any defect, tenders nonconforming goods to a buyer who properly rejects them, may avail itself of the cure provision of subdivision (2) of section 2–508 of the Uniform Commercial Code. We hold that, if seasonable notice be given, such a seller may offer to cure the defect within a reasonable period beyond the time when the contract was to be performed so long as it has acted in good faith and with a reasonable expectation that the original goods would be acceptable to the buyer.

The factual background against which we decide this appeal is based on either undisputed proof or express findings at Trial Term. In January, 1974, midst the fuel shortage produced by the oil embargo, the plaintiff (then known as Joc Oil USA, Inc.) purchased a cargo of fuel oil whose sulfur content was represented to it as no greater than 1%. While the oil was still at sea en route to the United States in the tanker *M T Khamsin*, plaintiff received a certificate from the foreign refinery at which it had been processed informing it that the sulfur content in fact was .52%. Thereafter, on January 24, the plaintiff entered into a written contract with the defendant (Con Ed) for the sale of this oil. The agreement was for delivery to take place between January 24 and January 30, payment being subject to a named independent testing agency's confirmation of quality and quantity. The contract, following a trade custom to round off specifications of sulfur content at, for instance, 1%, .5% or .3%, described that of the *Khamsin* oil as .5%. In the course of the negotiations, the plaintiff learned that Con Ed was then authorized to buy and burn oil with a sulfur content of up to 1% and would even mix oils containing more and less to maintain that figure.

When the vessel arrived, on January 25, its cargo was discharged into Con Ed storage tanks in Bayonne, New Jersey. In due course, the independent testing people reported a sulfur content of .92%. On this basis, acting within a time frame whose reasonableness is not in question, on February 14 Con Ed rejected the shipment. Prompt negotiations to adjust the price failed; by February 20, plaintiff had offered a price reduction roughly responsive to the difference in sulfur reading, but Con Ed, though it could use the oil, rejected this proposition out of hand. It was insistent on paying no more than the latest prevailing price, which, in the volatile market that then existed, was some 25% below the level which prevailed when it agreed to buy the oil.

The very next day, February 21, plaintiff offered to cure the defect with a substitute shipment of conforming oil scheduled to arrive on the *S.S. Appollonian Victory* on February 28. Nevertheless, on February 22, the very day after the cure was proffered, Con Ed, adamant in its intention to avail itself of the intervening drop in prices, summarily rejected this proposal too. The two cargos were subsequently sold to third parties at the best price obtainable, first that of the *Appollonian* and, sometime later, after extraction from the tanks had been accomplished, that of the *Khamsin*.

There ensued this action for breach of contract, which, after a somewhat unconventional trial course, resulted in a nonjury decision for the plaintiff in the sum of $1,385,512.83.... To arrive at this result, the Trial Judge, while ruling against other liability theories advanced by the plaintiff, which, in particular, included one charging the defendant with having failed to act in good faith in the negotiations for a price adjustment on the *Khamsin* oil (Uniform Commercial Code, § 1–203), decided as a matter of law that subdivision (2) of section 2–508 of the Uniform Commercial Code was available to the plaintiff even if it had no prior knowledge of the nonconformity. Finding that in fact plaintiff had no such belief at the time of the delivery, that what turned out to be a .92% sulfur content was "within the range of contemplation of reasonable acceptability" to Con Ed, and that seasonable notice of an intention to cure was given, the court went on to hold that plaintiff's "reasonable and timely offer to cure" was improperly rejected (sub nom. Joc Oil USA v. Consolidated Edison Co. of N.Y., 107 Misc.2d 376, 390, 434 N.Y.S.2d 623 [Shanley N. Egeth, J.]). The Appellate Division, 84 A.D.2d 970, 447 N.Y.S.2d 572, having unanimously affirmed the judgment entered on this decision, the case is now here by our leave....

In support of its quest for reversal, the defendant now asserts that the trial court erred (a) in ruling that the verdict on a special question submitted for determination by a jury was irrelevant to the decision of this case, (b) in failing to interpret subdivision (2) of section 2–508 of the Uniform Commercial Code to limit the availability of the right to cure after date of performance to cases in which the seller knowingly made a nonconforming tender and (c) in calculating damages on the basis of the resale of the nonconforming cargo rather than of the substitute offered to replace it. For the reasons which follow, we find all three unacceptable.

## I

[The court rejected objection (a).]

## II

We turn then to the central issue on this appeal: Fairly interpreted, did subdivision (2) of section 2–508 of the Uniform Commercial Code require Con Ed to accept the substitute shipment plaintiff tendered? In approaching this question, we, of course, must remember that a seller's right to cure a defective tender, as allowed by both subdivisions of section 2–508, was intended to act as a meaningful limitation on the absolutism of the old perfect tender rule, under which, no leeway being allowed for any imperfections, there was, as one court put it, just "no room ... for the doctrine of substantial performance" of commercial obligations (Mitsubishi Goshi Kaisha v. Aron & Co., 16 F.2d 185, 186 [Learned Hand, J.]; see Note, Uniform Commercial Code, § 2–508; Seller's Right to Cure Non–Conforming Goods, 6 Rutgers—Camden L.J. 387–388).

In contrast, to meet the realities of the more impersonal business world of our day, the code, to avoid sharp dealing, expressly provides for the liberal construction of its remedial provisions (§ 1–102) so that "good faith" and the "observance of reasonable commercial standards of fair dealing" be the rule rather than the exception in trade (see § 2–103, subd. [1], par. [b]), "good faith" being defined as "honesty in fact in the conduct or transaction concerned" (Uniform Commercial Code, § 1–201, subd. [19]). As to section 2–508 in particular, the code's Official Comment advises that its mission is to safeguard the seller "against surprise as a result of sudden technicality on the buyer's part" (Uniform Commercial Code, § 2–106, Comment 2;....

Section 2–508 may be conveniently divided between provisions for cure offered when "the time for performance has not yet expired" (subd. [1]), and ones which, by newly introducing the possibility of a seller obtaining "a further reasonable time to substitute a conforming tender" (subd. [2]), also permit cure beyond the date set for performance. ...

Since we here confront circumstances in which the conforming tender came after the time of performance, we focus on subdivision (2). On its face, taking its conditions in the order in which they appear, for the statute to apply (1) a buyer must have rejected a nonconforming tender, (2) the seller must have had reasonable grounds to believe this tender would be acceptable (with or without money allowance), and (3) the seller must have "seasonably" notified the buyer of the intention to substitute a conforming tender within a reasonable time.

In the present case, none of these presented a problem. The first one was easily met for it is unquestioned that, at .92%, the sulfur content of the *Khamsin* oil did not conform to the .5% specified in the contract and that it was rejected by Con Ed. The second, the reasonableness of the seller's belief that the original tender would be acceptable, was supported not only by unimpeached proof that the contract's .5% and the refinery certificate's .52% were trade equivalents, but by testimony that, by the time the contract was made, the plaintiff knew Con Ed burned fuel with a content of up to 1%, so that, with appropriate price adjustment, the *Khamsin* oil would have suited its needs even if, at delivery, it was, to the plaintiff's surprise, to test out at .92%. Further, the matter seems to have been put beyond dispute by the defendant's readiness to take the oil at the reduced market price on February 20. Surely, on such a record, the trial court cannot be faulted for having found as a fact that the second condition too had been established.

As to the third, the conforming state of the Appollonian oil is undisputed, the offer to tender it took place on February 21, only a day after Con Ed finally had rejected the *Khamsin* delivery and the *Appollonian* substitute then already was en route to the United States, where it was expected in a week and did arrive on March 4, only four days later than expected. Especially since Con Ed pleaded no prejudice (unless the drop in prices could be so regarded), it is almost impossible, given the flexibility of the Uniform Commercial Code definitions of "seasonable" and "reasonable"

..., to quarrel with the finding that the remaining requirements of the statute also had been met.

Thus lacking the support of the statute's literal language, the defendant nonetheless would have us limit its application to cases in which a seller *knowingly* makes a nonconforming tender which it has reason to believe the buyer will accept. For this proposition, it relies almost entirely on a critique in Nordstrom, Law of Sales (§ 105), which rationalizes that, since a seller who believes its tender is conforming would have no reason to think in terms of a reduction in the price of the goods, to allow such a seller to cure after the time for performance had passed would make the statutory reference to a money allowance redundant.[8] Nordstrom, interestingly enough, finds it useful to buttress this position by the somewhat dire prediction, though backed by no empirical or other confirmation, that, unless the right to cure is confined to those whose nonconforming tenders are knowing ones, the incentive of sellers to timely deliver will be undermined. To this it also adds the somewhat moralistic note that a seller who is mistaken as to the quality of its goods does not merit additional time (Nordstrom, *loc. cit.*). Curiously, recognizing that the few decisions extant on this subject have adopted a position opposed to the one for which it contends, Con Ed seeks to treat these as exceptions rather than exemplars of the rule (e.g., Wilson v. Scampoli, 228 A.2d 848 (D.C.App.) [goods obtained by seller from their manufacturer in original carton resold unopened to purchaser; seller held within statute though it had no reason to believe the goods defective]; Appleton State Bank v. Lee, 33 Wis.2d 690, 148 N.W.2d 1 [seller mistakenly delivered sewing machine of wrong brand but otherwise identical to one sold; held that seller, though it did not know of its mistake, had a right to cure by substitution]).

That the principle for which these cases stand goes far beyond their particular facts cannot be gainsaid. These holdings demonstrate that, in dealing with the application of subdivision (2) of section 2–508, courts have been concerned with the reasonableness of the seller's belief that the goods would be acceptable rather than with the seller's pretended knowledge or lack of knowledge of the defect (Wilson v. Scampoli, supra; compare Zabriskie Chevrolet v. Smith, 99 N.J.Super. 441, 240 A.2d 195).

It also is no surprise then that the aforementioned decisional history is a reflection of the mainstream of scholarly commentary on the subject (e.g., 1955 Report of N.Y.Law Rev.Comm., p. 484; White & Summers, Uniform Commercial Code [2d ed.], § 8–4, p. 322; 2 Anderson, Uniform Commercial Code [2d ed.], § 2–508:7; Hogan, The Highways and Some of the Byways in

---

8. The premise for such an argument, which ignores the policy of the code to prevent buyers from using insubstantial remedial or price adjustable defects to free themselves from unprofitable bargains (Hawkland, Sales and Bulk Sales Under the Uniform Commercial Code, pp. 120–122), is that the words "with or without money allowance" apply only to sellers who believe their goods will be acceptable with such an allowance and not to sellers who believe their goods will be acceptable without such an allowance. But, since the words are part of a phrase which speaks of an otherwise unqualified belief that the goods will be acceptable, unless one strains for an opposite interpretation, we find insufficient reason to doubt that it intends to include both those who find a need to offer an allowance and those who do not.

the Sales and Bulk Sales Articles of the Uniform Commercial Code, 48 Cornell L.Q. 1, 12–13; Note, Uniform Commercial Code, § 2–508: Seller's Right to Cure Non–Conforming Goods, 6 Rutgers–Camden L.J. 387, 399; Note, Commercial Law—The Effect of the Seller's Right to Cure on the Buyer's Remedy of Rescission, 28 Ark.L.Rev. 297, 302–303).

White and Summers, for instance, put it well, and bluntly. Stressing that the code intended cure to be "a remedy which should be carefully cultivated and developed by the courts" because it "offers the possibility of conforming the law to reasonable expectations and of thwarting the chiseler who seeks to escape from a bad bargain" (op. cit., at pp. 322–324), the authors conclude, as do we, that a seller should have recourse to the relief afforded by subdivision (2) of section 2–508 of the Uniform Commercial Code as long as it can establish that it had reasonable grounds, tested objectively, for its belief that the goods would be accepted (ibid., at p. 321). It goes without saying that the test of reasonableness, in this context, must encompass the concepts of "good faith" and "commercial standards of fair dealing" which permeate the code (Uniform Commercial Code, § 1–201, subd. [19]; §§ 1–203, 2–103, subd. [1], par. [b]).[10]

\* \* \*

Judgment affirmed.

NOTES

**(1) Sellers' Power to Cure After Rejections of Goods.** In a substantial departure from prior law, UCC Article 2 authorizes a seller to make a second tender or delivery of goods if the first is rightfully rejected. UCC 2–508(1). Complementing UCC 2–508 is the estoppel provision in UCC 2–605(1), which has the effect of requiring rejecting buyers to inform sellers of non-conformities that were reasonably ascertainable by inspection and that could have been cured. To what extent do these provisions overcome the vices perceived by critics of the perfect tender rule?

**(2) Substitute Goods as Cure.** When a seller exercises the right to cure by making a tender of substitute goods, the buyer has a second opportunity to accept or reject these goods. With respect to the quality of the goods, what standard applies to buyer's option on a second tender? May a buyer reject the new goods if they do not conform to the contract *in every respect*? With respect to the time of seller's second tender, UCC 2–508(1)

---

**10.** Except indirectly, on this appeal we do not deal with the equally important protections the code affords buyers. It is as to buyers as well as sellers that the code, to the extent that it displaces traditional principles of law and equity (§ 1–103), seeks to discourage unfair or hypertechnical business conduct bespeaking a dog-eat-dog rather than a live-and-let-live approach to the marketplace (e.g., §§ 2–314, 2–315, 2–513, 2–601, 2–608). Overall, the aim is to encourage parties to amicably resolve their own problems (Ramirez v. Autosport, 88 N.J. 277, 285, 440 A.2d 1345; compare Restatement, Contracts 2d, Introductory Note to Chapter 10, p. 194 ["the wisest course is ordinarily for the parties to attempt to resolve their differences by negotiations, including clarification of expectations [and] cure of past defaults"]).

differs from UCC 2–508(2). A second tender of goods under subsection (1) conforms to the time term of the contract. A second tender under subsection (2) may not. What is the policy justification for requiring some buyers to accept late deliveries? Comment 2 refers to avoidance of injustice to the seller by reason of a "surprise rejection" by the buyer. What is a "surprise rejection"?

In *T.W. Oil*, buyer was found to have rejected the *Khamsin* oil rightfully, but its subsequent rejection of the *Appollonian* oil was wrongful. The opinion stated that "the conforming state of the *Appollonian* oil is undisputed." Did this statement mean more than that the oil conformed to the sulfur-content term of the sales contract? The opinion did not indicate the nature of the time term of the contract. Delivery of the *Khamsin* oil, which was made on January 25, was not challenged as untimely. Tender of the *Appollonian* oil, which was made on February 21, was rejected, presumably because it believed that the time for performance had expired. The court implicitly agreed (perhaps on concession of seller's counsel) that the February 21 tender was non-conforming with respect to the time term and proceeded to the question whether seller was allowed added time under UCC 2–508(2).

The principal issue decided by the court involved interpretation of the statutory predicate for allowing sellers more time to perform than would have been permitted under their contracts. The predicate in UCC 2–508(2) is that the seller, when making the original non-conforming tender, "had reasonable grounds to believe [that the non-conforming tender] would be acceptable with or without monetary allowance." Was the court's construction of this language sound? The court did not agree with the view, attributed to Professor Nordstrom, that its decision would undermine the incentive of sellers to perform within the time limits set by contracts. Was the court correct on this point? The court did not consider the consequences its decision would have on the legislative intent manifest in the structure of UCC 2–508(1) and (2). In light of *T.W. Oil* what is the effect of lapse of the time to cure under UCC 2–508(1)? Under what circumstances would any seller be barred from claiming the right to added time under UCC 2–508(2)? Does the predicate in UCC 2–508(2) have any meaning?

The consequence of the court's decision in *T.W. Oil* was the determination that the buyer's rejection of the *Appollonian* oil was wrongful and the buyer was therefore in breach. The portion of the opinion dealing with seller's remedy was omitted here. We will consider sellers' remedies for wrongful rejection later in this Chapter.

**(3) Repair of Goods or Replacement of Components as Cure.** In a sale of a manufactured product that is rejected for non-conformity with respect to quality, would seller's repair of the goods or replacement of a defective component a cure under UCC 2–508? In circumstances where non-conforming goods are repaired or have new components installed, do buyers have a second opportunity to accept or reject the goods? With respect to the quality of the goods, what standard applies to buyer's option? May a buyer reject the new goods if they do not conform to the contract *in* *every respect*? What is the time allowed for repair or component replacement? Should the statute be construed to permit cure by repair or replacement of components more liberally in sales of business equipment than in sales of consumer goods?

Should it matter whether the person that does the repair or installs the replacement component is the manufacturer or the retailer? Suppose that a new automobile was rejected by a consumer because of transmission problems and the car dealer replaced the transmission in its own service department. Must buyer accept the car on second tender? See Zabriskie Chevrolet, Inc. v. Smith, 99 N.J.Super. 441, 240 A.2d 195 (1968) (dealer's replacement did not effect cure).

**(4) Cure and Warranty Service.** How does sellers' repair or replacement of rightfully rejected goods under UCC 2–508 relate to sales contracts under which sellers or manufacturers undertake to repair or replace goods during a specified warranty period?

**(5) Price Adjustment as Cure.** In some trade settings, particularly sales of fungible goods, sellers offer take a lower price when goods may be rightfully rejected and buyers agree. Could a practice of this kind be the basis for concluding that trade usage permits sellers to cure defective tenders by price adjustment? Counsel for seller in *T.W. Oil* argued, in the trial court, that buyer should be held liable for breach of a duty to bargain in good faith for a price adjustment on the *Khamsin* oil. This argument was rejected by the trial court and is mentioned only in passing by the court of appeals. Does this argument have force under the present Code? Should Article 2 be amended to provide generally that sellers may cure by price adjustment?

**(6) Sellers' Power to Cure After Rejections of Tenders of Documents.** UCC 2–508 is not limited to rejections of goods. Subsection (1) applies also to rejections of documents tendered in documentary transactions. Buyers' obligation to disclose ascertainable non-conformities, under UCC 2–605, is not limited to rejections of goods. Recall also the discussion of the responsibilities of presenting banks under UCC 4–503 to use diligence to ascertain the reasons for dishonor of documentary drafts. What would constitute cure of non-conformities in documents? Should the added time provisions of UCC 2–508(2) be applied after rejection of documents?

## Midwest Mobile Diagnostic Imaging v. Dynamics Corp. of America

United States District Court, Western District of Michigan, 1997.
965 F.Supp. 1003.

■ ENSLEN, CHIEF JUDGE.

### I.  INTRODUCTION

Plaintiff Midwest Mobile Diagnostic Imagining, L.L.C. [hereinafter "MMDI"] brings this diversity action against defendant Ellis & Watts,

d/b/a Dynamics Corporation of America [hereinafter "E & W"], seeking damages for . . . breach of a sales contract for the purchase of four mobile MRI units[1]. . . . Defendant, the seller, counterclaims for damages, alleging that the buyer is in breach. Having considered the evidence submitted and the legal arguments of the parties made during a three-day bench trial, and having reviewed the exhibits submitted, the Court enters the following Findings of Fact and Conclusions of Law pursuant to Federal Rule of Civil Procedure 52(a). . . .

\* \* \*

## III.   CONTENTIONS OF THE PARTIES

MMDI contends that, after its rightful rejection of a nonconforming trailer tendered by E & W on December 13, 1995, E & W repudiated the contract in its entirety. E & W's repudiation whether anticipatory or not, destroyed whatever right to cure E & W may have had and gave MMDI the right to cancel the contract, which it then did. Having rightfully canceled the contract, MMDI argues it is entitled to damages.

E & W counters that its tender on December 13, 1995 was both timely and in conformity with contract specifications. Consequently, MMDI's rejection was wrongful. E & W continues that, even if the trailer were not conforming, E & W had a right to cure pursuant to Uniform Commercial Code [hereinafter "UCC"] § 2–508, and MMDI could not cancel the contract without first requesting adequate assurances from E & W in writing pursuant to UCC § 2–609. Since plaintiff did not satisfy § 2–609 and a reasonable time for performance had not expired, MMDI's cancellation of the contract on December 18, 1995 constituted anticipatory repudiation.

## IV.   FACTS

Plaintiff Midwest Mobile Diagnostic Imaging, L.L.C. ("MMDI") is a Delaware limited liability company, with offices in Kalamazoo, Michigan, engaged in the business of furnishing equipment and personnel for magnetic resonance imaging (MRI) scans to hospitals in southwestern Michigan. In 1995, MMDI had three mobile MRI units servicing area facilities.

Defendant Ellis & Watts ("E & W") is a New York corporation whose principal place of business is in Cincinnati, Ohio, which engineers, designs, and manufactures trailers for mobile medical uses, including mobile MRI systems. . . .

In April 1995, plaintiff commenced negotiations with defendant to purchase four mobile MRI trailers, each designed to house a state-of-the-art, ACS NT 1.5T MR scanner system, which plaintiff would purchase separately from Philips. During these initial negotiations, E & W became aware that MMDI had an immediate need for the first trailer because of

---

**1.** A mobile MRI unit is, in effect, a mobile MRI clinic. It is a semi tractor trailer which contains an MRI scanner and the computer equipment necessary to operate such a machine. It is designed to function as a temporary extension of the hospital which it is serving, with an interior which generally matches the hospital environment.

the growing demand for its services. As a consequence, the parties agreed that delivery of the first trailer would occur in September 1995 with the rest to follow in monthly installments. However, during final negotiations in Kalamazoo on August 10, 1995, the parties agreed to delete a clause in the written contract requiring that all four trailers be delivered in 1995. While no specific delivery dates were ultimately included in the written contract, E & W understood that early delivery of the first trailer was of great importance to MMDI. At the time of signing, the parties expected delivery of the trailers to occur in October, November, December, 1995 and January, 1996. The delivery dates were, however, contingent upon coordination with Philips and agreement of the parties.

In addition to the timing of the project, during negotiations the parties also made representations concerning the design of the trailer. On April 17, 1995, Robert Freudenberger of E & W, faxed a signed purchase agreement to Jerry Turowski of MMDI. Attached to the form contract were two drawings. One of the drawings depicted a three-dimensional illustration of the interior of a mobile MRI system trailer upon which was written: "Spacious, efficient layout with clean, aesthetically pleasing interior." In addition, these drawings, and all others reviewed by MMDI both before and after contract signing, did not depict a bracing structure surrounding the scanner magnet.

On August 10, 1995, Mr. Turowski and Mr. Freudenberger executed a purchase agreement for four E & W trailers. With the signing of the contract, MMDI paid E & W a deposit in the amount of $63,000. On August 11, 1995, Mr. Andrew Pike, President of E & W, countersigned the purchase agreement in Cincinnati, Ohio. Under the parties' agreement, E & W was to construct the four trailers in accordance with Philips' specifications. Once certified by Philips, the trailers could be delivered.

On September 7, 1995, plaintiff and defendant met in Kalamazoo to discuss the delivery schedule. On September 21, 1995, MMDI sent a letter indicating that, as a result of that meeting, MMDI expected delivery of the first trailer on November 6, 1995. The letter also noted the parties' understanding that the trailer would be "show" ready for MMDI's open house in Kalamazoo, Michigan, on November 3, 1995. E & W did not respond to this letter. During the course of construction, the parties discussed several alterations to the trailer and consequently, again renegotiated the delivery date for the first trailer. Ultimately, the parties agreed upon a December 1, 1995 delivery date. Under the expectation that the trailer would be delivered on that date, MMDI scheduled patients assuming the trailer would be ready for use beginning December 4, 1995.

On November 3, 1995, indicating that the trailer was cosmetically complete, E & W presented the trailer to MMDI to show at its open house in Kalamazoo, during which representatives of MMDI and many of its customers, inspected the trailer. At that time, the scanner magnet was free from any metal, bracing structures. The trailer was then returned to E & W for final adjustments and testing.

As of mid-November 1995, the first E & W trailer was fully fabricated and substantially all equipment was installed and ready for testing by Philips. In anticipation of the December 1 delivery date, E & W invoiced MMDI on November 10, 1995 for the full purchase price of the first trailer. On November 16, 1995, E & W sent a follow-up letter requesting payment prior to shipment of the trailer on November 30 in accordance with the purchase agreement. MMDI paid $321,500 to E & W on November 17, 1995.

On November 28, 1995, the first trailer failed to meet contract specifications in a test conducted by Philips. The test indicated that the trailer did not comply with Philips' specifications for magnetic shielding in the sidewalls of the trailer. This failure occurred despite the fact that, throughout the construction of the trailer, Philips had repeatedly noted the importance of the proper fabrication of this feature in its correspondence with E & W.

When the parties discovered that the trailer had failed the test, they met to discuss potential solutions to the situation. At that time, E & W stated unequivocally that: 1) the trailer was defective; 2) the defect was entirely its fault and responsibility; and 3) it would cure the problem. E & W also indicated a willingness to reimburse MMDI for at least part of the expenses it might incur in renting another trailer to substitute for the one that E & W had not completed. As a result of the need for a cure, E & W failed to tender a conforming trailer on the December 1 delivery date and MMDI was forced to cancel appointments which had been scheduled with patients for December 4, 1995.

During the following two weeks, E & W designed a reinforcement structure to contend with the wall-flexing problem. The solution consisted of multiple, large, steel beams placed around the scanner magnet in a cage-like structure which prevented removal of the magnet's outer covers and dramatically changed its appearance. Such a bracing structure had never been used with a mobile MRI scanner by any manufacturer. During this period, E & W exchanged multiple letters and sketches with Philips in which Philips' representatives indicated several concerns with the bracing structure. E & W made adjustments to address some of these concerns. Ultimately, Philips approved the design as a temporary solution to the wall-flexing problem.

On December 7, 1995, E & W sent MMDI a schedule indicating that the decision whether to proceed with this design would be made on December 12, 1995. The letter indicated: "if no go at this point, alternate plans established." Although MMDI had reviewed drawings of the interior during the course of construction, E & W did not include a sketch of the reinforcement design in this correspondence.

On December 12, 1995, Philips' representatives retested the trailer with the bracing structure in place and found that the flexing problem had been remedied. Thus, the trailer was approved for use on a temporary basis. However, because the structure impaired service of the scanner magnet, Philips would not certify the trailer for permanent use with the structure in place.

On December 13, 1995, Mr. Turowski of MMDI arrived at E & W to inspect the new design for the first time. After viewing the trailer and speaking with Philips' representatives, Mr. Turowski concluded that the bracing structure was unacceptable for several reasons. Mr. Turowski and Mr. Andrew Pike of E & W then placed a telephone conference call to Dr. Azzam Kanaan and Dr. Ilydio Polachini at MMDI. At that time, Mr. Turowski indicated that, with the bracing structure, the trailer did not conform to the contract obligations because: 1) service of the scanner magnet would be impeded and, in cases, would be more dangerous; 2) its appearance was objectionable; and 3) the resale value of the trailer would be diminished.

Mr. Pike countered that the structure in place conformed to the parties' agreement, that this was the design that met the Philips' specification, that it had been approved by Philips, and told MMDI to accept it the way it was. Further, Mr. Pike stated that the materials had already been purchased to install this design in the second trailer, that this was the best design that one could come up with, and that he did not know if it could be done it any differently. Finally, Mr. Pike refused to pay rent for a replacement unit or to refund MMDI's previous payment.

The following day, December 14, 1995, Mr. Pike sent a letter to Dr. Kanaan at MMDI, indicating that E & W was working with "this design" to see if it could be made more aesthetically pleasing. The letter made no reference to the servicing problems, safety concerns, or concerns about a potential diminution in resale value resulting from the use of the bracing structure. Mr. Pike again asserted the validity of the contract, and refused to refund MMDI's payment for the trailer.

On December 18, 1995, acting in good faith, MMDI advised E & W in writing that the Purchase Agreement was canceled. On December 19, 1995, MMDI rented a mobile MRI unit to replace the one it had expected to receive from E & W. On December 21, 1995, MMDI executed a contract with a third party for the manufacture and construction of two trailers to house two of the Philips 1.5T MR scanner systems.

On December 22, 1995, Mr. Freudenberger sent a letter to Mr. Turowski, reiterating that the first trailer was ready for shipment and requesting instructions on how to ship it. In addition, the letter indicated that E & W was finalizing the design for an alternative bracing structure which would neither impede the servicing of the magnet components nor negatively impact the aesthetics of the trailer interior. Mr. Freudenberger also suggested that, after final testing and seeking MMDI's input regarding the aesthetics of the design, the design "would be considered the permanent solution" for the trailer. The design would then be incorporated into the second trailer at which time the first trailer would be returned to E & W and retrofitted with the new design at no cost to MMDI. E & W, however, maintained that the purchase agreement was still effective and continued to refuse to refund MMDI's payment. Soon after this correspondence, the parties ceased communication. Ultimately, E & W did remove the offending reinforcement structure and replaced it with an alternative design which was approved for permanent use by Philips. In the time since this replacement solution was fabricated and installed, E & W has sold two of the trailers to a third party.

On January 9, 1996, MMDI filed the instant suit for damages resulting from breach of contract and misrepresentation. E & W retained payments made by MMDI in the amount of $384,500. Further, MMDI incurred expenses in the amount of $185,250 for the lease of a mobile MRI scanner and trailer between December 19, 1995 and April 20, 1996.

## V.  ANALYSIS

### A.  Breach of contract

The primary issue for resolution by the Court is whether MMDI rightfully rejected E & W's tender of the first trailer and then subsequently canceled the contract, or if its actions in mid-December constituted anticipatory repudiation of the contract. Having previously determined that Michigan law controls in the instant case, the Court simply notes that the Michigan version of the Uniform Commercial Code [hereinafter the "UCC"] applies to this sales contract. MCLA §§ 440.1101 et seq.

### 1.  Installment Contract

Before turning to the specific questions of rejection and cancellation, the Court must first resolve a threshold issue. Under the UCC, the parties' rights to reject, cure, and cancel under an installment contract differ substantially from those defined under a single delivery contract. Consequently, resolution of whether the contract is an installment contract is of primary concern. Section 2–612(1) defines an "installment contract" as "one which requires or authorizes the delivery of goods in separate lots to be separately accepted. . . ." The commentary following this section emphasizes that the "definition of an installment contract is phrased more broadly in this Article [than in its previous incarnation as the Uniform Sales Act] so as to cover installment deliveries tacitly authorized by the circumstances or by the option of either party." § 2–612, cmt. 1.

Plaintiff argues that the contract between itself and E & W does not constitute an installment contract because it authorizes delivery in commercial units, and not lots, as required by subsection (1). However, upon review of the Code section defining those terms, it becomes clear that those terms are not mutually exclusive. Section 2–105 defines a "lot" as a "parcel or single article which is the subject matter of a separate sale or delivery, whether or not it is sufficient to perform the contract." The same section defines a commercial unit as "such a unit of goods as by commercial usage is a single whole for purposes of sale and division of which materially impairs its character or value on the market or in use. A commercial unit may be a single article (as a machine) or a set of articles (as a suite of furniture or an assortment of sizes) or a quantity (as a bale, gross, or carload) or any other unit treated in use or in the relevant market as a single whole." Thus, a lot, which is the measure of goods that the contract states will be delivered together in one installment, can be a single commercial unit. Consequently, § 2–612 applies wherever a contract for multiple items authorizes the delivery of the items in separate groups at different times, whether or not the installment constitutes a commercial unit.

The contract between MMDI and E & W for the sale of four trailers authorizes the delivery of each trailer separately. While the written contract does not explicitly state this delivery schedule, it does authorize separate delivery. Paragraph 2 of the contract assumes separate delivery dates by setting out a payment schedule wherein the balance for each unit is due at the time of shipment. Furthermore, based on the parties testimony it is clear that both parties understood the trailers would be delivered in separate installments. Indeed, neither party disputes that they agreed to have the trailers delivered at four separate times. Therefore, the Court finds that the contract in dispute is an installment contract.

### 2. Right of Rejection

Section 2–612, therefore, is the starting point for the Court's analysis of MMDI's actions on December 13, 1995. ... Under § 2–612, the buyer's right to reject is far more limited than the corresponding right to reject under a single delivery contract defined under § 2–601. Under § 2–601, a buyer has the right to reject, "if the goods or tender of delivery fail in any respect to conform to the contract...." Known as the "perfect tender" rule, this standard requires a very high level of conformity. Under this rule, the buyer may reject a seller's tender for any trivial defect, whether it be in the quality of the goods, the timing of performance, or the manner of delivery. To avoid injustice, the Code limits the buyer's correlative right to cancel the contract upon such rejection by providing a right to cure under § 2–508. § 2–508, cmt. 2. Under § 2–508, the seller has a right to cure if s/he seasonably notifies the buyer of the intent to do so, and either 1) the time for performance has not yet passed, or 2) the seller had reason to believe that the goods were in conformity with the contract. Thus, § 2–508's right to cure serves to temper the buyer's expansive right to reject under a single delivery contract. ...

Section 2–612 creates an exception to the perfect tender rule. ... Under subsection (2), a buyer may not reject nonconforming tender unless the defect substantially impairs the value of the installment. In addition, "if the nonconformity is curable and the seller gives adequate assurances of cure," the buyer must accept the installment. § 2–612, cmt. 5. But even if rejection is proper under subsection 2, cancellation of the contract is not appropriate unless the defect substantially impairs the value of the whole contract. § 2–612(3), cmt. 6. Because this section significantly restricts the buyer's right to cancel under an installment contract, there is no corresponding necessity for reference to § 2–508; the seller's right to cure is implicitly defined by § 2–612.[6]

---

6. Courts of other jurisdictions have reached differing conclusions with regard to the interaction between §§ 2–612 and 2–508. See, e.g., Arkla Energy Resources v. Roye Realty &

### a.  Delivery Date

Before proceeding with the analysis of MMDI's December 13 rejection, the Court initially notes that E & W's tender on December 13 constituted a cure attempt for the wall-flexing defect which delayed the delivery of the first trailer beyond the agreed upon delivery date. Although under § 2–612 the delivery date does not cut off the seller's right to cure, it does have an effect on the rights of the parties. . . .

In the instant case, the original, written contract included no definite delivery date. Instead, the contract left the delivery term to be agreed upon at a later date. At the time of execution, the parties both expected delivery of the first trailer to take place in October. During the months after the execution of the contract, however, the parties modified the deadline for the first installment of the contract on several occasions. As noted above, upon review of the testimony and documentary evidence, the Court finds that, whatever delivery date the parties had agreed upon prior to November 1995, by early November they had renegotiated their agreement to establish a December 1, 1995 delivery date. See § 2–209 (sales contract may be modified by oral or written agreement without consideration, so long as agreement does not state otherwise).

Defendant argues, however, that, even if the parties had at one point agreed upon a December 1, 1995 deadline, when the first trailer failed the Philips road test on November 28, 1995, the parties renegotiated the delivery term to allow E & W a reasonable time to cure the defect. While E & W is correct that, as of December 1, it had a reasonable time in which to cure the wall-flexing problem, the Court disagrees that MMDI's willingness to wait for a cure constitutes an agreement to extend the delivery deadline. Because the parties believed that the defect was curable and E & W, without solicitation, unequivocally promised to cure it, under § 2–612, MMDI had no choice but to accept an offer of cure. To reject the installment on November 28 would have constituted a violation of § 2–612. The Court, therefore, finds that any negotiations the parties engaged in regarding delivery after discovery of the wall-flexing problem, did not constitute a modification of the delivery date for the first installment, but rather involved negotiation regarding cure. Since no specific date for delivery of a cure was agreed upon during those negotiations, under section 2–309(1), E & W had a reasonable time to effectuate a cure. Although there is some question as to whether further delay would have been reasonable, the Court finds that, as of December 13, 1995, a reasonable time had not yet passed. Therefore, defendant's tender of a cure was timely.

---

Dev., Inc., 9 F.3d 855 (10th Cir.1993); Bodine, 493 N.E.2d at 713; Bevel–Fold, Inc. v. Bose Corp., 9 Mass. App. Ct. 576, 402 N.E.2d 1104, 1108 (Mass.App.Ct.1980); Continental Forest Prods., Inc. v. White Lumber Sales, Inc., 256 Ore. 466, 474 P.2d 1, 4 (Or.1970). This Court does not find the arguments of these other courts persuasive, however, and notes that their decisions are not binding on this Court. Nevertheless, the Court also notes that, since the time for delivery of the first installment had already passed on December 1, 1995 (see infra § 2(a)) and defendant could not have reasonably believed and, in fact, did not believe that the trailer was in conformity with the contract on that date, defendant had no right to cure under § 2–508.

b.  Substantial Impairment of the Installment

The Court's conclusion that E & W's December 13 tender was an attempt to cure the November 28 breach raises another question: which standard of conformity applies to cure under an installment contract, perfect tender or substantial impairment? Looking to the rationale behind § 2–612, the Court notes that the very purpose of allowing the seller time to cure under this section is to permit it additional time to meet the obligations of the contract. The assumption is that, because the parties have an ongoing relationship, the seller should be given an opportunity to make up the deficiency. This section was not designed to allow the seller to have a never-ending series of chances to bring the item into conformity with the contract. Nor was it enacted to force the buyer to accept a nonconforming product as satisfaction of the contract. Consequently, it is logical that a tender of cure should be required to meet the higher "perfect tender" standard. On its face, however, § 2–612, which generally defines a buyer's right to reject goods under an installment contract, requires only substantial impairment in this context as well. Thus, there is some question as to which is the appropriate standard. The answer is not crucial, however, since the trailer in this case fails under both standards. Because a decision on this point will not effect the ultimate outcome in this case, the Court declines to address the issue. Instead, the Court proceeds with the substantial impairment analysis provided by § 2–612.

To establish substantial impairment of the value of an installment, the buyer " 'must present objective evidence that with respect to its own needs, the value of the goods was substantially impaired.' " Arkla Energy Resources v. Roye Realty & Dev., Inc., 9 F.3d 855, 862 (10th Cir.1993) (quoting Bodine Sewer, Inc. v. Eastern Illinois Precast, Inc., 143 Ill. App. 3d 920, 493 N.E.2d 705, 713, 97 Ill. Dec. 898 (Ill. App. Ct. 1986)). See also § 2–612, cmt 4. The existence of such nonconformity depends on the facts and circumstances of each case, and "can turn not only on the quality of the goods but also on such factors as time . . ., and the like." § 2–612, cmt. 4. . . . Finally, whether nonconformity rises to the level of substantial impairment may be judged by reference to the concept of material breach under traditional contract law. . . .

In the instant case, plaintiff alleges several aspects in which defendant's December 13 tender failed to conform to contract obligations. Plaintiff contends that the trailer tendered on December 13 with the bracing structure did not conform to the parties' agreement because: 1) it was not and could not be certified by Philips without conditions for use with the 1.5T scanner and 2) its interior design did not conform with the parties' agreements. Because of these defects, MMDI argues that the value of trailer was reduced substantially. Defendant, on the other hand, contends that the contract required only that the trailer meet the technical specifications provided by Philips, and that, therefore, the December 13 trailer was in complete compliance with its terms.

The written contract signed by the parties in this case is relatively skeletal and thus, requires interpretation. The Court's fundamental purpose in interpreting the terms of the contract is to give effect to the intent of the parties as it existed at the time the agreement was made. . . . " 'The meaning of the agreement of the parties is to be determined by the language used by them and by their action, read, and interpreted in the light of commercial practices and other surrounding circumstances.' " 1 WILLISTON ON SALES § 10–2, 431 (quoting 1 CORBIN ON CON-TRACTS § 2.9 (Rev. Ed.)). See also § 1–203 (setting out the requirement of good faith and requiring the Court to interpret "contracts within the commercial context in which they are created, performed, and enforced[]"). Furthermore, the Code explicitly authorizes courts to look to the parties' course of dealings and performance and to the usage of terms in trade in interpreting the terms of the contract. §§ 1–205, 2–202, and 2–208.

As instructed by the commentary to § 2–612, the Court begins the substantial impairment analysis by looking to the "normal and specifically known purposes of the contract." § 2–612, cmt. 4. Reviewing the evidence presented, the Court finds that the primary purpose of the contract was to provide the plaintiff with four trailers for use with the Philips 1.5T scanner. With that in mind, the parties agreed that the trailers would be constructed in accordance with the specifications provided by Philips and that the trailer would be not be ready for delivery until Philips certification had been received. Philips did not, however, ever certify the trailer for unconditional use with the bracing structure. Because the bracing structure prevented normal service of the scanner magnet, it was only approved as a temporary fix.

The general rule in cases where third party approval is required as a condition of performance is one of strict compliance. See generally J. Calamari and J. Perillo, THE LAW OF CONTRACTS 399, § 11–17 (2d ed. 1977). Such conditions will only be excused where the third party acts in bad faith or dishonestly. Id. In the instant case, there was no credible evidence presented that Philips acted in bad faith by withholding approval. On the contrary, there was extensive evidence presented detailing the inherent problems with the long-term use of such a bracing solution, which demonstrated the reasonableness of Philips' refusal to certify the trailer. The bracing structure's shape and orientation prevented removal of the outer panels from the scanner magnet and made some repairs to the magnet more difficult and more dangerous. Furthermore, in order to perform certain repairs, the steel brace would have to be unbolted and removed. Once removed, the scanner magnet would have to be recalibrated and retested. Consequently, Philips' decision to refuse certification was entirely justified. Having found no evidence of bad faith or dishonesty on the part of Philips, the Court finds that defendant's failure to meet this condition constituted a breach of the parties' agreement. . . . Given that the central purpose of the trailer was to house a Philips 1.5T scanner, the failure to meet the standard for Philips' certification substantially impaired the value of the trailer. The Court, therefore, finds that this failure to conform to the parties' agreement, in and of itself, constituted a material breach.

In addition to violating the requirement that the trailer receive certification from Philips, plaintiff correctly asserts that defendant breached yet another term of the contract. The Court notes that the bracing structure also violated the parties' implied agreement regarding the design of the interior of the trailer. During the course of the parties' dealings both before and after the contract signing, MMDI reviewed numerous representations of the trailer's interior layout and design. Many of these drawings showed the location of the scanner and detailed the location of every structure in the trailer. None of them, however, depicted a cage-like brace made up of multiple, large, steel beams surrounding the scanner magnet. These drawings, when coupled with E & W's own statement that the trailer was cosmetically complete without the brace when it was presented at the open house, convince the Court that there was an implied agreement that the trailer would not have such a structure.

Furthermore, it is clear that, when the contract was executed, the parties both understood that the trailer's interior was meant to be aesthetically pleasing. It is the very nature of a mobile MRI trailer to function as an extension of the hospital it services. Since E & W was in the business of constructing trailers for mobile medical uses, it no doubt understood that the appearance of the trailer's interior could impact the comfort of MMDI's patients. Indeed, it is apparent that E & W realized such aesthetics were important to the value of the trailer, since, in its initial negotiations with MMDI, E & W included a cut-away drawing of the interior of a mobile unit which read: "Spacious, efficient layout with clean, aesthetically pleasing interior." The Court, therefore, finds that the agreement between the parties required that the interior of the trailer be aesthetically pleasing.

Such a condition of satisfaction by one of the parties to the contract will only be excused if approval is withheld unreasonably. ... In the instant case, upon review of photographs of the bracing structure and testimony of those experienced in this industry, and in light of the fact that the interior of the trailer should match that of a hospital and not a construction site, the Court finds that plaintiff's refusal to approve the aesthetics of the design was commercially reasonable. Given that an integral aspect of the trailer's function is to serve as a clinic for patients undergoing medical procedures, and given MMDI's clients' expectations after having viewed the trailer at the open house, such a defect in the trailer's interior also reduced the value of the trailer substantially.

Upon review of the evidence, the Court finds that the bracing structure substantially impaired the value of the first trailer. Although the trailer met the express technical Philips' specifications for wall-flexing, it was never certified by the manufacturer. The failure of this condition does not relieve defendant of liability because it was defendant's failure to properly construct the trailer that prevented certification. In light of the specific facts and circumstances of this case, the Court finds that this deficiency substantially impaired the value of the installment. When coupled with the trailer's failure to conform with the aesthetic requirements of the contract and the delay caused by the cure attempt, the Court holds that the cure attempt clearly constitutes a substantial breach within the meaning of § 2–612(2).

Substantial impairment, however, does not in itself justify rejection of the installment. As noted above, the buyer must still accept tender if the defect can be cured and the seller gives adequate assurances. Under § 2–612, as opposed to § 2–609, it is incumbent upon the seller to assure the buyer that cure would be forthcoming. ... Defendant has failed in this regard. The Court notes that neither E & W's statements during the December 13 conference call nor the letter sent the following day constituted adequate assurances. On the contrary, during the December 13 conference call, Andrew Pike, the President of E & W denied the existence of a defect, disclaimed any continuing obligation to cure under the contract, and stated that he did not believe a better design could be made which would remedy the wall-flexing problem. Furthermore, on December 14, Mr. Pike again ignored the servicing problems that the bracing structure had caused, ignored the fact that the bracing structure had not been approved for permanent use by Philips, and reiterated his doubt that the design could be constructed in a more aesthetically pleasing manner. Under these circumstances, the Court finds that MMDI's rejection of E & W's cure on December 13 constituted a rightful rejection under § 2–612(2).[10]

### 3. Cancellation

#### a. Substantial Impairment of Contract as a Whole

The fact that rejection of one installment is proper does not necessarily justify cancellation of the entire contract. Under § 2–612(3) the right to cancel does not arise unless the nonconforming goods substantially impair the value of the entire contract. Indeed, as noted above, the very purpose of the substantial impairment requirement of § 2–612(3) is to preclude parties from canceling an installment contract for trivial defects. Emanuel Law Outlines v. Multi–State Legal Studies, 899 F. Supp. 1081, 1088 (S.D.N.Y. 1995).

Whether a breach constitutes "substantial impairment" of the entire contract is a question of fact. ... Ultimately, "whether the non-conformity in any given installment justifies cancellation as to the future depends, not on whether such non-conformity indicates an intent or likelihood that future deliveries will also be defective, but whether the non-conformity substantially impairs the value of the whole contract." § 2–612, cmt. 6.

---

**10.** Defendant argues that, as of December 13, it still had a right to cure under § 2–508 and that it was not required to give assurances unless plaintiff requested them in writing under § 2–609. The Court reiterates that, under § 2–508, defendant's right to cure was cut off on December 1. Furthermore, § 2–612, unlike § 2–609, does not require the aggrieved party to request assurances. In an installment contract, where the seller's right to cure is more expansive it stands to reason that the burden would fall on the seller to show that it had the present ability and the intent to cure any remaining defect. ... In the instant case, defendant gave no indication that it either had the capability to satisfy the contract or the will to do so. On the contrary, E & W's President, gave MMDI the impression that cure was not possible and indicated clearly that he was not required to do anything more under the contract. Under such circumstances, MMDI's rejection was rightful.

Thus, the question is one of present breach which focuses on the importance of the nonconforming installment relative to the contract as a whole. If the nonconformity only impairs the aggrieved party's security with regard to future installments, s/he "has the right to demand adequate assurances but [] not an immediate right to cancel the entire contract." § 2–612, cmt. 6. The right to cancel will be triggered only if "material inconvenience or injustice will result if the aggrieved party is forced to wait and receive an ultimate tender minus the part or aspect repudiated." § 2–610, cmt.3 (noting the test for anticipatory repudiation under § 2–610 is the same as the test for cancellation under § 2–612(3)).

In the instant case, there is substantial evidence that one of the primary purposes of this contract was to provide MMDI with a fourth mobile MRI trailer so that it could meet the growing demand for its services. Thus, impairment of one of the four installments would have a substantial negative impact on MMDI. Moreover, an early delivery time was of primary importance to MMDI, as E & W was well aware. By failing to cure the November 28 breach on the first installment, E & W substantially delayed completion of the remainder of the contract which delayed MMDI's ability to begin use of the 1.5T MRI trailer it had promised to its customers at the open house on November 3. Having found that substantial injustice would be done to plaintiff if it were required to accept the remaining three trailers after substantial delay as satisfaction of the contract, the Court finds that plaintiff rightfully canceled the contract on December 18, 1995.

### 4. Damages

Having found that plaintiff rightfully rejected defendant's tender of cure on December 13, 1995, and subsequently properly canceled the contract, the Court finds that plaintiff is entitled to damages. Plaintiff has requested reimbursement of the amount it already paid for the nonconforming installment in the amount of $384,500 as well as damages in the amount of $185,250 incurred for the lease of a rental mobile MRI trailer between December 19, 1995 and April 20, 1996, to replace the trailer E & W failed to produce. Under § 2–711, a buyer who has rightfully canceled a contract may recover, among other things: 1) the amount that has already been paid, 2) damages for "cover" as defined in § 2–712, and 3) any damages of nondelivery, including consequential and incidental damages, as defined by § 2–715. Under § 2–715, incidental damages include "any [] reasonable expense incident to the delay or other breach." Thus, plaintiff is clearly entitled to return of the amount already paid for the item it never received. Plaintiff is also entitled to recover the amount paid for a replacement rental unit. Though this amount does not constitute cover it is allowable as incidental to the delay produced by E & W's breach. Had E & W made conforming tender on December 13, 1995, plaintiff would not have been forced to contract with another company for the trailers and to wait until spring for the first one. The Court, therefore, finds plaintiff is entitled to both expectation and consequential damages under the Code and awards plaintiff a sum total of $569,250 for the breach of contract claim.

* * *

## VI. CONCLUSION

For the foregoing reasons, plaintiff is awarded expectation and incidental damages in the amount of $569,250. . . .

## NOTES

**(1) Installment Sales: A Different Set of Standards.** The standard governing buyer's power to reject tendered goods changes dramatically if the sales contract "requires or authorizes the delivery of goods in separate lots to be separately accepted," UCC 2–612(1), language which the drafters of the Code intended to have considerable breadth.[16] Such sales, termed "installment contracts," are not governed by the perfect tender rule in UCC 2–601. As each lot is tendered in a simple, two-party sale, a buyer may reject that lot only if "the non-conformity substantially impairs the value of that installment and cannot be cured." UCC 2–612(2).[17] Section 2–612(3) deals with a different matter, cancellation of the "whole contract." Although the meaning of "whole contract" is somewhat uncertain, the most obvious meaning is the current installment and prospective installments that have not yet been tendered.

**(2) History of the Installment Sales Rules.** The Uniform Sales Act had a provision analogous to UCC 2–612(3), but had no antecedent to UCC 2–612(2). USA § 45(2) allowed installment contract buyers, when sellers have made one or more defective deliveries, to refuse to proceed further and sue for damages for breach of the entire contract if the breach was sufficiently material. Buyer's power to reject a single installment, like buyer's power to reject goods in a single-delivery contract, was not codified. Karl Llewellyn, principal drafter of UCC Article 2, believed that some buyers should have limited power to reject single installments.[18]

---

**16.** Section 2–307 permits delivery in several lots "where the circumstances give either party the right to make or demand delivery in lots." The issue in 2–307, whether a seller may demand payment for partial deliveries, is not the same as the issue in 2–612(1), whether a seller may demand acceptance of partial deliveries. Comment 1 to 2–612 states that drafters of the Code intended to define installment contracts more broadly than did pre-Code law, and Comment 2 adds that provision for separate payment for each lot is not essential to an installment contract.

**17.** In an unusual "belt and suspenders" style of drafting, 2–612(2) continues to define circumstances in which a buyer "must accept an installment." Conceptually under the Code, buyers must accept goods that they may not reject. Therefore, the criteria for "may reject" should be the same as the criteria for "must accept." However, as stated the drafters failed to make the two clauses complementary. Consider a tender of non-conforming goods by a seller who has the ability to cure the non-conformity but who fails to give adequate assurance of doing so.

**18.** Llewellyn wrote: "Except for open term contracts, market risks are invariably placed upon the buyer. The installment contract runs over a longer period than does the single

**(3) Rejection or Acceptance of an Installment: Cure.** UCC 2–612(2) is a single sentence with two independent clauses that pose interpretative difficulties. The operative language in the clause that precedes the semicolon is that a seller "may reject" an installment under certain circumstances. The operative language in the clause that follows the semicolon is that a seller "must accept" an installment under certain circumstances. The circumstances in the two clauses are not the same. This leads to a series of analytic problems in *Midwest Mobile Diagnostic Imaging*.

With respect to the tender on November 28, the court applied the first clause and concluded that the buyer could not reject the goods. The court did not discuss the second clause. Did the "must accept" clause apply to the events on November 28? If the buyer had accepted the goods on November 28, may the buyer reject those goods on December 13? What is the application to accepted installments of the provision on revocation of acceptance in UCC 2–608?

The court seemed to treat the issue of cure, in this installment sale, as if the issue was one of cure following rejection of a single delivery under UCC 2–601. The court found that the seller's offer of cure had been volunteered, rather than induced by buyer's rejection, and was binding on the buyer without determining whether the non-conformity was of a nature that it could not be cured under the first clause or whether the offer of cure was an "adequate assurance" under the second clause. The court also found that the expiration of the time term of the contract did not foreclose seller's later cure without determining whether the conditions of UCC 2–508(2) had been met. If the court had focused on these issues under UCC 2–612(2) and UCC 2–508(2), how would the analysis have changed?

The court held that buyer had the option, under the first clause of UCC 2–612(2), to reject seller's second tender of the goods on December 13. Did the facts show an effective rejection of the goods tendered on December 13? Does UCC 2–612(2) provide any support for the court's determination that buyers have the option to reject goods after sellers' attempt to cure?

The court's reasoning led to the question of the standard to be applied in rejection after seller's attempt to cure. Without reference to UCC 2–612, the court suggested that the perfect tender rule might apply, but declined to decide that question because the goods tendered on December 13 could be rejected under the substantial-impairment-of-value standard of the first clause of UCC 2–612. How persuasive were the court's findings on the level

delivery agreement. The longer the parties are bound, the greater the possibility of market variation during the contract term. A problem presents itself. If B attempts rejection of a shipment admittedly, but not grossly, defective, which (as evidenced by his conduct in prior installments) he would have accepted had the market behaved as he expected, it there not good reason for the court to limit him to damages? ... The other policy aspects of the question are fairly clear: is S to lose his whole contract, without chance to repair damage, because of one or two minor technical defaults, which the course of business justifies him in assuming that B would treat as negligible. or at least, as only founding a claim for adjustment?" K. Llewellyn, Cases and Materials on the Law of Sales 543 (1930).

of impairment of the first installment? If the non-conformities in the goods tendered on December 13 had not been grave enough to impair the value substantially, should the buyer have been permitted to reject the goods?

Seller's counsel argued that seller had a further right to cure after buyer's putative rejection of the goods tendered on December 13. In footnote 10 of the opinion, the court gave several reasons for its rejection of that argument. The court declared that the time for cure had lapsed on December 1. Was that correct? The court declared that seller had the burden of showing present ability and intent to cure any remaining defect. Was that correct?

**(4) Cancellation of the Whole Contract.** UCC 2–612(3) deals with the power of installment buyers to cancel contracts. The power to reject an installment and the power to cancel the whole are different powers. One manifestation of the difference would be transactions in which repeated tenders of non-conforming installments, no one of which was or could have been rejected, might in the aggregate be sufficient to justify cancellation of further deliveries.

In *Midwest Mobile Diagnostic Imaging*, buyer advised seller in writing on December 18 that the purchase agreement was canceled. The court declared that the standard for cancellation of future installments was not the same as the standard for rejection of an installment that had been tendered. How persuasive were the court's findings on the grounds for cancellation of the whole contract?

**(5) Damages.** *Midwest Mobile Diagnostic Imaging* is the first case in this section to consider buyer's recovery of damages after rightful rejection of goods. In prior cases, the primary claim litigated was an action by a seller for the unpaid price of the goods. Although references were made to counterclaims by some of those buyers, the substance of the counterclaims was not determined. Where market prices have fallen, buyers that succeed in rightful rejection of goods do not have a claim for expectation damages resulting from sellers' breach; released from their contract obligations, the buyers can obtain substitute goods at prevailing market prices that are lower than the contract prices.

The rejection of the first installment in *Midwest Mobile Diagnostic Imaging* occurred after the price had been paid and did not occur in a falling market. The procedural posture was therefore quite different. Buyer sought to recover the price paid and, in addition, damages based on a temporary replacement of the goods. The Code provisions mentioned by the court were UCC 2–711, UCC 2–712, and UCC 2–715. The court found that the rental cost of the replacement unit was not recoverable as "cover" under UCC 2–712. Was the court correct? Are rental costs for temporary replacements properly recoverable under UCC 2–715?

**Problem 3.** Sellers that sell goods in quantities that could be delivered at once can escape from the rigors of the perfect tender rule by eliciting from buyers express or tacit consent to divide full performance into more than one "lot." In making such arrangements, buyers may or may not be aware that they are surrendering a significant amount of leverage over the sellers when the time comes for performance. If you were counsel to a firm regularly engaged in selling or buying goods in quantities that could be divided, what advice would you give on standard contracting terms?

**Problem 4.** Seller and Buyer have a long-term trading pattern whereby Buyer submits orders frequently for goods to be delivered some time later. Within the delivery time necessary for an order, Buyer usually makes one or more additional orders. Each purchase order results in a single delivery by Seller. Is Buyer's right to reject tendered goods governed by UCC 2–601 or 2–612(2)?

## 3.   REVOCATION OF ACCEPTANCE

A buyer who accepts goods is not necessarily required to keep them and pay for them. In limited circumstances, buyers are permitted to revoke their acceptances. The governing law is UCC 2–608. We considered this matter previously, in Chapter 4, where several cases involved buyers' attempts to revoke acceptance. It is appropriate to revisit some of that material here.

### Hemmert Ag. Aviation, Inc. v. Mid–Continent Aircraft Corp.

[Reread this case, p. 181 supra]

NOTES

**(1) Time and Manner of Revocation of Acceptance.** Revocation of acceptance occurs when a buyer gives notice of it to the seller. This is by inference from the statute, which states that a revocation is "not effective until" a buyer gives notice. UCC 2–608(2).

The Code provides that buyers must give notice "within a reasonable time" after they discovered or should have discovered the grounds for revocation. In goods bought for use rather than resale, the non-conforming qualities may become manifest only after the goods have been used for some time. Was Hemmert Ag. Aviation's notice timely under this contract?

In many transactions, before buyers elect to revoke acceptance, they complain to the sellers. Sellers often try to satisfy their customers by modifying or adjusting the goods. Should the time involved in these accommodative actions be taken into consideration in a determination that a notice of revocation is timely? Is there any statutory basis for tolling the running of the "reasonable time" during such events? The answer may lie, in part, in the alternative situations in which buyers may revoke acceptance. Buyers may revoke their acceptance of some goods that they accepted earlier with full knowledge that the goods were nonconforming because they were assured by the sellers that the non-conformities would be "cured." UCC 2–608(1)(a). The power to revoke should not elapse while a seller is engaged in efforts to cure a non-conformity. Buyers may also revoke their acceptance of goods when the non-conformities become manifest after acceptance. UCC 2–608(1)(b). Sellers are never obligated to try to "cure" non-conformities, but they may choose to do so. Is there a way to read UCC 2–608(2) so that buyers that allow sellers to try to "cure" non-conformities are not penalized if they decide to revoke acceptance subsequently?

The statute is silent on the content of an effective notice and the manner of its communication. Must a buyer use the specific legal words, e.g., I revoke my acceptance of the goods? In *Hemmert*, the notice was formulated and sent to the seller by the buyer's attorney, who sent the message by certified letter. Was that necessary? Must a buyer give the reasons for the revocation? Comment 5 provides:

> 5. The content of the notice under subsection (2) is to be determined ... by considerations of good faith, prevention of surprise, and reasonable adjustment. More will generally be necessary than the mere notification of breach required under [UCC 2–607]. On the other hand the requirements of the section on waiver of [a rejecting] buyer's objections [UCC 2–605] do not apply here. ... Following the general policy of this Article, the requirements of the content of notification are less stringent in the case of a non-merchant buyer.

Is this Comment warranted by the text of the section?

Buyers are not required to tender the goods back to sellers as a condition of revoking acceptance. Buyers who have paid all or part of the price have security interests in the goods that entitle them to retain the goods and, if necessary, to sell the goods to recover the amounts to which they are entitled. UCC 2–608(3), 2–711(3). Note how the buyer's security interest was handled in *Hemmert*.

**(2) Buyer's Monetary Remedies After Revocation of Acceptance.** UCC 2–608(3) declares that a buyer who has rightfully revoked acceptance of goods has the same remedial rights as a buyer who rightfully rejected goods. These include the right to recover so much of the price has been paid. UCC 2–711(1). In addition to this restitutionary relief, a buyer has the right to expectation damages under UCC 2–712 and 2–713. Both of these provisions allow recovery of incidental and consequential damages under UCC 2–715. The *Hemmert* noted that seller was ordered to pay a substantial sum of money but did not recount the elements of the damages that were allowed.

**(3) Buyer's Use of the Goods After Revocation of Acceptance.** Notice of revocation of acceptance, when effective, revests title to the goods in the seller. Often, however, buyers who have been using the goods before the notice continue to use them thereafter. UCC 2–608 has no provision that allows buyers to go on using goods. Rather, subsection (3) incorporates by reference buyers' duties with respect to rejected goods, which include the prohibition, in UCC 2–602(2)(a), of any "exercise of ownership," and the duty, under UCC 2–602(2)(b), "to hold" the goods for the seller. Without legislative basis, some courts have found that buyers' use of goods after revocation of acceptance is not inconsistent with the revocations. E.g.,

A.O. Smith Corp. v. Elbi S.p.A., 123 Fed. Appx. 617 (5th Cir. 2005); McCullough v. Bill Swad Chrysler–Plymouth, Inc., 5 Ohio St.3d 181, 449 N.E.2d 1289 (1983). A rationale for these decisions is that the buyers, having paid for the goods, have no practical alternative and that the predicaments are not of their own making.

Courts that allow continued use of goods are unwilling to permit the buyers to so without charge. In actions by revoking buyers to recover damages, the buyers may be assessed for the use-value of the goods. The measurement of this is sometimes difficult. See Deere & Co. v. Johnson, 67 Fed. Appx. 253 (5th Cir. 2003); Johnson v. G.M. Corp., 233 Kan. 1044, 668 P.2d 139 (1983).

**(4) Revocation of Acceptance in Actions Against Manufacturers.** Buyers dissatisfied with goods with substantial problems that cannot be repaired may elect to revoke their acceptance of the goods and seek to recover the purchase price. We had a case of that kind in Section 2, *Hemmert Ag. Aviation v. Mid–Continent Aircraft.* The retail seller was the defendant in that case. Buyers sometimes try to revoke acceptance and recover the purchase price from manufacturers, in addition to or instead of suing the immediate sellers. Does UCC 2–608 or the MMWA contemplate or authorize buyers to bring revocation-of-acceptance price-recovery actions against manufacturers? Courts deciding the issue are sharply divided.[19] One set of commentators argues that revocation of acceptance and price recovery from remote sellers should be permitted:

> There is certainly nothing in Article 2 that would be inconsistent with such an approach. Moreover, the concept of "remote revocation" is gaining a foothold elsewhere. In the Magnuson–Moss Federal Warranty Act, a manufacturer who markets consumer products under a "full warranty" heading must permit the consumer/buyer to elect either a refund of the full purchase price or replacement goods if the product contains a "defect" or "malfunction" that cannot be cured after a "reasonable number of attempts" by the manufacturer. Thus, revocation against the remote manufacturer is a remedy under *federal* law in some situations. Similarly, a number of state legislatures are enacting "lemon" statutes that give revocation rights against the manufacturer

---

**19.** *Compare* Andover Air Ltd. Partnership v. Piper Aircraft Corp., 1989 WL 110453, 7 U.C.C. Rep. Serv. 2d 1494 (D.Mass.1989); Gasque v. Mooers Motor Car Co., 227 Va. 154, 313 S.E.2d 384 (1984); Seekings v. Jimmy GMC of Tucson, Inc., 130 Ariz. 596, 638 P.2d 210 (1981); Edelstein v. Toyota Motors Distributors, 176 N.J.Super. 57, 422 A.2d 101 (1980); Conte v. Dwan Lincoln–Mercury, Inc., 172 Conn. 112, 374 A.2d 144 (1976); Voytovich v. Bangor Punta Operations, Inc., 494 F.2d 1208 (6th Cir.1974), *with* Deere & Co. v. Johnson, 67 Fed. Appx. 253 (5th Cir. 2003); Fode v. Capital RV Center, Inc., 575 N.W.2d 682 (N.D.1998); Gochey v. Bombardier, Inc., 153 Vt. 607, 572 A.2d 921 (1990); Costa v. Volkswagen of America, 150 Vt. 213, 551 A.2d 1196 (1988); Ford Motor Credit Co. v. Harper, 671 F.2d 1117 (8th Cir.1982); Volkswagen of America v. Novak, 418 So.2d 801 (Miss.1982); Murray v. Holiday Rambler, Inc., 83 Wis.2d 406, 265 N.W.2d 513 (1978); Volvo of America v. Wells, 551 S.W.2d 826 (Ky.App.1977); Durfee v. Rod Baxter Imports, Inc., 262 N.W.2d 349 (Minn.1977); Asciolla v. Manter Oldsmobile–Pontiac, Inc., 117 N.H. 85, 370 A.2d 270 (1977).

of a defective motor vehicle without regard to limits in the written warranty accompanying the goods.

B. Clark & C. Smith, The Law of Product Warranties ¶ 7.03(3)(d) (1984). Cf. J. White & R. Summers, Uniform Commercial Code 330–331 (5th ed. 2000).

# Car Transportation Brokerage Co. v. Blue Bird Body Co.

United States Court of Appeal, Eleventh Circuit, 2009.
322 Fed. Appx. 891.

■ Before Edmondson, Chief Judge, Dubina and Kravitch, Circuit Judges.

■ Per Curiam:

CAR Transportation Brokerage Company (hereinafter the "Buyer") appeals the district court's grant of summary judgment on its revocation of acceptance claim brought under O.C.G.A. § 11–2–608(1)(b). At issue is whether the district court properly granted summary judgment on this claim where the Buyer of a defective motor coach provided the seller with only one opportunity to cure the defects in the coach prior to revoking acceptance.

## I.  BACKGROUND

The relevant facts of this case, as supported by the evidence construed in the light most favorable to the non-moving party, are as follows:

On December 31, 2004, the Buyer, a company located in Springdale, Arkansas, purchased a 2005 Blue Bird Wanderlodge LXi motor coach (the "Coach") from John Bleakley R.V. of Douglasville, Georgia (the "Seller") for $650,000. One month prior to this sale, the Seller had discovered that the Coach's electrical system was "going haywire" and had returned the Coach to the manufacturer for repairs. After the manufacturer returned the Coach, the Seller did not confirm that the problem had been solved. The Seller did not tell the Buyer about the prior repair work performed on the Coach.

Because the Buyer did not arrive on the lot until almost five p.m. on December 31st and the Buyer was already familiar with vehicles like the Coach, the Seller did not perform its customary pre-delivery inspection and customer product orientation prior to delivering possession to the Buyer. The Seller, however, represented that the Coach was new and in working condition. The parties executed a purchase agreement, in which the Seller disclaimed all warranties, including any warranty for merchantability or for fitness for a particular purpose. The manufacturer provided a limited warranty, which the Seller gave to the Buyer pursuant to the purchase agreement. This warranty limited the manufacturer's obligation to the repair or replacement of parts which, under normal use and service, were defective in workmanship or material.

On the day of the purchase, as the Buyer was driving back to Arkansas from Douglasville, Georgia, it noted that the Coach's low-beam headlights were not working and that the step-cover had come **\*893** out. It returned the Coach to the Seller the next morning for repairs. The Seller's service technicians found and repaired several electrical issues on the Coach. On January 5th, the Buyer, accompanied by the Seller's service technician, drove the Coach approximately thirty-five miles without incident. During this drive, the Seller's service technician told the Buyer that he had no experience repairing this particular model of motor coach. The Buyer then re-took possession of the Coach and returned home to Arkansas.

Over the next two months, however, the Coach had several other problems, including other issues with its electrical system. Because the Seller's service technician had told the Buyer that he was unfamiliar with this model of motor coach, the Buyer decided to take the Coach to the manufacturer for repairs, instead of returning it to the Seller. The manufacturer returned the Coach to the Buyer on February 18, without having completely repaired the electrical system. The manufacturer told the Buyer that a "circuit board" was required to fix the defect and assured the Buyer that the required part would be ordered, but the Buyer heard nothing more from the manufacturer regarding this potential fix.

On March 22, 2005, the Buyer's attorney wrote a letter to the Seller purporting to revoke acceptance of the Coach because "the vehicle has failed to perform in the manner required for a motor coach and thus is not merchantable." The Seller did not respond to the revocation letter.

The parties do not dispute that, as early as March 2005, the manufacturer was aware that the inverters of the 450 LXi coach were defective and would cause random operation of the coach's electrical components, such as was seen in the Coach. On November 30, 2005, the manufacturer discovered an inverter that would resolve the LXi coach's defect, but it did not notify its dealers of either the defect or the solution until March 10, 2006.

On July 24, 2006, the Buyer brought suit against the Seller[24] asserting claims for fraud, negligent misrepresentation, revocation of acceptance under O.C.G.A. § 11–2–608(1)(b), breach of implied warranty of merchantability, and violations of the Georgia Fair Business Practices Act. After discovery, the Seller moved for summary judgment on all of the claims and the Buyer moved for summary judgment on the issue of revocation.

The district court granted the Seller's motion and denied the Buyer's motion. The district court found, *inter alia,* that the Buyer was not entitled to revoke its acceptance of the Coach because the "limited opportunity to cure" provided by the Buyer was insufficient to satisfy "the Georgia law that before a buyer may bring a revocation claim, it must give the seller an opportunity to cure all known defects." The Buyer appeals, challenging only the grant of summary judgment on its revocation of acceptance claim.

---

**24.** The Buyer also named the manufacturer, Blue Bird Company, as a defendant in the original complaint. On August 28, 2006, however, the parties agreed to dismiss Blue Bird as a defendant.

The Buyer asserts that the district court erred in finding that it was required by statute O.C.G.A. § 11–2–608(1)(b) to provide the Seller with an opportunity to cure prior to revoking. In the alternative, the Buyer argues that if it was obliged to give the Seller an opportunity to repair, there is at least a jury question as to whether the Buyer satisfied this requirement.

The Seller responds that although O.C.G.A. § 11–2–608 does not require an opportunity to cure in all situations, the district court properly found that the Buyer was required to provide the Seller with an opportunity to cure in *this* case and that the Buyer failed to satisfy this requirement. The Seller also asserts that, even if the court erred by requiring an opportunity for repair, the district court could have granted summary judgment on the alternate ground that the Buyer performed acts after the alleged revocation which were inconsistent with the Seller's ownership of the Coach.

\* \* \*

## III. DISCUSSION

### A. *Opportunity to Cure*

This case hinges on whether the district court erred in finding that, under Georgia law and the facts of this case, the Buyer was required to provide the Seller with an opportunity to seasonably cure the defects in the Coach prior to revoking its acceptance.

\* \* \*

On appeal, the Buyer asserts that because it accepted the Coach without discovery of its nonconformity and the nonconformity was not apparent, its revocation claim arose under § 11–2–608(1)(b), not subsection (1)(a), and it was therefore not required to provide the Seller with an opportunity to cure prior to revoking.

On its face, the plain language of O.C.G.A. § 11–2–608 requires a pre-revocation opportunity to cure only where a buyer knew about the nonconformity prior to acceptance and reasonably assumed that the nonconformity would be cured. Courts in a majority of jurisdictions, therefore, take the position that a seller has no right to cure nonconformities prior to revocation under UCC § 2–608(1)(b), that is, where the goods are accepted by the buyer without knowledge that it fails to conform to the sales contract. See, e.g., Preston Motor Co. v. Palomares, 133 Ariz. 245, 650 P.2d 1227, 1231 (Ariz.1982); Werner v. Montana, 117 N.H. 721, 378 A.2d 1130, 1136–37 (1977); American Honda Motor Co., Inc. v. Boyd, 475 So.2d 835, 839–40 (Ala.1985) (holding that where buyer purchased a car, believing it to be new, and in fact the car was previously damaged and repaired, and buyer did not discover this until after it had accepted car, the case fell under UCC § 2–608(1)(b), and therefore, there was no right to cure); U.S. Roofing, Inc. v. Credit Alliance Corp., 228 Cal.App.3d 1431, 279 Cal.Rptr. 533, 540 (Cal.App.3d Dist.1991) (categorically stating that "[we] believe that the right to cure under [UCC § 2–508] does not apply to situations where the buyer seeks to revoke his acceptance under [UCC § 2–608]''); Jensen v. Seigel Mobile Homes Group, 105 Idaho 189, 668 P.2d 65, 69–70 (1983) (holding that right to cure is relevant only when there has been a rejection of goods; following acceptance there is no right to cure, citing authorities for the proposition that cure is not available following the buyer's acceptance of goods); Head v. Phillips Camper Sales & Rental, Inc., 234 Mich. App. 94, 593 N.W.2d 595, 600 (1999) (adopting majority view that "a seller has no right to cure a defect that was not discoverable when the buyer accepted the goods"); Bowen v. Foust, 925 S.W.2d 211, 215 n. 6 (Mo.Ct. App.S.D.1996) (noting that this remains the majority view, although the more recent cases allow opportunity to cure more willingly following an acceptance). Accordingly, where a buyer's acceptance is as described in UCC § 2–608(1)(b), the majority rule is that he may revoke the acceptance without waiting for a cure, seasonable or otherwise, by the seller.

A minority of state courts, however, interpret UCC § 2–608 as imposing upon the buyer a duty to provide notice and an opportunity to cure in *all* cases of revocation. These courts point to UCC § 2–608(3) which provides that a purchaser revoking his acceptance "has the same rights and duties with regard to the goods involved as if he had rejected them," and note that a seller has a general right to cure nonconformities in rejected goods under UCC § 2–508. By analogy, then, they hold that a similar duty to provide notice and opportunity to cure exists in the context of revocation. See, e.g., Conte v. Dwan Lincoln–Mercury Inc., 172 Conn. 112, 374 A.2d 144, 149 (1976); David Tunick, Inc. v. Kornfeld, 838 F.Supp. 848, 850 (S.D.N.Y.1993) (explaining that, through UCC § 2–608(3), the UCC § 2–508(2)'s requirement that a buyer provide notice and opportunity to cure nonconforming goods is generally applicable in the case of a revocation of acceptance); Tucker v. Aqua Yacht Harbor Corp., 749 F.Supp. 142, 145 (N.D.Miss.1990) ("Although a seller seems to have the right to cure only when the buyer rejects goods, the Mississippi Supreme Court, by analogy to § 75-2–508 and as a matter of public policy, has determined that before a buyer may revoke acceptance under § 75-2–608, the seller must be afforded a reasonable opportunity to cure."). In these jurisdictions, revocation is only appropriate after the seller has been afforded a reasonable opportunity to cure, regardless of whether the buyer accepted the goods with or without knowledge of the nonconformity.

Georgia courts have not addressed the issue; therefore, it is not clear that the district court-which appears to have adopted the minority view-erred. We need not decide this issue, however, because, as described more fully below, the Buyer invited the alleged error or waived its right to raise the issue on appeal.

## B. *Invited Error*

"It is a cardinal rule of appellate review that a party may not challenge [an error] invited by that party." . . . "Having induced the court to rely on a particular erroneous proposition of law or fact, a party in the normal case may not at a later stage of the case use the error to set aside the immediate consequences of the error." . . .

In this case, the Buyer stated in its motion for summary judgment that the Seller was entitled to an opportunity to repair prior to revocation under O.C.G.A. § 11–2–608(1)(b), but argued that it had satisfied this requirement. Specifically, the Buyer claimed that the Seller "made multiple failed attempts to cure, thus satisfying the *statutory requirement* that a seller be allowed to attempt to cure." (emphasis added). Then, in reply to the Seller's responsive argument that a revocation claim required evidence of a "refusal to remedy within a reasonable time, or lack of success in the attempts to remedy," the Buyer restated its position that it had satisfied the "statutory requirement that a seller be allowed to attempt to cure" because the Seller made "several attempts to cure the very serious electrical defects in the Motor Coach before revocation, but it failed to do so." Furthermore, although the Seller argued in its motion that summary judgment on the Buyer's revocation claim was appropriate because the Buyer did not give it "either notice or opportunity to address the new issues that arose" after the initial repairs, the Buyer did not assert in response that an opportunity to cure was not required. The district court, in making its decision, adopted without discussion the Buyer's assertion that a reasonable opportunity to cure was a prerequisite for revocation. It disagreed, however, with the Buyer's claim that it had satisfied this requirement and, therefore, granted summary judgment to the Seller on this ground.

Now, on appeal, the Buyer claims for the first time that the district court erred when it "read into the statute that notice and opportunity to cure must be given prior to notice of revocation[; s]uch a requirement does not exist in the plain language of the statute." Because the Buyer itself stated that its revocation claim required proof that the Seller had been given a reasonable opportunity to cure, it invited the district court to make this error-if error it be-and may not now assert that the district court incorrectly interpreted the law. . . .

Even if the Buyer had not invited the alleged error, this court will not, as a general rule, consider issues presented in the first instance on appeal in civil actions. . . . The Buyer failed to raise its current argument either in its own motion for summary judgment or in response to the Seller's assertion that revocation was foreclosed by the Buyer's failure to provide "notice or opportunity to address the new issues that arose" after the initial repairs. Admittedly, the rule foreclosing review of issues not presented below is not jurisdictional and may be abrogated in certain exceptional circumstances. . . . In its brief on appeal, however, the Buyer not only fails to acknowledge its lack of objection in the district court to the law applied, but it also fails to argue for the application of one of the exceptions to our rule regarding a party's waiver of an issue raised for the first time on appeal. . . . Consequently, we must conclude that the Buyer is precluded in this case from arguing that it was not required to provide the Seller with an opportunity to seasonably cure prior to revocation. We therefore turn to the question of whether the opportunity to cure provided by the Buyer was, as a matter of law, insufficient.

### C.   Sufficiency of the Opportunity to Cure

The Buyer argues that if it was required to provide the Seller with an opportunity to seasonably cure prior to revocation, there is at least a triable issue of fact as to whether it satisfied this requirement. It further asserts that even if it had returned the Coach to the Seller after the initial repairs, any further attempts at repair would have been futile because the "cure" for the electrical defect was not discovered by the manufacturer until November 2005 (nearly eight months after revocation). Accordingly, the Buyer asserts that it should be excused from the requirement of providing the Seller with another opportunity to cure because the statute should not be construed so as "to require [it] to do a futile and useless thing." BDI Distrib., Inc. v. Beaver Computer Corp., 232 Ga.App. 316, 501 S.E.2d 839, 841 (1998).

We disagree. Although the statutory opportunity to "seasonably cure" does not entitle a seller to *unlimited* attempts to cure a defect, it does require a buyer to provide a seller with a reasonable time in which to attempt to make repairs. O.C.G.A. § 11-1-204(3) (explaining that an action is taken "seasonably" when it is taken "at or within a reasonable time"). What constitutes a reasonable time in which to cure depends on the nature, purpose, and circumstances of a particular case. O.C.G.A. § 11-1-204(2). . . . In this case, the evidence taken in the light most favorable to the Buyer shows that the Buyer gave the Seller one opportunity to cure after the defect in the electrical system first became apparent. After these initial repairs, the Buyer did not inform the Seller when the Coach continued to have additional problems; rather, it returned the Coach to the manufacturer for repairs. Nearly three months after acceptance, after the manufacturer also had made one failed attempt to correct the defect, the Buyer informed the Seller that it was revoking its acceptance of the Coach. Based upon this undisputed evidence, we agree with the district court that, as a matter of law, the Buyer provided the Seller with an insufficient opportunity to cure. Providing only one opportunity to repair-before the extent of the defect was truly apparent-is not reasonable, especially where the product in question is as complicated as a motor coach. . . . At the least, the Seller was entitled to notice of the additional problems and an opportunity to attempt to repair them at some time during the three months prior to the Buyer's purported revocation. The Buyer's failure to provide this notice and opportunity bars the revocation claim as a matter of law.

The Buyer's argument that it was excused from providing the Seller with an opportunity to cure because attempts to repair would have been futile is not supported by the evidence. Certainly, we should not read an "opportunity to cure" requirement so as to "require[ ] a party to whistle in the wind," . . . but, in this case, there is no evidence that the Buyer *knew* prior to revocation that the Seller would have been unable to repair the Coach. As such, the Buyer's failure to provide the Seller with another opportunity to cure was not, and could not have been, based on the perceived futility of providing such an opportunity.

## IV.  CONCLUSION

We conclude that, under the limited circumstances of this case, the Buyer is barred by the doctrine of invited error from denying that it was required to provide the Seller with an opportunity to seasonably cure any nonconformities in the Coach prior to revocation. Because we agree with the district court that the one opportunity the Buyer provided was insufficient to satisfy this requirement, we AFFIRM the grant of summary judgment in this case.

## NOTES

**(1) Cure and Revocation of Acceptance.** The first prong of UCC 2–608(1) expressly incorporates the concept of seller's cure of a nonconformity in goods that had been tendered and accepted. The second prong does not. The two situations differ significantly

Upon tender or delivery of goods, if a buyer's inspection reveals a nonconformity in the quality or quantity of the goods, the buyer has the power to reject them under UCC 2–601 (or under UCC 2–612 if the nonconformity is sufficiently grave). That would trigger the seller's power to cure under UCC 2–508. Buyer, instead of rejecting, may inform the seller of the non-conformity and be induced to accept the goods (e.g., by so signifying under UCC 2–206(1)) by seller's assurance that it would cure the nonconformity forthwith. Such an acceptance might be characterized as a conditional acceptance. UCC 2–608(1)(a) does not use that characterization, but reaches essentially the same result by authorizing a buyer to revoke the acceptance if seller fails to cure, but only if the substantial impairment test is met.

UCC 2–608(1)(b) contemplates a buyer's discovery of a serious nonconformity after acceptance. Like the power to reject, the power to revoke acceptance is not contingent on any prior communication with the seller before the buyer exercises the power. If a buyer revokes acceptance without communicating with the seller, the subsection is silent on whether a seller may proffer a cure *after* the revocation. The UCC provision on cure *after* rejection, UCC 2–508, is silent on cure *after* revocation. The contract time for seller's performance would very likely have passed. The UCC 2–508 provisions that address this issue are not likely to be appropriately analogous to cure *after* revocation.

Neither prong of UCC 2–608(1) contemplates a possible (or even probable) course of events whereby a buyer discovers a serious nonconformity after acceptance and so informs the seller, who undertakes to address the issue; at some later time, the buyer, still dissatisfied, revokes acceptance of the goods. In a sense, such a buyer gives seller a chance to cure *before* revocation. The course of events is consistent with the likelihood that the decision to revoke is made upon advice of counsel, advice that would not be sought until the buyer's attempt to work things out with the seller had failed. Should courts create a power to cure *before* revocation? If so, should the onus be placed on the buyer to give the seller sufficient time and opportunity to cure? Would that be consistent with UCC 2–508? What did the courts do in the instant case?

**(2) Nature of Non–Conformity and Revocation.** The discussion segment of the Court of Appeals' opinion characterized the retail dealer's obligation as a warranty of merchantability. The court upheld a judgment that buyer was not entitled to relief based on revocation of acceptance. The court's characterization of the dealer's obligation was unnecessary to the outcome. It is dubious, on the facts stated by the court, that the dealer that a warranty of merchantability existed in this case,[20] breach of such a warranty, if severe enough to meet the substantial impairment test, would open the possibility of a buyer's revocation of acceptance. That, in turn, would lead to consideration of cure in connection with revocation.

The bus manufacturer's stated obligations were in its remedial promise if defects in materials and workmanship were found. The buyer initially sued the manufacturer as well as the dealer, but dropped the case against the manufacturer a month after the complaint had been filed. The description of the bus indicates defects in materials and workmanship by the manufacturer. What might explain the decision of buyer's counsel to dismiss the claim against the manufacturer?

**(3) Buyer's Remedy; UCC 2–608(3).** As in *Hemmert* this case is an action for monetary relief, probably including all or part of the $650,000 purchase price plus damages for breach of warranty. This follows from UCC 2–608(3). If buyer had proceeded against the manufacturer and prevailed, would this remedy be appropriate?

**(4) "Invited Error."** The express ground for the Court of Appeals judgment was a finding that buyer's counsel has misled the trial court on the applicable legal standard (sellers had the right to cure before revocation) and then argued on appeal that a different standard (seller had no right to cure before revocation) was correct. Not surprisingly, appellate courts are not tolerant of what appears to them to be advocacy that "invites error" by trial courts. Was the Court of Appeals too harsh in applying the "invited error" rule to this case?

The law on cure and revocation is unsettled. UCC 2–608 is not clear in text or comment. In the court's analysis, precedents in cases outside of Georgia are in conflict, with majority and minority views, and moreover the case law is in flux. No Georgia state court decisions exist to guide this federal court in this diversity of citizenship case, which is governed by Georgia law. Adding to the confusion is the uncertainty of the law regard-

---

**20.** The retail dealer's obligations were in the documented contract of sale, which was described by the court as containing disclaimer of all warranties, including the warranty of merchantability. (The bus is not a "consumer good"; thus the MMWA does not prohibit the disclaimer.) It is possible that the seller's oral statement describing the quality if the bus at the time of delivery would constitute an warranty, but the court did not discuss that.

ing revocation of acceptance in circumstances where the party primarily responsible for causing the qualitative deficiency and for remedying it is the manufacturer, not a party to the sales contract.

At the trial level, counsel for both parties knew or could have known of the considerable legal uncertainties and ferment. The amount in controversy, while not trivial, was not sufficient to justify large legal fees and costs on either side, fees and costs possibly not recoverable even in any event of a successful outcome. Could buyer's litigation position be described as saying: even if a seller has the right to try to cure before a buyer revokes acceptance, the seller had an opportunity and failed? Litigators often use the logical tactic of assuming a rule *arguendo*. If that had been buyer's counsel's tactic, should he or she be precluded from arguing that the proper rule is otherwise?

## (B) INTERNATIONAL SALES LAW

The Convention on International Sale of Goods does not use the concepts of rejection or acceptance of goods, or revocation of acceptance of goods by buyers. CISG also has no provision for sellers' cure of rejected goods or goods after acceptance has been revoked. The Convention has no special provisions for rejection or revocation of acceptance for installment sales.

The CISG provision that might be compared to the UCC Article 2 provisions for rejection or revocation of acceptance is CISG 49 which permits certain aggrieved buyers to *avoid* contracts.[21] Avoidance, as used in CISG however, is more comparable to the concept of *cancellation* in the Commercial Code. See UCC 2–106(4), 2–720. Under Article 2, cancellation is an option that a buyer in installment contracts where a seller's default substantially impairs the value of the whole contract. UCC 2–612(3).

*Avoidance: Fundamental Breach.* CISG 49(1)(a) permits buyers to avoid contracts on the ground that the goods delivered are non-conforming if the non-conformities are sufficiently grave as to constitute *fundamental breach*. A breach is *fundamental* if the detriment in performance substantially deprives the aggrieved party of what it was entitled to expect under the contract. CISG 25. The effects of avoidance are set forth in CISG 81–84.[22]

Professor Honnold noted that, in the discussions leading to the Convention, there was no significant support for allowing buyers to avoid contracts for insubstantial deviations from contracts:[23]

---

**21.** The word "reject" is used in CISG 86(1) and 86(2), but probably refers to buyer's refusal to keep goods after avoidance of contracts. See J. Honnold, Uniform Law for International Sales § 455 (3d ed. 1999).

**22.** CISG contemplates that buyers and sellers may avoid contracts. In this section, we are concerned with avoidance by buyers.

**23.** J. Honnold, Uniform Law for International Sales § 181.2 (3d ed. 1999).

Stricter avoidance (or "rejection") rules in some domestic laws failed to take account of the special circumstances of international trade, such as the fact that claims that the goods are defective often are made only after expensive transport to the buyer's place of business when avoidance for immaterial defects might needlessly lead to wasteful reshipment or redisposition of the goods in a foreign country. Moreover, the power to avoid the contract for immaterial defects in performance may tempt the ... buyer (after a price decline) to avoid the contract and thus reverse the allocation of the effect of price changes which the contract contemplated.

Of course, these factors will not always be present and in many cases only avoidance will adequately protect the aggrieved party. In transactions where a party is concerned that Article 25 is too lax or too strict or that a tribunal might improperly apply the law, the contract can provide for stricter (or looser) grounds for avoidance (Article 6).

*Effects of Avoidance by Buyers.* If a buyer elects to avoid a sales contract, it must return the goods to the seller and may demand refund of the price paid. A buyer loses the right to avoid a contract, even if there has been fundamental breach, if it cannot or does not make restitution of the goods substantially in the condition in which they were received. CISG 82(1). Exceptions exist (1) if the buyer is unable to return the goods and the impossibility is not due to its act or omission, or (2) if the goods were sold in the normal course of business or consumed or transformed by the buyer before it discovered or ought to have discovered the lack of conformity, or (3) if the goods deteriorated or perished as a result of the buyer's examination of them. CISG 82(2).

A buyer must act, on behalf of the seller, to preserve goods in the buyer's possession or placed at its disposal at their shipping destination. CISG 86. The buyer may warehouse the goods. CISG 87.

A buyer need not return goods if seller fails to repay the price or the cost of preservation of the goods. CISG 88(1). If a seller delays unreasonably in taking the goods back, the buyer may sell them by any appropriate means, CISG 88(1), and must do so if the goods are subject to rapid deterioration or their preservation would involve unreasonable expense. CISG 88(2).

*Remedies After Avoidance.* CISG allows a buyer to recover damages for the seller's default, whether or not the breach is fundamental. CISG 74. See also CISG 50. A buyer that is unable or unwilling to return the goods may proceed to seek damages under that article. If a buyer rightfully avoids a contract, the buyer is entitled not only to recover any price paid, but may also obtain damages. CISG 81(1) provides that avoidance releases both parties from their obligations under the contract "subject to any damages which may be due." Special rules for measurement of damages after avoidance are found in CISG 75 and 76.

We considered cases involving avoidance and claims for damages when sellers delivered non-conforming goods in Chapter 4. It is useful to review that material.

### Schmitz–Werke Gmbh & Co. v. Rockland Industries, Inc.

[Reread this case, p. 197 supra]

### Delchi Carrier SpA v. Rotorex Corp.

[Reread this case, p. 202 supra]

### Medical Marketing Int'l. v. Internazionale Medico Scientifica

[Reread this case, p. 209 supra]


## Decision of the Bundesgerichtshof, Germany

CLOUT Abstract No. 171, UNILEX D. 1996–4.

The Dutch plaintiff was the assignee of a Dutch company, which had sold four different quantities of cobalt sulphate to the [buyer], a German company. It was agreed that the goods should be of British origin and that the plaintiff should supply certificates of origin and of quality. After the receipt of the documents, the [buyer] declared the contracts to be avoided since the cobalt sulphate was made in South Africa and the certificate of origin was wrong. The [buyer] also claimed that the quality of the goods was inferior to what was agreed upon. The plaintiff demanded payment. The German Supreme Court held that there were no grounds for avoidance of the contract and thus found for the plaintiff.

According to the Court, the declaration of avoidance could not be based on article 49(1)(b) CISG since the plaintiff had effected delivery. The delivery of goods which do not conform with the contract either because they are of lesser quality or of different origin does not constitute non-delivery.

The Court also found that there was no fundamental breach of contract since the [buyer] failed to show that the sale of the South African cobalt sulphate in Germany or abroad was not possible (article 49(1)(a) CISG). Thus, the [buyer] failed to show that it was substantially deprived of what it was entitled to expect under the contract (article 25 CISG).

Lastly, the Court held that the delivery of wrong certificates of origin and of quality did not amount to a fundamental breach of contract since the [buyer] could obtain correct documents from other sources. Accordingly, the [buyer] could not refuse payment under article 58.

———

*Manner of Avoiding.* If goods received are so non-conforming that a seller's performance amounts to fundamental breach, the buyer may declare the contract avoided. CISG 49(1). For a declaration of avoidance to be effective, it must be made by notice to the seller. CISG 26. Notices under the Convention are effective, whether or not received, if dispatched "by means appropriate in the circumstances." CISG 27. The CISG does not prescribe the contents of an effective declaration of avoidance.

*Time of Avoidance.* A buyer's time to decide whether to declare a contracted avoided for fundamental breach is determined by the time needed to discover the deficiency. Power to avoid for quality or quantity defects expires a reasonable time after buyer knew or ought to have known of the breach. CISG 49(2)(b)(I). Power to avoid for late delivery that constitutes fundamental breach expires a reasonable time after buyer has become aware that delivery has been made. CISG 49(2)(a).

*Cure of Non-conforming Deliveries.* In contracts governed by the CISG, buyers are without power to reject goods and have only limited power to avoid contracts. Buyers are, therefore, not in a strong position to use self-help to compel sellers to cure non-conforming deliveries. However, the Convention permits buyers to seek court orders compelling sellers to perform. CISG 46(1). Article 46 differentiates between court orders to compel delivery of substitute goods and court orders to repair the goods that were delivered. Substitute goods may be ordered only if the deficiency in the original delivery was a fundamental breach. CISG 46(2). An order to repair is permitted unless repair is unreasonable in the circumstances. CISG 46(3).

The Convention's authorization of court-ordered relief may be of little value to buyers in the United States or other common-law nations where equitable relief, by injunction or specific performance, is denied if the aggrieved party has an adequate remedy at law, i.e. monetary damages. See, e.g., UCC 2–716. The Convention accepts that some nations' laws limit parties' access to specific relief. CISG 28.

Even if not faced with buyers' avoidance or not ordered to cure non-conforming deliveries, sellers may elect to try to remedy failures in their performances. Buyers must permit sellers to do so if the sellers act without unreasonable delay and without causing buyers unreasonable inconvenience. CISG 48(1). What might motivate sellers to act in this way? Professor Honnold explained:[24]

> It would be easy to over-estimate the importance of the Convention's rules on "requiring" performance. Buyers seldom need to coerce sellers to replace or repair defective goods.... Replacement and repair are opportunities sought by sellers—to preserve good will, reduce damage liability and avoid the drastic remedy of avoidance of the contract.

**Problem 5.** Telecommunications Company (TCo) in an African country contracted to buy a high power microwave amplifier (HPA) from a United States supplier (SCo). The agreement contained extensive technical specifications for the HPA. The agreement provided, further, that SCo

---

24.  J. Honnold, Uniform Law for International Sales § 286 (3d ed. 1999).

would install and test the HPA at the site in Africa within 15 months. When the HPA had been manufactured, TCo inspected it at the factory and found that it met the contract specifications. SCo installed the HPA in Africa. Before the HPA was operational, TCo again inspected the equipment and indicated that it was satisfactory. After six months of SCo's effort to get the HPA into service, SCo realized that it would not work because it had been designed for a grounded neutral power supply system, whereas the power supply at the site was an isolated neutral power system. The contract specifications were silent on the nature of the power supply. Rebuilding the HBA to operate with the available power supply would delay installation for more than a year. Assuming that the contract is governed by the CISG, may TCo avoid the contract?[25]

**Problem 6.** Buyer and seller contracted for sale of a computer. Seller shipped the computer to buyer. On arrival, buyer discovered that three major components of the equipment were defective. Buyer immediately informed seller of the defects and of its election to avoid the contract. Seller wired back: "All defects can promptly and completely corrected. Will send top-level team next week." Assume that the deficiencies in the computer, as delivered, would constitute fundamental breach. If the seller has the ability to correct the problems without unreasonable delay and without causing buyer unreasonable convenience, may it do so despite buyer's declaration of avoidance? What is the meaning of "subject to article 49" in CISG 48(1)? According to Professor Honnold:[26]

> "[T]he seller's right to cure should also be protected if, ... where cure is feasible, the buyer hastily declares the contract avoided before the seller has an opportunity to cure the defect. ... [W]here cure is feasible and where an offer of cure can be expected, one cannot conclude that the breach is 'fundamental' until one knows the answer to this question: Will the seller cure?"

**Problem 7.** In performance of a contract for the sale of sugar with an average polarization of 78, seller shipped sugar which buyer tested and determined to average 73. Buyer immediately wired seller a notice that the sugar received did not conform to contract specifications on polarization. What purpose would this notice serve? Recall CISG 39(1). Would this notice constitute an effective declaration of avoidance under CISG 26? May sellers combine, in one communication, notice of a lack of conformity and declaration of avoidance? What content would such a communication have? Must a buyer use the word "avoid"? Professor Honnold offered this analysis:[27]

> A notice specifying a "lack of conformity" in accordance with Article 39 would not, without more, constitute a "declaration of avoidance"

---

**25.** See Awards of June 1984 and May 1985 in Case No. 4567, 11 Yearbook Commercial Arbitration 143 (1986). This ICC arbitration case, on the facts set forth in the Problem, was decided under United States law. The arbitration panel, one member dissenting, found that the buyer was entitled to revoke its acceptance of the HPA and to recover damages.

**26.** J. Honnold, Uniform Law for International Sales § 296 (3d ed. 1999).

**27.** J. Honnold, Uniform Law for International Sales § 187.2 (3d ed. 1999).

under Article 26. A buyer who specifies non-conformity ... may, and often does, choose to retain the goods and claim a reduction in the price or other damages to compensate for the deficiency. Avoidance of the contract is a different and much more drastic remedy. In the setting of tender of delivery of defective goods "avoidance of the contract" by the buyer means that the buyer will not accept or keep the goods, and that the seller has the responsibility to take over their disposition A buyer's declaration of *avoidance*, to be effective under Article 26, must inform the seller that the buyer will not accept or keep the goods.

**Problem 8.** Buyer received goods that are sufficiently deficient in quality that seller has committed a fundamental breach. Buyer sent notice to the seller specifying the lack of conformity (CISG 39) and declaring the contract avoided (CISG 26). One week later, buyer sought a court order directing the seller to deliver substitute goods on the ground that seller had delivered goods whose lack of conformity constitutes a fundamental breach and that buyer was entitled to "require" seller to deliver substitute goods under CISG 46(2). Seller counters that its obligations under the contract were released when buyer declared the contract avoided. Is seller correct? See J. Honnold, Uniform Law for International Sales § 440.2 (3d ed. 1999).

*Litigation After Avoidance.* Price actions are likely to be less frequent in international sales transactions than in domestic United States transactions. International sales transactions are commonly structured by the parties so that the price is paid by banks that issued letters of credit payable on submission of documents. In such transactions, buyers' right to avoid arises in the circumstance that sellers have the money. After avoidance, buyers would have to sue the sellers for restitution of the price and, if appropriate, damages.

*Installment Contracts.* The Convention provides special rules for installment contracts in CISG 73. There is no definition of "instalment contract."[28] Like UCC Article 2, the Convention differentiates between breach with respect to an individual installment, breach with respect to future installments, and breach with respect to past deliveries. Only breaches that are "fundamental" trigger remedies under CISG 73.[29]

---

**28.** The UNCITRAL Digest states: "An instalment contract is one that provides for delivery of goods in separate lots. The goods do not have to be fungible so that an instalment contract may cover delivery of different kinds of goods in each instalment (e.g., men's lambskin coats and women's lambskin coats.) ... Several decisions have characterized separate contracts between parties that have an on-going relationship as an instalment contract governed by article 73 or have concluded that the aggrieved party might act under either article 73 or another article, such as article 71 or article 72. One decision also applies article 73 to separate yearly supply contracts between the same parties for the supply of aluminum. Another decision, however, distinguishes an instalment contract from a distribution or framework agreement, which may provide for non-sales matters such as exclusive representation in a geographical area or an agreement without any determinable quantity." UNCITRAL Digest of Case Law on the CISG, Article 73 (8 June 2004).

**29.** For commentary, see J. Honnold, Uniform Law for International Sales § 399 (3d ed. 1999).

If there is a fundamental breach with respect to an installment, the aggrieved party may declare the contract avoided with respect to that installment only. CISG 73(1). One has to take care to understand that, under the Convention, an avoidance of a contract may be avoidance as to only a part of the contract.

CISG 73(2) deals with avoidance of a contract with respect to future installments. The power of an aggrieved party to avoid the contract in this respect arises if the aggrieved party has "good grounds to conclude that a fundamental breach will occur with respect to future instalments."

When an aggrieved party elects to avoid a contract with respect to an installment, avoidance with respect to past deliveries (as well as future deliveries) is permitted if, by reason of their interdependence, those deliveries could not be used for the purpose contemplated at the time the contract was formed. CISG 73(3).

## Section 3.   Buyers' Wrongful Rejection: Sellers' Damages

### (A) Domestic United States Law

If buyers reject wrongfully and have not paid the full contract price, sellers are entitled to various remedies, catalogued in UCC 2–703.

*Price Actions.* One of the remedies that is sometimes available is the UCC 2–709 price remedy, which we considered in Section 1. Sellers that elect to pursue the price remedy are committed, at least initially, to deliver or redeliver the goods to the buyers. If buyers are compelled to pay the price, they are entitled to receive the goods. UCC 2–709(2). The Code does not require a seller to hold on to goods pending the ultimate judgment in a price action. A sellers is permitted to sell the goods "if resale becomes possible." Proceeds of the resale are credited against the judgment for the price.

*Actions for Damages.* Sellers have another set of remedies that are premised on the outcome that the rejected goods, even though wrongfully rejected, remain under the sellers' control. In these circumstances, aggrieved sellers make alternative disposition of the goods and seek monetary damages from the buyers.

UCC Article 2 provides two remedies based upon sellers' actual or possible substitute transactions. A seller may resell the goods and recover monetary damages measured by the differential between the contract price and the net proceeds of the resale, UCC 2–706, or measured by the difference between the contract price and the market price of the goods, UCC 2–708(1).

The "wild card" remedy available to aggrieved sellers under the Code is recovery of damages measured by the "profit" the seller would have made if buyer had not rejected. UCC 2–708(2). "Profit" under this section is akin to the accounting formula of contract price less variable costs-of-goods-sold; "overhead" or so-called fixed costs are not included in calculating "profit."

## Apex Oil Co. v. The Belcher Co. of New York, Inc.

United States Court of Appeals, Second Circuit, 1988.
855 F.2d 997.

■ Winter, Circuit Judge:

This diversity case, arising out of an acrimonious commercial dispute, presents the question whether a sale of goods six weeks after a breach of contract may properly be used to calculate resale damages under Section 2–706 of the Uniform Commercial Code, where goods originally identified to the broken contract were sold on the day following the breach. Defendants The Belcher Company of New York, Inc. and Belcher New Jersey, Inc. (together "Belcher") appeal from a judgment, entered after a jury trial before Judge McLaughlin, awarding plaintiff Apex Oil Company ("Apex") $432,365.04 in damages for breach of contract and fraud in connection with an uncompleted transaction for heating oil. Belcher claims that the district court improperly allowed Apex to recover resale damages and that Apex failed to prove its fraud claim by clear and convincing evidence. We agree and reverse.

### BACKGROUND

Apex buys, sells, refines and transports petroleum products of various sorts, including No. 2 heating oil, commonly known as home heating oil. Belcher also buys and sells petroleum products, including No. 2 heating oil. In February 1982, both firms were trading futures contracts for No. 2 heating oil on the New York Mercantile Exchange ("Merc"). In particular, both were trading Merc contracts for February 1982 No. 2 heating oil—i.e., contracts for the delivery of that commodity in New York Harbor during that delivery month in accordance with the Merc's rules. As a result of that trading, Apex was short 315 contracts, and Belcher was long by the same amount. Being "short" one contract for oil means that the trader has contracted to deliver one thousand barrels at some point in the future, and being "long" means just the opposite—that the trader has contracted to purchase that amount of oil. If a contract is not liquidated before the close of trading, the short trader must deliver the oil to a long trader (the exchange matches shorts with longs) in strict compliance with Merc rules or suffer stiff penalties, including disciplinary proceedings and fines. A short trader may, however, meet its obligations by entering into an "exchange for physicals" ("EFP") transaction with a long trader. An EFP allows a short trader to substitute for the delivery of oil under the terms of a futures contract the delivery of oil at a different place and time.

Apex was matched with Belcher by the Merc, and thus became bound to produce 315,000 barrels of No. 2 heating oil meeting Merc specifications in New York Harbor. Those specifications required that oil delivered in

New York Harbor have a sulfur content no higher than 0.20%. Apex asked Belcher whether Belcher would take delivery of 190,000 barrels of oil in Boston Harbor in satisfaction of 190 contracts, and Belcher agreed. At trial, the parties did not dispute that, under this EFP, Apex promised it would deliver the No. 2 heating oil for the same price as that in the original contract—89.70 cents per gallon—and that the oil would be lifted from the vessel Bordeaux. The parties did dispute, and vigorously so, the requisite maximum sulfur content. At trial, Belcher sought to prove that the oil had to meet the New York standard of 0.20%, while Apex asserted that the oil had to meet only the specifications for Boston Harbor of not more than 0.30% sulfur.

The Bordeaux arrived in Boston Harbor on February 9, 1982, and on the next day began discharging its cargo of No. 2 heating oil at Belcher New England, Inc.'s terminal in Revere, Massachusetts. Later in the evening of February 10, after fifty or sixty thousand barrels had been offloaded, an independent petroleum inspector told Belcher that tests showed the oil on board the Bordeaux contained 0.28% sulfur, in excess of the New York Harbor specification. Belcher, nevertheless continued to lift oil from the ship until eleven o'clock the next morning, February 11, when 141,535 barrels had been pumped into Belcher's terminal. After pumping had stopped, a second test indicated that the oil contained 0.22% sulfur—a figure within the accepted range of tolerance for oil containing 0.20% sulfur. (Apex did not learn of the second test until shortly before trial.) Nevertheless, Belcher refused to resume pumping, claiming that the oil did not conform to specifications.

After Belcher ordered the Bordeaux to leave its terminal, Apex immediately contacted Cities Service. Apex was scheduled to deliver heating oil to Cities Service later in the month and accordingly asked if it could satisfy that obligation by immediately delivering the oil on the Bordeaux. Cities Service agreed, and that oil was delivered to Cities Service in Boston Harbor on February 12, one day after the oil had been rejected by Belcher. Apex did not give notice to Belcher that the oil had been delivered to Cities Service.

Meanwhile, Belcher and Apex continued to quarrel over the portion of the oil delivered by the Bordeaux. Belcher repeatedly informed Apex, orally and by telex, that the oil was unsuitable and would have to be sold at a loss because of its high sulfur content. Belcher also claimed, falsely, that it was incurring various expenses because the oil was unusable. In fact, however, Belcher had already sold the oil in the ordinary course of business. Belcher nevertheless refused to pay Apex the contract price of $5,322,200.27 for the oil it had accepted, and it demanded that Apex produce the remaining 48,000 barrels of oil owing under the contract. On February 17, Apex agreed to tender the 48,000 barrels if Belcher would both make partial payment for the oil actually accepted and agree to negotiate as to the price ultimately to be paid for that oil. Belcher agreed and sent Apex a check for $5,034,997.12, a sum reflecting a discount of five cents per gallon from the contract price. However, the check contained an endorsement stating that "[t]he acceptance and negotiation of this check constitutes full payment and final settlement of all claims" against Belcher. Apex refused the check, and the parties returned to square one. Apex demanded full payment; Belcher demanded that Apex either negotiate the check or remove the discharged oil (which had actually been sold) and replace it with 190,000 barrels of conforming product. Apex chose to take the oil and replace it, and on February 23 told Belcher that the 142,000 barrels of discharged oil would be removed on board the Mersault on February 25.

By then, however, Belcher had sold the 142,000 barrels and did not have an equivalent amount of No. 2 oil in its entire Boston terminal. Instead of admitting that it did not have the oil, Belcher told Apex that a dock for the Mersault was unavailable. Belcher also demanded that Apex either remove the oil *and* pay terminalling and storage fees, or accept payment for the oil at a discount of five cents per gallon. Apex refused to do either. On the next day, Belcher and Apex finally reached a settlement under which Belcher agreed to pay for the oil discharged from the Bordeaux at a discount of 2.5 cents per gallon. The settlement agreement also resolved an unrelated dispute between an Apex subsidiary and a subsidiary of Belcher's parent firm, The Coastal Corporation. It is this agreement that Apex now claims was procured by fraud.

After the settlement, Apex repeatedly contacted Belcher to ascertain when, where and how Belcher would accept delivery of the remaining 48,000 barrels. On March 5, Belcher informed Apex that it considered its obligations under the original contract to have been extinguished, and that it did not "desire to purchase such a volume [the 48,000 barrels] at the offered price." Apex responded by claiming that the settlement did not extinguish Belcher's obligation to accept the 48,000 barrels. In addition, Apex stated that unless Belcher accepted the oil by March 20, Apex would identify 48,000 barrels of No. 2 oil to the breached contract and sell the oil to a third party. When Belcher again refused to take the oil, Apex sold 48,000 barrels to Gill & Duffus Company. This oil was sold for delivery in April at a price of 76.25 cents per gallon, 13.45 cents per gallon below the Belcher contract price.

On October 7, 1982, Apex brought this suit in the Eastern District, asserting breach of contract and fraud. The breach-of-contract claim in Apex's amended complaint contended that Belcher had breached the EFP, not in February, but in March, when Belcher had refused to take delivery of the 48,000 barrels still owing under the contract. The amended complaint further alleged that "[a]t the time of the breach of the Contract by Belcher the market price of the product was $.7625 per gallon," the price brought by the resale to Gill & Duffus on March 23. ... In turn, the fraud claim asserted that Belcher had made various misrepresentations—that the Bordeaux oil was unfit, and unusable by Belcher; and that consequently Belcher was suffering extensive damages and wanted the oil removed—upon which Apex had relied when it had agreed to settle as to the 142,000 barrels lifted from the Bordeaux. Apex asserted that as a result of the alleged fraud it had suffered damages of 2.5 cents per gallon, the discount agreed upon in the settlement.

The case went to trial before Judge McLaughlin and a jury between February 3 and February 13, 1986. As it had alleged in its pleadings, Apex asserted that its breach-of-contract claim was based on an alleged breach occurring *after* February 11, 1982, the day Belcher rejected the oil on board the Bordeaux. Judge McLaughlin, however, rejected this theory as a matter of law. His view of the case was that Belcher's rejection of the Bordeaux oil occurred under one of two circumstances: (I) either the oil conformed to the proper sulfur specification, in which case Belcher breached; or (ii) the oil did not conform, in which case Apex breached. Judge McLaughlin reasoned that, if Belcher breached on February 11, then it could not have breached thereafter. If on the other hand Apex breached, then, Judge McLaughlin reasoned, only under the doctrine of cure, see N.Y.U.C.C. § 2–508 (McKinney 1964), could Belcher be deemed to have breached. Apex, however, waived the cure theory by expressly disavowing it (perhaps because it presumes a breach by Apex). Instead, Apex argued that, regardless of whether the Bordeaux oil had conformed, Belcher's refusal throughout February and March 1982 to accept delivery of 48,000 barrels of conforming oil, which Belcher was then still demanding, had constituted a breach of contract. Judge McLaughlin rejected this argument, which he viewed as simply "an attempt to reintroduce the cure doctrine."

In a general verdict, the jury awarded Apex $283,752.94 on the breach-of-contract claim, and $148,612.10 on the fraud claim, for a total of $432,365.04. With the addition of prejudgment interest, the judgment came to $588,566.29.

Belcher appeals from this verdict. Apex has not taken a cross-appeal from Judge McLaughlin's dismissal of its post-February 11 breach theories, however. The parties agree, therefore, that as the case comes to us, the verdict concerning the breach can be upheld only on the theory that, if Belcher breached the contract, it did so only on February 11, 1982, and that the oil sold to Gill & Duffus on March 23 was identified to the broken contract.

## DISCUSSION

\* \* \*

Belcher's principal argument on appeal is that the district court erred as a matter of law in allowing Apex to recover resale damages under Section 2–706. Specifically, Belcher contends that the heating oil Apex sold to Gill & Duffus in late March of 1982 was not identified to the broken contract. According to Belcher, the oil identified to the contract was the oil aboard the Bordeaux—oil which Apex had sold to Cities Service on the day after the breach. In response, Apex argues that, because heating oil is a fungible commodity, the oil sold to Gill & Duffus was "reasonably identified" to the contract even though it was not the same oil that had been on board the Bordeaux. We agree with Apex that, at least with respect to fungible goods, identification for the purposes of a resale transaction does not necessarily require that the resold goods be the exact goods that were rejected or repudiated. Nonetheless, we conclude that as a matter of law the oil sold to Gill & Duffus in March was not reasonably identified to the contract breached on February 11, and that the resale was not commercially reasonable.

Resolving the instant dispute requires us to survey various provisions of the Uniform Commercial Code. ... The Bordeaux oil was unquestionably identified to the contract under Section 2–501(b), and Apex does not assert otherwise. Nevertheless, Apex argues that Section 2–501 "has no application in the context of the Section 2–706 resale remedy," because Section 2–501 defines identification only for the purpose of establishing the point at which a buyer "obtains a special property and an insurable interest in goods." N.Y.U.C.C. § 2–501. This argument has a facial plausibility but ignores Section 2–103, which contains various definitions, and an index of other definitions, of terms used throughout Article 2 of the Code. With regard to "[i]dentification," Section 2–103(2) provides that the "definition[] applying to *this Article*" is set forth in Section 2–501. Id. § 2–103 (emphasis added).

Section 2–501 thus informs us that the Bordeaux oil was identified to the contract. It does not end our inquiry, however, because it does not exclude as a matter of law the possibility that a seller may identify goods to a contract, but then substitute, for the identified goods, *identical* goods that are then identified to the contract. ... Belcher relies upon Section 2–706's statement that "the seller may resell the *goods concerned*," N.Y.U.C.C. § 2–706(1) (emphasis added), and upon Section 2–704, which states that "[a]n aggrieved seller ... may ... identify to the contract conforming goods *not already identified* if at the time he learned of the breach they are in his possession or control." Id. § 2–704(1) (emphasis added). According to Belcher, these statements absolutely foreclose the possibility of reidentification for the purpose of a resale. Apex, on the other hand, points to Section 2–706's statement that "it is not necessary that the goods be in existence or that any or all of them have been identified to the contract before the breach." Id. § 2–706(2). According to Apex, this language shows that "[t]he relevant inquiry to be made under Section 2–706 is whether the resale transaction is reasonably identified to the breached contract and not whether the goods resold were originally identified to that contract." Apex Br. at 25.

None of the cited provisions are dispositive. First, Section 2–706(1)'s reference to reselling "the goods concerned" is unhelpful because those goods are the goods identified to the contract, but which goods are so identified is the question to be answered in the instant case. Second, as to Section 2–704, the fact that an aggrieved seller may identify goods "not already identified" does not mean that the seller may not identify goods as substitutes for previously identified goods. Rather, Section 2–704 appears to deal simply with the situation described in Section 2–706(2) above, where the goods are not yet in existence or have not yet been identified to the contract. Belcher thus can draw no comfort from either Section 2–704 or Section 2–706(1). Third, at the same time, however, Section 2–706(2)'s reference to nonexistent and nonidentified goods does not mean, as Apex suggests, that the original (prebreach) identification of goods is wholly irrelevant. Rather, the provision regarding nonexistent and nonidentified goods deals with the special circumstances involving anticipatory repudiation by the buyer. See N.Y.U.C.C § 2–706 comment 7. Under such circumstances, there can of course be no resale remedy unless the seller is allowed to identify goods to the contract after the breach. That is obviously not the case here.

\* \* \*

[F]ungible goods resold pursuant to § 2–706 must be goods identified to the contract, but need not always be those *originally* identified to the contract. In other words, at least where fungible goods are concerned, identification is not always an irrevocable act and does not foreclose the possibility of substitution. ... Nevertheless, as [§ 2–706] expressly states, "[t]he resale must be *reasonably* identified as referring to the broken contract," and "every aspect of the sale including the method, manner, time, place and terms must be commercially reasonable." Moreover, because the purpose of remedies under the Code is to put "the aggrieved party ... in as good a position as if the other party had performed," id. § 1–106(1), the reasonableness of the identification and of the resale must be determined by examining whether the market value of, and the price received for, the resold goods "accurately reflects the market value of the goods which are the subject of the contract." Servbest [Foods, Inc. v. Emessee Industries, Inc., 82 Ill. App. 3d 662,] 671, [403 N.E.2d 1], 8.

\* \* \*

Apex's delay of nearly six weeks between the breach on February 11, 1982 and the purported resale on March 23 was clearly unreasonable, even if the transfer to Cities Service had not occurred. Steven Wirkus, of Apex, testified on cross-examination that the market price for No. 2 heating oil on February 12, when the Bordeaux oil was delivered to Cities Service, was "[p]robably somewhere around 88 cents a gallon or 87." (The EFP contract price, of course, was 89.70 cents per gallon.) Wirkus also testified on redirect examination that the market price fluctuated throughout the next several weeks:

> Q.  Sir, while you couldn't remember with particularity what the price of oil was on a given day four years ago, is it fair to say that prices went up and down?
>
> A.  Definitely that's fair to say.
>
> Q.  From day-to-day?
>
> A.  Yes.
>
> Q.  Towards the end of February prices went down?
>
> A.  That's correct.

Q.  Then in early March it went back up?

A.  In early March, yes.

Q.  Then they went back down again towards the middle of March; isn't that correct?

MR. GILBERT: I object to the form of this, your Honor, on redirect.

THE COURT: Yes.

Q.  Did they go back down in mid March, Mr. Wirkus?

A.  My recollection, yes.

Q.  In late March what happened to the price?

A.  Market went back up.

Moreover, Wirkus testified that, on March 23, in a transaction unrelated to the resale, Apex purchased 25,000 barrels of No. 2 oil for March delivery at 80.50 cents per gallon, and sold an equivalent amount for April delivery at 77.25 cents per gallon. Other sales on March 22 and 23 for April delivery brought similar prices: 100,000 barrels were sold at 76.85 cents, and 25,000 barrels at 76.35 cents. The Gill & Duffus resale, which was also for April delivery, fetched a price of 76.25 cents per gallon—some eleven or twelve cents below the market price on the day of the breach.

In view of the long delay and the apparent volatility of the market for No. 2 oil, the purported resale failed to meet the requirements of Section 2–706 as a matter of law. . . .

. . . Apex's only asserted justification, which the district court accepted in denying Belcher's motion for judgment notwithstanding the verdict, was that the delay was caused by continuing negotiations with Belcher. We find that ruling to be inconsistent with the district court's view that Belcher's breach, if any, occurred on February 11. The function of a resale was to put Apex in the position it would have been on that date by determining the value of the oil Belcher refused. The value of the oil at a later date is irrelevant because Apex was in no way obligated by the contract or by the Uniform Commercial Code to reserve 48,000 gallons for Belcher after the February 11 breach. Indeed, that is why Apex's original theory, rejected by the district court and not before us on this appeal, was that the breach occurred in March.

The rule that a "resale should be made as soon as practicable after . . . breach," . . . should be stringently applied where, as here, the resold goods are not those originally identified to the contract. In such circumstances, of course, there is a significant risk that the seller, who may perhaps have already disposed of the original goods without suffering any loss, has identified new goods for resale in order to minimize the resale price and thus to maximize damages. That was not the case in Servbest, for example, where the resale consisted of the first sales made after the breach. See 82 Ill. App. 3d at 675, 403 N.E.2d at 11. Here, by contrast, the oil originally identified to the contract was sold the day after the February 11, 1982 breach, and no doubt Apex sold ample amounts thereafter in the six weeks before the purported resale. . . . Because the sale of the oil identified to the contract to Cities Service on the next day fixed the value of the goods refused as a matter of law, the judgment on the breach-of-contract claim must be reversed.

We turn finally to Apex's fraud claim. . . . Belcher claims that the evidence was insufficient to support the jury's finding that Apex, in agreeing to the settlement with Belcher, had relied upon Belcher's misrepresentations in ignorance of their falsity and had suffered injury accordingly.

In support of the finding of reliance, Apex relies primarily, if not exclusively, upon the testimony of its president, Anthony Novelly. Novelly testified that he had delegated the task of negotiation to in-house counsel, Harold Lessner. Lessner nevertheless kept Novelly abreast of Belcher's various demands and representations because it was Novelly, as president, "who had to approve the settlement ultimately." To this effect, Novelly testified as follows:

Q.  During your discussion with Mr. Lesner [sic], did he say anything to you concerning whether Belcher had used the oil?

A.  No, he said the oil was off spec and not useable.

Q.  He said that is what Belcher had told him?

A.  Correct.

Q.  During your conversation with Mr. Lesner [sic], did he tell you anything about whether Belcher was claiming damages, as a result of the delivery?

A.  Yes, they were.

Q.  And did you rely on all the matters that were conveyed to you in approving the settlement?

A.  Yes, I did.

According to Apex, this testimony regarding its alleged reliance is "unrebutted." That may be true so far as other witnesses are concerned, but Novelly candidly modified his testimony on cross-examination as follows:

Q.  At the time you approved the settlement, one of the terms was that Belcher was going to get a discount off the agreed price for the BORDEAUX oil of two and a half cents per gallon, is that correct?

A.  Yes.

Q.  Did you believe they were intitled [sic] to a two and a half cent per gallon discount based on the facts you know?

MR. WEINER: Objection.

THE COURT: Overruled.

A.  Not really.

Q.  You did not believe that?

A.  No.

Q.  Did you believe they were intitled [sic] to any discount?

A.  I wouldn't have thought so.

Q.  You agreed to the settlement for other reasons, did you not?

A.  I agreed to the settlement to get the thing settled.

Q.  You wanted to get it behind you, is that correct?

A.  Yes.

Q.  You had a number of items?

A.  Whole bunch of them.

Q.  You didn't like to leave all these open items?

A.  I didn't want a mess hanging around.

Q.  You wanted to get everything cleaned up?

A.  That's correct.

Q.  You had another idea—withdrawn. You had another motivation, didn't you sir?

A.  Coastal [Belcher's parent] was a big company, I don't like to have problems with big companies. I try to settle things and avoid litigation.

Q.  You want to get all the open items closed, for you to do business with Coastal and its subsidiaries, is that correct?

A.  That is a good statement, yes.

\* \* \*

Q.  At the time you were discussing the settlement with Mr. Lesner [sic] or anybody else you talked about it with, did you have the belief that the oil delivered to Belcher aboard the BORDEAUX was in fact not useable by Belcher?

A.  I never had that belief, no.

However much this display of refreshing candor ought to be rewarded, we must conclude that, in light of the concessions that Novelly was seeking a compromise of all outstanding disputes and did not believe Belcher's misrepresentations as to the oil delivered on February 11, a reasonable jury could not find by clear and convincing evidence that Apex believed and relied upon Belcher's misrepresentations.

Reversed.

NOTES

(1) **Commodities Futures.** This case illustrates how products may be traded through "exchanges" that permit buyers and sellers to anticipate future deliveries of certain standardized products. Many participants in these futures markets have no expectation of either delivering or receiving goods under their contracts; before the closing date, these traders take

offsetting buy-sell positions so that no performance occurs. These participants may be investors seeking profits from changes in market prices of the commodities or merchants "hedging" planned transactions against shifts in market prices. The buyer and seller in *Apex Oil* did not close out their positions and were "matched" by the N.Y. Mercantile Exchange as seller and buyer. Once "matched" the parties became obligated as if they had chosen to contract with each other. Thereafter, they negotiated a modification of the place of performance for part of the oil.

**(2) Construction of UCC 2–706 and 2–708.** Seller's counsel sought unsuccessfully to fix damages under UCC 2–706 by the March 23 sale to Gill & Duffus. Why was that claim denied? When a seller claims but fails to qualify for relief under 2–706, may recovery be had under UCC 2–708(1)? Under 2–708(2)? See Comment 2 to UCC 2–706. See also Annot., Resale of Goods Under UCC 2–706, 101 A.L.R.5th 563 (2004).

Should counsel for a seller-plaintiff draft the initial pleading as a claim for damages under all possible statutory provisions in the alternative? Should counsel introduce evidence on each of the alternative claims?

The segment of the opinion dealing with damages was omitted in *T.W. Oil v. Consolidated Edison*, which we read in the previous section. In that case, the buyer rightfully rejected the initial delivery of oil from the *Khamsin* but wrongfully rejected the substitute delivery of the *Appollonian* oil. The trial judge measured seller's damages as the difference between the contract price and the proceeds of resale of the *Khamsin* oil more than two months after wrongful rejection of the *Appollonian* oil.[1] Was this an appropriate application of UCC 2–706? The Court of Appeals declined to entertain appeal on the issue of damages because the issue had not be properly presented to the appellate court.[2]

**Problem 1.** Suppose seller in *Apex* had sought damages measured by UCC 2–708(1). Buyer countered that seller's damages should be measured, under UCC 2–706, by the price of the resale to Cities Service. Is there any statutory basis for an argument that seller may not recover a larger amount under 2–708(1) than it would be entitled to receive if damages were measured by 2–706? See J. Sebert, Remedies Under Article Two of the

---

1. Joc Oil USA, Inc. v. Consolidated Edison Co., 107 Misc.2d 376, 434 N.Y.S.2d 623 (1980).

2. "As to the damages issue raised by the defendant, we affirm without reaching the merits. At no stage of the proceedings before the trial court did the defendant object to the plaintiff's proposed method for their calculation, and this though the plaintiff gave ample notice of that proposal by means of a preliminary statement and pretrial memorandum filed with the court. So complete was defendant's acquiescence in the theory thus advanced that the plaintiff was permitted to introduce its proof of the *Khamsin* resale alone, and without opposition. Furthermore, in consensually submitting the four jointly framed advisory questions that went to the jury, the language of one of them, which was damages-related, indicates that both parties were acting on the assumption that the *Khamsin* oil was the one with which the court was to be concerned. And, even after the decision at nisi prius revealed that the Judge had acted on such an assumption, so far as the record shows, no motion was ever made to correct it." 57 N.Y.2d 587.

Uniform Commercial Code: An Agenda for Review, 130 U. Pa. L. Rev. 360, 380–383 (1981).

## R.E. Davis Chemical Corp. v. Diasonics, Inc.

United States Court of Appeals, Seventh Circuit, 1987.
826 F.2d 678.

■ CUDAHY, CIRCUIT JUDGE.

Diasonics, Inc. appeals from the orders of the district court denying its motion for summary judgment and granting R.E. Davis Chemical Corp.'s summary judgment motion. . . . We . . . reverse the grant of summary judgment in favor of Davis and remand for further proceedings.

### I.

Diasonics is a California corporation engaged in the business of manufacturing and selling medical diagnostic equipment. Davis is an Illinois corporation that contracted to purchase a piece of medical diagnostic equipment from Diasonics. On or about February 23, 1984, Davis and Diasonics entered into a written contract under which Davis agreed to purchase to equipment. Pursuant to this agreement, Davis paid Diasonics a $300,000 deposit on February 29, 1984. . . . Davis . . . [subsequently] refused to take delivery of the equipment or to pay the balance due under the agreement. Diasonics later resold the equipment to a third party for the same price at which it was to be sold to Davis.

Davis sued Diasonics, asking for restitution of its $300,000 down payment under section 2–718(2) of the Uniform Commercial Code (the "UCC" or the "Code"). Ill. Rev. Stat. ch. 26, para. 2–718(2) (1985). Diasonics counterclaimed. Diasonics did not deny that Davis was entitled to recover its $300,000 deposit less $500 as provided in section 2–718(2)(b). However, Diasonics claimed that it was entitled to an offset under section 2–718(3). Diasonics alleged that it was a "lost volume seller," and, as such, it lost the profit from one sale when Davis breached its contract. Diasonics' position was that, in order to be put in as good a position as it would have been in had Davis performed, it was entitled to recover its lost profit on its contract with Davis under section 2–708(2) of the UCC. Ill. Rev. Stat. ch. 26, para. 2–708(2) (1985). . . .

The district court . . . entered summary judgment for Davis. The court held that lost volume sellers were not entitled to recover damages under 2–708(2) but rather were limited to recovering the difference between the resale price and the contract price along with incidental damages under section 2–706(1). Ill. Rev. Stat. ch. 26, para. 2–706(1) (1985). . . . Davis was awarded $322,656, which represented Davis' down payment plus prejudgment interest less Diasonics' incidental damages. Diasonics appeals the district court's decision respecting its measure of damages as well as the dismissal of its third-party complaint.

### II.

We consider first Diasonics' claim that the district court erred in holding that Diasonics was limited to the measure of damages provided in 2–706 and could not recover lost profits as a lost volume seller under 2–708(2). Surprisingly, given its importance, this issue has never been addressed by an Illinois court, nor, apparently, by any other court construing Illinois Supreme Court would resolve this issue if it were presented to it. Courts applying the laws of other states have unanimously adopted the position that a lost volume seller can recover its lost profits under 2–708(2). Contrary to the result reached by the district court, we conclude that the Illinois Supreme Court would follow these other cases and would allow a lost volume seller to recover its lost profit under 2–708(2).

We begin our analysis with 2–718(2) and (3). Under 2–718(2)(b), Davis is entitled to the return of its down payment less $500. Davis' right to restitution, however, is qualified under 2–718(3)(a) to the extent that Diasonics can establish a right to recover damages under any other provision of Article 2 of the UCC. Article 2 contains four provisions that concern the recovery of a seller's general damages (as opposed to its incidental or consequential damages); 2–706 (contract price less resale price); 2–708(1) (contract price less market price); 2–708(2) (profit); and 2–709 (price). The problem we face here is determining whether Diasonics' damages should be measured under 2–706 or 2–708(2). To answer this question, we need to engage in a detailed look at the language and structure of these various damage provisions.

The Code does not provide a great deal of guidance as to when a particular damage remedy is appropriate. The damage remedies provided under the Code are catalogued in section 2–703, but this section does not indicate that there is any hierarchy among the remedies. One method of approaching the damage sections is to conclude that 2–708 is relegated to a role inferior to that of 2–706 and 2–709 and that one can turn to 2–708 only after one has concluded that neither 2–706 nor 2–709 is applicable.[6] Under

---

**6.** Evidence to support this approach can be found in the language of the various damage sections and of the official comments to the UCC. See § 2–709(3) ("a seller who is held not entitled to the price under this Section shall nevertheless be awarded damages for non-acceptance under the preceding section [§ 2–708]"); UCC comment 7 to § 2–709 ("if the action for the price fails, the seller may nonetheless have proved a case entitling him to damages for non-acceptance [under § 2–708]"); UCC comment 2 to § 2–706 ("failure to act properly under this section deprives the seller of the measure of damages here provided and relegates him to that provided in Section 2–708"); UCC comment 1 to § 2–704 (describes § 2–706 as the "primary remedy" available to a seller upon breach by the buyer); see also Commonwealth Edison Co. v. Decker Coal Co., 653 F. Supp. 841, 844 (N.D.Ill.1987) (statutory language and case law suggest that "§ 2–708 remedies are available only to a seller who is not entitled to the contract price" under § 2–709); Childres & Burgess, Seller's Remedies: The Primacy of UCC 2–708(2), 48 N.Y.U. L. Rev. 833, 863–64 (1973). As one commentator has noted, 2–706 "is the Code section drafted specifically to define the damage rights of aggrieved reselling sellers, and there is no suggestion within it that the profit formula of section 2–708(2) is in any way intended to qualify or be superior to it." Shanker, The Case for a Literal Reading of UCC Section 2–708(2) (One Profit for the Reseller), 24 Case W. Res. 697, 699 (1973).

this interpretation of the relationship between 2–706 and 2–708, if the goods have been resold, the seller can sue to recover damages measured by the difference between the contract price and the resale price under 2–706. The seller can turn to 2–708 only if it resells in a commercially unreasonable manner or if it cannot resell but an action for the price is inappropriate under 2–709. The district court adopted this reading of the Code's damage remedies and, accordingly, limited Diasonics to the measure of damages provided in 2–706 because it resold the equipment in a commercially reasonable manner.

The district court's interpretation of 2–706 and 2–708, however, creates its own problems of statutory construction. There is some suggestion in the Code that the "fact that plaintiff resold the goods [in a commercially reasonable manner] does *not* compel him to use the resale remedy of § 2–706 rather than the damage remedy of § 2–708." Harris, A Radical Restatement of the Law of Seller's Damages: Sales Act and Commercial Code Results Compared, 18 Stan. L. Rev. 66, 101 n.174 (1965) (emphasis in original). Official comment 1 to 2–703, which catalogues the remedies available to a seller, states that these "remedies are essentially cumulative in nature" and that "whether the pursuit of one remedy bars another depends entirely on the facts of the individual case." See also State of New York Report of the Law Revision Comm'n for 1956, 396–97 (1956).[7]

Those courts that found that a lost volume seller can recover its lost profits under 2–708(2) implicitly rejected the position adopted by the district court; those courts started with the assumption that 2–708 applied to a lost volume seller without considering whether the seller was limited to the remedy provided under 2–706. None of those courts even suggested that a seller who resold goods in a commercially reasonable manner was limited to the damage formula provided under 2–706. We conclude that the Illinois Supreme Court, if presented with this question, would adopt the position of these other jurisdictions and would conclude that a reselling seller, such as Diasonics, is free to reject the damage formula prescribed in 2–706 and choose to proceed under 2–708.

---

**7.** UCC comment 2 to 2–708(2) also suggests that 2–708 has broader applicability than suggested by the district court. UCC comment 2 provides: "This section permits the recovery of lost profits in all appropriate cases, which would include all standard priced goods. The normal measure there would be list price less cost to the dealer or list price less manufacturing cost to the manufacturer."

The district court's restrictive interpretation of 2–708(2) was based in part on UCC comment 1 to 2–704 which describes 2–706 as the aggrieved seller's primary remedy. The district court concluded that, if a lost volume seller could recover its lost profit under 2–708(2), every seller would attempt to recover damages under 2–708(2) and 2–706 would become the aggrieved seller's residuary remedy. This argument ignores the fact that to recover under 2–708(2), a seller must first establish its status as a lost volume seller. . . .

The district court also concluded that a lost volume seller cannot recover its lost profit under 2–708(2) because such a result would negate a seller's duty to mitigate damages. This position fails to recognize the fact that, by definition, a lost volume seller cannot mitigate damages through resale. Resale does not reduce a lost volume seller's damages because the breach has still resulted in its losing one sale and a corresponding profit. . . .

Concluding that Diasonics is entitled to seek damages under 2–708, however, does not automatically result in Diasonics being awarded its lost profit. Two different measures of damages are provided in 2–708. Subsection 2–708(1) provides for a measure of damages calculated by subtracting the market price at the time and place for tender from the contract price.[9] The profit measure of damages, for which Diasonics is asking, is contained in 2–708(2). However, one applies 2–708(2) only if "the measure of damages provided in subsection (1) is inadequate to put the seller in as good a position as performance would have done...." Ill. Rev. Stat. ch. 26, para. 2–708(2) (1985). Diasonics claims that 2–708(1) does not provide an adequate measure of damages when the seller is a lost volume seller. To understand Diasonics' argument, we need to define the concept of the lost volume seller. Those cases that have addressed this issue have defined a lost volume seller as one that has a predictable and finite number of customers and that has the capacity either to sell to all new buyers or to make the one additional sale represented by the resale after the breach. According to a number of courts and commentators, if the seller would have made the sale represented by the resale whether or not the breach occurred, damages measured by the difference between the contract price and market price cannot put the lost volume seller in as good a position as it would have been in had the buyer performed. The breach effectively cost the seller a "profit," and the seller can only be made whole by awarding it damages in the amount of its "lost profit" under 2–708(2).

We agree with Diasonics' position that, under some circumstances, the measure of damages provided under 2–708(1) will not put a reselling seller in as good a position as it would have been in had the buyer performed because the breach resulted in the seller losing sales volume. However, we disagree with the definition of "lost volume seller" adopted by other courts. Courts awarding lost profits to a lost volume seller have focused on whether the seller had the capacity to supply the breached units in addition to what it actually sold. In reality, however, the relevant questions include, not only whether the seller could have produced the breached units in addition to its actual volume, but also whether it would have been profitable for the seller to produce both units. Goetz & Scott, Measuring Sellers' Damages: The Lost–Profits Puzzle, 31 Stan. L. Rev. 323, 332–33, 346–47 (1979). As one commentator has noted, under the economic law of diminishing returns or increasing marginal costs[,] ... as a seller's volume increases, then a point will inevitably be reached where the cost of selling each additional item diminishes the incremental return to the seller and eventually makes it entirely unprofitable to conclude the next sale. Shank-

---

**9.** There is some debate in the commentaries about whether a seller who has resold the goods may ignore the measure of damages provided in 2–706 and elect to proceed under 2–708(1). Under some circumstances the contract-market price differential will result in overcompensating such a seller. See J. White & R. Summers, Handbook of the Law under the Uniform Commercial Code § 7–7, at 271–73 (2d ed. 1980); Sebert, Remedies under Article Two of the Uniform Commercial Code: An Agenda for Review, 130 U. Pa. L. Rev. 360, 380–83 (1981). We need not struggle with this question here because Diasonics has not sought to recover damages under 2–708(1).

er, supra, at 705. Thus, under some conditions, awarding a lost volume seller its presumed lost profit will result in overcompensating the seller, and 2–708(2) would not take effect because the damage formula provided in 2–708(1) does place the seller in as good a position as if the buyer had performed. Therefore, on remand, Diasonics must establish, not only that it had the capacity to produce the breached unit in addition to the unit resold, but also that it would have been profitable for it to have produced and sold both. . . .

One final problem with awarding a lost volume seller its lost profits was raised by the district court. This problem stems from the formulation of the measure of damages provided under 2–708(2) which is "the profit (including reasonable overhead) which the seller would have made from full performance by the buyer, together with any incidental damages provided in this Article (Section 2–710), due allowance for costs reasonably incurred and due credit for payments or *proceeds of resale*." Ill. Rev. Stat. ch. 26, para. 2–708(2) (1985) (emphasis added). The literal language of 2–708(2) requires that the proceeds from resale be credited against the amount of damages awarded which, in most cases, would result in the seller recovering nominal damages. In those cases in which the lost volume seller was awarded its lost profit as damages, the courts have circumvented this problem by concluding that this language only applies to proceeds realized from the resale of uncompleted goods for scrap. See, e.g., Neri, 30 N.Y.2d at 399 & n.2, 285 N.E.2d at 314 & n.2; see also J. White & R. Summers, Handbook of the Law under the Uniform Commercial Code § 7–13, at 285 ("courts should simply ignore the 'due credit' language in lost volume cases") (footnote omitted). Although neither the text of 2–708(2) nor the official comments limit its application to resale of goods for scrap, there is evidence that the drafters of 2–708 seemed to have had this more limited application in mind when they proposed amending 2–708 to include the phrase "due credit for payments or proceeds of resale." We conclude that the Illinois Supreme Court would adopt this more restrictive interpretation of this phrase rendering it inapplicable to this case.

We therefore reverse the grant of summary judgment in favor of Davis and remand with instructions that the district court calculate Diasonics' damages under 2–708(2) if Diasonics can establish, not only that it had the capacity to make the sale to Davis as well as the sale to the resale buyer, but also that it would have been profitable for it to make both sales. Of course, Diasonics, in addition, must show that it probably would have made the second sale absent the breach.

\* \* \*

NOTES

**(1) Construction of UCC 2–708(2).** As indicated in the court's opinion, the academic debate about the proper reading of UCC 2–708(2) has been vigorous. Some explanation must be found for the enormous difference in the damages recoverable in a case like *Davis*, under 2–708(2)

($453,000), under 2–706 ($–0–), under 2–708(1) (probably $–0–). The remarkably laconic Comment to 2–708(2) gives no indication of appreciating the sheer force of this section. Much of the academic debate is in the mode of law-and-economics analysis, based upon models of "lost volume" sellers. Others argue that the basic remedial principle requires putting an aggrieved seller into as good a position as buyer's performance would have done, UCC 1–106, and that market-based damages under 2–706 and 2–708(1) fail to mirror full performance.

Although the UCC 2–708 Comments state that the section is a rewriting of a provision in the Uniform Sales Act, that act had no provision comparable to UCC 2–708(2). The cited section, USA 64, provided generally for recovery of loss resulting in the ordinary course of events from buyer's breach (USA 64(2)) and stated the specific formula of market-based damages in USA 64(3); it added in USA 64(4):

> (4) If, while labor or expense of material amount are necessary on the part of the seller to enable him to fulfill his obligations under the contract to sell or the sale, the buyer repudiates the contract or the sale, or notifies the seller to proceed no further therewith, the buyer shall be liable to the seller for no greater damages than the seller would have suffered if he did nothing towards carrying out the contract or the sale after receiving notice of the buyer's repudiation or countermand. The profit the seller would have made if the contract or the sale had been fully performed shall be considered in estimating such damages.

The Commercial Code revised the USA 64(4) allocation of risk if a manufacturing seller elects, upon repudiation, to complete the process. UCC 2–704(2). The manufacturer who exercises reasonable commercial judgment for the purposes of avoiding loss and "effective realization" is protected even if the value added thereby is less than the costs incurred.

Is it accurate to describe UCC 2–708 as a rewriting of USA 64?

**(2) Subsequent Decision.** On remand, Diasonics proved its average costs of manufacturing through expert testimony by accountants. It introduced evidence that the contract price was $1,500,000 but offered no specific evidence of the cost of manufacturing the equipment intended for Davis and resold to the third party. Using average cost data, the district court found that Diasonics profit would have been $453,000. The court of appeals affirmed. 924 F.2d 709 (7th Cir.1991).

# The Colonel's Inc. v. Cincinnati Milacron Marketing Co.

United States Court of Appeals, Sixth Circuit, 1998.
149 F.3d 1182.

■ NORRIS, CIRCUIT JUDGE.

This dispute arises out of a transaction involving the sale of equipment between plaintiff The Colonel's Inc., a Michigan corporation, and defendant Cincinnati Milacron Marketing Company, an Ohio corporation. Plaintiff appeals the district court's grant of summary judgment to defendant on both plaintiff's breach of contract claim and defendant's counterclaim. Defendant cross-appeals the district court's damages calculation and its denial of attorney fees, costs, and interest. We affirm.

## I.

Plaintiff and defendant entered into a written contract under which plaintiff agreed to purchase two plastic injection molding machines to assist in the production of automobile replacement parts (hereinafter "Machine 1" and "Machine 2"). Machine 1 was a typical plastic injection molding machine, but Machine 2 was uniquely configured. To be usable where it would be placed in plaintiff's plant, the operator's controls were located opposite and ten feet higher than where defendant usually placed them. Machine 2 was the only machine defendant ever manufactured with this configuration. Both machines were designed to have 140.2 inches of "daylight," the opening necessary to allow molds to be inserted and finished parts removed. Plaintiff contracted to purchase each machine for $1,290,871. Delivery of Machine 1 was scheduled for December 1993, and Machine 2 was to be delivered the following February. Plaintiff made an advance payment on each machine.

After receiving shipment of Machine 1, plaintiff discovered that because 140.2 inches of daylight was not available when the machine's ejector box was in place, the machine would not open far enough to accommodate fabrication of the company's largest automobile parts. Accordingly, it rejected Machine 1 and refused to accept Machine 2, claiming that the machines did not conform to the specifications outlined in the sales agreement, and refused to pay the balance due for the two machines. Plaintiff then sued defendant in Michigan state court, seeking two machines that conformed with their specifications. Defendant removed the case to federal court based upon diversity of citizenship.

Defendant notified its sales personnel that it had a configured injection molding machine and to offer Machine 2 to their customers. Because the machine was uniquely designed for plaintiff, it was difficult to market. After efforts to resell Machine 2 failed, defendant filed a counterclaim for the contract price. The parties settled their dispute over Machine 1. Defendant ultimately rebuilt Machine 2 for an existing customer, selling it for more than plaintiff's contract price.

Defendant moved for summary judgment on plaintiff's complaint for specific performance, arguing that the parol evidence rule barred any extrinsic evidence that the two machines did not conform to the parties' agreement. The district court agreed and dismissed plaintiff's claims.

Defendant then sought summary judgment on its counterclaim, arguing that the earlier summary judgment removed any defense plaintiff could raise regarding its right to reject the machines. The district court once again granted summary judgment in favor of defendant. The district court then concluded that because defendant had resold Machine 2 for more than it had bargained for with plaintiff, even after allowing for the additional costs of reconfiguration, it was owed no damages. The court later awarded defendant pre-judgment interest and denied attorney fees.

Leaving no stone unturned, the parties appeal each adverse ruling by the district court.

## II.

The first two issues on appeal concern the summary judgments dismissing plaintiff's breach of contract claim and finding plaintiff liable on defendant's counterclaim for breach of contract. We review the district court's grant of summary judgment de novo. ... We will affirm the district court if the evidence, viewed in the light most favorable to the non-moving party, shows that no dispute of material fact exists and that the moving party is entitled to judgment as a matter of law. ... We review the district court's interpretation of Ohio law de novo. ...

Plaintiff's breach of contract claim rests upon its contention that the agreement entered into by the parties includes ambiguous language. Plaintiff asserts that it relied upon one of defendant's publications which, in mentioning maximum daylight of 140.2 inches, is unclear as to whether that clearance exists only when the ejector box is not used. In view of that ambiguity, plaintiff argues, the court should have looked to parol evidence, including statements allegedly made by defendant's sales representative, to determine the specifications called for by the parties' agreement. Plaintiff then argues that a reasonable person could conclude that, in light of comments made by defendant's sales representative, the machines were to have 140.2 inches of daylight when the ejector box was in place.

Under Ohio law, when a court determines whether a contract is ambiguous, it is to consider the whole instrument and give the words in the contract their natural and ordinary meaning. ... A contract is ambiguous only if its terms are susceptible to more than one meaning so that reasonable persons may fairly and honestly differ in their construction of the terms. ... A contract is not ambiguous merely because the parties disagree over its meaning. ... While parol evidence may be used to clarify an ambiguous contract, a party cannot use parol evidence to create an ambiguity or to show that an obligation is other than that expressed in the written instrument. ...

The sales agreement provided that defendant would provide two injection molding machines as described in the customer order and the proposal to purchase the machines. The proposal included specifications that point out that the maximum daylight available with an ejector box installed would be 111.6 inches, 140.2 inches with the ejector box left out. Plaintiff's controller, who signed the sales contract, acknowledged that he read all of the pertinent documents and that they were in accordance with what plaintiff intended to order. Because the agreement is clear on its face, parol evidence cannot be used to read into the contract something which it does not say.

Further, parol evidence cannot be used to modify or contradict the unambiguous terms of a written contract purporting to incorporate the whole agreement between the parties. ... The contract between plaintiff and defendant contained an integration clause, which is a strong indication that the parties intended for the agreement to be complete and final. ... Under these circumstances, we conclude that the contract was complete and unambiguous and that, under the terms of the contract, the machines were delivered in an acceptable configuration.

Because plaintiff's only evidence in opposition to defendant's counter-claim consists of the parol evidence underlying its breach of contract claim, we also affirm the district court's summary judgment on the counterclaim.

\* \* \*

### IV.

We next consider defendant's claim that the district court erred in refusing to award damages pursuant to U.C.C. § 2–708(2), the lost volume seller provision. Defendant claims on appeal that § 2–709, the provision the district court relied upon in calculating damages, does not provide an adequate measure of damages when the seller is a lost volume seller, and that, thus, the district court erred.

Article 2 contains four provisions that concern the recovery of a seller's general damages (as opposed to its incidental or consequential damages): § 2–706 (contract price less resale price); § 2–708(1) (contract price less market price); § 2–708(2) (profit); and § 2–709 (price). Section 2–709 allows the seller to recover the price of the goods if the goods have been identified to the contract and after reasonable efforts fail to result in a sale of the goods at a reasonable price. Further, § 2–709(3) provides that the seller can pursue a remedy under § 2–708 only if he is not entitled to bring an action for the price under § 2–709.

In its counterclaim, defendant sought the full price of Machine 2. Several weeks later, after settling several other claims with plaintiff, defendant still maintained that it was suing for payment in full and that its counterclaim was an "action for the price." Subsequently, defendant identi-fied Machine 2 to the Davidson Textron contract, and partially disassem-bled and reconfigured the machine. Nevertheless, defendant did not at-tempt to amend or supplement its pleadings. It was not until almost a year later, when filing its proposed joint pretrial order, that defendant an-nounced its intention to seek damages pursuant to § 2–708.

Defendant originally sought the full price of Machine 2 pursuant to § 2–709, and never attempted to introduce its "lost volume seller" theory until over a year after discovery had begun. Under these circumstances, we are unable to say that the district court erred in concluding that defendant was bound by its election to pursue remedies under § 2–709.

\* \* \*

## VI.

For the reasons outlined above, the orders of the district court are affirmed.

## NOTES

**(1) Election of Remedies.** The primary reason given by the court for denial of seller's claim for damages under UCC 2–708(2) was that seller's counsel initially sought to recover the full contract price under UCC 2–709 and continued on that path through the period of discovery. In what way might the buyer have been prejudiced by the subsequent amendment of the claim to seek damages under UCC 2–708(2)?

**(2) The Price Remedy and Resale.** The original litigation strategy of seller's counsel was to seek the price under UCC 2–709(1)(b): goods identified to the contract that the seller was unable to resell at a reasonable price. Thereafter, it appears, the seller was able to resell the machine, after making modifications, to "an existing customer" for more than the original contract price. What would be the effect of that change in circumstances under UCC 2–709(3)? Can UCC 2–709(3) and UCC 2–708(2) be reconciled?

## (B) INTERNATIONAL SALES LAW

Sellers' remedies under CISG when buyers' wrongfully declare contracts avoided or, without making a declaration, refuse to take and pay for the goods, are similar to sellers' remedies under UCC Article 2. For convenience, we will use the term "wrongful avoidance" to refer to situations in which buyers declared contracts avoided without justification as well as situations in which buyer received goods but refused to accept and pay for them. The structure of the remedies provisions of the Convention is quite different from the structure of the remedies provisions in the Commercial Code. Two fundamental differences should be noted. First, CISG combines buyers' and sellers' damages remedies in the same articles. Second, many of CISG's remedies articles apply only to contracts that have been avoided.

CISG 61(1) summarizes the remedies of a seller if the buyer "fails to perform any of his obligations under the contract or this Convention." One of the remedies, in CISG 62, allows an aggrieved seller to recover the contract price. This CISG remedy is not conditioned in the way that the Code limits price actions under domestic United States law. In circumstances of wrongful avoidance by buyers that have not paid the price, it is reasonable to expect that counsel for sellers will seek a remedy under CISG 62. This is particularly likely if the goods have been shipped to the buyer and are in the buyer's possession or control at the time of the purported avoidance.

If sellers have possession or control of the goods and elect not to seek the price, their basic damages remedies, listed in CISG 61(1)(b), are provided in CISG 74 to 77. These formulae in these four articles apply to buyers' and sellers' damages, but our concern here is for the application of these articles to sellers' claims. The most basic provisions are CISG 74 and CISG 77. Both apply to all situations of breach. The former states a general formula for measurement of damages; the latter states the principle of mitigation of damages. Under CISG 74, an aggrieved seller is entitled to "a sum equal to the loss, including loss of profit, suffered . . . as a consequence of the breach." Professor Honnold referred to this standard as "brief but powerful."[3] Under CISG 77, an aggrieved seller "must take such measures as are reasonable in the circumstances to mitigate the loss, including loss of profit, resulting from the breach."

The basic damages provision of CISG 74 is complemented by two other damages provisions, CISG 75 and CISG 76, that apply only if an aggrieved seller has avoided the contract.[4] CISG 75 allows an aggrieved seller that has resold the goods to recover "the difference between the contract price and the price in the substitute transaction." CISG 76(1), which applies if a seller has not made a resale under CISG 75, allows an aggrieved seller to recover "the difference between the price fixed by the contract and the current price at the time of avoidance." "Current price" is defined in CISG 76(2) to mean, primarily, the prevailing price at the place where delivery of the goods should have been made.

Both CISG 75 and CISG 76 allow sellers to recover further damages under CISG 74. These CISG remedies resemble the resale remedy under UCC 2–706 and the market-damages remedy under UCC 2–708(1), but careful reading of the CISG and Code provisions reveals important differences. UCC 2–706 has significant conditions on a seller's right to fix damages by resale that are not contained in CISG 75. UCC 2–708(1) measures market damages at the time and place of tender, while CISG 76 uses the time of avoidance and the place of delivery. UCC 2–708(1).

The mitigation principle in CISG 77 applies to sellers claims of damages under CISG 74, CISG 75, and CISG 76. Application of the mitigation requirement to aggrieved sellers in possession or control of goods means that sellers must make reasonable efforts to redispose of the goods and credit the net proceeds to reduce the loss. That result is explicit in the damages measure of CISG 75 and implicit in the credit for current price in CISG 76(1). Mitigation by resale can be applied without difficulty to the general "loss suffered" standard of CISG 74.

---

**3.**  J. Honnold, Uniform Law for International Sales § 403 (3d ed. 1999).

**4.**  An aggrieved seller is not allowed to claim damages under CISG 75 or CISG 76 unless the seller has declared the contract avoided. A seller has he right to avoid a contract, under CISG 64(1)(a), if the buyer's failure to perform its obligations amounts to a fundamental breach of the contract. A buyers' wrongful avoidance is likely to be sufficiently serious as to constitute a fundamental breach. But avoidance is not automatic. Under CISG 26, avoidance does not occur unless the aggrieved party declares the contract avoided and gives a required notice. Sellers aggrieved by buyers' wrongful avoidance are likely to meet the procedural requirements of CISG 26 only in conjunction with arbitration or litigation proceedings.

What, then, is the CISG remedy for a lost-volume seller of the kind that is allowed to recover under UCC 2–708(2)? CISG 74 refers to loss of profit, but that phrase, drafted to cover sellers' and buyers' damages, has its most obvious application to buyers' consequential damages. Moreover, CISG 77 requires mitigation of any loss, including loss of profit. There is no general mitigation requirement in the Commercial Code. UCC 2–708(2) damages are not consistent with a strong general mitigation principle. However, Professor Honnold espoused the view that lost-volume sellers may have a remedy under CISG that is comparable to the profit recovery allowed by UCC 2–708(2).[5]

---

## Section 4. Performance Under Letters of Credit

Performance issues in letter of credit transactions arise on each of the three independent contracts that form the triad of all payment letter of credit transactions: the bank-beneficiary contract embodied in the letter of credit, the customer-bank contract that causes a bank to agree to issue a letter of credit, and the sales contract in which the buyer agrees to make payment by letter of credit. If more than one bank is involved in performance of a letter of credit transaction, issues arise in the relationship between the issuing bank and a confirming bank, or between the issuing bank and an advising bank.

Letter of credit practice is substantially affected by the existence of the Uniform Customs and Practices for Commercial Credits (UCP), promulgated from time to time by the International Chamber of Commerce. Banks engaged in letter of credit transactions, whether domestic or international in scope, commonly require that the letter be issued subject to the UCP. The UCP is not a body of legislative law, but incorporation by reference to the UCP in banks' letters has the effect of making the UCP provisions part of the banks' contractual obligations. Domestic courts typically use the UCP to determine the banks' obligations. The current edition of the UCP, UCP 600, was promulgated by the ICC in 2007.

## (A) Domestic United States Law

### Hanil Bank v. PT. Bank Negara Indonesia (Persero)

United States District Court, Southern District of New York, 2000.
2000 WL 254007, 41 U.C.C. Rep. Serv. 2d 618.

■ JOHN F. KEENAN, UNITED STATES DISTRICT JUDGE:

Before the Court are cross-motions for summary judgment, pursuant to Fed. R. Civ. P. 56. For the reasons discussed below, the Court grants Defendant's motion for summary judgment and denies Plaintiff's motion for summary judgment.

---

5. See J. Honnold, Uniform Law for International Sales § 415 (3d ed. 1999).

## The Parties

Plaintiff Hanil Bank ("Hanil") was, at all times relevant to this action, a banking corporation organized under the laws of the Republic of Korea, with an agency in New York, New York.

Defendant PT. Bank Negara Indonesia (Pesero) ("BNI") is a banking corporation organized under the laws of Indonesia, with an agency located in New York, New York.

## Background

On July 27, 1995, PT. Kodeco Electronics Indonesia ("Kodeco") applied to BNI to issue a letter of credit (the "L/C") for the benefit of "Sung Jun Electronics Co., Ltd." ("Sung Jun"). On July 28, 1995, BNI issued the L/C ... in the amount of $170,955.00 but misspelled the name of the beneficiary as "Sung Jin Electronics Co. Ltd." The beneficiary did not request amendment of the L/C to change the name of the beneficiary. On August 2, 1995 Sung Jun negotiated the L/C to Hanil. Hanil purchased the L/C and the documents submitted by Sung Jun thereunder from Sung Jun for $157,493.00, the face amount of the draft, less Hanil's commission. On August 2, 1995, Hanil submitted the documents, a draft, a commercial invoice, bill of lading, insurance policy, a packing list, and a fax advice, to BNI for payment. On August 16, 1995, BNI rejected the documents tendered by Hanil and refused to pay under the L/C. BNI alleges that it compared the documents with the L/C and identified four discrepancies, and based upon those discrepancies, refused the documents and demand for payment. The alleged discrepancies are as follows:

1.  The Name of the Beneficiary: The L/C identifies the beneficiary as Sung Jin Electronics Co. Ltd. instead of Sung Jun Electronics Co. Ltd.

2.  The Packing List: BNI claims that the packing list did not show the contents of each carton as required by the L/C.

3.  "Export Quality": BNI claims that the packing list also fails to specify that the goods were of "export quality."

4.  The Bill of Lading: BNI claims that Hanil supplied a "Freight Bill of Lading" instead of the required "Ocean Bill of Lading."

BNI alleges that before it issued its notice of refusal on August 16, 1995, it contacted Kodeco to ask whether it would accept the discrepancies and approve the requested payment, but Kodeco declined to do so. BNI further alleges that it continued to ask Kodeco to waive the discrepancies after August 16, but that Kodeco continued to refuse to waive the discrepancies. BNI then returned the entire original package of documents back to Hanil on September 4, 1995.

Hanil contends that BNI decided to reject the documents presented by Hanil after consulting with, and on the instructions of, Kodeco. In support of this contention, Hanil points to a letter from BNI to Hanil, dated October 4, 1995, which stated that "we are acting at the request and on the instruction of the applicant, i.e., PT. Kodeco Electronics Indonesia. We will, anyhow make a final attempt to have the applicant reconsider their determination and to accept the discrepancies and give as the approval [sic] for payment of the documents." BNI denies the contention that it acted on the instructions of Kodeco when BNI refused to pay because of the alleged discrepancies.

Plaintiff brought suit in New York State court on April 19, 1996, asserting claims for breach of contract, breach of the Uniform Customs and Practice for Documentary Credits (1993 Revision) International Chamber of Commerce Publication No. 500 (the "UCP"), unjust enrichment, and breach of an implied covenant of good faith and fair dealing, and seeking $157,493 in damages, plus interest. Defendant then removed the case to this Court. Both parties now move for summary judgment.

Discussion

* * *

Letters of Credit and the UCP

The principles of letter of credit law are embodied in the Uniform Customs and Practice for Documentary Credits (1993 Revision) International Chamber of Commerce Publication No. 500 (the "UCP"). The UCP is a compilation of internationally accepted commercial practices. . . . Although it is not law, the UCP commonly governs letters of credit by virtue of its incorporation into most letters of credit. See id. In this case, the L/C provides that it is governed by the UCP and both parties agree that the provisions of the UCP govern the L/C in this case. The New York Uniform Commercial Code (the "U.C.C.") provides that if a letter of credit is subject in whole or part to the UCP, as in this case, the U.C.C. does not apply. See N.Y. U.C.C. § 5–102(4).

Typically, in a letter-of-credit transaction, the letter of credit substitutes the credit of the opening bank for that of the account party. International letters of credit permit quick and easy financing of international transactions by reducing the risks of non-payment. . . .

A fundamental tenet of letter of credit law is that the obligation of the issuing bank to honor a draft on a credit is independent of the performance of the underlying contract. . . . See Marino Indus. v. Chase Manhattan Bank, N.A., 686 F.2d 112, 115 (2d Cir.1982); E & H Partners, 39 F. Supp. 2d at 280. "The duty of the issuing bank to pay upon the submission of documents which appear on their face to conform to the terms and conditions of the letter of credit is absolute, absent proof of intentional fraud. . . ." E & H Partners, 39 F. Supp. 2d [275,] at 280 [S.D.N.Y 1998], (citing Beyene v. Irving Trust Co., 762 F.2d 4, 6 (2d Cir.1985)). Because the credit engagement is concerned only with documents, "the essential requirements of a letter of credit must be strictly complied with by the party entitled to draw against the letter of credit, which means that the papers, documents and shipping description must be as stated in the letter." Marino Indus., 686 F.2d at 114 . . . Even under the strict compliance rule, however, "some variations . . . might be so insignificant as not to relieve the issuing or confirming bank of its obligation to pay," for example, if there were a case where "the name intended is unmistakably clear despite what is obviously a typographical error, as might be the case if, for example, 'Smith' were misspelled 'Smithh.'" Beyene, 762 F.2d at 6. The Court will now consider the alleged discrepancies in this case.

The Name of the Beneficiary

As set out above, the name of the beneficiary in this case was Sung Jun. Kodeco's application to BNI for the issuance of the L/C requested that the L/C be issued to Sung Jun. BNI, however, issued the L/C identifying the beneficiary as Sung Jin. BNI argues that under Beyene v. Irving Trust Co., 762 F.2d 4 (2d Cir.1985) and Mutual Export Corp. v. Westpac Banking Corp., 983 F.2d 420 (2d Cir.1993) this discrepancy was a proper basis to reject the letter of credit presentation. Hanil argues, however, that the strict compliance rule does not permit an issuing bank to dishonor a letter of credit based on a discrepancy such as the misspelling in this case which could not have misled or prejudiced the issuing bank. For the reasons discussed below, the Court agrees with BNI.

In *Beyene*, Plaintiffs brought suit seeking damages for the alleged wrongful refusal of the defendant trust company, Irving Trust Co. ("Irving"), to honor a letter of credit. The district court granted Irving's motion for summary judgment because the bill of lading presented to Irving misspelled the name of the person to whom notice was to be given of the arrival of the goods, listing the name of the party as Mohammed Soran instead of Mohammed Sofan. As a result, the district court found that the bill of lading failed to comply with the terms of the letter of credit and that Irving was under no obligation to honor the letter of credit. The Second Circuit agreed, finding that "the misspelling in the bill of lading of Sofan's name as 'Soran' was a material discrepancy that entitled Irving to refuse to honor the letter of credit" and stating that "this is not a case where the name intended is unmistakably clear despite what is obviously a typographical error, as might be the case if, for example, 'Smith' were misspelled 'Smithh.'" 762 F.2d at 6. The Second Circuit also noted that it was not claimed that in the Middle East, where the letter of credit was issued, that "Soran" would be obviously recognized as a misspelling of the surname "Sofan." The Court finds the misspelling in the present case to be similar to the misspelling in *Beyene* and notes that Hanil likewise does not claim that Sung "Jin" would be obviously recognized as a misspelling of Sun "Jun."

Plaintiff argues that *Beyene* is distinguishable from the present case because in *Beyene* the beneficiary made the error, while in the present case, the issuing bank made the error. However, the Second Circuit has made it clear that under letter of credit law, "the beneficiary must inspect the letter of credit and is responsible for any negligent failure to discover that the credit does not achieve the desired commercial ends." Mutual Export, 983 F.2d at 423. Thus, in *Mutual Export*, even though the issuing bank had issued a letter of credit with an incorrect termination date, the Second

Circuit reversed the district court's finding that the letter of credit should be reformed to reflect the appropriate date, and held that the beneficiary was responsible for failure to discover the error. The *Mutual Export* court explained that this rule is important because

> the beneficiary is in the best position to determine whether a letter of credit meets the needs of the underlying commercial transaction and to request any necessary changes.... "it more efficient to require the beneficiary to conduct that review of the credit before the fact of performance than after it, and the beneficiary that performs without seeing or examining the credit should bear the costs."

See id. (citation omitted).

Pursuant to *Beyene* and *Mutual Export*, this Court concludes that BNI properly rejected payment on the ground that the documents improperly identified the beneficiary of the letter of credit. Although Hanil contends that BNI should have known that the intended beneficiary was Sung Jun, not Sung Jin, based on the application letter in BNI's own file, the Second Circuit has stated that in considering whether to pay, "the bank looks solely at the letter and the documentation the beneficiary presents to determine whether the documentation meets the requirements in the letter." See Marino Indus., 686 F.2d at 115; see also UCP 500 Art. 13(a) (stating that compliance is to be determined from the face of the documents stipulated in the letter of credit).

Although Plaintiff argues that Bank of Montreal v. Federal Nat'l Bank & Trust Co., 622 F. Supp. 6 (W.D.Okla.1984), allowed recovery when the error was greater than the misspelling of a single letter, in *Bank of Montreal*, the letter of credit contained two, internally inconsistent, statements of the name of one of the entities whose indebtedness was secured. The letter of credit referred to "Blow Out Products, Ltd." in its first paragraph and to "Blow Out Prevention, Ltd." in its second paragraph. Based on this inconsistency on the face of the letter of credit itself, the court found that the letter of credit was ambiguous and resolved the ambiguity against the issuer. There is no internal inconsistency or ambiguity in the L/C at issue in the present case, however.

Having found that BNI properly refused payment based on the improper identification of the beneficiary of the L/C, the Court need not address the three remaining alleged discrepancies.

Finally, as to Hanil's argument that BNI dishonored the L/C at the instruction of Kodeco and thereby violated its duty of good faith and fair dealing, the Court again disagrees. As noted above, the issuing bank's obligation under the letter of credit is independent of the underlying commercial transaction. Thus, BNI had an obligation to independently review Hanil's submissions to determine if there were any discrepancies. However, under the UCP, BNI is permitted to approach the payor of the letter of credit, in this case Kodeco, for a waiver of any discrepancies with or without the beneficiary's approval. See UCP, Art. 14(c); E & H Partners, 39 F. Supp. 2d at 284; see also Alaska Textile [Co., Inc. v. Chase Manhattan

Bank, N.A., 982 F.2d 813,] at 824 (2d Cir.1992) (noting that allowing the issuer to seek waiver from the payor is efficient because the account party typically waives the discrepancies and authorizes payment). In this case there is no evidence that BNI communicated with Kodeco other than to ask whether Kodeco would accept the discrepancies and approve the requested payment. As a result, the Court finds that Hanil has not set forth facts showing there is a genuine issue as to whether BNI breached its duty of good faith and fair dealing by dishonoring the L/C. Summary judgment for BNI is therefore appropriate.

### Conclusion

For the reasons discussed above, the Court grants BNI's motion for summary judgment and denies Hanil's motion for summary judgment. . . .

### NOTES

**(1) Choice of Forum; Choice of Law.** The bank that issued the letter of credit was an Indonesian bank, acting on the application of an Indonesian company, which had bought goods from the beneficiary. The beneficiary, apparently a Korean firm, had sold goods to the Indonesian buyer. What might explain the plaintiff's choice to sue in a federal district court in the United States? The federal district court proceeded on the premise that the law governing this letter of credit was New York law. What might explain the court's assumption that New York law governed?[1]

**(2) The New York Version of UCC Article 5.** New York adopted the original UCC Article 5 with a non-uniform exception providing that Article 5, in its entirety, did not apply to letters of credit that incorporated the ICC Uniform Customs and Practices for Documentary Credits (UCP). The letter of credit in this case incorporated the UCP and, therefore, the court held that the case was not within the New York version of Article 5. The governing law was therefore the common law of New York.

**(3) UCP 500.** The court noted that the letter of credit was subject to UCP 500, but did not quote or cite any UCP provision in its analysis of the sufficiency of the documents submitted to the issuing bank. UCP 13(a) provided:

> Banks must examine all documents stipulated in the Credit with reasonable care, to ascertain whether or not they appear, on their face, to be in compliance with the terms and conditions of the Credit.

---

**1.** Original UCC Article 5 did not contain a provision on choice of law. UCC 1–105(1), the Commercial Code's general choice of law provision, allowed parties to a Code transaction to choose the law of a state, such as New York, if the transaction bears a reasonable relation to that state. Revised Article 5 has a quite different choice of law provision, UCC 5–116. Parties to a letter of credit transaction are permitted to choose the law of any jurisdiction, whether or not that jurisdiction has any relation to the transaction. Absent agreement, however, UCC 5–116(b) provides that the liability of an issuing bank is governed by the law of the jurisdiction in which the bank is located. The subsection adds that a bank is located at the address indicated in the letter of credit.

Compliance of the stipulated documents on their face with the terms and conditions of the Credit, shall be determined by international standard banking practice as reflected in these Articles.

The issuing bank communicated with the applicant before refusing to honor the draft presented to it. UCP 14(c), cited by the court, allows issuing banks to do this. It provided:

If the Issuing Bank determines that the documents appear on their face not to be in compliance with the terms and conditions of the Credit, it may in its sole judgment approach the Applicant for a waiver of the discrepancy(ies). This does not, however, extend the period mentioned in sub-Article 13(b).

Sub–Article 13(b) provided:

The Issuing Bank ... shall ... have a reasonable time, not to exceed seven banking days following the date of receipt of the documents, to examine the documents and determine whether to take up or refuse the documents and to inform the party from which it received the documents accordingly.

Why was UCP 14(c) drafted to give issuing banks discretion to decide whether to approach applicants with respect to non-conforming documents? Do banks have an interest in the performance or failure of the transactions underlying letters of credit? Would applicants prefer that issuing banks approach them in these circumstances?

In *Hanil Bank* the issuer approached the applicant, Kodecko, and Kodecko refused to waive the non-conformities. What might explain Kodecko's decision? Is it likely that the Kodecko would have acted on the basis of the misspelled name alone? From Kodecko's perspective, how serious were the various non-conformities?

**(4) Transfer of the Letter of Credit.** The plaintiff in *Hanil Bank* was not the beneficiary of the letter of credit. The opinion noted that the letter of credit, together with the supporting documents, had been sold to Hanil Bank, which paid the face amount of the draft less the bank's commission. Beneficiaries of letters of credit commonly use intermediary banks to present requests for payment to issuing banks. In this case, the beneficiary not only used an intermediary bank, but the bank also discounted the draft and made payment to the beneficiary before presentment to the issuing bank. Hanil Bank's right to payment of the letter of credit by the issuing bank was no stronger than the beneficiary's right to payment.

**(5) Aftermath of Dishonor.** Upon dishonor by BNI, Hanil Bank elected to sue BNI on the ground that BNI's dishonor was wrongful and the court ultimately held for BNI. What alternatives actions were available to Hanil Bank? What might have led Hanil Bank to sue BNI rather than proceed against Sung Jun?

After an issuing bank rightfully dishonors a draft drawn on a letter of credit, what happens to the bill of lading and the other documents presented to the issuer? The payment term of the underlying sales contract has not been performed. What are the respective rights and obligations of the seller and buyer under that contract?

Upon an issuing bank's dishonor of a draft, what is the effect on the applicant's duty to reimburse the issuing bank?

# Petra Int'l Banking Corp. v. First Amer. Bank of Va.

United States District Court, Eastern District of Virginia, 1991.
758 F.Supp. 1120.

■ ELLIS, DISTRICT JUDGE.

This dispute grows out of the use of two documentary letters of credit to finance the purchase of T-shirts by a Virginia corporation from the manufacturer in Amman, Jordan. In essence, following the delivery of poor quality T-shirts, the purchaser refused to pay the issuing bank and the issuing bank then refused to pay the confirming bank, which had honored drafts drawn under the letters of credit. The purchaser and the issuing bank rely on their receipt of technically nonconforming documents under the letters as grounds for nonpayment. The purchaser and the manufacturer settled their dispute over the poor quality T-shirts, but the remaining parties were not able to resolve their differences. Thus, here the confirming bank seeks recovery against the issuing bank and the purchaser for payments it made under the letters of credit, and the issuing bank seeks recovery against the purchaser for any sums it must pay to the confirming bank.

Before the Court are cross-motions for summary judgment. The motions raise, inter alia, the seldom litigated issue of what remedy an account customer has when an issuing bank inadvertently accepts nonconforming documents under a letter of credit. All material facts are undisputed. These facts, the terms of the letters of credit, other relevant contractual agreements, and existing law require that defendant First American Bank, the issuer of the letters, reimburse the confirming bank for payments made under the letters, and that First American Bank's account customer, the purchaser of the T-shirts, reimburse First American. Both First American and the purchaser, by failing to object to documentary inconsistencies in timely fashion, have waived their right to do so. All other issues raised in this case with the exception of costs and attorney's fees are also disposed of on summary judgment.

*Facts*

In 1987 Dameron International, Inc., a Virginia corporation ("Dameron"), purchased T-shirts from National Marketing–Export Co. ("National Marketing") of Amman, Jordan. To facilitate the transaction, Dameron sought issuance of two letters of credit by First American Bank of Virginia ("First American"). To this end, Dameron executed two documents, each entitled Application and Agreement for International Commercial Letter of Credit ("the Agreements"), and signed two commercial notes, each in the amount of $135,000.00, to secure the letters of credit. Richard Pitts, the president of Dameron, and his wife, son, and daughter-in-law, executed continuing guaranties to further secure any debts of Dameron owed to First American. First American issued its Irrevocable Letters of Credit Nos. 1–629 and 1–630 ("the Letters"), each for $135,000, on December 17, 1987. The Letters stated that they were issued "in favor of National Marketing–Export Co.," of Amman, Jordan and "for the account of Dameron Intl., Inc." of McLean, Virginia. The Letters authorized drafts to be drawn on First American within thirty days of submission to First American of specific, listed documents. At the request of National Marketing and National's bank in Jordan, Petra Bank, the Letters were amended on December 22, 1987, to provide that drafts under the Letters could be drawn directly on Petra International Banking Corporation of Washington, D.C. ("PIBC"), Petra's American affiliate. In the vernacular of letters of credit transactions, PIBC became a "confirming bank," First American an "issuing bank," Dameron the "account customer," and National Marketing the "beneficiary" of the Letters.

When initially issued, the Letters required that an "inspection certificate from [an] independent inspector certifying number and quality of pieces per sample" of the T-shirts be among the documents presented for payment. This provision subsequently was amended to require both a certificate from a specific independent inspection company and a "statement by the beneficiary," National Marketing, attesting to the quality of the T-shirts.

Dameron received several T-shirt shipments from National Marketing in 1988. Several corresponding payments were made under the Letters by PIBC to National Marketing. In late September 1988, another shipment was begun and National Marketing made a demand for payment under the Letters. This demand was relayed from Petra Bank in Amman to PIBC as two documentary time drafts drawn against the Letters in the aggregate amount of $95,904. PIBC sent a telex to First American on October 7, 1988, noting certain discrepancies between the documents submitted and those required by the Letters, including the fact that the certificate from the independent inspection company was missing. First American forwarded PIBC's telex to Dameron, which waived the discrepancies listed by PIBC on condition that the drafts were drawn 150 days from the date of the bill of lading, i.e., from the date of shipment. First American sent a telex message to PIBC on October 19, 1988, stating "ACCOUNT PARTY HAS WAIVED ALL DISCREPANCIES PROVIDED DRAFTS ARE DRAWN AT 150 DAYS BILL OF LADING." First American sent a second telex message on October 24, 1988, stating in relevant part: "DISCREPANCIES HAVE BEEN WAIVED BY A/P [i.e., Dameron]. PLEASE ACCEPT DRAFT AND FORWARD DOCS TO US." Between receipt of the first and second telexes, on October 21, 1988, PIBC discounted and accepted the documentary time drafts. On October 25, 1988, PIBC sent a telex to First American that confirmed receipt of First American's telex of October 24th, informed First American that the drafts had been accepted with the proviso that they be drawn 150 days from the date of the bill of lading, i.e., on February 21, 1989, and transmitted the documents to First American. First American forwarded the documents to Dameron shortly after receiving them. Dameron kept the documents and took possession of the T-shirts. On November 16, 1988, First American sent an acknowledgment letter to PIBC stating that the documentary drafts for $95,904 were "accepted and, at maturity, we will remit proceeds according to your cover letter."

Dameron was dissatisfied with the quality of the T-shirts received from National Marketing. It undertook negotiations with National concerning the $95,904 payment. As the February 21, 1989 deadline for drawing on the time drafts approached, Dameron requested that First American obtain an extension of payment. First American then sent a telex to PIBC requesting an extension to May 21, 1989. The telex stated that National Marketing had agreed to this delay in receiving payment. PIBC informed First American that it would delay and refinance the payment provided that First American pay interest during the delay at the prime rate plus two percent. Dameron and First American agreed. As the new May 21, 1989 deadline drew near, Dameron requested that First American seek an additional extension of thirty days. First American requested the extension, explaining that "SPECIAL ARRANGEMENTS REGARDING THESE PAYMENTS WERE MADE BY BUYERS AND SELLERS ALLOWING THE 30 DAY EXTENSION." PIBC agreed to this second extension on the condition that it continue to receive interest at prime plus two percent, and First American and Dameron accepted this requirement.

In June or July, 1989, Richard Pitts informed First American that Dameron did not want to pay National Marketing because of the poor quality of the T-shirts. William von Berg of First American informed Pitts that First American would be obligated to pay under the Letters unless the bank were sued by Dameron and enjoined from doing so. While the parties are uncertain as to when this conversation occurred, it is clear that in late June, when Dameron requested a third extension, Dameron and National Marketing continued to be hopeful that they would settle their differences concerning the $95,904. Dameron planned to obtain additional T-shirts of suitable quality from National at a reduced price, and it so informed First American. On June 20, 1989, Richard Pitts requested that First American seek a third extension. On the same day, Bassem Farouki, the principal of National Marketing, informed PIBC that Dameron would be requesting an additional thirty-day extension. Although PIBC initially took the position that First American should finance Dameron, it eventually agreed to an extension to July 21, 1989, under the same interest payment conditions as were attached to the previous two extensions.

Dameron's negotiations with National Marketing did not bear fruit. On July 20, 1989, Dameron obtained an Order of Attachment from the Fairfax County Circuit Court, directing First American not to pay PIBC under the Letters. First American claims that it did not immediately learn of the existence of the writ. Nevertheless, First American did not pay PIBC on July 21, 1989. Rather, on that day, at Dameron's request, First American requested an extension of payment to the following week. PIBC responded by demanding payment. Payment was not made. Instead, on July 28th,

First American informed PIBC that it had been enjoined by the Fairfax County Circuit Court from making payments under the Letters until further notice.

From July 20, 1989 until April 13, 1990, Dameron pursued a law suit against National Marketing in the Fairfax County Circuit Court. In the course of this litigation, and more than one year after its receipt of the documents, Dameron noticed and then informed First American that the "Statement of the Beneficiary" was not among the documents that First American forwarded pertaining to the $95,904 shipment. First American informed Dameron that it had forwarded all documents it had received. The absence of the Statement of the Beneficiary from the documents was not noted as a discrepancy by PIBC or First American when each had examined the documents. Both Dameron and First American agree that the Statement of the Beneficiary was never among the documents presented by National Marketing to PIBC, and that PIBC, First American, and Dameron each inadvertently failed to notice the missing Statement of the Beneficiary when each received the documents.

Dameron and National Marketing eventually settled their suit. Dameron kept the T-shirts, but received an undisclosed amount of cash from National Marketing related, it appears, to the shipment here at issue and to other shipments and disputes between the parties. The precise terms of the settlement remain confidential and have not been disclosed to the Court. On April 13, 1990, the Fairfax County Circuit Court vacated the Order of Attachment. On the same day, PIBC requested payment from First American of $95,904 of principal and $14,079.24 of interest. First American has refused to make the payment, relying primarily on PIBC's alleged failure to note the missing Statement of the Beneficiary. Dameron, in turn, has refused to reimburse First American if payment is made under the Letters, despite having signed the Agreements and commercial notes, kept the documents accompanying the relevant drafts, taken possession of the T-shirts, and recovered settlement compensation from National Marketing. The Pitts, in turn, have refused First American's demands for reimbursement under the Continuing Guarantees.

\* \* \*

## I. First American's Obligation to Pay PIBC

PIBC requests summary judgment on Count I of its Complaint, which alleges that First American wrongfully refused to honor the Letters and pay the $95,904 plus interest to PIBC. First American contends that PIBC's failure to note the missing Statement of the Beneficiary relieves it of any obligation to honor the drafts drawn under the Letters. The threshold issue is the choice of governing law. The Letters state on their face that they are to be governed by the Uniform Customs and Practices for Documentary Credits (1983 Revision), International Chamber of Commerce Publication No. 400 ("the UCP"). Given this, the Court finds that the UCP should be applied in this case. Neither PIBC nor First American objects to application of the UCP, though they differ in interpreting its provisions.

The pertinent UCP provision is Article 16, which states that if an issuing bank desires to "refuse documents," it must do so "without delay" by stating the discrepancies it has found and "holding the documents at the disposal of, or . . . returning them to, the presentor (remitting bank or the beneficiary, as the case may be)." If the issuing bank fails to perform these requirements, it "shall be precluded from claiming that the documents are not in accordance with the terms and conditions of the credit."[26] Numerous courts have held that Article 16 and its predecessor, Article 8 of the 1974 UCP, preclude an issuing bank from asserting the noncompliance of documents presented by a beneficiary where the bank delays in raising this claim. Bank of Cochin v. Manufacturers Hanover Trust Co., 808 F.2d 209 (2d Cir.1986), a case precisely on point, presents a striking example of this principle in operation between an issuing and a confirming bank. There, the issuing bank, on the very day of its receipt of a documentary draft from the confirming bank, telexed its intention to dishonor the draft. But the issuing bank did not supply the confirming bank with a reason for the dishonor until twelve-to-thirteen-days later. This delay, the Court found, violated Article 8(d)'s command that an issuing bank intending to dishonor a documentary draft "notify [the confirming bank] 'expeditiously' and 'without delay' of specific defects and of the disposition of the documents, and . . . precluded [the issuing bank] from asserting noncompliance. . . ." Id. at 213. The same result should obtain here because the issuing bank's notice was delayed even longer than in Bank of Cochin. In the instant case,

---

**26.** The full text of Article 16 of the UCP is as follows:

(a) If a bank so authorized effects payment, or *incurs a deferred payment undertaking*, or accepts or negotiates *against documents which appear on their face to be in accordance with the terms and conditions of a credit*, the party giving such authority *shall be bound* to reimburse the bank which has effected payment, or incurred a deferred payment undertaking, or has accepted or negotiated, and *to take up the documents*.

(b) If, upon receipt of the documents, the issuing bank considers that they appear on their face not to be in accordance with the terms and conditions of the credit, *it must determine, on the basis of the documents alone, whether to take up such documents, or to refuse them* and claim that they appear on their face not to be in accordance with the terms and conditions of the credit.

(c) The issuing bank shall have *a reasonable time* in which to examine the documents and to determine as above whether to take up the documents or to refuse the documents.

(d) *If the issuing bank decides to refuse the documents. it must give notice to that effect without delay* by telecommunication or, if that is not possible, by other expeditious means, to the bank from which it received the documents (the remitting bank), or to the beneficiary, if it received the documents directly from him. *Such notice must state the discrepancies* in respect of which the issuing bank refuses the documents *and must also state whether it is holding the documents at the disposal of, or is returning them to, the presentor* (remitting bank or the beneficiary, as the case may be). The issuing bank shall then be entitled to claim from the remitting bank any refund of any reimbursement which may have been made to that bank.

(e) *If the issuing bank fails* to act in accordance with the provisions of paragraphs (c) and (d) of this article and/or fails *to hold the documents at the disposal of*, or to return them to, *the presentor, the issuing bank shall be precluded from claiming that the documents are not in accordance with the terms and conditions of the credit.*

(Emphasis added.)

First American received the documents on or about October 25, 1988. Not only did it fail to note any discrepancies or to hold the documents at PIBC's disposal, it transferred the documents to its account customer and formally notified PIBC on November 16, 1988 that "the transaction was accepted and, at maturity, we will remit proceeds...." First American did not mention any discrepancies to PIBC until more than one year after receipt of the documents. In the interim, it made several promises to pay in exchange for extensions of time. First American is therefore precluded by Article 16 from asserting noncompliance.

First American seeks to avoid application of Article 16 by arguing that Article 16 applies to drafts passing from beneficiaries or advising banks to issuing banks, but not to drafts passing from confirming banks to issuing banks. In support, First American points to Virginia Code § 8.5–107(2), which states that a confirming bank "becomes directly obligated on the credit to the extent of its confirmation, *as though it were its issuer* and acquires the rights of an issuer." (Emphasis added.) From this, First American argues that it should be viewed as PIBC's account customer in the transaction at issue, while PIBC should be deemed to be the issuing bank subject to Article 16. It is true that PIBC, upon becoming a confirming bank, has the rights and duties of an issuing bank and is therefore subject to Article 16. It is also true that First American may be viewed as PIBC's customer. Even so, neither of these points changes First American's status as an issuing bank nor relieves it from its Article 16 duties. In short, as one or more confirming banks are inserted in the chain between the original issuing bank and the beneficiary, each bank, including the original issuer, is an issuing bank subject to Article 16. This conclusion finds support in the language of Article 16 and makes good commercial sense. On its face, Article 16 uses broad language, the plain meaning of which covers documentary draft transfers between confirming and issuing banks. Sensible policy considerations support this construction. To hold otherwise and accept First American's reading of Article 16 would render the UCP devoid of standards governing transactions between confirming and issuing banks. This would make no business sense. For similar reasons, the Court rejects First American's odd claim that PIBC's acceptance of the documentary drafts before First American had received and reviewed the documents should absolve First American of its obligation to honor the draft.[32] Finally, even if the Court were to find that First American should be treated as a

---

**32.** Under the scheme of Article 16, it appears that a confirming bank becomes obligated to pay a documentary credit when it transfers documents on to the issuing bank. The confirming bank may, if it finds discrepancies, dishonor a documentary draft and return the documents to the beneficiary or to a prior confirming or advising bank in the chain of transfer. The confirming bank, like the issuing bank, appears to be required to accept or reject the documents "on the basis of the documents alone." Article 16(b). It is not permitted to pass them on perfunctorily to the issuing bank to obtain that bank's opinion on the documents' compliance with the letter of credit. If it could so operate, it would be no more than an advising bank. Furthermore, First American can claim no harm from PIBC's acceptance of the draft before First American received the documents. Under Article 16, First American was still entitled to review the documents upon receipt and to reject and return them as nonconforming to PIBC. ...

"customer" of PIBC, First American would still be liable for the reasons given below in Part III for holding Dameron liable to reimburse First American.

\* \* \*

### III.  Dameron's Obligation to Reimburse First American

Having found that PIBC has a legal right to payment from First American, . . . the Court turns next to First American's claim that Dameron must reimburse it for any amount it must pay PIBC under the Letters. First American relies on the Agreements executed by Dameron to obtain the Letters. In the Agreements, Dameron pledged to indemnify First American for the latter's acts with respect to the Letters as long as such acts were taken in good faith. And, First American correctly notes that Dameron has not shown any bad faith on the part of First American with respect to accepting the documents. Dameron argues, however, that the good faith standard in the Agreements violates Virginia law and hence is void. Therefore, Dameron continues, First American's failure to note the missing Statement of the Beneficiary, though not a breach of good faith, nevertheless relieves Dameron of any obligation to reimburse First American.

It is not necessary to reach the unsettled, thorny question whether the Agreements, which appear to be standard form contracts employed by First American, violate Virginia law. Even assuming first that the Agreements run afoul of Virginia law, next that First American is obligated, as Dameron contends, by Virginia Code § 8.5–109(2) to "examine documents with care so as to ascertain that on their face they appear to comply with the terms" of the Letters, and finally that First American breached this duty by failing to note the absence of the Statement of the Beneficiary, the Virginia UCC and the common law of letters of credit still bar Dameron's claim because Dameron accepted the documents and used them to gain control of the T-shirts. Under these circumstances, Dameron cannot rely on documentary discrepancies to avoid honoring its Agreements with First American.

The Agreements between First American and Dameron state that they shall be governed by Virginia law. Title 8.5 of Virginia's UCC, which pertains to Letters of Credit, contains no provision governing an account customer's remedies for wrongful honor by an issuing bank. Section 8.5–102(3), however, frankly admits that Title 8.5 "deals with some but not all of the rules and concepts of letters of credit. . . ." The section invites the application of "rules or concepts . . . developed prior to this act or . . . hereafter" to "a situation not provided for . . . by this title." Id. . . . Thus, in ascertaining Dameron's remedies as an account customer for First American's wrongful honor, this Court is directed by Virginia law to apply the "fundamental theory" of letters of credit and the "canon of liberal interpretation" in Virginia Code § 8.1–102. . . .

A review of the few existing, apposite cases indicates that under the common law of letters of credit an account customer, by accepting documents from the issuing bank and subsequently "surrendering the documents [to shippers or customs officials] and accepting a substantial portion of the goods . . . waives its right to seek strict enforcement of the letter of credit." Dorf Overseas Inc. v. Chemical Bank, 91 A.D.2d 895, 457 N.Y.S.2d 513, 514 (N.Y.App.Div.1983). This result "is the only one consistent with principle and common sense." H. Harfield, Bank Credits and Acceptances 107 (5th ed. 1974). Fundamental to letter of credit transactions is the principle that both the letter of credit and also the separate agreement between account customer and issuing bank are transactions in documents entirely independent from the underlying sale of goods. . . . An account customer, if it desires to claim discrepancies, has a duty to return documents to the issuing bank rather than use them to obtain control over the goods. The documents provide some compensation to a bank which has inadvertently honored nonconforming documents. "The bank's loss will be the amount of the payment which it has made under the credit less any amount which it may realize from disposition of the documents which it has purchased." Id. at 105. The result is equitable. The beneficiary/seller is paid by the bank for the goods; the bank owns the documents and title to the goods; and the account customer has avoided paying for goods that, because of discrepancies in the documents, it feared accepting. This rule also avoids the inequitable result of a windfall for the account customer in the form of obtaining goods never paid for. While some commentators have favored less stringent rules with respect to an account customer's acceptance of documents,[42] the rule just stated has gained the widest acceptance

---

**42.**   Harfield, quoted in the text, presents the most in-depth analysis found of an account customer's remedies for an issuing bank's inadvertent acceptance of nonconforming documents. Harfield's conclusion, discussed supra, is that an account party must reject and return nonconforming documents within a reasonable period or be deemed to have waived its right to object to documentary inconsistencies. . . . Some commentators have favored other rules.

In an early treatise, Finkelstein contended that an account customer should be able to accept nonconforming documents, reimburse the issuing bank, but deduct any direct or consequential damages flowing from the bank's acceptance of nonconforming documents. Finkelstein likened this to a buyer's ability to keep nonconforming goods, retain its right of action against the seller for breach of contract, and recover consequential damages. Finkelstein, Legal Aspects of Commercial Letters of Credit 195–97 (1930). . . .

More recently, Kozolchyk took a middle ground between Finkelstein and Harfield. Kozolchyk, Commercial Letters of Credit in the Americas 322–26 (1966). Kozolchyk . . . believed . . . that an account customer might be permitted to receive "direct and foreseeable" damages, and urged American courts to adopt the practice found in some other countries of permitting an account customer to accept documents while expressly reserving a right of action against the bank for document inconsistencies. Id. at 316, 324. See also J. White and R. Summers, Handbook of the Law Under the Uniform Commercial Code § 19–8 at 864–65 (3d ed. 1988) (suggesting that an account customer might recover damages pertaining to defective goods from an issuing bank that wrongfully honors a draft, but providing no case law or reasons for this conclusion and observing that "because customers are so infrequently successful in suing issuing banks for wrongful honor, the law here is quite undeveloped"); Dolan, The Law of Letters of Credit para. 9.03 at 9–35, 9–36 (1984) (observing merely that disputes between issuing banks and account parties should be governed by "contract remedy rules" unless such rules are inadequate). . . .

in American case law and best reflects the fundamental theory underlying letters of credit.

The undisputed facts of this case are that shortly after October 25, 1988, First American transferred the documents at issue to Dameron. Dameron did not note any discrepancies; rather, it used the documents to take possession of the T-shirts. Until July 1989, when it brought suit against National Marketing, Dameron attempted to sell the T-shirts, apparently with disappointing results, and to work out a deal with National to compensate Dameron for the nonconforming goods. On three occasions during this period, Dameron pledged to reimburse First American for honoring the drafts related to the T-shirts in exchange for extensions of time for payment. Furthermore, Dameron obtained a court order attaching payment of the drafts, which order was not lifted until Dameron had settled its law suit with National Marketing. The terms of this settlement have been kept confidential by Dameron, although it stated that it received some monetary compensation under the settlement. It is reasonable to assume that a portion of the settlement was intended to compensate Dameron for the substandard quality of the T-shirts. Not until approximately a year or more after receipt of the documents and goods, did Dameron raise the issue of the missing Statement of the Beneficiary. The undisputed facts therefore show that Dameron delayed informing First American of any discrepancies for more than a reasonable period of time. It failed to return the documents to First American and instead took control of the goods. By these acts, Dameron waived its right to reject nonconforming documents and bound itself to reimburse First American for the amount of the drafts. ... First American's cross-claim against Dameron should be granted, and Dameron will be ordered to reimburse First American for the amount of the drafts plus interest.

\* \* \*

NOTES

**(1) Issuing and Confirming Banks.** This case illustrates the role of confirming banks in letter of credit transactions. As originally structured, letters of credit were issued by First American Bank of Virginia (First American) in favor of National Marketing Export Co. of Amman, Jordan. The seller's bank in Jordan, Petra Bank, was not a party to the letter of credit, but seller probably anticipated that Petra Bank would transmit

---

[E]ven if the Court were to accept the notion that an account customer should be able to accept documents and goods and then sue for direct damages resulting from a bank's acceptance of nonconforming documents, it would not permit Dameron to reduce the payment owed to First American by any damages stemming from National Marketing's delivery of faulty goods. Such damages stem from the seller's breach, not First American's. Moreover, even if the court were to hold that an account customer could receive damages from the issuing bank stemming from the receipt of faulty goods, Dameron has already been compensated for such receipt through its settlement with National Marketing. There is no reason in this case for Dameron not to reimburse First American for the full amount First American paid for the goods.

documents, through banking channels, to First American. The letter of credit arrangement was altered to add a confirming bank, Petra International Banking Corp. (PIBC), an American affiliate of Petra Bank. With the addition of a confirming bank, that bank became the entity to which seller would submit the documents required under the letter of credit. Undoubtedly, Petra Bank in Jordan determined that it would be more efficient to have the seller's documents submitted to its American affiliate. The typical reason for introducing a confirming bank into a transaction is to facilitate the beneficiary's access to the banks.

Original UCC 5–107(2) declared: "A confirming bank by confirming a credit becomes directly obligated on the credit to the extent of its confirmation as though it were its issuer and acquires the rights of an issuer." Revised UCC 5–107(a) is similar. These provisions are mirrored in the UCP.

Both the issuing bank and the confirming bank were involved in handling the presentment of seller's drafts and supporting documents in *Petra*. The confirming bank, PIBC, noted discrepancies in the documents and telexed the issuing bank, First American, which in turn telexed the applicant, Dameron. Dameron's waiver, conditioned on change in the time of payment, was communicated to First American, which informed PIBC. Based on this message, PIBC accepted seller's drafts. PIBC then forwarded the supporting documents to First American, which turned them over to Dameron. Among the documents was the bill of lading that Dameron surrendered to the carrier in exchange for the goods.

Neither the UCP nor the Commercial Code deals with the right or the duty of confirming banks to seek guidance from issuing banks when nonconforming documents are presented to the confirming banks. UCP 500 14(c), which we considered in *Hanil Bank*, refers only to issuing banks approaching applicants. What might explain PIBC's decision to telex First American to seek guidance on whether to accept the non-conforming documents?

**(2) Time and Sight Drafts; Accepted Drafts.** The letters of credit first issued in this case did not call for immediate payment by the issuing bank, but rather for payment within 30 days of submission of specified documents. Subsequently, at the request of the applicant, the letters of credit were modified to require payment 150 days after the date of the bill of lading. As provided in the letters of credit, the beneficiary presented time drafts, negotiable instruments that called for the bank's future payment. On presentment of the time drafts, after the exchange of telex messages, the confirming bank "accepted" them. Acceptances of time drafts, defined in UCC 3–409, creates an obligation to pay the amount of the drafts under UCC 3–413(a). The legal liability of a bank that has accepted a time draft is independent of the bank's obligation under a letter of credit. If a letter of credit requires a bank to accept a time draft, the bank's obligation under the letter of credit is discharged by acceptance of a draft. UCC 3–310(c).

Letter of credit transactions that permit the use of time drafts delay payment for the periods of time stated in the drafts. Why would sellers, having contracted for buyers' payment by letter of credit, be willing to allow use of time drafts rather than sight drafts? Without any release of funds, buyers obtain the documents of title that give them control or possession of the goods. As this case indicates, time drafts can be dishonored when presented for payment. What explains sellers' willingness to hand over goods to buyers while this risk exists? Note that the obligation to pay an accepted time draft is the unconditional obligation of the bank, not of the buyer, and the bank's obligation is not contingent on buyer's willingness or ability to reimburse the bank. Banks are not prone to dishonor their legal obligations.

PIBC did not dishonor the accepted time drafts in *Petra* when the drafts were presented for payment. The court stated, somewhat inaccurately, that PIBC made payments under its letter of credit. The payments were made pursuant to the independent obligation of the accepted time drafts.

**(3) Bank-to-Bank Relationships.** The principal claim in the case is by PIBC against First American. The precise nature of the claim is somewhat unclear.

The *Petra* court relied on Article 16 of UCP 400, which it set forth in full in a footnote with much emphasis of certain words and phrases. Article 16 dealt generally with the obligation of issuing banks when presented with documents by remitting banks or by beneficiaries directly, particularly the obligations to give notice of discrepancies without delay and the consequence of failure to act. Nothing in that Article refers explicitly to the relationship between a confirming bank and an issuing bank. Counsel for First American argued, therefore, that Article 16 did not authorize a claim by a confirming bank. The court rejected the argument: "To ... accept First American's reading of Article 16 would render the UCP devoid of standards governing transactions between confirming banks and issuing banks. This would make no business sense." Was the court's analysis sound? Was it First America's reading of Article 16 or the language of the Article itself that rendered UCP 400 devoid of standards governing transactions between confirming banks and issuing banks?

If the UCP is silent on the rights of issuing and confirming banks *inter sese*, the issue becomes one for the law underlying the transaction. If domestic United States law applies, the legal rule may be found in UCC Article 5. The *Petra* court referred to UCC 5–107(2), but that section provides only for the duties of confirming banks. It is as silent as the UCP was on the rights of confirming banks.

Revised Article 5 adds a new provision, in UCC 5–107(a):

> The confirmer also has rights against and obligations to the issuer as if the issuer were the applicant and the confirmer had issued the letter of credit at the request and for the account of the issuer.

If this provision had been in effect in *Petra*, would it have been a basis for PIBC's claim against First American? First American's letters of credit called for presentment of time drafts. Did PIBC present time drafts to First American? As noted, PIBC ultimately paid against its accepted time drafts.

Those payments were not documentary conditions in First American's letter of credit.

**(4) Nature of Terms Conditioning Banks' Obligations.** In theory, the parties to letter of credit transactions could make any fact or event the condition that unlocks a bank's conditional duty to pay or accept a demand for payment. Banking practice, however, has strongly favored limiting the fact or event to the presentation of described documents.

The parties in *Petra* established a documentary requirement that seller provide a statement from a specified independent inspection company certifying the number and quality of the goods per sample and the seller's own statement that the goods shipped were of the quality of the samples on which buyer had relied.

The statement of the independent inspection company was a document of potentially great importance to the buyer, since the letters of credit would be honored before the buyer had any opportunity to inspect the goods shipped. The statement was not presented. When informed of this by the issuing bank, the buyer waived the discrepancy. What might explain the buyer's decision to waive this requirement?

The second statement, which the court refers to as the Statement of the Beneficiary, was also not presented to PIBC. This, too, was waived by the buyer. Of what value to buyer would such a documented statement be?

**Problem 1.** Seller, in London, agreed to sell "Coromandel groundnuts" to a Danish buyer. Pursuant to the contract Bank opened a letter of credit in Seller's favor. Seller tendered documents to Bank which included a commercial invoice that described the goods as "Coromandel groundnuts" in the manner called for in the letter of credit. The bill of lading tendered to Bank described the goods as "machine shelled groundnut kernels." Bank refused to honor Seller's draft because of the discrepancy between the bill of lading and the letter of credit. In action by Seller against the Bank, Seller proved that, in the London produce market, the two terms referred interchangeably to the same commodity.[2] Should the Bank be held liable? See UCC 5–108(a) and (e).

**(5) Bank–Customer Relationships.** The second part of *Petra* was the claim of the issuing bank against the applicant. The court noted that this was primarily a matter of the agreement between the bank and the applicant when the latter sought to obtain the letters of credit. The UCP is silent on bank-customer relationships. So, too, was original UCC Article 5. The court was persuaded to follow the general principles of interpretation in UCC 1–102.

Revised UCC 5–108(i) adds a subsection on the rights of issuers that have rightfully honored a presentation. Such an issuer "(1) is entitled to be reimbursed by the applicant in immediately available funds not later than the date of its payment of funds." If this provision had been in effect in

---

2. See Rayner & Co. v. Hambros Bank, [1942] 2 All E.R. 694 (C.A.).

*Petra*, would it have been a basis for First American's claim against Dameron?

# Mid–America Tire, Inc. v. PTZ Trading Ltd.

Supreme Court of Ohio, 2002.
95 Ohio St.3d 367, 768 N.E.2d 619.

■ ALICE ROBIE RESNICK, J.

## I. FACTS

### A. Overview

These appeals arise out of an action brought in the Clermont County Court of Common Pleas to enjoin payment under a letter of credit ("LC") on the basis of fraud in the underlying transaction. The underlying transaction involved extensive overseas negotiations toward an agreement to import blemished Michelin tires for sale in the United States. A blemished or "blem" tire is one that is cosmetically but not operationally affected by a surface imperfection.

The gravamen of the fraud claim is that the overseas seller's agents made certain false promises and representations concerning the sale of more lucrative summer tires in order to induce the American buyers to purchase and open an LC securing the purchase of less lucrative mud and snow tires, many of which could not legally be imported or sold in the United States. The buyers claim that they discovered the fraud after the LC was issued and instructed the seller not to ship the tires, but the seller went ahead with shipment anyway and presented its invoice and shipping documents for payment under the supporting LC. The buyers then instituted this action pursuant to *[UCC 5–109(b)]*, alleging that honoring the LC in this case would facilitate and consummate the seller's fraud.

### B. Parties and Participants

Given the multilateral nature of the negotiations and arrangements in this case, it is beneficial to provide a working list of the various parties and key participants and their relationships to one another and the transactions at hand.

The American parties and participants are as follows:

(1) Plaintiff-appellant and cross-appellee, Mid–America Tire, Inc. ("Mid–America"), is an Ohio corporation doing business as a tire wholesaler. Mid–America provided the financing for the purchase of the tires in this case and was the named applicant by whose order and for whose account the LC was issued.

(2) Arthur Hine is the president of Mid–America and signatory to the LC application.

(3) Plaintiff-appellant and cross-appellee, Jenco Marketing, Inc. ("Jenco"), is a Tennessee corporation doing business as a tire whole-

saler. Jenco formed a joint venture with Mid–America to purchase the tires at issue.

(4) Fred Alvin "F.A." Jenkins is the owner of Jenco and also acted as Mid–America's agent in the underlying negotiations.

(5) Paul Chappell is an independent tire broker who resides in Irvine, California. Chappell works as an independent contractor for Tire Network, Inc., a company owned by his wife, and acted throughout most of the negotiations as an agent for Jenco.

(6) First National Bank of Chicago ("First National"), on behalf of NBD Bank Michigan, is the issuer of the LC in this case. First National was a defendant below, but is not a party to this appeal.

The European parties and participants are as follows:

(1) Defendant-appellee and cross-appellant, PTZ Trading Ltd. ("PTZ"), is an offshore import and export company established in Guernsey, Channel Islands. PTZ is the seller in the underlying transaction and the beneficiary under the LC.

(2) Gary Corby is an independent tire broker operating as Corby International, a trading name of Corby Tyres (Wholesale) Ltd., in Wales, United Kingdom. Corby was the initiator of the underlying negotiations. The trial court's findings with regard to Corby's status as PTZ's agent form the subject of PTZ's cross-appeal.

(3) John Evans is the owner of Transcontinental Tyre Company located in Wolverhampton, England, and PTZ's admitted agent in the underlying negotiations.

(4) Aloysius Sievers is a German tire broker to whom PTZ owed money from a previous transaction unconnected to this case. Sievers, also an admitted agent for PTZ, procured and shipped the subject tires on behalf of PTZ, and signed and presented the draft for payment under the LC.

(5) Patrick Doumerc is the son of the proprietor of Doumerc SA, a French company that is authorized to sell Michelin overstock or surplus tires worldwide. Doumerc is the person from whom Sievers procured the mud and snow tires for sale to Jenco and Mid–America.

(6) Barclays Bank PLC in St. Peter Port, Guernsey, is the bank to which Sievers presented the invoice and shipping documents for payment under the supporting LC. Barclays Bank was a defendant below, but is not a party to this appeal.

C.   Events Leading to the Issuance of the LC

In October 1998, Corby approached Evans about obtaining large quantities of Michelin winter tires. Evans contacted Sievers, to whom PTZ owed money. Evans knew that Sievers had a relationship with a sole distributor of Michelin surplus tires out of France. Eventually, an arrangement was worked out under which Sievers would buy the tires from Doumerc's warehouse in France and Evans would sell them on behalf of PTZ through Corby to an American purchaser.

Meanwhile, Corby contacted Chappell in California and asked whether he was interested in importing Michelin tires on the gray market for sale in the United States. "Gray imports" are tires that are imported without the knowledge or approval of a manufacturer into a market that the manufacturer serves, at a greatly reduced price. Corby told Chappell that he had a large client who negotiated an arrangement directly with Michelin to handle all of its overstock blem tires from France and who could offer 50,000 to 70,000 Michelin tires per quarter at 40 to 60 percent below the United States market price on an exclusive and ongoing basis. Chappell contacted Jenkins in Tennessee, who called Hine in Ohio, and it was arranged that Jenco and Mid–America would pursue the deal through Chappell.

On October 28, 1998, Corby faxed Chappell a list of Michelin mud and snow tires that were immediately available for shipment and Chappell forwarded the list to Jenkins. The list was arranged in columns for quantity, size, pattern, and other designations applicable to the European market with which Chappell and Jenkins were unfamiliar. In particular, many of the tires on the list bore the designation "DA/2C." Chappell and Jenkins understood that DA meant "defective appearance," a European marking for a blem, but they were not familiar with the "/2C" portion of the designation. When they asked for clarification, Corby told Chappell that "DA/2C" means the same thing as "DA," but since all of the listed tires are not warehoused at a single location, "/2C" is used merely to indicate that those blemished tires are located in a different warehouse.

Chappell also asked Corby whether he could procure and offer summer or "highway" tires, along with the winter tires. Chappell, Jenkins, and Hine had no interest in purchasing strictly snow tires, as it was already too late in the season to market them profitably. However, they would have an interest in buying both winter and highway tires and marketing them together as a package deal.

Corby told Chappell that 50,000 to 70,000 highway tires would be made available on a quarterly basis at 40 to 60 percent below the United States market price. However, when Chappell received another list of available tires from Corby on November 11, 1998, he complained to Corby that this list contained no summer tires and nowhere near 50,000 units. Corby responded that Michelin was anxious to get rid of these tires first, as the market for snow tires in Europe was coming to a close, that a list of summer highway tires would be made available over the next few weeks, and that Chappell and appellants would not have an opportunity to procure the highway tires unless they first agreed to purchase the snow tires. Corby explained that Michelin does not list available summer tires in the mid-month of a quarter. Instead, it waits for these tires to accumulate in a warehouse and then puts out the list at the end of the month. Thus, a list of summer tires would be available over the next few weeks.

In a transmission dated November 13, 1998, Corby wrote to Chappell:

"The situation is as I explained yesterday, there are no summer tyres available at all but, if, and a very big if, this deal goes ahead we will get all surplus stocks at the end [of] each quarter from now on, but if this deal does not go, then I know we can kiss any future offers good buy [sic]."

On November 20, 1998, Corby faxed Chappell a list of summer tires available for immediate shipment, but the listed units were not priced, were composed of many small "odd ball sizes" unmarketable in the United States, and did not approach the 50—to 70,000—range in aggregate quantity. In his cover letter, Corby assured Chappell that "I have of course been in contact with Michelin regarding the list of summer tyres" and "they have confirmed that in the next three/four weeks we have exclusive to us the new list of Michelin summer tyres, quantity unknown as yet, but they believe to be anything from 50,000/70,000 tyres, which would not be too bad for Jan sales." The letter also stated that Michelin was offering the tires at "the price of $1.50 per tyre more than the M & S tyres * * * based on taking the whole lot."

On November 23, 1998, Corby faxed the following letter to Jenkins:

"Subject: Michelin Tyre Programme.

"Dear F.A.

"I would just like to confirm our current position with the Off-Shore marketing company that have been authorized to sell all Michelin factory 'Over Stock' tyres. That is, from now on the tyres will only be offered for sale to us through PTZ Trading Ltd., these tyres will come available every two/three months which I have been informed by my contact the next large consignment (not including the current stock of winter/summer tyres) will be in the next three/four weeks time of around 50,000/70,000 tyres.

"If our business with the winter tyres goes well, then I see this as [an] extremely excellent opportunity to tap into large consignments of tyres direct from the factory on a regular long term basis.

"Just to confirm once again, I have been assured by PTZ Trading who are acting on behalf of the factory that we will have exclusivity to all tyres that come available from now on."

On December 1, 1998, Evans faxed a letter and "pro forma invoice" (an invoice that sets out in rough terms what the eventual invoice will look like) to Jenkins. The letter stated, "We understand from Gary Corby that you are now about to open the Letter of Credit for the Michelin M & S Tyres."

However, Chappell and Jenkins were hesitant to have Hine proceed with the financing for the winter tires because they had not yet received concrete information as to the cost and availability of the initial 50,000 to 70,000 summer tires. As Chappell and Jenkins held out for the list of summer tires, Corby and Evans pressed for the LC. While continually assuring Chappell and Jenkins that large stocks of Michelin summer tires would be made available in a short time, Corby and Evans became increasingly insistent about conditioning the offer of summer tires upon the issuance of an acceptable LC in favor of PTZ for the winter tires.

From early December 1998, through late January 1999, Corby made repeated, often daily, telephone calls to Chappell insisting that Jenkins confirm the issuance of the LC or forfeit the deal entirely. During this time, Corby also sent a number of faxes to Chappell, each one proclaiming that without confirmation of the LC by the end of the day, the offer for the winter tires would be withdrawn and there would be no future offers for winter or summer tires.

In addition, Evans faxed two messages to Jenkins on January 7, 1999. In the first, Evans wrote:

> "There are large stocks of Michelin summer pattern tyres being made available within the next 7/10 days and we will be pleased to offer these to you when an acceptable Letter of Credit is received for the winter pattern tyres. We will be very happy to work with you on Michelin tyres on a long term basis and give you first option on offers.

> "May we once again stress the urgency of letting us have the Letter of Credit for the Michelin winter tyres so that we can commence business on a long term basis."

In the second message, Evans informed Jenkins:

> "Further to our fax of today we understand that you would like clarification on future offers made by PTZ Trading Ltd. of Michelin tyres.

> "As we have already indicated we wish to commence a long term business relationship with Jenco Marketing Ltd. [sic.] We assure you that we will not offer any Michelin tyres that we obtain to any other party in the United States of America provided Jenco Marketing Inc. agree to purchase in a reasonable time."

D.   The Issuance of the LC

By the end of January 1999, Jenkins and Hine were convinced that they had to open the LC for the winter tires as a show of good faith towards the quarterly acquisition of summer tires and that, upon doing so, PTZ would honor its end of the bargain.

Effective February 1, 1999, and expiring in Guernsey, Channel Islands, on April 2, 1999, First National issued an irrevocable credit at Hine's request in favor of PTZ and for the account of Mid–America in the amount of $517,260.33. The LC provided, among other things:

> "COVERING SHIPMENT OF:" 14,851 MICHELIN TYPES AT USD 34.83 PER TIRE IN ACCORDANCE WITH SELLER'S PROFORMA INVOICE 927–98 DATED 11–19–98

> "SHIPPING TERMS: EXWORKS ANY EUROPEAN LOCATION

> " * * *

"THE CREDIT IS SUBJECT TO THE UNIFORM CUSTOMS AND PRACTICE FOR DOCUMENTARY CREDITS (1993 REVISION), INTERNATIONAL CHAMBER OF COMMERCE—PUBLICATION 500."

E.  Events Following the Issuance of the LC

Over the next month, Corby and Evans pushed for shipping arrangements under the supporting LC for the winter tires, while Chappell and Jenkins continued to insist on a conforming price list for the summer tires. As the final LC shipping date approached, and several nonconforming lists of summer tires emerged, the negotiations grew increasingly volatile until they were hostilely terminated.

A week after the issuance of the LC, Chappell wrote to Corby, "Without the list and pricing [for the summer tires], we are at a standstill with the clock ticking on the winters. Please make every effort to send list during your workday, so we can compile our list for combined sales of both winter and summer units." Corby then faxed Chappell a list of summer tires but, as before, this list contained no prices and fell considerably short of 50,000 units. When Chappell complained, Corby sent another list, which he noted to be six out of 15 sheets of an "original list from Michelin." The other nine sheets, however, were never sent. In any event, this list once again failed to contain the promised quantities of tires, and a considerable number of the listed units were snow tires. Although this list did set forth unit prices, those prices were represented in French francs, and when the French francs were converted into United States dollars, it became apparent that the prices for these units were equal to or in excess of the maximum market prices for a like product in the United States.

On the morning of February 17, 1999, Evans telephoned Jenkins to inform him that no price list for summer tires would be sent until Barclays Bank received the LC for the winter tires. This caught Jenkins by surprise, as the LC had been in place since the first of the month and all information pertaining thereto had previously been sent to Evans, but Jenkins nevertheless faxed Evans the LC confirmation number. Throughout that day, Evans made repeated requests for Jenkins to provide him with shipping instructions and orders to release the winter tires. Jenkins responded with several letters that he faxed to Evans on February 17. In these letters, Jenkins informed Evans that he would not authorize the shipment of any winter tires in the absence of a conforming list of summer tires, that any attempt by Evans to ship the winter tires without Jenkins's written consent would be met with legal action, and that the deal would be voided and the LC recalled unless a complete list of competitively priced summer tires arrived in Jenkins's office by February 19.

On February 19, 1999, Evans faxed the following message to Jenkins:

"We appreciate your feeling of frustration at the delay in giving you the price for the Summer Tyres but assure you it is only in your best interests to obtain the most favorable prices. * * *

"Further urgent negotiations are due to take place with Michelin on Monday February 22nd 1999 to see if we can arrive at an acceptable packaged price but of course the final desission [sic] is yours.

"In the meantime in the interests of all concerned please do not give a specific time for completion if you want us to obtain the most favorable price."

On February 23, 1999, Corby faxed Chappell another list of summer tires, but this list was illegible in places and irreconcilable with the previous list. Chappell complained and Corby sent another list the following day. However, once again, this list fell well short of 50,000 units, contained many European sizes not used in the United States and various tires not manufactured by Michelin, and stated prices that were often higher than the cost of purchasing the tires one at a time from most United States dealers. The list also provided that, in addition to the stated prices, appellants were required to pay all shipping, handling, duty, and freight charges. Moreover, Jenkins was now informed that he could no longer pick and choose from among the listed tires, but instead must purchase the entire lot or none at all.

On March 1, 1999, Jenkins wrote to Evans, "We are with drawing [sic] our offer effective immediately to purchase the snow package, as PTZ has failed to meet their agreed commitment on the Michelin summer tire offer." (Emphasis deleted.) Jenkins stated that the listed prices for the tires are "not competitive" and "TOTALLY UNACCEPTABLE," and that "we have gone from a reported 50,000 tires to a total offer of about 12,000 tires of which approximately 2,500 of those are TRX tires not sold in this country."

Between March 1 and March 5, 1999, Chappell and Jenkins discovered that it was Doumerc, not PTZ, who all along had the direct and exclusive relationship with Michelin to sell all of its overstock and blem tires. They also discovered that Corby had misrepresented the "DA/2C" designation, which attached to many of the tires on the summer lists as well as on the original winter list. Rather than indicating the warehousing location for those tires, "/2C" actually meant that the Department of Transportation serial numbers had been buffed off those units, rendering them illegal for import or sale in the United States.

During this time, Jenkins informed Evans that he would notify the United States Customs Service if the DA/2C tires were shipped, and Evans confirmed that he would not ship those tires to the United States. Also, Chappell informed Doumerc of the entire course of events, and Doumerc agreed not to ship the tires until Chappell and Jenkins had the opportunity to come to France, inspect the tires, and resolve the situation.

Chappell and Jenkins made arrangements to fly to France, but when they called Doumerc on March 11, Sievers answered the phone. They explained the entire matter to Sievers and offered to extend the LC expiration date in order to allow for a peaceful resolution. Sievers rejected the offer, however, stating that the winter tires belonged to him, not

Doumerc, that he did not care what Doumerc had agreed to, and that "I have a letter of credit and I am shipping the tires."

The following day, Mid–America instituted the present action to enjoin payment under the LC. The complaint was later amended to add Jenco as a plaintiff. The trial court granted a temporary restraining order on March 16, 1999, and a preliminary injunction on April 8, 1999.

On July 14 and 15, 1999, a trial was held on appellants' motion for a permanent injunction. In a final judgment entry dated October 8, 1999, the trial court granted a permanent injunction against honor or presentment under the LC pursuant to [UCC 5–109(b)]. In its separate findings of fact and conclusions of law, the trial court found that the documents presented to Barclays Bank on behalf of PTZ appeared on their face to be in strict compliance with the terms and conditions of the LC. However, the court also found by clear and convincing evidence that PTZ, acting through Evans and Corby, fraudulently induced appellants to open the LC, and that such fraud was sufficient to vitiate the LC. In this regard, the trial court was "satisfied that fraud in the inducement of the issuance of a letter of credit is grounds for a court to grant injunctive relief against the payment of such letter of credit to the beneficiary who perpetrated such fraud."

In a split decision, the court of appeals reversed the judgment of the trial court. ... The cause is now before this court pursuant to the allowance of a discretionary appeal and cross-appeal.

* * *

## III.   MID–AMERICA AND JENCO'S APPEAL

### A.   Inadequate Legal Remedy

PTZ argues, and the court of appeals held, that appellants should be denied injunctive relief under [UCC 5–109(b)] because they have an adequate remedy at law. ...

In the present case, an action to recover damages for fraud would not be an adequate legal remedy because it would not be as prompt, efficient, and practical as the injunction issued by the trial court, and would not provide appellants with certain and complete relief in a single action. The pursuit of such a remedy would likely entail a multiplicity of suits against a number of defendants in several jurisdictions. The damages that appellants might seek to recover in an action for fraud would be difficult to estimate because of the near impossibility of determining the quantity of winter and summer tires that could or would have been seasonally marketed together and separately, the quantity of the "DA/2C" and other tires not marketable in the United States that could have been sold overseas, and the appropriate market conditions, cost/price differential, and quantity of offered or promised units. While it may be true, as PTZ argues, that appellants accepted some risk of pursuing damages in another nation's courts, it cannot be found that appellants assumed the risk of having to pursue an inadequate legal remedy.

* * *

Thus, we find that injunctive relief should not be refused in this case on the basis that Mid–America has an adequate remedy at law. Accordingly, the judgment of the court of appeals is reversed as to this issue.

B. Governing Law

R.C. Chapter 1305 is Ohio's version of Article 5 of the Uniform Commercial Code ("UCC"). It was enacted in its current form, effective July 1, 1998, to reflect the 1995 revision of Article 5, and is applicable to any LC that is issued on or after its effective date. See 1997 H.B. No. 338, uncodified Section 4.

* * *

The parties in this case have specifically adopted the UCP as applicable to the present undertaking. In fact, "many letters of credit, domestic and international, state that they shall be governed by the UCP." 3 White & Summers, Uniform Commercial Code (4th Ed. 1995) 122, Section 26–3. "When rules of custom and practice are incorporated by reference, they are considered to be explicit terms of the agreement or undertaking." UCC 5–103, Official Comment 2.

The question that naturally arises from such an incorporation is whether and to what extent R.C. Chapter 1305 will continue to apply to the undertaking. In other words, when a particular LC states that it is subject to the UCP, what is the resulting relationship between the UCP and R.C. Chapter 1305 with regard to that transaction?

* * *

It is only when the UCP and R.C. Chapter 1305 contain overlapping inconsistent provisions on the same issue or subject that the UCP's terms will displace those of R.C. Chapter 1305. Thus, when a particular LC states that it is subject to the UCP, the UCP's terms will replace those of R.C. Chapter 1305 only to the extent that "there is a direct conflict between a provision of the UCP and an analogous provision of R.C. Chapter 1305." . . .

The UCP . . . adopts the independence principle, but does not provide for a fraud exception. Article 3(a) of the UCP states:

> "Credits, by their nature, are separate transactions from the sales or other contract(s) on which they may be based and banks are in no way concerned with or bound by such contract(s), even if any reference whatsoever to such contract(s) is included in the Credit. Consequently, the undertaking of a bank to pay, accept and pay Draft(s) or negotiate and/or to fulfill any other obligation under the Credit, is not subject to claims or defences by the Applicant resulting from his relationships with the Issuing Bank or the Beneficiary."

Article 4 explains, "In Credit operations all parties concerned deal with documents, and not with goods, services and/or other performances to which the documents may relate."

\* \* \*

[T]he overwhelming weight of authority is to the effect that Article 5's fraud exception continues to apply in credit transactions made subject to the UCP. ...

PTZ concedes that these cases were correctly decided under former UCP Publication No. 400 (1983), which was silent on the issue of fraud. According to PTZ, however, "UCP 500 art. 3, which controls this action, is no longer silent on the fraud exception." Instead, PTZ argues that the last sentence in Article 3 of UCP 500, which did not appear in UCP 400, "specifically speaks to the fraud exception, [and provides that] a fraud claim may not be interposed to bar the collection of [an] L/C." In fact, relying on Documentary Credits, UCP 500 & 400 Compared, International Chamber of Commerce Publication No. 511 (1993), PTZ contends that Article 3 was amended in 1993 for the express purpose of breaking the UCP's long-standing silence on the issue of fraud in order to counteract the effect of the foregoing decisions.

PTZ's arguments regarding the amended UCP are ingenious but unavailing. ...

[T]he official comments to UCP 511 do not support the notion that Article 3 has now addressed the issue of fraud. The word "fraud" does not even appear in the commentary quoted by PTZ. To the contrary, the Working Group states specifically that the new text of Article 3 operates to deter "the Applicant's demand that payment should be stopped because of the Beneficiary's *breach of his contractual obligations* to the Applicant." (Emphasis added.) Reporting further, the Working Group explains, "This new language in UCP 500 Article 3 clarifies that neither the Beneficiary nor the Applicant can avail himself of any underlying *contractual relationship*." (Emphasis added.)

The UCP has been amended approximately every ten years since 1962. See 7A Lawrence (Rev.2001) 428, fn. 32, Section 5–101:22. If the current version had finally broken the UCP's longstanding silence on the issue of fraud, one would expect at least a mention of that fact somewhere in the amendatory text or commentary. ...

We hold, therefore, that when a letter of credit expressly incorporates the terms of the UCP, but the UCP does not contain any rule covering the issue in controversy, the UCP will not replace the relevant provisions of R.C. Chapter 1305. Since the UCP does not contain any rule addressing the issue of injunctive relief where fraud occurs in either the credit documents or the underlying transaction, [UCC 5–109(b)] remains applicable in credit transactions made subject to the UCP.

Accordingly, the rights and obligations of the parties in this case are governed by [UCC 5–109(b)], and the judgment of the court of appeals is reversed as to this issue.

C.   Establishing Fraud Under [UCC 5–109(b)]

Having determined the applicability of [UCC 5–109(b)], we must now consider its boundaries. In this regard, we have been asked to decide whether an issuer may be enjoined from honoring a presentation on the basis of beneficiary's fraud in the underlying transaction and to characterize the fraudulent activity justifying such relief.

1.   Fraud in the Underlying Transaction

May the issuer be enjoined from honoring a presentation under [UCC 5–109(b)] on the basis of the beneficiary's fraudulent activity in the underlying transaction? The short answer is yes, since [UCC 5–109(b)] authorizes injunctive relief where "honor of the presentation would facilitate a material fraud by the beneficiary on the * * * applicant." ...

* * *

We hold, therefore, that material fraud committed by the beneficiary in either the letter of credit transaction or the underlying sales transaction is sufficient to warrant injunctive relief under [UCC 5–109(b)]. Accordingly, the judgment of the court of appeals is reversed as to this issue.

2.   Measure of Fraud

Another controversy that surrounded the "fraud in the transaction" language of UCC 5–114(2) involved the degree or quantity of fraud necessary to warrant injunctive relief. ...

However, UCC 5–109(b) clarifies that only "material fraud" by the beneficiary will justify an injunction against honor. ...

Thus, we hold that "material fraud" under [UCC 5–109(b)] means fraud that has so vitiated the entire transaction that the legitimate purposes of the independence of the issuer's obligation can no longer be served.

* * *

3.   PTZ's Actions

The trial court found the following facts to have been established by clear and convincing evidence:

"6.   Gary Corby represented to F.A. Jenkins that PTZ Trading, Ltd. was in fact the sole distributor for surplus Michelin tires and that there was a direct relationship between PTZ Trading, Ltd. and Michelin. Corby further represented to Jenkins that there would be 50,000 to 70,000 summer tires available to Jenco per quarter at a price 40 to 60 percent below the U.S. market price within weeks of Jenco showing good faith by purchasing in excess of five hundred thousand dollars worth of mud and snow tires currently offered by PTZ Trading, Ltd.

"7.   The Court further finds that John Evans, as agent for PTZ Trading, Ltd., was aware that Corby was making such representations to Jenco and that such representations were false. Mr. John Evans, as an agent for PTZ, knew that Jenco considered the purchase of the summer tires to be necessary in order to make the winter snow and mud tires saleable in the U.S. market. Mr. Evans did nothing to correct Mr. Corby's misrepresentations. Mr. Evans affirmed the misrepresentations and attempted to buttress them in correspondence with Jenco.

"8.   Mr. Evans conveyed this information to Mr. Sievers who also acknowledged that he understood that the purchase of the summer tires by Jenco was critical to the conclusion of the sale of the mud and snow tires and without which the winter tire sale would not occur.

"9.   John Evans and Aloysius Sievers also knew that a large portion of the mud and snow tires they were attempting to sell were not capable of being imported into the United States or sold here because the United States Department of Transportation identification number had been 'buffed' off of such tires. Both Sievers and Evans knew that Jenco and Mid America Tire intended to sell the snow tires in the United States, but neither advised Jenco or Mid America Tire of the existence of the 'buffed' tires.

"10.   Prior to the issuance of the letter of credit, John Evans knew Mid America Tire, Inc. and Jenco were operating under intentionally false and inaccurate representations made by Corby and reinforced by John Evans. * * *

"12.   The Court finds, specifically, that the representation that PTZ had a direct relationship with Michelin Tire, the representation that PTZ was the exclusive distributor for surplus Michelin Tires, the representation that a substantial quantity of between fifty and seventy thousand tires would be available quarterly on an exclusive basis to Jenco and Mid America Tire, Inc. at 40 to 60 percent of the U.S. market price were all material statements inducing Plaintiffs to issue the underlying letter of credit and were in fact false and made with knowledge of their falsity."

* * *

Given these facts, we are compelled to conclude that PTZ's actions in this case are sufficiently egregious to warrant injunctive relief under the "material fraud" standard of [UCC 5–109(b)]. The trial court's findings demonstrate that PTZ sought to unload a large quantity of surplus winter tires on appellants by promising a large number of bargain-priced summer tires, without which the winter tires would be virtually worthless to appellants. Keenly aware that appellants would not agree to purchase the winter tires without the summer tires, PTZ made, participated in, and/or failed to correct a series of materially fraudulent promises and representations regarding the more lucrative summer tires in order to induce appellants to commit to purchasing the winter tires and to open an LC in PTZ's favor to secure payment. Dangling the prospect of the summer tires just beyond appellants' reach, PTZ sought first the issuance of the LC, and then shipping instructions, in an effort to cash in on the winter deal before appellants could discover the truth about the "DA/2C" tires and PTZ's lack of ability and intention ever to provide summer tires at the price and quantity represented. Indeed, when appellants learned of PTZ's fraud after opening the LC, and PTZ was no longer able to stall for shipping instructions with nonconforming lists of summer tires, Sievers proclaimed, "I have a letter of credit and I am shipping the tires."

Under these facts, it can truly be said that the LC in this case was being used by PTZ as a vehicle for fraud and that PTZ's actions effectively deprived appellants of any benefit in the underlying arrangement. . . .

PTZ's demand for payment under these circumstances has absolutely no basis in fact, and it would be pointless and unjust to permit PTZ to draw the money. PTZ's conduct has so vitiated the entire transaction that the only purpose served by invoking the independence principle in this case would be to transform the LC into a fraudulent seller's Holy Grail, which once obtained would provide cover for fraudulent business practices in the name of commercial expedience. Accordingly, we reverse the court of appeals' judgment as it bears on this issue.

### IV.   PTZ's CROSS–APPEAL

In its five separate cross-propositions of law, PTZ essentially argues that Corby was not its agent and that, in any event, appellants could not have justifiably relied on Corby's representations.

### A.   Corby's Status

PTZ argues that because appellants "had no direct evidence of PTZ having made Corby its agent," they sought to meet their burden "by pointing to a series of inferences drawn from neutral facts." . . . We disagree.

PTZ has succeeded in showing only that the evidence going to Corby's status in the underlying transaction is circumstantial and would have been sufficient to support differing conclusions. But not all circumstantial evidence is conjectural, and not every inference is speculative. The difference lies essentially in the distinction between a reasonable inference and a guess. . . .

With regard to Corby's status in the underlying transaction, the trial court found as follows:

> "Mr. Evans' admission that Corby did the negotiating on behalf of PTZ constitutes an admission that Corby had authority to deal for PTZ, an admission of *actual agency*, although Mr. Evans denies that was the actual relationship with Corby. However, in light of his admission that Corby negotiated on behalf of PTZ, including corresponding for PTZ with Plaintiffs and that Corby "knew of the pricing levels' for PTZ, knowledge which it would certainly be odd for a competitor's agent to have possession of in a negotiation, the Court

concludes that Corby acted as the agent of PTZ in this transaction. At the very least, Evans knew Corby was negotiating on behalf of PTZ and representing himself as having the ability to do that, and Evans allowed Corby to do so and did nothing to correct the situation, leading to agency by estoppel." (Emphasis sic.)

In addition, Jenkins testified that whenever he "would call Mr. Evans and leave a message or * * * send a fax to Mr. Evans, Mr. Corby would either return the call or a fax would come back from Mr. Corby with the answer." Jenkins also testified that at one point he requested to deal directly with Evans rather than through Corby, but Evans responded that "he was not cutting [Corby] out of the deal."

On the other hand, Evans testified that Corby had corresponded with Chappell "on behalf of PTZ." However, when asked whether Corby "handled the negotiations for PTZ with regard to this transaction," Evans stated that "at no time was Mr. Corby acting as PTZ. * * * He was not acting on behalf of PTZ." Evans then stated that Corby negotiated on behalf of PTZ only "in so far as that Corby did the negotiations with Mr. Chappell and the price was then agreed between Mr. Corby and myself." Later in his testimony, when asked whether he had previously stated that "Mr. Corby did the negotiations for this deal on behalf of PTZ," Evans replied, "No, sir, I didn't say that. I said that Mr. Corby was negotiating with PTZ on behalf of Jenco and Mr. Chappell."

Considering the totality of the evidence going to Corby's status and the circumstances surrounding his role in the underlying negotiations, we find that in resolving this issue, the trial court did no more than what factfinders are generally charged with doing, which is to draw reasonable inferences from established facts, "view the witnesses and observe their demeanor, gestures and voice inflections, and use these observations in weighing the credibility of the proffered testimony." . . .

B.  Justifiable Reliance

The gist of PTZ's justifiable reliance argument is that appellants should have known prior to applying for the LC that Corby was lying about the "DA/2C" designation, the availability and cost of the summer tires, and PTZ's relationship with Michelin. PTZ reasons that because of the "repeated stonewalling in providing information" to appellants about the summer tires, appellants should have perceived a danger of possible fraud and sought to confirm the veracity of all of Corby's representations. Having failed to do so, appellants cannot show justifiable reliance.

The arguments presented on both sides of this issue are lengthy, primarily factual, and supported extensively by evidentiary material that has already been set forth in detail throughout this opinion. We find it wholly unnecessary to revisit these facts and reproduce them anew for purposes of resolving this issue. Suffice it to say that no fraudulent activity, no misrepresentation, and no false promise were discovered or reasonably discoverable by appellants or Chappell prior to the issuance of the LC. It may be true that appellants were hesitant to open the LC because of the nonconforming lists of summer tires, but they certainly did request and receive confirmation from PTZ on all relevant matters. While hindsight reveals that appellants may have been somewhat too generous or premature with their trust, we cannot say as a matter of law that appellants acted unreasonably at the time, that they failed to exercise due diligence in their dealings with PTZ, or that they should have been alerted to the danger that awaited them. Given the circumstances, it was perfectly reasonable for appellants to accept that PTZ was merely seeking a show of good faith on their part and that conforming summer tire lists would be forthcoming upon the issuance of the LC. There is sufficient evidence from which to conclude that it was not appellants' lack of diligence that failed to expose the fraud in this case, but PTZ's adeptness at keeping it concealed.

## V.   CONCLUSION

Based on all of the foregoing, the judgment of the court of appeals is hereby reversed, and the permanent injunction as granted by the trial court is reinstated.

Judgment reversed.

## NOTES

**(1) Injunction Against Payment Under a Letter of Credit.** The Commercial Code allows some buyers a slim chance of stopping payment by an issuing bank. The opportunity is predicated on a showing by a buyer that it is the potential victim of fraudulent activities by the seller. Prospective breach of the underlying sales contracts is not sufficient. The harm must be the result of serious fault. The problem is addressed under domestic United States law in UCC 5–109(b). Was the Ohio Supreme Court correct in concluding that the seller's conduct was sufficiently egregious to warrant the issuance of the injunction?

**(2) The UCP and Seller's Misconduct.** The letter of credit in this case was issued subject to the UCP 500. The beneficiary contended that the UCP, which became part of the letter of credit contract, superseded UCC 5–109(b). Section 5–116(c) states a general rule regarding the relationship between the UCP and the Commercial Code: "If . . . the relevant undertaking incorporates rules of custom and practice and . . . there is conflict between this article and those rules as applied to that undertaking, those rules govern except to the extent of any conflict with the nonvariable provisions specified in Section 5–103(c)." The Ohio court held that the UCP was silent on the consequences of fraud in contracts underlying the issuance of letters of credit. Was the Ohio court's decision consistent with the UCP and UCC 5–116(c)?

**(3) Other Injunctive Remedies; Attachment of Proceeds of Letters of Credit.** Some aggrieved buyers proceed on multiple remedial paths: injunction against the bank to stop payment as well as injunction against the beneficiary from drawing against a letter of credit. It is clear from the opinion in *Mid–America Tire* that the injunction in that case was issued against the issuing bank and the beneficiary. The court noted that issuing bank, First National Bank of Chicago, was a party to the trial court proceedings, but was not a party to the appeal. The appeal was taken by the beneficiary.

An aggrieved buyer may also seek to seize a seller's bank account, including proceeds of an issuing bank's payment of a letter of credit before transmission of the funds to the seller. See Daye Nonferrouse Metals Co. v. Trafigura Beheer B.V., 1997 WL 375680 (S.D.N.Y. 1997), vacated in part, 152 F.3d 917 (2d Cir. 1998).

## (B) INTERNATIONAL SALES LAW

The ICC Uniform Customs and Practices for Documentary Credits (UCP) are a compilation of international banking practices for letter of credit transactions, but the UCP provisions are not positive law. They apply to letter of credit transactions by agreement of the parties to letters of credit. The Convention on Contracts for International Sale of Goods has no provisions on performance of letter of credit transactions. There is no body of international commercial law comparable to Article 5 of the Uniform Commercial Code.

## SECTION 5.   CASUALTY TO GOODS; RISK OF LOSS

## (A) DOMESTIC UNITED STATES LAW

### 1.   INTRODUCTION

Casualty to goods—as by fire, theft, or flood—may occur at any one of several stages in the performance of the sales contract. Goods may be lost or stolen. The casualty or loss may occur while the goods are on the seller's premises, either after the making of a contract for the sale of specific (identified) goods or after the seller has identified goods as those intended for performance of the contract. More frequently, the loss occurs while the goods are in transit or after their arrival but before the buyer takes possession. Problems can arise even after the buyer receives the goods if casualty occurs during a period of testing or inspection, or following the buyer's rejection (or revocation of acceptance) of the goods on the ground that they were not in conformity with the contract.

Dispute between the seller and buyer is often avoided by the widespread existence of insurance coverage, and sometimes by the legal responsibility of the carrier for damage occurring during transit. Even in these situations, problems may arise as to whether the seller or the buyer has the responsibility to take over and salvage damaged goods, press a claim against the insurer or carrier, and bear any loss from inadequacy in insurance coverage or from limitations on the liability of the carrier.

In addition, rules on risk of loss may determine whether the seller has performed its warranty and other contractual obligations. Suppose, for instance, that a contract calls for No. 1 wheat and that water damage during the rail shipment reduces the wheat grade to No. 4. In such a case the rules on risk of loss in transit will determine whether the buyer has a claim against the seller for breach of a quality warranty. UCC Article 2 does not express the obvious relationship between rules on risk and quality warranties. CISG is more articulate: "The seller is liable . . . for any lack of conformity which exists at the time when the risk passes to the buyer, even though the lack of conformity becomes apparent only after that time."[1]

*Historical Background.* English law, at an early stage, concluded that risk of loss did not pass from a seller to a buyer until the goods had been delivered. Such was the view expressed in the thirteenth century by Bracton in De Legibus, ". . . because in truth, he who has not delivered a thing to the purchaser, is still himself the lord of it;" Bracton illustrated the point with the death of an ox and the burning of a house prior to delivery to the buyer.[2]

Long before the first codification of British sales law, a different approach had developed. This change probably was not designed to accelerate the transfer to buyers of risk of loss, but rather to strengthen buyers' remedies against sellers who refused to deliver goods. The difficulty stemmed from the fact that buyers had no common-law remedy to take the goods from recalcitrant sellers, or from third persons (such as a seller's creditors), unless buyers could be said to have "property" or "title." A claim for damages against a seller who is plagued by creditors is, of course, of little value; what is needed is a remedy to seize the goods, or a legal claim (e.g., for conversion) against a third person that is not judgment-proof. There is evidence that, to mitigate this deficiency in the common-law remedial system, courts at an early date developed the view that when a contract is made for the sale of specific (identified) goods, the buyer thereupon has the "property."[3]

Once it was concluded that a buyer had "property" in the goods, it seemed to follow that it bore the risk if "its" goods were destroyed. A famous 1827 King's Bench decision in Tarling v. Baxter involved the sale of a stack of hay which burned prior to the time for delivery and payment.[4] The opinion by Bayley, J., opened with the basic premise: "It is quite clear that the loss must fall upon him in whom the property was vested at the time when it was destroyed by fire." All that remained was to find where

---

**1.**   CISG 36(1); see also CISG 36(2), 66.

**2.**   Bracton, De Legibus, Twiss Ed. 1878, Ch. XXVII, p. 493. Compare Glanville, Laws and Customs (cir. 1187–89) Book X, Ch. XIV, 216 (Beames ed. 1900). The joint treatment of goods and realty did not survive later developments in the common law, but to some extent has persisted in civil law formulations.

**3.**   Holdsworth, History of English Law 355–56 (3d ed. 1923). Holdsworth suggests that such remedies led to "the doctrine that a contract of sale of specific goods passes the property in the goods." See also: Blackburn, The Contract of Sale 188–189 (1845); 2 Pollock & Maitland, History of English Law 210 (2d ed. 1898); P. Atiyah, The Rise and Fall of Freedom of Contract 103, 106 (1979) (present ownership, with possession postponed, used as tool for effective future planning).

**4.**   6 B & C 360, 108 Eng.Rep. 484 (K.B.1827).

the abstraction, "the property," was located. The answer was that "the property" vested in the buyer when the contract was made, even though the buyer did not have possession and would not have even the right to possession until he paid (or tendered) the price. The opinion recognized that more was at stake than risk of loss: "*All* the consequences resulting from the vesting, of the property follow, *one* of which is, that if it be destroyed, the loss falls upon the vendee." (Emphasis added.)

*"Property" and Risk of Loss in the Sale of Goods Act and the Uniform Sales Act.* The use of the "property" concept was brought to the New World as part of the common-law heritage, and dominated the handling of sales problems in both England and the United States long before the onset of codification. Mackensie Chalmers conscientiously transcribed the case-law rules in preparing the British Sale of Goods Act (1893). Under Section 20, unless the parties have agreed otherwise, when "the property" in goods "is transferred to the buyer, the goods are at the buyer's risk whether delivery has been made or not." Under Section 17, where there is a contract for the sale of "specific or ascertained" goods, the property is transferred when the parties so intend. Section 18 laid down five rules (when no different intention appears) "for ascertaining the intention of the parties as to the time at which the property in the goods is to pass to the buyer." Rule 1 codified the approach of *Tarling v. Baxter*:

> Where there is an unconditional contract for the sale of specific goods, in a deliverable state, the property in the goods passes to the buyer when the contract is made, and it is immaterial whether the time of payment or the time of delivery, or both, be postponed.

In preparing the Uniform Sales Act, the reporter, Samuel Williston, closely followed the British model. The general rule that risk of loss passes when "the property" is transferred was placed in USA 22; the rules for ascertaining the parties' intent appear in USA 19–with the rule of *Tarling* reproduced as Rule 1.[5] The USA retained the crucial role of "property" in other settings. For example, under USA 66, where the property has passed, the buyer may "maintain any action allowed by law to the owner of goods of similar kind when wrongfully converted or withheld;" under USA 63(1) the seller may bring an action to recover the price (as contrasted with damages for breach of contract) where "the property has passed to the buyer." Thus, the solution of a congeries of sales problems under the USA was entangled with the question whether "the property" in the goods remained with the seller or whether "it" had passed to the buyer.

*Difficulty with the "Property" Concept.* "Property" in goods is, of course, a legal conclusion and can serve as a tool for decision only when it is implemented by rules referring to events, such as the making of a contract, completion of an agreed performance, delivery to a carrier, or receipt by a buyer. The "property" concept was highly malleable, and

---

**5.** The Uniform Sales Act made a significant (and unfortunate) deviation from the British Act by adding as Rule 5 a provision holding risk in transit on the seller where the contract "requires the seller to deliver the goods to the buyer ... or to pay the freight or cost of transportation to the buyer. ..."

probably would have served as well as any other label for the development of rules addressed to a single problem such as risk of loss. Difficulty, however, developed because one concept was employed to solve several problems which called for different solutions. There was reason to speed the passage of "property" to buyers to provide them with effective remedies against recalcitrant sellers. Very different practical considerations bear on the question as to who should bear casualty loss while the goods are still held by sellers.

*Risk of Loss Under UCC Article 2.* The most radical departure of UCC Article 2 from the approach of the Uniform Sales Act was the Article's virtual abandonment of "property" (or "title") as a vehicle for deciding sales controversies.[6] Instead, the Article provided separate rules to govern risk, replevin rights, recovery of the full price, and other problems which the Uniform Sales Act referred to the "property" concept. The UCC Article 2 provisions on risk of loss are found in UCC 2–509 and UCC 2–510.

## 2.  LOCAL TRANSACTIONS

We begin with losses that occur in the performance stage of local transactions, that is, transactions in which the goods are to be delivered by a seller to a buyer directly without the use of an independent carrier. It may be helpful to consider a few illustrative problem situations.

**Problem 1.** John Smith, a dairy farmer, usually grows a small amount of alfalfa hay to feed to his dairy cows. This summer his alfalfa field did unusually well and he found he had a stack of hay he did not need. On June 1, a neighbor, Brown, came and looked at the stack of hay in Smith's field, and they made a contract for the sale of the stack to Brown for $400; Brown was to pay for the hay and remove it during the first week in July. On June 15, the stack burned.

(a) Smith sues Brown to recover the agreed price of $400. What result? See UCC 2–509; 2–104(1).

(b) At the trial, Smith's lawyer calls Smith to the stand and asks questions that would elicit testimony that Brown specifically requested and received assurances that Smith "would hold the hay in the pasture for Brown and would not sell it to anyone else." Brown's lawyer objects to the evidence as irrelevant. Smith's lawyer answered that the evidence was relevant to show that Brown had received the goods under UCC 2–509(3). What ruling? See UCC 2–103(1)(c).

(c) Suppose the fire had occurred on July 10? See UCC 2–503, 2–510.

(d) Assume that the fire (as in (c), above) occurred on July 10, but that the seller is the Smith Alfalfa Company. What result?

---

**6.** Professor Williston characterized this step as "the most objectionable and irreparable feature" of the Sales Article; even apart from other objections, this was sufficient reason for rejecting Article 2. S. Williston, The Law of Sales in the Proposed Uniform Commercial Code, 63 Harv.L.Rev. 561, 569–71 (1950). Most commentators came to a different conclusion. E.g., A. Corbin, The Uniform Commercial Code—Sales; Should it be Enacted? 59 Yale L.J. 821, 824–27 (1950).

# Martin v. Meland's Inc.

Supreme Court of North Dakota, 1979.
283 N.W.2d 76.

■ Erickstad, Chief Justice.

The narrow issue on this appeal is who should bear the loss of a truck and an attached haystack mover that was destroyed by fire while in the possession of the plaintiff, Israel Martin (Martin), but after certificate of title had been delivered to the defendant, Melland's Inc. (Melland's). The destroyed haymoving unit was to be used as a trade-in for a new haymoving unit that Martin ultimately purchased from Melland's. Martin appeals from a district court judgment dated September 28, 1978, that dismissed his action on the merits after it found that at the time of its destruction Martin was the owner of the unit pursuant to Section 41–02–46(2), N.D.C.C. (Section 2–401 U.C.C.). We hold that Section 41–02–46(2), N.D.C.C., is inapplicable to this case, but we affirm the district court judgment on the grounds that risk of loss had not passed to Melland's pursuant to Section 41–02–57, N.D.C.C. (Section 2–509 U.C.C.).

On June 11, 1974, Martin entered into a written agreement with Melland's, a farm implement dealer, to purchase a truck and attached haystack mover for the total purchase price of $35,389. Martin was given a trade-in allowance of $17,389 on his old unit, leaving a balance owing of $18,000 plus sales tax of $720 or a total balance of $18,720. The agreement provided that Martin "mail or bring title" to the old unit to Melland's "this week." Martin mailed the certificate of title to Melland's pursuant to the agreement, but he was allowed to retain the use and possession of the old unit "until they had the new one ready." The new unit was not expected to be ready for two to three months because it required certain modifications. During this interim period, Melland's performed minor repairs to the trade-in unit on two occasions without charging Martin for the repairs.

Fire destroyed the truck and the haymoving unit in early August, 1974, while Martin was moving hay. The parties did not have any agreement regarding insurance or risk of loss on the unit and Martin's insurance on the trade-in unit had lapsed. Melland's refused Martin's demand for his new unit and Martin brought this suit. The parties subsequently entered into an agreement by which Martin purchased the new unit, but they reserved their rights in any lawsuit arising out of the prior incident.

The district court found "that although the Plaintiff [Martin] executed the title to the ... [haymoving unit], he did not relinquish possession of the same and therefore the Plaintiff was the owner of said truck at the time the fire occurred pursuant to [UCC 2–401]."

Martin argues that the district court erroneously applied ... [§ 2–401 U.C.C.], regarding passage of title, to this case and that ... [§ 2–509 U.C.C.], which deals with risk of loss in the absence of breach, should have been applied instead. Martin argues further that title (apparently pursuant to [UCC 2–401(1)]) and risk of loss passed to Melland's and the property was then merely bailed back to Martin who held it as a bailee. Martin submits that this is supported by the fact that Melland's performed minor repairs on the old unit following the passage of title without charging Martin for the repairs. Melland's responds that [UCC 2–401(2)], governs this case and that the district court's determination of the issue should be affirmed.

One of the hallmarks of the pre-Code law of sales was its emphasis on the concept of title. The location of title was used to determine, among other things, risk of loss, insurable interest, place and time for measuring damages, and the applicable law in an interstate transaction. This single title or "lump" title concept proved unsatisfactory because of the different policy considerations involved in each of the situations that title was made to govern. Furthermore, the concept of single title did not reflect modern commercial practices, i.e. although the single title concept worked well for "cash-on-the-barrelhead sales," the introduction of deferred payments, security agreements, financing from third parties, or delivery by carrier required a fluid concept of title with bits and pieces held by all parties to the transaction.

Thus the concept of title under the U.C.C. is of decreased importance. The official comment to Section 2–101 U.C.C. [§ 41–02–01, N.D.C.C.] provides in part:

> The arrangement of the present Article is in terms of contract for sale and the various steps of its performance. The legal consequences are stated as following directly from the contract and action taken under it without resorting to the idea of when property or title passed or was to pass as being the determining factor. The purpose is to avoid making practical issues between practical men turn upon the location of an intangible something, the passing of which no man can prove by evidence and to substitute for such abstractions proof of words and actions of a tangible character. Uniform Commercial Code (U.L.A.) § 2–101.

Section 41–02–46, N.D.C.C. (§ 2–401 U.C.C.), which the district court applied in this case, provides in relevant part:

> Each provision of this chapter with regard to the rights, obligations and remedies of the seller, the buyer, purchasers or other third parties applies irrespective of title to the goods except where the provision refers to such title. Insofar as situations are not covered by the other provisions of this chapter and matters concerning title become material the following rules apply . . .

[UCC 2–509] is an "other provision of this chapter" and is applicable to this case without regard to the location of title. Comment one to Section 2–509 U.C.C. provides that "the underlying theory of these sections on risk of loss is the adoption of the contractual approach rather than an arbitrary shifting of the risk with the 'property' in the goods."

\* \* \*

Before addressing the risk of loss question in conjunction with [UCC 2–509], it is necessary to determine the posture of the parties with regard to the trade-in unit, i.e. who is the buyer and the seller and how are the responsibilities allocated. It is clear that a barter or trade-in is considered a sale and is therefore subject to the Uniform Commercial Code. . . . It is also clear that the party who owns the trade-in is considered the seller. [UCC 2–304] provides that the "price can be made payable in money or otherwise. If it is payable in whole or in part in goods each party is a seller of the goods which he is to transfer." . . .

Martin argues that he had already sold the trade-in unit to Melland's and, although he retained possession, he did so in the capacity of a bailee (apparently pursuant to [UCC 2–509(2)]). White and Summers in their hornbook on the Uniform Commercial Code argue that the seller who retains possession should not be considered bailee within Section 2–509:

> The most common circumstance under which subsection (2) will be applied is that in which the goods are in the hands of a professional bailee (for instance, a warehouseman) and the seller passes a negotiable or a non-negotiable document of title covering the goods to the buyer. That case is simple enough. One question remains, however. Can the seller ever be a 'bailee' as the word is used in subsection (2)? The facts in a pre-Code case . . . well illustrate the problem. There seller had reached an agreement with buyer for the sale of a colt. The parties had agreed that the seller would hold the colt for the buyer and, depending upon the terms of the payment of the price, would or would not charge him a fee for stabling the colt. The colt was killed without any fault on the part of the seller, and the seller sued the buyer for the purchase price. In such a case the seller could certainly argue that he was a bailee and that risk had passed since he had acknowledged the buyer's "right" to possession of goods under (2)(b). The case would be a particularly appealing one for that argument if the seller were receiving payment from the buyer for the boarding of the horse.
>
> We believe that such an interpretation of the word bailee should be rejected by the courts, and except in circumstances which we cannot now conceive, a seller should not ever be regarded as a bailee. To allow sellers in possession of goods already sold to argue that they are bailees and that the risk of loss in such cases is governed by subsection (2) would undermine one of the basic policies of the Code's risk of loss scheme. As we have pointed out, the draftsmen intended to leave the risk on the seller in many circumstances in which the risk would have jumped to the buyer under prior law. The theory was that a seller with possession should have the burden of taking care of the goods and is more likely to insure them against loss.
>
> If we accept such sellers' arguments, that is, that they are bailees under subsection (2) because of their possession of the goods sold or because of a clause in the sale's agreement, we will be back where we started from, for in bailee cases the risk jumps under (2)(b) on his

"acknowledgment" of the buyer's right to possession. By hypothesis our seller has acknowledged the buyer's right and is simply holding the goods at buyer's disposal. Thus, to accomplish the draftsmen's purpose and leave risk on the seller in possession, we believe that one should find only non-sellers to be "bailees" as that term is used in 2–509(2). Notwithstanding the fact that a seller retains possession of goods already sold and that he has a term in his sale's contract which characterizes him as a "bailee" we would argue that he is not a bailee for the purposes of subsection (2) of 2–509 and would analyze his situation under subsection (1) or subsection (3) of 2–509.

J. White & R. Summers, Handbook of the Law Under the Uniform Commercial Code, 144–45 (1972) . . .

It is undisputed that the contract did not require or authorize shipment by carrier pursuant to [UCC 2–509(1)]; therefore, the residue section, subsection 3, is applicable:

> In any case not within subsection 1 or 2, the risk of loss passes to the buyer on his receipt of the goods if the seller is a merchant; otherwise the risk passes to the buyer on tender of delivery.

Martin admits that he is not a merchant; therefore, it is necessary to determine if Martin tendered delivery of the trade-in unit to Melland's. Tender is defined in [UCC 2–503(1)]. . . .

It is clear that the trade-in unit was not tendered to Melland's in this case. The parties agreed that Martin would keep the old unit "until they had the new one ready." . . .

We hold that Martin did not tender delivery of the trade-in truck and haystack mover to Melland's pursuant to (§ 2–509 U.C.C.); consequently, Martin must bear the loss.

We affirm the district court judgment.

## NOTES

**(1) Relevance of Insurance Coverage.** Comment 3 to UCC 2–509 declares that the underlying theory of subsection (3) is based on expectations as to probable casualty insurance coverage on the goods. Merchants, it is said, can be expected to have effective coverage on merchandise in their possession, while buyers cannot be expected to have insurance on property purchased but not yet delivered. This follows from standard fire and casualty insurance policies, sold to business concerns, that provide broad coverage for specified buildings that includes, generally, all contents of those buildings. Policies typically include coverage for "property sold but not removed."[7]

Casualty insurance policies rarely cover the full market value of the property insured. One reason is the concern, commonly referred to as moral

---

7. In recent years, business concerns have had access to even broader insurance coverage through "multiple line" or "package" policies.

hazard, that insureds who do not bear some of the risk of loss may not take sufficient care to protect the property and, in extreme circumstances, may cause casualties to occur. Does the text of UCC 2–509(3) or the Comment's theoretical explanation state or imply that merchant-sellers that have insurance should obtain relief for losses from their insurance carriers primarily? Exclusively?

The "seller" of the trade-in haystack mover in *Martin* was not a merchant-seller of the kind envisioned in Comment 3. He was a farmer who, at the time of the contract of sale, had insurance coverage on that equipment. He allowed the insurance to lapse while he continued to use it. Therefore, when the fire occurred, the seller had no insurance. It is reasonable to infer that the dealer also lacked insurance that covered the equipment in the farmer's possession. The dealer's insurance on buildings and contents would not apply to property located elsewhere. The property in this situation was therefore uninsured. Should UCC 2–509(3) be adapted to take into account the lack of insurance and the reasons for that?

The opinion notes that the sales contract lacked any terms on insurance or risk of loss. What commercially reasonable terms might have been added to the contract? Should either the dealer or the farmer be responsible for the omission of such terms?

The property in *Martin* was covered by a "certificate of title." Pursuant to the sales contract, the farmer had delivered the certificate to the dealer before the fire. This fact was mentioned by the court but was not significant to the court's analysis. Why did the buyer require that seller surrender the certificate of title? Should this have played a part in allocation of the risk of loss?

The message of *Martin* for lawyers who counsel clients on transactional matters is quite clear. In many circumstances, insurance and risk of loss clauses are essential terms of sales contracts.

**(2) Insurable Interest in the Goods.** Counselors should also be aware that persons in the position of the dealer in *Martin* can obtain insurance on goods that they have bought but have not yet received. UCC 2–501(1) declares that a buyer obtains an "insurable interest" in goods when the goods are "identified" to the contract and continues with rules on when identification occurs. For reasons related to concerns for moral hazard, only persons with something at stake, i.e., an insurable interest, may obtain casualty insurance on goods. During the performance stage of sales contracts, both sellers and buyers may have an insurable interest in the goods. UCC 2–501(1) specifies when a buyer's insurable interest arises, often a date well before the delivery date under the contract.

**(3) Litigation Posture; Price Actions.** Risk of loss cases commonly arise when buyers refuse to pay the price of goods destroyed in the performance stage of sales contracts. UCC 2–709(1)(a) provides that a seller has an action for the price of conforming goods lost or damaged after risk of their loss has passed to the buyer.

The litigation posture in *Martin* is complicated by the offsetting contracts for sale of the new equipment and trade-in of the old equipment. The farmer-seller of the old equipment demanded that the dealer-buyer credit the agreed price of the trade-in against the higher price of the new equipment. In trade-in transactions, however, each party is both a seller and buyer of the separate goods involved. See UCC 2–304(1). When the dealer refused to pay for the trade-in, the parties entered into a new contract which allowed the farmer to obtain the new equipment without giving up the right to sue for the price of the trade-in.

**(4) Insurance Carrier Subrogation.** A seller who suffers loss or casualty to goods on which it has effective insurance coverage is likely to submit a claim under the insurance policy even if the risk of loss has passed to the buyer. If an insurance company pays a claim, it may seek to be subrogated to seller's claim for the price under UCC 2–709(1)? Would a seller be entitled to the proceeds of the policy from its insurance company and recovery of the price from the buyer? Should it matter whether the buyer caused the loss or casualty? These interrelated questions have been answered most clearly in the context of real property transactions. In an executory contract, if only the vendor has effective insurance on property that suffers loss or casualty after risk of loss has passed to the vendee, the vendor's insurance should ultimately benefit the vendee. See R. Keeton & A. Widiss, Insurance Law 324 (1988).

**(5) Construction of UCC 2–509(3).** The *Martin* court held that the governing law was UCC 2–509(3), accepted the contention of the farmer that he was not a merchant, and therefore concluded that risk of loss passed upon tender of delivery of the trade-in equipment. Without analysis, the court declared that it was "clear" that the trade-in unit had not been tendered. Do you agree that this proposition was "clear"? Tender of delivery, under UCC 2–503(1), occurs when a seller puts and holds goods at the buyer's disposition. Did the farmer put and hold the trade-in equipment at the dealer's disposition? What delayed the "let go" of those goods? If a non-merchant seller tenders conforming goods and the buyer does not tender the price, does risk of loss pass to the buyer? Was the dealer's failure to tender the new equipment tantamount to failure to tender the price?

The *Martin* court characterized the farmer's assertion that he was not a merchant as an "admission." Would the farmer's case under UCC 2–509(3) have been stronger or weaker if he were deemed to be a merchant?[8]

**(6) Seller in Possession of Goods Sold as Bailee; UCC 2–509(2).** The litigation strategy of counsel for the farmer was to escape from UCC 2–509(3) rather than rely on that section. Counsel argued that the case was governed by UCC 2–509(2). The court, after quoting extensively from a treatise, rejected that argument. Should this argument have prevailed?

---

**8.** The Permanent Editorial Board Study Group on UCC Article 2 recommended that the Commercial Code be revised to eliminate the distinction between merchant and non-merchant sellers. "We assume that the non-merchant seller in possession will be in a much better position than the buyer to obtain insurance." Preliminary Report 148 (1990).

**(7) Effect of Casualty on Sellers' Contract Obligations: UCC 2–613.** The Commercial Code does not declare, in UCC 2–509, that sellers are discharged of obligation to deliver because certain goods have been lost or damaged while the risk of loss was on sellers. Under contracts of sale, there are a number of possibilities that bear on the question of discharge. (a) The goods lost or damaged were the only goods that the seller might have tendered properly under the contract. (b) The goods lost or damaged were part of a supply of substitutable goods, any of which the seller might have tendered properly under the contract, but the seller had identified the specific goods lost or damaged as those it planned to deliver. (c) The goods lost or damaged were among a supply of substitutable goods, but the seller had not yet identified any specific goods lost or damaged as those it planned to deliver. Should seller be discharged from its contractual obligation in any or all of these circumstances?

The Code provides a partial answer in UCC 2–613, which provides that contracts may be totally or partially "avoided" depending upon the degree of the physical loss. When contracts are avoided, according to Comment 1, the parties are relieved from obligation. Section 2–613 fits, to large extent, the first of the three circumstances we hypothesized. Would UCC 2–613 apply on the facts of *Martin*? If so, did the dealer have a claim against the farmer for breach of his promise to deliver the used haystack mover?

What line of reasoning leads to the conclusion that the dealer should be excused from performing its promise to deliver the new haystack mover? If the farmer had not allowed the insurance coverage to lapse and had tendered the insurance proceeds plus $18,720 (the agreed cash balance owed) to the dealer, could the dealer have refused to deliver the new haystack mover without being in breach of contract?

What happens to the contract obligations of sellers who bear the risk of loss of goods but whose contracts are not avoided under 2–613. See UCC 2–615.

**Problem 2.** S Company made a contract for the sale to B of a specified machine tool which S had been using in its manufacturing operations; prior to this transaction S had never sold a machine tool. The contract permitted B to remove the tool within a month. One week after the contract was made, the tool was destroyed by a fire in S's plant. Both S and B are insured under the standard fire policy. How should the interests of the parties be adjusted?

# United Air Lines v. Conductron Corp.

Appellate Court of Illinois, First District, 1979.
69 Ill.App.3d 847, 26 Ill.Dec. 344, 387 N.E.2d 1272.

■ GOLDBERG, PRESIDING JUSTICE:

United Air Lines, Inc. (plaintiff), brought an action for breach of contract against Conductron Corporation, McDonnell Douglas Electronics

Company, a subsidiary of McDonnell Douglas Corporation, and McDonnell Douglas Corporation (defendants). . . . The case involves sale by defendants to plaintiff of an aircraft flight simulator. This machine was destroyed by fire while on plaintiff's property. [At the time of the fire, plaintiff had paid $1,043,434.33 as partial payment of the purchase price. Plaintiff sought recovery of its payments, liquidated damages for defendants' breach of contract, and interest.] The trial court entered summary judgment in favor of plaintiff for $1,326,573.20. Defendants appeal.

Defendants contend that the trial court erred in entering summary judgment for plaintiff because the risk of loss of the simulator was upon plaintiff at the time of its destruction. . . .

Plaintiff contends that at the time the simulator was destroyed the risk of loss was upon defendants. In this regard, plaintiff urges that defendants defaulted under the terms of the contract by failing to deliver a conforming aircraft flight simulator; this default was never cured; the simulator was never accepted by plaintiff because of its deficiencies and plaintiff at all times retained the right of rejection. . . .

Many of the facts which appear from the pleadings, interrogatories, depositions, and affidavits are undisputed. The purchase agreement between plaintiff and defendants, some 65 pages in length, was executed on December 30, 1966. The agreement contains 19 articles and was supplemented by a number of change orders. It required defendants to deliver a Boeing 727 digital flight simulator to plaintiff on January 13, 1968. A flight simulator is a highly sophisticated electro-mechanical device operated by computers. It is designed to simulate the experiences of a pilot in the cockpit of a jet airplane during flight. As flight simulators are used for training pilots, they must meet the requirements necessary for approval by the Federal Aviation Administration (FAA). The contract so provided. In addition the contract provided that the simulator would conform to plaintiff's specifications.

The original contract provided for inspection and testing of the simulator by plaintiff at defendants' plant prior to its shipment to plaintiff's Flight Training Center in Denver, Colorado. The defendants agreed to correct any deficiency or discrepancy appearing from such inspection. The agreement further provided that when delivery of the simulator was made title would pass to plaintiff but that such delivery would not constitute acceptance of the simulator by plaintiff. Final acceptance by plaintiff was subject to satisfactory completion and also to certification by the FAA.

Defendants failed to complete fabrication of the simulator by the agreed upon date. This resulted in a request by plaintiff that the simulator be delivered to the plaintiff's training center in Colorado for the testing process which, under the original agreement, could have been completed at defendants' plant. On February 20, 1969, the parties entered into a modification of the contract referred to as Change Order Number 3. This order provided for disassembly of the machine, its delivery to plaintiff by common carrier not later than February 28, 1969, and reassembly by defendants on plaintiff's premises not later than March 15, 1969. From July 1, 1969 to August 1, 1969, the simulator was to be available to plaintiff for demonstration purposes and for correction by defendants of deviations noted by plaintiff in the above mentioned testing. The documents stated that in the event the defendants were unable satisfactorily to correct all deviations prior to November 1, 1969, the plaintiff would have the right to cancel the agreement and receive a refund of all payments made to the defendants as buyer plus liquidated damages. The Change Order also gave plaintiff the right to use the simulator for personnel training purposes.

While the simulator was still in possession of defendants upon their facilities, plaintiff's personnel noted some 647 deficiencies in its operation. These difficulties were recorded and reported to defendants by means of written reports referred to as "squak sheets." The simulator was delivered to plaintiff's facility and was reassembled by defendants on March 14, 1969, in accordance with Change Order Number 3. Since the machine had not received FAA approval, it could not be used as an aircraft flight simulator. It was used for training purposes to acquaint and familiarize pilots with instrument location in the cabin of a Boeing 727 aircraft.

On April 18, 1969, the simulator was tested for 10 hours by two of plaintiff's test pilots. About 10 p.m. a fire was discovered in the machine. The simulator was substantially damaged. The origin of the fire is unknown. After the fire, plaintiff requested that defendants dismantle and ship the simulator back to their plant for repairs at plaintiff's expense. On May 16, 1969, plaintiff notified defendants that they considered there was a breach by defendants of the warranties contained in the purchase agreement. On June 4, 1969, the parties amended the agreement by Change Order Number 4. This document provided that the plaintiff would receive $60,000 as liquidated damages for the late delivery of the simulator to be deducted from the remaining payments due defendants. Plaintiff commenced this action on May 11, 1973, seeking rescission of the contract and damages. On January 28, 1977, plaintiff filed Count VII as an amendment to the complaint. This amendment alleged that the risk of loss of the simulator was upon defendants at the time it was destroyed.

. . . Summary judgment in favor of plaintiff was entered by the trial court based on the theory that the simulator had never been accepted by plaintiff and, therefore, the risk of loss remained upon defendants. The order allowed plaintiff $1,043,434.33 as a refund of partial payments made, $60,000 as liquidated damages for delay and prejudgment interest of $223,138.78; a total of $1,326,573.20. No issue is raised on computation of these damages.

* * *

### III.

We turn next to the merits of summary judgment in favor of plaintiff based on the theory that defendants should bear the risk of loss for the destruction of the simulator. . . .

To evaluate the risk of loss issue, attention must be given to the impact of both the Uniform Commercial Code and the contract terms. Section 2–510 of the Code (Ill.Rev.Stat.1977, ch. 26, par. 2–510(1)), provides:

> (1) Where a tender or delivery of goods so fails to conform to the contract as to give a right of rejection the risk of their loss remains on the seller until cure or acceptance.

Few cases involve this section of the Code and those that do merely cite the Code with little explanation. ... The official Uniform Commercial Code Comment provides some guidance by stating that the purpose of this section is to make clear that "the seller by his individual action cannot shift the risk of loss to the buyer unless his action conforms with all the conditions resting on him under the contract." (S.H.A. ch. 26, par. 2–510(1) at page 398.) Of primary importance, then, is the determination of whether or not the simulator so failed to conform to the contract provisions as to vest the right of rejection in plaintiff and whether or not there was acceptance of the simulator by plaintiff.

The purchase agreement provided in part that the simulator would "accurately and faithfully simulate the configuration and performance of ..." a certain specified Boeing aircraft and that final acceptance of the simulator would be "subject to satisfactory completion of the reliability demonstration requirements ..." and to Federal Aviation Administration certification. The affidavit of John Darley, an employee of plaintiff who tests and evaluates flight simulators to determine whether they meet plaintiff's and the FAA specifications, states that the simulator at no time met those requirements and that plaintiff was never able to begin acceptance testing. His affidavit states clearly that the machine was destroyed by fire "before that time when United [plaintiff] was to begin acceptance testing ..." The affidavit of Phil C. Christy, employed by plaintiff as a technical assistant regarding simulators, reaffirms that as late as February 1969 there were "numerous discrepancies" in the operation of the simulator. These affidavits stand uncontradicted by counteraffidavit. Therefore they "are admitted and must be taken as true." ... On February 23, 1977, J.M. Gardner, Director of Contracts & Pricing for defendant McDonnell Douglas Electronics Company wrote a letter to plaintiff's attorney in which he stated that the simulator was "destroyed prior to final acceptance."

Defendants contend that Change Order Number 3, which provided for delivery of the simulator at plaintiff's training center in Denver, resulted in waiver of plaintiff's right to object to predelivery nonconformities. We reject this contention. The Change Order simply provides that the testing and inspection, which under the original agreement would have occurred at defendants' plant, would take place in Denver. Sections of the original agreement which provide that delivery does not constitute acceptance remain unchanged by this Change Order Number 3. Also, the language of the Change Order that testing and inspection would be completed in Denver and that the seller would have access to the simulator to demonstrate compliance are inconsistent with the idea that plaintiff had waived the right to object to nonconformity of the simulator.

Defendants do not contest the fact that there were technical difficulties with the simulator, as evidenced by the hundreds of discrepancy reports, actually 645, prepared by plaintiff's employees during the testing period. Instead, defendants stress the complex nature of the device and urge that plaintiff accepted the simulator despite its manifest deficiencies. In support of this contention defendants look to the six week period of inspection of the simulator in Denver and cite Uniform Commercial Code section 2–606 (Ill.Rev.Stat.1977, ch. 26, par. 2–606), which provides:

Acceptance of goods occurs when the buyer

(a) after a reasonable opportunity to inspect the goods signifies to the seller that the goods are conforming or that he will take or retain them in spite of their non-conformity; or

(b) fails to make an effective rejection (subsection (1) of Section 2–602), but such acceptance does not occur until the buyer has had a reasonable opportunity to inspect them; or

(c) does any act inconsistent with the seller's ownership; but if such act is wrongful as against the seller it is an acceptance only if ratified by him.

Defendants thus wish this court to hold that plaintiff had a reasonable opportunity to inspect the simulator and to reject it prior to its destruction. This approach completely ignores the terms of the contract. The purpose of the Uniform Commercial Code is set forth in section 1–102 (Ill.Rev.Stat. 1977, ch. 26, par. 1–102), which states that the provisions of the act may be varied by agreement. This court expressed the same principle in First Bank & Trust Co., Palatine v. Post (1973), 10 Ill.App.3d 127, 131, 293 N.E.2d 907, 910, where we stated:

[t]he Uniform Commercial Code was enacted to provide a general uniformity in commercial transactions conducted in this state and was never intended to be used by courts to create a result that is contrary to the clearly understood intentions of the original parties.

The clear intent of the parties before this court, as stated in the purchase agreement, was that physical delivery of the simulator and payments received by the defendants were not to constitute acceptance of the simulator. Acceptance was to be predicated on successful completion of acceptance testing and also upon receipt of FAA certification. The contract terms definitely anticipated and sanctioned use of the simulator by plaintiff to enable it to determine whether this complex and expensive device met the contract specifications. If use of goods is necessary to allow proper evaluation of them, such use does not constitute acceptance. . . .

This record shows that the simulator at no time conformed to the specifications agreed to in the purchase agreement and it remained nonconforming until its destruction. Although plaintiff had use and possession of the simulator for six weeks that arrangement was expressly sanctioned by the contract to allow testing. Retention of the simulator for testing purposes did not constitute acceptance so as to shift the risk of loss to the plaintiff. The simulator was destroyed before completion of acceptance testing and before receipt of FAA certification. Both were conditions precedent to acceptance of the simulator. In this situation the risk of loss remained on the defendants as seller. On the issue of risk of loss, there is no genuine issue regarding any material fact. On the contrary, in our opinion, plaintiff's right to summary judgment in this regard is clear beyond question. We conclude that the plaintiff is entitled to summary judgment as a matter of law.

\* \* \*

Judgment affirmed.

NOTES

**(1) Risk of Loss After Buyers Have Received Goods.** Assuming that UCC 2–509(3) governs passage of the risk of loss on the facts of *United Air Lines*, the merchant-seller provision provides that risk passes to the buyer on "receipt of the goods." "Receipt" means "taking physical possession" of goods. UCC 2–103. Without referring to UCC 2–509, the court analyzed the case not in terms of buyer's *receipt* of the simulator, but in terms of buyer's *acceptance* of it. On what basis could the court determine that risk of loss remained upon sellers until buyer accepted the simulator? Should UCC 2–509(3) be read to mean that risk of loss passes to a buyer only upon receipt of *conforming* goods? See the caption to UCC 2–509 and UCC 1–107.

The court in *United Air Lines* based its opinion on UCC 2–510(1). Does this section apply to the facts of that case? When Conductron delivered the simulator to United Air Lines pursuant to Change Order Number 3, did the parties expect that it would conform to the contract requirements? Was Conductron then in breach? Was Conductron in breach when the fire occurred on April 18? If Conductron was not in breach, is UCC 2–510 pertinent? (We will consider UCC 2–510 further after the following case.)

If neither UCC 2–509(3) nor UCC 2–510(1) is applicable, what risk of loss rule does apply?

**(2) Alternative Analysis Under UCC 2–711(1).** Why should risk-of-loss analysis be used at all in a case like *United Air Lines*? Buyer seeks to recover so much of the price as has been paid plus damages, remedies available under UCC 2–711(1) "where the seller fails to make delivery . . . or the buyer rightfully rejects [the goods]." United Air Lines would not accept the fire-damaged simulator; if Conductron tendered the simulator in that condition, United Air Lines would almost certainly reject it. If Conductron fails to tender a conforming simulator within the time permitted under the contract, it will have failed to make delivery. Is application of UCC 2–711(1) affected by risk-of-loss rules?

**Problem 3.** B agreed to buy a mobile home of S. In accordance with the agreement, S put the mobile home in place on B's lot and made the sewer and gas connections. B moved into the home. S had not yet made the furnace and electrical hook-ups when a gas explosion and an ensuing fire destroyed the mobile home. Who bears the loss?[9]

**Problem 4.** The S Chevrolet Company delivered a car to B under an instalment sales contract. B paid S $3,700 in cash and agreed to pay the balance of $25,000 in 36 monthly installments. The contract provided that S held a security interest in the car which S could exercise to enforce its right to receive payment. In addition, the contract provided:

> It is expressly understood and agreed that the title to the above-described automobile shall remain in the seller until the aforesaid sums of money shall be paid as herein provided, and that the seller may at any time, either personally or by agent, using so much force as is necessary, enter in or upon the premises where said automobile may be, with or without the issuance of any writ of replevin, and take possession of said automobile on default in any of the payments herein provided or on failure to comply with one or all of the conditions of this contract.

A month after delivery, the car is wrecked beyond repair without any fault by B. Must he continue to make the payments to S? Does the language of the sales contract evidence an intent by the parties to exercise their power, under UCC 1–302, to vary by agreement the Article 2 rules on risk of loss? Can the policy of the Code be drawn, by analogy, from UCC 2–505; UCC 2–509(1)(a); UCC 1–201(35) (second sentence)? What, apart from constructional aids in the statute, is the most sensible reading of this language?

In normal commercial practice, unless there has been some mishap in the drafting, printing or assembling of the forms typically used in instalment sales contracts, the documents will provide expressly that the buyers bears all casualty risks and agree to maintain fire and casualty insurance.

# Ron Mead T.V. & Appliance v. Legendary Homes, Inc.

Oklahoma Court of Appeals, Division Three, 1987.
746 P.2d 1163.

■ HANSEN, PRESIDING JUDGE.

Plaintiff, Ron Mead, is a retail merchant selling household appliances. Defendant, Legendary Homes, is a home builder. Defendant purchased appliances from Plaintiff for installation in one of its homes. The appliances were to be delivered on February 1, 1984. At five o'clock on that day the appliances had not been delivered. Defendant closed the home and left. Sometime between five and six-thirty Plaintiff delivered the appliances. No

---

9. See Southland Mobile Home Corp. v. Chyrchel, 255 Ark. 366, 500 S.W.2d 778 (1973); Wilke v. Cummins Diesel Engines, 252 Md. 611, 250 A.2d 886 (1969).

one was at the home so the deliveryman put the appliances in the garage. During the night someone stole the appliances.

Defendant denied it was responsible for the loss and refused to pay Plaintiff for the appliances. This suit resulted.

After a non-jury trial the court issued a "Memorandum Opinion" finding § 2–509 of the Uniform Commercial Code, 12A 0.S. 1981 controlled. This section provides: "The risk of loss passes to the Buyer on his receipt of the goods." The trial court found Defendant had not received the goods, thus the risk of loss remained with Plaintiff. Plaintiff appeals the judgment rendered in favor of Defendant.

\* \* \*

Plaintiff ... submits the trial court erred in concluding Plaintiff did not establish usage of trade in leaving appliances unattended at a building site. The trial court found the record was void of any evidence which would show the method of delivery used by Plaintiff was pursuant to a "course of dealing" between the parties which would waive or excuse the requirements of 12A O.S. 1981 § 2–503.

Section 1–205(2) defines "usage of trade" as any "practice or method of dealing having such regularity of observance in a place, vocation or trade as to justify an expectation that it will be observed with respect to the transaction in question." Although there was testimony some builders allow deliveries to be made to unattended job sites, nothing indicated such practice was uniformly observed after working hours unless specifically agreed to by the parties.

Although there was conflicting testimony between witnesses whether Defendant advised Plaintiff to deliver the appliances before noon, nothing appears in the record to indicate there was any agreement the appliances would be accepted after hours.

Section 2–103 defines "receipt" of goods as taking physical possession of them. We agree with the trial court "(t)he act by the deliveryman of placing the goods in an unlocked garage, in a house under construction, and then locking the door did not give the Buyer the opportunity to take physical possession (of them)."

Credibility of witnesses and weight and value to be given to their testimony is for the trial court on waiver of a jury, and conclusions there reached will not be disturbed on appeal, unless appearing clearly to be based upon caprice or to be without any reasonable foundation. Accordingly, the trial court is affirmed.

\* \* \*

NOTES

**(1) Basis of the Decision: Analytical Confusion.** The problem presented in this case can be analyzed in three ways: under the rules for tender of delivery or under the two rules allocating risk of loss. The Oklahoma courts, and presumably the lawyers arguing the case, did not resolve which of these rules they were applying.

If seller had not made a tender of delivery, buyer had no duty to pay the price. UCC 2–507(1). Seller tried and failed to establish a course of dealing or trade usage that permitted tender of delivery by the method it employed. Thus, buyer's duty to pay the price never matured under UCC 2–507.

Alternatively, the case can be analyzed under the risk of loss rules in UCC 2–509(3). Since seller unquestionably was a merchant, risk of loss would pass only on receipt of the goods. The appellate court, citing UCC 2–103, concluded that "receipt" had not occurred. Seller's action for the price depended on risk of loss passing. UCC 2–709(1)(a). Absent receipt, risk of loss did not pass, and the price action must fail.

A third line of analysis has been offered:

> Although the court manages to properly conclude that the risk of loss had not passed to the buyer, it does so despite misapplication of the Code's risk of loss provisions. Both the trial court and the court of appeals incorrectly cited section 2–509 as the controlling section. Because of the improper tender by the seller, the risk of loss issue in this case should have been resolved by application of section 2–510(1). Regardless of whether the goods have been received, under section 2–510(1) the buyer does not bear risk of loss where the tender is no nonconforming as to give a right of rejection. . . . One must wonder how this case would have ended if, all other things being the same, the court had decided that the buyer had received the goods. In view of the court's apparent ignorance of both section 2–510 and the immateriality of the possession issue, it would seem that, notwithstanding the defective tender, the seller would have wrongfully prevailed.

D. Frisch and J. Wladis, Uniform Commercial Code Annual Survey: General Provisions, Sales, Bulk Transfers, and Documents of Title, 44 Bus. Law. 1445, 1467 (1989).

Which of these lines of analysis is more sound?[10]

**(2) Sellers' Price Action.** The remedy sought in *Ron Mead* was the contract price for the appliances. On what basis could seller seek to recover the price of the stolen appliances? See UCC 2–709(1)(a). Could seller argue successfully that it was entitled to the price on the ground that the appliances were "conforming goods" even though the manner of their tender did not conform to the contract?

---

**10.** The Permanent Editorial Board Study Group on UCC Article 2 found numerous flaws in 2–510 and recommended that it be repealed. Preliminary Report 149 (1990). The Study Group noted that the section requires no showing of any causal connection between the breach and the loss and may allocate risk from the party in the best position to insure the goods to the party who is not. Moreover, the Study Group declared, the section is "complex, incomplete and difficult to apply." Id.

# Multiplastics v. Arch Industries

Supreme Court of Connecticut, 1974.
166 Conn. 280, 348 A.2d 618.

■ Bogdanski, J.

The plaintiff, Multiplastics, Inc., brought this action to recover damages from the defendant, Arch Industries, Inc., for the breach of a contract to purchase 40,000 pounds of plastic pellets. From a judgment rendered for the plaintiff, the defendant has appealed to this court.

The facts may be summarized as follows: The plaintiff, a manufacturer of plastic resin pellets, agreed with the defendant on June 30, 1971, to manufacture and deliver 40,000 pounds of brown polystyrene plastic pellets for nineteen cents a pound. The pellets were specially made for the defendant, who agreed to accept delivery at the rate of 1000 pounds per day after completion of production. The defendant's confirming order contained the notation "make and hold for release. Confirmation." The plaintiff produced the order of pellets within two weeks and requested release orders from the defendant. The defendant refused to issue the release orders, citing labor difficulties and its vacation schedule. On August 18, 1971, the plaintiff sent the defendant the following letter: "Against P.O. 0946, we produced 40,000 lbs. of brown high impact styrene, and you have issued no releases. You indicated to us that you would be using 1,000 lbs. of each per day. We have warehoused these products for more than forty days, as we agreed to do. However, we cannot warehouse these products indefinitely, and request that you send us shipping instructions. We have done everything we agreed to do." After August 18, 1971, the plaintiff made numerous telephone calls to the defendant to seek payment and delivery instructions. In response, beginning August 20, 1971, the defendant agreed to issue release orders but in fact never did.

On September 22, 1971, the plaintiff's plant, containing the pellets manufactured for the defendant, was destroyed by fire. The plaintiff's fire insurance did not cover the loss of the pellets. The plaintiff brought this action against the defendant to recover the contract price.

The trial court concluded that the plaintiff made a valid tender of delivery by its letter of August 18, 1971, and by its subsequent requests for delivery instructions; that the defendant repudiated and breached the contract by refusing to accept delivery on August 20, 1971; that the period from August 20, 1971, to September 22, 1971, was not a commercially unreasonable time for the plaintiff to treat the risk of loss as resting on the defendant under General Statutes § 42a–2–510(3), and that the plaintiff was entitled to recover the contract price plus interest.

General Statutes § 42a–2–510, entitled "Effect of breach on risk of loss," reads, in pertinent part, as follows: "(3) Where the buyer as to conforming goods already identified to the contract for sale repudiates or is otherwise in breach before risk of their loss has passed to him, the seller may to the extent of any deficiency in his effective insurance coverage treat the risk of loss as resting on the buyer for a commercially reasonable time."

The defendant contends that § 42a–2–510 is not applicable because its failure to issue delivery instructions did not constitute either a repudiation or a breach of the agreement. The defendant also argues that even if § 42a–2–510 were applicable, the period from August 20, 1971, to September 22, 1971, was not a commercially reasonable period of time within which to treat the risk of loss as resting on the buyer. The defendant does not claim that the destroyed pellets were not "conforming goods already identified to the contract for sale," as required by General Statutes § 42a–2–510(3), nor does it protest the computation of damages. With regard to recovery of the price of goods and incidental damages, see General Statutes § 42a–2–709(1)(a).

The trial court's conclusion that the defendant was in breach is supported by its finding that the defendant agreed to accept delivery of the pellets at the rate of 1000 pounds per day after completion of production. The defendant argues that since the confirming order instructed the defendant to "make and hold for release," the contract did not specify an exact delivery date. This argument fails, however, because nothing in the finding suggests that the notation in the confirming order was part of the agreement between the parties. Since, as the trial court found, the plaintiff made a proper tender of delivery, beginning with its letter of August 18, 1971, the plaintiff was entitled to acceptance of the goods and to payment according to the contract. General Statutes §§ 42a–2–507(1), 42a–2–307.

The defendant argues that its failure to issue delivery instructions did not suffice to repudiate the contract because repudiation of an executory promise requires, first, an absolute and unequivocal renunciation by the promisor, and, second, an unambiguous acceptance of the repudiation by the promisee. ... Anticipatory repudiation is now governed by General Statutes §§ 42a–2–609 to 42a–2–611, which in some respects alter the prior law on the subject. The present case does not involve repudiation of an executory promise, however, since the defendant breached the contract by failing to accept the goods when acceptance became due.

The defendant next claims that the plaintiff acquiesced in the defendant's refusal to accept delivery by continuing to urge compliance with the contract and by failing to pursue any of the remedies provided aggrieved sellers by General Statutes § 42a–2–703. In essence, the defendant's argument rests on the doctrines of waiver and estoppel, which are available defenses under the Uniform Commercial Code. General Statutes §§ 42a–1–103, 42a–1–107, 42a–2–209; Mercanti v. Persson, 160 Conn. 468, 477–79, 280 A.2d 137. ... The defendant has not, however, shown those defenses to apply. Waiver is the intentional relinquishment of a known right. ... Its existence is a question of fact for the trier. ... The trial court did not find that the plaintiff intentionally acquiesced in the defendant's breach of their agreement, thereby waiving its right to take advantage of that breach. Indeed, the plaintiff's repeated attempts to secure compliance seem inconsistent with the possibility of waiver. ...

Nor has the defendant made out a case of estoppel. "The two essential elements of estoppel are that 'one party must do or say something which is intended or calculated to induce another to believe in the existence of certain facts and to act on that belief; and the other party, influenced thereby, must change his position or do some act to his injury which he otherwise would not have done.' Dickau v. Glastonbury, 156 Conn. 437, 441, 242 A.2d 777; Pet Car Products, Inc. v. Barnett, 150 Conn. 42, 53, 184 A.2d 797." Mercanti v. Persson, supra, 477. Neither element of estoppel is present in the record of this case. The plaintiff's requests for delivery instructions cannot be said to have misled the defendant into thinking that the plaintiff did not consider their contract breached. In fact, General Statutes § 42a–2–610, entitled "Anticipatory repudiation," specifically provides that the aggrieved seller may "resort to any remedy for breach as provided by section 42a–2–703 . . ., even though he has notified the repudiating party that he would await the latter's performance and has urged retraction." Although the present case is not governed by General Statutes § 42a–2–610, that section does demonstrate that the plaintiff's conduct after the defendant refused to accept delivery was not inconsistent with his claim that the contract was breached.

The remaining question is whether, under General Statutes § 42a–2–510(3), the period of time from August 20, 1971, the date of the breach, to September 22, 1971, the date of the fire, was a "commercially reasonable" period within which to treat the risk of loss as resting on the buyer. The trial court concluded that it was "not, on the facts in this case, a commercially unreasonable time," which we take to mean that it was a commercially reasonable period. The time limitation in § 42a–2–510(3) is designed to enable the seller to obtain the additional requisite insurance coverage. . . . The trial court's conclusion is tested by the finding. . . . Although the finding is not detailed, it supports the conclusion that August 20 to September 22 was a commercially reasonable period within which to place the risk of loss on the defendant. As already stated, the trial court found that the defendant repeatedly agreed to transmit delivery instructions and that the pellets were specially made to fill the defendant's order. Under those circumstances, it was reasonable for the plaintiff to believe that the goods would soon be taken off its hands and so to forego procuring the needed insurance.

We consider it advisable to discuss one additional matter. The trial court concluded that "title" passed to the defendant, and the defendant attacks the conclusion on this appeal. The issue is immaterial to this case. General Statutes § 42a–2–401 states: "Each provision of this article with regard to the rights, obligations and remedies of the seller, the buyer, purchasers or other third parties applies irrespective of title to the goods except where the provision refers to such title." As one student of the Uniform Commercial Code has written: "The single most important innovation of Article 2 [of the Uniform Commercial Code] is its restatement of . . . [the parties'] responsibilities in terms of operative facts rather than legal conclusions; where pre-Code law looked to "title" for the definition of rights and remedies, the Code looks to demonstrable realities such as custody, control and professional expertise. This shift in approach is central to the whole philosophy of Article 2. It means that disputes, as they arise, can focus, as does all of the modern law of contracts, upon actual provable circumstances, rather than upon a metaphysical concept of elastic and endlessly fluid dimensions. Peters, "Remedies for Breach of Contracts Relating to the Sale of Goods Under the Uniform Commercial Code: A Roadmap for Article Two," 73 Yale L.J. 199, 201.

There is no error.

In this opinion the other judges concurred.

## NOTES

**(1) Breach of Contract, Risk of Loss, and Action for the Price.** The outcome of this case depends upon whether the buyer was in breach of the sales contract before the fire. If the case was determined by UCC 2–509, captioned Risk of Loss in the Absence of Breach, risk of loss "passes [from a merchant-seller] to a buyer on his receipt of the goods." UCC 2–509(3). The seller was undoubtedly a merchant, UCC 2–104, and the goods never left the seller's warehouse. Risk of loss would not have passed when the goods perished in the fire. A merchant-seller can shift the risk of loss to a buyer not in possession only by invoking UCC 2–510, Effect of Breach on Risk of Loss.

If risk of loss is on the buyer when the goods are destroyed, the seller is entitled to recover the contract price. UCC 2–709(1)(a). That was the seller's contention in this case.[11] In an action for compensatory damages, what would the seller have been entitled to recover for the buyer's alleged breach of contract? Buyer's breach was an element of the seller's case only to shift the risk of loss to the buyer. Buyer's breach was not an element of the statutory right to the price.

This has been the basis for trenchant criticism of UCC 2–510(3). Under that subsection, any breach by a buyer, whether serious or trivial, and for which compensatory damages might be small, shifts the risk of loss and results in heavy costs to a buyer compelled the pay the price for goods that have perished or suffered severe injury.

**(2) Terms of the Contract; Breach.** The court faced a difficult legal challenge in determining whether the buyer was in breach on or before the date of the fire. The original agreement may have been made orally. In any event its terms apparently contemplated that the buyer would control the time of delivery. Buyer's confirming order, a document, contained the notation: make and hold for release. Seller's post-contract August 18 letter acknowledged that it had agreed to warehouse the products pending buyer's release order. The trial court held that the buyer breached on August 20. What was the basis for that holding? Did the Supreme Court

---

**11.** In the first paragraph of the opinion, the court described the action as one "to recover damages . . . for breach of a contract." Later the court characterized the claim as one to recover the price. This is a not uncommon error, but an action for the price is not an action for damages. A price action is more akin to specific performance of a contract than to recovery of compensation for breach of contract.

affirm that breach occurred on that date? The Supreme Court declared that the confirmation was not part of the agreement. Was that correct? See UCC 2–207(1). Was that consistent with seller's August 18 letter? Was that determination necessary to the court's decision?

The Supreme Court's analysis veered abruptly away from analysis of the time term of the agreement into consideration of the law of anticipatory repudiation. See UCC 2–610.This was the result, apparently, of the litigation strategy of buyer's counsel, who argued that buyer had not repudiated the agreement before the date of the fire. The premise of this argument appears to have been that, absent repudiation by the buyer, the buyer was not in breach. Was that premise correct? How did the court respond to the argument?

Buyer's counsel argued that seller had acquiesced in buyer's conduct. The Supreme Court characterized that as an argument of waiver or estoppel. Was the court correct in its characterization of the argument? Assuming that buyer claimed that seller had waived performance of a time term, under UCC 2–209(4), how well did the Supreme Court deal with that contention?[12] Assuming that the buyer raised the issue of estoppel, what would be the nature of that argument? The law of estoppel is not codified in Article 2, see UCC 1–103(b), and remains a matter of common law. How well did the Supreme Court deal with the estoppel argument? Note that the court returned to the law of anticipatory repudiation. Was that relevant?

The Connecticut court and counsel struggled to find a way to put the contract question into a recognizable legal frame. Is it fair to say that their efforts were unsatisfactory? Was there any way that a court might have made a more satisfactory application of the Article 2 doctrine that shifts risk of loss to buyers at the moment of their breach of sales contracts, particularly where the only alleged breaches are of the time terms of those contracts?

**(3) Construction of UCC 2–510(3); Insurance Coverage.** The final argument made by buyer's counsel was that risk of loss, having shifted to buyer, shifted back to seller under UCC 2–510(3). What is the legislative purpose of the limitation of a "commercially reasonable time"? The Comments are silent. The Connecticut Supreme Court declared that the limitation was designed to enable a seller to obtain insurance coverage. Does that make commercial sense? Recall the policy rationale with respect to casualty insurance that underlies the basic risk of loss rules in UCC 2–509. What explanation can be offered for the seller's failure in this case to have any insurance on goods in its warehouse? Section 2–510(3) deals explicitly with the gap when seller's effective insurance coverage is less than the value of the goods; section 2–709(1)(a) deems that value to be the contract price. If a seller elected to have *no* insurance coverage, should Article 2 allow the consequences of that assumption of risk to be shifted to

---

**12.** We considered the law of waiver earlier in Chapter 2, particularly in *BMC Industries v. Barth Industries* where the issue of common-law or statutory waiver was litigated.

a buyer as a result of a finding of buyer's breach of an ephemeral time term?

## 3. SHIPMENT CONTRACTS

Sellers are commonly authorized or required to ship goods to buyers via carriers. While en route, goods may suffer loss or damage. The principal subject in this subsection is the allocation of risk of such losses between sellers and buyers. A subordinate question is the extent of the carriers' liability for goods that suffer casualty while in their possession.

*Shipment and Destination Contracts.* In Chapter 6, we learned that sales contracts that contemplate delivery of goods by carrier are generally characterized as place-of-shipment or at-a-particular-destination contracts. In the former, the cost of transportation is borne by the buyer; in the latter, freight charges are paid by the seller. Risk of loss is allocated in the same characterization. UCC 2–509(1).

Under UCC 2–319, sales contracts that use the F.O.B. term are shipment contracts if the term is F.O.B. the place of shipment; seller bears the risk of putting the goods into the carrier's possession. UCC 2–319(1)(a). Risk passes to the buyer when the goods are duly delivered to the carrier. UCC 2–509(1)(a). Conversely, if the contract term is F.O.B. the place of destination, seller must at its own risk transport the goods to that place. UCC 2–319(1)(b). Risk passes to the buyer when the goods are there duly tendered. UCC 2–509(1)(b).

Shipping terms commonly associated with deep water transport pose difficult problems for risk of loss. Even though the price includes the cost of transportation, sellers expressly bear the risk of putting the goods into the carriers' possession, loading the goods on board, or delivering them alongside a vessel, as the terms require. UCC 2–319(1)(b) and (2), 2–320(2) and (3). Contracts that use the terms F.O.B. vessel or F.A.S. can be recognized as shipment contracts; thus the risk passing provision of UCC 2–509(1)(a) applies. However contracts that use the terms C.I.F. and C. & F. cannot easily be characterized as shipment contracts. Nor is it plausible to construe them as destination contracts with risk passing at the place of destination.[13] A different result follows if the term used is "delivery ex-ship." UCC 2–322.

Risk of loss and contract performance problems tend to arise when sales contracts are ambiguous as to whether they are shipment or destination contracts.

**Problem 5.** Seller Manufacturing Company, in Sellersville, Pennsylvania, has distributed a catalogue giving descriptions and prices for a line of garden tractors which Seller makes and sells. Buyer Garden Supply Company, in Birmingham, Alabama, an enterprise with stores in various cities in Alabama, wired Seller, "Please ship to us in Birmingham, 10 Garden

---

**13.** The Code provision on the C.I.F. term imposes a duty on sellers to contract for casualty insurance for the benefit of the buyers. UCC 2–320(2)(c).

Tractors, Catalogue No. 103X, priced at $4,430 each." Seller replied: "Order accepted. Tractors being shipped this week." Neither the catalogue nor the correspondence dealt with methods or costs of delivery.

Seller promptly hauled the 10 garden tractors in his truck to the freight station of the CSX Railroad in Sellersville and delivered them to the freight agent in the freight yards. Seller received a "straight" (non-negotiable) bill of lading providing that the goods were "Consigned to Buyer Garden Supply Co., Birmingham, Ala." Freight costs of $910 were noted on the bill of lading as "C.O.D." (Collect on Delivery).

One of the tractors was stolen from the CSX freight yard in Sellersville. Another was damaged in a freight car en route to Birmingham.

(a) Buyer paid for eight tractors, but refused to pay for the tractor that was stolen or for the damaged tractor. Seller sues for the price of the two tractors. Buyer interposes all available defenses to the price action and, in addition, counterclaims for the freight costs of $910 which he had to pay the railroad in order to receive delivery of the tractors. What result? See UCC 2–509, UCC 2–504, UCC 2–709(1)(a).

(b) Suppose Seller's truck had overturned and burned while the tractors were being taken from Seller's factory to the freight yards. May Seller recover the price for the tractors destroyed by fire?

## Pestana v. Karinol Corp.

District Court of Appeal of Florida, Third District, 1979.
367 So.2d 1096.

■ HUNNART, JUDGE.

This is an action for damages based on a contract for the sale of goods. The defendant seller and others prevailed in this action after a non-jury trial in the Circuit Court for the Eleventh Judicial Circuit of Florida. The plaintiff buyer appeals.

The central issue presented for review is whether a contract for the sale of goods, which stipulates the place where the goods sold are to be sent by carrier but contains (a) no explicit provisions allocating the risk of loss while the goods are in the possession of the carrier and (b) no delivery terms such as F.O.B. place of destination, is a shipment contract or a destination contract under the Uniform Commercial Code. We hold that such a contract, without more, constitutes a shipment contract wherein the risk of loss passes to the buyer when the seller duly delivers the goods to the carrier under a reasonable contract of carriage for shipment to the buyer. Accordingly, we affirm.

### A

The critical facts of this case are substantially undisputed. On March 4, 1975, Nahim Amar B. [the plaintiff Pedro P. Pestana's decedent herein] who was a resident of Mexico entered into a contract through his authorized representative with the Karinol Corporation [the defendant herein] which is an exporting company licensed to do business in Florida and operating out of Miami. The terms of this contract were embodied in a one page invoice written in Spanish and prepared by the defendant Karinol. By the terms of this contract, the plaintiff's Amar agreed to purchase 64 electronic watches from the defendant Karinol for $6,006. A notation was printed at the bottom of the contract which, translated into English, reads as follows: "Please send the merchandise in cardboard boxes duly strapped with metal bands via air parcel post to Chetumal. Documents to Banco de Commercio De Quintano Roo S.A." There were no provisions in the contract which specifically allocated the risk of loss on the goods sold while in the possession of the carrier; there were also no F.O.B., F.A.S., C.I.F. or C & F terms contained in the contract. See §§ 672.319, 672.320, Fla.Stat. (1977). A 25% downpayment on the purchase price of the goods sold was made prior to shipment.

On April 11, 1975, there is sufficient evidence, although disputed, that the defendant Karinol delivered the watches in two cartons to its agent American International Freight Forwarders, Inc. [the second defendant herein] for forwarding to the plaintiff's decedent Amar. The defendant American insured the two cartons with Fidelity & Casualty Company of New York [the third defendant herein] naming the defendant Karinol as the insured. The defendant American as freight forwarder strapped the cartons in question with metal bands and delivered them to TACA International Airlines consigned to one Bernard Smith, a representative of the plaintiff's decedent, in Belize City, Belize, Central America. The shipment was arranged by Karinol in this manner in accord with a prior understanding between the parties as there were no direct flights from Miami, Florida to Chetumal, Mexico. Mr. Smith was to take custody of the goods on behalf of the plaintiff's decedent in Belize and arrange for their transport by truck to the plaintiff's decedent Amar in Chetumal, Mexico.

On April 15, 1975, the cartons arrived by air in Belize City and were stored by the airline in the customs and air freight cargo room. Mr. Smith was duly notified and thereupon the plaintiff's decedent made payment on the balance due under the contract to the defendant Karinol. On May 2, 1975, Mr. Smith took custody of the cartons after a certain delay was experienced in transferring the cartons to a customs warehouse. Either on that day or shortly thereafter, the cartons were opened by Mr. Smith and customs officials as was required for clearance prior to the truck shipment to Chetumal, Mexico. There were no watches contained in the cartons. The defendant Karinol and its insurance carrier the defendant Fidelity were duly notified, but both eventually refused to make good on the loss.

The plaintiff Pedro P. Pestana, as representative of the Estate of Nahim Amar B., deceased, filed suit against the defendant Karinol as the seller, the defendant American as Karinol's agent freight forwarder, and the defendant Fidelity as the defendant Karinol's insurer. The complaint alleged that the defendant Karinol entered into a contract to ship merchandise from Miami, Florida to Chetumal, Mexico with the plaintiff's decedent, that the defendant American as freight forwarder and agent of the defendant Karinol accepted shipment of such merchandise, that the merchandise was lost, stolen or misplaced while in the care and custody of the defendant Karinol and the defendant American, that the defendants Karinol and American failed to make delivery to the plaintiff's decedent at Chetumal, Mexico, and that there existed a liability policy with the defendant Fidelity for the benefit of the plaintiff's decedent. The complaint sought damages together with court costs and reasonable attorneys fees. All the defendants duly filed answers to the complaint wherein liability was denied. The defendant Karinol filed a cross-complaint against the defendant American. The trial court after a non-jury trial found for all of the defendants in this cause. This appeal follows.

## B

There are two types of sales contracts under Florida's Uniform Commercial Code wherein a carrier is used to transport the goods sold: a shipment contract and a destination contract. A shipment contract is considered the normal contract in which the seller is required to send the subject goods by carrier to the buyer but is not required to guarantee delivery thereof at a particular destination. Under a shipment contract, the seller, unless otherwise agreed, must: (1) put the goods sold in the possession of a carrier and make a contract for their transportation as may be reasonable having regard for the nature of the goods and other attendant circumstances, (2) obtain and promptly deliver or tender in due form any document necessary to enable the buyer to obtain possession of the goods or otherwise required by the agreement or by usage of the trade, and (3) promptly notify the buyer of the shipment. On a shipment contract, the risk of loss passes to the buyer when the goods sold are duly delivered to the carrier for shipment to the buyer. §§ 672.503 (Official U.C.C. comment 5), 672.504, 672.509(1), Fla.Stat. (1977). . . .

A destination contract, on the other hand, is considered the variant contract in which the seller specifically agrees to deliver the goods sold to the buyer at a particular destination and to bear the risk of loss of the goods until tender of delivery. This can be accomplished by express provision in the sales contract to that effect or by the use of delivery terms such as F.O.B. (place of destination). Under a destination contract, the seller is required to tender delivery of the goods sold to the buyer at the place of destination. The risk of loss under such a contract passes to the buyer when the goods sold are duly tendered to the buyer at the place of destination while in the possession of the carrier so as to enable the buyer to take delivery. The parties must explicitly agree to a destination contract; otherwise the contract will be considered a shipment contract. §§ 672.319(1)(b), 672.503 (Official U.C.C. comment 5), 672.509(1), Fla.Stat. (1977). . . .

Where the risk of loss falls on the seller at the time the goods sold are lost or destroyed, the seller is liable in damages to the buyer for non-delivery unless the seller tenders a performance in replacement for the lost or destroyed goods. On the other hand, where the risk of loss falls on the buyer at the time the goods sold are lost or destroyed, the buyer is liable to the seller for the purchase price of the goods sold. White and Summers, Uniform Commercial Code 134 (1972).

### C

In the instant case, we deal with the normal shipment contract involving the sale of goods. The defendant Karinol pursuant to this contract agreed to send the goods sold, a shipment of watches, to the plaintiff's decedent in Chetumal, Mexico. There was no specific provision in the contract between the parties which allocated the risk of loss on the goods sold while in transit. In addition, there were no delivery terms such as F.O.B. Chetumal contained in the contract.

All agree that there is sufficient evidence that the defendant Karinol performed its obligations as a seller under the Uniform Commercial Code if this contract is considered a shipment contract. Karinol put the goods sold in the possession of a carrier and made a contract for the goods safe transportation to the plaintiff's decedent; Karinol also promptly notified the plaintiff's decedent of the shipment and tendered to said party the necessary documents to obtain possession of the goods sold.

The plaintiff Pestana contends, however, that the contract herein is a destination contract in which the risk of loss on the goods sold did not pass until delivery on such goods had been tendered to him at Chetumal, Mexico § an event which never occurred. He relies for this position on the notation at the bottom of the contract between the parties which provides that the goods were to be sent to Chetumal, Mexico. We cannot agree. A "send to" or "ship to" term is a part of every contract involving the sale of goods where carriage is contemplated and has no significance in determining whether the contract is a shipment or destination contract for risk of loss purposes. ... As such, the "send to" term contained in this contract cannot, without more, convert this into a destination contract.

It therefore follows that the risk of loss in this case shifted to the plaintiff's decedent as buyer when the defendant Karinol as seller duly delivered the goods to the defendant freight forwarder American under a reasonable contract of carriage for shipment to the plaintiff's decedent in Chetumal, Mexico. The defendant Karinol, its agent the defendant American, and its insurer the defendant Fidelity could not be held liable to the plaintiff in this action. The trial court properly entered judgment in favor of all the defendants herein.

Affirmed.

### NOTES

**(1) Allocation of Freight Costs as Allocation of Risk of Loss.** If freight from Sellersville to Buyersville is $12 per ton, quotations of "$100 F.O.B. Sellersville," "$112 F.O.B. Buyersville," and "$112 F.O.B. Sellersville, freight allowed" all have the same effect with respect to the buyer's costs. However, the first and third allocate transit risk to the buyer, while the second allocates transit risk to the seller. It seems likely that the parties, in negotiating the contract, are more likely to concentrate on immediate cost and return factors rather than on the relatively unusual aspect of risk of loss. Hence, there is ground for skepticism that choice among the above forms of quotation reflects an intentional agreement as to risk.

Price quotations that include freight may, on occasion, be employed to meet competition from a seller that is close to the buyer. If a seller wishes to be in a position to quote prices that include freight, but with transit risk allocated to the buyer, how could the order forms be structured? Would it be adequate to include a form clause dealing with risk of loss? Since negotiating agents cannot be expected to remember technical instructions, should the form include a special notation at the point where the price is to be inserted? What would you recommend?

**(2) Policy Considerations Relevant to Risk Allocation Rules.** Comment 5 to UCC 2–503 regards the "shipment" contract as normal and the "destination" contract as a variant. Under UCC 2–509(1) the "normal" shipment contract places transit risks on the buyer. Are there considerations of policy that bear on this result?

In considering risk allocation while sellers remain in possession, we considered whether sellers or buyers have the better opportunity to guard against casualty and to insure against loss. Are these considerations significant in transportation cases? It has been suggested that sellers should bear transit loss since they are in a better position to select and bargain with carriers. In evaluating this argument would it be relevant to inquire into the amenability of railways, truckers and ocean carriers to negotiate concerning the terms and conditions for transport?

Would it be relevant to consider which party can more readily cope with the consequences of in-transit damage? At which point in the transaction will in-transit damage be discovered? Are sellers or buyers in a better position to salvage the goods, assess the damage, and press a claim against the carriers or insurers? Would the answer be the same for (a) raw materials, such as cotton shipped to a textile manufacturer and (b) a complex machine manufactured by a seller?

Note that considerations of policy as to who can most efficiently handle in-transit losses is relevant not only in the construction of ambiguous contracts but also in the process of negotiating and drafting contract provisions.

**Problem 6.** Seller agreed to sell Buyer an accumulation of brass scrap, with terms "f.o.b. Seller's city, payable by sight draft on arrival." Seller shipped and took a bill of lading running to "Seller or order." The brass was stolen during transit. Must Buyer pay the price? Does the fact that the bill of lading is a "document of *title*" and ran in Seller's name affect the risk of loss? See UCC 2–509(1)(a) ("even though the shipment is under reservation").

What considerations of policy underlie this result?

**Problem 7.** Seller in Seattle, Washington, and Buyer in Boise, Idaho, made a contract calling for Seller to ship Buyer one hundred bags of "No. 1 Cane Sugar," F.O.B. Seattle. When the shipment was unloaded at Buyer's place of business Buyer inspected the sugar and immediately wired Seller "Sugar grades No. 2, will hold you responsible for reduced value of shipment." The next day the sugar was destroyed by a fire in the buyer's warehouse.

(a) On the above facts, who has risk of loss? See UCC 2–510(1), UCC 2–606(1)(a).

(b) Suppose the buyer had wired: "Sugar grades No. 2. Will reject sugar unless you allow price reduction of 50 cents per hundredweight." If the casualty occurred before Seller replied, who would bear the risk?

**Problem 8.** Seller is a sugar refiner located in San Francisco, California; Buyer is a Boston, Massachusetts, candy manufacturer. Seller and Buyer made a contract for the sale to Buyer of 1000 tons of No. 1 beet sugar at $560 per ton. The contract terms were "C.I.F. Boston, ocean carriage via the Panama Canal. Shipment during June; payment 60 days after arrival of ship in Boston."

During the ocean voyage, water leaked into the hold and seriously damaged half of the sugar. On arrival Buyer noticed not only the water damage, but also concluded that the sugar had been poorly refined and that it contained excessive impurities, so that the sugar graded No. 2 and was unsuitable for use in making candy. The sugar undamaged by water would bring $610 per ton; the water-soaked sugar was worthless. Buyer rejected the entire shipment and refused to pay the price.

(a) Seller sues for the price, and claims that the sugar conformed to the contract when it was loaded on board in San Francisco. Seller also contends that, in any event, the loss from the water damage fell on the Buyer, and that the Buyer may not reject since he cannot return the goods to the Seller in the same condition as when risk of loss passed to the Buyer. What result? See UCC 2–320, UCC 2–509, UCC 2–510, UCC 2–601, UCC 2–709(1)(a).

(b) Assume that Seller delivered No. 1 sugar to the ocean carrier, but had completed delivery to the ship on July 3. As in the above problem, the sugar is seriously damaged in transit by ocean water. Seller sues Buyer for the price. What result?

**Problem 9.** Rheinberg, a German wine exporter, and Vineyard, a North Carolina wine distributor, made a contract for Rheinberg to sell 620 cases of wine to Vineyard. The contract called for Rheinberg to ship the wine to Vineyard, but Vineyard was to pay the freight. The sales contract also provided: "Insurance to be covered by purchaser." On 29 November, Rheinberg delivered a container containing the wine to an ocean carrier for shipment to Wilmington, Delaware, freight payable by Vineyard at destination. Early in December the shipment left Germany via the M.S. Munchen, which in mid-December was lost in the North Atlantic with all hands and cargo. Vineyard received no notice of the shipment until after the ship and cargo had been lost.

Vineyard refused to pay for the wine, and Rheinberg sued for the price in a North Carolina court. Assume that domestic United States law applies. What should be the outcome? See UCC 2–504(c); Rheinberg–Kellerei GMBH v. Vineyard Wine Co., 53 N.C.App. 560, 281 S.E.2d 425 (1981). In *Rheinberg–Kellerei,* judgment for the buyer was affirmed by the Court of Appeals. The transfer of risk of loss to buyer was negated by UCC 2–504(c) since the seller did not "promptly notify the buyer of the shipment." It would not be practical "to attempt to engraft into [2–504] a rigid definition of prompt notice ... which must be determined on a case-by-case basis, under all the circumstances." However, in this case Vineyard was not notified "within the time in which its interest could have been protected by insurance or otherwise"; the notice had not been "prompt."

The opinion in *Rheinberg–Kellerei* did not discuss the ambiguities latent in the last phrase of UCC 2–504(c): "if material loss or delay *ensues.*" On these facts, would loss have ensued from the failure to notify if the buyer had been covered by insurance under a blanket policy? Or did loss ensue from the loss at sea of the ship and cargo? Who should have the burden to show that loss had ensued?

**(3) Liability of Domestic United States Carriers; UCC 2–722.** When goods suffer casualty or loss while in the custody of a carrier, the carrier may be liable for some or all of the loss. The legal obligations of carriers vary with the kinds of carriers involved. Many of the laws on duties of carriers are complex and cannot be considered in any depth in these materials.

When a carrier is liable for injury to goods that are the subject of a sales contract, the carrier's liability can be enforced by the seller or the buyer. The party that bears the risk of loss under the contract of sale is more likely to be the claimant against the carrier. Article 2 provides, in UCC 2–722(a), that a right of action is in either party to the sales contract that has title or a special property or an insurable interest in the goods. The section adds that, if the goods have been destroyed or converted, a right of action is in the party that either bore the risk of loss under the contract for sale or that has assumed that risk as against the other party to the contract. UCC 2–722(c) provides that either seller or buyer may, with the consent of the other, sue a carrier for the benefit of "whom it may concern."

**(4) Insurers v. Carriers.** The seller or the buyer may have insurance that covers damage to the goods that occurs during transit. In cases where rules of law provide that the carrier is also responsible for the damage, interesting jockeying for position has occurred to determine whether the loss should fall ultimately on the insurer or on the carrier. The situation was summarized by Professors Robert E. Keeton and Alan I. Widiss as follows:

For many years insurers and common carriers (such as truckers and railroads) engaged in an extended struggle with regard to the insurers' assertion of claims against carriers for damage to goods covered by insurance obtained by shippers. The following description of some main events in this struggle indicates the nature of the controversy and its relation to subrogation.

One of the early events in the conflict was the adoption by carriers of a bill-of-lading clause giving a carrier the benefit of insurance effected by a shipper. Insurers responded to this clause in the bill-of-lading with a policy clause providing for nonliability of an insurer upon shipment under a bill of lading that gave a carrier the benefit of a shipper's insurance. Since carriers then had nothing to gain and shippers had much to lose by retention of the clause previously used in bills of lading, the carriers modified the bill-of-lading clause to give a carrier the benefit of any insurance effected on the goods so far as this did not defeat the insurer's liability. This strategic retreat by the carriers still left the insurers with a problem. If an insurer paid a shipper, would it be a "volunteer" and therefore not entitled to subrogation to the shipper's claim against the carrier? If it did not pay the shipper, how could it maintain good business relations with an insured who wanted prompt payment from somebody and did not like waiting for the carrier and insurer to resolve a dispute as to ultimate responsibility for the loss? To avoid this problem, insurers resorted to loan receipts: an insurer paid a shipper an amount equal to the promised insurance benefits, but the transaction was cast as a loan repayable out of the prospective recovery from the carrier. The effectiveness of a loan receipt in preserving rights against a common carrier has been recognized in a number of judicial decisions. Thus, at least as reflected in such precedents, the insurers prevailed in the struggle with carriers over form provisions concerning responsibility for losses of insured property during shipment. And this result is also fortified by decisions that a "benefit of insurance" clause in a bill of lading is invalid under statutory prohibitions against rate discrimination, since a carrier would be receiving greater compensation from a shipper who had insurance than from one who did not.

R. Keeton & A. Widiss, Insurance Law 250–251 (1988).[14]

## (B) INTERNATIONAL SALES LAW

The CISG provisions on risk of loss are found in Chapter IV of the Convention. The most important articles are CISG 67 and CISG 69. Article 67 applies when the sales contract involves carriage of goods; the special situation of goods sold while in transit is covered in CISG 68. Article 69 applies when the sales contract requires the buyer to come to the seller for the goods.[15]

---

**14.**  Copied with permission of the authors and of the West Publishing Company.

**15.**  For a useful account of the Convention's rules, see P. Roth, The Passing of Risk, 27 Am. J. Comp. L. 291 (1979). See also Berman & Ladd, Risk of Loss or Damage in Documentary

### 1.  LOCAL TRANSACTIONS

Sales transactions that do not involve shipment of goods by carriers, while not typical of international sales, may nonetheless occur in some circumstances. The Convention establishes risk of loss rules for this type transaction in Article 69. The general principle is that risk passes when a buyer "takes over the goods." CISG 69(1). This phrase is more clear in its connotation of positive buyer action than is Article 2's "receipt." Recall, for example, the conceptual difficulty posed in applying UCC 2–509(3) in the *United Air Lines* case. Moreover the Convention standard applies to all sellers. The Convention does not contemplate non-merchant sellers.

The Convention also addresses the possibility that buyers, having opportunity to do so, will fail to "take over" goods. Although the Convention does not generally use the concepts of tender of delivery, it incorporates a similar idea here only for the purpose of allocating risk of loss to such buyers. Risk of loss thus remains on sellers until buyers' failure to take over goods placed at their disposal is breach of contract. How would the problem in *Multiplastics v. Arch Industries* be resolved if the transaction were governed by CISG?

*Nachfrist provisions.* The Convention allows party to sales contracts to use a procedure during the performance stage of a contract that lacks a firm delivery date to fix a date certain for the performance of the other party. Thus, a seller may fix an additional period of time of reasonable length for the performance of a buyer's obligations. CISG 63(1). If the buyer fails to perform within that time, the seller may declare the contract avoided. CISG 64(1)(b). (Similar provisions apply on the other side. See CISG 47(1), 49(1)(b).) These provisions are not addressed specifically to risk of loss, but allow sellers to deal conclusively with the buyers that are dilatory in taking delivery of goods.

The Convention relates buyers' duty to pay to the risk of loss rules. Buyers' duty to pay is not discharged if casualty or loss occurs after risk of loss has passed. CISG 66. An inference can be drawn that payment obligations are discharged if risk of loss had not passed.[16] The Convention has no counterpart provision that relates sellers' duty to deliver to the rules of risk of loss. However, the Convention provides broadly that sellers (and buyers) may not be liable for failures to perform if the failures were due to impediments beyond their control. CISG 79.[17]

**Problem 10.** On June 1, Seller handed over goods to Buyer. Buyer's inspection on June 2 disclosed that the goods were not in conformity with the quality term of the contract. On June 3 a fire in Buyer's warehouse injured the goods.

---

Transactions Under the Convention on the International Sale of Goods, 21 Cornell Int'l L.J. 423 (1988).

**16.**  Under CISG 66, a buyer is discharged from the obligation to pay the price if the loss or damage is due to an act or omission of the seller.

**17.**  CISG 79 adds other conditions that sellers must meet to be protected from liability.

(a) Buyer claims damages from Seller for the non-conformity of the goods and for the injury to the goods. What result under CISG? See CISG 36(1), 69(1), 74.

(b) Buyer contends that the non-conformity was so substantial as to constitute a fundamental breach and, on June 4, declares the contract avoided. Assuming that Buyer is correct in characterizing the non-conformity as a fundamental breach, to what remedies is Buyer entitled under CISG? See CISG 70, CISG 81, and CISG 84. See also J. Honnold, Uniform Law for International Sales § 383 (3d ed. 1999).

## 2.   SHIPMENT CONTRACTS

Under CISG 67(1), risk of loss passes to the buyer "when the goods are handed over to the first carrier for transmission to the buyer in accordance with the contract of sale" in a transaction involving carriage of goods and the seller is "not bound to hand them over at a particular place."

**Problem 11.** Seller in San Francisco, California, made a contract with Buyer in Bombay, India, for the sale of a machine to Buyer. The contract included the provision: "Price $30,000. CIF Bombay." The machine was damaged during the ocean voyage. If CISG applies, which party to the sales contract bears the risk of loss? For purposes of applying CISG 67(1), is Seller "bound to hand [the goods] over at a particular place," i.e., Bombay? Compare CISG 31.

*Incoterms.* The matter is dealt with more clearly if the parties have incorporated the ICC Incoterms into their sales contracts. The most recent version is Inconterms 2000. Incoterms specify when risk of loss passes in three categories of common shipping terms, which the ICC categorizes as "F" terms, "C" terms, and "D" terms. The "F" category are the terms in which the contract price does not include cost of carriage (e.g., FOB or FAS). In the "C" category are terms under which sellers must paid the costs of carriage (e.g., CFR and CIF). Under any of the "F" or the "C" terms of CFR and CIF, risk of loss passes at the time of shipment. A different result follows if the parties use other "C" terms, such as CPT (carriage paid to place of destination) or CIP (carriage and insurance paid to place of destination) or "D" terms, such as DES (delivered ex ship), DEQ (delivered ex quay), and DDP (delivered duty paid). Sellers bear risk of loss until the goods are delivered at the specified place.

Incoterms also allocate the responsibility to obtain insurance on the goods while enroute.

## BP Oil Int'l, Ltd. v. Empresa Estatal Petroleos de Ecuador

United States Court of Appeals for the Fifth Circuit, 2003.
332 F.3d 333.

■ JERRY E. SMITH, CIRCUIT JUDGE:

Empresa Estatal Petroleos de Ecuador ("PetroEcuador") contracted with BP Oil International, Ltd. ("BP"), for the purchase and transport of gasoline from Texas to Ecuador. PetroEcuador refused to accept delivery, so BP sold the gasoline at a loss. BP appeals a summary judgment dismissing PetroEcuador and Saybolt, Inc. ("Saybolt"), the company responsible for testing the gasoline at the port of departure. We affirm in part, reverse in part, and remand.

## I.

PetroEcuador sent BP an invitation to bid for supplying 140,000 barrels of unleaded gasoline deliverable "CFR" to Ecuador. "CFR," which stands for "Cost and Freight," is one of thirteen International Commercial Terms ("Incoterms") designed to "provide a set of international rules for the interpretation of the most commonly used trade terms in foreign trade." Incoterms are recognized through their incorporation into the Convention on Contracts for the International Sale of Goods ("CISG"). . . .

BP responded favorably to the invitation, and PetroEcuador confirmed the sale on its contract form. The final agreement required that the oil be sent "CFR La Libertad–Ecuador." A separate provision, paragraph 10, states, "Jurisdiction: Laws of the Republic of Ecuador." The contract further specifies that the gasoline have a gum content of less than three milliliters per one hundred milliliters, to be determined at the port of departure. PetroEcuador appointed Saybolt, a company specializing in quality control services, to ensure this requirement was met.

To fulfill the contract, BP purchased gasoline from Shell Oil Company and, following testing by Saybolt, loaded it on board the M/T TIBER at Shell's Deer Park, Texas, refinery. The TIBER sailed to La Libertad, Ecuador, where the gasoline was again tested for gum content. On learning that the gum content now exceeded the contractual limit, PetroEcuador refused to accept delivery. Eventually, BP resold the gasoline to Shell at a loss of approximately two million dollars.

BP sued PetroEcuador for breach of contract and wrongful draw of a letter of guarantee. After PetroEcuador filed a notice of intent to apply foreign law pursuant to *FED. R. CIV. P. 44.1*, the district court applied Texas choice of law rules and determined that Ecuadorian law governed. BP argued that the term "CFR" demonstrated the parties' intent to pass the risk of loss to PetroEcuador once the goods were delivered on board the TIBER. The district court disagreed and held that under Ecuadorian law, the seller must deliver conforming goods to the agreed destination, in this case Ecuador. The court granted summary judgment for PetroEcuador.

BP also brought negligence and breach of contract claims against Saybolt, alleging that the company had improperly tested the gasoline. Saybolt moved for summary judgment, asserting a limitation of liability defense and waiver of claims based on the terms of its service contract with BP. The court granted Saybolt's motion, holding that BP could not sue in tort, that BP was bound by the waiver provision, and that Saybolt did not take any action causing harm to BP. Pursuant to FED. R. CIV. P. 54(b), the court entered final judgment in favor of PetroEcuador and Saybolt.

## II.

We review a summary judgment using the same standards as did the district court; thus our review is de novo. . . .

## III.

BP and PetroEcuador dispute whether the domestic law of Ecuador or the CISG applies. After recognizing that federal courts sitting in diversity apply the choice of law rules of the state in which they sit, . . . the district court applied Texas law, which enforces unambiguous choice of law provisions. . . . Paragraph 10, which states "Jurisdiction: Laws of the Republic of Ecuador," purports to apply Ecuadorian law. Based on an affidavit submitted by PetroEcuador's expert, Dr. Gustavo Romero, the court held that Ecuadorian law requires the seller to deliver conforming goods at the agreed destination, making summary judgment inappropriate for BP.

## A.

Though the court correctly recognized that federal courts apply the choice of law rules of the state in which they sit, it overlooked its concurrent federal question jurisdiction that makes a conflict of laws analysis unnecessary. The general federal question jurisdiction statute grants subject matter jurisdiction over every civil action that arises, inter alia, under a treaty of the United States. *28 U.S.C. § 1331(a)*. The CISG, ratified by the Senate in 1986, creates a private right of action in federal court. Delchi Carrier v. Rotorex Corp., 71 F.3d 1024, 1027–28 (2d Cir. 1995). The treaty applies to "contracts of sale of goods between parties whose places of business are in different States . . . when the States are Contracting States." CISG art. 1(1)(a). BP, an American corporation, and PetroEcuador, an Ecuadorian company, contracted for the sale of gasoline; the United States and Ecuador have ratified the CISG.

As incorporated federal law, the CISG governs the dispute so long as the parties have not elected to exclude its application. CISG art. 6. PetroEcuador argues that the choice of law provision demonstrates the parties' intent to apply Ecuadorian domestic law instead of the CISG. We disagree.

A signatory's assent to the CISG necessarily incorporates the treaty as part of that nation's domestic law. BP's expert witness as to Ecuadorian law, Xavier Rosales–Kuri, observed that "the following source of Ecuadorian law would be applicable to the present case: (I) United Nations Convention on the International Sale of Goods. . . ." PetroEcuador's expert did not disagree with this assessment. Given that the CISG is Ecuadorian law, a choice of law provision designating Ecuadorian law merely confirms that the treaty governs the transaction.

Where parties seek to apply a signatory's domestic law in lieu of the CISG, they must affirmatively opt-out of the CISG. In *Asante Techs., Inc. v. PMC–Sierra, Inc., 164 F. Supp. 2d 1142, 1150 (N.D. Cal. 2001)*, the court held that a choice-of-law provision selecting British Columbia law did not, without more, "evince a clear intent to opt out of the CISG.... Defendant's choice of applicable law adopts the law of British Columbia, and it is undisputed that the CISG is the law of British Columbia."

Similarly, because the CISG is the law of Ecuador, it governs this dispute. "If the parties decide to exclude the Convention, it should be expressly excluded by language which states that it does not apply and also states what law shall govern the contract." RALPH H. FOLSOM, ET AL., INTERNATIONAL BUSINESS TRANSACTIONS 12 (2d ed. 2001). An affirmative opt-out requirement promotes uniformity and the observance of good faith in international trade, two principles that guide interpretation of the CISG. CISG art. 7(1).

### B.

The CISG incorporates Incoterms through article 9(2), which provides:

The parties are considered, unless otherwise agreed, to have impliedly made applicable to their contract or its formation a usage of which the parties knew or ought to have known and which in international trade is widely known to, and regularly observed by, parties to contracts of the type involved in the particular trade concerned.

Even if the usage of Incoterms is not global, the fact that they are well known in international trade means that they are incorporated through article 9(2).

PetroEcuador's invitation to bid for the procurement of 140,000 barrels of gasoline proposed "CFR" delivery. The final agreement, drafted by PetroEcuador, again specified that the gasoline be sent "CFR La Libertad–Ecuador" and that the cargo's gum content be tested pre-shipment. Shipments designated "CFR" require the seller to pay the costs and freight to transport the goods to the delivery port, but pass title and risk of loss to the buyer once the goods "pass the ship's rail" at the port of shipment. The goods should be tested for conformity before the risk of loss passes to the buyer. FOLSOM, supra, at 41. In the event of subsequent damage or loss, the buyer generally must seek a remedy against the carrier or insurer. *In re Daewoo Int'l (Am.) Corp., 2001 U.S. Dist. LEXIS 19796, at \*8 (S.D.N.Y. Dec. 3, 2001).*

In light of the parties' unambiguous use of the Incoterm "CFR," BP fulfilled its contractual obligations if the gasoline met the contract's qualitative specifications when it passed the ship's rail and risk transferred to PetroEcuador. CISG art. 36(1). Indeed, Saybolt's testing confirmed that the gasoline's gum content was adequate before departure from Texas. Nevertheless, in its opposition to BP's motion for summary judgment, PetroEcuador contends that BP purchased the gasoline from Shell on an "as is" basis and thereafter failed to add sufficient gum inhibitor as a way to "cut corners." In other words, the cargo contained a hidden defect.

Having appointed Saybolt to test the gasoline, PetroEcuador "ought to have discovered" the defect before the cargo left Texas. CISG art. 39(1). Permitting PetroEcuador now to distance itself from Saybolt's test would negate the parties' selection of CFR delivery and would undermine the key role that reliance plays in international sales agreements. Nevertheless, BP

could have breached the agreement if it provided goods that it "knew or could not have been unaware" were defective when they "passed over the ship's rail" and risk shifted to PetroEcuador. CISG art. 40.

Therefore, there is a fact issue as to whether BP provided defective gasoline by failing to add sufficient gum inhibitor. The district court should permit the parties to conduct discovery as to this issue only.

## IV.

BP raises negligence and breach of contract claims against Saybolt, alleging that the company improperly tested the gasoline's gum content before shipment. These claims amount to indemnification for BP's losses suffered on account of PetroEcuador's refusal to accept delivery. Our conclusion that PetroEcuador is liable so long as BP did not knowingly provide deficient gasoline renders these claims moot. Summary judgment was therefore proper, though we need not review the district court's reasoning.

If PetroEcuador improperly refused CFR delivery, it is liable to BP for any consequential damages. In its claims against Saybolt, BP pleaded "in the alternative"; counsel also acknowledged, at oral argument, that beyond those damages stemming from PetroEcuador's refusal to accept delivery, BP has no collateral claims against Saybolt. If Saybolt negligently misrepresented the gasoline's gum content, PetroEcuador (not BP) becomes the party with a potential claim.

Even if PetroEcuador is not liable because BP knowingly presented gasoline with an inadequate gum content, BP's claims drop out. BP alleges that Saybolt "negligently misrepresented the quality" of the gasoline before its loading in Texas; it also claims that Saybolt's improper testing was "a proximate cause of the gasoline to be refused by PetroEcuador and/or the gum content to increase which caused BP to suffer pecuniary loss." BP's claims depend on the fact that Saybolt misrepresented the quality of the gasoline. It goes without saying, however, that if BP knew that the gasoline was deficient, it could not have relied on Saybolt's report to its detriment.

The judgment dismissing PetroEcuador is REVERSED and REMAND-ED for proceedings consistent with this opinion. The judgment dismissing Saybolt is AFFIRMED.

NOTES

**(1) Incoterms and the CISG.** The contract used the term CFR but did not provide any definition. The Court of Appeals held that the contract implicitly incorporated the ICC's Incoterms and applied the meaning of CFR as an Incoterm which provides that title and risk pass to the buyer when goods pass the ship's rail. The Court of Appeals relied upon CISG 9(2) for its determination that the contract referred tacitly to the Incoterms. What alternative definitional source might have been used to give meaning to "CFR"? Would CISG 67(1) have been sufficient to resolve the dispute in this case?

**(2) Risk of Loss and Conformity of Goods.** CISG relates its provisions on passing of risk of loss with its provisions on determination whether the goods conform qualitatively to the contract. CISG 36(1) provides that the quality of the goods at the time risk passes is the quality that also determines whether the goods are conforming. Does this case turn on the passing of risk of loss or the fulfillment of seller's quality obligations? It appears that the goods deteriorated (gum content increased) while in transit. The Court of Appeals declared that the seller's obligations of quality were fulfilled or not fulfilled depending upon the quality of the oil when it passed the ship's rail in Texas. This also the moment when risk of loss passed to the buyer.

Buyer's counsel apparently made two claims: that risk of loss did not pass until the oil arrived in Ecuador and that, whenever risk passed, the oil did not conform to the contract. With regard to risk of loss, the Court of Appeals rejected the contention that risk passed after the voyage. Insofar as deterioration in quality occurred after the oil was loaded, under risk of loss analysis, the loss fell on the buyer. But buyer's second argument survived the summary judgment proceeding. Passing of risk of loss does not absolve a seller of breach. If the deterioration in the quality of the oil was the result of a nonconformity at the time of shipment, seller might be liable for damages. This question turns upon whether the oil had sufficient gum inhibitor when it passed the ship's rail. The Court of Appeals remanded that issue for further litigation.

*Liability of Carriers in International Transport Under International Law.* A substantial body of international law deals with the liability of carriers. Attempts to establish the liability of ocean carriers culminated, at the Fifth International Conference on Maritime Law held in Brussels in 1924, in an international convention usually called the "Hague Rules." The United States Government and many other countries signed this Convention. In 2008, under the auspices of UNCITRAL, a new Convention on Contracts for the International Carriage of Good, called the "Rotterdam Rules," was completed. Within a short time, more than 20 countries signed the convention. As of this date, there have been no ratifications, but the convention is supported by affected commercial interests and progress toward implementation is expected.

Rules for liability for international air shipments were prescribed by the Warsaw Convention of 1929. The Convention has now been accepted by the United States and over 90 other countries.

# SECTION 6.   NON-PERFORMANCE

## (A) DOMESTIC UNITED STATES LAW

### 1.   BREACH BY FAILURE TO GIVE PERFORMANCE WHEN DUE

Disputes arise occasionally when a performance is due but has not occurred. In the life of sales transactions, non-performance may occur because one of the parties decides not to perform. If that party communicates that fact, the law of sales characterizes the communication as an *anticipatory repudiation*. This section deals with the legal consequences that follow from anticipatory repudiations. Non-performance may also occur, in effect, when one party's performance is tendered, rightfully rejected, and cure is not made. This section also deals with the legal consequences of non-performance after rightful rejections.

Disputes of this kind are relatively rare. This sparsity of disputes may be explained by the realities of the circumstances of the aggrieved parties. They may elect, sensibly, to do nothing. The harm may be only disappointment, pursuing a legal remedy is costly, attaining a favorable outcome in court is uncertain, and enforcing a judgment is problematic. Another explanation that makes sense to many merchants is that an ongoing business relationship is valuable enough to allow a trading partner to walk away from a deal on occasion. Seventy-five years ago, Karl Llewellyn noted that "business understandings commonly permit wide cancellations of what to the court are flatly enforceable contracts to buy."[1] On March 26, 1974, the Wall Street Journal published a major article under the headline: "Broken Promises: Many Contracts Aren't Worth the Paper They're Printed On." The article reported a combination of soaring prices, shortages of materials, and strong demand had produced "a rash of what is no more than welshing on contracts [by sellers]." The article noted that some buyers threaten to sue, but relatively few follow through. On December 12 of the same year, the Journal featured another article, on the same subject, but with a different aspect. Market conditions had changed drastically. The article recounted a wave of buyers' cancellations of accepted orders. The article did not cover the anticipated litigation fall-out, but sellers, like buyers, tend not to sue regular customers.

Occasionally, however, the disappointed parties elect to seek their remedies at law. This section considers what remedies exist and how they are applied.

*Remedies for Breach by Nonperformance.* UCC Article 2 provides remedies for buyers and for sellers where the performances they contracted for are not made when due. We already considered these remedies, but it may be helpful to review them.

*Market-based damages.* One set of these remedies is market-based. When a buyer does not perform, an aggrieved seller is entitled to recover damages based upon the difference between the contract price and the (lower) market value of the goods that a buyer has wrongfully refused to accept and to pay for. UCC 2–708(1). When a seller does not perform, an aggrieved buyer is entitled to recover damages based upon the difference between the contract price and the (higher) market value of the goods that a seller failed to deliver or that a buyer rightfully rejected. UCC 2–713(1).[2]

---

**1.** K. Llewellyn, Contract: Institutional Aspects, 4 Encyclopedia of the Social Sciences 332 (1930).

**2.** The statutory formulae do not make clear whether market prices are higher or lower than contract prices, but common-sense tells us that a seller is not injured by buyer's

*Damages based on substitute transactions.* Another set of remedies is based on substitute transactions. An aggrieved seller may resell the goods in a commercially reasonable manner and recover damages based upon the difference between the contract price and the (lower) resale price. UCC 2–706. An aggrieved buyer may buy substitute goods from a third part ("cover") and recover damages based upon the difference between the contract price and the (higher) cover price.

*Damages measured by lost profits.* The symmetry is broken by the "wild card" remedy for some sellers, damages based upon the profit that an aggrieved seller would have made from buyer's performance. UCC 2–708(2).

*Specific performance; replevin.* In some circumstances, an aggrieved buyer can obtain specific relief. UCC 2–716 provides that a buyer may obtain a court decree of specific performance by a seller "when the goods are unique or in other proper circumstances." If goods have been identified to the contract (UCC 2–501), and the buyer is unable to effect cover after reasonable effort or the circumstances indicate that such effort would be unavailing, a buyer has a right of replevin.

*Price action.* An aggrieved seller may have the right to recover the contract price under UCC 2–709 for goods identified to the contract if the seller is unable to resell them at a reasonable price after reasonable effort or circumstances indicate that such effort would be unavailing.

## 2.  ANTICIPATORY REPUDIATION

A decision by a party to a sales contract that it will not perform its obligations may be made at the time performance is due, but the decision could be made earlier. If the period of time between closing of the agreement and the due date for performance is short, there is not much difference between an early repudiation or non-performance. However, when a contract period is longer, a repudiation may occur well before performance is due. In contract law generally, and in commercial law specifically, such a repudiation is called an "anticipatory repudiation," signaling an event that occurs before the contract due date.

Our concern here is with anticipatory repudiations of obligations under contracts of sale in which there is a significant period of time between dates of formation and the dates for performance. For this purpose, UCC Article 2 contains a set of legal rules of unusual difficulty. The Code does not define "anticipatory repudiation,"[3] but provides for the legal consequences.

---

nonperformance when the market price is higher than the contract price, and vice versa. On the contrary, the breach allows the "aggrieved" party to escape from what turned out to be a bad economic bargain.

**3.**  Some parties may flatly declare their intention not to perform, but others may signal their intentions by their conduct. If the signals are troublesome but ambiguous, the Commercial Code allows the party that has been made insecure to demand adequate assurance of performance. UCC 2–609(1). Failure to provide that assurance is a repudiation. UCC 2–609(4). If the statute fails to provide a definition, the principles of common-law contract would apply. UCC 1–103 [R1–103(b)].

The aggrieved party may suspend its performance, may await performance by the repudiating party for a commercially reasonable time, and may resort to any remedy for breach. UCC 2–610.

Note that the Code does not declare that a repudiation is a breach of contract. This is more than semantics. UCC 2–610 allows the aggrieved party to try to keep the contract alive (wait for performance). UCC 2–611 permits a repudiating party to retract its repudiation. A retraction reinstates the repudiating party's rights under the contract as well as the other party's duties. If reinstatement does not happen, the Code states that aggrieved party may "resort to any remedy for breach."

*Remedies for Anticipatory Repudiation.* UCC Article 2 has no separate remedies for the party to a sales contract aggrieved by an anticipatory repudiation. The Code provides, rather, that the parties aggrieved by repudiations have the remedies that the law provides for contract breach. This creates severe problems in some circumstances. The principal difficulty that arises when ordinary remedies for breach are applied to anticipatory repudiations is one of fixing the time for measurement of damages based on market values. The statutory formulae for market-based damages in cases of breach specify the time to look to market data. Sellers' damages, under UCC 2–708(1), are determined as of the time for tender. For buyers' damages, under UCC 2–713(1), the time is when the buyer learned of the breach. These time provisions were designed for the circumstance of breaches occurring when performances are due. UCC 2–713(1) use of the time when buyer learned of a breach because in some circumstances, e.g., shipment contracts, buyers may not become aware of the breach at the time the sellers fail to perform. The statute moves the date forward to take into account when a buyer can reasonably react to a seller's non-performance.

In anticipatory repudiation situations, however, the time when an aggrieved party is allowed resort to a remedy may be earlier, perhaps much earlier, than the date when performance is due. Should the damages for repudiation be fixed at or near the time of repudiation rather than at or near to the time for contract performance? If the market value for the goods in question is volatile, can an aggrieved party "play the market" at the expense of the repudiating party? Should the general common-law contract mitigation principle that disallows recovery for harm that could have been avoided be applied in repudiation cases? If the dispute comes to trial before the contract due date, how can future market values be predicted? These questions require courts to go outside the plain language of the statute.

Coupled with these difficult questions is the role of UCC 2–708(2) in cases of a buyer's anticipatory repudiation. Are there any circumstances in which a seller should be required to take damages based on lost profit where that is less than would be market-based damages? As we have seen, UCC 2–708(2) is designed to apply when market-based damages under UCC 2–708(1) are "inadequate." In the context of anticipatory repudiation, can a seller be denied market-based damages because they would be, on some criteria, excessive?

Courts have struggled with these grizzly questions of statutory interpretation in a number of cases. Some of these may be familiar from your study of contract law. We will consider first a case where a buyer sought market-based damages for a seller's repudiation. Then we will consider the analogous situation for seller's damages.

## Trinidad Bean and Elevator Co. v. Frosh

Nebraska Court of Appeals, 1992.
1 Neb.App. 281, 494 N.W.2d 347.

■ CONNOLLY, JUDGE.

This is a case regarding the sale of goods brought under the Uniform Commercial Code. Trinidad Bean and Elevator Company (Trinidad) brought suit against Elmo Frosh for damages based on breach of a contract for the sale of beans. Trinidad appeals a jury verdict for Elmo Frosh. We affirm.

FACTS

Trinidad is a Colorado corporation which owns and operates an elevator located in Imperial, Nebraska. Elmo Frosh is an individual engaged in the business of farming.

On or about April 26, 1988, Elmo Frosh entered into a written contract with Trinidad, whereby Trinidad agreed to buy and Frosh agreed to sell 1,875 hundredweight of dried, edible navy beans, which were to be delivered to Trinidad at Imperial upon completion of the harvest of the 1988 crop. . . .

Elmo Frosh testified that on approximately May 1, 1988, he told Larry Peterson, the elevator manager at Imperial, to tear up the contract. Larry Peterson testified that Elmo Frosh never made the statement. . . . It is . . . undisputed that on or about May 1, the contract and market prices for edible navy beans were the same.

On August 31, 1988, Elmo Frosh went to the elevator office and asked Buffington whether the contract had been torn up. On September 8, Elmo Frosh sent a letter to James Peterson at the Denver office, in which letter Frosh stated that he felt the contract was void.

Harvest was completed in mid-October, and no beans were delivered as promised in the contract. Because of drought conditions, the price of navy beans rose during the 1988 growing season from $16 per hundredweight in April, to $32 per hundredweight in late August to early September, and to $36 per hundredweight in late September, when Trinidad purchased beans from other sources.

The court instructed the jury that a contract existed, that the measure of damages was the price of the beans at the time of performance minus the contract price, that the time of performance was harvest time, and that Elmo Frosh might be entitled to the defenses of mitigation of damages and Trinidad's failure to "cover" within a commercially reasonable time after repudiation. The jury returned a general verdict for Elmo Frosh. Trinidad filed a motion for judgment notwithstanding the verdict or, in the alternative, for new trial, which motion was overruled. Trinidad now appeals to this court.

## ASSIGNMENTS OF ERROR

On appeal, Trinidad assigns that the district court erred (1) in not sustaining Trinidad's motion for directed verdict; (2) in not sustaining Trinidad's posttrial motion for new trial or for judgment notwithstanding the verdict, for the reason that the verdict rendered by the jury was contrary to law and contrary to the evidence; and (3) in instructing the jury that Trinidad had a duty to mitigate damages.

## MEASURE OF DAMAGES

In its first assignment of error, Trinidad claims that the court erred in not sustaining its motion for directed verdict. This assignment will be considered together with the second assignment, which is based on the trial court's failure to sustain Trinidad's posttrial motion for judgment notwithstanding the verdict and new trial.

\* \* \*

Anticipatory repudiation centers upon an overt communication of intention or an action which renders performance impossible or demonstrates a clear determination not to continue with performance. However, it is not necessary for repudiation that performance be made literally and utterly impossible. Repudiation can result from action which reasonably indicates a rejection of the continuing obligation.

Trinidad argues that the court ought to have sustained its motion for judgment notwithstanding the verdict or new trial for two reasons: (1) the jury could easily have ascertained the amount of Trinidad's damages at the time of harvest, since exhibit 3 was in evidence to show that at the time of harvest in mid-October 1988, edible beans were selling for $37 to $38 per hundredweight and (2) the jury was wrongly instructed that it should apply the defense of mitigation of damages to reduce Trinidad's recovery.

These assignments of error require us to determine the measure of a buyer's damages under Neb. U.C.C. § 2–713(1) (Reissue 1980) upon anticipatory repudiation, a question which "presents one of the most impenetrable interpretive problems in the entire Code." 1 James J. White & Robert S. Summers, Uniform Commercial Code § 6–7 at 320 (3d ed. 1988). Specifically, the question is whether the language "at the time when the buyer learned of the breach," § 2–713(1), refers to the time when the seller repudiated or the time when the performance came due.

\* \* \*

Neb. U.C.C. § 2–610 (Reissue 1980) provides that an aggrieved party may

(a) for a commercially reasonable time await performance by the repudiating party; or

(b) resort to any remedy for breach (Section 2–703 or Section 2–711), even though he has notified the repudiating party that he would await the latter's performance and has urged retraction; and

(c) in either case suspend his own performance. . . .

Section 2–610(b) provides a remedy for breach of contract before the time of performance has arrived. If a buyer chooses to treat the repudiation as a breach, he may proceed under Neb. U.C.C. § 2–711 (Reissue 1980). Section 2–711(1) provides that the buyer may cancel and recover any amount paid to the seller, as well as seek damages for cover, see Neb. U.C.C. § 2–712 (Reissue 1980), or the contract-market differential, see Neb. U.C.C. § 2–713 (Reissue 1980). Upon the breach of a contract for the sale of an article, a buyer is not required to effect the remedy of cover under § 2–712, but may recover damages for nondelivery.

In this case, Trinidad chose not to cover and sought damages for the contract-market differential under § 2–713(1), which provides:

Subject to the provisions of this article with respect to proof of market price (Section 2–723), the measure of damages for nondelivery or repudiation by the seller is the difference between the market price *at the time when the buyer learned of the breach* and the contract price. . . . (Emphasis supplied.)

The key question this court must determine on appeal is whether "learned of the breach" refers to time of repudiation or time of performance. The trial court found that damages were to be measured at the time of performance and so instructed the jury; however, the court also instructed the jury to consider whether Trinidad awaited performance unreasonably after Elmo Frosh's anticipatory repudiation.

\* \* \*

The word "breach" as used in § 2–713(1) is ambiguous and must be interpreted within its statutory setting. There are essentially two views as to how the ambiguity is to be interpreted: (1) "learned of the breach" refers to time of repudiation or (2) "learned of the breach" refers to time of performance under the terms of the parties' contract. But see *First Nat. Bank of Chicago v. Jefferson Mtg. Co., 576 F.2d 479 (3d Cir. 1978)* (adopting a third approach). Plausible arguments support both interpretations.

Time of Repudiation.

The most common interpretation, accepted by a majority of courts, is that Code § 2–713(1) refers to time of repudiation. This interpretation was adopted in the leading case of *Oloffson v. Coomer, 11 Ill. App. 3d 918, 296 N.E.2d 871 (1973).* In Oloffson, the buyer contracted with the seller-farmer for delivery of corn in 1970. In June 1970, the seller notified the buyer that he was not planting corn because of weather conditions and that he would not deliver. In September, the buyer again asked the seller about delivery of the corn, and the seller repeated that he would not be able to deliver. The buyer refused to cover and urged performance even though he knew there would be none. The Illinois Appellate Court refused to award damages based on the September price, but based its award on the price of corn on the June date, when the seller notified the buyer that he would not deliver. In so doing, the court pointed out that there was an easily accessible market for purchase of the grain and that the words "for a commercially reasonable time," appearing in Code § 2–610(a), relating to anticipatory repudiation "must be read relatively to the obligation of good faith that is defined in Section 2–103(1)(b) and imposed expressly in Section 1–203." *11 Ill. App. 3d at 922–23, 296 N.E.2d at 875.*

Time of Performance.

The performance date measurement is preferred by White and Summers. See 1 White & Summers, supra. The performance date measurement was adopted in *Cargill, Inc. v. Stafford, 553 F.2d 1222 (10th Cir. 1977),* in which the court reasoned that before the adoption of the Code, damages were measured from the time when performance was due and not from the time when the buyer learned of repudiation.

The court also noted that in Code § 2–723(1), providing for the measure of damages in a suit for anticipatory repudiation which comes to trial before the time for performance, the drafters stated, " 'Any damages based on market price . . . shall be determined according to the price of such goods prevailing at the time when the aggrieved party learned of the repudiation.' " (Emphasis omitted.) *Cargill, Inc., 553 F.2d at 1226.* The court reasoned that when the Code drafters intended to base damages on the date a party "learned of the repudiation," they did so by explicit language.

Analysis of the Alternatives.

Since the Code's vocabulary is not consistent, both of these interpretations appear equally plausible. However, for the following reasons, we conclude that the repudiation date interpretation gives the provisions their best combined effect.

It must be conceded that the performance date interpretation has the advantage of achieving consistency between § 2–713 and Neb. U.C.C. § 2–708 (Reissue 1980), the section containing the seller's market-based remedy for a buyer's anticipatory repudiation. Section 2–708 establishes the performance date as the proper time for measuring a seller's damages. The performance date argument draws additional support from Neb. U.C.C. § 2–723 (Reissue 1980), which expressly refers to both § 2–708 and § 2–713.

The shortcoming of the performance date interpretation is that it fails to explain § 2–610(a), which appears to allow an aggrieved party to await performance only "for a commercially reasonable time." As one court has said: "If buyer is entitled to market-contract damages measured at the time of performance, it is difficult to explain why the anticipatory repudiation section limits him to a commercially reasonable time to await performance." *Cosden Oil v. Karl O. Helm Aktiengesellschaft, 736 F.2d 1064, 1072 (5th Cir. 1984).*

We are also persuaded that pre-Code law is irrelevant. Under the common law, a buyer in anticipatory repudiation cases was privileged to await a seller's performance until the date performance was scheduled under the contract. See *Fahey v. Updike Elevator Co., 102 Neb. 249, 166 N.W. 622 (1918).* An aggrieved buyer was under no duty to enter into substitute transactions such as buyer's cover or seller's resale. See, e.g., *Reliance Cooperage Corp. v. Treat, 195 F.2d 977, 983 (8th Cir. 1952).* This was also the rule under § 67 of the Uniform Sales Act. However, prior law was changed by § 2–610(a), which allows an aggrieved party to await performance only "for a commercially reasonable time." Section 2–610(a) substitutes a commercial standard for a legal standard.

Moreover, the policy behind the commercial reasonableness of § 2–610(a) is to compensate a buyer based on the prevailing market. The goal in sales contract cases should be to compensate an aggrieved buyer in whole and this is accomplished by the Code's policy on cover. "Measuring buyer's damages at the time of performance will tend to dissuade the buyer from covering, in hopes that market price will continue upward until performance time." *Cosden Oil, 736 F.2d at 1072.* When a performance measure is applied, an aggrieved buyer in a rising market will speculate that prices will continue to rise. If the market falls after repudiation, the buyer will obtain the same goods at a price lower than under the contract. The effect is to overcompensate the buyer and penalize the seller. See Thomas H. Jackson, "Anticipatory Repudiation" and the Temporal Element of Contract Law: An Economic Inquiry into Contract Damages in Cases of prospective Nonperformance, *31 Stanford L. Rev. 69 (1978).*

Our interpretation is also influenced by § 2–712, under which a buyer may cover by making in good faith any reasonable purchase of substitute goods, so long as he does not delay unreasonably. See *Farmer's Union Co-op Company of Mead v. Flamme Brothers, 196 Neb. 699, 245 N.W.2d 464 (1976).* If the performance measure is correct, then "in a rising market, no reason would exist for requiring the buyer to act 'without unreasonable delay' when he seeks to cover following an anticipatory repudiation." *Cosden Oil, 736 F.2d at 1072.*

Holding.

We conclude that best effect is given to the statutes if "learned of the breach," in § 2–713(1), refers to the time the buyer learned of the seller's repudiation. Therefore, we hold that the measure of damages for a buyer upon anticipatory repudiation by the seller is the difference between the contract price and the price of the goods on the date of repudiation, so long as it would be commercially reasonable for the buyer to cover on the date of repudiation. Conditioning the repudiation date measurement on commercial reasonableness is required by § 2–712(3): "Failure of the buyer to effect cover within this section does not bar him from any other remedy." However, an aggrieved buyer ought to bear the burden of showing that it was commercially unreasonable for him to cover on the repudiation date.

Application.

Having determined that date of repudiation is the correct date for measurement of damages, we must determine when repudiation took place in the case at bar.

Comment 1 to § 2–610 states that "anticipatory repudiation centers upon an overt communication of intention or an action which renders performance impossible or demonstrates a clear determination not to continue with performance." *Crowder v. Aurora Co-op Elev. Co., 223 Neb. 704, 712–13, 393 N.W.2d 250, 257 (1986).* See, also, Annot., *1 A.L.R.4th 527 (1980).*

According to Elmo Frosh's testimony, he entered the Imperial facility in early May and directed Larry Peterson to tear up the contract because Frosh wanted no contract. If true, Elmo Frosh's testimony proves that an overt communication of intention not to continue with the contract occurred in May. Therefore, repudiation would have occurred in early May.

The gist of Trinidad's argument for directed verdict and judgment notwithstanding the verdict is that it was insignificant that Elmo Frosh repudiated because, even if he did, Trinidad was entitled to await performance under § 2–713. Further, damages were to be calculated at the time Trinidad learned of the breach. Trinidad argues that the breach occurred when performance was due and that Trinidad thereafter had a reasonable time to cover.

Since the factual issues of the time of Elmo Frosh's repudiation and the reasonableness of Trinidad's delay could not be decided as a matter of law, a directed verdict was not warranted. Moreover, since on a motion for judgment notwithstanding the verdict, the moving party is deemed as having admitted as true all relevant evidence favorable to the nonmoving party and the nonmoving party must be given the benefit of every favorable inference, Elmo Frosh's repudiation occurred in early May, when the contract and market price were identical. The jury's finding in favor of Elmo Frosh was not clearly wrong.

\* \* \*

Finally, Trinidad argues in its brief that even if the jury found that repudiation occurred in early May, it would be commercially reasonable for Trinidad to wait 4 months because the futures market for edible beans was fluctuating daily. "Because of the nature of forward contracting any commodity, the reasonableness of purchasing commodities to cover the amount of a commodity in a repudiated contract will always be questionable." Brief for appellant at 29. We are not persuaded by Trinidad's argument.

We have held that if an aggrieved buyer claims it was reasonable to delay after repudiation, he has the burden of showing that it was commercially unreasonable to cover on the date of repudiation. As we interpret the Code, its policy is to make an aggrieved buyer whole. The Code was not enacted to encourage or reward speculative behavior. As long as a well-ordered market is accessible, cover would be commercially reasonable at the earliest time following repudiation. Since Trinidad has not shown that it could not gain access to the futures market for edible beans in early May, it has not shown that it was commercially unreasonable to cover on the date of repudiation.

Accordingly, these assignments of error are without merit.

\* \* \*

AFFIRMED.

NOTES

**(1) Nature of Seller's "Repudiation."** The seller's conduct in this case was equivocal. What did it mean when he told the buyer's manager on May 1 "to tear up the contract"? What did it mean when he wrote on September 8 that he "felt the contract was void"? Were either of these acts an anticipatory repudiation of the April 26 sales contract? How was the question tried in the lower court? How did the appellate court conclude that there had been an anticipatory repudiation? Consider the litigation strategy of buyer's counsel on appeal. Did buyer's counsel contend that there had been no anticipatory repudiation? Should they?

**(2) Mitigation of Damages.** In the trial court, the instructions to the jury included a general charge that the seller was not liable for any damages that could reasonably have been prevented by the buyer. The jury returned a general verdict for the seller. The only possible basis for this verdict, given the trial judge's other instructions that the seller was in breach and on the applicable statutory measure of damages under UCC 2–708(1), was the instruction on mitigation of damages. On appeal, buyer's counsel argued that it was error for the trial judge to give this instruction. What would be the basis for this argument? Does Part 7 of Article 2 have any general provision on mitigation of damages? Compare UCC 2–715(2). Is the statute's silence on mitigation generally a meaningful silence? Does the silence override the common-law contract doctrine on mitigation of damages?

On the trial judge's legal analysis of damages, buyer's breach occurred at the time for buyer's performance of his contract obligations in mid-October. If damages were limited by mitigation that was reasonably possible at that time, was the jury's verdict for the buyer coherent? Does the mitigation doctrine become applicable before a breach occurs?

A segment of the appellate court's opinion not reproduced above held that the trial judge's instruction on mitigation of damages was error, but that buyer was not prejudiced thereby. The court arrived at this conclusion

after holding that buyer's market-based damages were fixed under the Code at the date of the repudiation.

**(3) Remedy for Anticipatory Repudiation.** The bulk of the appellate court's opinion deals with the difficulties of fashioning a remedy for repudiation from the Code's remedy provisions for breach? Was the court's reasoning persuasive? How did the court deal with the issue of the right of the non-repudiating party to await performance for a period of time? Consider again the effectiveness of the litigation strategy of buyer's counsel.

## Purina Mills, L.L.C. v. Less

United States District Court, N. D. Iowa, 2003.
295 F. Supp. 2d 1017.

■ BENNETT, CHIEF JUDGE.

### MEMORANDUM OPINION AND ORDER

### I.   INTRODUCTION

#### A.   Procedural Background

On October 28, 2002, Purina Mills, L.L.C. ("Purina") filed a complaint with this court claiming that defendants Kenneth Less and Karla Less ("Lesses") breached the Producer Pass–Through Agreement ("Agreement") they entered into with Purina. Specifically, Purina alleges that the Lesses breached the agreement by failing to pay for goods they accepted, and by repudiating the remainder of the contract. In its complaint Purina requests relief in the form of monetary damages resulting from the repudiation, monies still owing Purina on the goods already accepted, prejudgment interest, costs and any other equitable relief the court deems appropriate. The defendants timely filed their answer on January 3, 2003, which included an affirmative defense that Purina had failed to state a claim upon which relief could be granted. . . .

\* \* \*

#### B.   Pertinent Factual Background

Purina is a limited liability company engaged primarily in the business of manufacturing and selling animal feed and nutrition products. As an offshoot of its primary business activities, Purina also sells feeder pigs and weanling pigs to its feed customers. . . . Defendants Kenneth Less and Karla Less operate a large hog farm in Merill, Iowa.

On November 25, 1997, the Lesses and Purina's predecessor, Purina Mills, Inc., entered into a contract titled Producer Pass–Through Agreement ("Agreement"). In the Agreement, Purina Mills, Inc., is referred to as "Purina," and the Lesses are referred to as "Producer." The objectives of the Agreement are spelled out in the opening paragraph:

> WHEREAS, Purina sells feed which is suitable in the industry for the growing of weanling pigs to slaughter weight and wants an assured market for the sale of such feed; and

> WHEREAS, Purina has entered into a contract to purchase weanling pigs from a single source for sale to Producer.

> WHEREAS, Producer desires to purchase such weanling pigs from Purina for the sole purpose of growing them to slaughter weight.

> WHEREAS, Producer desires that Purina purchase the weanling pigs from Perennial Pork, LLP for purpose of sale to Producer. However if weanling pigs are not available from Perennial Pork, LLP, Purina, at is own discretion, will purchase weanling pigs from another single source for sale to Producer.

The Agreement provided that the Lesses would purchase approximately 15,000 weanling pigs each year from Purina Mills, Inc., for a period commencing on November 25, 1997, through December 31, 2007. The 15,000 weanling pigs were to be delivered in approximately 28 deliveries over the course of the year. Upon delivery, the weanling pigs were to be graded by the Lesses as either "grade one," "substandard" or "rejected." The Lesses were then to regrade the initially graded "substandard" and "rejected" weanling pigs approximately 48 hours after delivery. The grading system is described in the Agreement as follows:

> Pigs weighing 8 pounds or more will be classified as grade one. Pigs weighing less than 8 pounds will be classified as substandard. Sick, crippled, damaged or dead pigs not acceptable to Producer are to be classified as rejects and upon regrading shall be destroyed and not counted as party of the quantity delivered to Producer.

> If a weanling pig was regraded "substandard" then the Lesses could elect to either: (1) reject the substandard weanling pig, in which case the Lesses would not have to pay for that pig; or (2) accept the substandard weanling pig and pay a reduced price for that pig. The Agreement requires the Lesses pay $32.00 per "grade one" weanling pig and $24.00 per weanling pig that is regraded as "substandard" and that the Lesses elect to accept. If the Lesses chose not to feed the weanlings Purina products, then the price of each accepted weanling pig, whether graded "grade one" or "substandard," would increase by $3.00:

> 15.   FEED AGREEMENT. Producer acknowledges that Purina's interest in entering into this Agreement is to supply nutritional products and programs.

>     a.   Producer, therefore, agrees to feed nutritional products manufactured and supplied by Purina to all pigs furnished under this Agreement. If Producer fails to feed the pigs Purina products, the price per pig shall be increased by three dollars ($3.00) each. Producer

agrees to furnish to Purina all data and other Documentation as Purina deems necessary to complete and verify group closeouts.

\* \* \*

On November 25, 1997, the same day as the Purina—Less agreement was entered into, Purina Mills, Inc. entered into a contract with Perennial Pork, L.L.P. ("Perennial Pork"). . . . This contract provided that Purina would purchase 530 weanling pigs per week from Perennial Pork. The same "grading" system described in the Purina—Less Agreement was employed in this contract. Purina agreed to pay $32.00 for each "grade one" weanling pig, and $24.00 for each "substandard weanling pig" that Purina chose to accept. Under the "Delivery" section, the contract states: "It is Purina's intent to deliver the pigs to Ken Less' nursery and to the nursery used by Kingsley Producers, L.C. so long as those parties are not in default with Purina." Further, as part of this contract, Perennial Pork was required to purchase from Purina the amount of feed necessary to produce the weanling pigs Purina purchased. . . . This contract ran for approximately a ten-year period; from November 25, 1997 through December 31, 2007—the same term as the Purina—Less Agreement.

\* \* \*

On August 14, 2002, the Lesses accepted delivery of 306 grade one weanling pigs at $32.00 a head, and 4 substandard weanling pigs at $24.00 a head, from Purina Mills, L.L.C., for a total price of $9,888.00. Also on August 14, 2002, the Lesses prepaid their account with Purina by VISA in the amount of $15,000.00. On August 16, 2002, the Lesses accepted delivery of 203 grade one weanling pigs at $32.00 per head, and 2 substandard weanling pigs at $24.00 a head, from Purina Mills, L.L.C. for a total price of $6,544.00. After taking into account the amount the Lesses prepaid by VISA, a balance of $1,432.00 remained. To date, the Lesses have not paid Purina the amount left outstanding on their account.

On August 21, 2002, the Lesses did not accept a scheduled delivery of weanling pigs from Purina because of alleged financial difficulties. The Lesses have not purchased any more weanling pigs from Purina since the last accepted delivery on August 16, 2002.

In a letter dated August 26, 2002, and addressed to the Lesses, Purina's attorney Kevin D. Schluender, references the Agreement, and notes their nonpayment of amounts due and their rejection of additional shipments of weanling pigs. The letter further states that the Lesses' actions constitute a material breach of the Agreement under paragraph 16, and informs them that they must cure the breach within 15 days of receipt of the letter or Purina would exercise its right to terminate the Agreement.

On September 1, 2002, Perennial Pork and Purina Mills, L.L.C., entered into a "Consent to Assignment and Release Agreement" in which Purina consented to Perennial Pork's assignment of the agreement to Concord Valley Pork, L.L.C. ("Concord Pork"), and released Perennial Pork from its obligations under the Purina—Perennial Pork agreement.

This assignment was executed in conjunction with Concord Pork's acquisition of all of Perennial Pork's assets, including the Purina–Perennial Pork agreement—thus, the supply contract then became the Purina–Concord Pork Agreement. At this time Concord Pork offered Purina the option of "buying out" of the supply agreement between the parties for a lump sum price of $100,000.00. Purina refused this offer.

Finally, in a letter dated October 2, 2002, Mr Schluender, on behalf of Purina, again wrote the Lesses. This letter detailed the Lesses' breach of the Agreement, and noted that the Lesses had not taken any action to cure the breach within the 15 days allowed for under the Agreement. The letter concluded as follows:

> Since the cure period has expired, and the breach remains, Purina hereby gives notice that ... it has terminated the Agreement. Purina intends to pursue all of the remedies available to it....

This litigation followed.

\* \* \*

## III.   LEGAL ANALYSIS

\* \* \*

### C.   Damages

\* \* \*

### 2.   General damage provisions under the U.C.C.

\* \* \*

Section 2–703 of the UCC sets forth a catalog of the remedies the seller may pursue when the buyer wrongfully rejects goods, fails to make payment, or repudiates the contract. See *IOWA CODE § 554.2703*. n.7 The UCC rejects Purina's claim to a right to select the remedy of its choosing in Comment 1 to § 2–703:

> This section is an index section which gathers together in one convenient place all of the various remedies open to a seller for any breach by the buyer. This Article rejects any doctrine of election of remedy as a fundamental policy and thus the remedies are essentially cumulative in nature and include all of the available remedies for breach. Whether the pursuit of one remedy bars another depends entirely on the facts of the individual case.

\* \* \*

### 3.   Damages for weanling pigs accepted before the Lesses' repudiation

Purina claims it is entitled to the outstanding amount on the Lesses account pursuant to the following language of section 2–709. ... As a matter of law, Purina is entitled to the $1,432.00 outstanding on the weanling pigs delivered to the Lesses on August 14, 2002 and August 16, 2002. . . .

4.  Damages for the Lesses' repudiation on August 21, 2002

What at first glance, in determining which provision applies, appears to be a dispute easily resolved through a banausic application of the UCC damages provisions, becomes a delicate balancing of the wording of the UCC provisions, the principles underlying the UCC provisions, and the molding of UCC provisions to a fact scenario unanticipated by the drafters of the UCC.

The debate over the amount of damages Purina is entitled to due to the Lesses' repudiation centers around section 2–708 of the UCC. . . . Purina claims that it is entitled to damages under subsection (1); the difference between the contract price and the market price ("contract/market") at the time that Purina learned of the Lesses' repudiation. [Purina asserts a market price of $18.38 per weanling pig, evidenced by the fact that the United States Department of Agriculture ("USDA") quoted the market price of a weanling pig at $18.38 for the week ending August 16, 2001—the reported price allegedly closest in time to when Purina learned of the Lesses' repudiation on or about August 21, 2001.] Multiplying the difference between the contract price, $35.00, and the market price, $18.38, by the number of weanling pigs the Lesses were to buy under the remainder of the contract, 76,250, the court arrives at a damages award, under this measure of damages, of $1,267,275.00. The Lesses claim that using the contract/market formula would result in a windfall to Purina, and that Purina should instead be restricted to the "lost profits" remedy under subsection (2) of section 2–708. Purina responds to the Lesses' attempt to restrict it to lost profits by pointing out the contract/market formula adequately compensates Purina, and that the statute expressly states that the lost profits formula is not available unless the contract/market formula is inadequate to compensate the seller.

Generally, the seller is not restricted to any particular formula, and is awarded the damages they would have received under the contract/market formula as long as the seller has adequately established the market price and the unpaid contract price. . . . In fact, courts in most instances reject the application of the lost profits formula unless there is a showing that the contract/market formula results in an inadequate, or lesser, recovery for the seller. . . .

a.  When is the contract/market formula under § 2–708(1) inadequate?

Courts have routinely recognized that the contract/market remedy is inadequate, and that the lost profits formula is applicable, in three situations. First, where the goods to be sold, and that are the subject of the breached or repudiated contract, are specially-manufactured goods for which there is no readily accessible market. . . .

The second situation is where the seller is a "lost volume seller," which is defined as:

"... one who upon a buyers breach of contract, resells the article to a second purchaser at the price agreed to by the first purchaser. The second purchaser, however, would have purchased a similar article notwithstanding the first purchaser's breach. Under such circumstances, when the seller resells the article, he is still not made whole because he will have lost one sale, one profit, over the course of the year."

*Tigg Corp., 962 F.2d at 1130* (quoting *Storage Tech. Corp. v. The Trust Co. of N.J., 842 F.2d 54, 56 n.2 (3rd Cir. 1988))* (quotations omitted). ... A lost volume seller is not adequately compensated by the contract/market formula because it would result in damages less than the profit the seller expected to make from both sales; he would be reimbursed only for one profit, rather than the two profits he would have earned if there had been no breach. ...

The third, and final, category of sellers recognized as inadequately compensated under the contract/market formula are sellers who are "jobbers." According to the Eighth Circuit Court of Appeals, to be classified as a "jobber" a seller must: (1) never acquire the contract goods; and (2) his decision not to acquire the goods after learning of the breach must be commercially reasonable. *Blair Intn'l, Ltd. v. LaBarge, Inc., 675 F.2d 954, 960 (8th Cir. 1982)*; see also *Nobs Chemical, U.S.A., Inc. v. Koppers Co., Inc., 616 F.2d 212, 215 (5th Cir. 1980)* (defining a "jobber" under the same two factors); *Mid-South Materials [**49] Co. v. Ellis, 1988 Tenn. App. LEXIS 107, No. 87–314–II, 1988 WL 23914, at *2 (Tenn. Ct. App. Mar. 16, 1988)* (citing Blair for requirements for classification as a "jobber"); *Copymate Mktg., Ltd. v. Modern Merch., Inc., 34 Wn. App. 300, 660 P.2d 332, 333 (Wash. Ct. App. 1983)* (finding lost profits remedy applicable where seller never obtained possession of the goods, and cancellation of purchase contract whereby seller would have obtained the goods was commercially reasonable); *67A Am. Jur. 2D Sales § 1008* (listing same requirements for classification as a "jobber," and referencing Blair). ...

By listing the three categories of sellers that are routinely granted a lost profits remedy under § 2–708 the court is in no way asserting that these are the only types of sellers entitled to the lost profits remedy. The lost profits remedy is in no way restricted to these three categories, these are just the three categories of sellers that are most widely recognized as inadequately compensated by the contract/market remedy—hence, making lost profits damages the appropriate remedy. ... Importantly, the court notes that Purina does not comfortably fit within any of these three categories of sellers. It cannot qualify as a "jobber" as it has acquired, and is contractually obligated to acquire, the weanling pigs it was to sell to the Lesses from Perennial Pork. Purina also does not fit into the "lost volume" seller category as it would not have been able to sell the weanling pigs it was supposed to sell to the Lesses to a third party regardless of the Lesses' repudiation of the contract. Finally, and quite obviously, weanling pigs are not specialty goods for which there is no easily identifiable market.

b. Should Purina be restricted to a lost profits remedy, even though the contract/market formula would result in a greater damages award?

In spite of the wording of section 2–708 making the lost profits formula available only in the cases where the contract/market formula is inadequate, courts have, in three instances, found factual circumstances that warrant restricting an aggrieved seller to lost profits damages. This court finds these rare cases particularly instructive in determining the appropriate damages formula to apply to this matter, and as such concludes it necessary to provide recaps of the four cases dealing specifically with the question before the court in this matter: should Purina be forced to take damages under a lost profits formula, even where the contract/market formula would yield a greater damages award?

i. Nobs Chemical, U.S.A., Inc. v. Koppers Co., Inc. In *Nobs Chemical, U.S.A., Inc. v. Koppers Co., Inc., 616 F.2d 212 (5th Cir. 1980)*, the Fifth Circuit Court of Appeals became the first court to publicly address whether a seller's damages for breach of contract by the buyer should be calculated under the lost profits formula or the "market/contract" formula. In this case, Koppers Company ("Koppers") contracted with Nobs Chemical, U.S.A., Inc. ("Nobs Chemcial") and Calmon–Hill Trading Corporation ("Calmon–Hill") to purchase 1000 metric tons of cumene. *Id. at 214.* Koppers breached the contract. Nobs Chemical and Calmon–Hill had made arrangements to purchase the cumene from a Brazilian supplier for a fixed price, but at the time of the breach Nobs Chemical was not contractually bound to purchase the cumene. Id. The district court found that Nobs Chemical was entitled only to its lost profits, or $95,000.00. Nobs Chemical appealed this decision to the Fifth Circuit Court of Appeals, asserting that it was entitled to the contract/market formula for calculating its damages. Id. Under the contract/market formula, Nobs would have received approximately $300,000, or three times more than it would under the lost profits formula. See id.

The court first noted that Nobs Chemical and Calmon–Hell met both of the requirements for categorization as "jobbers" as they had never acquired the contract goods, and the decision not to acquire the contract goods was commercially reasonable. *Id. at 215.* Then, drawing heavily on the White & Summers treatise on the UCC as no other jurisdiction had directly addressed the issue, the court ultimately restricted Nobs Chemical and Calmon–Hill to lost profits damages under § 2–708(2):

(a) as a liquidated damage clause available to a plaintiff-seller regardless of his actual damages. There have been some commentators who agree with this philosophy ... White and Summers conclude that statutory damage formulas do not significantly affect the practices of businessmen and therefore "breach deterrence," which would be the purpose of the statutory liquidated damages clause, should be rejected in favor of a standard approximating actual economic loss. WHITE & SUMMERS, supra, § 7–12, at 232. No one insists, and we do not think they could, that the difference between the fallen market price and the contract price is necessary to compensate the plaintiffs for the breach. Had the transaction been completed, their "benefit of the bargain" would not have been affected by the fall in market price, and they would not have experienced the windfall they otherwise would receive if the market price-contract price rule contained in § 2–708(a) is followed. Thus the premise contained in § 1–106 and Texas case law is a strong factor weighing against application of § 2–708(a).

*Id. at 215–16.* The court affirmed the district court's use of the lost profits formula to calculate Nobs Chemical's and Calmon–Hill's damages for Kopper's breach of contract.

   ii.   Trans World Metals, Inc. v. Southwire Company. Though the case of *Trans World Metals, Inc. v. Southwire Company, 769 F.2d 902 (2d Cir. 1985),* illustrates a case in which the court refused to force the plaintiff-seller to take damages under the lost profits formula where the seller had proved the necessary elements for obtaining contract/market damages, *Id. at 907–09,* it is valuable in that it helps illuminate factual situations in which it is inappropriate to force the seller to take lost profit damages. In Trans World, the plaintiffs Trans World Metals, Inc., Trans–World Metals & Co., Ltd. and Trans World Metals, Ltd (collectively "Trans World") entered into a contract with Southwire Company ("Southwire") in March 1981, in which Trans World was to deliver 2,205,000 pounds of aluminum monthly, from January 1982 through December 1982. *Id. at 904.* In exchange, Southwire would pay Trans World approximately $0.77 per pound. Id. In March 1982, the price of aluminum fell dramatically and Southwire repudiated the contract in its entirety. *Id. at 905.* In May 1982, Trans World filed suit against Southwire for breach of contract in New York State court. Id. The jury awarded Trans World $6,702,529.00 for the repudiation, using the contract/market formula, and $419,232.84 for shipments that were accepted by Southwire, but never paid for. *Id. at 906.* The district court denied Southwire's motions for judgment notwithstanding the verdict and for a new trial, and an appeal to the Second Circuit Court of Appeals followed. Id.

   On appeal, Southwire raised numerous points of contention, but in regard to the formula used to calculate Trans World's damages, Southwire relied on Nobs Chemical and argued that the lost profits formula should be used as the contract/market formula would overcompensate Trans World. The Second Circuit Court of Appeals outright rejected Southwire's contentions for the following reasons:

   ... nothing in the language or history of section 2–708(2) suggests that it was intended to apply to cases in which section 2–708(1) might overcompensate the seller. See WHITE & SUMMERS § 7–12, at 283. Nor has Southwire cited any New York case that interprets section 2–708(2) as Southwire urges us to interpret it. As a federal court sitting in diversity, we will not extend the application of this state law.

   Nor are we convinced that Trans World has been overcompensated. No measure other than the contract/market price differential will award Trans World the "benefit of its bargain," that is, the "amount necessary to put [it] in as good a position as [it] would have been if the defendant had abided by the contract." *Western Geophysical Co. of America, Inc. v. Bolt Associates, Inc., 584 F.2d 1164, 1172 (2d Cir. 1978)* (quoting Perma Research & Development Co. v. Singer Co., 402 F. Supp. 881, 898 (S.D.N.Y. 1975), aff'd, *542 F.2d 111 (2d Cir.)*, cert. denied, *429 U.S. 987, 97 S. Ct. 507, 50 L. Ed. 2d 598 (1976))*. The contract at issue in this case is an aluminum supply contract entered into eight months prior to the initial deliveries called for by its terms. The last of the anticipated deliveries of aluminum would not have been completed until a full twenty months after the negotiations took place. *It simply could not have escaped these parties that they were betting on which way aluminum prices would move. Trans World took the risk that the price would fall. Under these circumstances, Trans World should not be denied the benefit of its bargain, as reflected by the contract/market price differential. Cf. Apex Oil Co. v. Vanguard Oil & Service Co., 760 F.2d 417 (2d Cir. 1985)* (defaulting seller obligated to pay damages based on contract/market price differential).

*Id. at 908* (emphasis added and footnotes omitted). The court differentiated the Nobs Chemical case by noting that in Nobs Chemical the plaintiff-sellers had contractually insulated themselves against market price fluctuation by entering into a second fixed-price contract with their Brazilian supplier. The result of this second contract was that the plaintiffs contractually fixed their "market price." Id. In this case, unlike Nobs Chemical, Trans World did not enter into any adjacent contracts to fix their market price, and therefore since "Trans World accepted the risk that the prices would rise, it is entitled to benefit from their fall" through an award under the contract/market formula. *Id. at 909*.

iii. Union Carbide Corporation v. Consumers Power Company. The case of *Union Carbide Corporation v. Consumers Power Company, 636 F. Supp. 1498 (E.D. Mich. 1986)*, involved two contracts: (1) A contract between Petrosar Limited and Union Carbide in which Union Carbide was to acquire residual fuel oil from Petrosar Limited; and (2) a contract between Union Carbide and Consumers Power Company in which Consumers would purchase 10,000 barrels of residual fuel oil a day from September 5, 1980 through December 31, 1987. *Id. at 1499*. The execution of these two simultaneous contracts resulted in the "Consumer [Power Company] always pa[ying] Union Carbide more per barrel than Union Carbide paid to Petrosar [Limited]." *Id. at 1500*. Following a dramatic drop in the price of residual fuel oil, Consumers Power Company refused to accept any more deliveries of fuel oil from Union Carbide after December 31, 1981. Id. Union Carbide cancelled the contract with Consumers Power Company, and paid Petrosar Limited, pursuant to a clause in the Union Carbide–Petrosar Limited contract, to keep the oil that Petrosar was to deliver to Union Carbide. Id. Union Carbide sued Consumers Power Company for breach of contract, alleging that it was entitled to damages under the contract/market formula. *Id. at 1501*. Consumers Power Company asserted that Union Carbide should be restricted to the lost profits formula for calculating damages, as awarding damages under the contract/market formula would result in Union Carbide receiving more than it would have received had the contract been performed. Id. In this case the lost profits damages amounted to $30 million, while the contract/market damages came to around $120 million. *Id. at 1503.*

The court first defined "inadequate" in the following manner in order to give it meaning both where the contract/market formula undercompensates and overcompensates the aggrieved seller:

> ... the court believes that inadequate should be interpreted to mean incapable or inadequate to accomplish the stated purpose of the UCC remedies of compensating the aggrieved person but not overcompensating that person or specially punishing the other person. The measure of damages provided in section 1 will be incapable of putting the seller in as good a position as performance whenever it does not fairly measure the damages suffered by the aggrieved party. This interpretation is more flexible in that it provides the damages under section 1 can be *too great or too small.*

*Id. at 1501* (emphasis added). As the facts of Union Carbide were analogous to those presented in Nobs Chemical, the court derived support for its position from the Nobs Chemical holding. *Id. at 1501–02.* The court noted that for the period of time that Union Carbide sought damages, it was acting as a "jobber" in that it did not acquire the residual fuel oil after Consumers Power Company repudiated the contract, and that the decision not to acquire any more fuel oil was commercially reasonable. *Id. at 1503.* The court adopted the rationale proffered in Nobs that use of the contract/market formula, where it would clearly overcompensate the plaintiff-seller, flies in the face of the UCC's philosophy embodied in § 1–106(1) that the aggrieved party should be placed in "as good as" a position as performance would have done, but no better. Id. The court concludes that it should restrict Union Carbide to lost profits damages under § 2–708(2) because it did not assume the risks of a market fluctuation in the price of oil, and because the contract/market formula would overcompensate it:

> Most importantly, this court finds that here, as in Nobs Chemical, had the transaction between Union Carbide and Consumers been completed, Union Carbide's "benefit of the bargain" *would not have been affected by changes in the market price of oil.* The price formula which set the contract price paid by Consumers traced the price that union Carbide paid to Petrosar. No matter what happened to Petrosar's prices, Union Carbide could pass through the change in prices to Consumers. *It was guaranteed its fixed profit on the contract and no more.* Any windfall gains that might arise from rapid price changes would be realized by Petrosar, not Union Carbide. For this court to fundamentally alter this allocation of contractual benefits between the parties by giving Union Carbide vastly greater returns than were provided for by its contract with Consumers would fly in the face of the UCC's basic premises and be manifestly unjust. In short Union Carbide was *guaranteed a riskless, fixed profit* under the terms of the contract

and they should not receive the benefit of price fluctuations whose risk they did not assume.

Finally, the court finds that market price damages will overcompensate Union Carbide. By overcompensation, the court means that Union Carbide would receive greatly more than the riskless benefit of the bargain they would have received if the contract had been performed.

Id. (emphasis added). The court distinguished the Trans World decision in that, unlike this case, the Trans World parties had expressly bargained for the allocation of the risk of market price changes—thereby making the Trans World opinion irrelevant to the case at hand. Id. at 1504. The court concluded by requiring that Union Carbide's damages be calculated under the lost profits formula of § 2–708(2). Id.

iv.  Diversified Energy, Inc. v. Tennessee Valley Authority. The final and most recent case dealing with the specific problem of when it is appropriate to 'force' an aggrieved seller to take lost profits damages under § 2–708(2) where § 2–708(1) would overcompensate the seller is *Diversified Energy, Inc. v. Tennessee Valley Authority, 339 F.3d 437 (6th Cir. 2003)*. In Diversified Energy, the plaintiff, Diversified Energy, Inc. ("Diversified") entered into a long-term coal supply contract with Tennessee Valley Authority ("TVA") in which Diversified was to supply TVA with 10,000 tons of coal per week from August 1990 through March 27, 1996. *Id. at 440.* According to the agreement, Diversified was to obtain the coal required to fulfill the contract only from Sigmon Coal Company ("Sigmon"). Id. Diversified entered a simultaneous contract with Sigmon in which Diversified was paid a fixed commission of $0.98 per ton of coal delivered to TVA. Id. Diversified was then obligated to pay $0.22 for each ton delivered to TVA, Billy Evans as compensation for assigning Diversified the contract in June 1980. n13 *Id. at 446.* TVA repudiated the contract on March 19, 1993. *Id. at 440.* Pursuant to the Diversified–TVA contract, the matter was submitted to a Disputes Contracting Officer. Id. Diversified claimed two specific proposed measures of damages: (1) the contract/market differential of $5.13 per ton, resulting in approximately $8 million in damages; and (2) $14 per ton for the 1,570,000 tons remaining, totaling approximately $21 million, which represented the liquidated damages Diversified would be entitled to if TVA was found to have unilaterally terminated the contract. Id. The Disputes Contract Officer rejected most of Diversified's proposed damages calculations and further found that Diversified had violated a provision of the contract which gave TVA the right to terminate the agreement Id. In March 1997, Diversified appealed the Disputes Contracting Officer's decision to the United States District Court for the Eastern District of Tennessee. *Id. at 441.* Though procedurally the case becomes complex and convoluted at this point, for purposes of this case summary it is important only to note that eventually the district court, on a motion for summary judgment, awarded Diversified $1,193,200.00, plus interest, reflecting the $0.98 per ton commission it would have received from Sigmon if TVA had performed less the $0.22 per ton that Diversified was obligated to pay to Billy Evans. *Id. at 443.* Among other things, Diversified appealed this damage award to the Sixth Circuit Court of Appeals. Id. [The Court of Appeals for the Sixth Circuit affirmed.]

\* \* \*

v.  Application. The cases discussed illustrate some factors a court should consider when trying to determine if the plaintiff-seller should be forced to take lost profits damages when contract/market damages would give the seller a windfall. As gleaned from the summarized cases above that have addressed this issue, the key reasons for restricting an aggrieved seller to lost profits damages are: (1) contract/market damages would clearly overcompensate the seller; (2) the seller has insulated itself from changes in the market price by entering into a contract with a supplier to fix its market price; (3) the seller's expectation interest is more accurately met by lost profits damages than contract/market damages; (4) the seller doesn't currently have possession of the goods remaining to be delivered under the contract; and (5) the seller is not contractually obligated to accept goods from its supplier, or could pay the supplier to retain the goods pursuant to the seller's contract with the supplier. On the other hand, Trans World provides the court with factors dictating when lost profits damages should not be imposed on the seller: (1) where it isn't clear that the contract/market formula would, in fact, overcompensate the seller; (2) the seller is not contractually insulated from fluctuations in market price; and (3) the state in which the federal court sits has not interpreted § 2–708 to allow for the imposition of "lost profit" damages where the seller has proven the elements necessary for entitlement to contract/market damages.

\* \* \*

A close examination of the Agreement in this case, and the accompanying Purina–Perennial Pork contract, shows that the factual situation is similar, though not identical, to those detailed in *Nobs Chemical, Union Carbide* and *Diversified Energy*. This case is unique in that the court could find no other case involving the appropriate damage award of a seller who bargained to be insulated from market fluctuations, yet knowing that the buyers had repudiated, refused an option extended by the supplier to buy out of the third-party agreement, and therefore remained contractually bound to accept the contract goods from its supplier after the buyer's breach. Like the sellers in Nobs Chemical, Union Carbide and Diversified Energy, Purina, by entering into a fixed-price contract with Perennial Pork for purchase of the weanling pigs at $32.00 each, effectively insulated itself from any fluctuation in the market price of weanling pigs. Purina did not assume any risk that the market price of weanling pigs would fluctuate throughout the term of the Agreement with the Lesses. See *Diversified Energy, 339 F.3d at 447.* If all parties had performed their roles, the only party who would be affected by fluctuations in the market price would be the supplier, Perennial Pork and/or Concord Pork. Had the Lesses performed, Purina's expected "benefit of the bargain" would not have been affected by a fluctuation in the market price of weanling pigs. See *Union Carbide, 636 F. Supp. at 1503.* The fact that Purina contractually insulated itself from market fluctuations puts it in contention for restriction to lost profits damages—but in assessing the appropriate measure of damages the court must also consider Purina's expectancy interest in remaining insulated from the market in tandem with the buyout option offered by Concord mere days after the Lesses' repudiation.

The court will first consider Purina's expectancy interest standing alone. When Purina simultaneously entered into Agreements with the Lesses and Perennial, Purina's expected "benefit of the bargain" was to either sell the Lesses all of the feed products necessary to raise the weanling pigs they purchased to slaughter weight, or, if the Lesses decided not to use Purina feed products, to receive an additional $3.00 per weanling pig. Additionally, regardless of whether the Lesses used Purina feed and nutritional products, [Purina also expected to recoup, from the Lesses,] the purchase price of $32.00 per weanling pig that it paid to acquire the weanling pig from Perennial Pork. One key difference in this case that makes Purina unlike the sellers in Nobs Chemical, Union Carbide and Diversified Energy, is that Purina is contractually obligated to purchase the weanling pigs from Perennial Pork at $32.00 a head, for the remainder of the term of the contract—through December 2007. n15 Purina is not excused from performance under its contract with Perennial merely because the Lesses' repudiated their contract with Purina. The fact that Purina is contractually bound to purchase the weanling pigs that it was to sell the Lesses necessitates consideration of an additional expectancy interest that was part of Purina's "benefit of the bargain": Purina's expectation that it would remain insulated from market fluctuations. Consideration of this expectation interest did not come into play in Nobs Chemical, Union Carbide or Diversified Energy because in those cases the plaintiff-sellers were not required to accept the contract goods from their suppliers; hence, the breach by the buyers did not compromise the sellers' expected market insulation. In this case the Lesses' repudiation resulted in Purina losing its "contracted for" market insulation, in that Purina, in order to recoup the cost of the weanling pigs it had to purchase from Perennial Pork, is now required to resell the weanling pigs subject to the market for weanling pigs; subject to the very market fluctuations that it expected to be insulated against as a benefit of its bargain with the Lesses. Regardless of the Lesses' repudiation, Purina is still contractually required to pay a flat $32.00 purchase price for the weanling pigs to its supplier, and in order to break even it must sell these weanling pigs at whatever the market dictates they are worth at the time—whether that be $8.00 each or $38.00 each. The Lesses' repudiation stripped Purina of its contracted for security from market price fluctuations. If there were no other factors to consider, the court would comfortably find that Purina was entitled to contract/market damages as the Lesses' repudiation destroyed Purina's expectancy interest and Purina was helpless to stop it.

However, looking at Purina's expectancy interest in tandem with the buyout offer by Concord Pork it becomes clear that the Lesses are not the keepers of Purina's expectancy interest—almost serindiputously, mere days after learning of the Lesses' repudiation, Purina was given the option by

Concord Pork to buy out of the remainder of the contract between Purina and Concord for the sum of $100,000.00. Dave Hoffman, president of Concord Pork, testified that on September 1, 2002, the day that he purchased Concord Pork, and the day that Concord Pork acquired the rights and obligations of the Purina–Perennial Agreement through a purchase of all of Perennial Pork's assets, Concord offered Purina the option of buying out of the supply agreement:

> A:  When I bought Concord there was a discussion and we felt at the time that the contract has some value to us as a purchaser, and so we asked Purina for $100,000 for the contract and that was not accepted, so we left the contract in place ...
>
> Q:  Do I understand your testimony correctly then that at the time of the closing you offered to let Purina out of the contract for $100,000?
>
> A:  Yes.

Though the Lesses' repudiation thrust Purina into the market, Purina remained the master of its own destiny, as it could have chosen to take the buyout offer by Concord and preserved its expected market insulation. Curiously, rather than accept the buyout offer by Concord—which would have insured protection of Purina's expectancy interests—Purina made the choice to remain vulnerable to the market in spite of the fact that it knew that the Lesses would not be able to fulfill their end of the contract bargain. Purina said it best: "There was no way to know whether [Purina] would be able to find another buyer or, if not, whether it would make or lose money be re-selling the pigs on the open market." While it is true that the Lesses' repudiation initially forced Purina into the uncertain ebb and flow of the marketplace, Purina, with full knowledge that the Lesses were financially unable to accept any more weanling pigs, made the conscious choice to remain in this position by refusing the buyout option offered by Concord. In this instance, where Purina itself distinctly declined the opportunity to protect its expectancy interest in market insulation, the court finds no reason why it should protect the expectancy interest Purina perfunctorily cast aside through an award of contract/market damages.

Some scholars have worried that restricting an aggrieved seller to lost profits damages would lead to opportunistic breaching by the buyer, ... however in this instance it appears as though not restricting Purina to lost profits damages would encourage large, corporate sellers not to mitigate their damages, but rather hold out for "guaranteed" contract/market damages—as appears to be the case in this instance. Key in this determination is the fact that Purina opted to continue receiving weanling pigs from Concord Pork, with full knowledge that it would have to sell, subject to the market, the weanling pigs the Lesses could no longer purchase to a third party. Further enforcing the decision to award only lost profits is the fact that the Lesses' repudiation and the buyout offer occurred mere days apart—thus the Lesses' repudiation unilaterally affected Purina's expected market insulation for only a handful of days. If Purina were granted contract/market damages, Purina would receive the $3.00 profit per weanling pig, the contract/market differential of $16.62 per weanling pig and any amount Purina would receive for selling the weanling pigs to a third-party rather than to the Lesses—this surely would constitute a windfall to a seller, such as Purina, that chose not to protect its expected market insulation. ... The only actual loss caused by the Lesses' repudiation, in light of Concord's almost simultaneous buyout offer, is Purina's lost profits. The Lesses are not responsible for Purina's election to remain contractually bound to receive weanling pigs from Concord, and consequently Purina's assumption of the risk of selling those pigs subject to a fluctuating market. In summary, the court has found that: (1) by simultaneously entering into agreements with both Perennial Pork (now Concord Pork) and the Lesses, Purina effectively insulated itself from market fluctuations; (2) less than a month after the Lesses' repudiation, Purina was given the option to buyout of the contract with its supplier; and (3) an award of contract/market damages would clearly overcompensate a seller in Purina's position. Therefore, like the courts in Nobs Chemical, Union Carbide and Diversified Energy, this court finds that based on undisputed material facts, considerations of equity require that Purina be restricted to lost profits damages.

\* \* \*

## IV. CONCLUSION

For the reasons stated above, Purina's motion for summary judgment is granted. IT IS ORDERED AND ADJUDGED that plaintiff Purina shall recover as follows:

1. Damages against the Lesses, jointly and severally, under *Iowa Code § 554.2709* for the price of goods accepted by the Lesses in the amount of $1,432.00 with interest to accrue at a rate of 3.24% per annum from October 28, 2002.

2. Damages against the Lesses, jointly and severally, under *Iowa Code § 554.2708(2)* for the Lesses' repudiation in the amount of $57,639.49 with interest to accrue at a rate of 3.24% per annum from October 28, 2002.

3. Future Damages against the Lesses, jointly and severally, under *Iowa Code § 554.2708(2)* for the Lesses' repudiation in the amount of $158,452.66 with interest to accrue at a rate of 3.24% per annum from December 22, 2003.

IT IS SO ORDERED.

## NOTES

(1) **Nature of Buyer's "Repudiation."** Was this case one of anticipatory repudiation under UCC 2–610? The 10–year sales contract in this case provided for multiple deliveries and acceptances of goods and payments each year. Buyer defaulted by nonpayment for certain deliveries and refusal to receive other tenders of delivery. Did buyer's acts constitute an anticipatory repudiation of the balance of the 10–year contract? Installment contracts are governed by UCC 2–612. Subsection (3) provides that a party

aggrieved by default with respect to one or more installments may treat those facts as a breach of the whole contract only if the past defaults substantially impair the value of the whole contract. Was UCC 2–612(3) relevant to this case? Can an aggrieved party treat defaults in early installments of a long-term contract as an anticipatory repudiation of the whole contract even if the defaults are not sufficiently substantial to impair the value of the whole contract?

**(2) Remedies for Buyer's Repudiation.** The bulk of the court's opinion deals with the measure of damages that seller could recover for an anticipatory repudiation. What was the legal position of seller's counsel on this issue? Why did counsel concede that "learned of the breach" in UCC 2–708(1) was equivalent to "learned of the repudiation"? See UCC 2–723(1).

The court adopted the legal position of buyer's counsel that the seller was not entitled to damages under UCC 2–708(1) and 2–723(1). The opinion recapitulated the case law on situations when sellers may claim lost-profit damages. Were these cases relevant to the decision that compelled this seller to forego the market-based damages that it preferred? The opinion restated at length four former cases in which courts had considered whether to compel sellers to take damages based on UCC 2–708(2) and elected to do so in this case. Did the court's decision conform to the law as declared in the statute? Was departure from the statute justifiable?

**(3) Remedies for Breach of the Whole Installment Contract.** Would seller's claim to market-based damages have prevailed if seller had elected to proceed under UCC 2–612(3)?

## (B) INTERNATIONAL SALES LAW

### 1. REMEDIES FOR NONPERFORMANCE

We start with a review of the remedies under the Convention on Contracts for International Sale of Goods.

*Market-based damages.* Damages for nonperformance are provided generally under the Convention in CISG 74 and 77. CISG 74 uses the general formula of "loss suffered as a consequence of breach"; parenthetically, CISG 74 includes "loss of profit" within "loss." Professor Honnold refers to CISG 74 as a "brief but powerful" provision.[4] A conventional way of measuring loss is by reference to the market value at the time for performance and the contract price.[5] CISG 77 allows reduction in damages by the amount by which a loss, or loss of profit, should have been mitigated.

---

**4.** J. Honnold, Uniform Law for International Sales 445 (3d ed. 1999).

**5.** When the aggrieved party has rightfully avoided the contract of sale, that party may be able to measure market value ("current price") as of the date of avoidance rather than as of the date for performance. CISG 76(1).

*Damages measured by substitute transactions.* Under the Convention, a party can claim damages based on a substitute transaction only if the aggrieved party has rightly avoided the contract. CISG 75.

*Buyer's right to specific performance.* CISG 46(1) provides that a buyer may require performance by the seller unless the buyer has resorted to another inconsistent remedy. This article reflects civil law theory of contract remedies. For common-law jurisdictions, where specific relief is exceptional, CISG 28 declares that courts are not bound to enter judgments for specific performance if the courts would not do so in domestic transactions.

*Seller's price action.* CISG 62 provides that a seller may require the buyer to pay the price unless the seller has resorted to another inconsistent remedy. There are no legal conditions on the right to recover the price.

## 2.  ANTICIPATORY BREACH

The Convention does not use the phrase "anticipatory repudiation" and has no provision directly analogous to UCC 2–610. Rather the Convention provides for what it calls "anticipatory breach,"[6] a quite different concept. CISG 73(1) provides:

> (1) If prior to the date for performance of the contract it is clear that one of the parties will commit a fundamental breach of the contract, the other party may declare the contract avoided.

Note that the article applies only to circumstances of "fundamental breach." Note further the provision that the evidence of impending breach must be "clear."

*Remedies for Anticipatory Breach.* The aggrieved party who rightfully avoids a contract under CISG 73 is entitled to fix its market-based damages as of the date of the avoidance rather than as of the date for performance. CISG 76(1). That article is stated in permissive rather than mandatory language. There is an inference that the aggrieved party may claim damages based on the market as of the date performance is due. Is this inference countered by the general mitigation principle of CISG 77? Professor Honnold asserts that the answer should be "no." "The aggrieved party has no general obligation under Article 77 to attempt to mitigate damages by 'accepting repudiation' by the other party."[7] Do you agree?

# Magellan Int'l Corp. v. Salzgitter Handel GmbH

United States District Court, N.D. Ill., 1999.
76 F. Supp. 2d 919.

■ Milton I. Shadur, Senior District Judge.

### MEMORANDUM OPINION AND ORDER

Salzgitter Handel GmbH ("Salzgitter") has filed a motion pursuant to *Fed.R.Civ.P. ("Rule") 12(b)(6)* ("Motion"), seeking to dismiss this action

---

6.  The caption to CISG Chapter 5, Section 1, refers to "anticipatory breach."

7.  J. Honnold, Uniform Law for International Sales 459 (3d ed. 1999).

brought against it by Magellan International Corporation ("Magellan"). Because the allegations in Complaint Counts I and II state claims that are sufficient under Rule 8(a), Salzgitter's Motion must be and is denied as to those claims. . . .

Facts

In considering a Rule 12(b)(6) motion to dismiss for failure to state a claim, this Court accepts all of Magellan's well-pleaded factual allegations as true, as well as drawing all reasonable inferences from those facts in Magellan's favor. . . . What follows is the version of events set out in the Complaint, when read in that light.

Offers, Counteroffers and Acceptance

Magellan is an Illinois-based distributor of steel products. Salzgitter is a steel trader that is headquartered in Dusseldorf, Germany and maintains an Illinois sales office. In January 1999 Magellan's Robert Arthur ("Arthur") and Salzgitter's Thomas Riess ("Riess") commenced negotiations on a potential deal under which Salzgitter would begin to act as middleman in Magellan's purchase of steel bars—manufactured according to Magellan's specifications—from a Ukrainian steel mill, Dneprospetsstal of Ukraine ("DSS").

By letter dated January 28, Magellan provided Salzgitter with written specifications for 5,585 metric tons of steel bars, with proposed pricing, and with an agreement to issue a letter of credit ("LC") to Salzgitter as Magellan's method of payment. Salzgitter responded two weeks later (on February 12 and 13) by proposing prices $5 to $20 per ton higher than those Magellan had specified.

On February 15 Magellan accepted Salzgitter's price increases, agreed on 4,000 tons as the quantity being purchased, and added $5 per ton over Salzgitter's numbers to effect shipping from Magellan's preferred port (Ventspills, Latvia). Magellan memorialized those terms, as well as the other material terms previously discussed by the parties, in two February 15 purchase orders. Salzgitter then responded on February 17, apparently accepting Magellan's memorialized terms except for two "amendments" as to prices. Riess asked for Magellan's "acceptance" of those two price increases by return fax and promised to send its already-drawn-up order confirmations as soon as they were countersigned by DSS. Arthur consented, signing and returning the approved price amendments to Riess the same day.

On February 19 Salzgitter sent its pro forma order confirmations to Magellan. But the general terms and conditions that were attached to those confirmations differed in some respects from those that had been attached to Magellan's purchase orders, mainly with respect to vessel loading conditions, dispute resolution and choice of law.

Contemplating an ongoing business relationship, Magellan and Salzgitter continued to negotiate in an effort to resolve the remaining conflicts between their respective forms. While those fine-tuning negotiations were under way, Salzgitter began to press Magellan to open its LC for the transaction in Salzgitter's favor. On March 4 Magellan sent Salzgitter a draft LC for review. Salzgitter wrote back on March 8 proposing minor amendments to the LC and stating that "all other terms are acceptable." Although Magellan preferred to wait until all of the minor details (the remaining conflicting terms) were ironed out before issuing the LC, Salzgitter continued to press for its immediate issuance.

On March 22 Salzgitter sent amended order confirmations to Magellan. Riess visited Arthur four days later on March 26 and threatened to cancel the steel orders if Magellan did not open the LC in Salzgitter's favor that day. They then came to agreement as to the remaining contractual issues. Accordingly, relying on Riess's assurances that all remaining details of the deal were settled, Arthur had the $1.2 million LC issued later that same day.

Post–Acceptance Events

Three days later (on March 29) Arthur and Riess engaged in an extended game of "fax tag" initiated by the latter. Essentially Salzgitter demanded that the LC be amended to permit the unconditional substitution of FCRs [Freight-forwarders' Certificates of Receipt] for bills of lading—even for partial orders—and Magellan refused to amend the LC, also pointing out the need to conform Salzgitter's March 22 amended order confirmations to the terms of the parties' ultimate March 26 agreement. At the same time, Magellan requested minor modifications in some of the steel specifications. Salzgitter replied that it was too late to modify the specifications: DSS had already manufactured 60% of the order, and the rest was under production.

Perhaps unsurprisingly in light of what has been recited up to now, on the very next day (March 30) Magellan's and Salzgitter's friendly fine-tuning went flat. Salzgitter screeched an ultimatum to Magellan: Amend the LC by noon the following day or Salzgitter would "no longer feel obligated" to perform and would "sell the material elsewhere." On April 1 Magellan requested that the LC be canceled because of what it considered to be Saltzgitter's breach. Salzgitter returned the LC and has since been attempting to sell the manufactured steel to Magellan's customers in the United States.

Magellan's Claims

Complaint Count I posits that—pursuant to the Convention (CISG)—a valid contract existed between Magellan and Salzgitter before Salzgitter's March 30 ultimatum. Hence that attempted ukase is said to have amounted to an anticipatory repudiation of that contract, entitling Magellan to relief for its breach.

Count II seeks specific performance of the contract or replevin of the manufactured steel. That relief is invoked under the Illinois version of the Uniform Commercial Code ("UCC," specifically *810 ILCS 5/2–716*) because Magellan is "unable to 'cover' its delivery commitments to its customers without unreasonable delay."

\* \* \*

Count I: Breach of Contract

Choice of Law

... Because the transaction involves the sale and purchase of steel—"goods"—the parties acknowledge that the governing law is either the Convention or the UCC. Under the facts alleged by Magellan, the parties agreed that Convention law would apply to the transaction, and Salzgitter does not now dispute that contention. That being the case, this opinion looks to Convention law.

\* \* \*

[T]he requisite contractual joinder could reasonably be viewed by a factfinder as having jelled on March 26. ... [A]t the very least, a jury could find consistently with Magellan's allegations that the required indication of complete (mirrored) assent occurred when Magellan issued its LC on March 26. So much, then, for the first element of a contract: offer and acceptance.

Next, the second pleading requirement for a breach of contract claim—performance by plaintiff—was not only specifically addressed by Magellan but can also be inferred from the facts alleged and from Magellan's prayer for specific performance. Magellan's performance obligation as the buyer is simple: payment of the price for the goods. Magellan issued its LC in satisfaction of that obligation, later requesting the LC's cancellation only after Salzgitter's alleged breach. Moreover, Magellan's request for specific performance implicitly confirms that it remains ready and willing to pay the price if such relief were granted.

As for the third pleading element—Salzgitter's breach—[the] Complaint alleges:

> Salzgitter's March 30 letter demanding that the bill of lading provision be removed from the letter of credit and threatening to cancel the contract constitutes an anticipatory repudiation and fundamental breach of the contract.

It would be difficult to imagine an allegation that more clearly fulfills the notice function of pleading.

Convention Art. 72 addresses the concept of anticipatory breach:

> (1) If prior to the date for performance of the contract it is clear that one of the parties will commit a fundamental breach of contract, the other party may declare the contract avoided.

(2) If time allows, the party intending to declare the contract avoided must give reasonable notice to the other party in order to permit him to provide adequate assurance of his performance.

(3) The requirements of the preceding paragraph do not apply if the other party has declared that he will not perform his obligations.

And Convention Art. 25 states in relevant part:

A breach of contract committed by one of the parties is fundamental if it results in such detriment to the other party as substantially to deprive him of what he is entitled to expect under the contract....

That plain language reveals that under the Convention an anticipatory repudiation pleader need simply allege (1) that the defendant intended to breach the contract before the contract's performance date and (2) that such breach was fundamental. Here Magellan has pleaded that Salzgitter's March 29 letter indicated its pre-performance intention not to perform the contract, coupled with Magellan's allegation that the bill of lading requirement was an essential part of the parties' bargain. That being the case, Salzgitter's insistence upon an amendment of that requirement would indeed be a fundamental breach.

Lastly, Magellan has easily jumped the fourth pleading hurdle—resultant injury. [The] Complaint alleges that the breach "has caused damages to Magellan."

Count II: Specific Performance or Replevin

Convention Art. 46(1) provides that a buyer may require the seller to perform its obligations unless the buyer has resorted to a remedy inconsistent with that requirement. As such, that provision would appear to make specific performance routinely available under the Convention. But Convention Art. 28 conditions the availability of specific performance:

If, in accordance with the provisions of this Convention, one party is entitled to require performance of any obligation by the other party, a court is not bound to enter judgment for specific performance unless the court would do so under its own law in respect of similar contracts of sale not governed by this Convention.

Simply put, that looks to the availability of such relief under the UCC. And in pleading terms, any complaint adequate to provide notice under the UCC is equally sufficient under the Convention.

Under *UCC § 2–716(1)* a court may decree specific performance "where the goods are unique or in other proper circumstances." That provision's Official Commentary instructs that inability to cover should be considered "strong evidence" of "other proper circumstances." *UCC § 2–716* was designed to liberalize the common law, which rarely allowed specific performance.... Basically courts now determine whether goods are replaceable as a practical matter—for example, whether it would be difficult to obtain similar goods on the open market....

Given the centrality of the replaceability issue in determining the availability of specific relief under the UCC, a pleader need allege only the difficulty of cover to state a claim under that section. Magellan has done that.

\* \* \*

Conclusion

It may perhaps be that when the facts are further fleshed out through discovery, Magellan's claims against Salzgitter will indeed succumb either for lack of proof or as the consequence of some legal deficiency. But in the current Rule 12(b)(6) context, Salzgitter's motion as to Counts I and II is denied, and it is ordered to file its Answer to the Complaint on or before December 20, 1999. . . .

NOTES

**(1) Anticipatory Breach.** Although the decision was based entirely on the sufficiency of the buyer's complaint, it is useful to consider whether the allegations meet the standards of CISG 72(1). Was the evidence "clear"? Did the seller's conduct constitute fundamental breach? The key factor in the court's analysis was seller's request that it be allowed to obtain payment under the letter of credit by submitting certificates of receipt issued by freight forwarders (CFRs), rather than ocean bills of lading issued by carriers. Freight forwarders are intermediaries that offer specialized services to seller that want to ship goods. Among other things, freight forwarders consolidate goods from various shippers in order to better utilize the capacity of a vessel or other transportation media. CFRs are not conventional documents of title and, since they are not issued by carriers, do not entitle buyers to demand delivery of goods by carriers.[8]

**(2) Specific Relief.** The court followed CISG 46(1) and 28 to the conclusion that domestic United States law governed the buyer's request for specific performance. The court's determination that specific relief was warranted under the facts alleged may be questioned. The goods involved were manufactured to contract specifications. It is not clear that the goods were unique or that there were other circumstances that made specific performance proper. There is no indication that the buyer sought or obtained a preliminary injunction or restraining order.

---

8.  It appears that, in this transaction, the buyer undertook to arrange for the vessel that would carry the steel from Latvia to the United States. How does that affect the seller's effort to use CFRs rather than bills of lading as the documents for collection under the letter of credit?

# APPENDIX

The Table below presents an overview of the principal cases in this book, including the subject matter of the contracts, the status of the buyers, and the legal provisions that the tribunals applied. The sellers were, in all but a very few instances, business corporations.

The most common type of goods involved in the controversies was manufacturing equipment. These are about one-third of the total. In four instances the sellers undertook to design and build unique equipment, a contract-type that is especially prone to performance failure. Two other large groups involved sales of raw materials and sales of inventory. Each is about one-fifth of the total. Ten cases arose out of sales to consumers of consumer goods, usually relatively expensive durable goods.

The case collection reflects the widely held view that litigation tends to arise when contracting parties do not have a strong, continuing commercial relationship. Such relationships are likely to arise between inventory or materials suppliers and their regular customers. The commercial value of such relationships to both parties leads them to make mutually satisfactory commercial accommodations when issues arise rather than to "go to law." The business relationships in the cases involving inventory and raw materials in this Table do not appear to have had that character.

The case collection also reflects the view that the potential costs of commercial litigation, particularly attorney fees that usually are not recoverable, are an impediment to using litigation as a way of resolving disputes unless there is a substantial amount of money at stake. Although the Magnuson Moss Warranty Act and the laws of some states allow plaintiffs who prevail to ask for attorney fees and court costs, there is no indication that this significantly increased the likelihood of litigation involving consumer goods.

## TABLE OF PRINCIPAL CASES

| Cases | Pg | Subject Matter | Buyer | UCC | CISG | Other law |
|---|---|---|---|---|---|---|
| **CHAPTER 2.  BASIC PRINCIPLES** | | | | | | |
| **BMC Industries, Inc. v. Barth Industries, Inc.** U.S. Court of Appeals, 11th Cir., 1998 | 31 | Eyeglass lens equipment Design-build | Business Corporation | 2–102 2–105(1) 2–209 | | |
| **Advent Systems Lyd. V. Unisys Corp.** U.S. Court of Appeals, 3d Cir., 1991 | 47 | Computer software Design-build | Business Corporation | 1–102 2–102 2–201(a) 2–204 | | |

| Cases | Pg | Subject Matter | Buyer | UCC | CISG | Other law |
|---|---|---|---|---|---|---|
| **MCC-Marble Ceramic Center v. Ceramics** <br> U.S. Court of Appeals, 11th Cir. 1998 | 72 | Ceramic tiles | Business Corporation | 2–201 | 8(1) <br> 11 | |
| **CHAPTER 3. TITLE** | | | | | | |
| **Colton v. Decker** <br> South Dakota Supreme Court, 1996 | 84 | Rebuilt truck | Business <br> Individual | 2–312 <br> 2–714 <br> 2–715 | | |
| **Frank Arnold Contractors, Inc. v. Vilsmeier Auctions Co.** <br> U.S. Court of Appeals, 3d Cir. 1986 | 94 | Construction equipment | Business Corporation | 2–312 | | |
| **Pacific Sunwear of Calif., Inc. v. Olaes Enterprises, Inc.** <br> California Court of Appeal, 4th App. Dist., 2008 | 99 | T-shirts | Business Corporation | 2–312(3) | | |
| **Kotis v. Nowlin Jewelry, Inc.** <br> Texas Court of Appeals, 14th Dist., 1992 | 113 | Rolex watch | Business Corporation | 2–403(1) <br> 1–201(b)((29) <br> 1–204 | | |
| **Porter v. Wertz** <br> New York Court of Appeals, 1981 | 122 | Utrillo painting | Business <br> Individual | 2–403(2) <br> 1–201(b)(9) | | |
| **Madrid v. Bloomington Auto Co.** <br> Indiana Court of Appeals, 4th Dist., 2003 | 127 | Lincoln Navigator | Consumer | 2–403(2) | | Certificate of Title Act |
| **CHAPTER 4. SELLERS' WARRANTIES** | | | | | | |
| **Royal Business Machines v. Lorraine Corp.** <br> U. S. Court of Appeals, 7th Cir., 1980. | 147 | Copy machines | Business Corporation | 2–313 <br> 2–314 <br> 2–315 | | Common-law fraud |
| **McDonnell Douglas Corp. v. Thiokol Corp.** <br> U. S. Court of Appeals, 9th Cir., 1997. | 157 | Motors for space module | Business Corporation | 2–313 | | |

| Cases | Pg | Subject Matter | Buyer | UCC | CISG | Other law |
|---|---|---|---|---|---|---|
| **Sidco Products Marketing, Inc. v. Gulf Oil Corp.**<br>U. S. Court of Appeals, 5th Circuit, 1988. | 165 | Middle layer emulsion | Business Corporation | 2–313<br>2–314 | | Environmental law |
| **Chatlos Systems v. National Cash Register Corp.**<br>U. S. Court of Appeals, 3d Cir., 1982. | 172 | Compter system Design–build | Business Corporation | 2–714 | | |
| **Hemmert Ag. Aviation, Inc. v. Mid–Continent Aircraft Corp.**<br>U. S. District Court, Dist. Kan., 1987 | 181 | Crop spraying plane | Business Corporation | 2–313<br>2–608<br>2–711<br>2–715<br>2–715 | | |
| **Carnation Company v. Olivet Egg Ranch**<br>California Court of Appeal, 1986. | 190 | Chickenfeed | Business Corporation | 2–715 | | |
| **Schmitz-Werke Gmbh & Co. v. Rockland Industries, Inc.**<br>U. S. Court of Appeals, 4th Cir., 2002. | 197 | Drapery Lining Fabric | Business Corporation | | 35 | |
| **Delchi Carrier SpA v. Rotorex Corp.**<br>U. S. Court of Appeals, 2d Cir., 1995. | 202 | Air conditioner compressors | Business Corporation | | 7<br>25<br>35<br>36<br>46<br>49<br>74 | |
| **Medical Marketing Int'l v. Internazionale Medico Medico Scientifica**<br>U. S. District Court, E. D. La., 1999. | 209 | Mammography units | Business Corporation | | 7<br>25<br>35<br>49 | Federal Arbitration Act |
| **AWARD IN CASE NO. 3779 OF 1981**<br>ICC Arbitral Awards 1974–85 | 213 | Whey powder | Business Corporation(?) | | | |
| **AWARD OF SEPTEMBER 27, 1983, CASE NO. 3880** | 218 | 159,000 pairs ladies' boots | Business | | | |

| Cases | Pg | Subject Matter | Buyer | UCC | CISG | Other law |
|---|---|---|---|---|---|---|
| **Insurance Co. of North America v. Automatic Sprinkler Corp.**<br>Ohio Supreme Court, 1981. | 221 | Components for dry chemical fire protection system | Business Corporation | 2–316<br>2–719(3) | | Subrogation law |
| **Universal Drilling Co. v. Camay Drilling Co.**<br>U. S. Court of Appeals, 10th Cir., 1984. | 228 | Two used drilling rigs | Business Corporation | 2–313<br>2–316 | | |
| **Western Industries, Inc. v. Newcor Canada Limited**<br>U. S. Court of Appeals, 7th Cir., 1984. | 233 | Welding machines Design-build | Business Corporation | 2–316 | | |
| **Kunststoffwerk Alfred Huber v. R.J. Dick, Inc.**<br>U. S. Court of Appeals, 3d Cir., 1980. | 236 | Nylon cord belting | Business Corporation | 2–209<br>2–719 | | |
| **Hill v. Gateway 2000, Inc.**<br>U. S. Court of Appeals, 7th Cir., 1997. | 243 | Computer | Consumers | 2–204<br>2–206<br>2–207 | | |
| **Milgard Tempering, Inc. v. Selas Corp.**<br>U. S. Court of Appeals, 9th Cir., 1990. | 253 | Glass tempering furnace Design-build | Business Corporation | 2–719(2) | | |
| **Smith v. Navistar International Transportation Corp.**<br>U. S. Court of Appeals, 7th Cir., 1992. | 261 | Truck | Business Individual | 2–719(2) | | |
| **Castro v. QVC Network, Inc.**<br>U. S. Court of Appeals, 2d Cir., 1998. | 272 | Roasting pan | Consumer | 2–314 | | Strict tort liability |
| **M.K. Associates v. Stowell Products, Inc.**<br>U. S. District Court, D. Maine, 1988. | 279 | Dowels | Business Corporation | 2–607(3)(a)<br>2–717 | | |
| **FINAL AWARD IN CASE NO. 5713 OF 1989**<br>ICC 15 Y.B. Comm. Arb. 70 (1990) | 287 | Unspecified product | Business | | 38<br>39 | |

| Cases | Pg | Subject Matter | Buyer | UCC | CISG | Other law |
|---|---|---|---|---|---|---|
| **UNCITRAL CLOUT Abstract No. 285** <br> Oberlandesgericht, Koblenz, Germany, 1998. | 290 | Raw material for manufacture of PVC tubes | Business | | 39 <br> 44 | |

### CHAPTER 5. MANUFACTURERS' WARRANTIES

| Cases | Pg | Subject Matter | Buyer | UCC | CISG | Other law |
|---|---|---|---|---|---|---|
| **Martin Rispens & Son v. Hall Farms, Inc.** <br> Indiana Supreme Court, 1993 | 300 | Watermelon seed | Business | 2–302 <br> 2–313 | | |
| **Caterpillar, Inc. v. Usinor Industeel** <br> U. S. District Court, N.D. Illinois, 2005. | 317 | Steel for dump truck bodies | Business Corporation | 2–313 <br> 2–315 | | |
| **Hyundai Motor America, Inc. v. Goodin** <br> Indiana Supreme Court., 2005. | 343 | New car | Consumer | 2–318 | | MMWA |
| **Beard Plumbing and Heating, Inc. v. Thompson Plastics, Inc.** <br> U. S. Court of Appeals, 4th Circuit, 1998. | 355 | Polyvinyl plumbing components | Business Corporation | 2–314 <br> 2–315 <br> 2–318 <br> 2–714 <br> 2–715 | | Certified question |
| **Cooley v. Big Horn Harvestore Systems, Inc.** <br> Colorado Supreme Court, 1991 | 363 | Grain storage and distribution system | Farmers Individuals | 2–607(3)(a) <br> 2–714 <br> 2–719 | | |
| **U.S. Tire–Tech, Inc. v. Boeran, B.V.** <br> Texas Court of Appeals, 1st District, 2003 | 377 | Tire liner to seal punctures | Business Corporation | 2–313 <br> 2–318 <br> 1–607(3)(a) | | Deceptive Trade Practices Act |
| **Tittle v. Steel City Oldsmobile GMC Truck, Inc.** <br> Alabama Supreme Court, 1989. | 382 | New car Oldsmobile | Consumer | 2–725 | | MMWA |
| **Nationwide Insurance Co. v. General Motors Corp.** <br> Pennsylvania Supreme Court, 1993. | 390 | New car Chevrolet Corvette | Consumer | 2–725 | | MMWA <br><br> Subrogation |

| Cases | Pg | Subject Matter | Buyer | UCC | CISG | Other law |
|-------|-----|----------------|-------|-----|------|-----------|
| **Joswick v. Chesapeake Mobile Homes, Inc.** | 402 | Mobile home | Consumer | 2–725 | | |
| Maryland Court of Appeals, 2001. | | | | | | |

## CHAPTER 6. EXECUTION OF CONTRACTS

| Cases | Pg | Subject Matter | Buyer | UCC | CISG | Other law |
|-------|-----|----------------|-------|-----|------|-----------|
| **Mendelson–Zeller Co. v. Joseph Wedner & Son Co.** | 422 | Cantaloupes and lettuce | Business Corporation | 2–309 2–504 | | Perishable Agricultural Commodities Act |
| U.S. Department of Agriculture, 1970. | | | | | | |

## CHAPTER 7. PERFORMANCE STAGE CONTROVERSIES

| Cases | Pg | Subject Matter | Buyer | UCC | CISG | Other law |
|-------|-----|----------------|-------|-----|------|-----------|
| **Moulton Cavity & Mold v. Lyn–Flex Industries** | 455 | Innersole molds | Business Corporation | 2–601 | | Common law contract Substantial performance |
| Maine Supreme Judicial Court, 1979 | | | | | | |
| **Plateq Corp. v. Machlett Laboratories** | 461 | Two leadcovered steel tanks | Business Corporation | 2–602 2–606 2–709 | | |
| Connecticut Supreme Court, 1983. | | | | | | |
| **T.W. Oil, Inc. v. Consolidated Edison Co.** | 465 | Cargo of fuel oil | Business Corporation | 2–508 | | |
| New York Court of Appeals, 1982. | | | | | | |
| **Midwest Mobile Diagnostic Imaging v. Dynamics Corp. of America** | 472 | Four mobile MRI units | Business Corporation | 2–508 2–612 2–711 2–712 2–715 | | |
| U. S. District Court, W. D. Michigan, 1997. | | | | | | |
| **Hemmert Ag. Aviation, Inc. v. Mid–Continent Aircraft Corp.** | 488 | | | | | |
| (See page 181) | | | | | | |
| **Car Transportation Brokerage Co. v. Blue Bird Body Co.** | 491 | Motor coach | Business Corporation | 2–608 | | |
| U. S. Court of Appeal, 11th Circuit, 2009 | | | | | | |

| Cases | Pg | Subject Matter | Buyer | UCC | CISG | Other law |
|---|---|---|---|---|---|---|
| **Schmitz-Werke Gmbh & Co. v. Rockland Industries, Inc.** (See page 197) | 501 | | | | | |
| **Delchi Carrier SpA v. Rotorex Corp.** (See page 202) | 501 | | | | | |
| **Medical Marketing Int'l. v. Internazionale Medico Scientifica** (See page 209) | 501 | | | | | |
| **Decision of the Bundesgerichtshof, Germany** CLOUT Abstract No. 171 | 501 | Cobalt sulfate | Business Corporation | | 25 49 | |
| **Apex Oil Co. v. The Belcher Co. of New York, Inc.** U. S. Court of Appeals, 2d Cir., 1988. | 506 | Futures contracts for heating oil | Business Corporation | 2–704 2–706 2–708 | | Rules NY Mercantile Exchange |
| **R.E. Davis Chemical Corp. v. Diasonics, Inc.** U. S. Court of Appeals, 7th Cir., 1987. | 516 | Medical diagnostic equipment | Business Corporation | 2–706 2–708 2–718 | | |
| **The Colonel's Inc. v. Cincinnati Milacron Marketing Co.** U. S. Court of Appeals, 6th Cir., 1998. | 521 | Plastic injection molding machines | Business Corporation | 2–708 2–709 | | |
| **Hanil Bank v. PT. Bank Negara Indonesia (Persero)** U. S. District Court, S. D. New York, 2000. | 527 | Unspecified electronic goods | Business Corporation | 5–102 | | UCP |
| **Petra Int'l Banking Corp. v. First Amer. Bank of Va.** U. S. District Court, E. D. Virginia. 1991. | 534 | T shirts | Business Corporation | 5–107 | | UCP |
| **Mid-America Tire, Inc. v. PTZ Trading Ltd.** Ohio Supreme Court, 2002. | 546 | Michelin winter tires | Business Corporation | 5–109 | | UCP |

| Cases | Pg | Subject Matter | Buyer | UCC | CISG | Other law |
|---|---|---|---|---|---|---|
| **Martin v. Meland's Inc.** North Dakota Supreme Court, 1979. | 565 | Truck and hay-mowing unit | Farmer Individual | 2–401 2–509 2–709 | | |
| **United Air Lines v. Conductron Corp.** Illinois Appellate Court, 1st Dist., 1979. | 571 | Aircraft flight simulator | Business Corporation | 2–509 2–510 2–606 | | |
| **Ron Mead T.V. & Appliance v. Legendary Homes, Inc.** Oklahoma Court of Appeals, Div. Three, 1987. | 577 | Household appliances | Business Corporation | 2–507 2–509 2–709 | | |
| **Multiplastics v. Arch Industries** Connecticut Supreme Court, 1974. | 580 | Plastic polytyrene pellets | Business Corporation | 2–401 2–510 2–609–611 2–709 | | |
| **Pestana v. Karinol Corp.** Florida District Court of Appeal, 3d Dist., 1979. | 586 | 64 electronic watches | Business Individual | 2–503 2–509 | | |
| **BP Oil Int'l, Ltd. v. Empresa Estatal Petroleos de Ecuador** U. S. Court of Appeals, 5th Cir., 2003. | 595 | Bulk gasoline | Business Corporation | | 9(2) 36 67 | INCOTERMS |
| **Trinidad Bean and Elevator Co. v. Frosh** Nebraska Court of Appeals, 1992. | 604 | Dried navy beans | Business Corporation | 2–610 2–712 2–713 2–723 | | |
| **Purina Mills, L.L.C. v. Less** U. S. District Court, N. D, Iowa, 2003. | 611 | Weanling pigs | Business Individuals | 2–610 2–703 2–708 2–723 | | |
| **Magellan Int'l Corp. v. Salzgitter Handel GmbH** U. S. District Court, N.D. Ill., 1999. | 627 | Steel bars | Business Corporation | | 25 28 46 72 | |

†